PSY
BETHEL COLL

Y0-AQM-164

American Psychology in Historical Perspective

G. Stanley Hall (*1892*)
First President of the American
Psychological Association

American Psychology in Historical Perspective

Addresses of the Presidents of the American Psychological Association, 1892-1977

Edited by Ernest R. Hilgard

American Psychological Association, Inc.

This book is sponsored by the Publications and Communications Board of the American Psychological Association in commemoration of the centennial of the founding of the first psychology laboratory in 1879.

Library of Congress Cataloging in Publication Data
Main entry under title:
American psychology in historical perspective.

Bibliography: p.
Includes index.
1. Psychology—United States—History—Addresses, essays, lectures. 2. American Psychological Association—History—Addresses, essays, lectures. I. Hilgard, Ernest Ropiequet, 1904–
BF108.U5A43   150′.973   78–15672
ISBN 0–912704–05–5 (clothbound)
ISBN 0–912704–07–1 (paperbound)

Published by the American Psychological Association, Inc.
1200 Seventeenth Street, N.W., Washington, D.C. 20036.
Copyright © 1978 by the American Psychological Association.
All rights reserved.

Printed in the United States of America.

Contents

Preface / vii

Part Three   Psychology After World War II

Part Four   The Recent Years

Preface

Suggestions that a collection of reprinted addresses of the presidents of the American Psychological Association (APA) would be a desirable contribution to the history of American psychology came from various sources to the Publications and Communications Board of APA. After consideration of other proposals, the Board decided that APA might make the project its own. The invitation was extended to me to proceed as I saw best, gaining the advice and help from those whom I wished to have join me in the venture.

The addresses available were too many for a book of reasonable size, so some selection was necessary. After preliminary correspondence with Arthur W. Melton, the Chief Editorial Adviser, and my colleagues Gardner Lindzey and Robert R. Sears, I decided to take advantage of the perspective that would be added by asking the living APA presidents to rate the addresses. Prior to the ratings, we decided to aim to publish about 20 addresses and not to publish any from the last 10 years because of their accessibility. Of the 17 presidents who returned their ballots, 9 agreed on 17 addresses to be included. I therefore selected these for republication in full. For reasons of historical significance, I took the liberty of selecting 4 other addresses, although with slightly less agreement from the presidents, bringing the total to 21. Lindzey, Sears, and I, prior to the selection, agreed to exclude our own addresses.

Within this framework it was possible for me to proceed with the task. I prepared a background chapter on the history of the APA and some introductory materials on the several periods into which the addresses are divided. For each of the presidential addresses—whether or not they are included in this volume—I supplied brief biographical material on the president who gave the address and an abstract of the address, as an invitation to those who might wish to seek out the original. These editorial supplements have been reviewed and revised on the basis of valuable comments from Albert Hastorf, Gardner Lindzey, Arthur Melton, Robert Sears, and John Sullivan, whose help I gratefully acknowledge.

vii

A great deal of assistance has been given in assembling materials and photographs and in seeing the manuscript through the press by the staff of the Central Office of the APA, particularly by Patricia Walsh, Managing Editor of Special Publications, and her assistants, Jeanne McManus and Melissa Maholick. I am thankful for all they have done.

Ernest R. Hilgard
Stanford University

Introduction

Chapter 1

The American Psychological Association and Its Presidents

The American Psychological Association (APA) was founded in 1892—a most opportune time not only in the history of psychology but also in the history of American universities. The PhD degree had not long been given in any field of scholarship, although the frequency of its granting was slowly accelerating. The first American PhD in any area of study had been granted by Yale University in 1861, the second by the University of Pennsylvania in 1870, and the third by Harvard University in 1873. The founder of the APA, G. Stanley Hall, who was awarded a degree at Harvard in 1878, was the first person in America to receive what might be considered a psychology degree; moreover, his degree was only the eighteenth PhD granted by Harvard among all fields of study. Hall was also the only person to grant PhDs in psychology to others until 1893. In that year, the University of Pennsylvania granted its first PhD in psychology, and Yale University granted its first two.

The timing of APA's founding was opportune also because Americans had previously flocked to Germany for their PhDs. Students of psychology usually sought out Wilhelm Wundt at the University of Leipzig. In addition to his professorship in philosophy, Wundt had

3

established a psychological laboratory in the modern spirit, rich with apparatus, and his students founded many of the original laboratories in America and Canada. Wundt's influence was more important for providing a stimulus to organize laboratories than for persuading Americans to adopt his psychology. The first American laboratory, a rather informal one, had been developed by William James at Harvard University, but in 1892 it was taken over by a student of Wundt, Hugo Münsterberg. The second American laboratory was founded by G. S. Hall at Johns Hopkins University in 1883. Hall, although a Harvard PhD, had also studied with Wundt. The next university laboratories in North America followed rapidly in the years 1887–1892—in chronological order, at the University of Pennsylvania, Indiana University, University of Wisconsin, Clark University, University of Nebraska, University of Michigan, University of Iowa, Columbia University, University of Toronto, Cornell University, Wellesley College, Brown University, University of Illinois, University of Kansas, Catholic University, Yale University, University of Chicago, Princeton University, University of Minnesota, and Stanford University (Garvey, 1929). Among these laboratories, students of Wundt had founded those at Pennsylvania, Nebraska, Iowa, Cornell, Catholic, Yale, and Stanford. E. B. Titchener, another of Wundt's students, came to Cornell late in 1892, after Frank Angell, the founder of the Cornell laboratory, moved to Stanford University to found his second laboratory. This chronology was the background when Hall called together a group of recognized psychologists to begin the American Psychological Association (Fernberger, 1932).

The first organizational meeting was held at Clark University on July 8, 1892, and was followed by the first regular meeting at the University of Pennsylvania on December 27, 1892. Records of the organizational meeting are incomplete, but a fairly representative group attended. Hall, the host and senior member was then age 48. G. S. Fullerton, who presided, was 33; J. Jastrow, the secretary, was 29.

The members elected the remainder of the charter members from among those Hall had invited to the first organizational meeting and a few more (Dennis & Boring, 1952; Sokal, 1973). The roster of charter members, with their university or other affiliation in 1892, is as follows:

Angell, Frank (Stanford University)

Baldwin, J. M. (University of Toronto)

Bryan, W. S. (Indiana University)

Burnham, W. H. (Clark University)

Cattell, J. McK. (Columbia University)

Cowles, E. (McLean Hospital, Waverly, Massachusetts)

Delabarre, E. B. (Brown University)

Dewey, John (University of Michigan)

Fullerton, G. S. (University of Pennsylvania)

Gilman, B. I. (Clark University)

Griffin, E. H. (Johns Hopkins University)

Hall, G. S. (Clark University)

Hume, J. G. (Toronto University)

Hyslop, J. H. (Columbia University)
James, William (Harvard University)
Jastrow, Joseph (University of Wisconsin)
Krohn, W. O. (Clark University)
Ladd, G. T. (Yale University)
Nichols, Herbert (Harvard University)
Noyes, William (McLean Hospital, Waverly, Massachusetts)
Patrick, G. T. W. (University of Iowa)
Royce, Josiah (Harvard University)
Sanford, E. C. (Clark University)
Scripture, E. W. (Yale University)
Witmer, Lightner (University of Pennsylvania)
Wolfe, H. K. (University of Nebraska)

Five new members were added before the December 1892 meeting: T. W. Mills (McGill University), Hugo Münsterberg (Harvard University), A. T. Ormond (Princeton University), E. A. Pace (Catholic University), and E. B. Titchener (Cornell University).

A Council of seven members was chosen to guide the new APA: William James, G. T. Ladd, and G. S. Hall, the senior members (all near age 50), and four energetic younger men, Baldwin, Cattell, Fullerton, and Jastrow (none older than 32). Each of these seven Council members was later elected to the APA presidency, as were other charter members— Bryan, Dewey, Münsterberg, Royce, and Sanford; thus, 12 of the original 31 members were elected to the presidency.

Although the probability of being chosen to head the APA was greater when the membership was smaller, one cannot help but be impressed by the level of distinction of this early group. Among those never elected to the presidency, E. B. Titchener was one of the most distinguished, but the fact that he was never president was in part a matter of his own choosing. (He was reelected to *membership* in the APA in 1897 and in 1910 because his membership lapsed when he failed to pay dues.) He arrived from Europe after the first organizational meeting had been held, and he soon found himself at odds with some APA leaders. Hence he was only a nominal member of the APA and never was an active participant. By 1904 he had formed his own group of disciples and friends, known as the "Experimentalists," and they met separately from APA. After his death in 1927, the group changed its name to the Society of Experimental Psychologists and broadened its base of membership. It carried on the tradition of separate meetings, but its members remained active in the APA.

Annual Meetings and Annual Conventions

The first Annual Meeting of the American Psychological Association was held in December 1892, and until 1930 all following meetings were held between Christmas and New Year's Day. (One exception was made in 1929 when the meeting was held in September at New Haven because of conflict with the meeting of the International Congress of Psychology, where Karl S. Lashley gave his presidential address.) Since 1930 all meetings have been held in late summer, usually over the Labor Day weekend.

The month December was originally chosen by APA because it coincided with the December meeting of the American Association for the Advancement of Science (AAAS) and other societies that were likely to meet jointly with APA. The time and place chosen by AAAS became the time and place of APA meetings until 1914, when APA decided to meet with the AAAS on alternate years. Hotels eventually became too crowded, and the alternation of years was ended, soon to be replaced by the APA's meeting in late summer.

The matter of joint meetings is also of interest from another viewpoint. In the early years of psychology, the distinction between psychology and philosophy was not sharp. Many years passed before some psychology departments were completely divorced from philosophy departments in universities such as Harvard and Yale. Hence some of the early programs at annual meetings were devoted specifically to philosophy. In 1896 the psychologist Witmer moved that only psychological papers be accepted for the annual meeting. Energetic young psychologists seemed to be better organizers than the philosophers, and, in part at their instigation, a separate organization, the American Philosophical Association, was established for the philosophers in 1900, a few years after the founding of the APA. The two associations were entirely cordial, and for some years they commonly met at the same time and place, with overlapping programs. After the philosophical association came into being, the strictly philosophical papers almost disappeared from the programs at the APA annual meetings.

With the exception of some years in which World War I and World War II disrupted professional gatherings, APA has held an annual meeting each year since 1892. In 1946, when the new APA constitution was adopted, the name Annual Meeting was changed to Annual Convention to reflect the relative autonomy of the APA divisions, some of which were also separate societies.

Ingrained habits take precedence over formal labels, however, and some older psychologists are likely to ask the question, "Are you going to the APA *meeting* this year?" instead of, "Are you going to the APA *convention*?"

Growth of APA

Members of a scientific or professional organization who share common interests do value both the exchange of information at face-to-face meetings and the incident sociability. When the membership of an organization is small, this meeting yields an in-group feeling, a sense of identification with common purposes, and provides sustaining support, whereas, closer to home, there may be few who are so like-minded.

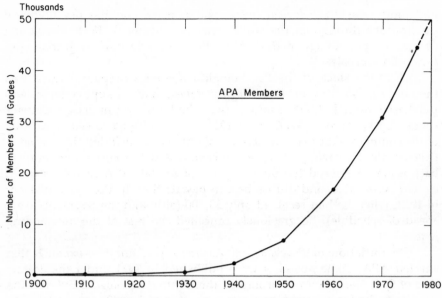

Figure 1. Growth (and projected growth) of APA membership.

These interests, and others, become more difficult to satisfy as the organization grows, and consequently changes have to be made.

Membership

The success of American psychology, reflected in the growth of APA, has accentuated the difficulty of providing satisfaction to all members through APA's annual gathering. The growth in membership has been exponential, as shown in Figure 1. Growth was steady until 1925, with nearly equal increments each year; then positive acceleration began. This acceleration was only in part a post World War I phenomenon, although psychology had gained in public stature after the psychological testing of American soldiers during World War I.

Journals

APA did not at first publish its own journals, although early APA leaders had been active in the creation of several journals. The *American Journal of Psychology* was started by G. S. Hall in 1887 while he was still at Johns Hopkins University. He also initiated the *Pedagogical Seminary* (later renamed the *Journal of Genetic Psychology*), among others, but neither of these journals, although still published, ever became an APA journal. The *Psychological Review,* started in 1894, was edited by J. McK. Cattell and J. Mark Baldwin, with a monograph supplement (which became *Psychological Monographs*) edited by C. H. Judd and a literature section (which became *Psychological Bulletin*), edited by Cattell, H. C. Warren, and Judd. The *Psychological Index,* which listed by title psychological publications throughout the world, was also begun in 1894. The young science of psychology had these outlets, in addition to British and European journals.

All of the stock of the Psychological Review Company, which was the holding company for *Psychological Review* and its supplements, was purchased from J. Mark Baldwin (who had earlier purchased Cattell's shares) by Howard C. Warren. In 1922 Warren offered to sell to APA all of the company's journals, which by this time also included the *Journal of Experimental Psychology.* For these journals and the entire inventory of back issues, he asked the modest price of $5,500. APA raised its dues, elected Associates, and did its best to pay its debt to Professor Warren; in 1929, when he had received only $3,500 (although the payments were ahead of schedule), he graciously cancelled the rest of the outstanding notes.

The initiation of *Psychological Abstracts* was another expense that affected APA. Some abstracts were published in 1921 under the editorship of S. I. Franz, who incorporated them into *Psychological Bulletin;* the new journal, *Psychological Abstracts,* was started in 1927 with Walter S. Hunter as editor. *Psychological Abstracts* received a subsidy of $76,500 over an 11-year period from the Laura Spelman Rockefeller Memorial. Hence, *Psychological Index* was discontinued in 1930. Other psychological journals had also appeared, and a number of them were acquired by the APA; for example, in 1925 Morton Prince gave his *Journal of Abnormal Psychology* to APA. Although the history of APA's journal acquisition and initiation is too long to complete here, it is useful to know that APA now publishes 18 psychological journals, a monthly newspaper, and offers a variety of communications services.

Management of APA Affairs: The Central Office

For many years the affairs of APA were managed through the devoted efforts of its secretary and its treasurer, operating through their own offices. Their universities provided the space and facilities essential for storing records and dealing with correspondence. The burdens increased as the membership grew and as more journals were published, but the situation remained unchanged for more than 50 years, until the reorganization of APA in 1945 (Wolfle, 1946). The last officers to serve before reorganization were Willard C. Olson of the University of Michigan (Secretary, 1938–1945) and Willard L. Valentine of Northwestern University (Treasurer and Manager of Publications, 1937–1945; Treasurer through the transitional years until 1947). As noted later, after the reorganization in 1945 a Central Office, with an executive secretary, was established.

The transition was made less difficult by taking advantage of psychology's representation in Washington at the Office of Psychological

Personnel, established during World War II and headed by Donald G. Marquis, then of Yale University. Prior to his move to the University of Michigan, Marquis aided in the transition by serving as Recording Secretary of the APA during the transition year, while Dael Wolfle, the first Executive Secretary, organized the Central Office.

When Wolfle began in 1945, the APA's central staff occupied space divided between the building of the National Academy of Sciences and some rooms at American University. In February of 1946 APA leased space at 1227 Nineteenth Street, N.W., and then moved in the fall of 1946 to quarters in the new building of the American Association for the Advancement of Science, at 1515 Massachusetts Avenue, N.W. That site remained the APA headquarters for six years, until the APA purchased and then refurbished the first building of its own, at 1333 Sixteenth Street, N.W. This building was occupied in the fall of 1952, but APA soon outgrew it. In 1963 APA sold it to the Republic of Nigeria. A new APA building had been planned, was already under construction at 1200 Seventeenth Street, N.W., and was ready for occupancy in the fall of 1964. It was expected to fulfill APA's needs for many years, and was large enough not only to accommodate APA but to have excess space to be rented until APA needed to expand further. In 1977, however, APA purchased another building in Arlington, Virginia, at 1400 Uhle Street and also retained ownership of the building in Washington. The newly constructed subway will permit access between the two buildings. That situation prevails as this account is written; the future can be expected to bring further changes.

When the Central Office was established, following the reorganization described in the next section, a limited term was assigned to the Executive Secretary (the name later changed to Executive Officer). APA has been fortunate in the succession of its Executive Officers: Dael Wolfle (1946–1950), Fillmore H. Sanford (1950–1956), Roger W. Russell (1956–1959), John G. Darley (1959–1962), Arthur H. Brayfield (1962–1968), Kenneth B. Little (1969–1974), and Charles A. Kiesler, the incumbent since 1974.

Science and Profession: The Reorganization of APA

From the early years, APA members wanted more than annual meetings and journals from their association. Of particular interest was the standardization and regulation of psychological testing and other services related to clinical and applied psychology (Wallin, 1960). These interests sometimes clashed with the interests of members who were more experimental- and academic-minded. A few historical highlights are recounted here that led to the reorganization of the APA and to the establishment of a Central Office.

A committee on mental and physical tests was appointed as early as 1895, consisting of J. McK. Cattell, J. M. Baldwin, E. C. Sanford, and L. Witmer, with H. C. Warren later replacing Witmer. It recommended in

1896 that a group of 27 mental and physical tests be given systematically to college students. In 1897 the APA annual meeting was large enough to be divided into simultaneous sessions. One afternoon session was devoted entirely to mental and physical tests, while the other simultaneous session covered more general psychological topics. Another committee on tests was appointed in 1906, consisting of J. R. Angell, C. H. Judd, W. B. Pillsbury, C. E. Seashore, and R. S. Woodworth. Although these committees had little influence, their existence showed at least a respectable early interest in individual differences.

APA's task became more difficult when practitioners began to ask APA to certify those psychologists competent to serve the public. In 1915 APA passed a resolution that ended with these words: "Be it Resolved, That this Association discourage the use of mental tests for practical diagnosis by individuals psychologically unqualified for the work." This statement was too ambiguous, and in 1917 some interested psychologists formed their own association, the American Association of Clinical Psychologists. To avoid dismemberment of APA, the Association of Clinical Psychologists was transformed by APA into a section of clinical psychology, recognized in the APA constitution along with a Division of Consulting Psychology. For a few years (1921–1927), certification of competence was attempted by APA, but the practice was discontinued because only 25 members elected to become certified. Those certified included some well-known practicing psychologists and as many academic ones. Among the "certified psychologists" were W. F. Dearborn, J. E. Downey, A. Gesell, L. S. Hollingworth, B. J. Johnson, B. M. Luckey, L. J. Martin, J. B. Miner, R. Pintner, L. M. Terman, F. L. Wells, and H. T. Wooley. The Division of Consulting Psychology was deleted from the APA constitution in 1932, although the section of clinical psychology persisted, even if it was not very active.

Professional psychologists did not disappear with the elimination of the division. A committee consisting of R. G. Bernreuter, F. N. Maxfield, D. Paterson (then Secretary of the APA), M. L. Reymert, and D. H. Fryer, as Chairman, met at Dartmouth in 1936 and organized the American Association for Applied Psychology (AAAP). The new AAAP met formally for the first time in connection with the 1937 APA annual meeting in Minneapolis, with Fryer as President and H. B. English as Executive Secretary. They began publishing the *Journal of Consulting Psychology*, which flourished immediately. Although retaining a loose affiliation with the APA, the new organization was very vigorous, and member loyalties moved toward it and away from the APA as the parent organization.

But World War II mobilized psychologists, brought the academics out of their ivory towers, and created a sense of unity and social purpose because the war was felt to be a righteous one. An Emergency Committee on Psychology had been meeting under the chairmanship of K. M. Dallenbach, and it in turn appointed a Subcommittee on Survey and Planning, under the chairmanship of R. M. Yerkes, who had taken so much responsibility for psychology in World War I. The other members were E. G. Boring, A. I. Bryan, E. A. Doll, R. M. Elliott, E. R. Hilgard, C. R. Rogers, and C. P. Stone, a group of psychologists who were evenly divided between experimental and applied interest areas. They began to meet for long weekends in Vineland, New Jersey, to consider psychology's future after the war. They recognized the danger that the AAAP might withdraw its members from the APA, a danger called to their attention by Alice Bryan, who was then Secretary of the AAAP, and they noted other centrifugal tendencies within psychology. Hence a Constitution Convention was proposed and met in the Pennsylvania Hotel in New York City, May 29–31, 1943, under the chairmanship of E. G. Boring. APA was invited to send delegates, as an equal constituent with the AAAP, the Psychometric Society, the Society for the Psychological Study of Social Issues, and a number of other scientific and professional societies composed primarily of psychologists. The issue was initially left open whether the APA should be replaced by some other type of organization or confederation. By vote of the delegates, and subsequent appropriate ratification by the constituent bodies, the APA was retained as the parent organization but its constitution was drastically revised with a diverse divisional structure that recognized the plurality of psychological interests, scientific and professional. The AAAP was voted out of existence and its *Journal of Consulting Psychology* became an APA journal. (In 1968 its name was changed to *Journal of Consulting and Clinical Psychology*.) The transition was completed by September 1945 when the central office was established with Dael Wolfle as the first Executive Secretary. The new journal designed for the entire membership, the *American Psychologist*, was published in January 1946. It appeared that unification had been restored and that psychologists were pleased to meet under one tent. The revised constitution has remained for over 30 years, and the only changes made were those provided for when the constitution was written to insure that it keep abreast of the changing times.

If before 1945 the members of the AAAP as an applied group resented the power of academic psychologists within the APA, the situation may now be reversed. At least some academics believe that professional problems, such as certification, licensing, malpractice insurance, and policy-making roles of state associations, demand too much of APA's time. The largest single organization of psychologists outside the APA structure now is the Psychonomic Society, which sees its role to be that of conserving the scientific side of psychology.

An equilibrium in a large and dynamic organization of scientists and professionals in any field is a delicate one, and the viability of such an organization depends on its internal mechanisms for adapting to new conditions by changing itself appropriately. The new constitution of APA provided for a Policy and Planning Board whose obligation is to take the long-range view, to recognize centers of conflict and tension, and to advise about appropriate changes. Its role is distinguished from that of the Council of Representatives and the Board of Directors, whose members deal with matters of immediate importance. The Policy and

Planning Board recommends changes to keep the organization from becoming rigid and stereotyped, and the Association's members, through referendums, are able to accept or reject the Board's recommendations. A detailed review of the history might show that initiatives in recent years have more often been proposed by the Council and Board of Directors than by the Policy and Planning Board, but the concept of a review and planning agency not pressed for immediate decisions still appears to be sound.

Fortunately members can express their special interests outside the APA and to do so need not withdraw from it. Special interest groups may form in great variety, some in fields of research that are newly opened. These like-minded psychologists meet on their own for discussion and exchange of information. The special interest groups constitute no threat to the APA. In a study conducted a few years ago, Paul Woods (1964) showed great overlap (a) in divisional memberships within APA and (b) between membership in APA and memberships in other societies to which psychologists belong. With 92% of the members of the Psychonomic Society retaining APA membership, for example, that society, which obviously fulfills important needs for its members, is not depleting the ranks of APA. Of course when a society is essentially interdisciplinary, the proportion of APA members is lower; for example, it is not surprising that the Society for Psychophysiological Research has only 56% APA members, or, at the other extreme, that the Professional Group on Human Factors in Electronics has only 9% APA members. When psychological interests are preeminent, then APA is likely to retain a strong interest, as in the Psychonomic Society and in the group known as Psychologists in Private Practice (of whom 99% belong to the APA).

The Presidents

When the new constitution was adopted and made operative in 1945, each division began to have its own presidential address, in addition to the one given by the APA president. This arrangement wisely permitted more members of the APA to have the kudos that result when one has been elected to an office by peers.

The sheer growth in membership of the APA means that many distinguished psychologists cannot be elected to the presidency. But who does get elected? The answer is not straightforward: nomination procedures have changed through the years, topics have changed in their priorities, and social climate makes some leaders more visible and acceptable than others. The sample of presidents is probably too small to make any significant generalizations, but the addresses presented and summarized in this volume might pique the curiosity of anyone who wishes to try to explain the process of choice.

An interesting exercise would be to determine the relationship between the supervisor of the PhD and the frequency of election to the presidency (Boring & Boring, 1948). A very high proportion of those elected to the presidency worked for their degrees under a prior APA president. Starting with J. Jastrow in 1900, PhDs from Johns Hopkins University, who worked under the supervision of Hall, began to be elected; of the next 30 presidents elected, 22 had studied under a previous APA president. Of the remaining 8, 3 had European degrees, 4 had studied under Titchener (the equivalent in prestige of an APA president), and only one, C. L. Hull, worked toward his PhD with a nonpresident. But it would be misleading to conclude that the way to become an APA president is to study under a previous president; the probabilities have to be corrected. Of the 81 PhDs who studied under Hall at Clark University, only 2 who received the degree later became APA presidents (Bryan and Terman). A close examination of the facts shows that for many years those who supervised PhDs in most major universities were APA presidents or were later elected president.

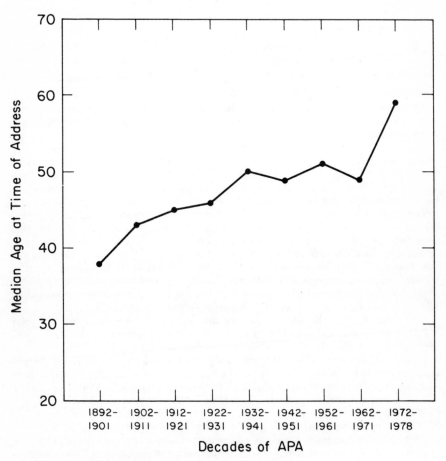

Figure 2. Median age (in years) of APA presidents at time of presidential address.

The situation has now changed, and scores of universities offer the PhD. To determine now the probability of election of any one person as president, careful analysis would be required of personality factors, distinctiveness of contributions, prior recognition that led to a broad base of support before the election, and social pressures at the time of nomination and election; in addition, analysis would include where and under whom the candidate had studied or the department, agency, or area in which the candidate became known.

Presidents have usually been selected near the height of their careers: they are neither too young to be unknown nor too old to be passed over in favor of promising and energetic younger members. As the membership of APA has grown, its presidents have been selected at slightly older ages, perhaps because the larger the organization, the longer it takes to become prominent. The median presidential ages, when plotted by decades, show this trend (see Figure 2).

The presidential addresses represent one time sample of the changing interests of psychologists (Gibson, 1972). They show the history of psychology represented by those selected as its leaders.

ANNOTATED BIBLIOGRAPHY

Biographies of APA Presidents and Other Distinguished Psychologists

A convenient source for biographical information on historically important psychologists is E. G. Boring, *A History of Experimental Psychology*, Second Edition (New York: Appleton-Century-Crofts, 1950).

Short biographies, pictures, and lists of other sources of biographical data on 526 eminent deceased psychologists throughout the world can be found in *Names in the History of Psychology: A Biographical Sourcebook* by Leonard Zusne (Washington, D.C.: Hemisphere; distributed by Halstead/Wiley, 1975). The primary publications of psychologists have been listed by Robert I. Watson in *Eminent Contributions to Psychology. Volume 1: A Bibliography of Primary References* (New York: Springer, 1974). Zusne's and Watson's books discuss many of the same psychologists because, despite some editorial discretion, they were both based primarily on a common list in which the names were rated for eminence. These eminence ratings are also included in both books. The original source of these lists and eminence ratings was an article authored by E. L. Annin, E. G. Boring, and R. I. Watson, "Important Psychologists, 1600-1967," which appeared in the *Journal of the History of the Behavioral Sciences*, 1968, *4*, 303-315. Zusne has deleted some names included by Watson and added a few (without eminence ratings) who died after 1967.

An earlier volume gives brief biographical data and essentially complete bibliographies of 2,400 psychologists living in 1932 from 40 countries: *The Psychological Register*, Volume III; C. Murchison (Ed.); Worcester, Mass.: Clark University Press, 1932.

More extensive biographies of individual psychologists may also be found. Special attention should be called to the collection of volumes entitled *A History of Psychology in Autobiography*. These books were initiated under the editorship of Carl Murchison in 1930, and he edited the next two volumes in 1932 and 1936. They were published by Clark University Press. The later volumes, under other editorships, appeared in 1952 (published by Clark University Press), 1967 (published by Appleton-Century-Crofts), and 1974 (published by Prentice-Hall). A seventh volume under Gardner Lindzey's editorship is now in preparation. The six published volumes contain the autobiographies of 35 ex-presidents of the APA, among selected psychologists from around the world.

A related series of autobiographies was undertaken by T. S. Krawiec, entitled *The Psychologists* (New York: Oxford University Press, Vol. I, 1972; Vol. II, 1974; Vol. III, 1978. Brandon, Vt.: Clinical Psychology Publishing Company. Eight APA presidents appear among the 35 published biographies. The index to the first two volumes contains a brief biographical introduction to all psychologists cited in the autobiographies.

For biographies of eminent Americans generally, the volumes of the *Dictionary of American Biography* (New York: Scribners) are valuable. Supplementary volumes appear from time to time, with indexes to the earlier ones. The volumes of *Who Was Who in America* help on matters of dates of birth and death and employment histories, and through them the appropriate volumes of *American Men of Science* can be located.

REFERENCES

Boring, M. D., & Boring, E. G. Masters and pupils among American psychologists. *American Journal of Psychology*, 1948, *61*, 527–534.

Clark, K. E. *America's psychologists*. Washington, D.C.: American Psychological Association, 1957.

Dallenbach, K. M. The Emergency Committee of Psychology, National Research Council. *American Journal of Psychology*, 1946, *49*, 496–582.

Dennis, W., & Boring, E. G. The founding of the APA. *American Psychologist*, 1952, *7*, 95–97.

Fernberger, S. W. The American Psychological Association: A historical summary, 1892–1930. *Psychological Bulletin*, 1932, *29*, 1–88.

Garvey, C. R. List of American psychology laboratories. *Psychological Bulletin*, 1929, *26*, 652–660.

Gibson, K. *The conceptual bases of American psychology: A content analysis of the presidential addresses of the American Psychological Association, 1892–1970*. Ann Arbor, Mich.: University Microfilms, 1972.

Sokal, M.M. APA's first publication: Proceedings of the American Psychological Association, 1892–1893. *American Psychologist*, 1973, *28*, 277–292.

Wallin, J. E. W. History of the struggles within the American Psychological Association to attain membership requirements, test standardization, certification of practitioners, and professionalization. *Journal of General Psychology*, 1960, *63*, 287–308.

Wolfle, D. The reorganized American Psychological Association. *American Psychologist*, 1946, *1*, 3–6.

Woods, P. J. Psychological organizations: Their nature and membership patterns. *American Psychologist*, 1964, *19*, 130–132.

Part One

The First Twenty-Five Years

Presidents of the
American Psychological Association
1892–1916

G. Stanley Hall, *1892*

George T. Ladd, *1893*

William James, *1894*

J. McKeen Cattell, *1895*

G. S. Fullerton, *1896*

J. M. Baldwin, *1897*

Hugo Münsterberg, *1898*

John Dewey, *1899*

Joseph Jastrow, *1900*

Josiah Royce, *1901*

E. C. Sanford, *1902*

William L. Bryan, *1903*

William James, *1904*

Mary W. Calkins, *1905*

James R. Angell, *1906*

Henry R. Marshall, *1907*

George M. Stratton, *1908*

Charles H. Judd, *1909*

Walter B. Pillsbury, *1910*

Carl E. Seashore, *1911*

Edward L. Thorndike, *1912*

Howard C. Warren, *1913*

R. S. Woodworth, *1914*

John B. Watson, *1915*

Raymond Dodge, *1916*

Chapter 2

The Presidents and Their Messages

1892–1916

Early psychologists were closely affiliated with philosophy until experimental psychology became better established. G. Stanley Hall, the first president of the APA, had had a theological training and had studied philosophy in Europe before he took his PhD at Harvard University under the physiologist H. P. Bowditch and the psychologist William James. Perhaps he was the first American to receive a degree in the "new" experimental psychology. Hall founded the *American Journal of Psychology* in 1887 at Johns Hopkins University, and, although he was given the title "Professor of Psychology and Pedagogics," J. McK. Cattell at the University of Pennsylvania is said to have held the first chair actually named "Psychology" in 1888. Several of the first APA presidents were authors of books on philosophy as well as on psychology. Among these were George T. Ladd, William James, G. S. Fullerton, John Dewey, Josiah Royce, and Mary W. Calkins. Although these were the formative years in which psychology as a science was still finding itself, each president was strongly identified with psychology in order to have been elected. Some of the later presidents were also trained in philosophy, but they "belonged" distinctly to the science of psychology.

The new science of psychology was recognized early as fitting within the tradition of natural science. Eleven of the first 25 presidents became members of the National Academy of Sciences. They were elected by a membership consisting primarily of physical and biological scientists.

The topics of these first APA presidential addresses varied widely, from a discussion of psychology's proper role to debates over theoretical issues, such as Titchener's structuralism, Angell's functionalism, and Watson's behaviorism. The substantive topics of experimental psychology were little represented until later.

In the remainder of this chapter, and in later chapters introducing each of the historical periods into which the addresses have been divided, the following information is supplied, where possible, for each president: the full name of the president and dates of birth and death; the title of the address and the reference citation for the published version of the address; the annual meeting at which the address was delivered and the site and year of the presentation; the university at which the president's doctorate was received and the year of receipt; a short biographical account of the president's career, including important publications; and an abstract of the presidential address. Only some of the addresses are presented here *in toto* but all are abstracted; those fully presented are so noted after the reference citation to the address.

Granville Stanley Hall (1844–1924)

PhD, Harvard University, 1878 (under W. James and H. P. Bowditch).

The History and Prospects of Experimental Psychology in America. (No published version of this address is extant.)

Presented at the First Annual Meeting of the American Psychological Association, Philadelphia, Pennsylvania, 1892.

After receiving his PhD, Hall was the first of many Americans to study with Wilhelm Wundt at the University of Leipzig. His laboratory (second in chronology only to that of William James at Harvard University) was founded in 1883 at Johns Hopkins University, where among his students and associates were four subsequent APA presidents: Cattell, Dewey, Jastrow, and Sanford. He became president of Clark University in 1889 where he continued actively until 1920 and where 81 PhDs were granted under his direction. His most important works are the two-volume book *Adolescence* (1904) and the book *Senescence* (1922).

George Trumbull Ladd (1842–1921)

BD, Andover Theological Seminary, 1869; DD, Andover Theological Seminary, 1879.

President's Address Before the New York Meeting of the American Psychological Association. *Psychological Review,* 1894, *1*, 1–21.

Presented at the Second Annual Meeting of the American Psychological Association, New York, New York, 1893.

After spending a few years in the ministry, Ladd taught at Bowdoin College from 1879 to 1881, then transferred to Yale University where he spent the rest of his career and became emeritus in 1905. He authored *Elements of Physiological Psychology* (1887), which was the first book written in English that was in the Wundtian tradition. Ladd revised this influential book with R. S. Woodworth in 1911.

This address, the first published APA presidential address, was appropriately the lead article of the new journal, *Psychological Review,* founded and edited by Cattell and Baldwin. Ladd intended his address to serve as a "cheering reminder that this Association should enter upon its career with a sufficiently generous estimate of its privileges and its responsibility."

William James (1842–1910)

MD, Harvard University, 1868.

The Knowing of Things Together. *Psychological Review*, 1895, *2*, 105–124.

Presented at the Third Annual Meeting of the American Psychological Association, Princeton, New Jersey, 1894. *(See Chapter 3.)*

James traveled widely and was so well read that he may not have been specifically influenced by his Harvard professors. He did have the opportunity, however, to study chemistry under Charles W. Eliot (later president of Harvard) and he traveled on a naturalist's expedition to the Amazon with the distinguished biologist Louis Agassiz. He also studied for a year and a half in Germany.

In 1872 he began to teach physiology at Harvard but soon moved to psychology and then to philosophy. His *Principles of Psychology* (1890) appeared in two volumes and remains influential today. A shorter version, *Psychology: Briefer Course,* was published in 1892. Other books of James that are of most interest to psychologists are *Talks to Teachers* (1899) and *Varieties of*

Religious Experience (1902). His importance to philosophy lies in his espousal of pragmatism or radical empiricism.

In his address, James discussed an important question in cognitive psychology: Is a complex experience—"knowing things together"—made up of separate parts or is there some initial unity in the knowing of the whole? Many of his views anticipated the later Gestalt attacks on the associationist position of how mental events appear. James here modified his position from that taken in *Principles of Psychology* and stated that mental contents can be called complex if it is recognized that mental states involve a complexity in unity.

James McKeen Cattell (1860–1944)

PhD, University of Leipzig, 1886 (first American PhD under W. Wundt).

Address of the President. *Psychological Review*, 1896, *3*, 134–148.

Presented at the Fourth Annual Meeting of the American Psychological Association, Philadelphia, Pennsylvania, 1895. (*See Chapter 4*, where address is presented *in toto* with the more informative chapter title "The Progress of Psychology as an Experimental Science.")

Cattell lectured at Bryn Mawr College, the University of Pennsylvania, and Cambridge University in England. In 1888 he became a professor at the University of Pennsylvania and then moved to Columbia University, where he stayed for the rest of his academic career (1891–1917). He served as head of the department of anthropology and the department of philosophy at Columbia University.

Always independent in his views, Cattell sought greater participation of the Columbia faculty in university affairs and came into conflict with Columbia's president, Nicholas Murray Butler. In keeping with his views, Cattell assisted in the founding of the American Association of University Professors. At the age of 57 Cattell was fired by Butler, who made the trivial charge that after the United States had entered World War I Cattell had used Columbia University letterhead to urge that draftees not be sent overseas against their will. The concealed charge against Cattell was directed at his pacifist stance, and other members of the faculty, such as historian Charles A. Beard, resigned from Columbia in protest. (Butler received the Nobel Peace Prize in 1931, shared with Jane Addams.)

Cattell continued his energetic life as editor of *Science*, *Scientific Monthly*, *School and Society*, *American Naturalist*, and the first six editions of *American Men of Science*. He was also the founder and an officer of the Psychological Corporation.

Cattell authored numerous journal articles, both as reports of research and as essays and addresses. His papers are collected in two volumes under the editorship of A. T. Poffenberger: *James McKeen Cattell: Man of Science* (1947).

In his address, Cattell traced the rise of experimental psychology by citing areas where progress had been made and by noting the precision of measurement achieved. He gently refuted James' attacks on psychophysics by pointing out the amount of experimentation that was represented in James' *Principles of Psychology*. Cattell noted that even philosophy will benefit from experimental psychology: "The twilight of philosophy can be changed into its dawn only by the light of science, and psychology can contribute more light than any other science."

George Stuart Fullerton (1859–1925)

MA, University of Pennsylvania, 1882.

The Knower in Psychology. *Psychological Review*, 1897, *4*, 1–26.

Presented at the Fifth Annual Meeting of the American Psychological Association, Boston, Massachusetts, 1896.

In 1883 Fullerton taught at the University of Pennsylvania and then moved to Columbia University, where he taught philosophy (1904–1913). He went to Europe on leave in 1913, never to return to Columbia, and was an exchange professor of philosophy at the University of Vienna (1913–1914), where he was awarded the title of Honorary Professor. Caught in Europe at the beginning of World War I, he was unable to return to the United States until 1918. Then in frail health, he began some lecturing at Vassar College.

He is best known in psychology for an important monograph published jointly with Cattell entitled *On the Perception of Small Differences with Special Reference to the Extent, Force and Time of Movement* (1892). His philosophical works include *Sameness and Identity* (1890) and *The Philosophy of Spinoza* (1894).

In his address Fullerton faced the persistent problem of the status of the self as knower. He believed that psychologists, in addressing this problem, should rely on empirical information. Most of the actual experience of selfhood arises out of bodily experience; even in a dream, it is the body that seems to move about and serve as a locus of the experiences. Fullerton attempted to show that to add some implied self to these experiences leads to contradictions. "To attempt to explain the ultimate nature of consciousness by the assumption of hypothetical entities not to be found in consciousness, or by ascribing inconceivable virtues to hypostatized activities, seems to me an unprofitable task."

James Mark Baldwin (1861–1934)

PhD, Princeton University, 1889, in philosophy (under James McCosh).

On Selective Thinking. *Psychological Review,* 1898, *5,* 1–24.

Presented at the Sixth Annual Meeting of the American Psychological Association, Ithaca, New York, 1897.

Baldwin founded a psychological laboratory at the University of Toronto in 1889 and at Princeton University in 1893. He then moved to Johns Hopkins University (1903), before beginning a career outside the United States (1909), first in Mexico and then in Paris. He was co-founder with Hall of the APA. His books *Mental Development in the Child and the Race* (1895) and *Social and Ethical Interpretations in Mental Development* (1897) placed human development in evolutionary perspective. He wrote *The Story of the Mind* (1898) at about the time he delivered his presidential address. His work of most lasting usefulness may be *Dictionary of Philosophy and Psychology,* which he edited with collaborators (two volumes, 1901–1902; the third volume, a bibliography, 1905).

In his address, Baldwin sought to show how the stream of thought is directed. He decided that the level of organization already achieved determines the later organization or direction. His use of the ideas (and the words) *accommodation* and *assimilation* anticipated Piaget's genetic theory.

Hugo Münsterberg (1863–1916)

PhD, University of Leipzig, 1885 (under W. Wundt).

Psychology and History. *Psychological Review,* 1899, *6,* 1–31.

Presented at the Seventh Annual Meeting of the American Psychological Association, New York, New York, 1898.

In addition to his PhD, Münsterberg received an MD from the University of Heidelberg (1887) and taught at the University of Freiburg in Germany. His experimental work attracted the attention of William James, who brought him to Harvard University at first temporarily (1892–1895) and then permanently (1897–1916). It was expected that Münsterberg would be an exponent of the new experimental psychology at Harvard, as reported in his four-volume book *Beiträge zur Experimentelle Psychologie* (1888), which was based on his research in Germany. Instead, he turned his interests to applied psychology and wrote a book on testimony entitled *On the Witness Stand* (1908); he also authored *Psychology and the Teacher* (1909) and *Psychotherapy* (1909). His book

Psychology and Industrial Efficiency (1913) helped to launch that field of psychology. At the same time he maintained a theoretical and philosophical interest, as reflected in his presidential address.

The title of Münsterberg's address may be slightly misleading. By "psychology" Münsterberg meant the standard study of lawful relationships, as in any other *nomothetic* discipline; by "history" he meant the life-history approach, as in an *idiographic* discipline. The terms *nomothetic* and *idiographic,* which Münsterberg used, were later made familiar in America by Gordon Allport, who attributed them to the German philosopher Wilhelm Windelband. Münsterberg also felt that psychology could learn both from natural history and from experimental investigation.

John Dewey (1859-1952)

PhD, Johns Hopkins University, 1884, in philosophy (influenced by G. Stanley Hall).

Psychology and Social Practice. *Psychological Review*, 1900, 7, 105-124.

Presented at the Eighth Annual Meeting of the American Psychological Association, New Haven, Connecticut, 1899. *(See Chapter 5.)*

Dewey taught philosophy at the University of Michigan (1884-1894) before moving to the University of Chicago (1894-1904). At Chicago he founded his Laboratory School, the beginning of the movement known as Progressive Education. This interest was in the foreground at the time he gave his presidential address. He completed his academic career at Columbia University (1904-1929) and retired in 1929.

His text entitled *Psychology,* written in 1886, preceded the texts of G. T. Ladd and William James. It was successful enough to be printed in three editions (last edition, 1891), but it was too philosophical to survive the competition of the more experimental and physiological texts that followed. Although Dewey authored some articles on psychology while he was at Chicago and was one of the founders of functionalism, he had little taste for experimental methods, even though his philosophy sometimes bore the name of "experimentalism." His interest in education fit into his larger interests in social reform, and both are reflected in his presidential address.

His works on philosophy and education, such as *How We Think* (1910) and *Human Nature and Conduct* (1922) bear directly on psychology. *School and Society* (1900) is one of his best-known educational texts, and *Experience and Nature* (1925) is an influential text in philosophy. In his ninetieth year, he was still writing in the field of philosophy and he co-authored *Knowing and the Known* (1949) with A. F. Bentley.

In his address, Dewey discussed the bearing of psychology on education to illustrate the way in which psychology impinges on social problems. Education illustrates well the need for a "linking science" between basic psychology on the one hand and the task of the teacher on the other. "While the psychological theory would guide and illuminate the practice, acting upon the theory would immediately test it, and thus criticize it, bringing about its revision and growth." He ended the address with a discussion of the problems of ethical values in applying psychology to the broader aspects of social life.

Joseph Jastrow (1863–1944)

PhD, Johns Hopkins University, 1886 (first PhD given under G. Stanley Hall).

Some Currents and Undercurrents in Psychology. *Psychological Review*, 1901, *8*, 1–26.

Presented at the Ninth Annual Meeting of the American Psychological Association, Baltimore, Maryland, 1900.

Jastrow taught at the University of Wisconsin (1888–1927) until he retired and moved to the New School for Social Research (1927–1933). He was known as a popularizer of psychology, as evidenced by the exhibit that he arranged for the Chicago World's Fair in 1893.

Although some of his experimental work was of conventional value, his books were primarily on such topics as *Fact and Fable in Psychology* (1900), *Keeping Mentally Fit: A Guide to Everyday Psychology* (1928), *The House that Freud Built* (1932), and *The Betrayal of Intelligence: A Preface to Debunking* (1938).

Jastrow, in his address, expressed disappointment that research in psychology had not led to more significant results. He felt that the increased recognition of the practical significance of psychological science ("a science of mental functions") was both a prominent and a fortunate development.

Josiah Royce (1855–1916)

PhD, Johns Hopkins University, 1878, in philosophy (dissertation approved by Noah Porter, President of Yale University).

Recent Logical Inquiries and their Psychological Bearings. *Psychological Review*, 1902, *9*, 105–133.

Presented at the Tenth Annual Meeting of the American Psychological Association, Chicago, Illinois, 1901.

After some graduate work in Germany, Royce received his PhD, then returned to his native California to teach at the University of California, Berkeley (1878-1882). He next moved to Harvard University, where he spent the rest of his career (1882-1916). Although he wrote *Outlines of Psychology* (1903) he was known primarily as an idealistic philosopher. His other books include *The Spirit of Modern Philosophy* (1892), *The Philosophy of Loyalty* (1908), and *Lectures on Modern Idealism* (1919, edited by J. Loewenberg).

Royce considered two logical problems in his presidential address: first, the natural history of logical phenomena in general; second, a new examination of the logic of the special sciences. He attempted to make his remarks bear upon problems of the psychology of thinking and upon psychology's own logic as a science.

Edmund Clark Sanford (1859-1924)

PhD, Johns Hopkins University, 1888 (under G. Stanley Hall).

Psychology and Physics. *Psychological Review*, 1903, *10*, 105-119.

Presented at the Eleventh Annual Meeting of the American Psychological Association, Washington, D.C., 1902.

In 1889 Sanford followed G. Stanley Hall to Clark University, where he directed the laboratory. In addition, he served as president of Clark College (1909-1920) and continued as professor of psychology and education at Clark University until the time of his death.

He was best known for his laboratory work and for his laboratory equipment inventions, such as the vernier pendulum chronoscope. His laboratory manual *A Course in Experimental Psychology* (1894) was widely used.

Sanford noted in his address that psychology is influenced by physics, perhaps even to an embarrassing extent, and that psychology is to some extent anthropomorphic. In a discussion of the body-mind problem, Sanford stated that interaction was more sensible than parallelism. He also noted that psychology cannot solve some of the ultimate problems of philosophy; therefore alternative solutions must be treated with equal favor.

William Lowe Bryan (1860–1955)

PhD, Clark University, 1892 (under G. Stanley Hall).

Theory and Practice. *Psychological Review,* 1904, *11,* 71–82.

Presented at the Twelfth Annual Meeting of the American Psychological Association, St. Louis, Missouri, 1903.

Before receiving his PhD in psychology, Bryan first taught Greek at Indiana University (1884–1885) and then began to teach philosophy. On leave from Indiana University, he spent a year in Berlin, Germany (1886–1887) and returned to teach philosophy until he entered graduate study in psychology at Clark University. He took leave again to study at the University of Paris and the University of Würzburg but was soon elected to the presidency of Indiana University (1902–1937, followed by emeritus status), a position he held at the time of his presidential address.

He is best known to students in psychology for an early study of the learning of the telegraphic language, which he formulated in collaboration with N. Harter (1894 and 1897) and which featured a plateau in the learning curve.

Because Bryan was a university president, the emphasis of his APA presidential address may have been partly autobiographical. He stressed the role of the scholar as statesman, one who bridges abstract science and the arts of practice. "The scholar may at a great price become a statesman. When this occurs, whether on a great scale or on a small one, whether at court or in a village school, we have at last a solution of the ancient problem of theory and practice."

William James (1842–1910)

MD, Harvard University, 1868.

The Experience of Activity. *Psychological Review,* 1905, *12,* 1–17.

Presented at the Thirteenth Annual Meeting of the American Psychological Association, Philadelphia, Pennsylvania, 1904.

Elected to the presidency of APA for the second time, at the age of 62 (10 years after election to his first term), James addressed "our two associations," thereby recognizing the American Philosophical Association, which was meeting jointly with APA. He stressed the prominence at that time of pragmatism, a position that was under the leadership of John Dewey and to which James had given the name "radical empiricism." In his address, he applied this approach to the problem of activity, particularly the problems of causation and originality. (William James' first presidential address is reproduced in Chapter 3; his second presidential address was reprinted in James' posthumous *Essays in Radical Empiricism* [1967].)

Mary Whiton Calkins (1863–1930)

AM, Smith College, 1887.

A Reconciliation Between Structural and Functional Psychology. *Psychological Review*, 1906, *13*, 61–81.

Presented at the Fourteenth Annual Meeting of the American Psychological Association, Cambridge, Massachusetts, 1905.

Calkins attended Radcliffe College (1885–1886; 1890–1891); was a "guest" at Harvard University (1890–1895), where she studied with William James; and attended the University of Leipzig, where she studied with Wundt (1886–1887). Although all of her degree requirements were satisfied, Harvard refused to grant a PhD to a woman. Calkins later rejected a PhD from Radcliffe.

She began her teaching career at Wellesley College (1887), set up the first laboratory there (1891), and spent her entire career there until her death. Concerned with philosophical as well as psychological issues, she wrote *The Persistent Problems of Philosophy* (1907; fifth edition, 1925). She authored two psychology texts, *An Introduction to Psychology* (1901) and *A First Book in Psychology* (1909; fourth edition, 1914). She was the first woman elected to the presidency of APA.

In her address, Calkins defended the self-psychology for which she became famous and argued that there is no consciousness without self-consciousness. From this standpoint, she believed that a union is required between the structural psychology of E. B. Titchener and the functional psychology of J. R. Angell.

James Rowland Angell (1869–1949)

MA, University of Michigan, 1891 (under John Dewey); MA, Harvard University, 1892 (under William James).

The Province of Functional Psychology. *Psychological Review*, 1907, *14*, 61–91.

Presented at the Fifteenth Annual Meeting of the American Psychological Association, New York, New York, 1906. (*See Chapter 6.*)

After receiving his degree at Harvard University, Angell continued his graduate study in Germany. He chose to study in Berlin and Halle but did not finish his dissertation because, it is said, he chose to return to the United States to be married. He is credited with founding the psychology laboratory at the University of Minnesota (1893-1894). He arrived at the University of Chicago as professor of psychology in 1894, the same year that Dewey came from the University of Michigan (where Angell's father had been the president since 1871). Angell left teaching for administrative work (1919-1921) and became the acting president of the University of Chicago. He was also president of Yale University (1921-1937). He retired in 1937.

Best known for his leadership in functional psychology, he was the author of *Psychology: An Introductory Study of the Structure and Functions of Human Consciousness* (1904). His later books include *Chapters from Modern Psychology* (1912) and *An Introduction to Psychology* (1918). His lectures reflecting his period as an administrator are collected in *American Education: Addresses and Articles* (1937).

Angell's presidential address is an elegant demonstration of a literate debater at his best. He demolished with surgical finesse those with whom he disagreed, but always in gentlemanly fashion; he stated his position boldly but denied being dogmatic. "[Functionalism] means today a broad and flexible and organic view in psychology. The moment it becomes dogmatic and narrow its spirit will have passed and undoubtedly some worthier successor will fill its place."

Henry Rutgers Marshall (1852-1927)

AM, Columbia University, 1875, in architecture.

The Methods of the Naturalist and Psychologist. *Psychological Review*, 1908, *15*, 1-24.

Presented at the Sixteenth Annual Meeting of the American Psychological Association, Chicago, Illinois, 1907.

Marshall was the first president of APA who was not employed in an institution of higher learning. He was a practicing architect all of his life and also wrote a number of books on esthetics and psychology, of which the best known is *Pain, Pleasure, and Esthetics* (1894). He also was the author of *Mind and Conduct* (1910).

In 1907, APA abandoned its joint meeting with the American Philosophical Association and chose to meet with the American Association of Naturalists. Marshall probably chose the title of his address to recognize this particular meeting, but it does not reflect well the content of his message. In his address, he proposed a search for the more fundamental aspects of conscious experience (in that sense, more "naturalistic" than the search for elements by introspection). He noted that a presentation to consciousness has the characteristics of intensity, manifoldness, realness, algedonic quality, and time quality.

George Malcolm Stratton (1865-1957)

PhD, University of Leipzig, 1896 (under W. Wundt).

Toward the Correction of Some Rival Methods in Psychology. *Psychological Review*, 1909, *16*, 67-84.

Presented at the Seventeenth Annual Meeting of the American Psychological Association, Baltimore, Maryland, 1908.

After receiving his PhD, Stratton went to the University of California, Berkeley, where he founded the psychology laboratory (1896). Except for a few years at Johns Hopkins University (1904-1908), he spent the remainder of his career at Berkeley, where he retired in 1935. His writings covered a wide range of topics, for example, *Experimental Psychology and Its Bearing upon Culture* (1903); *Theophrastus and the Greek Physiological Psychology Before Aristotle* (1917), which included both the Greek text and Stratton's translation; and *The Social Psychology of International Conduct* (1929). But he is best remembered for his article in *Psychological Review* (1897), "Vision Without Inversion of the Retinal Image." This article introduced the method of wearing distorting lenses to study learning in perception.

In his address Stratton pointed to the need for a broad functional analysis, in which the study of relations and modes of interaction is required along with analysis and description: "The mental world is not a whit less spacious than the physical, and the full explication of the mind will call for as many sciences as the physical world requires. What we call psychology is really a writhing brood of young sciences, and he can have no feeling for the future who would try to stifle any of them."

Charles Hubbard Judd (1873-1946)

PhD, University of Leipzig (under W. Wundt).

Evolution and Consciousness. *Psychological Review*, 1910, *17*, 77-97.

Presented at the Eighteenth Annual Meeting of the American Psychological Association, Cambridge, Massachusetts, 1909.

Judd taught at Wesleyan University (1896-1898), at New York University (1898-1901), at the University of Cincinnati (1901-1902), and at Yale University (1902-1909). He moved to the University of Chicago in 1909, where he was affiliated at the time of his presidential address. At Chicago, he served as professor of psychology and director of the psychological laboratory, professor and head of the department of education, director of the school of education, and, for a few years, chairman of the department of psychology.

His many books include *Genetic Psychology for Teachers* (1903) (in the days when "genetic" meant "developmental"), *Psychology: General Introduction* (1907), *Introduction to the Scientific Study of Education* (1918), *Education as the Cultivation of the Higher Mental Processes* (1936), and *Educational Psychology* (1939).

In his address, Judd asserted that consciousness is of positive importance in the evolutionary process. "Psychology will boldly assert its right to existence as the science which deals in a broad way with the evolutionary processes by which consciousness arose and through which the trend of life has been changed from organic adaptation to intelligent conquest."

Walter Bowers Pillsbury (1872–1960)

PhD, Cornell University, 1896 (under E. B. Titchener).

The Place of Movement in Consciousness. *Psychological Review*, 1911, *18*, 83–99.

Presented at the Nineteenth Annual Meeting of the American Psychological Association, Minneapolis, Minnesota, 1910.

Pillsbury can be considered the first of the second generation of APA presidents whose teachers had studied with Wundt (if we do not count G. Stanley Hall as a student of Wundt). His career was spent entirely at the University of Michigan (1897–1942). His best known book (apart from his textbooks), *L'Attention* (1906), appeared first in French and then was translated into English in 1908. Other books include *The Psychology of Reasoning* (1910), *The Essentials of Psychology* (1911), *The Fundamentals of Psychology* (1916; third edition, 1934), and *The History of Psychology* (1929).

In his address, Pillsbury said that the "motor theory of consciousness" had gone too far in leading to the conviction that there is nothing in consciousness but movement. He believed that complete explanation of any phase of consciousness can be neither in terms of sensation nor in terms of movement, but must include both.

Carl Emil Seashore (1866–1949)

PhD, Yale University, 1895 (under E. W. Scripture).

The Measure of a Singer. *Science*, 1912, *35*, 201–212.

Presented at the Twentieth Annual Meeting of the American Psychological Association, Washington, D.C., 1911.

The first of Yale's PhDs in psychology (in the second generation of psychologists from Wundt), Seashore was first a laboratory assistant at Yale, and then spent his career at the University of Iowa (1897–1936) until his first retirement at the age of 70. He was called back from retirement in 1942 and served through the World War II years until his second retirement at the age of 80. As dean of the graduate college of the University of Iowa from 1908, he continued to be productive in research and publication along with his administrative duties. He had written a laboratory manual, *Elementary Experiments in Psychology* (1908), before he delivered his presidential address and was already known for his experimental and test studies. His manual was revised later (1935) in collaboration with his son, Robert H. Seashore. His other books include *The Psychology of Musical Talent* (1919), *Introduction to Psychology* (1923), *Psychology of Music* (1938), a collection of his articles, *In Search of Beauty in Music* (1947), and an autobiography, *Pioneering in Psychology* (1942).

Seashore's address called attention to the rise of the applied psychological sciences, and he used his work on music to illustrate mental measurement. He listed measurements of sensory and motor functions related to pitch, intensity, and time; he listed measurements of associational functions of imagery, memory, and ideation; and, finally, he listed measurements of affective reactions. He believed that applied psychology "must recognize itself, its diversities, its stupendous difficulties, its essential limitations and withal its promise and worth."

Edward Lee Thorndike (1874–1949)

PhD, Columbia University, 1898 (under J. McK. Cattell; influenced by William James).
Ideo-Motor Action. *Psychological Review*, 1913, *20*, 91–106.

Presented at the Twenty-First Annual Meeting of the American Psychological Association, Cleveland, Ohio, 1912. (*See Chapter 7.*)

After spending one year (1898–1899) at Wesleyan University, Thorndike returned to Columbia University for the rest of his career and retired in 1940. Thorndike was a prodigious worker and prolific writer; a sample of his book titles includes *Animal Intelligence* (1911; expanded from his 1898 dissertation), *An Introduction to the Theory of Mental and Social Measurements* (1904), *The Elements of Psychology* (1905), *Educational Psychology* (three volumes, 1913–1914), *The Psychology of Arithmetic* (1922, with others), *The Measurement of Intelligence* (1926), *The Psychology of Wants, Interests, and Attitudes* (1935), *Human Nature and the Social Order* (1940), and *The Teacher's Word Book of 30,000 Words* (1944).

As in the case of other productive psychologists elected to the APA presidency, Thorndike's presidential address does not ideally represent his beliefs. At the same time he delivered his address he was also writing his monumental book, *Educational Psychology*. But the address did represent his beliefs in that as a connectionist he believed that situations and responses could be directly connected without the intervention of ideas. This theme was represented in his denial of ideo-motor action. The law of effect is there if it is looked for.

He twice repeated in his address: "An image, idea or any other mental fact, has, apart from connections made by heredity, use and satisfying results, no stronger tendency to produce any other movement whatsoever, no stronger tendency to produce it than ideas of dollars and earthquakes have to produce them."

Howard Crosby Warren (1867–1934)

PhD, Johns Hopkins University, 1917 (under J. B. Watson).

The Mental and the Physical. *Psychological Review*, 1914, *21*, 79–100.

Presented at the Twenty-Second Annual Meeting of the American Psychological Association, New Haven, Connecticut, 1913.

Although Warren had studied at the University of Leipzig, he had not remained to receive a PhD. By special arrangement, one of his book manuscripts was accepted as a dissertation at Johns Hopkins University several years after he had become an APA president, although he was never in residence at Johns Hopkins. Warren's academic career was spent at Princeton University (1890–1934). He was influenced greatly by Baldwin, his predecessor at Princeton, from whom Warren later purchased the *Psychological Review* publications. His books include *Human Psychology* (1919), *A History of the Association Psychology* (1921), *Elements of Human Psychology* (1922; revised with Leonard Carmichael, 1930), and *Dictionary of Psychology* (1934).

In his address, Warren dealt directly with the mind-body problem. He found that the most satisfactory formulation was the double-aspect view, which leads naturally to a two-aspect psychology—the psychology of introspection and the psychology of behavior.

Robert Sessions Woodworth (1869–1962)

PhD, Columbia University, 1899 (under J. McK. Cattell; influenced by William James).

A Revision of Imageless Thought. *Psychological Review*, 1915, *22*, 1–27.

Presented at the Twenty-Third Annual Meeting of the American Psychological Association, Philadelphia, Pennsylvania, 1914. (*See Chapter 8.*)

Woodworth was an instructor in mathematics at Washburn College, Kansas (1893–1895) before attending graduate school at Harvard University. At Harvard he assisted in physiology (1897–1898) while earning a master's degree. After receiving his PhD, he was an instructor in physiology at Bellevue Hospital (1899–1902) and worked with C. S. Sherrington at the University of Liverpool as a demonstrator in physiology (1902–1903). The remainder of his career (1903–1942) was spent at Columbia University until his official retirement in 1942. He continued to lecture, however, until 1958 at the age of 89. His last book, *Dynamics of Behavior* (1958), updated his historically important *Dynamic Psychology* (1918). His other books include *Le Mouvement* (1903), the collaborative revision of Ladd's *Elements of Physiological Psychology* (1911), *Psychology* (1921; appearing as a fifth edition in collaboration with Donald G. Marquis, 1947), and *Experimental Psychology* (1938; revised in collaboration with Harold Schlosberg, 1960).

The controversial concept of imageless thought ultimately was to lead to the decline of a strictly sensationist psychology. In his address, Woodworth took a functional position that recall is never, in a strict sense, of sensory content only. He developed what he called a perceptual reaction theory—that a perception is an inner reaction to sensation.

John Broadus Watson (1878–1958)

PhD, University of Chicago, 1903 (under J. R. Angell).

The Place of the Conditioned-Reflex in Psychology. *Psychological Review*, 1916, *23*, 89–116.

Presented at the Twenty-Fourth Annual Meeting of the American Psychological Association, Chicago, Illinois, 1915. *(See Chapter 9.)*

After receiving his PhD, Watson remained on the faculty of the University of Chicago in charge of the animal laboratory (1903–1908). He then moved to Johns Hopkins University where he ended his academic career in 1920 but remained influential through his later writings on behaviorism. He was active as an officer in advertising agencies until retiring in 1946. He initiated behaviorism in a paper which appeared in *Psychological Review*, entitled "Psychology as the Behaviorist Views It" (1913); his presidential address was delivered shortly thereafter. His earliest book was *Animal Education: The Psychical Development of the White Rat* (1903), but his more widely used text was *Behavior: An Introduction to Comparative Psychology* (1914). The general textbook *Psychology from the Standpoint of a Behaviorist* (1919) represented his new approach. His later books, which were more popular and reached audiences outside the psychological profession, include *Behaviorism* (1924) and *Psychological Care of the Infant and Child* (1928, with Rosalie R. Watson).

Watson's address focuses on the effort to find an objective method for studying the more conventional topics in human psychology. Watson believed that the conditioned reflex as described by Bekhterev, is in some respects more convenient than Pavlov's salivary method, although Watson preferred Pavlov's terminology to that of Bekhterev. He described a number of preliminary experiments, with specimen records, to show the possible methods.

Raymond Dodge (1871–1942)

PhD, University of Halle (under philosopher B. Erdmann).

The Laws of Relative Fatigue. *Psychological Review*, 1917, *24*, 89–113.

Presented at the Twenty-Fifth Annual Meeting of the American Psychological Association, New York, New York, 1916.

Dodge remained at Halle for a year after he received his degree to complete a pioneering monograph with Erdmann on experimental studies in reading. He then taught one year at Ursinus College before he moved to Wesleyan University (1898–1924). On invitation from Angell, then president of Yale University, he went to Yale in 1924 with R. M. Yerkes to establish a new Institute of Psychology (the forerunner of the Institute of Human Relations) where he remained until retirement in 1936. A pioneer in the recording of eye movements, he aided in the invention and the development of psychological apparatus; his best known invention was the mirror tachistoscope.

Because Dodge was inhibited by Erdmann's advice that book writing was not Dodge's forte, he remained a psychologist's psychologist—he was well known by his colleagues but unknown outside this small circle of co-workers. In addition to his monographs that reported experimental findings, he wrote two small books late in his career, *Conditions and Consequences of Human Variability* (1931) and *The Craving for Superiority* (1931, with Eugen Kahn).

For his presidential address, Dodge chose to discuss a problem that had long interested him for its theoretical significance. He insisted that the problems of mental fatigue have an importance independent of questions of practical expediency, such as the role of rest pauses in industrial work. His address was illustrated by records of eye movements studied by the corneal reflection method that he invented.

Reprinted with permission
from *Psychological Review*,
1895, 2, 105–124.

Chapter 3

The Knowing of Things Together

William James
Harvard University

I

The nature of the synthetic unity of consciousness is one of those great underlying problems that divide the psychological schools. We know, say, a dozen things singly through a dozen different mental states. But on another occasion we may know the same dozen things together through a single mental state. The problem is as to the relation of the previous many states to the later one state. In physical nature, it is universally agreed, a multitude of facts always remain the multitude they were and appear as one fact only when a mind comes upon the scene and so views them, as when H–O–H appear as "water" to a human spectator. But when, instead of extramental "things," the mind combines its own "contents" into a unity, what happens is much less plain.

The matters of fact that give the trouble are among our most familiar experiences. We know a lot of friends and can think of each one singly. But we can also think of them together, as composing a "party" at our house. We can see single stars appearing in succession between the clouds on a stormy night, but we can also see whole constellations of

---

Read as the President's Address before the American Psychological Association at Princeton, December, 1894, and reprinted with some unimportant omissions, a few slight revisions, and the addition of some explanatory notes.

those stars at once when the wind has blown the clouds away. In a glass of lemonade we can taste both the lemon and the sugar at once. In a major chord our ear can single out the *c, e, g,* and *c'*, if it has once become acquainted with these notes apart. And so on through the whole field of our experience, whether conceptual or sensible. Neither common sense nor commonplace psychology finds anything special to explain in these facts. Common sense simply says the mind "brings the things together," and common psychology says the "ideas" of the various things "combine," and at most will admit that the occasions on which ideas combine may be made the subject of inquiry. But to formulate the phenomenon of knowing things together thus as a combining of ideas, is already to foist in a theory about the phenomenon simply. Not so should a question be approached. The phenomenon offers itself, in the first instance, as that of *knowing things together*; and it is in those terms that its solution must, in the first instance at least, be sought.

"Things," then; to "know" things; and to know the "same" things "together" which elsewhere we knew singly—here, indeed, are terms concerning each of which we must put the question, "What do we *mean* by it when we use it?"—that question that Shadworth Hodgson lays so much stress on, and that is so well taught to students, as the beginning of all sound method, by our colleague Fullerton. And in exactly ascertaining what we do mean by such terms there might lie a lifetime of occupation.

For we do mean something; and we mean something true. Our terms, whatever confusion they may connote, denote at least a fundamental fact of our experience, whose existence no one here present will deny.

II

What, then, do we mean by "things"? To this question I can only make the answer of the idealistic philosophy. For the philosophy that began with Berkeley, and has led up in our tongue to Shadworth Hodgson, things have no other nature than thoughts have, and we know of no things that are not given to somebody's experience. When I see the thing white paper before my eyes, the nature of the thing and the nature of my sensations are one. Even if with science we supposed a molecular architecture beneath the smooth whiteness of the paper, that architecture itself could only be defined as the stuff of a farther possible experience, a vision, say, of certain vibrating particles with which our acquaintance with the paper would terminate if it were prolonged by magnifying artifices not yet known. A thing may be my phenomenon or some one else's; it may be frequently or infrequently experienced; it may be shared by all of us; one of our copies of it may be regarded as the original, and the other copies as representatives of that original; it may appear very differently at different times; but whatever it be, the stuff of which it is made is thought-stuff, and whenever we speak of a thing that is out of our own mind, we either mean nothing; or we mean a thing that was or will be in our own mind on another occasion; or, finally, we mean a thing in the mind of some other possible receiver of experiences like ours.

Such being "things," what do we mean by saying that we "know " them?

There are two ways of knowing things, knowing them immediately or intuitively, and knowing them conceptually or representatively. Although such things as the white paper before our eyes can be known intuitively, most of the things we know, the tigers now in India, for example, or the scholastic system of philosophy, are known only representatively or symbolically.

Suppose, to fix our ideas, that we take first a case of conceptual knowledge; and let it be our knowledge of the tigers in India, as we sit here. Exactly what do we *mean* by saying that we here know the tigers? What is the precise fact that the cognition so confidently claimed is *known-as*, to use Shadworth Hodgson's inelegant but valuable form of words?

Most men would answer that what we mean by knowing the tigers is having them, however absent in body, become in some way present to our thought; or that our knowledge of them is known as presence of our thought to them. A great mystery is usually made of this peculiar presence in absence; and the scholastic philosophy, which is only common sense grown pedantic, would explain it as a peculiar kind of existence, called *intentional inexistence,* of the tigers in our mind. At the very least, people would say that what we mean by knowing the tigers is mentally *pointing* towards them as we sit here.

But now what do we mean by *pointing,* in such a case as this? What is the pointing known-as, here?

To this question I shall have to give a very prosaic answer—one that traverses the prepossessions not only of common sense and scholasticism, but also those of nearly all the epistemological writers whom I have ever read. The answer, made brief, is this: The pointing of our thought to the tigers is known simply and solely as a procession of mental associates and motor consequences that follow on the thought, and that would lead harmoniously, if followed out, into some ideal or real context, or even into the immediate presence, of the tigers. It is known as our rejection of a jaguar, if that beast were shown us as a tiger; as our assent to a genuine tiger if so shown. It is known as our ability to utter all sorts of propositions which don't contradict other propositions that are true of the real tigers. It is even known, if we take the tigers very seriously, as actions of ours which may terminate in directly intuited tigers, as they would if we took a voyage to India for the purpose of tiger-hunting and brought back a lot of skins of the striped rascals which we had laid low. In all this there is no self-transcendency in our mental images taken by themselves. They are one physical fact; the tigers are another; and their pointing to the tigers is a perfectly commonplace physical relation, if you once grant a connecting world to be there. In short, the ideas and the tigers are in themselves as loose and separate, to use Hume's language, as any two things can be; and pointing means here an operation as external and adventitious as any that nature yields.[1]

I hope you may agree with me now that in representative knowledge there is no special inner mystery, but only an outer chain of physical or mental intermediaries connecting thought and thing. *To know an object is here to lead to it through a context which the world supplies.* All this was most instructively set forth by our colleague Miller, of Bryn Mawr, at our meeting in New York last Christmas, and for re-confirming my sometime wavering opinion, I owe him this acknowledgment.[2]

Let us next pass on to the case of immediate or intuitive acquaintance with an object, and let the object be the white paper before our eyes. The thought-stuff and the thing-stuff are here indistinguishably the same in nature, as we saw a moment since, and there is no context of intermediaries or associates to stand between and separate the thought and thing. There is no "presence in absence" here, and no "pointing," but rather an allround embracing of the paper by the thought; and it is clear that the knowing cannot now be explained exactly as it was when the tigers were its object. Dotted all through our experience are states of immediate acquaintance just like this. Somewhere our belief always does rest on ultimate data like the whiteness, smoothness, or squareness of this paper. Whether such qualities be truly ultimate aspects of being or only provisional suppositions of ours, held-to till we get better informed, is quite immaterial for our present inquiry. So long as it is believed in, we see our object face to face. What now do we mean by "knowing" such a sort of object as this? For this is also the way in which we should know the tiger if our conceptual idea of him were to terminate by having led us to his lair?

This address must not become too long, so I must give my answer in the fewest words. And let me first say this: So far as the white paper or other ultimate datum of our experience is considered to enter also into some one else's experience, and we, in knowing it, are held to know it there as well as here; so far again as it is considered to be a mere mask for hidden molecules that other now impossible experiences of our own might some day lay bare to view; so far it is a case of tigers in India again—the things known being absent experiences, the knowing can only consist in passing smoothly towards them through the intermediary context that the world supplies. But if our own private vision of the paper be considered in abstraction from every other event, as if it constituted by itself the universe (and it might perfectly well do so, for

---

1. A stone in one field may "fit," we say, a hole in another field. But the relation of "fitting," so long as no one carries the stone to the hole and drops it in, is only one name for the fact that such an act may happen. Similarly with the knowing of the tigers here and now. It is only an anticipatory name for a further associative and terminative process that may occur.

2. See also Dr. Miller's article on Truth and Error, in the *Philosophical Review*, July, 1893.

aught we can understand to the contrary), then the paper seen and the seeing of it are only two names for one indivisible fact which, properly named, is *the datum, the phenomenon, or the experience.* The paper is in the mind and the mind is around the paper, because paper and mind are only two names that are given later to the one experience, when, taken in a larger world of which it forms a part, its connections are traced in different directions.[3] *To know immediately, then, or intuitively, is for mental content and object to be identical.* This is a very different definition from that which we gave of representative knowledge; but neither definition involves those mysterious notions of self-transcendency and presence in absence which are such essential parts of the ideas of knowledge, both of common men and of philosophers. Is there no experience that can justify these notions, and show us somewhere their original?

I think the mystery of presence in absence (though we fail to find it between one experience and another remote experience to which it points, or between the "content" and "object" of any one experience falsely rent asunder by the application to it of these two separate names) may yet be found, and found between the parts of a single experience. Let us look for it, accordingly, in its simplest possible form. What is the smallest experience in which the mystery remains? If we seek, we find that there is no datum so small as not to show the mystery. The smallest effective pulse of consciousness, whatever else it may be consciousness of, is also consciousness of passing time. The tiniest feeling that we can possibly have involves for future reflection two sub-feelings, one earlier and the other later, and a sense of their continuous procession. All this has been admirably set forth by Mr. Shadworth Hodgson,[4] who shows that there is literally no such datum as that of the present moment, and no such content, and no such object, except as an unreal postulate of

---

3. What is meant by this is that "the experience" can be referred to either of two great associative systems, that of the experiencer's mental history, or that of the experienced facts of the world. Of both of these systems it forms part, and may be regarded, indeed, as one of their points of intersection. One might let a vertical line stand for the mental history; but the same object, O, appears also in the mental history of different persons, represented by the other vertical lines. It thus ceases to be the private property of one experience, and becomes, so to speak, a shared or public thing. We can track its outer history in this way,

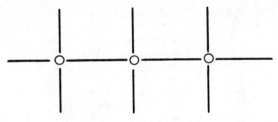

and represent it by the horizontal line. (It is also known representatively at other points of the vertical lines, or intuitively there again, so that the line of its outer history would have to be looped and wandering, but I make it straight for simplicity's sake.) In any case, however, it is the same *stuff* that figures in all the sets of lines.

4. *Philosophy of Reflection,* Vol. 1, p. 248 ff.

abstract thought. The *passing* moment is the only thing that ever concretely was or is or shall be; and in the phenomenon of elementary memory, whose function is to apprehend it, earlier and later are present to each other in an experience that feels either only on condition of feeling both together.

We have the same knowing together in the matter that fills the time. The rush of our thought forward through its fringes is the everlasting peculiarity of its life. We realize this life as something always off its balance, something in transition, something that shoots out of a darkness through a dawn into a brightness that we know to be the dawn fulfilled. In the very midst of the alteration our experience comes as one continuous fact. "Yes," we say at the moment of full brightness, *this* is what I meant. No, we feel at the moment of the dawning, this is not yet the meaning, there is more to come. In every crescendo of sensation, in every effort to recall, in every progress towards the satisfaction of desire, this succession of an emptiness and fulness that have reference to each other and are one flesh is the essence of the phenomenon. In every hindrance of desire the sense of ideal presence of what is absent in fact, of an absent, in a word, which the only function of the present is to *mean*, is even more notoriously there. And in the movement of thoughts not ordinarily classed as involving desire, we have the same phenomenon. When I say *Socrates is mortal*, the moment *Socrates* is incomplete; it falls forward through the *is* which is pure movement, into the *mortal*, which is indeed bare mortal on the tongue, but for the mind, is *that mortal*, the *mortal Socrates*, at last satisfactorily disposed of and told off.

Here, then, inside of the minimal pulse of experience which, taken as object, is change of feeling, and, taken as content, is feeling of change, is realized that absolute and essential self-transcendency which we swept away as an illusion when we sought it between a content taken as a whole and a supposed objective thing outside. *Here in the elementary datum of which both our physical and our mental worlds are built, we find included both the original of presence in absence and the prototype of that operation of knowing many things together which it is our business to discuss.*[5] For the fact that past and future are already parts of the least

---

5. It seems to me that we have here something like what comes before us in the psychology of space and time. Our original intuition of space is the single field of view; our original intuition of time covers but a few seconds; yet by an ideal piecing together and construction we frame the notions of immensity and eternity, and suppose dated events and located things therein, of whose actual intervals we grasp no distinct idea. So in the case before us. The way in which the constituents of one undivided datum drag each other in and run into one, saying *this* is what *that* means, gives us our original intuition of what knowing is. That intuition we extend and constructively build up into the notion of a vast tissue of knowledge, shed along from experience to experience until, dropping the intermediary data from our thought, we assume that terms the most remote still know each other, just after the fashion of the parts of the prototypal fact. Cognition here is only constructive, as we have already seen. But he who should say, arguing from its nature here, that it nowhere is direct, and seek to construct it without an originally given pattern, would be like those psychologists who profess to develop our idea of space out of the association

experience that can really be, is just like what we find in any other case of an experience whose parts are many. Most of these experiences are of objects perceived to be simultaneous and not to be immediately successive as in the heretofore considered case. The field of view, the chord of music, the glass of lemonade are examples. But the gist of the matter is the same—it is always knowing-together. You cannot separate the consciousness of one part from that of all the rest. What is given is pooled and mutual; there is no dark spot, no point of ignorance; no one fraction is eclipsed from any other's point of view. Can we account for such a being-known-together of complex facts like these?

The general *nature* of it we can probably never account for, or tell how such a unity in manyness can be, for it seems to be the ultimate essence of all experience, and anything less than it apparently cannot be at all. But the particular *conditions* whereby we know particular things together might conceivably be traced, and to that humble task I beg leave to devote the time that remains.

III

Let me say forthwith that I have no pretension to give any positive solution. My sole ambition now is, by a little classification, to smooth the ground somewhat so that some of you, more able than I, may be helped to advance, before our next meeting perhaps, to results that I cannot obtain.

Now, the first thing that strikes us in these complex cases is that the condition by which one thing may come to be known together with other things is an *event*. It is often an event of the purely physical order. A man walks suddenly into my field of view, and forthwith becomes part of it. I put a drop of cologne-water on my tongue, and, holding my nostrils, get the taste of it alone, but when I open my nostrils I get the smell together with the taste in mutual suffusion. Here it would seem as if a sufficient condition of the knowing of (say) three things together were the fact that the three several physical conditions of the knowing of each of them were realized at once. But in many other cases we find on the contrary that the physical conditions are realized without the things being known together at all. When absorbed in experiments with the cologne-water, for example, the clock may strike, and I not know that it has struck. But again, some seconds after the striking has elapsed, I may, by a certain shifting of what we call my attention, hark back to it and resuscitate the sound, and even count the strokes in memory. The

---

of data that possess no original extensity. Grant the *sort* of thing that is meant by presence in absence, by self-transcendency, by reference to another, by pointing forward or back, by knowledge in short, somewhere in our experience, be it in ever so small a corner, and the construction of pseudo-cases elsewhere follows as a matter of course. But to get along without the real thing *anywhere* seems difficult indeed.

condition of knowing the clock's striking is here an event of the mental order which must be added to the physical event of the striking before I can know it and the cologne-water at once. Just so in the field of view I may entirely overlook and fail to notice even so important an object as a man, until the inward event of altering my attention makes me suddenly see him with the other objects there. In those curious phenomena of dissociation of consciousness with which recent studies of hypnotic, hysteric and trance-states have made us familiar (phenomena which surely throw more new light on human nature than the work of all the psycho-physical laboratories put together), the event of hearing a "suggestion," or the event of passing into trance or out of it, is what decides whether a human figure shall appear in the field of view or disappear, and whether a whole set of memories shall come before the mind together, along with its other objects, or be excluded from their company. There is in fact no possible object, however completely fulfilled may be the outer condition of its perception, whose entrance into a given field of consciousness does not depend on the additional inner event called attention.

Now, it seems to me that this need of a final inner event, over and above the mere sensorial conditions, quite refutes and disposes of the associationist theory of the unity of consciousness. By associationist theory, I mean any theory that says, either implicitly or explicitly, that for a lot of objects to be known together, it suffices that a lot of conscious states, each with one of them as its content, should exist, as James Mill says, "synchronically." Synchronical existence of the ideas does not suffice, as the facts we now have abundantly show. Gurney's, Binet's and Janet's proofs of several dissociated consciousnesses existing synchronically, and dividing the subject's field of knowledge between them, is the best possible refutation of any such view.

Union in consciousness must be *made* by something, must be brought about; and to have perceived this truth is the great merit of the anti-associationist psychologists.[6] The form of unity, they have obstinately said, must be specially accounted for; and the form of unity the radical associationists have as obstinately shied away from and ignored, though their accounts of those preliminary conditions that supply the matters to be united have never been surpassed. As far as these go, we are all, I trust, associationists, and reverers of the names of Hartley, Mill, and Bain.

Let us now rapidly review the chief attempts of the anti-associationists to fill the gap they discern so well in the associationist tale.

---

6. In this rapid paper I content myself with arguing from the experimental fact that something *happens* over and above the realization of sensorial conditions, wherever an object adds itself to others already "before the mind." I say nothing of the logical self-contradiction involved in the associationist doctrine that the two facts, "A is known," and "B is known," *are* the third fact, "A + B are known together." Those whom the criticisms already extant in print of this strange belief have failed to convince, would not be persuaded, even though one rose from the dead. The appeal to the actual facts of dissociation may make impression, however, even on such hardened hearts as theirs.

1. *Attention.*   Attention, we say, by turning to an object, includes it with the rest; and the naming of this faculty in action has by some writers been considered a sufficient account of the decisive "event." [7] But it is plain that the act of Attention itself needs a farther account to be given, and such an account is what other theories of the event implicitly give.

We find four main types[8] of other theory of how particular things get known together, a physiological, a psychological, an animistic, and a transcendentalist type. Of the physiological or "psycho-physical" type many varieties are possible, but it must be observed that none of them pretends to assign anything more than an empirical law. A psycho-physical theory can couple certain antecedent conditions with their result; but an explanation, in the sense of an inner reason why the result should have the nature of one content with many parts instead of some entirely different nature, is what a psycho-physical theory cannot give.[9]

2. *Reminiscence.*   Now, empirically, we have learned that things must be known in succession and singly before they can be known together.[10] If A, B, and C, for example, were outer things that came for the first time and affected our senses all at once, we should get one content from the lot of them and make no discriminations. The content would symbolically point to the objects A, B, C, and eventually terminate there, but would contain no parts that were immediately apprehended as standing for A, B, and C severally. Let A, B, and C stand for pigments, or for a tone and its overtones, and you will see what I mean when I say that the first result on consciousness of their falling together on the eye or ear would be a single new kind of feeling rather than a feeling with

---

7. It might seem natural to mention Wundt's doctrine of "Apperception" here. But I must confess my inability to say anything about it that would not resolve itself into a tedious comparison of texts. Being alternately described as intellection, will, feeling, synthesis, analysis, principle and result, it is too "protean" a function to lend itself to any simplified account at second hand.

8. It is only for the sake of completeness that we need mention such notions of a sort of mechanical and chemical activity between the ideas as we find in Herbart, Steinthal and others. These authors see clearly that mere synchronical existence is not combination, and attribute to the ideas dynamic influences upon each other; pressures and resistances according to Herbart, and according to Steinthal "psychic attractions." But the philosophical foundation of such physical theories have been so slightly discussed by their authors that it is better to treat them only as rhetorical metaphors and pass on. Herbart, moreover, must also be mentioned later, along with the animistic writers.

9. We find this impotence already when we seek the conditions of the passing pulse of consciousness, which, as we saw, always involves time and change. We account for the passing pulse, physiologically, by the overlapping of dying and dawning brain-processes; and at first sight the elements time and change, involved in both the brain-processes and their mental result, gives a similarity that, we feel, might be the real reason for the psycho-physic coupling. But the moment we ask "metaphysical" questions—"Why not each brain-process felt apart?—Why just this amount of time, neither more nor less?" etc., etc.—we find ourselves falling back on the empirical view as the only safe one to defend.

10. The latest empirical contribution to this subject, with which I am acquainted, is Dr. Herbert Nichols' excellent little monograph, "Our Notions of Number and Space." Boston, Ginn & Co., 1894.

three kinds of inner part. Such a result has been ascribed to a "fusion" of the three feelings of A, B, and C; but there seems no ground for supposing that, under the conditions assumed, these distinct feelings have ever been aroused at all. I should call the phenomenon one of *indiscriminate knowing together*, for the most we can say under the circumstances is that the content resembles somewhat each of the objects A, B, and C, and knows them each potentially, knows them, that is, by possibly leading to each smoothly hereafter, as we know Indian tigers even whilst sitting in this room.

But if our memory possess stored-up images of former A-s, B-s, and C-s, experienced in isolation, we get an altogether different content, namely, one through which we know A, B, and C together, and yet know each of them in discrimination through one of the content's own parts. This has been called a "colligation" or *Verknüpfung* of the "ideas" of A, B, and C, to distinguish it from the aforesaid fusion. Whatever we may call it, we see that its physiological condition is more complex than in the previous case. In both cases the outer objects, A, B, and C, exert their effects on the sensorium. But in this case there is a cooperation of higher tracts of memory which in the former case was absent. *Discriminative knowing-together, in short, involves higher processes of reminiscence.* Do these give the element of manyness, whilst the lower sensorial processes that by themselves would result in mere "fusion," give the unity to the experience? The suggestion is one that might repay investigation, although it has against it two pretty solid objections: first, that in man the consciousness attached to infra-cortical centres is altogether subliminal, if it exist; and, second, that in the cortex itself we have not yet discriminated sensorial from ideational processes. Possibly the frontal lobes, in which Wundt has supposed an *Apperceptionsorgan*, might serve a turn here. In any case it is certain that, into our present rough notions of the cortical functions, the future will have to weave distinctions at present unknown.

3. *Synergy.* The theory that, physiologically, the oneness precedes the manyness, may be contrasted with a theory that our colleagues Baldwin and Münsterberg are at present working out, and which places the condition of union of many data into one datum, in the fact that the many pour themselves into one motor discharge. The motor discharge being the last thing to happen, the condition of manyness would physiologically here precede and that of oneness follow. A printed word is apprehended as one object, at the same time that each letter in it is apprehended as one of its parts. Our secretary, Cattell, long ago discovered that we recognize words of four or five letters by the eye as quickly, or even more quickly, than we recognize single letters. Recognition means here the motor process of articulation; and the quickness comes from the fact that all the letters in the particular combination unhesitatingly cooperate in the one articulatory act. I suppose such facts as these to lie at the base of our colleagues' theories, which probably differ in detail, and which it would be manifestly unjust to discuss or

guess about in advance of their completer publication. Let me only say that I hope the latter may not be long delayed.

These are the only types of physiological theory worthy of mention. I may next pass to what, for brevity's sake, may be called *psychological accounts* of the event that lets an object into consciousness, or, by not occurring, leaves it out. These accounts start from the fact that what figures as part of a larger object is often perceived to have relations to the other parts. Accordingly the event in question is described as an *act of relating thought*. It takes two forms.

4. *Relating to self.*   Some authors say that nothing can enter consciousness except on condition that it be related to the self. Not *object*, but *object-plus-me*, is the minimum knowable.

5. *Relating to other objects.*   Others think it enough if the incoming object be related to the other objects already there. To fail to appear related is to fail to be known at all. To appear related is to appear with other objects. If relations were correlates of special cerebral processes, the addition of these to the sensorial processes would be the wished-for event. But brain physiology as yet knows nothing of such special processes, so I have called this explanation purely psychological. There seem to be fatal objections to it as a universal statement, for the reference to self, if it exist, must in a host of cases be altogether subconscious; and introspection assures us that in many half-waking and half-drunken states the relations between things that we perceive together may be of the dimmest and most indefinable kind.

6. *The individual soul.*   So we next proceed to *the animistic account*. By this term I mean to cover every sort of individualistic soul-theory. I will say nothing of older opinions; but in modern times we have two views of the way in which the union of a many by a soul occurs. For Herbart, for example, it occurs because the soul itself *is* unity, and all its *Selbsterhaltungen* are obliged to necessarily share this form. For our colleague Ladd, on the other hand, to take the best recent example, it occurs because the soul, which *is* a real unity indeed, furthermore performs a unifying *act* on the naturally separate data of sense—an act, moreover, for which no psycho-physical analogon can be found. It must be admitted that much of the reigning bias against the soul in so-called scientific circles is an unintelligent prejudice, traceable far more to a vague impression that it is a theological superstition than to exact logical grounds. The soul is an "entity," and, indeed, that worst sort of entity, a "scholastic entity"; and, moreover, it is something to be damned or saved; so let's have no more of it! I am free to confess that in my own case the antipathy to the Soul with which I find myself burdened is an ancient hardness of heart of which I can frame no fully satisfactory account even to myself. I passively agree that if there were Souls that we could use as principles of explanation, the *formal* settlement of the questions now before us could run far more smoothly towards its end. I admit that a soul is a medium of union, and that brain-processes and ideas, be they never so "synchronical," leave all mediating agency out.

Yet, in spite of these concessions, I never find myself actively taking up the soul, so to speak, and making it do work in my psychologizing. I speak of myself here because I am one amongst many, and probably few of us can give adequate reasons for our dislike. The more honor to our colleague from Yale, then, that he remains so unequivocally faithful to this unpopular principle! And let us hope that his forthcoming book may sweep what is blind in our hostility away.[11]

But all is not blind in our hostility. When, for example, you say that A, B, and C, which are distinct contents on other occasions, are now on this occasion joined into the compound content ABC by a unifying act of the soul, you say little more than that now they *are* united, unless you give some hint as to *how* the soul unites them. When, for example, the hysteric women which Pierre Janet has studied with such loving care, go to pieces mentally, and their souls are unable any longer to connect the data of their experience together, though these data remain severally conscious in dissociation, what is the condition on which this inability of the soul depends? Is it an impotence in the soul itself? or it is an impotence in the physiological conditions, which fail to stimulate the soul sufficiently to its synthetic task? The *how* supposes on the Soul's part a constitution adequate to the act. An hypothesis, we are told in the logic-books, ought to propose a being that has some other constitution and definition than that of barely performing the phenomenon it is evoked to explain. When physicists propose the "ether," for example, they propose it with a lot of incidental properties. But the soul proposed to us has no special properties or constitution of which we are informed. Nevertheless, since particular conditions do determine its activity, it must have a constitution of some sort. In either case, we ought to know the facts. But the soul-doctrine, as hitherto professed, not only doesn't answer such questions, it doesn't even ask them; and it must be radically rejuvenated if it expects to be greeted again as a useful principle in psychological philosophy. Here is work for our spiritualist colleagues, not only for the coming year, but for the rest of their lives.[12]

---

11. I ought, perhaps, to apologize for not expunging from my printed text these references to Professor Ladd, which were based on the impression left on my mind by the termination of his Physiological Psychology. It would now appear from the paper read by him at the Princeton meeting, and his "Philosophy of Mind," just published, that he disbelieves in the Soul of old-fashioned ontology; and on looking again at the P.P., I see that I may well have misinterpreted his deeper meaning there. I incline to suspect, however, that he had himself not fully disentangled it when that work was written; and that between now and then his thought has been evolving somewhat, as Lotze's did, between his "Medical Psychology" and his "Metaphysic." It is gratifying to note these converging tendencies in different philosophers; but I leave the text as I read it at Princeton, as a mark of what one could say not so very unnaturally at that date.

12. The soul can be taken in three ways as a unifying principle. An already existing lot of animated sensations (or other psychic data) may be simply *woven* into one by it; in which case the form of unity is the soul's only contribution, and the original stuff of the Many remains in the One as its stuff also. Or, secondly, the resultant synthetic One may be regarded as an immanent *reaction* of the Soul on the preexisting psychic Many; and in this case the Soul, in addition to creating the new form, reproduces in itself the old stuff of the

7. *The world-soul.*   The second spiritualist theory may be named as that of *transcendentalism.* I take it typically and not as set forth by any single author. Transcendentalism explains things by an over-soul of which all separate souls, sensations, thoughts, and data generally are parts. To be, as it would be known together with everything else in the world by this over-soul, is for transcendentalism the *true* condition of each single thing, and to pass into this condition is for things to fulfill their vocation. Such being known together, since it is the innermost reality of life, cannot on transcendentalist principles be explained or accounted for as a work wrought on a previous sort of reality. The monadic soul-theory starts with separate sensational data, and must show how they are *made* one. The transcendentalist theory has rather for its task to show how, being one, they can spuriously and illusorily be made to appear separate. The problem for the monadic soul, in short, is that of unification, and the problem for the over-soul is that of insulation. The removal of insulating obstructions would sufficiently account for things reverting to their natural place in the over-soul and being known together. The most natural insulating or individualizing principle to invoke is the bodily organism. As the pipes of an organ let the pressing mass of air escape only in single notes, so do our brains, the organ pipes of the infinite, keep back everything but the slender threads of truth to which they may be pervious. As they obstruct more, the insulation increases, as they obstruct less it disappears. Now transcendental philosophers have as a rule not done much dabbling in psychology. But one sees no abstract reason why they might not go into psychology as fully as any one, and erect a psychophysical science of the conditions of more separate and less separate cognition which would include all the facts that psycho-physicists in general might discover. And they would have the advantage over other psycho-physicists of not needing to explain the nature of the resultant knowing-together when it should occur, for they could say that they simply begged it as the ultimate nature of the world.

This is as broad a disjunction as I can make of the different ways in which men have considered the conditions of our knowing things together. You will agree with me that I have brought no new insight to the subject, and that I have only gossiped to while away this unlucky presidential hour to which the constellations doomed me at my birth. But since gossip we have had to have, let me make the hour more gossipy still by saying a final word about the position taken up in my own *Principles of Psychology* on the general question before us, a position which, as you doubtless remember, was so vigorously attacked by our colleague from the University of Pennsylvania at our meeting in New

---

Many, superseding it for our use, and making it for us become subliminal, but not suppressing its existence. Or, thirdly, the One may again be the Soul's immanent reaction on a physiological, not on a mental, Many. In this case preexisting *sensations or ideas* would not be there at all, to be either woven together or superseded. The synthetic One would be a primal psychic datum with parts, either of which might know the same object that a possible sensation, realized under other physiological conditions, could also know.

York a year ago.[13] That position consisted in this, that I proposed to simply eliminate from psychology "considered as a natural science" the whole business of ascertaining *how* we come to know things together or to know them at all. Such considerations, I said, should fall to metaphysics. That we do know things, sometimes singly and sometimes together, is a fact. That states of consciousness are the vehicle of the knowledge, and depend on brain states, are two other facts. And I thought that a natural science of psychology might legitimately confine itself to tracing the functional variations of these three sorts of fact, and ascertaining and tracing what determinate bodily states are the condition when the states of mind know determinate things and groups of things. Most states of mind can be designated only by naming what objects they are "thoughts-of," i.e., what things they know.

Most of those which know compound things are utterly unique and solitary mental entities demonstrably different from any collection of simpler states to which the same objects might be singly known.[14] Treat them all as unique in entity, I said then; let their complexity reside in their plural cognitive function; and you have a psychology which, if it doesn't ultimately explain the facts, also does not, in expressing them, make them self-contradictory (as the associationist psychology does when it calls them many ideas fused into one idea) or pretend to explain them (as the soul-theory so often does) by a barren verbal principle.

---

13. Printed as an article entitled "The Psychological Standpoint," in this *Review*, Vol. 1, p. 113. (March, 1894.)

14. When they know conceptually they don't even remotely resemble the simpler states. When they know intuitively they resemble, sometimes closely, sometimes distantly, the simpler states. The sour and sweet in lemonade are extremely unlike the sour and sweet of lemon juice and sugar, singly taken, yet like enough for us to "recognize" these "objects" in the compound taste. The several objective "notes" recognized in the chord sound differently and peculiarly there. In a motley field of view successive and simultaneous contrast give to each several tint a different hue and luminosity from that of the "real" color into which it turns when viewed without its neighbors by a rested eye. The difference is sometimes so slight, however, that we overlook the "representative" character of each of the parts of a complex content, and speak as if the latter were a cluster of the original "intuitive" states of mind that, occurring singly, know the "object's" several parts in separation. Prof. Meinong, for example, even after the true state of things had been admirably set forth by Herr H. Cornelius (in the *Vierteljahrschrift f. wiss. Phil.*, 16, 404; 17, 30), returns to the defence of the radical associationist view (in the *Zeitschrift f. Psychologie*, 6, 340, 417). According to him, the single sensations of the several notes lie unaltered in the chord-sensations; but his analysis of the phenomenon is vitiated by his nonrecognition of the fact that the *same objects* (i.e., the notes) *can be known* representatively through one compound state of mind, and directly in several simple ones, without the simple and the compound states having strictly anything in common with each other. In Meinong's earlier work, Ueber Begriff und Eigenschaften der Empfindung (*Vierteljahrschrift*, vol. 12), he seems to me to have hit the truth much better, when he says that the aspect *color*, e.g., in a concrete sensation of *red*, is not an abstractable *part* of the sensation, but an *external relation of resemblance* between that sensation and other sensations to the whole lot of which we give the name of colors. Such, I should say, are the aspects of *c, e, g* and *c'* in the chord. We may call them *parts* of the chord if we like, but they are not *bits* of it, identical with *c*'s, *e*'s, *g*'s and *c''*'s elsewhere. They simply resemble the *c*'s, *e*'s, *g*'s and *c''*'s elsewhere, and know these contents or objects representatively.

My intention was a good one, and a natural science infinitely more complete than the psychologies we now possess could be written without abandoning its terms. Like all authors, I have, therefore, been surprised that this child of my genius should not be more admired by others—should, in fact, have been generally either misunderstood or despised. But do not fear that on this occasion I am either going to defend or to re-explain the bantling. I am going to make things more harmonious by simply *giving it up*. I have become convinced since publishing that book that no conventional restrictions *can* keep metaphysical and so-called epistemological inquiries out of the psychology books. I see, moreover, better now than then that my proposal to designate mental states merely by their cognitive function leads to a somewhat strained way of talking of dreams and reveries, and to quite an unnatural way of talking of some emotional states. I am willing, consequently, henceforward that mental contents should be called complex, just as their objects are, and this even in psychology. Not because their parts are separable, as the parts of objects are; not because they have an eternal or quasi-eternal individual existence, like the parts of objects; for the various "contents" of which they are parts are integers, existentially, and their parts only live as long as *they* live. Still, *in* them, we can call parts, parts.—But when, without circumlocution or disguise, I thus come over to your views, I insist that those of you who applaud me (if any such there be) should recognize the obligations which the new agreement imposes on yourselves. Not till you have dropped the old phrases, so absurd or so empty, of ideas "self-compounding" or "united by a spiritual principle"; not till you have in your turn succeeded in some such long inquiry into conditions as the one I have just failed in; not till you have laid bare more of the nature of that altogether unique kind of complexity in unity which mental states involve; not till then, I say, will psychology reach any real benefit from the conciliatory spirit of which I have done what I can to set an example.

Reprinted with permission
from *Psychological Review*,
1896, *3*, 134–148.

Chapter 4

The Progress of Psychology as an Experimental Science

J. McKeen Cattell

Columbia University

In the struggle for existence that obtains among the sciences psychology is continually gaining ground. We bear witness to the fact meeting here on terms of equality with the other natural sciences. This Association demonstrates the organic unity of psychology, while the wide range of our individual interests proves our adjustment to a complex environment.

While our confidence in the future of psychology rests on a knowledge of its intrinsic vitality, we are able for the convincing of others to offer the brute argument of material success. The academic growth of psychology in America during the past few years is almost without

[This address with the nonspecific title of Address of the President of the American Psychological Association was presented at the Fourth Annual Meeting of the American Psychological Association, Philadelphia, Pennsylvania, 1895.]

precedent. The work begun by James at Harvard, Ladd at Yale, and Hall at Johns Hopkins not more than about fifteen years ago has become an important factor in our universities. Psychology is a required subject in the undergraduate curriculum wherever studies are required, and among university courses psychology now rivals the other leading sciences in the number of students attracted and in the amount of original work accomplished.

In addition to the objective test of university recognition we may regard productiveness in publication. There are in America three journals of general science, in all of which psychology is treated as are the other sciences, and there are special journals as follows: mathematics, 3; astronomy, 3; physics, 1; chemistry, 2; geology, 2; botany, 2; zoology, 1; physiology, 0; psychology, 2. A comparison of these journals will not discredit those devoted to psychology; and it should be noted that we have in addition to these at least two journals of philosophy and two journals of education in which psychology occupies a prominent place. It would be difficult to select by an objective criterion the most important books published in America during the past ten years, but if we may regard the judgment of foreign nations as the most probable verdict of posterity, the books written by members of this Association will stand well to the front among American contributions to science.

We must admit that the rapid growth of psychology in America has been due to conditions of the soil as well as to vitality of the germ. The more complete absorption of the college president by executive work has made necessary the transferring of his former prerogative of teacher of philosophy to the special student, while the development of the university with elective courses has permitted the easy introduction of a new study.

It follows that a comparison of the progress of psychology in America with its progress in other countries is less flattering to our *amour propre* as psychologists than to our patriotism. Still Germany maintains its prestige in psychology, and psychology maintains its prestige in Germany. Psychological courses are an increasingly large part of the philosophical courses, and the laboratories of psychology are being acknowledged as equal in rank to those in other sciences. There are two excellent journals of psychology, one of which is attracting part of the best work formerly published in physiological and physical journals. In France the *Année psychologique* bears witness to much recent work in experimental psychology, while interest in social, individual and pathological psychology is unabated. In England the traditional psychology is being enriched by absorption of the most important foreign work, while new contributions are offered on the side of philosophy and on the side of the biological and the medical sciences. In Russia, in Scandinavia and in Italy professorships and laboratories are being established.

While the recent progress of our science has been great, we do not admit that psychology is a new science. It is not a "sport," not even a fortuitous variation. If science is to date from the year of "the master of those who know," then we may take pride in the beginnings of psychology whose foundations were more securely laid by Aristotle than those of any other science. Like the little boy answering the first question of the Catechism we may say "God made one foot big and I growed the rest." But with our superior knowledge of embryology we may further believe that we did not start even as an infant of the size of the famous one in "Midshipman Easy," but began our inarticulate growth long before "mewing and puking" we came hither.

Even the "new psychology" began at the beginning, and developed *pari passu* with the other sciences. Take, for example, a subject, not of leading importance, but typical of the problems studied in our laboratories—after-images. We have in after-images a case where we investigate the relations of the change in consciousness to the physical stimulus on the one hand and to the bodily organism on the other, where we make experiments and measurements on phenomena known to us only on the side of the individual consciousness, a case where we may hope for useful applications in education, in medicine, etc. We have in after-images phenomena related to and throwing light on a large range of mental activity—imagery, memory, hallucinations, space-perception, etc., and even of interest (see, for example, what Royce has to say in Vol. 3 of the *Philosophical Review*) in their bearing on epistemology and metaphysics. Now after-images, phenomena thus typical of modern experimental psychology, were described by Aristotle with such exactness that we may feel sure that he himself made experiments upon them, whereas he refers to them as though they were familiar to his readers. Experiments upon after-images have been made by men eminent in widely separated fields of mental activity—by Augustine, Newton, Buffon, the elder Darwin, Goethe and many more—long before the date usually assigned to the development of psychology as an experimental science. I have perhaps selected a favorable example, but I think there are but few subjects now in course of investigation in our laboratories whose origin and gradual development could not be traced a long way back.

I may mention parenthetically that the earliest explicit formulation of the problems of experimental psychology, as I understand them, is to be found not in Lotze, nor in Fechner, nor in Wundt, but in the most visionary and poetic of poets, himself a problem in heredity, character and intellect far beyond the reach of our psychology. Shelley wrote[1] about eighty years ago:

A scale might be formed, graduated according to the degrees of a combined scale of intensity, duration, connexion, periods of recurrence, and utility, which would be the standard, according to which all ideas might be measured, and an uninterrupted chain of nicely shadowed distinctions would be observed, from the faintest impression on the senses, to the most distinct combination of those impressions; from the simplest of those combinations, to that mass of knowledge which, including our own nature, constitutes what we call the universe.

---

1. Shelley's Works, Forman's Edition, 6, 285. *Speculations on Metaphysics.*

While psychology traces its descent through a long and noble line, we need not hesitate to mark a natural, but at the same time a notable, development under our own eyes and hands. A little while ago the psychologist might still say with Browning's *Cleon:*

> And I have written three books on the soul,
> Proving absurd all written hitherto,
> And putting us to ignorance again.

But we are past the time for systems of psychology; now handbooks of psychology are prepared. We have, like the other sciences, a small area lighted by ascertained fact and accepted theory, outside this is the penumbra, and beyond is darkness through which none of us pretends to see. We, indeed, estimate differently the importance of different departments and the hopefulness of different lines of research, but in this respect we only exhibit the human nature in whose study we are engaged. The student of mechanics proposes to account for all physical phenomena by Newton's laws, the student of electricity by electric vibrations, etc. An eminent chemist recently remarked that chemistry is evidently the basis of psychology.

It is, however, possible that we over-emphasize the differences that do exist. Certainly there is no member of this Association who believes that science should be a *tohu-wabohu* of facts, nor any who believes that reasonable theories can be devised without regard to facts. Probably none of us would claim that he could draw a straight line and say: "on this side is science, on that side is philosophy." Possibly none would say: "these observations have no scientific validity, because they rest on introspection," or "these determinations have no psychological interest, because they are mere measurements." Rather we all join in the admirable words of our President at the New York meeting:

> Let us all always be just; nay, let us be something more than merely just; let us be generous. And let our generosity include all workmen of all times, with their works, from Aristotle's *De Anima* to the latest thesis by the youngest aspirant for the degree of Doctor of Philosophy.

While science advances along many paths, there are certain highways most traveled and most direct. What these are in psychology at the present time the analogy of the other sciences may perhaps indicate. We cannot, I think, doubt, but that modern science is either quantitative or genetic. I say "either" because there is at present a partial divorce between the physical sciences in which the relative permanence of the phenomena makes the quantitative point of view easy and the genetic difficult, and the biological sciences in which the converse conditions obtain. This divorce is, however, due rather to our ignorance than to our knowledge. In the progress of science the physical sciences will become increasingly genetic and the biological sciences increasingly quantitative.

Astronomy learned the laws of Kepler before it learned the nebular hypothesis. The physicist could not find in the star-dust the problems of modern physics and chemistry. There is variation and survival in the inorganic as well as in the organic world. The biologist in turn should no longer rest content with describing the genesis of species and of individuals, but should measure variations and changes, and determine causal relations by the methods of exact science.

It would seem likely that methods prevailing in the other sciences should also hold in psychology, more especially as we must admit that most of these sciences have passed through the stage in which psychology now is—or until recently was—and have reached a clearer self-consciousness. But we do not need to depend exclusively on the often delusive argument from analogy. Recent work in psychology speaks with sufficient emphasis in favor of tracing the genesis and the degeneration of mental states on the one hand, and their quantitative definition on the other.

I think we may claim without undue self-assertion that the most important contributions to genetic psychology made during the past year have come from members of this Association. Baldwin has treated with an elaboration hitherto unequalled, the mental development of the child and of the race; Stanley has studied the evolutionary psychology of feeling; and Royce has analysed the genesis of the contents of the individual consciousness in its dependence on social environment and evolution with great acuteness. While much of the definite outcome is still *sub judice*, there is none to question the validity of the genetic method.

When we turn to the quantitative method in psychology we find, I fear, more difference of opinion. We have, indeed, our many laboratories, all of which are at least silent witnesses in its favor. But several of our leading members have expressed, at the meetings of this Association and in their published writings, doubts as to the validity, or at all events as to the value, of mental measurements.

Now it is easy to adopt a skeptical point of view in such a matter. By the nature of things men of science and students of philosophy are quit of the enthusiasm of the proselytizer and reformer. The every-day up-hill work of the laboratory is scarcely more stimulating than the routine of the factory or of the farm. Each, as Clough's *Dipsychus* tells us,

> Must slave, a meager coral-worm
> To build beneath the tide with excrement
> What one day will be island, or be reef,
> And will feed men, or wreck them.

But this skeptical point of view can be applied with equal success and equal futility to any science, or to the conduct of daily life. We may, if we see fit, wonder why anybody does anything. By common consent the discovery of argon in the atmosphere was the most important scientific advance of the past year, but it has not as yet been found that argon is of any practical use, and, so far from helping us to understand the universe, this substance but adds to its apparent complexity. Why not let the last decimal be, and enjoy the air in the springtime—or devise means to keep out of it if one happen to live near Boston?

Münsterberg has written: "Die Messung ist niemals Selbstzweck in der Psychologie, eben dadurch unterscheidet sie sich von der Physik." Now it seems to me, on the contrary, that measurements have just the same place in psychology as in the material sciences, except in so far as they have not been as yet so successfully prosecuted. The immediate end of science, whether physical or mental, is to describe the world—it may be added, and to explain it, though if we had a complete and unified description, it is not clear what would be left to explain. We wish to describe the world, partly because our knowledge can be applied in useful ways, and partly because the effort satisfies mental needs, as do art and religion. Measurements in the physical sciences are in a way means to the ends mentioned, but in so far as a description of the world is an end in itself, measurements are a part of this description, and by far the most exact, general and economical method of description hitherto devised.

It may be that in psychology the field for quantitative definition is more limited than in the case of the physical sciences. The lack of many or wide-reaching numerical formulas expressing mental relations may be due not so much to the recentness of our attempts to discover these as to the nature of the subject-matter with which we are dealing. Indeed it is evident that as a mere matter of definition we have to a large extent limited the physical sciences to a quantitative treatment of time, space and energy, relegating qualitative differences to consciousness. But it is also true that the quantitative point of view in physical science has only gradually and but recently emerged from a chaos of animistic and teleological conceptions. The unitary point of view developed by physical science is truly a matter for marvel. The awe inspired in the great mystic of rationalism by the starry heavens and the moral law may well pervade the student of physics in the presence of the unforeseen grandeur and simplicity of his own handiwork.

It is, indeed, true that measurements give as yet only a partial description even of the physical world, and the progress of science may make this less rather than more adequate. The ether, elastic and solid as it is supposed to be, seems on the point of breaking under the load laid upon it. Atoms are stumbling blocks, however small we may assume them. Ludwig, chiefly instrumental in establishing for a while a mechanical theory of living tissues, lived long enough to witness the emergence of a neo-vitalism. Indeed Ludwig himself, on being asked why he did not prepare a new edition of his *Physiology* said, "Such a work must be written by a young man; an old man is too well aware of his ignorance." We are as the earth in the Hebrew cosmogony, when the light had been separated from the darkness, but the sun had not yet been set in the firmament.

Both the success and the failure of material science may encourage the experimental psychologist. He may hope to accomplish much by measurements, even though he may foresee that he will not accomplish everything. Whether he be entrusted with one talent or with many, he can serve in better ways than in standing and waiting.

This commingling of hopeful endeavor and hopeless limitation drawn from the analogy of physical science may be more directly deduced from the work hitherto accomplished in the psychological laboratory. This has indeed been called trivial and pedantic, and has been wounded even in the house of its friends. Statistics, averages and probable errors seem remote from the complex fulness of human nature. There seems imminent danger from a neo-scholasticism with measurements in the place of definitions.

Now when it is said that nothing has been done beyond measuring time, intensity, and complexity of sensations, movements and mental processes, the reply may readily be made that nothing further can be desired. Physical science measures only time, space and energy. If psychology can do as much it has the same abundance of individual problems; if it need do no more it has the same great simplicity as its goal.

The use of averages and probable errors in psychology is not pedantic, except when attempted by those not acquainted with their meaning. The probable error tells us just how many experiments we ought to make and just what reliance may be placed upon them. The theory of probabilities, enabling us to measure both our knowledge and our ignorance, is one of the great achievements of the human intellect, and is equally applicable in sciences attaining varying degrees of exactness. It was, indeed, pedantic for Helmholtz to give the velocity of the nervous impulse as 37.4927 m. per second, when the average velocity and the individual variations are not known within tens of meters. But it is exactly an application of probable errors that would prevent such pedantry, and if the greatest of physicists has on occasion indulged in it, we need not too severely blame the student preparing his doctor's thesis for carrying his average a decimal beyond what is warranted by the theory of probabilities.

In some cases a very considerable degree of accuracy is attainable and necessary in psycho-physical measurements. Thus doubling the intensity of the stimulus shortens the reaction-time about 0.001 sec., and if we wish to determine the relation between intensity of stimulus and duration of reaction we must measure to the ten-thousandth of a second, and the averages and probable errors show that such a degree of accuracy is attainable. The apparatus used for the purpose in the psychological laboratory of Columbia College has this year been borrowed by professors in the physical department to measure the rate of fall of bodies in liquids, and it has resulted that the constancy of the physical motions is less than that of the psycho-physical processes.

Such problems—the correlations of quantities—are those ultimate in exact science, and in so far as they can be undertaken in psychology it becomes an exact science. It may be said that in the example given we are concerned with the nervous system rather than with consciousness. But even if this be exclusively the case it may be urged that a dynamics of the nervous system is essential to a final psychology. Further, the correlations of quantities may be investigated in cases in which we know the changes in consciousness, but are completely ignorant of the neural processes which may accompany them. Thus we all are familiar with the many investigations on the discrimination of differences in intensity. There is room for various interpretations of the meaning of a just noticeable difference, but by definition differences in sensation are equal if they be equally perceptible. We can find when differences are equally perceptible by determining the percentage of times in which they are in fact correctly perceived. But we can approach the problem from a new point of view, first defined, I believe, at the New York meeting of this Association, involving the correlation of mental magnitudes.

If differences be equally perceptible it takes equal times to discriminate them, and the less the difference in sensation the greater the time required. By measuring the time of discrimination it is possible to determine differences in the intensity of sensation. We can thus investigate the relation of the intensity of stimulus to the accuracy of discrimination (Weber's law), and can even use the method for the comparison of disparate sensations. We may find that the difference between red and blue is equal, say, to the difference between sensations due to lights from 10 to 1,000 candles, or even that the difference between the tones C and c is equal to the difference between certain visual sensations.

The appeal made to different minds by such problems as part of a worthy description of the world must of necessity vary with the individual mind. Our goals in religion, art, philosophy and science are not only wide apart, but they also shift even as we run. Our science and our philosophy are but as a doll in the arms of a little girl, who does not know what it means nor what the years will bring.

I think, however, that conclusive testimony may be advanced to prove that psychological experiment has had and will have both practical applications and an important share in psychology as a whole, whether regard be had to its individual development or to its relations with the other sciences.

Professor Burdon Sanderson, in his presidential address before the Ipswich meeting of the British Association, said that he was not aware of any useful application of experimental psychology, and Professor Morley, president of the American Association, said, at the recent Springfield meeting, "science cannot change human natures or the social order." These selected representatives of science in England and America, however, both hold that science has an adequate end in the satisfaction of intellectual curiosity. On the other hand Franklin, the father of American science, speaks of new discoveries as important only because they tend "to extend the power of man over matter, avert or diminish the evils he is subject to, or augment the number of his enjoyments." Franklin's point of view may be regarded as materialistic, but science for the sake of science is in turn in danger of dilettantism.

We may be glad that experimental psychology has practical applications in spite of quasi-official dicta to the contrary. In the United States more than one hundred and fifty million dollars, collected by enforced taxation, is spent annually on public schools in the attempt to "change human natures." President Eliot says that nothing is accomplished in these schools except the training of the memory, and his colleague, our retiring president, tells us that the memory cannot be trained.[2] Surely in education, which extends from birth to death, we can learn by experiments on the senses and the mind what may be done to fit the individual to his environment. It should not be forgotten that we not only hold the clay in our hands to mold for honor or dishonor, but we also have the ultimate decision as to what material we shall use. The physicist can turn his pig iron into steel, and so can we ours; but he cannot alter the quantities of gold and iron in his world, whereas we can in ours. Our responsibility is, indeed, very great. By one psychological experiment we injure the eyesight of our children in the schools, and by another psychological experiment we discover the defect and fit glasses to correct it. It seems to me certain that experimental psychology has wide-reaching practical applications, not only in education, but also in medicine, in the fine arts, in political economy and, indeed, in the whole conduct of life.

It also seems evident that experimental psychology has recently become an important factor in the development of psychology as a whole, both by its actual contributions and by the changes in method to which it has given rise. The psycho-physical camel will never be able to exclude the psychological Arab from his tent, but it must be welcomed, or at least tolerated. A comparison of modern text-books of psychology, such as those by James, Ladd, Baldwin, and Dewey, with older works bears irrefutable witness to the introduction of the results of physiological and psychological experiment. I shall undertake the *argumentum ad hominem* in the case of James, who said at our last meeting that "curious phenomena of the dissociation of consciousness. . . throw more new light on human nature than the work of all psycho-physical laboratories put together." On taking down James' *Psychology*—which has breathed the breath of life into the dust of psychology—and turning at random to the even hundred pages, I find that the first is entirely taken up with the measurement of the temperature of the brain in relation to thought; the second is on continuity of consciousness with time measurements; the third a description of the bodily movements giving the consciousness of self; the fourth on the relation of the two hemispheres of the brain and of bodily movements to self-consciousness; the fifth on the relative intensity of sensations and images; the sixth on the association of ideas; the seventh on observations and experiments on the mistaken interpretation

---

2. As Professor James said at the meeting, he only holds that native retentiveness is unchangeable. It was not, of course, intended in this paradox to adequately represent the views of President Eliot and Professor James.

of sense-stimuli; the eighth on the relation of movements of the eyes to the perception of space; the ninth on the factors distinguishing the perception of reality; the tenth on instinctive actions; the eleventh on muscular sensations; the twelfth on hypnotic suggestion. These topics illustrate very fairly the field covered by modern psychology. They nearly all rest upon psycho-physical observations and experiments, and in cases where observations predominate it is evident that they will soon be superseded by actual experiments from our laboratories yielding quantitative results.

Even in directions where experiment has not yet offered considerable contributions, it has performed an important service in setting a standard of carefulness and objectivity. It may also be urged that experiment serves as a stimulus and starting point for thought. Thus Wundt states that his theory of the development of the will and of its relation to "apperception" had its origin in observations made during the course of experiments on the reaction-time. It requires peculiar genius to sit down at a desk and write out observations and theories that are new and true; they are more likely to occur during actual work of some sort. Further, there are many who can carry out experiments in the laboratory who are incapable of constructive work. The data obtained by them may be seen by others in their larger relations. The generalizations of a Newton must be based upon the observations of a Flamsteed.

The introduction of experiment has also made the teaching of psychology easier and more useful. Laboratory work by students is by common consent an important part of their training. Whether the experiments be in chemistry or in psychology may not greatly matter. In the chemical laboratory, when the course is intended for liberal training, the experiments are meant to educate the senses and the mind, rather than to give information concerning metals and acids. When the object of an experiment is not to learn what happens when two solutions are mixed, but to teach the student to observe what happens, we may perhaps claim that a psychological experiment has been undertaken. Whether experiments directed to the senses and the mind would serve better or worse than others for the purpose in view, or whether it is practicable to introduce a new study into the preparatory school or the early college years, are matters that can themselves only be settled by experiment. It is, however, certain that such preliminary work, or, lacking it, some experiments introduced into the course in psychology commonly offered and even required in the junior year, would enable the average student to follow this course with greater interest and intelligence, so that he would be less likely to regard it as:

A tale
Told by an idiot, full of sound and fury,
Signifying nothing.

I venture to maintain that the introduction of experiment and measurement into psychology has added directly and indirectly new subject-matter and methods, has set a higher standard of accuracy and objectivity, has made some part of the subject an applied science with useful applications, and has enlarged the field and improved the methods of teaching psychology. In conclusion I wish to urge that experiment in psychology has made its relations with the other sciences more intimate and productive of common good.

In courses in physics, for example, certain psychological subjects, vision, hearing, etc., have always been included. The treatment has of necessity been inadequate, and the student, if not the teacher, may have left the subject with confused notions, e.g., as to the distinction between light as a mode of motion and color as sensation. Or it may be incidentally stated that color, pitch and warmth are "subjective," while matter in motion is alone "real." Now the treatment of certain subjects in common with physics has set for the psychologist a higher scientific standard, whereas it may be hoped that the physicist has learned that processes of perception and thought are part of the real world which science as a whole must take into account.

In physiology the treatment of certain subjects in common must ultimately result in mutual benefit. Our host Fullerton showed this morning how largely the physiology of the nervous system leaves its proper field for that of psychology. The physiologist must face the problem as to whether consciousness shall be assumed in causal interaction with the nervous system. It may not matter greatly to us whether cerebral functions are located here or there, but it would be a survival or an atavism to hold that we can fully treat processes of perception, ideation, feeling or will without regard to sense organs, movements, paths of conduction and nervous centers, or even apart from metabolism and circulation of the blood.

In general biology, whose great problem is the development of life, zoology-botany and psychology cannot advance excepting hand in hand. Darwin did not hesitate to use consciousness as a *vera causa* in the preservation of species, and Cope, now presiding over our sister society, urges that it is a preeminent cause in their origin. Sensations, movements, instincts and habits are prominent in any theory of the evolution of species, and they must be treated in common by physical zoology and psychology. The importance of these problems is borne witness to by the fact that we have selected them for special discussion to-morrow morning. For many the leading interest in organic evolution is in its application to social evolution, and it is scarcely necessary to mention the relation of psychology to sociology, which science is indeed simply collective psychology.

Psychology has long been and properly remains the gateway to architectonic philosophy. It may be that experiment cannot answer the final questions of philosophy, but the world-view of each of us depends increasingly on what the natural and exact sciences contribute to it. The white light of philosophy can only result from the proper commingling of the colors of the sciences. Systems of philosophy, elaborated prior to the development of modern science or without regard to this, may receive our admiration as poetry, but they cannot claim our adherence as truth. To allot to science those subjects concerning which we have knowledge, and to reserve for philosophy those questions concerning which we know nothing, is evidently subversive of philosophy. Epistemology, ethics, logic and aesthetics are regarded as philosophic disciplines, but they rest increasingly on psychology. Epistemology depends on the psychology of perception and may be nothing else. Works on ethics, logic and aesthetics take increasing account of psychological facts; indeed, as our knowledge increases, the distinction between a normative and a descriptive science becomes somewhat tenuous. The twilight of philosophy can be changed to its dawn only by the light of science, and psychology can contribute more light than any other science.

Reprinted with permission
from *Psychological Review*,
1900, 7, 105–124.

Chapter 5

Psychology and Social Practice

John Dewey

University of Chicago

In coming before you I had hoped to deal with the problem of the relation of psychology to the social sciences—and through them to social practice, to life itself. Naturally, in anticipation, I had conceived a systematic exposition of fundamental principles covering the whole ground, and giving every factor its due rating and position. That discussion is not ready to-day. I am loath, however, completely to withdraw from the subject, especially as there happens to be a certain phase of it with which I have been more or less practically occupied within the last few years. I have in mind the relation of Psychology to Education. Since education is primarily a social affair, and since educational science is first of all a social science, we have here a section of the whole field. In some respects there may be an advantage in approaching the more comprehensive question through the medium of one of its special cases. The absence of elaborated and coherent view may be made up for by a background of experience, which shall check the projective power of reflective abstraction, and secure a translation of large words and ideas into specific images. This special territory,

---

Address of the President before the American Psychological Association, New Haven, 1899.

moreover, may be such as to afford both sign-posts and broad avenues to the larger sphere—the place of psychology among the social sciences. Because I anticipate such an outcome, and because I shall make a survey of the broad field from the special standpoint taken, I make no apology for presenting this discussion to an Association of Psychologists rather than to a gathering of educators.

In dealing with this particular question, it is impossible not to have in mind the brilliant and effective discourses recently published by my predecessor in this chair. I shall accordingly make free to refer to points, and at times to words, in his treatment of the matter. Yet, as perhaps I hardly need say, it is a problem of the most fundamental importance for both psychology and social theory that I wish to discuss, not any particular book or article. Indeed with much of what Dr. Münsterberg says about the uselessness and the danger for the teacher of miscellaneous scraps of child study, of unorganized information regarding the nervous sytem, and of crude and uninterpreted results of laboratory experiment, I am in full agreement. It is doubtless necessary to protest against a hasty and violent bolting of psychological facts and principles which, of necessity, destroys their scientific form. It is necessary to point out the need of a preliminary working over of psychological material adapting it to the needs of education. But these are minor points. The main point is whether the standpoint of psychological science, as a study of mechanism, is indifferent and opposed to the demands of education with its free interplay of personalities in their vital attitudes and aims.

I

The school practice of to-day has a definite psychological basis. Teachers are already possessed by specific psychological assumptions which control their theory and their practice. The greatest obstacle to the introduction of certain educational reforms is precisely the permeating persistence of the underlying psychological creed. Traced back to its psychological ultimates, there are two controlling bases of existing methods of instruction. One is the assumption of a fundamental distinction between child psychology and the adult psychology where, in reality, identity, reigns; viz.: in the region of the motives and conditions which make for mental power. The other is the assumption of likeness where marked difference is the feature most significant for educational purposes; I mean the specialization of aims and habits in the adult, compared with the absence of specialization in the child, and the connection of undifferentiated status with the full and free growth of the child.

The adult is primarily a person with a certain calling and position in life. These devolve upon him certain specific responsibilities which he has to meet, and call into play certain formed habits. The child is primarily one whose calling is growth. He is concerned with arriving at specific ends and purposes—instead of having a general framework already developed. He is engaged in forming habits rather than in definitely utilizing those already formed. Consequently he is absorbed in getting that all around contact with persons and things, that range of acquaintance with the physical and ideal factors of life, which shall afford the background and material for the specialized aims and pursuits of later life. He is, or should be, busy in the formation of a flexible variety of habits whose sole immediate criterion is their relation to full growth, rather than in acquiring certain skills whose value is measured by their reference to specialized technical accomplishments. This is the radical psychological and biological distinction, I take it, between the child and the adult. It is because of this distinction that children are neither physiologically nor mentally describable as "little men and women."

The full recognition of this distinction means of course the selection and arrangement of all school materials and methods for the facilitation of full normal growth, trusting to the result in growth to provide the instrumentalities of later specialized adaptation. If education means the period of prolonged infancy, it means nothing less than this. But look at our school system and ask whether the 3 R's are taught, either as to subject matter or as to method, with reference to growth, to its present demands and opportunities; or as technical acquisitions which are to be needed in the specialized life of the adult. Ask the same questions about geography, grammar and history. The gap between psychological theory and the existing school practice becomes painfully apparent. We readily realize the extent to which the present school system is dominated by carrying over into child life a standpoint and method which are significant in the psychology of the adult.

The narrow scope of the traditional elementary curriculum, the premature and excessive use of logical analytic methods, the assumption of ready-made faculties of observation, memory, attention, etc., which can be brought into play if only the child chooses to do so, the ideal of formal discipline—all these find a large measure of their explanation in neglect of just this psychological distinction between the child and the adult. The hold of these affairs upon the school is so fixed that it is impossible to shake it in any fundamental way, excepting by a thorough appreciation of the actual psychology of the case. This appreciation cannot be confined to the educational leaders and theorists. No individual instructor can be sincere and whole hearted, to say nothing of intelligent, in carrying into effect the needed reforms, save as he genuinely understands the scientific basis and necessity of the change.

But in another direction there is the assumption of a fundamental difference: Namely, as to the conditions which secure intellectual and moral progress and power.[1] No one seriously questions that, with an

---

1. I owe this point specifically (as well as others more generally) to my friend and colleague, Mrs. Ella Flagg Young.

adult, power and control are obtained through realization of personal ends and problems, through personal selection of means and materials which are relevant, and through personal adaptation and application of what is thus selected, together with whatever of experimentation and of testing is involved in this effort. Practically every one of these three conditions of increase in power for the adult is denied for the child. For him problems and aims are determined by another mind. For him the material that is relevant and irrelevant is selected in advance by another mind. And, upon the whole, there is such an attempt to teach him a ready-made method for applying his material to the solution of his problems, or the reaching of his ends, that the factor of experimentation is reduced to the minimum. With the adult we unquestioningly assume that an attitude of personal inquiry, based upon the possession of a problem which interests and absorbs, is a necessary precondition of mental growth. With a child we assume that the precondition is rather the willing disposition which makes him ready to submit to any problem and material presented from without. Alertness is our ideal in one case; docility in the other. With one, we assume that power of attention develops in dealing with problems which make a personal appeal, and through personal responsibility for determining what is relevant. With the other we provide next to no opportunities for the evolution of problems out of immediate experience, and allow next to no free mental play for selecting, assorting and adapting the experiences and ideas that make for their solution. How profound a revolution in the position and service of text-book and teacher, and in methods of instruction depending therefrom, would be effected by a sincere recognition of the psychological identity of child and adult in these respects can with difficulty be realized.

Here again it is not enough that the educational commanders should be aware of the correct educational psychology. The rank and file, just because they are persons dealing with persons, must have a sufficient grounding in the psychology of the matter to realize the necessity and the significance of what they are doing. Any reform instituted without such conviction on the part of those who have to carry it into effect, would never be undertaken in good faith, nor in the spirit which its ideal inevitably demands; consequently it could lead only to disaster.

At this point, however, the issue defines itself somewhat more narrowly. It may be true, it is true, we are told, that some should take hold of psychological methods and conclusions, and organize them with reference to the assistance which they may give to the cause of education. But this is not the work of the teacher. It belongs to the general educational theorist: the middleman between the psychologist and the educational practitioner. He should put the matter into such shape that the teacher may take the net results in the form of advice and rules for action; but the teacher who comes in contact with the living personalities must not assume the psychological attitude. If he does he reduces persons to objects, and thereby distorts, or rather destroys, the ethical relationship which is the vital nerve of instruction (*Psychology and Life*, p. 122, and pp. 136–138).

That there is some legitimate division of labor between the general educational theorist and the actual instructor, there is of course no doubt. As a rule, it will not be the one actively employed in instruction who will be most conscious of the psychological basis and equivalents of the educational work, nor most occupied in finding the pedagogical rendering of psychological facts and principles. Of necessity, the stress of interest will be elsewhere. But we have already found reason for questioning the possibility of making the somewhat different direction of interest into a rigid dualism of a legislative class on one side and an obedient subject class on the other. Can the teacher ever receive "obligatory prescriptions"? Can he receive from another a statement of the means by which he is to reach his ends, and not become hopelessly servile in his attitude? Would not such a result be even worse than the existing mixture of empiricism and inspiration?—just because it would forever fossilize the empirical element and dispel the inspiration which now quickens routine. Can a passive, receptive attitude on the part of the instructor (suggesting the soldier awaiting orders from a commanding general) be avoided, unless the teacher, as a student of psychology, himself sees the reasons and import of the suggestions and rules that are proffered him?

I quote a passage that seems of significance:

Do we not lay a special linking science everywhere else between the theory and practical work? We have engineering between physics and the practical working-men in the mills; we have a scientific medicine between the natural science and the physician. (p. 138)

The sentences suggest, in an almost startling way, that the real essence of the problem is found in an *organic* connection between the two extreme terms—between the theorist and the practical worker—through the medium of the linking science. The decisive matter is the extent to which the ideas of the theorist actually project themselves, through the kind offices of the middleman, into the consciousness of the practitioner. It is the participation by the practical man in the theory, through the agency of the linking science, that determines at once the effectiveness of the work done, and the moral freedom and personal development of the one engaged in it. It is because the physician no longer follows rules, which, however rational in themselves, are yet arbitrary to him (because grounded in principles that he does not understand), that his work is becoming liberal, attaining the dignity of a profession, instead of remaining a mixture of empiricism and quackery. It is because, alas, engineering makes only a formal and not a real connection between physics and the practical workingmen in the mills that our industrial problem is an ethical problem of the most serious kind. The question of the amount of wages the laborer receives, of the purchasing value of this wage, of the hours and conditions of labor, are, after all, secondary. The problem primarily roots in the fact that the mediating science does not connect with his consciousness, but merely with his outward actions. He does not appreciate the significance and bearing of what he does; and he does not perform his work because of sharing in a larger scientific and social consciousness. If he did, he would be free. All other proper accompaniments of wage, and hours, healthful and inspiring conditions would be added unto him, because he would have entered into the ethical kingdom. Shall we seek analogy with the teacher's calling in the workingmen in the mill, or in the scientific physician?

It is quite likely that I shall be reminded that I am overlooking an essential difference. The physician, it will be said, is dealing with a body which either is in itself a pure object, a causal interplay of anatomical elements, or is something which lends itself naturally and without essential loss to treatment from this point of view; while the case is quite different in the material with which the teacher deals. Here is personality, which is destroyed when regarded as an object. But the gap is not so pronounced nor so serious as this objection implies. The physician after all is not dealing with a lifeless body; with a simple anatomical structure, or interplay of mechanical elements. Life functions, active operations, are the reality which confronts him. We do not have to go back many centuries in the history of medicine to find a time when the physician attempted to deal with these functions directly and immediately. They were so overpoweringly present, they forced themselves upon him so obviously and so constantly that he had no resource save a mixture of magic and empiricism: magic so far as he followed methods derived from uncritical analogy, or from purely general speculation on the universe and life; empiricism so long as he just followed procedures which had been found helpful before in cases which somewhat resembled the present. We have only to trace the intervening history of medicine to appreciate that it is precisely the ability to state function in terms of structure, to reduce life in its active operations to terms of a causal mechanism, which has taken the medical calling out of this dependence upon a vibration between superstition and routine. Progress has come by taking what is really an activity as if it were only an object. It is the capacity to effect this transformation of life activity which measures both the scientific character of the physician's procedure and his practical control, the certainty and efficacy of what he, as a living man, does in relation to some other living man.

It is an old story, however, that we must not content ourselves with analogies. We must find some specific reason in the principles of the teacher's own activities for believing that psychology—the ability to transform a living personality into an objective mechanism for the time being—is not merely an incidental help, but an organic necessity. Upon the whole, the best efforts of teachers at present are partly paralyzed, partly distorted, and partly rendered futile precisely from the fact that they are in such immediate contact with sheer, unanalyzed personality.

The relation is such a purely ethical and personal one that the teacher cannot get enough outside the situation to handle it intelligently and effectively. He is in precisely the condition in which the physician was when he had no recourse save to deal with health as entity or force on one side, and disease as opposing agency or invading influence upon the other. The teacher reacts *en bloc*, in a gross wholesale way, to something which he takes in an equally undefined and total way in the child. It is the inability to regard, upon occasion, both himself and the child as just objects working upon each other in specific ways that compels him to resort to purely arbitrary measures, to fall back upon mere routine traditions of school teaching, or to fly to the latest fad of pedagogical theorists—the latest panacea peddled out in school journals or teachers' institutes—just as the old physician relied upon his magic formula.

I repeat, it is the fundamental weakness of our teaching force to-day (putting aside teachers who are actually incompetent by reason either of wrong motives or inadequate preparation), that they react in gross to the child's exhibitions in gross without analyzing them into their detailed and constituent elements. If the child is angry, he is dealt with simply as an angry being; anger is an entity, a force, not a symptom. If a child is inattentive, this again is treated as a mere case of refusal to use the faculty or function of attention, of sheer unwillingness to act. Teachers tell you that a child is careless or inattentive in the same final way in which they would tell you that a piece of paper is white. It is just a fact, and that is all there is of it. Now it is only through some recognition of attention as a mechanism, some awareness of the interplay of sensations, images and motor impulses which constitute it as an objective fact that the teacher can deal effectively with attention as a function. And, of course, the same is true of memory, quick and useful observation, good judgment and all the other practical powers the teacher is attempting to cultivate.

Consideration of the abstract concepts of mechanism and personality is important. Too much preoccupation with them in a general fashion, however, without translation into relevant imagery of actual conditions is likely to give rise to unreal difficulties. The ethical personality does not go to school naked; it takes with it the body as the instrument through which all influences reach it, and through control of which its ideas are both elaborated and expressed. The teacher does not deal with personality at large, but as expressed in intellectual and practical impulses and habits. The ethical personality is not formed—it is forming. The teacher must provide stimuli leading to the equipment of personality with active habits and interests. When we consider the problem of forming habits and interests we find ourselves at once confronted with matters of this sort: What stimuli shall be presented to the sense organs and how? What stable complexes of associations shall be organized? What motor impulses shall be evoked, and to what extent? How shall they be induced in such a way as to bring favorable stimuli under greater control, and to lessen the danger of excitation from undesirable stimuli? In a word, the teacher is dealing with the psychical factors that are concerned with furtherance of certain habits, and the inhibition of others—habits intellectual, habits emotional, habits in overt action.

Moreover, all the instruments and materials with which the teacher deals must be considered as psychical stimuli. Such consideration involves of necessity a knowledge of their reciprocal reactions—of what goes by the name of causal mechanism. The introduction of certain changes into a net-work of associations, the reinforcement of certain sensori-motor connections, the weakening or displacing of others—this is the psychological rendering of the greater part of the teacher's actual business. It is not that one teacher employs mechanical considerations, and that the other does not, appealing to higher ends; it is that one does not know his mechanism, and consequently acts servilely, superstitiously and blindly, while the other, knowing what he is about, acts freely, clearly and effectively.[2]

The same thing is true on the side of materials of instruction—the school studies. No amount of exaltation of teleological personality (however true, and however necessary the emphasis) can disguise from us the fact that instruction is an affair of bringing a child into intimate relations with concrete objects, positive facts, definite ideas and specific symbols. The symbols are objective things in arithmetic, reading and writing. The ideas are truths of history and of science. The facts are derived from such specific disciplines as geography and language, botany and astronomy. To suppose that by some influence of pure personality upon pure personality, conjoined with a knowledge of rules formulated by an educational theorist, an effective interplay of this body of physical and ideal objects with the life of the child can be effective, is, I submit, nothing but an appeal to magic, plus dependence upon servile routine. Symbols in reading and writing and number, are both in themselves, and in the way in which they stand for ideas, elements in a mechanism which has to be rendered operative within the child. To bring about this influence in the most helpful and economical way, in the most fruitful and liberating way, is absolutely impossible save as the teacher has some power to transmute symbols and contents into their working psychical equivalents: and save as he also has the power to see what it is in the child, as a psychical mechanism, that affords maximum leverage.

Probably I shall now hear that at present the danger is not of dealing with acts and persons in a gross, arbitrary way, but (so far as what is called new education is concerned) in treating the children too much as mechanism, and consequently seeking for all kinds of stimuli to stir and attract—that, in a word, the tendency to reduce instruction to a merely agreeable thing, weakening the child's personality and indulging his mere love of excitement and pleasure, is precisely the result of taking the

---

2. That some teachers get their psychology by instinct more effectively than others by any amount of reflective study may be unreservedly stated. It is not a question of manufacturing teachers, but of reinforcing and enlightening those who have a right to teach.

psycho-mechanical point of view. I welcome the objection for it serves to clear up the precise point. It is through a partial and defective psychology that the teacher, in his reaction from dead routine and arbitrary moral and intellectual discipline, has substituted an appeal to the satisfaction of momentary impulse. It is not because the teacher has a knowledge of the psycho-physical mechanism, but because he has a partial knowledge of it. He has come to consciousness of certain sensations, and certain impulses, and of the ways in which these may be stimulated and directed, but he is in ignorance of the larger mechanism (just as a mechanism), and of the causal relations which subsist between the unknown part and the elements upon which he is playing. What is needed to correct his errors is not to inform him that he gets only misleading [help] from taking the psychical point of view; but to reveal to him the scope and intricate interactions of the mechanism as a whole. Then he will realize that while he is gaining apparent efficacy in some superficial part of the mechanism, he is disarranging, dislocating and disintegrating much more fundamental factors in it. In a word he is operating not as a psychologist, but as a poor psychologist, and the only cure for a partial psychology is a fuller one. He is gaining the momentary attention of the child through an appeal to pleasant color, or exciting tone, or agreeable association, but at the expense of isolating one cog and ratchet in the machinery, and making it operate independently of the rest. In theory, it is as possible to demonstrate this to a teacher, showing how the faulty method reacts unhappily into the personality, as it is to locate the points of wrong construction, and of ineffective transfer of energy in a physical apparatus.

This suggests the admission made by writers, in many respects as far apart as Dr. Harris and Dr. Münsterberg—that scientific psychology is of use on the pathological side—where questions of "physical and mental health" are concerned. But is there anything with which the teacher has concern that is not included in the ideal of physical and mental health? Does health define to us anything less than the teacher's whole end and aim? Where does pathology leave off in the scale and series of vicious aims and defective means? I see no line between the more obvious methods and materials which result in nervous irritation and fatigue; in weakening the power of vision, in establishing spinal curvatures; and others which, in more remote and subtle, but equally real ways, leave the child with, say, a muscular system which is only partially at the service of his ideas, with blocked and inert brain paths between eye and ear, and with a partial and disconnected development of the cerebral paths of visual imagery. What error in instruction is there which could not, with proper psychological theory, be stated in just such terms as these? A wrong method of teaching reading, wrong I mean in the full educational and ethical sense, is also a case of pathological use of the psycho-physical mechanism. A method is ethically defective that, while giving the child a glibness in the mechanical facility of reading, leaves him at the mercy of suggestion and chance environment to decide whether he reads the "yellow journal," the trashy novel, or the literature which inspires and makes more valid his whole life. Is it any less certain that this failure on the ethical side is repeated in some lack of adequate growth and connection in the psychical and physiological factors involved? If a knowledge of psychology is important to the teacher in the grosser and more overt cases of mental pathology is it not even more important in these hidden and indirect matters—just because they are less evident and more circuitous in their operation and manifestation?

The argument may be summarized by saying that there is controversy neither as to the ethical character of education, nor as to the abstraction which psychology performs in reducing personality to an object. The teacher is, indeed, a person occupied with other persons. He lives in a social sphere—he is a member and an organ of a social life. His aims are social aims; the development of individuals taking ever more responsible positions in a circle of social activities continually increasing in radius and in complexity. Whatever he as a teacher effectively does, he does as a person; and he does with and towards persons. His methods, like his aims, when actively in operation, are practical, are social, are ethical, are anything you please—save merely psychical. In comparison with this, the material and the data, the standpoint and the methods of psychology, are abstract. They transform specific acts and relations of individuals into a flow of processes in consciousness; and these processes can be adequately identified and related only through reference to a biological organism. I do not think there is danger of going too far in asserting the social and teleological nature of the work of the teacher; or in asserting the abstract and partial character of the mechanism into which the psychologist, as a psychologist, transmutes the play of vital values.

Does it follow from this that any attempt on the part of the teacher to perform this abstraction, to see the pupil as a mechanism, to define his own relations and that of the study taught in terms of causal influences acting upon this mechanism, are useless and harmful? On the face of it, I cannot understand the logic which says that because mechanism is mechanism, and because acts, aims, values are vital, therefore a statement in terms of one is alien to the comprehension and proper management of the other. Ends are not compromised when referred to the means necessary to realize them. Values do not cease to be values when they are minutely and accurately measured. Acts are not destroyed when their operative machinery is made manifest. The statement of the disparity of mechanism and actual life, be it never so true, solves no problem. It is no distinction that may be used off-hand to decide the question of the relation of psychology to any form of practice. It is a valuable and necessary distinction; but it is only preliminary. The purport of our discussion has, indeed, led us strongly to suspect any ideal which exists purely at large, out of relation to machinery of execution, and equally a machinery that operates in no particular direction.

The proposition that a description and explanation of stones, iron and mortar, as an absolutely necessary causal nexus of mechanical conditions, makes the results of physical science unavailable for purposes of practical life, would hardly receive attention to-day. Every sky-scraper, every railway bridge is a refutation, compared with which oceans of talk are futile. One would not find it easy to stir up a problem even if he went on to include, in this same mechanical system, the steam derricks that hoist the stones and iron, and the muscles and nerves of architect, mason and steel worker. The simple fact is still too obvious: the more thorough-going and complete the mechanical and causal statement, the more controlled, the more economical are the discovery and realization of human aims. It is not in spite of, nor in neglect of, but because of the mechanical statement that human activity has been freed, and made effective in thousands of new practical directions, upon a scale and with a certainty hitherto undreamed of. Our discussion tends to suggest that we entertain a similar question regarding psychology only because we have as yet made so little headway—just because there is so little scientific control of our practice in these directions; that at bottom our difficulty is local and circumstantial, not intrinsic and doctrinal. If our teachers were trained as architects are trained, if our schools were actually managed on a psychological basis as great factories are run on the basis of chemical and physical science; if our psychology were sufficiently organized and coherent to give as adequate a mechanical statement of human nature as physics does of its material, we should never dream of discussing this question.

I cannot pass on from this phase of the discussion without at least incidental remark of the obverse side of the situation. The difficulties of psychological observation and interpretation are great enough in any case. We cannot afford to neglect any possible auxiliary. The great advantage of the psycho-physical laboratory is paid for by certain obvious defects. The completer control of conditions, with resulting greater accuracy of determination, demands an isolation, a ruling out of the usual media of thought and action, which leads to a certain remoteness, and easily to a certain artificiality. When the result of laboratory experiment informs us, for example, that repetition is the chief factor influencing recall, we must bear in mind that the result is obtained with nonsense material—i.e., by excluding the conditions of ordinary memory. The result is pertinent if we state it thus: The more we exclude the usual environmental adaptations of memory the greater importance attaches to sheer repetition. It is dubious (and probably perverse) if we say: Repetition is the prime influence in memory.

Now this illustrates a general principle. Unless our laboratory results are to give us artificialities, mere scientific curiosities, they must be subjected to interpretation by gradual reapproximation to conditions of life. The results may be very accurate, very definitive in form; but the task of re-viewing them so as to see their actual import is clearly one of great delicacy and liability to error. The laboratory, in a word, affords no final refuge that enables us to avoid the ordinary scientific difficulties of forming hypotheses, interpreting results, etc. In some sense (from the very accuracy and limitations of its results) it adds to our responsibilities in this direction. Now the school, for psychological purposes, stands in many respects midway between the extreme simplifications of the laboratory and the confused complexities of ordinary life. Its conditions are those of life at large; they are social and practical. But it approaches the laboratory in so far as the ends aimed at are reduced in number, are definite, and thus simplify the conditions; and their psychological phase is uppermost—the formation of habits of attention, observation, memory, etc.—while in ordinary life these are secondary and swallowed up.

If the biological and evolutionary attitude is right in looking at mind as fundamentally an instrument of adaptation, there are certainly advantages in any mode of approach which brings us near to its various adaptations while they are still forming, and under conditions selected with special reference to promoting these adaptations (or faculties). And this is precisely the situation we should have in a properly organized system of education. While the psychological theory would guide and illuminate the practice, acting upon the theory would immediately test it, and thus criticize it, bringing about its revision and growth. In the large and open sense of the words psychology becomes a working hypothesis, instruction is the experimental test and demonstration of the hypothesis; the result is both greater practical control and continued growth in theory.

II

I must remind myself that my purpose does not conclude with a statement of the auxiliary relation of psychology to education; but that we are concerned with this as a type case of a wider problem—the relation of psychology to social practice in general. So far I have tried to show that it is not in spite of its statement of personal aims and social relations in terms of mechanism that psychology is useful, but because of this transformation and abstraction. Through reduction of ethical relations to presented objects we are enabled to get outside of the existing situation; to see it objectively, not merely in relation to our traditional habits, vague aspirations and capricious desires. We are able to see clearly the factors which shape it, and therefore to get an idea of how it may be modified. The assumption of an identical relationship of physics and psychology to practical life is justified. Our freedom of action comes through its statement in terms of necessity. By this translation our control is enlarged, our powers are directed, our energy conserved, our aims illuminated.

The school is an especially favorable place in which to study the availability of psychology for social practice; because in the school the formation of a certain type of social personality, with a certain attitude and equipment of working powers, is the express aim. In idea at least no other purpose restricts or compromises the dominance of the single purpose. Such is not the case in business, politics, and the professions. All these have upon their surface, taken directly, other ends to serve. In many instances these other aims are of far greater immediate importance; the ethical result is subordinate or even incidental. Yet as it profiteth a man nothing to gain the whole world and lose his own self, so indirectly and ultimately all these other social institutions must be judged by the contribution which they make to the value of human life. Other ends may be immediately uppermost, but these ends must in turn be means; they must subserve the interests of conscious life or else stand condemned.

In other words, the moment we apply an ethical standard to the consideration of social institutions, that moment they stand on exactly the same level as does the school, viz.: as organs for the increase in depth and area of the realized values of life. In both cases the statement of the mechanism, through which the ethical ends are realized, is not only permissible, but absolutely required. It is not merely incidentally, as a grateful addition to its normal task, that psychology serves us. The essential nature of the standpoint which calls it into existence, and of the abstraction which it performs, is to put in our possession the method by which values are introduced and effected in life. The statement of personality as an object; of social relations as a mechanism of stimuli and inhibitions, is precisely the statement of ends in terms of the method of their realization.

It is remarkable that men are so blind to the futility of a morality which merely blazons ideals, erects standards, asserts laws without finding in them any organic provision for their own realization. For ideals are held up to follow; standards are given to work by; laws are provided to guide action. The sole and only reason for their conscious moral statement is, in a word, that they may influence and direct conduct. If they cannot do this, not merely by accident, but of their own intrinsic nature, they are worse than inert. They are impudent impostors and logical self-contradictions.

When men derive their moral ideals and laws from custom, they also realize them through custom; but when they are in any way divorced from habit and tradition, when they are consciously proclaimed, there must be some substitute for custom as an organ of execution. We must know the method of their operation and know it in detail. Otherwise the more earnestly we insist upon our categorical imperatives, and upon their supreme right of control, the more flagrantly helpless we are as to their actual domination. The fact that conscious, as distinct from customary, morality and psychology have had a historic parallel march, is just the concrete recognition of the necessary equivalence between ends consciously conceived, and interest in the means upon which the ends depend. We have the same reality stated twice over: once as value to be realized, and once as mechanism of realization. So long as custom reigns, as tradition prevails, so long as social values are determined by instinct and habit, there is no conscious question as to the method of their achievement, and hence no need of psychology. Social institutions work of their own inertia, they take the individual up into themselves and carry him along in their own sweep. The individual is dominated by the mass life of his group. Institutions and the customs attaching to them take care of society both as to its ideals and its methods. But when once the values come to consciousness, when once a Socrates insists upon the organic relation of a reflective life and morality, then the means, the machinery by which ethical ideals are projected and manifested, comes to consciousness also. Psychology must needs be born as soon as morality becomes reflective.

Moreover, psychology, as an account of the mechanism of workings of personality, is the only alternative to an arbitrary and class view of society, to an aristocratic view in the sense of restricting the realization of the full worth of life to a section of society. The growth of a psychology that, as applied to history and sociology, tries to state the interactions of groups of men in familiar psychical categories of stimulus and inhibition, is evidence that we are ceasing to take existing social forms as final and unquestioned. The application of psychology to social institutions is the only scientific way of dealing with their ethical values in their present unequal distribution, their haphazard execution and their thwarted development. It marks just the recognition of the principle of sufficient reason in the large matters of social life. It is the recognition that the existing order is determined neither by fate nor by chance, but is based on law and order, on a system of existing stimuli and modes of reaction, through knowledge of which we can modify the practical outcome. There is no logical alternative save either to recognize and search for the mechanism of the interplay of personalities that controls the existing distributions of values, or to accept as final a fixed hierarchy of persons in which the leaders assert, on no basis save their own supposed superior personality, certain ends and laws which the mass of men passively receive and imitate. The effort to apply psychology to social affairs means that the determination of ethical values lies not in any set or class, however superior, but in the workings of the social whole; that the explanation is found in the complex interactions and inter-relations which constitute this whole. To save personality in all, we must serve all alike—state the achievements of all in terms of mechanism, that is, of the exercise of reciprocal influence. To affirm personality independent of mechanism is to restrict its full meaning to a few, and to make its expression in the few irregular and arbitrary.

The anomaly in our present social life is obvious enough. With tremendous increase in control of nature, in ability to utilize nature for the indefinite extension and multiplication of commodities for human use and satisfaction, we find the actual realization of ends, the enjoyment of values growing unassured and precarious. At times it seems as if we were caught in a contradiction; the more we multiply means, the less certain and general is the use we are able to make of them. No wonder a Carlyle or a Ruskin puts our whole industrial civilization under a ban, while a Tolstoi proclaims a return to the desert. But the only way to see the situation steadily, and to see it as a whole, is to keep in mind that the entire problem is one of the development of science, and of its application to life. Our control of nature with the accompanying output of material commodities is the necessary result of the growth of physical science—of our ability to state things as interconnected parts of a mechanism. Physical science has for the time being far outrun psychical. We have mastered the physical mechanism sufficiently to turn out possible goods; we have not gained a knowledge of the conditions through which possible values become actual in life, and so are still at the mercy of habit, of haphazard, and hence of force.

Psychology, after all, simply states the mechanism through which conscious value and meaning are introduced into human experience. As it makes its way, and is progressively applied to history and all the social sciences, we can anticipate no other outcome than increasing control in the ethical sphere—the nature and extent of which can be best judged by considering the revolution that has taken place in the control of physical nature through a knowledge of her order. Psychology will never provide ready-made materials and prescriptions for the ethical life, any more than physics dictates off-hand the steam-engine and the dynamo. But science, both physical and psychological, makes known the conditions upon which certain results depend, and therefore puts at the disposal of life a method for controlling them. Psychology will never tell us just what to do ethically, nor just how to do it. But it will afford us insight into the conditions which control the formation and execution of aims, and thus enable human effort to expend itself sanely, rationally and with assurance. We are not called upon to be either boasters or sentimentalists regarding the possibilities of our science. It is best, for the most part, that we should stick to our particular jobs of investigation and reflection as they come to us. But we certainly are entitled in this daily work to be sustained by the conviction that we are not working in indifference to or at cross-purposes with the practical strivings of our common humanity. The psychologist, in his most remote and technical occupation with mechanism, is contributing his bit to that ordered knowledge which alone enables mankind to secure a larger and to direct a more equal flow of values in life.

Reprinted with permission
from *Psychological Review*,
1907, 14, 61–91.

Chapter 6

The Province of Functional Psychology

James Rowland Angell

University of Chicago

Functional psychology is at the present moment little more than a point of view, a program, an ambition. It gains its vitality primarily perhaps as a protest against the exclusive excellence of another starting point for the study of the mind, and it enjoys for the time being at least the peculiar vigor which commonly attaches to Protestantism of any sort in its early stages before it has become respectable and orthodox. The time seems ripe to attempt a somewhat more precise characterization of the field of functional psychology than has as yet been offered. What we seek is not the arid and merely verbal definition which to many of us is so justly anathema, but rather an informing appreciation of the motives and ideals which animate the psychologist who pursues this path. His status in the eye of the psychological public is unnecessarily precarious. The conceptions of his purposes prevalent in non-functionalist circles range from positive

Delivered in substantially the present form as the President's Annual Address before the American Psychological Association at its fifteenth annual meeting held at Columbia University, New York City, December 27, 28 and 29, 1906.

and dogmatic misapprehension, through frank mystification and suspicion up to moderate comprehension. Nor is this fact an expression of anything peculiarly abstruse and recondite in his intentions. It is due in part to his own ill-defined plans, in part to his failure to explain lucidly exactly what he is about. Moreover, he is fairly numerous and it is not certain that in all important particulars he and his confreres are at one in their beliefs. The considerations which are herewith offered suffer inevitably from this personal limitation. No psychological council of Trent has as yet pronounced upon the true faith. But in spite of probable failure it seems worth while to hazard an attempt at delineating the scope of functionalist principles. I formally renounce any intention to strike out new plans; I am engaged in what is meant as a dispassionate summary of actual conditions.

Whatever else it may be, functional psychology is nothing wholly new. In certain of its phases it is plainly discernible in the psychology of Aristotle and in its more modern garb it has been increasingly in evidence since Spencer wrote his *Psychology* and Darwin his *Origin of Species*. Indeed, as we shall soon see, its crucial problems are inevitably incidental to any serious attempt at understanding mental life. All that is peculiar to its present circumstances is a higher degree of self-consciousness than it possessed before, a more articulate and persistent purpose to organize its vague intentions into tangible methods and principles.

A survey of contemporary psychological writing indicates, as was intimated in the preceding paragraph, that the task of functional psychology is interpreted in several different ways. Moreover, it seems to be possible to advocate one or more of these conceptions while cherishing abhorrence for the others. I distinguish three principal forms of the functional problem with sundry subordinate variants. It will contribute to the clarification of the general situation to dwell upon these for a moment, after which I propose to maintain that they are substantially but modifications of a single problem.

I

There is to be mentioned first the notion which derives most immediately from contrast with the ideals and purposes of structural psychology so-called.[1] This involves the identification of functional psychology with the effort to discern and portray the typical *operations* of consciousness under actual life conditions, as over against the attempt to analyze and describe its elementary and complex *contents*. The structural psychology of sensation, e.g., undertakes to determine the number and character of

---

1. The most lucid exposition of the structuralist position still remains, so far as I know, Titchener's paper, "The Postulates of a Structural Psychology," *Philosophical Review*, 1898 *(7)*, p. 499. Cf. also the critical-controversial papers of Caldwell, *Psychological Review*, 1899, p. 187, and Titchener, *Philosophical Review*, 1899 *(8)*, p. 290.

the various unanalyzable sensory materials, such as the varieties of color, tone, taste, etc. The functional psychology of sensation would on the other hand find its appropriate sphere of interest in the determination of the character of the various sense activities as differing in their *modus operandi* from one another and from other mental processes such as judging, conceiving, willing and the like.

In this its older and more pervasive form functional psychology has until very recent times had no independent existence. No more has structural psychology for that matter. It is only lately that any motive for the differentiation of the two has existed and structural psychology—granting its claims and pretensions of which more anon—is the first, be it said, to isolate itself. But in so far as functional psychology is synonymous with descriptions and theories of mental action as distinct from the materials of mental constitution, so far it is everywhere conspicuous in psychological literature from the earliest times down.

Its fundamental intellectual prepossessions are often revealed by the classifications of mental process adopted from time to time. Witness the Aristotelian bipartite division of intellect and will and the modern tripartite division of mental activities. What are cognition, feeling and will but three basally distinct modes of mental action? To be sure this classification has often carried with it the assertion, or at least the implication, that these fundamental attributes of mental life were based upon the presence in the mind of corresponding and ultimately distinct mental elements. But so far as concerns our momentary interest this fact is irrelevant. The impressive consideration is that the notion of definite and distinct forms of mental action is clearly in evidence and even the much-abused faculty psychology is on this point perfectly sane and perfectly lucid. The mention of this classic target for psychological vituperation recalls the fact that when the critics of functionalism wish to be particularly unpleasant, they refer to it as a bastard offspring of the faculty psychology masquerading in biological plumage.

It must be obvious to any one familiar with psychological usage in the present year of grace that in the intent of the distinction herewith described certain of our familiar psychological categories are primarily structural—such for instance as affection and image—whereas others immediately suggest more explicit functional relationships—for example, attention and reasoning. As a matter of fact it seems clear that so long as we adhere to these meanings of the terms structural and functional every mental event can be treated from either point of view, from the standpoint of describing its detectable contents and from the standpoint of characteristic mental activity differentiable from other forms of mental process. In the practice of our familiar psychological writers both undertakings are somewhat indiscriminately combined.

The more extreme and ingenuous conceptions of structural psychology seem to have grown out of an unchastened indulgence in what we may call the "states of consciousness" doctrine. I take it that this is in reality the contemporary version of Locke's "idea." If you adopt as your material for psychological analysis the isolated "moment of consciousness," it is very easy to become so absorbed in determining its constitution as to be rendered somewhat oblivious to its artificial character. The most essential quarrel which the functionalist has with structuralism in its thoroughgoing and consistent form arises from this fact and touches the feasibility and worth of the effort to get at mental process as it *is* under the conditions of actual experience rather than as it *appears* to a merely postmortem analysis. It is of course true that for introspective purposes we must in a sense always work with vicarious representatives of the particular mental processes which we set out to observe. But it makes a great difference even on such terms whether one is directing attention primarily to the discovery of the way in which such a mental process operates, and what the conditions are under which it appears, or whether one is engaged simply in teasing apart the fibers of its tissues. The latter occupation is useful and for certain purposes essential, but it often stops short of that which is as a life phenomenon the most essential, i.e., the *modus operandi* of the phenomenon.

As a matter of fact many modern investigations of an experimental kind largely dispense with the usual direct form of introspection and concern themselves in a distinctly functionalistic spirit with a determination of what work is accomplished and what the conditions are under which it is achieved. Many experiments in memory and association, for instance, are avowedly of this character.

The functionalist is committed *vom Grunde auf* to the avoidance of that special form of the psychologist's fallacy which consists in attributing to mental states without due warrant, as part of their overt constitution in the moment of experience, characteristics which subsequent reflective analysis leads us to suppose they must have possessed. When this precaution is not scrupulously observed we obtain a sort of *pâte de foie gras* psychology in which the mental conditions portrayed contain more than they ever naturally would or could hold.

It should be added that when the distinction is made between psychic structure and psychic function, the anomalous position of structure as a category of mind is often quite forgotten. In mental life the sole appropriateness of the term structure hinges on the fact that any moment of consciousness can be regarded as a complex capable of analysis, and the terms into which our analyses resolve such complexes are the analogues—and obviously very meager and defective ones at that—of the structures of anatomy and morphology.

The fact that mental contents are evanescent and fleeting marks them off in an important way from the relatively permanent elements of anatomy. No matter how much we may talk of the preservation of psychical dispositions, nor how many metaphors we may summon to characterize the storage of ideas in some hypothetical deposit chamber of memory, the obstinate fact remains that when we are not experiencing a sensation or an idea it is, strictly speaking, non-existent. Moreover, when we manage by one or another device to secure that which we designate the same sensation or the same idea, we not only have no guarantee that our second edition is really a replica of the first, we have a good bit of presumptive evidence that from the content point of view the original never is and never can be literally duplicated.

Functions, on the other hand, persist as well in mental as in physical life. We may never have twice exactly the same idea viewed from the side of sensuous structure and composition. But there seems nothing whatever to prevent our having as often as we will contents of consciousness which *mean* the same thing. They function in one and the same practical way, however discrepant their momentary texture. The situation is rudely analogous to the biological case where very different structures may under different conditions be called on to perform identical functions; and the matter naturally harks back for its earliest analogy to the instance of protoplasm where functions seem very tentatively and imperfectly differentiated. Not only then are general functions like memory persistent, but special functions such as the memory of particular events are persistent and largely independent of the specific conscious contents called upon from time to time to subserve the functions.

When the structural psychologists define their field as that of mental *process*, they really preempt under a fictitious name the field of function, so that I should be disposed to allege fearlessly and with a clear conscience that a large part of the doctrine of psychologists of nominally structural proclivities is in point of fact precisely what I mean by one essential part of functional psychology, i.e., an account of psychical operations. Certain of the official exponents of structuralism explicitly lay claim to this as their field and do so with a flourish of scientific rectitude. There is therefore after all a small but nutritious core of agreement in the structure-function apple of discord. For this reason, as well as because I consider extremely useful the analysis of mental life into its elementary forms, I regard much of the actual work of my structuralist friends with highest respect and confidence. I feel, however, that when they use the term structural as opposed to the term functional to designate their scientific creed they often come perilously near to using the enemy's colors.

Substantially identical with this first conception of functional psychology, but phrasing itself somewhat differently, is the view which regards the functional problem as concerned with discovering how and why conscious processes are what they are, instead of dwelling as the structuralist is supposed to do upon the problem of determining the irreducible elements of consciousness and their characteristic modes of combination. I have elsewhere defended the view that however it may be in other sciences dealing with life phenomena, in psychology at least the answer to the question "what" implicates the answer to the questions "how" and "why." [2]

Stated briefly the ground on which this position rests is as follows:

---

2. "The Relations of Structural and Functional Psychology to Philosophy," *Philosophical Review*, 1903 *(12)*, p. 203 ff.

In so far as you attempt to analyze any particular state of consciousness you find that the mental elements presented to your notice are dependent upon the particular exigencies and conditions which call them forth. Not only does the affective coloring of such a psychical moment depend upon one's temporary condition, mood and aims, but the very sensations themselves are determined in their qualitative texture by the totality of circumstances subjective and objective within which they arise. You cannot get a fixed and definite color sensation for example, without keeping perfectly constant the external and internal conditions in which it appears. The particular sense quality is in short functionally determined by the necessities of the existing situation which it emerges to meet. If you inquire then deeply enough what particular sensation you have in a given case, you always find it necessary to take account of the manner in which, and the reasons why, it was experienced at all. You may of course, if you will, abstract from these considerations, but in so far as you do so, your analysis and description is manifestly partial and incomplete. Moreover, even when you do so abstract and attempt to describe certain isolable sense qualities, your descriptions are of necessity couched in terms not of the experienced quality itself, but in terms of the conditions which produced it, in terms of some other quality with which it is compared, or in terms of some more overt act to which the sense stimulation led. That is to say, the very description itself is functionalistic and must be so. The truth of this assertion can be illustrated and tested by appeal to any situation in which one is trying to reduce sensory complexes, e.g., colors or sounds, to their rudimentary components.

II

A broader outlook and one more frequently characteristic of contemporary writers meets us in the next conception of the task of functional psychology. This conception is in part a reflex of the prevailing interest in the larger formulae of biology and particularly the evolutionary hypotheses within whose majestic sweep is nowadays included the history of the whole stellar universe; in part it echoes the same philosophical call to new life which has been heard as pragmatism, as humanism, even as functionalism itself. I should not wish to commit either party by asserting that functional psychology and pragmatism are ultimately one. Indeed, as a psychologist I should hesitate to bring down on myself the avalanche of metaphysical invective which has been loosened by pragmatic writers. To be sure pragmatism has slain its thousands, but I should cherish scepticism as to whether functional psychology would the more speedily slay its tens of thousands by announcing an offensive and defensive alliance with pragmatism. In any case I only hold that the two movements spring from similar logical motivation and rely for their vitality and propagation upon forces closely germane to one another.

The functional psychologist then in his modern attire is interested not alone in the operations of mental process considered merely of and by and for itself, but also and more vigorously in mental activity as part of a larger stream of biological forces which are daily and hourly at work before our eyes and which are constitutive of the most important and most absorbing part of our world. The psychologist of this stripe is wont to take his cue from the basal conception of the evolutionary movement, i.e., that for the most part organic structures and functions possess their present characteristics by virtue of the efficiency with which they fit into the extant conditions of life broadly designated the environment. With this conception in mind he proceeds to attempt some understanding of the manner in which the psychical contributes to the furtherance of the sum total of organic activities, not alone the psychical in its entirety, but especially the psychical in its particularities—mind as judging, mind as feeling, etc.

This is the point of view which instantly brings the psychologist cheek by jowl with the general biologist. It is the presupposition of every philosophy save that of outright ontological materialism that mind plays the stellar rôle in all the environmental adaptations of animals which possess it. But this persuasion has generally occupied the position of an innocuous truism or at best a jejune postulate, rather than that of a problem requiring, or permitting, serious scientific treatment. At all events, this was formerly true.

This older and more complacent attitude toward the matter is, however, being rapidly displaced by a conviction of the need for light on the exact character of the accommodatory service represented by the various great modes of conscious expression. Such an effort if successful would not only broaden the foundations for biological appreciation of the intimate nature of accommodatory process, it would also immensely enhance the psychologist's interest in the exact portrayal of conscious life. It is of course the latter consideration which lends importance to the matter from our point of view. Moreover, not a few practical consequences of value may be expected to flow from this attempt, if it achieves even a measurable degree of success. Pedagogy and mental hygiene both await the quickening and guiding counsel which can only come from a psychology of this stripe. For their purposes a strictly structural psychology is as sterile in theory as teachers and psychiatrists have found it in practice.

As a concrete example of the transfer of attention from the more general phases of consciousness as accommodatory activity to the particularistic features of the case may be mentioned the rejuvenation of interest in the quasi-biological field which we designate animal psychology. This movement is surely among the most pregnant with which we meet in our own generation. Its problems are in no sense of the merely theoretical and speculative kind, although, like all scientific endeavor, it possesses an intellectual and methodological background on which such problems loom large. But the frontier upon which it is pushing forward its explorations is a region of definite, concrete fact, tangled and confused and often most difficult of access, but nevertheless a region of fact, accessible like all other facts to persistent and intelligent interrogation.

That many of the most fruitful researches in this field have been achievements of men nominally biologists rather than psychologists in no wise affects the merits of the case. A similar situation exists in the experimental psychology of sensation where not a little of the best work has been accomplished by scientists not primarily known as psychologists.

It seems hardly too much to say that the empirical conceptions of the consciousness of the lower animals have undergone a radical alteration in the past few years by virtue of the studies in comparative psychology. The splendid investigations of the mechanism of instinct, of the facts and methods of animal orientation, of the scope and character of the several sense processes, of the capabilities of education and the range of selective accommodatory capacities in the animal kingdom, these and dozens of other similar problems have received for the first time drastic scientific examination, experimental in character wherever possible, observational elsewhere, but observational in the spirit of conservative non-anthropomorphism as earlier observations almost never were. In most cases they have to be sure but shown the way to further and more precise knowledge, yet there can be but little question that the trail which they have blazed has success at its farther end.

One may speak almost as hopefully of human genetic psychology which has been carried on so profitably in our own country. As so often in psychology, the great desideratum here, is the completion of adequate methods which will insure really stable scientific results. But already our general psychological theory has been vitalized and broadened by the results of the genetic methods thus far elaborated. These studies constantly emphasize for us the necessity of getting the longitudinal rather than the transverse view of life phenomena and they keep immediately in our field of vision the basic significance of growth in mental process. Nowhere is the difference more flagrant between a functional psychology and the more literal minded type of structural psychology. One has only to compare with the better contemporary studies some of the pioneer work in this field, conceived in the more static and structuralistic manner, as Preyer's for example was, to feel at once the difference and the immensely greater significance both for theory and for practice which issues from the functional and longitudinal descriptions.

The assertions which we have permitted ourselves about genetic psychology are equally applicable to pathological psychology. The technique of scientific investigation is in the nature of the case often different in this field of work from that characteristic of the other ranges of psychological research. But the attitude of the investigator is distinctly functionalistic. His aim is one of a thoroughly vital and generally practical kind leading him to emphasize precisely those considerations which our analysis of the main aspects of functional psychology disclose as the goal of its peculiar ambitions.

It is no purpose of mine to submerge by sheer *tour de force* the individuality of these various scientific interests just mentioned in the regnant personality of a functional psychology. But I am firmly convinced that the spirit which gives them birth is the spirit which in the realms of general psychological theory bears the name functionalism. I believe, therefore, that their ultimate fate is certain, still I have no wish to accelerate their translation against their will, nor to inflict upon them a label which they may find odious.

It should be said, however, in passing, that even on the side of general theory and methodological conceptions, recent developments have been fruitful and significant. One at least of these deserves mention.

We find nowadays both psychologists and biologists who treat consciousness as substantially synonymous with adaptive reactions to novel situations. In the writings of earlier authorities it is often implied that accommodatory activities *may be* purely physiological and non-psychical in character. From this view-point the mental type of accommodatory act supervenes on certain occasions and at certain stages in organic development, but it is no indispensable feature of the accommodatory process.[3]

It seems a trifle strange when one considers how long the fundamental conception involved in this theory has been familiar and accepted psychological doctrine that its full implication should have been so reluctantly recognized.[4] If one takes the position now held by all psychologists of repute, so far as I am aware, that consciousness is constantly at work building up habits out of coordinations imperfectly under control; and that as speedily as control is gained the mental direction tends to subside and give way to a condition approximating physiological automatism, it is only a step to carry the inference forward that consciousness immanently considered is *per se* accommodation to the novel. Whether conscious processes have been the precursors of our present instinctive equipment depends on facts of heredity upon which a layman may hardly speak. But many of our leaders answer strongly in the affirmative, and such an answer evidently harmonizes with the general view now under discussion.

To be sure the further assertion that no real organic accommodation

---

3. At this point there is obviously a possible ambiguity in the use of the term accommodatory. Any physiologically adequate process may be described as accommodatory. Respiration, for example, might be so designated. Clearly one needs a special term to designate accommodation to the novel, for this is the field of conscious activity. Of course if the contention be granted for which the view now under consideration stands, this could be called conscious accommodation and it would be understood forthwith that such accommodation was to the novel.

4. Cf. Mc Dougall striking papers in *Mind,* 1898, entitled "Contribution toward an Improvement in Psychological Method."

to the novel ever occurs, save in the form that involves consciousness, requires for its foundation a wide range of observation and a penetrating analysis of the various criteria of mentality. But this is certainly a common belief among biologists to-day. Selective variation of response to stimulation is the ordinary external sign indicative of conscious action. Stated otherwise, consciousness discloses the form taken on by primary accommodatory process.

It is not unnatural perhaps that the frequent disposition of the functional psychologist to sigh after the flesh-pots of biology should kindle the fire of those consecrated to the cause of a pure psychology and philosophy freed from the contaminating influence of natural science. As a matter of fact, alarms have been repeatedly sounded and the faithful called to subdue mutiny. But the purpose of the functional psychologist has never been, so far as I am aware, to scuttle the psychological craft for the benefit of biology. Quite the contrary. Psychology is still for a time at least to steer her own untroubled course. She is at most borrowing a well-tested compass which biology is willing to lend and she hopes by its aid to make her ports more speedily and more surely. If in use it prove treacherous and unreliable, it will of course go overboard.

This broad biological ideal of functional psychology of which we have been speaking may be phrased with a slight shift of emphasis by connecting it with the problem of discovering the fundamental utilities of consciousness. If mental process is of real value to its possessor in the life and world which we know, it must perforce be by virtue of something which it does that otherwise is not accomplished. Now life and world are complex and its seems altogether improbable that consciousness should express its utility in one and only one way. As a matter of fact, every surface indication points in the other direction. It may be possible merely as a matter of expression to speak of mind as in general contributing to organic adjustment to environment. But the actual contributions will take place in many ways and by multitudinous varieties of conscious process. The functionalist's problem then is to determine if possible the great types of these processes in so far as the utilities which they present lend themselves to classification.

The search after the various utilitarian aspects of mental process is at once suggestive and disappointing. It is on the one hand illuminating by virtue of the strong relief into which it throws the fundamental resemblances of processes often unduly severed in psychological analysis. Memory and imagination, for example, are often treated in a way designed to emphasize their divergences almost to the exclusion of their functional similarities. They are of course functionally but variants on a single and basal type of control. An austere structuralism in particular is inevitably disposed to magnify differences and in consequence under its hands mental life tends to fall apart; and when put together again it generally seems to have lost something of its verve and vivacity. It appears stiff and rigid and corpse-like. It lacks the vital spark. Functionalism tends just as inevitably to bring mental phenomena together, to show them focalized in actual vital service. The professional psychologist, calloused by long apprenticeship, may not feel this distinction to be scientifically important. But to the young student the functionalistic stress upon community of service is of immense value in clarifying the intricacies of mental organization. On the other hand the search of which we were speaking is disappointing perhaps in the paucity of the basic modes in which these conscious utilities are realized.

Ultimately all the utilities are possibly reducible to selective accommodation. In the execution of the accommodatory activity the instincts represent the racially hereditary utilities, many of which are under the extant conditions of life extremely anomalous in their value. The sensory-algedonic-motor phenomena represent the immediate short circuit unreflective forms of selective response. Whereas the ideational-algedonic-motor series at its several levels represents the long circuit response under the influence of the mediating effects of previous experience. This experience serves either to inhibit the propulsive power intrinsic to the stimulus, or to reinforce this power by adding to it its own dynamic tendencies. This last variety of action is the peculiarly human form of mediated control. On its lowest stages, genetically speaking, it merges with the purely immediate algedonic type of response. All the other familiar psychological processes are subordinate to one or more of these groups. Conception, judgment, reasoning, emotion, desire, aversion, volition, etc., simply designate special varieties in which these generic forms appear.

In facing the problem of classifying functions we may well turn for a moment to the experience of biologists for suggestions. It is to be remarked at once that the significance of function as a basis for biological classification varies greatly in different parts of the biological field. Among the more complex animal organisms, for example, function, as compared with structure, affords a relatively precarious basis of classification, since very divergent structures may subserve identical functions. Moreover, the functions merely as such often fail to indicate with the definiteness characteristic of the anatomical structure the genetic relations involved in the maturing of a form. But in the study of the lower orders of life such as the bacteria, where structural variations are so largely to seek, the functional chemico-physiological reactions are of the utmost significance for classificatory purposes. In the botanical field generally there has of late been an increasing disposition to employ functional similarity and difference for the illumination of plant relationships. Indeed, this transition from a purely taxonomic and morphological point of view to a physiological and functional point of view is the striking feature of recent progress in botanical theory.

The ultimate value of a psychological classification based on functions, if interpreted in the light of these considerations, would apparently hinge on one's conception of the analogy between consciousness and undifferentiated protoplasm. In the measure in which consciousness is immanently unstable and variable, one might anticipate that a functional classification would be more significant and penetrating than one based upon any supposedly structural foundation. But the analogy on which this inference rests is perhaps too insecure to permit a serious conclusion to be drawn from it. In any event it is to be said that functions as such seem to be the most stable characters in the biological field. They extend in a practically unbroken front from the lowest to the highest levels of life—allowing for a possible protest in certain quarters against including consciousness in this list. That they are not everywhere so useful as structures for classificatory purposes reflects on the aims of classification, not on the fundamental and relatively fixed character of functions.

A survey of current usage discloses two general types of functional categories. Of these, the one is in spirit and purpose dominantly physiological. It groups all the forms of life functions, whether animal or vegetable in manifestation, under the four headings of assimilation, reproduction, motion and sensibility. In such a schema assimilation is made to include digestion, circulation, respiration, secretion, and excretion, while motion in the sense here intended applies primarily to those forms of movement which enable the organism to migrate from place to place and thus accommodate itself to the exigencies of local conditions.

Another group of categories which concerns a deeper and more general level of biological interpretations is given by such terms as selection, adaptation, variation, accommodation, heredity, etc. These are categories of a primarily functional sort for they apply in a large sense to modes of behavior. Indeed, behavior may be said to be itself the most inclusive of these categories. But as compared with the members of the first group they have to do with the general trend of organic development and not with the specific physiological processes which may be concerned in any special case. This does not mean that a specific physiological setting cannot sometime be given these problems; but it does mean that at present the gaps in our knowledge of these matters are generally too large to be spanned with certainty.

Now it would appear that such general categories as selection and accommodation have a perfectly appropriate application to mental process. Indeed, as we have already remarked, not a few of our modern scientists regard the psychical as precisely synonymous with the selective—accommodatory activity as this appears in the life history of the individual; and we have, moreover, already pointed out certain limitations and certain merits of these categories when applied to the classification of mental phenomena. We have found them serving to magnify a certain community of organic service in the most various forms of psychical activity, but we have also found them rather too vague and general to afford a desirable scientific detail.

If on the other hand, we examine the familiar *physiological* functions with reference to their possible relations to mental functions, we are at once struck by certain similarities and certain disparities between the two. There are some mental operations which have repeatedly been designated as assimilative. So familiar is this characterization and so commonly accepted that we may without undue hesitation assume its appropriateness and relevancy. Under the physiological aspects of assimilation are commonly ranged such processes as respiration, circulation, secretion, excretion, etc. How far these processes find analogies in mental action is not altogether clear. Many of our psychologists are fond of describing "the stream of consciousness" and in so far as the metaphor is justifiable one may naturally think of the physiological circulation as its counterpart. But there are perhaps as many differences as there are resemblances between the two. Certainly the cyclical character of the circulation of the blood finds no precise analogue in the flow of psychical phenomena. Similarly the periodicity of respiration may suggest the fluctuation of attention, the storing of mental dispositions may be connected with secretion, the casting off of mental irrelevancies may be likened to excretion, etc. But these relations are so largely metaphorical in character that one can hardly assign them a larger consequence than springs from such amusement as they may afford.

It would perhaps be difficult to disprove the theory that reproduction can be regarded as a mental category quite as truly as a physiological category, not only in the sense in which one mind can be conceived as the parent of other minds, but also in the familiar sense in which the mind is thought of as recreating its own ideas from time to time.

Yet granting all this, it may safely be said that however numerous the analogies connecting the mental functions with the physiological functions may be, we are not at present in a position to take advantage of them in any very serious way. Motion is by common consent applicable to the physiological alone and sensibility is in the intent of the classification appropriate to the psychical alone. The basal categories utilized by physiologists seem therefore to render us but little assistance. This view is vigorously maintained by many modern writers, but generally on *a priori* grounds.

If we examine the historically conspicuous classifications of mental process made by psychologists, we discover, as was pointed out in an earlier paragraph, that they are frequently suggestive of definitely functional conceptions. The Aristotelian divisions, the so-called Kantian divisions, the divisions into higher and lower powers characteristic of the faculty psychologists (and many others not commonly ranked as such), and Brentano's and Stout's classifications, to mention no more, are all decidedly based on dynamic and functionalistic considerations. On the other hand, not a few of our contemporary authorities, notably Wundt, classify their material under the more statical and mechanical categories—"elements and compounds."

Professor Warren has recently suggested an interesting classification in which he proposes as the fundamental functional categories the following five: Sensibility, which gives us the sensory continuum; modification, which connotes our ability to become aware of intensive modifications in the continuum; differentiation, which covers our capacity to experience qualitative differences; association, which does not require interpretation, and discrimination, which refers to our ability to perform definite acts of rational apprehension and to articulate purposes.[5] These functions taken together will, he alleges, account for all forms of consciousness and they are not derivatives from phenomena of the material world which he regards as outside the pale. I do not propose at this time to offer any detailed criticism of Professor Warren's valuable paper. Indeed, until his views are more fully elaborated, extended criticism would be premature.

One distinction, however, to which he calls incidental attention as a biological distinction, is formulated in an admirable statement with which I fully agree. It presents a sort of functional analysis which seems to me at once pregnant and sound. He speaks of the three-fold division of cognition, affection and conative process as intrinsically biological in character and corresponding broadly to the differences among the external, the systemic and the kinaesthetic senses; the first reporting to us the outer world, the second our own general organic tone and the third supplying experiences of our motor activity by means of which voluntary control is developed.

Particularly significant is his remark that the "fundamental functions of consciousness and the kinds of experience" are something quite distinct from one another. It is because he believes that the "rise of any particular experience and its makeup as a datum of consciousness can be fully described in terms of certain mental functions" that he feels it possible to elaborate an independent natural science of psychology free from neurological, physiological and biological considerations. It is not clear that this conclusion flows from Professor Warren's premises any more exclusively than from the premises of the so-called structuralist's point of view. Nor is there any strictly logical impracticality in carrying out the program of such a pure psychology. But it is fair to emphasize the extremely pale, attenuated and abstract character of such a science as compared with one which should report upon conscious processes as they are really found amid the heat and battle of the actual mind–body life. It may be a pure science, but it is surely purity bought at a great price—i.e., truth to life.

All pure science must abstract in a measure from the actual circumstances of life, but in the so-called exact sciences the abstraction is always away from the irrelevant and disturbing. The type of abstraction which Professor Warren champions, in common with many other distinguished scholars, is one which appeals to me as an abstracting away from the more significant, with the consequent fixation of attention upon the relatively less important.

It is a commonplace of logic that classification is intrinsically teleological and that the merits of any special classification, assuming that it does not distort or misrepresent the facts, is to be tested by the success with which it meets the necessities for which it was devised. If one desires to emphasize the taxonomic and morphological features of

---

5. "The Fundamental Functions of Consciousness," *Psychological Bulletin*, 1906, p. 217.

mentality, no doubt some such division as Wundt employs, using the rubrics elements and compounds, is preferable. If one wishes primarily to emphasize qualitative similarities and dissimilarities, the Kantian principle of irreducibility is judicious; and if one wishes to bring out the dynamic character of consciousness, such a principle as Brentano's, based on the mode in which consciousness refers to its object, is effective. If functional psychology really possesses several distinct zones of interest, it is quite conceivable that different classifications may be necessary to fulfil most satisfactorily the demands in these several fields. In any case we must forego further discussion of the matter at this point and return to offer our description of the third of the main subdivisions of the functional problem.

III

The third conception which I distinguish is often in practice merged with the second, but it involves stress upon a problem logically prior perhaps to the problem raised there and so warrants separate mention. Functional psychology, it is often alleged, is in reality a form of psychophysics. To be sure, its aims and ideals are not explicitly quantitative in the manner characteristic of that science as commonly understood. But it finds its major interest in determining the relations to one another of the physical and mental portions of the organism.

It is undoubtedly true that many of those who write under functional prepossessions are wont to introduce frequent references to the physiological processes which accompany or condition mental life. Moreover, certain followers of this faith are prone to declare forthwith that psychology is simply a branch of biology and that we are in consequence entitled, if not indeed obliged, to make use where possible of biological materials. But without committing ourselves to so extreme a position as this, a mere glance at one familiar region of psychological procedure will disclose the leanings of psychology in this direction.

The psychology of volition affords an excellent illustration of the necessity with which descriptions of mental process eventuate in physiological or biological considerations. If one take the conventional analysis of a voluntary act drawn from some one or other of the experiences of adult life, the descriptions offered generally portray ideational activities of an anticipatory and deliberative character which serve to initiate immediately or remotely certain relevant expressive movements. Without the execution of the movements the ideational performances would be as futile as the tinkling cymbals of Scripture. To be sure, many of our psychologists protest themselves wholly unable to suggest why or how such muscular movements are brought to pass. But the fact of their occurrence or of their fundamental import for any theory of mental life in which consciousness is other than an epiphenomenon, is not questioned.

Moreover, if one considers the usual accounts of the ontogenesis of human volitional acts one is again confronted with intrinsically physiological data in which reflexes, automatic and instinctive acts are much in evidence. Whatever the possibilities, then, of an expurgated edition of the psychology of volition from which should be blotted out all reference to contaminating physiological factors, the actual practice of our representative psychologists is quite otherwise, and upon their showing volition cannot be understood either as regards its origin or its outcome without constant and overt reference to these factors. It would be a labor of supererrogation to go on and make clear the same doctrine as it applies to the psychology of the more recondite of the cognitive processes; so intimate is the relation between cognition and volition in modern psychological theory that we may well stand excused from carrying out in detail the obvious inferences from the situation we have just described.

Now if someone could but devise a method for handling the mind–body relationships which would not when published immediately create cyclonic disturbances in the philosophical atmosphere, it seems improbable that this disposition of the functional psychologist to inject physiology into his cosmos would cause comment and much less criticism. But even parallelism, that most insipid, pale and passionless of all the inventions begotten by the mind of man to accomplish this end, has largely failed of its pacific purpose. It is no wonder, therefore, that the more rugged creeds with positive programs to offer and a stock of red corpuscles to invest in their propagation should also have failed of universal favor.

This disposition to go over into the physiological for certain portions of psychological doctrine is represented in an interesting way by the frequent tendency of structural psychologists to find explanation in psychology substantially equivalent to physiological explanation.[6] Professor Titchener's recent work on *Quanitative Psychology* represents this position very frankly. It is cited here with no intent to comment disparagingly upon the consistency of the structuralist position, but simply to indicate the wide-spread feeling of necessity at certain stages of psychological development for resort to physiological considerations.

Such a functional psychology as I have been presenting would be entirely reconcilable with Miss Calkins' "psychology of selves" (so ably set forth by her in her presidential address last year) were it not for her extreme scientific conservatism in refusing to allow the self to have a body, save as a kind of conventional biological ornament. The real psychological self, as I understand her, is pure disembodied spirit—an admirable thing of good religious and philosophic ancestry, but surely

---

6. Cf. Münsterberg's striking pronunciamento to this effect in his paper entitled "Psychological Atomism," *Psychological Review,* 1900, p. 1. The same doctrine is incorporated in his "Grundzüge der Psychologie" and we await with interest the completion of that task in order to discover the characteristic features of a psychology consistently built on these foundations.

not the thing with which we actually get through this vale of tears and not a thing before which psychology is under any obligation to kotow.[7]

It is not clear that the functional psychologist because of his disposition to magnify the significance in practice of the mind–body relationships is thereby committed to any special theory of the character of these relationships, save as was said a moment since, that negatively he must seemingly of necessity set his face against any epiphenomenalist view. He might conceivably be an interactionist, or a parallelist or even an advocate of some wholly outworn creed. As a matter of fact certain of our most ardent functionalists not only cherish highly definite articles of faith as regards this issue, they would even go so far as to test functional orthodoxy by the acceptance of these tenets. This is to them the most momentous part of their functionalism, their holy of holies. It would display needless temerity to attempt within the limitations of this occasion a formulation of doctrine wholly acceptable to all concerned. But I shall venture a brief reference to such doctrine in the effort to bring out certain of its essentials.

The position to which I refer regards the mind–body relation as capable of treatment in psychology as a methodological distinction rather than a metaphysically existential one. Certain of its expounders arrive at their view by means of an analysis of the genetic conditions under which the mind–body differentiation first makes itself felt in the experience of the individual.[8] This procedure clearly involves a direct frontal attack on the problem.

Others attain the position by flank movement, emphasizing to begin with the insoluble contradictions with which one is met when the distinction is treated as resting on existential differences in the primordial elements of the cosmos.[9] Both methods of approach lead to the same

7. Miss Calkins' views on this matter, which are shared by many of our leading psychologists, have been lucidly expounded on several papers (particularly "Der doppelte Standpunkt in der Psychologie," and a "Reconciliation between Structural and Functional Psychology," *Psychological Review*, 1906, p. 61), to say nothing of their embodiment in her widely quoted *Introduction to Psychology*. She has done yeoman service in emphasizing the fundamental significance of the "self" consciousness for all psychological doctrine and I am in entire sympathy with her insistence on this fact. But she seems to me unduly to circumscribe the legitimate scope of this "self." Possibly I misinterpret her meaning, but the following sentences together with the procedure in her *Introduction to Psychology* seem to justify me. "By self as fundamental fact of psychology is not meant . . . the psychophysical organism, . . . the objection is, very briefly, that the doctrine belongs not to psychology at all, but to biology," *Psychological Review*, 1906, p. 66. After which reference is made to Professor Baldwin's *Development and Evolution* as a non-psychological treatise. Such a settlement of the issue is easy and logically consistent. But does it not leave us with a gulf set between the self as mind and the self as body, for the crossing of which we are forthwith obliged to expend much needless energy, as the gulf is of our own inventing?

8. The most striking attempt of this kind with which I am acquainted is Professor Baldwin's paper entitled "Mind and Body from the Genetic Point of View," *Psychological Review*, 1903, p. 225.

9. Cf. on this general issue Bawden, "Functional View of the Relation Between the Psychical and the Physical," *Philosophical Review*, 1902, (11), p. 474, and "Methodological Implications of the Mind–body Controversy," *Psychological Bulletin*, 1906, p. 321.

goal, however, i.e., the conviction that the distinction has no existence on the genetically lower and more naif stages of experience. It only comes to light on a relatively reflective level and it must then be treated as instrumental if one would avoid paralogisms, antinomies and a host of other metaphysical nightmares. Moreover, in dealing with psychological problems this view entitles one to reject as at least temporarily irrelevant the question whether mind *causes* changes in neural action and conversely. The previous question is raised by defenders of this type of doctrine if one insists on having such a query answered. They invite you to trace the lineage of your idea of causality, insisting that such a searching of one's intellectual reins will always disclose the inappropriateness of the inquiry as formulated above. They urge further that the profitable and significant thing is to seek for a more exact appreciation of the precise conditions under which consciousness is in evidence and the conditions under which it retires in favor of the more exclusively physiological. Such knowledge so far as it can be obtained is on a level with all scientific and practical information. It states the circumstances under which certain sorts of results will appear.

One's view of this functionalistic metaphysics is almost inevitably colored by current philosophical discussion as to the essential nature of consciousness. David Hume has been accused of destroying the reality of mind chiefly because he exorcised from it relationships of various kinds. If it be urged, as has so often been done, that Hume was guilty of pouring out the baby with the bath, the modern philosopher makes good the disaster not only by pouring in again both baby and bath, but by maintaining that baby and bath, mind and relations, are substantially one.[10] Nor is this unity secured after the manner prescribed by the good Bishop Berkeley. At all events the metaphysicians to whom I refer are not fond of being called idealists. But the psychological functionalist who emphasizes the instrumental nature of the mind–body distinction and the metaphysician who regards mind as a relation are following roads which are at least parallel to one another if not actually convergent.

---

10. To the simple-minded psychologist this saying, in which many authors indulge, that consciousness is merely a relation seems a trifle dark. The psychologist has no natural prejudice against relation, but in this special case he is as a rule given too little information concerning the terms between which this relation subsists. Possibly his vision has been darkened by a perverse logic, but relations imply termini in his usual modes of thought and before assenting too unreservedly to the "relation" philosophy of consciousness, he urges a fuller illumination as to the character and status of these supporting end terms.

The following well-known papers will introduce the uninitiated, if any such there be, into the thick of the battle. A complete bibliography would probably monopolize this issue of the *Review*. James, "Does Consciousness Exist?" *Journal of Philosophy, Psychology and Scientific Methods*, 1, p. 477. Woodbridge, "Nature of Consciousness," in the same *Journal*, 2, p. 119. Also Garman, "Memorial Volume," p. 137. Perry, "Conceptions and Misconceptions of Consciousness," *Psychological Review*, 1904, 11, p. 282. Bush, "An Empirical Definition of Consciousness," *Journal of Philosophy, Psychology and Scientific Methods*, 2, p. 561. Stratton, "Difference Between Mental and Physical," *Psychological Bulletin*, 1906, p. 1. "Character of Consciousness," *Ibid.*, p. 117.

Whether or not one sympathizes with the views of that wing of the functionalist party to which our attention has just been directed it certainly seems a trifle unfair to cast up the mind-body difficulty in the teeth of the functionalist as such when on logical grounds he is no more guilty than any of his psychological neighbors. No courageous psychology of volition is possible which does not squarely face the mind-body problem, and in point of fact every important description of mental life contains doctrine of one kind or another upon this matter. A literally pure psychology of volition would be a sort of hanging-garden of Babylon, marvelous but inaccessible to psychologists of terrestrial habit. The functionalist is a greater sinner than others only in so far as he finds necessary and profitable a more constant insistence upon the translation of mental process into physiological process and conversely.

IV

If we now bring together the several conceptions of which mention has been made it will be easy to show them converging upon a common point. We have to consider (1) functionalism conceived as the psychology of mental operations in contrast to the psychology of mental elements; or, expressed otherwise, the psychology of the how and why of consciousness as distinguished from the psychology of the what of consciousness. We have (2) the functionalism which deals with the problem of mind conceived as primarily engaged in mediating between the environment and the needs of the organism. This is the psychology of the fundamental utilities of consciousness; (3) and lastly we have functionalism described as psychophysical psychology, that is the psychology which constantly recognizes and insists upon the essential significance of the mind-body relationship for any just and comprehensive appreciation of mental life itself.

The second and third delineations of functional psychology are rather obviously correlated with each other. No description of the actual circumstances attending the participation of mind in the accommodatory activities of the organism could be other than a mere empty schematism without making reference to the manner in which mental processes eventuate in motor phenomena of the physiological organism. The overt accommodatory act is, I take it, always sooner or later a muscular movement. But this fact being admitted, there is nothing for it, if one will describe accommodatory processes, but to recognize the mind-body relations and in some way give expression to their practical significance. It is only in this regard, as was indicated a few lines above, that the functionalist departs a trifle in his practice and a trifle more in his theory from the rank and file of his colleagues.

The effort to follow the lead of the natural sciences and delimit somewhat rigorously—albeit artificially—a field of inquiry, in this case consciousness conceived as an independent realm, has led in psychology to a deal of excellent work and to the uncovering of much hidden truth. So far as this procedure has resulted in a focusing of scientific attention and endeavor on a relatively narrow range of problems the result has more than justified the means. And the functionalist by no means holds that the limit of profitable research has been reached along these lines. But he is disposed to urge in season and out that we must not forget the arbitrary and self-imposed nature of the boundaries within which we toil when we try to eschew all explicit reference to the physical and physiological. To overlook this fact is to substitute a psychology under injunction for a psychology under free jurisdiction. He also urges with vigor and enthusiasm that a new illumination of this preempted field can be gained by envisaging it more broadly, looking at it as it appears when taken in perspective with its neighboring territory. And if it be objected that such an inquiry however interesting and advantageous is at least not psychology, he can only reply; psychology is what we make it, and if the correct understanding of mental phenomena involves our delving in regions which are not at first glance properly mental, what recks it, provided only that we are nowhere guilty of untrustworthy and unverifiable procedure, and that we return loaded with the booty for which we set out, and by means of which we can the better solve our problem?

In its more basal philosophy this last conception is of course intimately allied to those appraisals of mind which emphasize its dominantly social characteristics, its rise out of social circumstances and the pervasively social nature of its constitutive principles. In our previous intimations of this standpoint we have not distinguished sharply between the physical and the social aspect of environment. The adaptive activities of mind are very largely of the distinctly social type. But this does not in any way jeopardize the genuineness of the connection upon which we have been insisting between the psychophysical aspects of a functional psychology and its environmental adaptive aspects.

It remains then to point out in what manner the conception of functionalism as concerned with the basal operations of mind is to be correlated with the other two conceptions just under discussion. The simplest view to take of the relations involved would apparently be such as would regard the first as an essential propaedeutic to the other two. Certainly if we are intent upon discerning the exact manner in which mental process contributes to accommodatory efficiency, it is natural to begin our undertaking by determining what are the primordial forms of expression peculiar to mind. However plausible in theory this conception of the intrinsic logical relations of these several forms of functional psychology, in practice it is extremely difficult wholly to sever them from one another.

Again like the biological accommodatory view the psycho-physical view of functional psychology involves as a rational presupposition some acquaintance with mental processes as these appear to reflective consciousness. The intelligent correlation in a practical way of physiological and mental operations evidently involves a preliminary knowledge of the conspicuous differentiations both on the side of conscious function and on the side of physiological function.

In view of the considerations of the last few paragraphs it does not seem fanciful nor forced to urge that these various theories of the problem of functional psychology really converge upon one another, however divergent may be the introductory investigations peculiar to each of the several ideals. Possibly the conception that the fundamental problem of the functionalist is one of determining just how mind participates in accommodatory reactions, is more nearly inclusive than either of the others, and so may be chosen to stand for the group. But if this vicarious duty is assigned to it, it must be on clear terms of remembrance that the other phases of the problem are equally real and equally necessary. Indeed the three things hang together as integral parts of a common program.

The functionalist's most intimate persuasion leads him to regard consciousness as primarily and intrinsically a control phenomenon. Just as behavior may be regarded as the most distinctly basic category of general biology in its functional phase so control would perhaps serve as the most fundamental category in functional psychology, the special forms and differentiations of consciousness simply constituting particular phases of the general process of control. At this point the omnipresent captious critic will perhaps arise to urge that the knowledge process is no more truly to be explained in terms of control than is control to be explained in terms of knowledge. Unquestionably there is from the point of view of the critic a measure of truth in this contention. The mechanism of control undoubtedly depends on the cognitive processes, to say nothing of other factors. But if one assumes the vitalistic point of view for one's more final interpretations, if one regards the furtherance of life in breadth and depth and permanence as an end in itself, and if one derives his scale of values from a contemplation of the several contributions toward this end represented by the great types of vital phenomena, with their apex in the moral, scientific and aesthetic realms, one must certainly find control a category more fundamental than the others offered by psychology. Moreover, it may be urged against the critic's attitude that even knowledge itself is built up under the control mechanism represented by selective attention and apperception. The basic character of control seems therefore hardly open to challenge.

One incidental merit of the functionalist program deserves a passing mention. This is the one method of approach to the problem with which I am acquainted that offers a reasonable and cogent account of the rise of reflective consciousness and its significance as manifested in the various philosophical disciplines. From the vantage point of the functionalist position logic and ethics, for instance, are no longer mere disconnected items in the world of mind. They take their place with all the inevitableness of organic organization in the general system of control, which requires for the expression of its immanent meaning *as psychic* a theoretical vindication of its own inner principles, its modes of procedure and their results.[11] From any other point of view, so far as I am aware, the several divisions of philosophical inquiry sustain to one another relations which are almost purely external and accidental. To the functionalist on the other hand they are and must be in the nature of the case consanguineous and vitally connected. It is at the point, for example, where the good, the beautiful and the true have bearing on the efficacy of accommodatory activity that the issues of the normative philosophical sciences become relevant. If good action has no significance for the enriching and enlarging of life, the contention I urge is futile, and similarly as regards beauty and truth. But it is not at present usually maintained that such is the fact.

These and other similar tendencies of functionalism may serve to reassure those who fear that in lending itself to biological influences psychology may lose contact with philosophy and so sacrifice the poise and balance and sanity of outlook which philosophy undertakes to furnish. The particular brand of philosophy which is predestined to functionalist favor cannot of course be confidently predicted in advance. But anything approaching a complete and permanent divorce of psychology from philosophy is surely improbable so long as one cultivates the functionalist faith. Philosophy cannot dictate scientific method here any more than elsewhere, nor foreordain the special facts to be discovered. But as an interpreter of the psychologist's achievements she will always stand higher in the functionalist's favor than in that of his colleagues of other persuasions, for she is a more integral and significant part of his scheme of the cosmos. She may even outgrow under his tutelage that "valiant inconclusiveness" of which the last of her long line of lay critics has just accused her.

A sketch of the kind we have offered is unhappily likely to leave on the mind an impression of functional psychology as a name for a group of genial but vaguer ambitions and good intentions. This, however, is a fault which must be charged to the artist and to the limitations of time and space under which he is here working. There is nothing vaguer in the program of the functionalist when he goes to his work than there is in the purposes of the psychologist wearing any other livery. He goes to his laboratory, for example, with just the same resolute interest to discover new facts and new relationships, with just the same determination to verify and confirm his previous observations, as does his colleague who calls himself perhaps a structuralist. But he looks out upon the surroundings of his science with a possibly greater sensitiveness to its continuity with other ranges of human interest and with certainly a

---

11. An interesting example of the possible developments in this direction is afforded by Professor G. H. Mead's paper entitled "Suggestions toward a Theory of the Philosophical Disciplines," *Philosophical Review* 1900, *9*, p. 1. My own paper referred to elsewhere on "Psychology and Philosophy," *Philosophical Review*, 1903, *12*, p. 243, contains further illustrative material.

Professor Baldwin's recent volume on genetic logic ("Thought and Things," etc., N. Y., 1906) is a striking case of functional psychology evolving into logic.

more articulate purpose to see the mind which he analyzes as it actually is when engaged in the discharge of its vital functions. If his method tempts him now and then to sacrifice something of petty exactitude, he is under no obligation to yield, and in any case he has for his compensation the power which comes from breadth and sweep of outlook.

So far as he may be expected to develop methods peculiar to himself—so far, indeed, as in genetic and comparative psychology, for example, he has already developed such—they will not necessarily be iconoclastic and revolutionary, nor such as flout the methods already devised and established on a slightly different foundation. They will be distinctly complementary to all that is solid in these. Nor is it in any way essential that the term functionalism should cling to this new-old movement. It seems at present a convenient term, but there is nothing sacrosanct about it, and the moment it takes unto itself the pretense of scientific finality its doom will be sealed. It means to-day a broad and flexible and organic point of view in psychology. The moment it becomes dogmatic and narrow its spirit will have passed and undoubtedly some worthier successor will fill its place.

Reprinted with permission
from *Psychological Review,*
1913, *20,* 91–106.

Chapter 7

Ideo-Motor Action

Edward L. Thorndike

Teachers College, Columbia University

$\mathbf{T}$he theory of ideo-motor action has been for a generation one of the stock "laws" of orthodox psychology. It is taught as almost axiomatic in standard treatises—is made the explanatory principle for phenomena of suggestion, hypnotism, obsessions and the like—and is used as the basis for recommended practices in education, psychiatry, religion—even in salesmanship and advertising.

In spite of contrary evidence brought forward by Kirkpatrick, Woodworth, Burnett, and others, probably nine out of ten of the members of this association believe, or think that they believe, in one or another form of this doctrine that an idea tends to produce the act which it represents or resembles or is "an idea of," or "has as its object."

Against this most respectable doctrine I early rebelled, and I somewhat greedily seize this occasion, which requires that in courtesy you listen to me for an hour, to justify this apostasy and convert you also, if I

[This address was presented at the Twenty-First Annual Meeting of the American Psychological Association, Cleveland, Ohio, 1912.]

can, to the view that the idea of a movement, or of any other response whatsoever, is, in and of itself, utterly impotent to produce it.

The course of the argument will be plainer if I state first what potency I do attach to ideas of movements, or of the resident and remote sensations produced by movements, or of other results of movements; or to any image or other inner state of awareness which represents, or means, or is like, or has as its object, a movement or act or, for that matter, anything else. Any such mental state has, in my opinion, no dynamic potency save that its physiological parallel will evoke whatever response is bound to it or to some part of it by inherited connections, or by the law of habit—including in the later the power of satisfying states of affairs to strengthen whatever connections they accompany or closely follow. I admit a slight tendency for a mental state which is produced immediately before and along with a movement—in one pulse of cerebral activity, as it were—to reinstate the movement by reinstating that total pulse of activity. The connections formed by the laws of habit work mainly forward, but slightly sidewise and even, indirectly, backward. The gist of my contention is that any idea or other situation tends to produce the response which heredity has connected with it or which has gone with it or some part of it with a satisfying or indifferent resulting state of affairs. An idea has no power to produce an act save the power of physiological connections born in man, or bred in him as the consequence of use, disuse, satisfaction and discomfort.

The doctrine of ideo-motor action, however stated, means that certain ideas or images have some further power than this—that between them and the responses which they represent, or have as their objects, or are "ideas of," or are similar to, some effective bond creates itself beyond what the connections made in the person's past can explain. Its classic statement by James reads, as you all know,

We may then lay it down for certain that every representation of a movement awakens in some degree the actual movement which is its object; and awakens it in maximum degree whenever it is not kept from so doing by an antagonistic representation present simultaneously to the mind.

Wundt asserts that the mere apperception of an image of a movement is followed by the movement unless some contrary force acts, and that in children and primitive men the presence of a vivid idea of a movement of their own bodies does therefore cause the movement to take place.

William McDougall writes to the same effect that:

In the special case in which the object to which we direct our attention by a volitional effort is a bodily movement, the movement follows immediately upon the idea, in virtue of that mysterious connection between them of which we know almost nothing beyond the fact that it obtains, and elsewhere, "the representation of a movement of one's own body . . . like all motor representations tends to realize itself immediately in movement."

Two intelligible meanings can be attached to the phrases—"the representation of a certain movement by an idea," an idea having a certain movement "as its object," an idea being "of a certain movement," "motor representation," and the like. The first is that the idea in question *is like* the movement—is to some extent a copy or correspondent of it in much the same way that the mental image of a square inch of red is like a square inch of red. The second is that the idea *means* the movement in much the same way that the thought of the words "square inch of red" means such a square. For the sake of clearness I shall in general restrict argument to the first of these meanings of the doctrine, it being an easy task to disprove it in the second sense once it has been disproved in the first.

That the kind of an idea which is supposed by the ideo-motor theory to be able by some "mysterious connection" to produce a movement is the idea which *is like* the movement appears more clearly in Miss Washburn's statement:

A movement idea is the revival, through central excitation, of the sensations, visual, tactile, kinesthetic, originally produced by the performance of the movement itself. And when such an idea is attended to, when, in popular language, we think hard enough of how the movement would "feel" and look if it were performed, then, so close is the connection between sensory and motor processes, the movement is instituted afresh. This is the familiar doctrine expounded by James.

Professor Calkins still more explicitly states that in voluntary action we arouse a certain response by getting in mind an idea that is *like* the response.

An "outer" volition being a volition to act in a certain way and an "inner" volition being a volition to think in a certain way,

the volition is the image of an action or of a result of action which is normally *similar* . . . to this same action or result. My volition to sign a letter is either an image of my hand moving a pen or an image of my signature written, and my volition to purchase something is an image of myself in the act of handing out money or an image of my completed purchase—golf stick or Barbédienne bronze.

"Inner volitions," she adds, "do not so closely resemble their results. The volitional image of an act may be, in detail, like the act as performed"; but the volitional image of a thought is followed by only a "partially similar" thought.

The issue is now clear. Does an idea tend to produce only the movements which it or some element of it *has* produced (or accompanied in one total response), or does it tend also to produce the movement by which the sensory stuff of which it is the image *was* produced, and which it resembles?

I shall try to prove that an idea of a movement has, apart from connections made by use and satisfying results, no stronger tendency to produce the movement which it resembles, than to produce any other movement whatsoever,—no stronger tendency to produce what it represents or has as its object than an idea of an event outside man's body has—that, apart from connections made by use and satisfying results, the idea of throwing a spear or of pinching one's ear, or of saying "yes" tends to produce the act in question no more than the idea of a ten-dollar bill or of an earthquake tends to produce that object or event.

Why should it? Why should the likeness between John Smith's mental image and some event in nature have any greater potency when that event is in the muscles of John Smith than when it is in the sky above or the earth beneath him? Why should McDougall's "mysterious connection" be allowed to "obtain" just here and not elsewhere?

The reasons why it should not are an attractive theme, but the evidence that it *does* not is our present concern.

First of all, an idea or image certainly *need* not arouse the movement which it represents, or "is of." Let each one of you now summon the most lively and faithful representation that he can of sneezing, then, after five seconds, of hiccoughing. Free your mind of any contradictory ideas, giving yourselves wholeheartedly to thinking hard of the "visual, tactile and kinesthetic sensations of sneezing." We hear no universal chorus of nasal outburst or diaphragmic spasm. Either ninety-nine out of a hundred of you cannot get such representations of these movements as the theory requires or the theory is at fault. But if the theory requires a representation which not one person in a hundred can get of so definite and frequent and interesting a movement as a sneeze, the theory seems very dubious. As a matter of fact a large percentage of you would report that you could get as vivid and faithful an image of a sneeze as of the movements of your hand in signing your name or in handing out money.

To retort that sneezing and hiccoughing are not subject to voluntary control is futile. By the ideo-motor theory they *should be*. The retort witnesses rather to the fact that for a movement to be subject to voluntary control means not "to be capable of representation in thought," but "to be connected as response by the laws of habit to some situation which one can summon at will."

In the second place, in at least a majority of the cases quoted to support the ideo-motor theory—cases where an idea of a movement does have the movement as its sequent,—the connection can be shown to have been built up by habit—by use and satisfying results. When one has the idea of going to bed and goes, or of writing the word "cat" and writes it, the explanation is found in the previous training that has connected the idea of going to bed with situations, such as being sleepy, to which the act is the original or accustomed sequent, or has otherwise connected the act of going to bed as response to the situation of thinking of so doing. The stock case most often quoted from James is that of a man getting out of bed—

The idea flashes across me, "Hollo! I must lie here no longer"—an idea which at that lucky instant awakens no contradicting or paralyzing suggestions, and consequently produces immediately its appropriate motor effects.

Here the idea is patently not a representation of the movement at all. The "Hollo" and "I must" show clearly that it is in words,[1] not in images of leg, trunk and arm movements. Its motor effects are appropriate, not in the sense of being in the least like it or represented by it, but in the sense of being the effects which that idea, when uncontested, had, by exercise and effect, come to produce in that man. The "Hollo! I must" is a lineal descendant of the sensory admonitions from others received during life and connected each with its response by use, satisfaction, and the discomforting punishment attached to opposite courses.

In the third place, the supposedly crucial cases in favor of the ideo-motor theory really show the person *making the movement in order to get the idea of it.* Some of you have doubtless instructed your students as follows:

Try to feel as if you were crooking your finger, whilst keeping it straight. In a minute it will fairly tingle with the imaginary change of position; yet it will not sensibly move because *its not really moving* is also a part of what you have in mind. Drop *this* idea, think of the movement purely and simply, with all brakes off; and, presto! it takes place with no effort at all. (James's "Principles," 2, p. 527)

Now the essential fact here is that when anybody is told to try to feel as if he were crooking his finger, he tends, in the case of many subjects, to respond by taking an obvious way to get that feeling, namely, by actually crooking his finger. He responds to the request, regardless of any ideas beyond his understanding of the words, by a strong readiness to crook his finger. Being forbidden, he restrains the impulse. The "tingling" is not from the *imaginary change* of the finger's position but from the *real restraint from* changing its position. The tingling occurs with individuals who cannot image the finger's movement. Far from showing that the imagined movement is adequate in and of itself to cause the movement, such cases show that it is unsafe to infer that the image comes first in cases where deliberately evoked images of movements are accompanied by the movements or parts thereof. If, in the experiment with ideas of sneezing, a stray individual does sneeze, it is

---

1. If by any sophistry it could be twisted into a representation of leg and trunk movements, it would be only the representation of lying still plus the idea of negation.

ten to one that he has the rare power to make himself sneeze and has done so, intentionally or unintentionally, in order to get a more adequate idea of how it feels to sneeze.

These facts have long seemed to me adequate evidence that an idea can produce only what it, in whole or in part, has produced in the past, not what it is like or what it means. And I venture to hope that, by realizing just what the somewhat cryptic terms—to represent, to have as object, to be an idea of—mean and by noting just what happens in even the most favored cases for the production of a movement by an idea's likeness to it, you are made somewhat suspicious of the "mysterious" and "so close" bond by which every "motor representation tends to realize itself immediately in movement."

I shall now attack the doctrine from within, showing first that its own apostles think more highly of it the less clearly and emphatically it is stated, and even believe that the power of an idea's likeness to a movement to produce that movement is in inverse ratio to the amount of likeness—that the power of an idea to arouse the movement it is like grows greater, the less alike they are!

Last spring many of the members of this association kindly ranked in order of truth from four to ten statements concerning the general power of ideas to produce the acts which they resemble, or the power of some particular idea to produce some particular act. I take this occasion to thank them for their cooperation. These rankings, to which reference will be made repeatedly in what follows, represent a collection of judgments that are expert and, so far as my argument is concerned, impartial. Whatever errors of carelessness in reading, writing and the like affect them are such as have no prejudicial effect upon any of the conclusions which will be drawn from them.

From them we can measure the relative acceptability of each of a series ranging from clear and emphatic to obscure and mild statements of the power of motor representations to realize themselves in movement.

Consider, for example, these four statements:

30. A movement idea is the revival, through central excitation, of the sensations, visual, tactile, kinesthetic, orginally produced by the performance of the movement itself. And when such an idea is attended to, when, in popular language, we think hard enough of how the movement would "feel" and look if it were performed, then, so close is the connection between sensory and motor processes, the movement is instituted afresh.

32. In the special case in which the object to which we direct our attention by a volitional effort is a bodily movement, the movement follows immediately upon the idea.

31. We may then lay it down for certain that every representation of a movement awakens in some degree the actual movement which is its object.

33. If a child or a primitive man has a vivid idea of a movement of his own body, that movement is thereby made unless it is prevented by some contrary idea.

The first two are obviously more emphatic statements of the doctrine of ideo-motor action than the last two, but they are less acceptable to a random picking from this association. Respect for the genius of James perhaps accounts for part of this, but other features of the returns show that the belief in ideo-motor action thrives on qualifications—turns gladly to "a child" or a "primitive man," "a vivid idea," "unless it is prevented," and the like.

Consider next what should be the effect of attention to an idea upon the strength of its tendency to arouse the movement which it represents, supposing it to have such a tendency. Should we not, on all general principles, expect with Miss Washburn that "when such an idea is attended to, when we think hard enough of how the movement would feel and look," its power would be increased? Such seems the inevitable inference from consistent use of the ideo-motor theory. But, as will be seen still more clearly later, there is in the adherents to the theory a struggle between its principles and their sense of actual concrete facts; and the result here is that, in their concrete judgments, they deny the implication of the theory and insist that attention to the idea *weakens* its tendency to arouse the movement which it represents.

For example, the second of the two statements which I shall presently read differs from the first by supposing the movement-idea to be attended to (and also by supposing the idea to be one which resembles the movement a little more closely). The first statement is:

6. To make your spear fly straight and pierce the breast of your enemy it is useful to call to mind the sensations you had when, on other occasions, you saw your spear hurtling through the air straight at an enemy and striking him full in the breast.

The second is:

9. To make your spear fly straight and pierce the breast of your enemy, it is useful to think hard of the visual sensations, originally produced by the performance of the movement itself.

This association would vote over three to one that the second statement was the less true or more false.

The same point can be tested by two other statements from those rated. These are:

8. To make your spear fly straight and pierce the breast of your enemy, it is useful to imagine the sensations you had when, on other occasions, you felt the spear leave your hand, saw it fly through the air straight at an enemy and strike him full in the breast.

11. To make your spear fly straight and pierce the breast of your enemy, it is useful to think hard of the visual, tactile and kinesthetic sensations originally produced by the performance of the movement itself.

As before, the second statement adds the element of attentiveness (and also makes the idea in question a closer representative of the movement and emphasizes the kinesthetic element). This association would vote over two to one that the second statement was less true or more false than the first.

Still more damaging to the theory that ideas tend to evoke the movements which they resemble is the fact that, within certain limitations, the more closely they resemble them the less likely they are, according to your own judgments, to evoke them.

Among the forty statements rated were eight forming a series beginning with:

4. "To make your spear fly straight and pierce the breast of your enemy, it is useful to imagine the spear striking him full in the breast,"

in which, as you see, the idea is of a very remote result of the movement, not at all clearly like it or representative of it more than of many other movements. From this the series proceeded by graduated differences, through cases of closer and closer resemblance to the movement, to number 11, which was an almost verbatim adaptation of Miss Washburn's general statement to this particular case, namely:

11. To make your spear fly straight and pierce the breast of your enemy, it is useful to think hard of the visual, tactile and kinesthetic sensations originally produced by the performance of the movement itself.

The ratings show that although nine out of ten members of this association assert the truth of one or another form of the ideo-motor theory, their sagacious sense of fact compels them to go dead against it by assigning an order of truth to these eight statements, directly opposite to that which the theory requires. You vote overwhelmingly that a mere picture of the spear striking the enemy is more likely to produce the proper cast of the spear than a full and exact representation of the movement itself. You vote that "any idea tends to produce that act which it resembles" but you vote that the more it resembles it the less it tends to produce it! The first vote you cast under pressure from the "steamroller" of traditional orthodoxy; the second is the result of the "direct primary" permitted by my questionnaire and reveals you as true progressives at heart.

If we let distance along a horizontal line FT stand for differences in truth, as judged by you, one foot equalling such a difference between two statements as seventy-five out of a hundred expert psychologists will distinguish correctly, No. 11, the statement concerning the close representative of the movement, is put nearly three feet *false* than No. 4.

Some of you may suspect that my earlier phrase "within certain limitations" conceals facts favorable to the ideo-motor theory. On the contrary, if time permitted, these limitations could be shown to be those expected by the habit-theory. The rule is that mere likeness does nothing; when, as here, an increase in likeness goes with a decrease in the strength of habit's bonds, likeness has the appearance of diminishing an idea's potency to arouse its act; when greater likeness of an idea to an act implies greater frequency of the idea as *situation leading to the act* in past behavior, then greater likeness has the appearance of increasing the tendency of the idea to arouse the act. Nor is the series quoted above a solitary or exceptional one. If one were free to get forty statements rated by each of you instead of four, one could report a dozen similar cases.

In general the ratings witness to a conflict in the minds of psychologists between adherence to the speculative doctrine that the conscious representation of a movement is, in and of itself, potent to produce it and a sense for concrete facts which insists that it is thus potent only when it has for some reason been in the past the situation leading to it. The theory claims that an idea produces what is like it; observation teaches that an idea produces what has followed it.

Why, then, one naturally asks, did the theory ever gain credence, and why is it still cherished? The answers to these questions which I shall try to justify furnish my last and perhaps strongest reason why it should be cherished no longer. My answers are that the ideo-motor theory originated some fifty thousand years ago in the form of the primitive doctrine of imitative magic, and is still cherished because psychology is still, here and there, enthralled by cravings for magical teleological power in ideas beyond what the physiological mechanisms of instinct and habit allow.

Shocking as it may seem, it can be shown that the orthodox belief of modern psychologists, that an idea of a movement tends to produce the movement which is like it, is a true child of primitive man's belief that if you sprinkle water in a proper way your mimicry tends to produce rain, that if you first drag a friend into camp as if he were a dead deer you will be more successful in the day's hunt, or that if you make a wax image of your enemy and stab it he will tend to sicken and die.

Evidence that the accepted doctrine of ideo-motor action is homologous to, and a lineal descendant or vestigial trace of, the crassest forms of imitative magic may be sought along two lines—the comparative and the historical or, as the biologists would say, the palaeontological. In comparative anatomy two forms of an individual or of an organ testify to a common ancestry—are rightly suspected of being homologous—in proportion as they are linked by intermediate forms and differ only, as we say, in degree. After a somewhat similar fashion I shall try to prove that the difference in falsity (or truth) between the absurdest magical superstition and the most approved form of the ideo-motor theory is one of degree only, and that the latter is linked to the former by a chain of intermediate forms.

As magical superstitions we may take the following:

1. "To make your spear fly straight and pierce the breast of your enemy it is useful to make a wax image of your enemy with a spear stuck through his breast."

24. "If a man draws secretly a picture of you with the words 'Yes, I will!' coming out of your mouth and then asks you 'Will you give me your coat?' you are more likely to answer 'Yes, I will' than you would have been if he had not drawn the picture."

As what is in fact the most approved of the stock statements of the ideo-motor theory we may take James's familiar statement:

31. "We may than lay it down for certain that every representation of a movement awakens in some degree the actual movement which is its object."

Either of the two assertions of magical potency would be voted false by the association with practical unanimity. James's statement would be voted true by a comfortable majority. We regard the doctrine of imitative magic as sheer nonsense and the doctrine of ideo-motor action as substantially true. But our own judgments indicate that the latter is close kin to the former, when we treat them as we treat any set of judgments of difference in measuring the discriminability of objects.

Indeed only two intermediate links are required to show and measure the kinship. Recall Professor Washburn's statement:

30. "A movement idea is the revival, through central excitation, of the sensations, visual, tactile, kinesthetic, originally produced by the performance of the movement itself. And when such an idea is attended to, when, in popular language, we think hard enough of how the movement would 'feel' and look if it were performed, then, so close is the connection between sensory and motor processes, the movement is instituted afresh."

And consider also this vague statement, that:

5. "To make your spear fly straight and pierce the breast of your enemy, it is useful to imagine the spear hurtling through the air straight at him and striking him full in the breast."

These five statements, James's, Miss Washburn's, the one about an

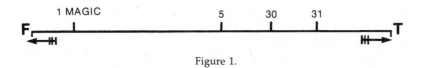

Figure 1.

image of a hurtling and striking spear, the one about contemplating a wax image, and the one about writing in secret the words you wish a man to speak, differ, in respect to truth, only in degree. For people are able to compare them as to truth nearly or quite as readily and confidently as they can compare in respect to truth any five dubious statements chosen at random from psychological treatises. And when they so compare them the results are as follows:

Let the line *FT* represent a scale for truth. Let the point marked 1. Magic represent the location on the scale of the truth (or falsity) of the statement (No. 1) about the potency of the wax image. Let each inch on the scale represent the amount of difference in truth necessary in order that seventy-five per cent of this association shall judge the difference correctly, one out of every four being in error. Then statements 5, 30 and 31 are located as shown in Fig. 1. For the difference in truth between statement 1 and statement 5 is 1.64. It is measured by the fact that of 37 psychologists who compared them, 28 judged that 5 was truer or less false, 5 rated them as equally true or false, and 4 judged 1 to be truer than 5. The difference between statement 5 and statement 30 is .53. It is measured by the fact that of 24 psychologists who compared them 14 judged that 30 was truer or less false, 2 that they were equally true, and 8 that 5 was truer than 30. The difference between statement 30 and statement 31 is .5. It is measured by the fact that of 17 psychologists who compared them 9 judged that 31 was truer or less false, 3 that it was equally true and 5 that 30 was truer than 31.

Thus the truth of statement No. 1—of the potency of fabricating a wax image of your enemy—is about $1\frac{2}{3}$ below the truth of statement No. 5—of the potency of vague thoughts about the spear striking him, $2\frac{1}{4}$ below the truth of Miss Washburn's statement and $2\frac{3}{4}$ below the truth of James's statement. The links are truly intermediate. The most approved statements of the ideo-motor theory are by their own advocates confessed to be only a little more truthful or less false than the rankest magical nonsense.

Using the same criterion of expert judgment in each case, the most approved statement of the ideo-motor theory is only about as far above a barefaced statement of the primitive superstition of imitative magic on a scale for truth as composition *B* is above composition *A* on a scale for merit in English writing; or as drawing *B* is above drawing *A* on a scale for merit in drawing.

A.

B.

Figure 2.

A

The book I refer to read is Ichabod Crane, it is an grate book and I like to rede it. Ichabod Crane was a man and a man wrote a book and it is called Ichabod Crane i like it because the man called it ichabod crane when I read it for it is such a great book.

B

First: De Quincys mother was a beautiful women and through her De Quincy inhereted much of his genius.

His running away from school enfluenced him much as he roamed through the woods, valleys and his mind became very meditative.

The greatest enfluence of De Quincy's life was the opium habit. If it was not for this habit it is doubtful whether we would now be reading his writings.

His companions during his college course and even before that time were great enfluences. The surroundings of De Quincy were enfluences. Not only De Quincy's habit of opium but other habits which were peculiar to his life.

His marriage to the woman which he did not especially care for.

The many well educated and noteworthy friends of De Quincy.

Some of you may be skeptical concerning this method of measuring differences of credibility in the minds of a given class of thinkers, harboring the suspicion that the individual reports were invalidated as measures of the individuals' opinions by the incommensurability of the statements. Some of you, indeed, refused to rate the statements. But, as a matter of fact, the main difficulty experienced with the various sets out of the forty-two statements which were issued was not that they were incommensurate as to truth, but that the differences were too small to be distinguished with any feeling of surety. I regret that the poll of this association is not complete, owing to the fact that some individuals refused, justly enough, to spend their time in grinding my axe, and that some canny ones refused to be drawn into any testifying that might conceivably be held against them later. It seems, however, certain that the membership of this association experienced—or would have experienced, had they tried to make the comparisons—no greater sense of incommensurability than they would have experienced in grading advertisements for "appeal," drawings for skill, or poems for beauty. Reports of such difficulties were very rare.

Whatever validity attaches to your belief that you know what you are about and mean something real when you judge that James's familiar statement is less false than the assertion about the potency of secretly writing "Yes I will" as a persuasive fetich, or that about the potency of wax constructions of one's enemy in warfare, attaches to all the comparisons that I have used. But had I asked for only this one comparison every member of the association would have made it with no sense of incommensurability or trickery, but only with a sad surprise that I should ask so foolish, because so easy, a question. This method of measuring differences in credibility in the minds of a defined group is in fact sound, and, I may add, is useful in the case of very many problems in the mental sciences.

In the present case it teaches us that our belief that an idea tends to produce the act which it is like, or represents, or "is an idea of" or "'has as its object," is kith and kin with our forebears' belief that dressing to look like a bear will give you his strength or that burning an effigy of the foe will make him die, and with the modern charlatan's belief that thinking one can walk will mend a broken bone. It is kith and kin with them, own grandchild of one and own brother to the other—and as false as either.

An image, idea or any other mental fact, has, apart from connections made by heredity, use and satisfying results, no stronger tendency to produce the movement which it resembles, or represents, or has as its object than to produce any other movement whatsoever—no stronger tendency to produce it than ideas of dollars and earthquakes have to produce them. Why should it? Why should the likeness between John Smith's mental image and an event in nature have any greater potency when that event is in the muscles of John Smith than when it is in the sky above or the earth beneath him? Why should McDougall's "mysterious connection" be allowed to "obtain" just here and not elsewhere?

It obtains nowhere. The connection whereby likeness or representative quality, in and of itself, created a bond between a thought and an act, would indeed be "mysterious" if it existed. But it does not exist.

Reprinted with permission
from *Psychological Review*,
1915, 22, 1-27.

Chapter 8

A Revision of Imageless Thought

R. S. Woodworth

Columbia University

Several years ago I was led by some experiments on voluntary movement to conclude that an act might be thought of without any representative or symbolic image, and further study led me to extend this conclusion to other thoughts. My attention was soon called, in a review of this work by Angell, to previous discussions of the same question, connected with Stout's assertion that there was nothing pyschologically absurd in the conception of imageless thought. Looking into the contemporary experimental literature, I then made the acquaintance of Binet and of Watt, Bühler and others of the Külpe school, and my own work soon fell into insignificance beside these extensive and many-sided contributions. Even the merit of independent confirmation was not specially important in this case, since such confirmation was forthcoming even from those who, like Wundt, were not at all in sympathy with the conclusions of the imageless thought party. It appeared that imageless thought, the mere gross fact of observation, had come to stay, and that the only question was what to do

Address of the President before the American Psychological Association, at Philadelphia, December, 1914.

with it. Some psychologists have assigned great importance to this fact as a demonstration of non-sensory content, while others have avoided so revolutionary a conclusion by explaining the fact away through one interpretation or another; others again have accepted the fact but minimized its importance, treating it as a mere limiting case; and some, while accepting the *gross* fact, have doubted that it would stand the test of more refined introspection. Meanwhile, my own views have been maturing as the result of continued thought and experiment, and the time is perhaps favorable for resuming the offensive, and endeavoring to uncover the weaknesses of the negative interpretations, and for offering a conception of the matter which may possibly appear superior to those hitherto presented, or at least worthy of some consideration.

Of the interpretations of imageless thought which explain the fact away without allowing it to modify existing systems of psychology, the most important is that of Wundt. It will be recalled that the method employed by the Külpe school in studying the thought processes was drastically criticized by Wundt, who objected to their experiments as being experiments in appearance only, and held that real thinking could not be done to order in the laboratory. He himself preferred to rely on incidental introspections during spontaneous thought, and in fact reports such observations of his own.[1] "In such self-observations," he writes,

it became perfectly clear to me that the thought was not formed during the process of its verbal expression, but was present as a whole in consciousness before the first word was reached. At first none of the verbal or other images, which subsequently appeared in running through the thought and giving it expression, was present in the focus of consciousness, but these parts of the thought appeared successively as the thought was allowed to develop.

With only this fact in mind, he admits, one might easily be led to regard the thought as a unit with a distinctive elementary character. But quite a different conclusion is reached when other facts are also taken into account, that of the narrowness of the field of attention, that of the existence of dim content in the background of consciousness, and that of the "total feeling," itself a unit, though generated by a complex of images. A thought, in Wundt's view, is essentially a complex of images, but these parts of the thought are too numerous to be present together in the field of attention. They are present at first only in the background and are not introspectively visible; but as the thought is dwelt upon and expressed, its constituent images come successively into view. What then was the apparently unitary thought with which the process started? This, explains Wundt, was a "total feeling," generated by the complex of images in the background, and itself occupying for an instant the center of the stage.

---

1. *Psychologische Studien*, 1907, *3*, 349.

It is obvious that such a position is almost inexpugnably entrenched. The extremely hypothetical nature of the ground renders a direct attack hopeless. So much as this may be ventured, that, if the words expressing a thought are really its constituent parts, it is curious that the same thought can be thought in different words, and even in different languages, and still more curious that the words to fit the thought are not always at hand. Apparently, the same complex may be composed of different elements, and may exist with some of its elements lacking. Further, it is curious to reflect that these verbal images in the background must somehow be present simultaneously and yet in proper sequence, since otherwise they might compose quite a different thought or no thought at all.

But the principal doubt to be raised concerns the "total feeling." This unitary feeling, present without observable images, and "adequate to the thought," would almost meet the demands of the opposing party, except for Wundt's insistence on its being a feeling, to the neglect of its noetic character. Certainly it is not a feeling, in any strict sense, that straightway finds expression in a statement of fact. Wundt's analysis leaves out of account the core of the whole experience, namely, the fact or supposition which was subsequently expressed in a sentence, but which was definitely and clearly present in mind in advance of the words.

Several writers have called attention to the presence of vague or apparently irrelevant imagery in moments that would otherwise appear imageless. The presence of kinesthetic sensations, habitually unattended to, has also been shown in many cases, and thus we have become wary of asserting that a given moment is really devoid of sensory content. Of course, no one has ever supposed that bodily sensation could be absent from the background of any conscious state, but it has been thought possible to distinguish between irrelevant content and content related to the topic of thought. We must, however, recognize the probability that apparently irrelevant sensations and images sometimes enter into the web of thinking. Especially has the attempt been made with some success to extend the James-Lange theory of emotions to cover the so-called "conscious attitudes"; and some would even extend it to cover the imageless awareness of definite facts, contending that every thought has its own peculiar motor expression, and that the sensations generated by the movement furnish the conscious content of the thought; but no one, as far as I know, has found empirical support for this extreme view.

It is worth remarking that the presence of images and sensations in many or most moments of thinking does not disconcert the supporter of imageless thought. He is perfectly willing to admit that such content is often or even usually present; and the only real importance of a few well-attested instances of thought without such content is that they furnish him his most direct evidence of the existence of other content. His main contention is that other content exists, and that it is the most essential and characteristic of all.

But some psychologists, while admitting the occasional occurrence of imageless thought, deny its evidential importance. It is merely the limiting case, they say, in a continuous gradation from thought in clear images, down through thought in medium and dim images, to thought in images at or near the zero mark. The most attractive form of this interpretation is that which sees in the graded series the progressive automatization of a thought through practise. When the thought is novel, it comes with abundant sensory content, but as it grows familiar and habitual it becomes less sensuous, that is to say, less conscious, until, just as it is about to become automatic and unconscious, it still shows a feeble spark of conscious life; and this feeble spark is pounced upon by the imageless thinker and rashly heralded forth as proof of some unrecognized species of conscious experience. In reality, imageless thought is imageless because it is all but unconscious. This genetic interpretation has been presented with most force by Titchener[2] and by Book.[3]

The undoubted attractiveness of this conception comes from its following so neatly from the law of practise, and its deficiencies arise from its taking account of only one side of the practise effect. There is much in practise besides the tendency toward automatism. Seldom does the course of training consist of repeating time after time the same performance, only with increasing smoothness and speed. Usually the process begins with varied and tentative reactions, and advances by selection and elimination. Moreover new forms of reaction, made possible by the progress in facility, make their appearance in the course of training. Thus the perfected act omits elements present at the start and contains elements not present at the start, and may be an entirely different means of reaching the same result. If therefore the first thinking on a given topic is fraught with imagery, while the practised thought on the same topic is bare of images, it does not in the least follow that the imageless thought is a condensation of the imaginal. It may be a more economical substitute. The imagery present at the start may have been due to a diffusion of excess energy such as is common in unpractised acts, or it may have furnished a round-about way of dealing with the problem and have given place with practise to the more direct attack represented by the imageless thought.

Practise experiments give little ground for believing that a series of part acts, by simply becoming very easy and swift, blend together into a total act in which the parts are lost to sight. Rather has it been found true that the more inclusive acts, such as dealing with words and phrases as units, in typewriting and telegraphy, arise suddenly as new forms of action, in the progress of training, and themselves make possible a great increase in the speed of the partial or lower-order acts. The partial acts do not blend to produce the inclusive act, but the latter is hit upon and causes the former to blend. Attention deserts the parts, which thus

---

2. "Experimental Psychology of the Thought Processes," 1909, pp. 173, 183, 187.
3. *Psychological Review*, 1910, 17, 381.

become automatic; but attention still remains keenly alive, being directed to the more inclusive acts. These higher acts are real units, and not mere blends; they are clearly conscious and yet not in imaginal form; indeed, they seem the very type of an imageless thought.

Observations of new ideas, at their first appearance in an individual, would be of interest in relation to the interpretation of imageless thought as exclusively old and well-drilled thought. In the hope of gathering such observations, I have sought to catch myself at moments when some new idea germinated in my mind. Unfortunately, opportunities have not presented themselves with the frequency that could be desired; but, in the few instances that I have collected the experience could be described as the dawning of some new meaning in things, sometimes with scrappy verbal and visual images, sometimes with none that were observable. When they occurred, the images were promptly forgotten, though the thought was firmly impressed on memory. So far from accepting the view that imageless thought is automatized thought, I should be inclined to believe that a new thought is characteristically imageless, and that it attaches itself secondarily to a word or other convenient symbol, and is more apt to occur with an image when it is somewhat familiar than when it is new.

Still another interpretation of imageless thought, or of the observations that purport to reveal it, presents a serious obstacle to our progress. Frequently such statements as these are contained in the subject's retrospective report: "I thought of such and such an object," or, "I thought that such and such was the case," this being the extent of the subject's description of his experience, except for the purely negative statement that no images were present. The objection has been raised by Dürr,[4] von Aster,[5] and Titchener,[6] that in such reports the subject is not playing the game. He has fallen from psychological description into the commonsense habit of telling what he has been thinking about. He has committed the Kundgabe or expression error: instead of describing his thoughts, he is expressing them. He has committed the stimulus or object error, and, instead of describing consciousness, is mentioning the objects with which consciousness was concerned. Confronted with this objection, the subject is apt to reply that he has done his best, that what was present in his mind was precisely the fact or object mentioned, and that if he is forbidden to refer to the object, all he can do is to hold his peace. Though this reply fails to satisfy the critic, there is something to say in the subject's behalf. Suppose, for the sake of argument, that the specific thought content exists: how would you propose to describe it? You offer the subject his choice of sensory terms, but these he rejects as not fitting the case. If then you exclude reference to objects, you have nothing further to offer him beyond a few vague and negative terms,

---

4. *Zeitschrift f. Psychol.*, 1908, *49*, 313–340.
5. *Ibid.*, 56–107.
6. *Op. cit.*, p. 147.

such as "imageless," "peculiar, unanalyzable state," etc. In fine, the objection has force only on the assumption that the state should be described in sensory terms, and that non-sensory content is non-existent. It prejudges the case.

It is curious that the presence of the stimulus error in reports of images is not treated with a similar seriousness. Seldom in the literature will you find an image really described. Instead of an analysis of the visual picture as composed of colors and shadings in a certain spatial arrangement, instead of an analysis of the auditory image as consisting of a sequence of elementary sounds, you read of "a visual image of a Massachusetts town," or of "an auditory image of the experimenter saying 'subordinate concept.' " If it is committing the stimulus error to report a "thought of" such and such an object, it is equally committing it to report an "image of" the object. A strictly descriptive regimen would require the subject, one would think, to exclude all reference to the object in the one case as in the other.

Yet consider the situation of an observer who is forbidden to refer to the object in describing his images. He would have to confine his report to such statements as "a bright, somewhat variegated spot against a dark ground," omitting to state that this was an image of his friend's face. Yet, if the image, whether faint or vivid, schematic or detailed, was for him, at the moment, an image of his friend's face, can he properly describe the consciousness of that moment without reference to his friend? No question of the logic of meaning is here involved, but a mere question of fact: Was or was not a reference to the object present in the momentary consciousness; and, if so, can the state be described without reference to the object?

The same question arises when we have a presented object instead of an image. I hear a noise from the street and say, "There is a horse galloping past." This is a commonsense reaction which makes no pretense of describing consciousness. But suppose I do attempt to describe consciousness. It is then, perhaps, in order for me to tell exactly what auditory sensations I had. If I do this as well as possible, and find nothing further, such as an image, to report—have I then, with my inventory of auditory sensations, fully accomplished my task of describing consciousness? It would seem not, if I actually was conscious of a galloping horse, while my report makes no mention of this object. It is all very well to warn me of the stimulus error if I show a tendency to go beyond my momentary experience and tell something about the horse which may be objectively a fact but was not present in my mind at the moment; but if I stick closely to the momentary experience, reference to the object is quite in order and in fact indispensable; for, as a matter of fact, reference to the object was probably the most prominent part of the experience. This is equally true in the case of an image, and I must conclude that an observer is perfectly justified in reporting an "image of his friend's face," and that he could not omit this reference to the object without badly mutilating the experience. If so, the observer who reports the "thought of such and such an object" is equally within his rights. He may have omitted something which a complete description should include, but he has, in all probability, reported the most prominent datum of his momentary consciousness.

One further important objection to the doctrine of imageless thought is contained in the teaching of such men as James, Ebbinghaus and Dewey. In speaking of non-sensory content, we have neglected to define sensation, or, worse yet, we have, according to these authors, fallen into the error of excluding relations, forms, patterns, meanings from our concept of sensation, and then being badly put to it to explain how they get into perception and thought. It is impossible, we are told, to draw a line in sense perception between what is sensation and what is perception; and there is therefore no excuse for speaking of non-sensory content in sense perception, nor for speaking of such content as present in thinking, unless we are ready to make the improbable assertion that positive content is vouchsafed us when withdrawn from the world of sense that can never be experienced in the presence of physical objects.

Instead of attempting to meet this objection directly, I propose to go on with a positive interpretation of imageless thought, in the hope that it may avoid the difficulty, and ultimately find a legitimate ground for the distinction between sensory and non-sensory.

To reach a positive interpretation that shall have any real significance, it is essential to turn away from the isolated fact thus far considered, and seek other facts which may be brought into relation to it. A hint as to the most profitable direction in which to seek for related facts is afforded by the following consideration. Thought deals largely with data derived from past experience. New ideas may certainly be generated in the process of thinking, but in very large measure the content of thought is provided by memory; and it is usually this memory content which appears in the imageless form. It may then be profitable to bring our rather extensive knowledge of memory into relation with the phenomenon of imageless thought; and it is in that direction that I propose to search.

On examining the way in which recalled facts present themselves, we are at once struck by something that broadens the outlook considerably. It is not only in thinking, properly so called, that facts come to mind without images, but in the most commonplace acts of memory. I recall, without visual, verbal or other observable images, what I have in my pockets, where I left my umbrella, whether my neighbor is at home today. This imageless recall is with some individuals quite the rule. The facts are clearly enough present in mind, but if there be any image it is so excessively dim as to elude detection. Such imageless recall is indicated though perhaps not fully demonstrated by some of Galton's results; and Miss Martin has recently[7] given a clear demonstration of the existence of memory content that is "unanschaulich."

In imageless thought, then, the imagelessness has nothing particular

---

7. *Zeitschrift f. Psychol.*, 1912, 65, 417–490.

to do with the thinking process; and we are permitted to drop, with some relief, the elevated tone that has sometimes seemed appropriate to the topic. Thought is imageless because its data are recalled in an imageless form, and not because it does not thrive in a sensory atmosphere. Much effective thinking occurs in the physical presence of its object. The use of the word "thoughts" to denote non-sensory content is unfortunate, for the words "thought" and "thinking" customarily denote a certain mental function or group of functions, and cannot easily be restricted to any particular sort of content. The best word would be one that suggested recall rather than thinking; but I am not at present prepared to suggest a suitable nomenclature.[8]

What, then, is it, in general, that is recalled? An old standard answer is that we recall our past experiences. Objection has several times been raised to this answer within the last two decades; but the following line of criticism is perhaps new. In experiments on testimony, or on "incidental memory," the subject is found to be incapable of recalling much that has been before his eyes, and even within the general scope of his attention. If he could call back his original experience, it would seem that he could give the testimony required of him. A specially instructive experiment, for our present purpose, is that of Thorndike,[9] who asked his subjects to call up an image of a certain scene, as of the front of a familiar building, and then, after they had estimated the vividness of their images, asked them specific questions, as to the number of pillars in the facade and similar details. He found a marked inability to answer the specific questions, even on the part of individuals with very lifelike

---

8. Unless the following suggestion can be seriously entertained. It has long appeared to me that we psychologists were on the wrong track in our selection of technical terms. Our custom is to choose some term of common usage that may convey to the uninitiated a suggestion of the technical meaning newly attached to it. The trouble is that the untechnical usage continues alongside of the technical and tends to cause confusion; until finally psychologists are driven to exclude the untechnical use from their discourse, and thus lose a very convenient tool of expression. It is nothing less than a scandal, for example, that the word "feeling" should have been so refined in usage that the psychologist can no longer speak of a "feeling of hesitation," and scarcely of a "feeling of familiarity," without an apology and the dread of being misunderstood by his colleagues. The older sciences, with their greater need for an extensive technical vocabulary, have gone to work in quite a different way. They either take unfamiliar Greek and Latin words and derivatives, or they set apart some proper name to serve the special purpose. Thus they have their watts and volts and ohms and amperes, terms regarding the meaning of which no one need ever be in doubt. Such terms are much better than "thoughts," or than "Bewusstseinslagen," with its doubtful translation of "conscious attitudes." I would propose, accordingly, to follow the lead of physics and chemistry; and since Bewusstseinslagen were first reported and defined in the work of Marbe and his associates, I would suggest calling them "marbs," the term to be defined for all time by reference to the original description by Marbe. Similarly, since the "thoughts" were gradually brought to light by the school of which Külpe was the guiding spirit, I would suggest calling them "kulps," defining this term similarly by reference to the original works. These terms are certainly beautifully compact and euphonious, and those who can bring themselves to use them will find them very convenient.

9. J. of Philos., 1907, 4, 324.

images; and, in fact, there was little or no correspondence between vividness of image and correctness of report on details. I have frequently repeated this experiment with the same results. I have never found an individual able to read off the number of pillars from his image. Only those could tell the number who had at some time counted them; and other subjects protested that it was not fair to expect them to find the number of pillars in the image, when they had never counted them in the original. All this seemed highly suggestive. It suggested that only that was recalled which had been noted in the original experience; and that even vivid images, described as being fully equal to the actual experience, were in fact something quite different.

I was thus prompted to undertake an examination of images and other content of recall, in order to see how far they could be described as revivals of past experiences, and how far they consisted of facts noted in the past. I set myself to recall events from my past life, and in other cases to recall persons, buildings, towns, and such specific facts as the exact colors of postage stamps, the quality of a friend's voice, the shapes, tastes, odors, etc., of a great variety of objects. What I got was sometimes to be called an image and sometimes not; but in all cases, with a few doubtful exceptions, it consisted of facts previously noted. When I say "facts," I do not mean verbal statements of facts, but a direct consciousness of some thing, quality, relation, action—of something which I had observed in the original experience. I did not get back experiences as concrete totals, but only facts which I had discriminated out of those totals. In the original experiences, those facts had had a concrete setting or background; but this setting was not recalled. The facts were recalled in isolation.

Often, indeed, a rudimentary setting was present, consisting of either a personal reference, or a spatial reference, or both. By "personal reference" is meant that the fact was recalled as my own experience, or that the relation of the fact to me, or my attitude to it, was recalled along with the fact. By "spatial reference" is meant that an object was recalled as being to the right or left, or in a certain town, or in a certain direction from my position at the time of recall. Spatial reference was more frequently present than personal. Neither was universally present; and, aside from them, no setting was recalled. It frequently happened that several facts derived from the same experience, or from different experiences, were recalled almost or quite simultaneously, so that the recall was richer than would be suggested by the expression, "Isolated fact." Nevertheless all of these facts had been previously noted, and they did not bring their concrete setting back with them.

As an example of my results, I will cite the recall of a colleague speaking in faculty meeting. What I got was a certain quality of voice and precise manner of enunciating, rather different from the conversational tone of this individual. There were no words nor particular vowel or consonantal sounds present in recall, but simply the quality of the voice and enunciation. I got also the fact that the speaker was speaking as chairman of a committee, and something of the rather critical attitude of the faculty towards him, these facts being recalled in the "imageless" way. Besides, I got a spatial reference, in that the speaker was located in a certain position with respect to my position in the meeting; and a vague personal reference amounting to an attitude of support or well-wishing. Beyond this, nothing. No visual background of faces or furniture, no auditory background of words spoken, no somesthetic background of myself sitting.

Among the facts thus recalled in relative isolation and without concrete setting were the following:

Of persons: shape of head or of nose, breadth of face, color of eye, curliness of hair, blotchiness of complexion, facial expression, tone of voice, trick of gesture, "smoothness" of manner, social position, ability, industry, relation to myself, as being friendly or unfriendly, a superior or dependent, agreeable, a bore, etc., or as having been seen recently or long ago.

Of buildings: location, size, color, material, architectural style.

Of towns: location, general topography, old or new style, abundance of shade, holiday atmosphere, quietness, association with certain events.

These facts run the gamut from simple to complex, and from sensory to abstrusely relational. They are so varied as to indicate that any observed fact can be recalled in isolation. Among the striking instances of isolation were recall of the color of an object without its shape, of its shape without its color, of its gloss or shading without either color or shape.

The following interpretation seems scarcely more than a restatement of these results. An actual situation presents an almost unlimited variety of facts or features, of which an observer notes a few, the rest remaining undiscriminated in the background and giving the concrete setting of the features noted. Later, he may "remember" the situation, but this is not to reinstate it in its original multiplicity and continuity. He recalls the features which he observed, or some of them, but not the great mass of material which remained in the background. Lacking this setting or background, he is not in a position to make any fresh observations in recall, and thus arises the weakness of incidental memory.

If generalized to cover all cases in all individuals, this statement does indeed go beyond the evidence at hand. But if the possibility of an occasional recall of the concrete setting is left open, and the assertion simply made that an observed fact is often recalled without its original setting, this conclusion, thought modest, is sufficient to furnish a positive interpretation of imageless recall.

Were it true that a recalled fact always brought with it its original setting, then, indeed, all recall would involve sensory imagery. But if a fact is recalled in isolation, it depends on the nature of the fact whether the recall would be called imaginal or imageless. If the fact lay as it were on the sensory surface of things, such as color or tone, its recall would usually be spoken of as an image. If the fact lay below the sensory surface, as the fact that a speaker was exaggerating, or speaking as chairman of a committee, an isolated recall of this fact would be unhesitatingly pronounced imageless, unless, to be sure, it were accompanied by a verbal or symbolic image derived perhaps from another source than the original setting of the fact. The definitely imaginal and the definitely imageless are the extremes of a series, between which lie many intermediate facts difficult to place in either class. The expression of a face, the composition of a painting, the style of a building or piece of music, recalled in an isolated way, are difficult to classify.

If you set yourself to discover what are the objects of your attention in a sensory experience, you will usually find that the actual sensations are less prominent than the things signified by them. You are more conscious of the horse galloping past than of the actual noises that you hear. When, therefore, you later recall hearing a horse gallop past, it is not surprising that the thing signified should be recalled more distinctly than the noises; and you are left in doubt whether to class the recall as an image or not. This is a type of numerous cases. An observed feature of a situation often lies partly "on the sensory surface" and partly below, and the observer does not take separate note of the sign and of the thing signified, but perceives them together as a single fact. His recall of the fact may then partake both of the sign and of the thing signified, though the sensory flavor is usually weakened in recall. The distinction between imaginal and imageless, between sensory and non-sensory, is not perfectly sharp, and appears, from our present point of view, to be of minor significance, the main principle being the isolated recall of observed facts.

I ought really to rest content with the conservative statements that precede, and leave imageless recall as an incident to the occasional, or frequent, recall in isolation of previously noted facts. But in the interests of a more clean-cut theory, I am tempted to more radical and general statements. I propose to strike out boldly and formulate a theory, hoping that, whether acceptable or not, it may prove a stimulus to thought and perhaps to experiment.

The first step towards this theory is to generalize the conclusion derived from observations already cited, and to offer the hypothesis that all recall is of facts previously noted, freed from the concrete setting in which they occurred when noted. This generalization I hold to be correct for my own case, and, though the testimony of many individuals regarding their imagery is on its face in flat contradiction with mine, the objective test of incidental memory seems to show that there is something radically wrong with their testimony. My generalization has the advantage of squaring with the facts of recall as objectively tested, and the only difficulty is to explain away the introspective reports of images "fully equivalent to actual experience," and of "living over the past as if it were present."

Without pretending to do full justice to this testimony, I must for the present content myself with a few remarks. Undoubtedly a person may become deeply absorbed in a remembered experience, because of its great interest for him. Now his present interest is probably the same as that which dominated him in the original experience and led him to observe and react to certain features. If, his interest reviving, he gets back these features and reactions, he has the essentials of the original experience from his own point of view, and satisfactorily lives it over again, even without the concrete background, the absence of which, in his absorption, he would not notice, any more than he noted its presence in the original experience.

As to the vivid image, said to be "in all respects equivalent to the actual scene," we undoubtedly have, in such a case, a revival of personal attitude and emotional value, which alone are enough to create a strong atmosphere of reality. We must also recognize that what an artist might call the general effect of a scene is as much a fact to be observed as any other. The features which can be analyzed out of a situation are not exclusively details, but include broad effects and syntheses and anything that can be the object of attention. If now you recall the emotional value and general effect of a scene, along with some of the colors and other previously noted details, you perhaps have enough to make you testify, rashly, that your image is in all respects equivalent to the actual scene. A test of incidental memory would soon convince you that the "equivalence" is an illusion.

It is also true that a person may observe a scene in such detail as to recall a great number of its features; and he might express the wealth of his recollection by asserting that he revived the entire experience; but, so long as what he recalls is what he previously observed, he offers no exception to the rule that has been formulated.

We have not yet by any means exhausted the relevant information to be derived from studies of memory. Evidently we should be much helped in any study of recall by having at hand a report of the process by which what is now recalled was originally learned. We should be helped in our present inquiry by knowing whether "impressing a thing on the memory" consists in simply standing before the thing and letting it "soak in," or whether it consists in reacting to the thing by observing its characteristic features. It may be said at once that studies of memorizing give little sign of a purely receptive attitude on the part of the learner, and much evidence of a reactive and analytical attitude. Meumann emphasized the importance of the "will to learn." A subject might attentively examine a list of nonsense syllables, and yet make little progress in memorizing it unless his will to learn were excited. Now the "will" can scarcely be conceived as acting without means or tools; and its tools consist of various specific reactions to the matter set for memorizing, the reactions varying with the material and with the test of memory that is to be met. Some of these reactions may properly be called motor; here would be classed the rhythm, accents, pauses and vocal inflections that are read into the list by the learner. But in large measure the reactions are of the perceptual sort, and consist in observing positions, relations, patterns, meanings, in the matter to be learned. The recent studies of Müller throw all these factors into clear relief. Memorizing is very largely a process of observation, of noting those features of the material that will serve to hold it together in the desired way. Some of these features, such as patterns and relations and the nearer-lying meanings, are, as it were, found in the material itself; while other features, the more far-fetched meanings and associative aids, are imported from without; but this distinction is only one of degree.

The reactions made in learning, it should once more be said, are specific, and adapted not only to the material learned but also to the kind of memory test that is anticipated. If the subject expects to recite a list of words or syllables throughout, he observes positions, sequences, patterns and relations that will serve to bind the whole list together. If he expects simply to respond to each of the odd-numbered words in the list by giving the following word, as in the method of paired associates, he takes each pair as a unit, and observes characteristics of the pair that bind it together, but neglects the sequence of pairs. If he expects to be called upon to recognize the individual words of the list, he fixes his attention on them singly, observing in each, as far as possible, some character that may serve to impress it. There is no one uniform process of learning, and the will to learn cannot be conceived as a general force or agency. What we find in memorizing is a host of specific reactions, largely of the perceptual sort.

I may be permitted to cite the results of a little experiment designed to test this matter. I read a list of twenty pairs of unrelated words to a group of 16 adult subjects, instructing them beforehand to learn the pairs so as to be able to respond with the second of each pair when the first should be given as stimulus. But, after reading the list three times, I told them that they should, if possible, give also the first word of the following pair on getting the second word of the preceding pair as stimulus. I then read the first word of the list, waited 5 seconds for the subject to recall and write the second word; then read this second word, and waited the same time for them to recall and write the third word, namely, the first word of the second pair; and so on through the list. The results were most definite: the second members of the pairs were correctly recalled in 74% of all the cases, but the first members were recalled in only 7% of the cases. The subjects reported that this great difference was apparently due to the fact that they had examined each pair with the object of finding some character or meaning in it; whereas they had neglected the sequence of pairs as being of no moment.

This result is instructive in several ways. It indicates, first, that the will to learn operates not by favoring a general receptive or memorizing attitude, but by leading to specific reactions of the observational type. It serves, next, to fortify the results of other experiments on "incidental memory." Here the objection cannot be raised that the incidental matter that is not recalled was never attended to; for the first words of the pairs were attended to as well as the second. The experiment also shows the unsatisfactory character of Ward's conception of the process of learning. He has said that associations are formed by the movement of attention from one to the other of the terms associated. But here attention moved from the first to the second member of a pair, and thence to the first member of the next pair; yet the first movement seems to have established a strong association, and the second, comparatively speaking, none. Evidently something much more specific than a mere movement of attention has been in play. The members of a pair are associated by the sequence, connection or meaning that is found in the pair. Finally, this experiment serves to strengthen doubts that have often been raised, especially by the work on incidental memory, regarding the adequacy of contiguity in experience as an associating force. Here the contiguity between the members of a pair was scarcely greater, in matter of time, than that between successive pairs; yet the association within pairs was strong, and that between successive pairs almost negligible. Since the associations within pairs gave 10 times as good a score as those between pairs, we may perhaps say that mere contiguity does not contribute more than one tenth of the whole associating force, the remaining nine tenths being contributed by the noting of suitable features in the material. Even the small fraction thus left to contiguity does not necessarily belong to it; for it is not improbable that the sequence and relation of successive pairs were sometimes observed. In fact, of the few correct recalls of first members, practically all occurred at the beginning or end of the list of twenty pairs; and it is quite likely that, in these favored positions, attention was occasionally directed to such incidental matters as the sequence of pairs or their positions in the list. Except at the ends of the list, the score for first members was only 1/85 as good as that for second members of the pairs; and this fraction, rather than 1/10, probably represents the proportion of the total associative force that should be assigned to mere contiguity; though even this is a doubtful concession.

It may be considered superfluous bravery in me to challenge the doctrine of association by contiguity, in addition to all the other enemies already on my hands; but, in reality, I have this doctrine on my hands at any rate. For if contiguity in a momentary experience is a strong and sufficient associative force, then any item that is later recalled will in turn recall its contiguous items and redintegrate the whole experience or a large part of it, and my hypothesis that what is recalled is observed facts without their setting would become untenable.

Now association by contiguity has played a worthy and important part in the development of psychology, and its attempt to absorb into itself all other laws of association has, in my opinion, been a success. Things become associated only when they are contiguous in experience. That is to say that contiguity is a necessary condition of association. But is it a sufficient condition? There is little in the experimental work on memory to indicate that it is sufficient, and much to indicate that it is not usually depended on to accomplish results. The things to be connected must be together, in order to arouse the reaction connecting them; but, unless they arouse some such reaction, they do not become connected, except it be very weakly. The reaction may be described in a general way as a reaction to the two things together; it is perhaps sometimes a purely motor reaction, but most often, I believe, is rather to be called a perceptual reaction, consisting in the observation of some relation between the two things, or some character of the whole composed of the two taken together. In any case, the reaction is specific; and it is this specific reaction, rather than any general factor like contiguity, or the movement of attention, or the will to learn, that does the work of association. To judge from the memory experiments, then, what is recalled is what has been noted—not past experiences in their totality, but definite reactions which occurred in those experiences.

This conclusion is perhaps even more clearly indicated by experiments in the learning of nonsense drawings than in the more usual work with linguistic materials. An instructive experiment is that of Judd and Cowling,[10] who exposed a rather simple drawing for successive periods of 10 seconds, requiring the subject to reproduce it as well as possible after each exposure. The results, both objective and introspective, showed that the subject usually got first the general character and shape of the figure, and, continuing his analysis, noted one fact after another, until a sufficient number of facts was known to make a satisfactory reproduction possible. There was no evidence of an inner reproduction of the entire sensory experience, from which the subject might read off such information as he required. In a somewhat similar experiment, T. V. Moore[11] called for the learning of a series of simple drawings. He supposed at the outset that a group of figures would be memorized by visual imagery, but experience taught him that there was another factor that was a powerful aid to memory. This was "a more or less complete analysis of the figures, an analysis which it is utterly unnecessary for the subject to put into words." It consisted in noting the parts and composition of the figures and their resemblances to familiar objects. He then undertook to compare the efficiency of memorizing by visualization with analysis excluded, and by analysis without visualization; and found a uniform superiority of the analytic method over the visualizing. But he also found that is was impossible to exclude analysis altogether. "Associations crop up spontaneously," he writes, "and one simply cannot exclude all analysis of the figure. . . . It is much easier to memorize by analysis to the exclusion of imagery than *vice versa.*" He believed, however, that learning by visualization, i.e., by forming an image which should be a "more or less perfect replica" of the visual sensation, was a real process. Under the circumstances, it was evidently impossible for him to prove this; for if analysis occurred spontaneously—and one has only to look at a drawing to realize how inevitable it is to note either details or broader characteristics—and if also analysis was a more powerful memorizing agency than visualization, it remains possible that all the learning was accomplished by analysis. The reality of the strictly visualizing or photographic process of learning is, I believe, still open to doubt. It is certainly impossible to avoid perceptual reactions, and to assume the purely receptive attitude of a photographic plate.

---

10. "Studies in Perceptual Development," *Psychol. Rev. Monograph 34*, 1907, 349-369.
11. "The Process of Abstraction," *Univ. of California Publications in Psychology*, 1910, 1, 139-153.

Miss Fernald's data on the memorization of pictures[12] show that even good visualizers depend largely, at least, on specific observations of the features which were later remembered; and her results on the recitation of letter-squares in changed orders[13] showed that even the best visualizers among her subjects were unable to do what it had been supposed was the prerogative of a visualizer to do, namely, "see the whole set of letters at once and simply read them off" in the changed order. She does not doubt the existence of persons able to accomplish this feat, but believes that they must be rare. This matter of visualization evidently requires further study, but the possibility is still open that even the best visualizer does not carry away a photograph of the scene, or replica of his visual sensation, but an image which amounts to a synthesis of specific observations, including observations of broad effects and observations of parts and their relations.

But it is time that I brought my theory out of hiding and placed it squarely before you. I call it, for lack of a better name, the mental reaction theory, or perhaps the perceptual reaction theory. Its basic idea is that a percept is an inner reaction to sensation. I call it a mental reaction to distinguish it from the motor reaction which several psychologists have put forward as being important in attention, perception, association and the like; for it appears to me that these suggestions, while on the right track in insisting that *reaction* is dynamically important, have mistaken the locus of the reaction, and so are unable to account for the conscious content that appears in these mental activities. This mental reaction is not, however, of the nature of an associated sensation, appearing as an image, as if the visual sensation of an orange, to give the percept orange, must reproduce the sensations of handling or tasting the orange. Nor, on the other hand, is the perceptual reaction an emphasis or pattern or meaning residing in the given sensations. It is something new, not present in the sensations, but, theoretically, as distinct from them as the motor reaction is. It adds new content which cannot be analyzed into elementary sensations; so that the sensory elements, which are often held to supply, along with the feelings, all the substance of consciousness, in reality furnish but a fraction of it, and probably a small fraction. Each perceptual reaction is specific, and contributes specific content. In recall, it is these perceptual reactions that are revived, and not sensation; and therefore the content of recall is never, in the strictest sense, sensory. Nevertheless, as was said before, some percepts lie, as it were, nearer to sensation than others, so that the distinction between an image and an imageless recall, while not perfectly sharp, is still legitimate.

It is possible that this theory may appear not so radical after all, and not worth the expenditure of so much breath; for all will perhaps admit that a percept is, in some sense, a reaction. It is therefore my duty to

---

12. *Psychol. Rev. Monograph 58,* 1912, 81ff.
13. *Ibid.,* p. 71.

show that the theory is worse than it seems, and this I shall attempt to do in the case of patterns or Gestaltqualitäten. It has long been known that the same pattern (for example, a melody) can sometimes be found in different sensory complexes, and it is also true that different patterns can be found in the same sensory complex, as in the case of the dot figure. A rather difficult problem is thus raised, for one would think that the compound would be determined by the elements. But the real crux of the difficulty is to get some conception of a pattern or of a compound, to show what is meant by the togetherness or grouping of the elements. There are three theories that attempt to solve this puzzle, that of synthesis, that of systasis or mere togetherness, and that of synergy, which is none other than the mental reaction theory. The synthesis theory brings in the subject or ego to put the elements together; the systasis theory rejects this deus ex machina, and says that the elements merely are together, or get together and so constitute the compound or pattern; the synergy theory holds that the elements act together, as stimuli, to arouse a further reaction which is the pattern. The synthetic theory occupies a weak position, since, unless the systatic theory succeeds in showing what is meant by the elements being together, there is no advantage in saying that something puts them so.

Now it is difficult to understand what can be meant by the elements being together or getting together so as to produce the group and pattern. If the group included the whole momentary content of consciousness, we could say that being together meant simply being simultaneously present, and speak of the pattern as a character of the whole conscious moment. But the group does not include the whole of consciousness, but—as in the case of three dots among a larger number, seen for an instant as a triangle—may occupy but a small part of the conscious field. The pattern is not the pattern of consciousness, but a pattern within consciousness. Nor will it help matters much to substitute for consciousness the field of attention; for the extent of a group may be either greater or smaller than that of this field; and, besides, a familiar pattern, such as a melody or arrangement of lines or dots, may come to consciousness quite outside the field of attention. Apperception, then, in the Wundtian sense, does not explain groups and patterns nor give them any intelligible meaning. But if we lay aside apperception and try to describe groups and patterns in terms of their constituent elements, we are in no better case. What is it that changes when the pattern changes, the elements remaining constant in quality, intensity and spatial position? This question is as serious for the synthetic theory as for the systatic. The synergy theory cuts the Gordian knot by admitting at once that there is no change in the elements. In fact, there is no real grouping or pattern of the elements; they neither get together nor are put together by some higher agency; but some of them simply act together, as a complex of stimuli, to arouse a perceptual reaction which constitutes the grouping and pattern. The pattern is numerically distinct from the elements, as a motor reaction is distinct from the complex of stimuli that arouses it. What pattern shall be aroused at any moment depends on the readiness of different perceptual reactions to be aroused, and thus on such factors as frequency and recency of past exercise, fatigue and present interest and control. In short, the synergy theory proposes to extend to patterns, and to all percepts, the same explanation that is accepted for such admittedly mental reactions as the sequence of one idea after another. No one doubts that one idea may represent a stimulus for the arousal of another idea, nor denies that the aroused idea is numerically distinct from the stimulus idea and adds new content to it. It is the same with sensation and perception, except that the reaction is usually very prompt and the perceptual content intimately fused with the sensational. The fusion is so complete that the pattern seems to lie right in or among the dots, as the galloping horse of an earlier illustration seemed to be actually heard in the series of noises.

But now, finally, I suspect that the party, which allowed me to proceed some time ago without coming to terms with their demand for a definition of sensation, will no longer be restrained. They will insist on taking the floor and addressing you as follows:

The speaker is certainly right in calling a percept a reaction; that is too obvious a fact to need discussion. But we ask, A reaction to what? And our answer is, To the physical stimulus. This "sensation" that the speaker has interpolated between the physical stimulus and the percept is pure gratuitous assumption. There is no warrant for it in introspection, for he himself admits that the sensation and the percept content are intimately fused. We regret that he has fallen into this obsolescent way of speaking, and would suggest that, in reviewing his remarks, you use the blue pencil of the censor wherever the word "sensation" occurs.

This objection is almost too serious to be dealt with in brief. I should freely admit that sensation and percept cannot be distinguished by direct introspection. Yet there are introspective facts that make the distinction appear legitimate. When we hear the galloping horse, we are not only aware of the horse, but we are able to state that we hear him. It is not quite correct to say that we get only the meaning, for we know also the sense by which we get the meaning. So, again, when we have changing percepts of the same stimulus, as in the case of the dot figure, the change of pattern does not amount to a complete change of the figure, but there is a constant substratum underlying the changes; and it seems appropriate to speak of this as sensation. In recall, even the best images lack something when compared with actual sensory experience. They lack body and incisiveness; and it appears probable that this lack is nothing more nor less than a lack of sensation, or, in other words, that the real sensory process is not resuscitated in the image.

But the concept of sensation might never have arisen in a purely introspective psychology. At bottom it is a physiological or psychophysical concept. Sensation is that conscious content which is in closest relation to the physical stimulus. It is the primary response to the stimulus, and may be followed by secondary responses. Neurology gives good ground for such a distinction, in tracing the sensory nerves to certain limited areas of the cortex, and finding the rest of the cortex to be only indirectly connected with the sense organs. Destruction of the cortical receiving station for any sense abolishes all conscious use of that sense, while destruction of neighboring areas, without making a person blind, for example, abolishes his power of reading, or his power of recognizing seen objects, or his power of orienting himself in visual space. Such perceptions are apparently secondary reactions, while the primary reaction, corresponding to the activity of the receiving station, is precisely that which distinguishes a person who is word-blind and object blind, from one who is totally blind. Here is a person who sees without perceiving, and here is one who does not see at all. The difference I would like to call sensation. Sensation, accordingly, would be the consciousness attending the activity of the sensory receiving stations of the brain, while percept-content would be the consciousness attending the activity of neighboring areas. Besides these secondary reactions, there are undoubtedly tertiary and further reactions, less and less directly connected with the incoming sensory impulses. They need not have a sharply limited localization in the cortex, yet they must be neurologically distinct, and it may well be that every distinct cerebral reaction is attended by its peculiar conscious content. I know of no reason in neurology or psychology for supposing that the elements of conscious content are contributed solely by the sensory receiving centers.

According to this theory, the sensation aroused by a physical stimulus must precede the secondary or perceptual reaction; but the interval need not be supposed to exceed a hundredth of a second, and could not be introspectively detected. The fusion of the primary and secondary reactions in consciousness is a fact which I cannot attempt to explain, since fusion is one of the fundamental peculiarities of consciousness as contrasted with its cerebral correlates. But I may perhaps make the whole conception a little more tangible by reverting to the similitude of photography.

A certain photographer found himself without sensitive plates, though with his camera, in the presence of a scene which he much desired to preserve. He therefore focused on the ground glass at the back of his instrument, and, stretching transparent paper over the glass, traced some of the outlines of the optical image. He thus created patterns, which lay really in his drawing and not in the optical image, but which were blended with the image as long as the image remained. He preserved his tracing, and found it to differ from a photograph in containing only the facts to which he had definitely reacted.

In this parable, the optical image is sensation, which is gone forever when the physical stimulus ceases. The tracing is perception, which may be preserved, though subject to decay. But the fusion of the two, depending in the case of the camera on the presence of the photographer's eye, is in the case of sensation and perception more deep-seated and inexplicable. Finally, the photographer was more restricted than is the process of perception, since he could only trace outlines and shadings and perhaps colors, and could not commit to his drawing the more remote relations and meanings which can be perceived, and, being later recalled, furnish the content of "imageless thought."

Reprinted with permission
from *Psychological Review*,
1916, 23, 89–116.

Chapter 9

The Place of the Conditioned Reflex in Psychology

John B. Watson

Johns Hopkins University

Since the publication two years ago of my somewhat impolite papers against current methods in psychology I have felt it incumbent upon me before making further unpleasant remarks to suggest some method which we might *begin* to use in place of introspection. I have found, as you easily might have predicted, that it is one thing to condemn a long-established method, but quite another thing to suggest anything in its place. I wish in my remarks tonight to report what progress has been made in this direction.

Probably the first question you will insist upon my answering is: "Why try to find a substitute for introspection? It is a pretty good method after all and has served us well." Rather than stop at this tempting place to enter into a controversy, I shall call your attention to

---

Address of the President, before the American Psychological Association, Chicago Meeting, December, 1915.

the naturalness of such a quest on the part of the students of animal psychology. The truth of the matter is that animal psychologists have become somewhat intoxicated with success. Finding that an amoeba will orient more quickly to certain rays of light than to others, and that a blind, anosmic rat can learn to thread its way through a maze, they begin to look at man with a covetous eye: "After all," they argue,

man is an animal; he moves in response to stimuli in his environment, or to the stimuli offered by the displacement of tissue within his own body. Furthermore, he moves in characteristic ways. Why cannot we study his behavior in the same way that we study the behavior of other animals, modifying our methods to suit this new genus?

We all admit that many problems in the two fields are similar if not identical. This is especially true of sensory problems. All of us alike wish to determine the various groups of stimuli to which our human or infra-human organism will respond; the various amounts of stimulation necessary to produce these responses, and the bodily areas upon which stimuli must impinge in order to be effective.

Now the animal psychologist has met with a certain degree of success in answering such questions. When we contrast animal psychology in 1900 with animal psychology in 1915 we are forced to admire the enormous strides which have been made in defining problems, in evaluating methods, and in refining apparatus. In 1900 we were content to study by crude methods the elementary features of habit formation in a few easily handled vertebrates. 1916 finds us prepared to carry out on animals as low in the scale as the worm far more delicately controlled experiments than were dreamed of in 1900. The present time likewise finds us prepared to undertake upon the higher vertebrates problems in behavior which in 1900 could hardly have been formulated in behavior terminology. In 1900 who thought of comparing visual acuity in different animals by the use of methods as delicate as those we use on the human being? Or who was bold enough then to assert that in a few years' time we should be using methods for studying vision, audition, and habit formation which are more refined than those which have been employed in the study of the human subject? We must admit, I think, that in the infra-human realm, at least, these years of constant effort have given the animal psychologist a right to look with yearning eyes at this proud genus *Homo*, the representatives of which he finds roaming everywhere, eating any kind of food and from almost any hand, and so resistant to climatic changes that only the lightest kind of covering is necessary to keep them in good condition.

Such in part are the motives which have led the animal behaviorist to push into gatherings to which he has not been especially invited. Whether we should condemn his enterprising spirit or accept him depends upon how he behaves after admittance. If he can justify his position by deeds, I believe he will be accepted, while possibly not to complete fellowship, at least as an individual who will not bring discredit upon his fellow scientists.

The behaviorist, while meeting no theoretical difficulties in his attempts thus to universalize his methods, does, at the very outset of his studies upon man, meet with very practical ones. In sensory problems when we ask such simple questions as, what is the smallest vibration difference between two tones that will serve as a stimulus to reaction in this particular man, or whether sweet and bitter can be reacted to differently by him, we find that there is no objective method ready at hand for answering them. We know how to employ objective methods in answering such questions with animals. But the animal methods are admittedly slow, and, from the standpoint of the human subject, cumbersome. Some years ago I suggested that we ought to begin to use human subjects in our so-called "discrimination boxes." As might have been surmised, no one took my advice. This was due in part at least to man's upright position, his size, and, I might add, his general unwillingness to work under the conditions which must be maintained in animal experimentation. One can scarcely blame the human subject for objecting to being kept for long stretches of time in a home box the door to which opens from time to time permitting him to pass to the right or left of a partition, and ultimately to reach one or the other of two differently colored surfaces below which he finds a food trough. That which makes the situation still more humiliating to him is the fact that if he has "backed" the wrong color he receives a stone in the guise of an electric shock, in place of the bread which he seeks.

I suggested this rather hopeless method of investigating the sensory side of human psychology because of the increasing desire on the part of many psychologists to see psychology begin to break away from the traditions which have held her bound hand and foot from the establishment of the first psychological laboratory. I believe that the time is here when the most conservative psychologists are willing to give a lenient hearing to even crude experimentation along lines which may possibly yield an objective approach to sensory problems. This belief has emboldened me to describe briefly our work at Hopkins upon the *conditioned reflex*.

Conditioned Reflexes

In discussing the subject of conditioned reflexes it is customary to make a distinction between (A) *conditioned secretion reflexes* and (B) *conditioned motor reflexes*. Whether there is any genuine distinction between the two types depends, I think, upon what ultimately will be found to be true about the *modus operandi* of the glands (i.e., whether under such conditions muscular activity is essential to glandular activity or whether control of the glands can be attained independently of the muscles through nervous mechanisms).

A. Conditioned Secretion Reflexes

Before taking up the conditioned motor reflex, with which I am most familiar, I wish briefly to call your attention to one of the most widely known conditioned secretion reflexes, viz., the salivary. The conditioned salivary reflex is well known in this country, thanks to the summaries of the researches in Pawlow's laboratory made by Yerkes and Morgulis, and more recently by Morgulis alone. In brief, this method, which has been under experimental control for some eighteen years, depends upon the following fact: If food (or some similar salivating agent) which produces a direct salivary reflex, and, e.g., a flash of light, are offered jointly for a number of times, the light alone will come finally to call out the salivary secretion. To bring this "reflex" under control it is necessary to fix upon some method for observing the flow of saliva. This is accomplished usually by first making a salivary fistula, and later attaching a glass funnel to the opening of the duct of the gland. The total flow of saliva may then be measured directly or the individual drops registered graphically. The use of food for arousing the direct flow of saliva has proved to be slow and not very satisfactory. Most of the work has been done by using acid (dilute HCl). The acid produces a salivary flow immediately and with great sureness.

The conditioned salivary reflex has at present no very wide sphere of usefulness or applicability. In the first place it can be used upon but few animals. Up to the present time it has been used largely upon dogs. Even when used upon these animals the method has very serious limitations. The use of acid for any appreciable time produces stomatitis, according to Burmakin. This makes it almost impossible to carry out investigations which extend over long periods of time. Unless some strong saliva-producing agent is used, the reflex quickly disappears and cannot easily be reinforced. In its present form the method (which calls for operative treatment of the subject) can not be used, of course, on man. Dr. Lashley has been making some tests looking towards an extension of the method. He is experimenting with a small disc grooved on one surface, so as to form two concentric but non-communicating chambers (Figure 1). The outer chamber, by means of a slender tube, communicates with a vacuum pump. When the air is exhausted the disc will cling to the inner surface of the cheek. The inner chamber, which is placed directly over the opening of the salivary gland, is likewise supplied with a slender tube which passes out through the mouth. The saliva passing out through this tube can be recorded in different ways. It is too early to make any predictions concerning the usefulness of such a method.

Of the possibility of extending investigation to other forms of secretion, little at present can be said. The work of Cannon, Carlson, Crile, and others, has opened our eyes to the extent to which glandular and muscular activity are called into play in the simplest forms of emotional response. The human psychologist has too long subordinated everything to the obtaining of a vocal response from the subject, while the animal psychologist has too long subordinated all to the obtaining of

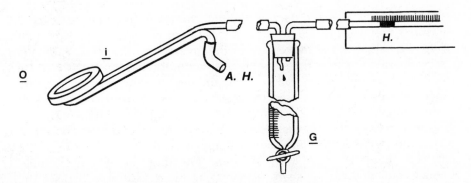

Figure 1. Apparatus for measuring salivary secretion in man (devised by K. S. Lashley). *o*, outer chamber connecting with vacuum pump, through tube at *AH*. When a vacuum is created the disc clings to the inner surface of the cheek. *i*, inner chamber which is placed over opening of parotid gland. Saliva flows into graduated flask *G* where the total flow of saliva can be measured. Another system of measurement is offered by reason of the fact that when a drop of saliva falls into *G*, air is forced out through a second opening in the flask. When a slender glass tube containing a drop of mercury is attached to this opening, the mercury drop is forced forward a short distance at each drop of saliva. A suitable scale placed behind the glass rod enables one to read and record the number of drops of saliva which fall during any part of the total reaction. (*Saliometer* is an appropriate name for this instrument.)

response in the muscles used in locomotion. Both have failed to work out methods for observing the finer changes that go on in that large class of actions that we call *emotional*. Until recent years we have been lacking proper indicators of such changes. I believe that the conditioned secretory reflex, in one form or another, can be made useful in these fields.

While recognizing the importance to all psychological students of Pawlow's work on secretion reflexes, our own work has centered around the conditioned motor reflex of Bechterew, since we find for his method an immediate and widespread usefulness.

B. The Conditioned Motor Reflex (Bechterew)

The *conditioned motor reflex*, while familiar in a general way to everyone, has not, so far as I know, engaged the attention of American investigators. This is not surprising in view of the fact that all of the researches have appeared in Russian and in periodicals which are not accessible at present to American students. At least we have not been able to obtain access to a single research publication. The German and French translations of Bechterew's "Objective Psychology" give the method only in the barest outline. Bechterew's summary was the only guide we had in our work at Hopkins.

We may give a few examples from daily life of conditioned *motor* reflexes. In the moving picture tragedies the suicide of the villain is often shown. Usually the hand only of this unfortunate individual is displayed grasping a revolver which points towards the place where his head ought to be. The sight of the movement of the hammer on the revolver brings out in many spectators the same defensive bodily reaction that the noise of the explosion would call out. Again we find in persons recently operated upon numerous reactions such as deep inspirations, cries of pain, pronounced muscular movements, the stimuli to which are the cut and torn tissues themselves. For many days after the disappearance of the noxious stimuli the reactions will appear at the slightest turn of the subject's body or even at a threat of touching the wound. Similar instances of this can be seen in many chronic cases. In such cases the charitable physician characterizes the patient as having "too great a sensitivity to pain." The patient, however, is not shamming in the ordinary sense: conditioned reflexes have been set up and the subject makes the same profound reactions to ordinary attendant stimuli that he would make to the noxious stimuli themselves.[1]

For almost a year Dr. Lashley and I have been at work upon the production and control of these reflexes. We are not ready to give any detailed report of the results. Our efforts have been confined rather to the general features of the method. We find little in the literature upon such important points as:

1. Technique of method;
2. Subjects upon which the method may be used;
3. Present range of application of method.

1. *Technique of method.* As Bechterew's students affirm, we find that a simple way to produce the reflex is to give a sound stimulus in conjunction with a strong electro-tactual stimulus. Bechterew's students use the reflex withdrawal of the foot: the subject sits with the bare foot resting on two metal electrodes. When the *faradic* stimulation is given the foot is jerked up from the metal electrodes. The movements of the foot are recorded graphically upon smoked paper. We modified this method slightly in our first experiments. We found that the reflex appeared more surely and quickly if the subject lay on his back with his leg raised and supported by a padded rod under the knee. This position leaves the muscles of the lower leg in a more flexible condition. As a further modification we placed one electrode having a large surface under the ball of the foot and a second electrode only one sixteenth of an inch in width under the great toe, and then strapped down the foot across the instep. When the electrical stimulation was given the great toe

---

1. I wish I had time here to develop the view that the concept of the conditioned reflex can be used as an explanatory principle in the psychopathology of hysteria and of the various "tics" which appear in so-called normal individuals. It seems to me that hysterical motor manifestations may be looked upon as conditioned reflexes. This would give a *raison d'etre* which has hitherto been lacking.

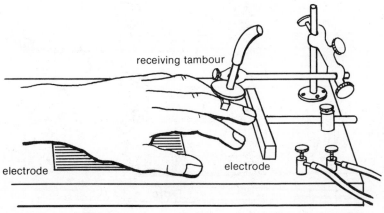

receiving tambour

electrode   electrode

secondary of inductorium

Figure 2. Method of recording finger movement and of giving faradic stimulation. A large electrode is placed under the hand, and a small electrode under the finger. When key, in the experimenter's room, is pressed down by the operator the secondary current from the inductorium causes the finger to rise from the small electrode. A receiving tambour, to the face of which a saddle-shaped button has been shellacked, enables a graphic record to . be made of such movements.

was raised from the narrow metal strip (toe reflex). This device made the recording of the reflex somewhat easier. While the use of the foot is fairly satisfactory it is inconvenient for general laboratory work. We found that the reflex appears in the finger as readily as in the toe. So satisfactory and convenient is this last method that we have adopted it in all of our later work with human subjects (Figures 2 and 3). A bank of keys is provided which enables the experimenter (he is in a different room, of course, from the subject) to give at will the sound of a bell coincidently with the current, or separate from the current. In beginning work upon any new subject we first sound the bell alone to see if it will directly produce the reflex. We have never yet been able to get the reflex evoked by the bell alone prior to the electro-tactual stimulation (Plate 1a). We give next the bell and shock simultaneously for about five trials; then again offer the bell. If the reaction does not appear, we give five more stimulations with the bell and current simultaneously—etc. The conditioned reflex makes its appearance at first haltingly, i.e., it will appear once and then disappear. Punishment is then again given. It may next appear twice in succession and again disappear. After a time it begins to appear regularly every time the bell is offered. In the best cases we begin to get a conditioned reflex after fourteen to thirty combined stimulations (Plate 1b). We have found several refractory subjects: subjects in which even the primary reflex will not appear in the toe when the current is strong enough to induce perspiration. Whether this is due to atrophy of the toe reflex through the wearing of shoes, or to some other cause, we have never been able to determine. In such cases, however, we can rely

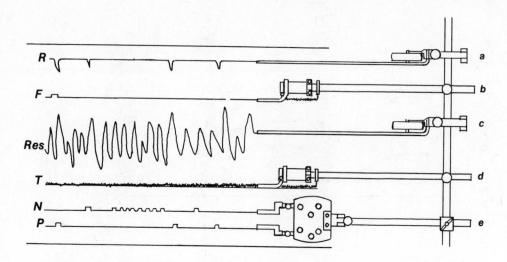

Figure 3. Showing system of making records. *a*, Marey tambour connected with the receiving tambour from the finger (see Figure 2). *b*, electromagnetic signal marker, connected with the key for giving faradic stimulations. *c*, Marey tambour connected with pneumograph. *d*, signal marker connected with seconds pendulum. *e*, double signal marker; one pointer moves when the negative stimulus (stimulus not to be reacted to) is given; second pointer moves only when the positive stimulus is given. The letters on the left refer as follows: *R*, conditioned reflex; *F*, faradic stimulation (punishment); *Res*, respiratory changes; *T*, time; *N*, negative stimulus; *P*, positive stimulus. These letters are used in an unchanging way in the illustrations which follow. A short schematic record of the ordinary curves obtained in the laboratory is shown. The eye should begin at the bottom and read up. The first record shows that the positive stimulus was given, that punishment was given simultaneously with it, and that the reflex occurred. The second record shows that the negative stimulus (different bell) was given, that no punishment was given with it, and that the reflex appeared (undifferentiated reflex). Then followed eight stimulations with the negative bell to produce fatigue to the negative stimulus. After fatigue to the negative bell, the positive bell is given. No punishment was given but the reflex appeared. Then the negative bell was given and no reflex appeared. Then the positive bell was given with the appearance of the reflex (differentiation). It will be noticed that respiratory changes show at every stimulation. Both bells cause a deep inspiration, increased amplitude, and a slowing in rate. When training is continued long enough, differentiation occurs in respiration just as it does in the finger movement (see Plate 2b); that is, in a short time, only the positive bell can produce the changes shown in this drawing.

upon the breathing which we record simultaneously with the reflex toe or finger movement. The breathing curve is very sensitive and a conditioned reflex appears very plainly upon its tracing.

Some General Characteristics of the Reflex

It is interesting at this point to treat of certain characteristics of the reflex. *First*, as regards the similarity and difference between the conditioned reflex and the primary reflex upon which it is grafted. However much they may differ so far as the central nervous pathway is concerned, the general and coarser motor features are closely similar. One watching the movements of a subject first beginning to show a conditioned reflex cannot tell whether he is being stimulated by the bell alone or by the bell and punishment combined. The conditioned motor reflex is usually sharp, quick, and widespread, the whole body as a rule being brought into the reaction at first. Gradually the reflex becomes more circumscribed. This appears clearly in Plates 2 and 9.

Second, as regards persistence of the reflex; after the reflex has once been thoroughly established it carries over from one day's experiments to the next for an indefinite period. Sometimes a single punishment at the beginning of a day's work is necessary to cause the reflex to make its appearance. We are not able to state over how long a period of time the unexercised reflex will persist. In one case we trained one subject thoroughly in May to the bell, then did not test him again until October. The reflex did not appear on the first ringing of the bell alone, but after the first administration of the combined stimuli (at which the subject disrupted the apparatus although the induction shock was very weak) the conditioned reflex appeared regularly to the bell alone.

Third. We had hoped to make some statements concerning the reaction times of the fundamental and the conditioned reflex. While we are at work upon this problem, we are not ready to make any report as yet.

Fourth. We know that the conditioned motor reflex can be made to undergo reinforcement and inhibition by factors such as those Yerkes has made us so familiar with in his work on the mutual relations of stimuli in the reflex movements of the leg of the frog. A few examples of the rôle such factors play in the control of the reflex may be of interest. Take first the fatigue of the reflex. A well trained subject will react regularly for an indefinite period of time to a stimulus given at an interval of four to five seconds. If now we give the stimulus, i.e., the bell, every two seconds for a short time, he may react for the first three times and then fail. If the interval is then lengthened, or a rest period introduced, the reflex will again appear.[2] It will be seen later that we utilize this principle of fatigue in setting up differential reactions. Oftentimes before the conditioned reflex is thoroughly set up, it will, after a time, begin to decrease in amplitude. Whether the time is increased is not known. When the reflex is beginning to vanish it can be strengthened in a variety of ways, the most usual way being the introduction of the current, but it can be reinforced also by throwing in simultaneously with the bell some other form of stimulation. I have dwelt at some length upon this subject for fear some might advance the view that the conditioned reflex is nothing more than the so-called "voluntary reaction." The fact, in addition to those cited above, which makes such a view less easily held, is the ease with which the condi-

---

2. Plates 3a and 3b.

tioned motor reflex can be set up in animals. The strongest argument against such a point of view is the fact that it apparently can be set up on processes which are presided over by the autonomic system. To test this we have made a series of experiments having for their object the establishment of a pupillary reflex by the combined stimuli of a very strong light and a sound (bell). We found that the diameter of the pupil under constant illumination with fixation is very steady after the first five minutes; consequently it is possible to make measurements upon the pupil. To ordinary stimulations (sounds, contacts, etc.) there is a slight but not constant change in diameter (at times changes follow evidently upon intra-organic stimulation). But to such stimulation the pupil may respond either by dilation or constriction. In the short time which we had for training subjects we found two individuals in which, after fifteen to twenty minutes' training, the sound alone would produce a small constriction of the pupil in about seventy-five per cent of the cases. In two subjects no such reflex could be built up in the time we had to devote to them.

The use of the pupil is thus not very satisfactory: first because it is very difficult to obtain the reflex in it; second, because, due to the fact that we have to induce the fundamental reflex by light, it is not possible to use light as a form of secondary stimulation; and third, because the method is very uncomfortable for the subject. Indeed the long training necessary to produce the reflex in refractory cases would probably be actually injurious to the eyes. Our interest in establishing a conditioned pupil reflex was entirely theoretical.

We have also made one brief attempt to establish the reflex on the heart beat; but on account of the fact that respiratory changes show so markedly on the tracing of the heart, we have been unable to convince ourselves that we have produced a genuine conditioned reflex.

Finally, we had hoped to combine this work with the so-called psycho-galvanic reflex in such a way as to produce a method which would yield quantitative results. It seemed a reasonable train of argument to suppose that the sound of an ordinary bell would not cause changes enough in the bodily resistance (or E.M.F.) to produce galvanometric deflections; but on the other hand, that the sound of the bell joined with the faradic stimulation of the foot (punishment) would produce an emotional change sufficient to show. We argued further that if punishment and bell were then given together for a sufficient number of times, the bell alone would come finally to produce bodily changes sufficient to show on the galvanometer and we would thus have our conditioned reflex. The only fault to be found with such a train of reasoning is that it does not work out when put to practical test. In the first place the bell, as we expected, does not produce observable changes (nor do other ordinary stimuli), but, and this was unexpected, neither does the combined stimulus of bell and electric shock. Violent stimulations such as the bursting of an electric light bulb, burning the subject with a cigarette, tickling with a feather, etc., do, in our set-up (which contains no battery), produce anywhere from ten mm. to one hundred mm. deflection. Furthermore, the movement of the galvanometer does not start until an appreciable time after the stimulus has been given; sometimes not until three or four seconds afterwards (showing that effect is a glandular change). Another difficulty is that after a deflection has been obtained the original reading of the galvanometer cannot again be duplicated (resistance of the body not going back to the same point). It was largely because of these factors that we temporarily discontinued our experiments in this direction.

Method of Using Reflex to Obtain Differential Reactions

As I have sketched the method of using the conditioned reflex it is suitable for working out many problems on reinforcement, inhibition, fatigue, intensity of stimulation necessary to call out response under different conditions, etc. The method, however, has a much wider sphere of usefulness. If we take a subject in whom such a reflex is established to a bell or a light, he will react to any sound or light not differing too widely in physical characteristics. By continued training it becomes possible to narrow the range of the stimulus to which the subject will react. For example, if we train on a given monochromatic light, using red until the reflex is well established, and then suddenly exhibit green or yellow, the reflex appears. The sudden throwing in of the green light will often cause the reflex to fail the next time the red light is given. We proceed then to differentiate the reflex. As was suggested above we bring about differentiation by punishment with the positive stimulus (red in this case) but never with the negative stimulus (green). The second step in the process of bringing about differentiation consists in exhausting the reflex to the negative stimulus (using the factor of fatigue). This can usually be done by giving the negative stimulus four or five times at intervals of about one to two seconds. After the reaction to the negative stimulus disappears we "rest" the subject for a few seconds, and then give the positive stimulus. If this procedure is continued long enough the differential reaction is finally perfected. The differential reaction can be so highly perfected that it becomes possible to use it with great accuracy in determining difference limens on human subjects. So far we have tested it out in the fields of light, sound, and contact with very encouraging results (see Plates 4–7 and 9).

As may readily be seen, this extension of the method gives us the possibility of objectively approaching many of the problems in sensory psychology. We give no more instruction to our human subjects than we give to our animal subjects. Nor do we care what language our subject speaks or whether he speaks at all. We are thus enabled to tap certain reservoirs which have hitherto been tapped only by the introspective method. The data which we collect in this way, while they have no bearing upon a Wundtian type of psychology, serve (as far as they go) every practical and scientific need of a truly functional psychology.

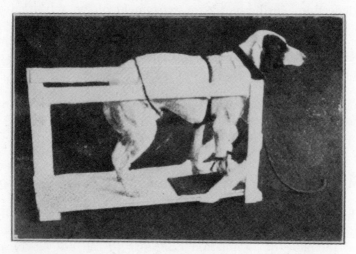

Figure 4. Shows method of obtaining reflex with the dog. A light spring keeps the foot of the dog pressed down upon the punishment grill. This spring is so light that the dog has no difficulty in pulling up the foot when the faradic stimulus is given. A small receiving device (made like a pneumograph over a coiled spring) or a lever system may be used for the recording of the foot movement.

2. *Subjects upon which the method may be used*. The range of subjects upon which the motor reflex method may be used is wide. We have tried it out in all upon eleven human subjects, one dog and seven chickens.

The method works in a very satisfactory way upon the particular dog with which we worked—a beagle of very mixed breed. In the case of the dog we stimulate the sole of the foot and record the resulting leg movement (Figure 4). Six out of the seven chicks showed the conditioned reflex in the respiratory curve (Plate 2). We failed to get the reflex in one chick. These animals are comfortably saddled with leg strapped to a punishment grill. The breathing is recorded by means of Rouse's device. Figure 5 shows the method in use with the great horned owl.

The adult human subjects used were chosen largely but not wholly from among the graduate students of psychology and biology. Three of the subjects used had never had any psychological training. As might be expected the ease with which the method may be used is not dependent upon the previous psychological training of the subject. We give the subjects no instructions or explanations of the purport of the experiment. It is unreasonable to suppose, however, that the adult psychologically trained subjects do not get the drift of what is expected of them as the experiment proceeds. Whether the bodily set or emotion which results from this plays any rôle in the ease with which the reaction may be obtained has not been determined. On the whole I am inclined to think now that students of physics will prove to be our best subjects since they have been trained to make fine observations of small differences in physical stimuli, without at the same time trying to make crude observations of the stimulations arising from the laryngeal or other vocal organs.

Figure 5. Method of obtaining respiratory reflex in all birds. The great horned owl is shown resting comfortably in a padded wooden saddle. Underneath the floor of this apparatus Rouse's respiratory apparatus is shown, sliding on vertical rods. A V-shaped button is shellacked to the receiving tambour, which is adjusted lightly against the bird's chest. The owl's feet are attached to a punishment grill.

Since we began to use the finger in place of the toe we have had only one subject fail to show the conditioned reflex (a graduate student of psychology). This subject also failed to give the conditioned toe reflex. We failed to obtain the great toe reflex (conditioned) upon one other subject, when we first began our work early in the year. We have had not an opportunity of retesting this individual with the finger reflex.

Whether the method can be used widely with children has not been determined. In the course of twenty minutes we obtained the reflex several times upon an eight-year-old boy. When first punished he cried and showed some reluctancy toward having the experiment continue. One of the experimenters then sat in the room with him, and, under promise of a moving picture show after the experiment, the series was completed with smiling fortitude. When once we get the reflex established thoroughly to the bell, our troubles with children ought to be over, since we can proceed to build up second order reflexes, that is, the bell may be used in place of the electric shock (Plate 8).

Much to our regret we have not been able during the year to find time to try the method out in pathological cases. We hope that during the coming year we may be able to try the method out thoroughly, especially upon cases to which language methods are not applicable.

3. *Present range of applicability of method.* For some time to come the "reflex method" will be used mainly by the animal psychologists. I shall point out here some of the advantages this method has over the "discrimination method" now almost exclusively used in studying the sensory side of animal behavior.

As may be easily seen from our description of the technique of the reflex method the secondary stimuli are offered to the subject serially. One of the greatest difficulties in the way of using the "discrimination method" upon animals arises from the fact that two or more stimuli must be given simultaneously. This in monochromatic light work, to take a single example, is very serious because it calls for very complicated slits, spacing prisms, methods of reversing the positions of the colors, etc. I shall not dwell upon the difficulties of the use of the discrimination method in other sense fields. They are well known. By using the "reflex method" it becomes possible at once to discard a mass of cumbersome machinery now used both in the manipulation of the stimuli and in the control of the animal. For a complete monochromatic light equipment we shall in the future need a single monochromatic illuminator, a smoked wedge or sector, thermal couple, and galvanometer. This replaces the entire outfit recommended in the Yerkes and Watson monograph. A similar simplification can be made in the apparatus of other sense fields, especially in audition and olfaction.

A great gain is likewise effected on account of the fact that both wild and vicious animals, and animals otherwise unsuited because of their large size, slowness of gait, etc., may be used. Another distinct gain comes from the fact that the record is made in complete and permanent form by the animal itself. The experimenter ceases to be a factor in influencing the animal's reactions. Possibly the greatest gain comes from the fact that, if our preliminary experiments may be trusted, dependable results may be reached in a fraction of the time required by the discrimination method. The differential reaction to the two bells shown in Plate 9 was obtained in the dog after four experiments, lasting twenty minutes each. Had the discrimination method been used it is probable that at least three to five hundred trials would have been required. Since only ten to twenty trials per day can be given by the discrimination method the experiments would not have been completed under fifteen to twenty-five days. A further conservation of time is effected by reason of the fact that a given animal may be used in more than one experiment on a given day. Where food is given after each individual trial, as in the discrimination method, this is absolutely impossible.

At the expense of possible repetition I shall enumerate some of the uses to which the method may be immediately applied.

1. To all forms of experimentation on light, size, form, visual acuity, etc. It is apparently the only method which will enable us to study visual after-images in animals.

2. It is apparently the only existing method of testing auditory acuity, differential sensitivity to pitch, range of pitch, timbre, etc., in any reasonable length of time.

3. It affords us, by reason of the fact that the stimuli may be given serially, a method of testing the rôle of olfaction. We know nothing now concerning olfactory acuity, differential sensitivity to olfactory stimuli, classification of stimuli, the effect of such stimuli on the emotional life of

the animal, etc. Nor is it very feasible to carry out such experiments by the discrimination method.

4. The method gives a reliable means of testing sensitivity to temperature and to contact and to the fineness of localization of such stimuli—factors which likewise cannot be determined by methods now in use.

When we recall that the reflex method can be used upon man, without modification, in solving many of the above and similar sensory problems, we must admit, I believe, that it will take a very important place among psychological methods. It may be argued, however, that this method is useful only in yielding results upon very simple sensory problems. Although I cannot here enter into the wider applications of the method, I am sure that its field will be a larger and wider one than I have indicated. I feel reasonably sure that it can be used in experimentation upon memory, and in the so-called association reaction work, and in determining the integrity of the sensory life of individuals who either have no spoken language or who are unable for one reason or another to use words—I have in mind deaf and dumb individuals, aphasics, and dementia praecox patients of the "shut in" type. If indications can be trusted the method ought to yield some valuable results on the localization and method of functioning of the various neural pathways.

In conclusion I must confess to a bias in favor of this method. Time may show that I have been over-enthusiastic about it. Certainly I have attempted here to evaluate a method which possibly cannot be evaluated properly until many investigators have had opportunity to subject it to prolonged tests.

Plate 1. Formation of conditioned motor reflex to sound of bell.

a. No reaction to bell alone.

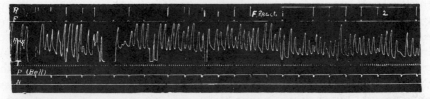

b. Reaction to bell alone (F. React.) after 13 combined stimulations (bell and punishment).

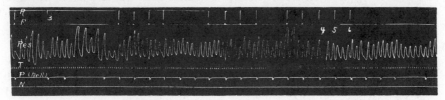

c. Reflex more firmly established as shown by three reflexes, 4, 5, 6, appearing in succession without punishment. (Further training is necessary.)

Plate 2. Conditioned respiratory reflex to sound (bell) in the fowl.

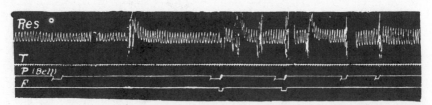

a. Conditioned reflex at beginning of training: Respiration obscured by general motor activity.

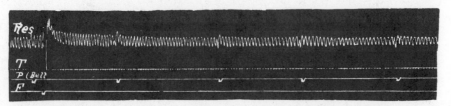

b. Restriction of reflex to respiratory movements after long training.

ate 3. Reinforcement of conditioned motor reflex. (These records are from trained subjects. Occasionally for one reason or another the reflex will disappear.)

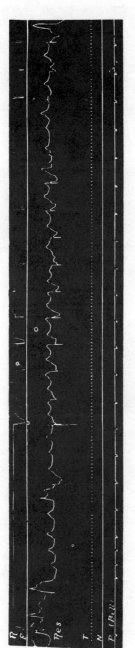

a. Reinforcement by single punishment.

b. Reinforcement by period of rest (between arrows).

Plate 4. Last stages in the formation of a differential reaction to sound of bells of different pitch.

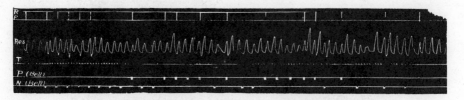

a. Fatigue of reaction to negative bell.

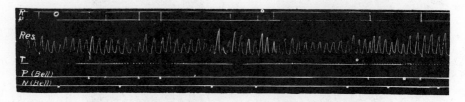

b. Differential not firmly established.

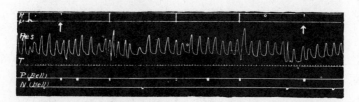

c. Reaction almost perfected after final punishment with positive bell. The arrows indicate that the reflex is present though small.

Plate 5. Differential reflex to pure tones. (Standard fork 256 v.d.)

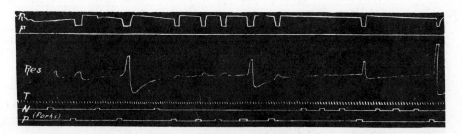

a. Perfect differentiation when the difference is 6 v.d.

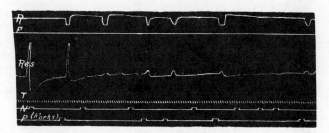

b. Perfect differentiation when the difference is 3 v.d.

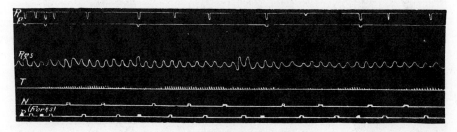

c. Differentiation, in another subject, when the difference is 6 v.d. (This subject failed when the difference was 3 v.d.)

Plate 6. Differential reflex to two contact stimulations on human forearm.

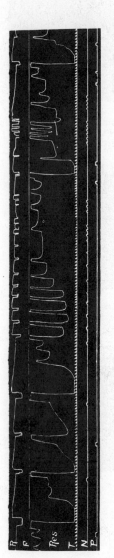

a. Reflex established but not differentiated: differentiation brought about by fatigue of reflex to negative stimulus.

b. Beginning of differentiation.

c. Differentiation established (arrow shows that reflex was present in tracing but too faint for reproduction).

Plate 7. Differential reflex to lights of different wave-length.

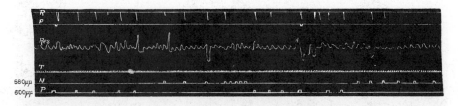

a. Reflex established but not differentiated.

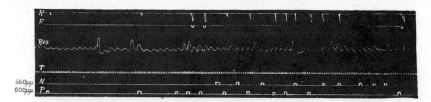

b. Progress toward differentiation. Example of reinforcement by rest.

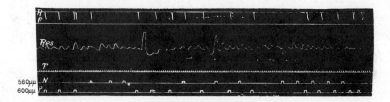

c. Differentiation perfect.

Plate 8. Formation of conditioned reflex to light by association with conditioned-reflex to sound. (The reflex to sound had been set up previously by the use of punishment.)

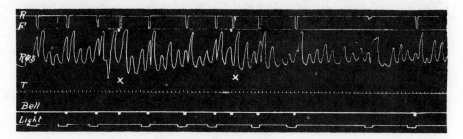

a. Light stimulus combined with sound. Reflex follows with light alone. (*Sound* stimulus *reinforced* by punishment at *x*.)

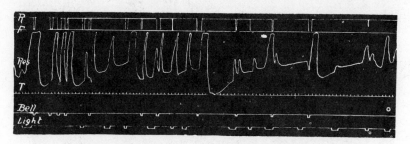

b. Later stages of training. Respiratory reflex well established.

Plate 9. Rise of differential reaction in the dog to two electric bells of different pitch. (R, reflex; upward jerk of forefoot.)

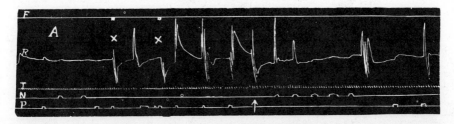

a. Undifferentiated reaction after punishment. (Punishment shown at x.) Arrow shows rhythmical reaction, no stimulus having been given.)

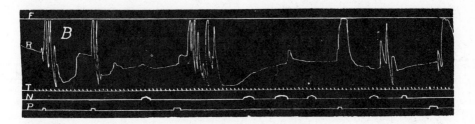

b. Beginning of differentiation.

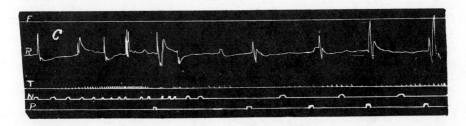

c. Differentiation established. (Prolonged stimulation with negative bell until fatigue. This seemed to complete the process of differentiation.)

Part Two

From World War I Through
World War II

Presidents of the
American Psychological Association
1917–1945

Robert M. Yerkes, *1917*

J. W. Baird, *1918*

Walter D. Scott, *1919*

Shepherd I. Franz, *1920*

Margaret F. Washburn, *1921*

Knight Dunlap, *1922*

Lewis M. Terman, *1923*

G. Stanley Hall, *1924*

Madison Bentley, *1925*

Harvey A. Carr, *1926*

H. L. Hollingworth, *1927*

E. G. Boring, *1928*

Wolfgang Köhler, *1959**

Karl S. Lashley, *1929*

Herbert S. Langfeld, *1930*

Walter S. Hunter, *1931*

Walter R. Miles, *1932*

L. L. Thurstone, *1933*

Joseph Peterson, *1934*

Albert T. Poffenberger, *1935*

Clark L. Hull, *1936*

Edward Chace Tolman, *1937*

John Frederick Dashiell, *1938*

Gordon W. Allport, *1939*

Leonard Carmichael, *1940*

Herbert Woodrow, *1941*

Calvin P. Stone, *1942*

John E. Anderson, *1943*

Gardner Murphy, *1944*

Edwin R. Guthrie, *1945*

---

* The address of Wolfgang Köhler, although delivered in 1959, for historical reasons is presented with the addresses of this time period, when Gestalt psychology became influential in America.

Chapter 10

The Presidents
and
Their Messages
1917–1945

World War I and World War II each had a profound influence on psychology. Because of the prestige attached to university positions and the tendency of universities to favor basic research, many able psychological scientists generally do not attempt to solve socially significant problems until a national emergency calls them into service. When they respond to that call, they commonly find that their training has indeed equipped them to do things they would not ordinarily have tried to do, or at least to quickly learn how to do what is expected of them.

A decade after World War I the economic depression was dramatized by the stock market crash of October 29, 1929. The disruptions that followed this national emergency greatly affected the lives of psychologists. Their services were called for—if they could find employment. Although reflections on the social meaning of the depression are rarely present in the presidential addresses of the time, the impact of the depression, like that of war, was bound to be reflected among psychologists generally, until World War II produced the next shock.

The largest single effort by psychologists in World War I was in the U.S. Army testing program, headed by Robert M. Yerkes, who is ordinarily identified with his leadership role in comparative psychology. Very able researchers from all aspects of psychology joined in the testing, some learning probability statistics for the first time and all having a new experience of organized group effort.

As R. M. Yerkes' presidential address recounts, a small group of friends of E. B. Titchener, known as the "Experimentalists," were meeting in Cambridge on April 6, 1917, when word came that World War I was declared. Immediately a committee consisting of Yerkes, W. V. Bingham, and R. Dodge was appointed to gather information on how psychologists might serve their country. The committee decided to turn the matter over to the APA, their representative organization, of which Yerkes was then president. He immediately invited the APA Council to an emergency meeting held in Philadelphia on April 21, 1917. By the time of the December APA Annual Meeting, Major Yerkes was able to report substantial progress, and his address is a fitting introduction to this period.

After World War I testing was recognized as one of psychology's major contributions to society. L. M. Terman's address reminded APA members that testing was not merely an applied technology but had always been a respectable psychological method. L. L. Thurstone's address showed the advances in methodology reflected in factor analysis, but he, and others, had extended the test method to many areas, such as the study of attitudes, personality, and vocational interests. Other addresses also showed applications of tests: W. R. Miles focused on the later years of life and J. E. Anderson concentrated on the developing years of childhood. Advances in testing were parallel to advances in other methods of applied psychology, and these areas were represented in the election to the presidency of W. D. Scott and A. T. Poffenberger.

The theoretical disputes over systematic viewpoints continued. It may be recalled that Watson's behaviorism was announced shortly before World War I, and his major text, *Psychology from the Standpoint of a Behaviorist* appeared in 1919, just after the war. Along with the dispute between functionalism and structuralism, this newcomer, behaviorism, became a position to attack or defend. Attacks on behaviorism appeared in the addresses of M. F. Washburn, M. Bentley, H. A. Carr, H. L. Hollingworth, and others. Behaviorism did not sweep the field of psychology immediately (as it appeared to do some years later); probably only W. S. Hunter, C. L. Hull, E. C. Tolman, J. F. Dashiell, and E. R. Guthrie (5 among the 30 presidents discussed in Part Two) would have consented to being called behaviorists, and even among them the kinds of behaviorism varied widely.

Gestalt psychology was also emerging as a theoretical contender after the visits of Kurt Koffka and Wolfgang Köhler to America and after the appearance of the English translations of their books. (Köhler's address is presented in Part Two, out of chronological order, so that it will fit into the decade in which its substance belongs.) M. Bentley was the earliest president to discuss Gestalt psychology seriously, even though he was dissatisfied with it. Later presidents, however, including K. S. Lashley and E. C. Tolman, had incorporated Gestalt ideas into their theories. E. G. Boring's address on the psychology of controversy shows the inevitability of these conflicts and the good that can come from them.

In the early 1930s controversies began to narrow from the larger systems to theoretical issues in the problems of learning. Ever since the time of William James the concept of habit had been central to American psychology. The concept was accepted with an increasing objectivity that was not confined to behaviorists. The older quarrels over sensation and perception for a time were diverted into competition among interpretations of learning. E. L. Thorndike (see Part One) had already defended his stimulus–response connectionism that had provided much of the background on learning theory until Pavlov's work became more familiar to Americans, particularly through the G. V. Anrep translation of Pavlov's book *Conditioned Reflexes* (1927). The addresses of J. Peterson, C. L. Hull, E. C. Tolman, and E. R. Guthrie represent the new perspectives on learning theory. Other important contributors, such as B. F. Skinner and K. W. Spence are not represented in either Part Two or Part Three since these men were never elected to the APA presidency.

Psychology has always had physiological leanings, and both W. Wundt and G. T. Ladd called their science physiological psychology. The brain extirpation method was discussed in the addresses of S. I. Franz and K. S. Lashley, who had started this work with Franz. Embryological development was L. Carmichael's topic, and C. P. Stone reviewed evolutionary contributions to the study of the inheritance of behavior (an early behavior genetics approach). Both Stone and J. E. Anderson made pleas for ecological investigation.

Although progress was being made in the field of social psychology, it is not heavily represented in this period. Its importance was recognized, however, and its development encouraged by K. Dunlap, W. S. Hunter, G. W. Allport, and G. Murphy.

The preceding summary should place in context all of the addresses except those of M. F. Washburn and H. S. Langfeld (whose discussions of the motor theory of consciousness came when the interest in consciousness was waning) and of H. Woodrow (whose mathematical model, even if unsuccessful, anticipated the mathematical psychology that was later to become prominent). Neither J. W. Baird nor G. S. Hall gave addresses—World War I interfered with the APA annual meeting at which Baird would have delivered his address, and Hall died before the annual meeting at which he would have made his presentation.

The nine addresses included in Part Two were selected as representing the trends in testing, theoretical controversy, physiological psychology, learning theory, and social psychology.

Robert Mearns Yerkes (1876–1956)

PhD, Harvard University, 1902 (under H. Münsterberg).

Psychology in Relation to the War. *Psychological Review*, 1918, *25*, 85–115.

Presented at the Twenty-Sixth Annual Meeting of the American Psychological Association, Pittsburgh, Pennsylvania, 1917. *(See Chapter 11.)*

Although he received his degree under H. Münsterberg, Yerkes was essentially a self-starter. He was an early leader in the field of comparative psychology and investigated a variety of organisms in the hope of revealing steps in the evolution of behavior and mind. He taught and was in charge of the animal laboratory at Harvard University until 1917 when he was invited to the University of Minnesota as professor of psychology and director of the laboratory. (He took charge in absentia but never served.) He filled various posts in Washington in connection with the war effort (1917–1924), then joined the newly formed Institute of Psychology at Yale University (1924), the forerunner of the Institute of Human Relations. Out of loyalty to his evolutionary interests he had his title changed from professor of psychology to professor of psychobiology. He remained at Yale until his retirement (1941). During World War II he again took a major part in the war effort, and the Survey and Planning Committee that he headed was responsible for a revised APA constitution.

Yerkes' animal experimentation covered a great variety of organisms, from earthworms, frogs, and kittens to chimpanzees and gorillas. He developed methods, such as the multiple-choice apparatus, that were adaptable to use with organisms of various sizes and abilities, including humans. His books reflect this range of interests: *The Dancing Mouse* (1907), *Introduction to Psychology* (1911), *The Great Apes* (1929, written with his wife, Ada W. Yerkes), and *Chimpanzees: A Laboratory Colony* (1943). His preparation for work with the Army testing program included his collaboration with J. W. Bridges and R. S. Hardwick on the development of an intelligence test, published as *A Point Scale for Measuring Mental Ability* (1915). After World War I he edited the massive book *Psychological Examining in the United States Army* (1921).

As president of the APA when World War I was declared in April 1917, Yerkes called a meeting of the APA Council, which was held in Philadelphia on April 21. By the time of his presidential address in December of 1917, Yerkes had been commissioned a Major in the U.S. Army's Surgeon General's Office and was able to describe in detail the plan for examining army recruits to eliminate the mentally unfit. These plans were the origin of the Army Alpha and Army Beta tests that were developed during the war under Yerkes' program. Although Yerkes' address does not represent him as a comparative psychologist, it is reprinted in full here for its historical significance and does indeed represent his leadership.

John Wallace Baird (1869–1919)

PhD, Cornell University, 1902 (under E. B. Titchener).

Because of World War I, the Twenty-Seventh Annual Meeting of the American Psychological Association was not held on a full scale; no presidential address was delivered.

Baird taught at Cornell University, Johns Hopkins University, and the University of Illinois; in 1910 he became director of the laboratory at Clark University, where he remained until his death. His monographic publication was entitled *The Color Sensitivity of the Peripheral Retina* (1905).

Walter Dill Scott (1869–1955)

PhD, University of Leipzig, 1900 (under W. Wundt).

Changes in Some of Our Conceptions and Practices of Personnel. *Psychological Review*, 1920, 27, 81–95.

Presented at the Twenty-Eighth Annual Meeting of the American Psychological Association, Cambridge, Massachusetts, 1919.

Most of Scott's academic career was spent at Northwestern University, where he taught psychology (1901–1920) and was president of the university from 1920 until his retirement (1939). During these years he also organized the Scott Company, a personnel firm over which he presided (1912–1921). He also directed salesmanship research at the Carnegie Institute of Technology (1916–1917), an interest that led to the postwar development of personnel psychology at Carnegie under Walter V. Bingham. Scott's interest also led him into Army personnel classification work during World War I.

His books represent his applied interests: *The Psychology of Public Speaking* (1907; second edition, 1926), *The Psychology of Advertising* (1908), *Increasing Human Efficiency in Business* (1911; revised, 1923), *Personnel Management* (1923; fifth edition with R. C. Clothier & W. R. Spriegel, 1954).

Scott indicated in his address that the notion of "putting square pegs into square holes" has been outmoded. The relation of the worker to his/her job must be seen as a "biological relationship," in which humans and their environment are not contrasted, and in which the industrial situation is "not men and over against them, jobs, but in reality *workers-in-their-work.*"

Shepherd Ivory Franz (1874–1933)

PhD, Columbia University, 1899 (under J. McK. Cattell).

Cerebral-Mental Relations. *Psychological Review*, 1921, *28*, 81–95.

Presented at the Twenty-Ninth Annual Meeting of the American Psychological Association, Chicago, Illinois, 1920.

Franz spent one year with W. Wundt at the University of Leipzig before receiving his PhD. He then taught physiology at Harvard University and Dartmouth College and served as a pathological psychologist at McLean Hospital in Worcester, Massachusetts. He then began a long service at St. Elizabeth's Hospital (1907–1924) and was appointed at the same time as a professor at George Washington University. His work on restitution of function after brain damage began at St. Elizabeth's, where he was joined by K. S. Lashley. He then moved to the University of California, Los Angeles, where he was professor of psychology (1924–1933). He wrote *Handbook of Mental Examination Methods* (1912) and *Nervous and Mental Re-Education* (1924). In his last year he also authored a book on a case of multiple personality, *Persons One and Three* (1933). The building that houses the Department of Psychology at the University of California, Los Angeles, is named for him.

Franz chose for his address one of the oldest topics in psychology, the relation of mind to brain. As a practical matter he recognized that (a) many facts regarding the nervous system may be discussed without reference to terms that connote mental processes; (b) many facts regarding the mind are associated together without knowledge of probable or possible cerebral intervention; (c) some mental states are known to occur when there are changes in the brain or in the nervous system; (d) when there are defects in the brain, concomitant variations from the usual or the normal states are frequently observed; (e) mental differences exist without known structural or functional nervous alterations; and (f) certain brain variations are not accompanied by known mental variation. He found fault with earlier observers who believed that the structure of the brain "statically symbolizes . . . all that may occur in consciousness."

As a corrective, he considered various aspects of motor and sensory aphasia and pointed to many instances of substantial recovery, even if the condition arose initially from gunshot wounds. The fact of recovery, without tissue restitution, argues against the view of strict cerebral localization.

Margaret Floy Washburn (1871-1939)

PhD, Cornell University, 1894 (first degree awarded under E. B. Titchener).

Introspection as an Objective Method. *Psychological Review*, 1922, *29*, 89-112.

Presented at the Thirtieth Annual Meeting of the American Psychological Association, Princeton, New Jersey, 1921.

Washburn taught at Wells College, Cornell University and the University of Cincinnati before going to Vassar College (1903) as an associate professor of philosophy in charge of psychology. Her title was changed to professor of psychology (1908), and she remained at Vassar until her retirement. She was the second woman elected to the presidency of APA. She was honored also by election to the National Academy of Sciences and was the second woman in any field of science to become a member.

Her book *Animal Mind* (1908; last edition, 1936) was a literature review that was the standard text in that area. Her more theoretical and controversial book, *Movement and Mental Imagery* (1916) advocated a motor theory of consciousness that W. B. Pillsbury had discussed in his earlier address and that H. S. Langfeld was to turn to later.

Washburn's address focused on the battle between structuralism and behaviorism. She noted that in some respects she preferred behaviorism to functionalism because behaviorism, like the structuralism in which she had been trained, accepted physical science as a closed system. Expressing her objection to the manner in which behaviorism substitutes language behavior for introspection, she proposed that the behaviorist should use an expression such as "symptomatic language behavior," and be concerned with what such language is symptomatic of. She also defended the trustworthiness of introspection.

Knight Dunlap (1875-1949)

PhD, Harvard University, 1903 (under H. Münsterberg).

The Foundations of Social Psychology. *Psychological Review*, 1923, *30*, 81-102.

Presented at the Thirty-First Annual Meeting of the American Psychological Association, Cambridge, Massachusetts, 1922.

After an instructorship at the University of California, Berkeley, Dunlap moved to Johns Hopkins University (1904-1936), where he was affiliated at the time of his APA presidential address. In 1936 he moved to the

University of California, Los Angeles, to head the department of psychology and remained until his retirement in 1947. Prior to his election as APA president, he authored books on many topics, including *An Outline of Psychobiology* (1914; new edition, 1917) and *Mysticism, Freudianism, and Scientific Psychology* (1920). The preparation of his book *Social Psychology* (1925) may have influenced his APA presidential address. His book *Habits: Their Making and Unmaking* (1932) was influential because of its emphasis on negative practice.

The popular social psychology at the time of Dunlap's address was that of William McDougall and was based on instincts. Dunlap had early taken a strong position against instincts, and he was also against McDougall's position on the group mind. Recognizing that social psychology is a vital and respectable subject, Dunlap hoped that it might be studied under controlled conditions. He recommended the study of audience responses to theatrical performances as a useful approach that is natural but that also has aspects of a true experiment.

Lewis Madison Terman (1877–1956)

PhD, Clark University, 1905 (under G. Stanley Hall and E. C. Sanford).

The Mental Test as a Psychological Method. *Psychological Review*, 1924, *31*, 93–117.

Presented at the Thirty-Second Annual Meeting of the American Psychological Association, Madison, Wisconsin, 1923. *(See Chapter 12.)*

After teaching at the Los Angeles State Normal School, Terman spent his academic career at Stanford University, first in the school of education (1910–1922) and then as head of the department of psychology (1922–1942). His prominence as a psychologist at the time of his election as president of APA rested on his revision and extension of the Binet-Simon intelligence scale (known as the Stanford-Binet), which was published as *The Measurement of Intelligence* (1916). This work prepared him to take a leading role in the preparation of the U.S. Army tests in World War I and led him to establish enduring friendships with R. M. Yerkes and E. G. Boring.

In addition to later revisions of the Stanford-Binet, Terman undertook a long-range study of children who scored high on intelligence tests. His results were published as a series of volumes entitled *Genetic Studies of Genius* (Volume 1, 1925; Volume 2, 1926; Volume 3, 1930; and Volume 4, 1947; Volume 5 appeared in 1959, after his death, through the efforts of his collaborator, M. H. Oden). Terman also co-authored *Sex and Personality* (1936, with C. C. Miles) and *Psychological Factors in Marital Happiness* (with other authors, 1938).

His presidential address provided a history and defense of mental tests as part of general psychology and refuted the idea that such tests were merely an applied innovation that had come to prominence at that time.

Granville Stanley Hall (1844–1924)

PhD, Harvard University, 1878 (under W. James and H. P. Bowditch).

Because Hall died before he could deliver a second presidential address, his colleague, W. H. Burnham, delivered a tribute to him entitled, "The Man, G. Stanley Hall." *Psychological Review*, 1925, *32*, 89–102.

Presented at the Thirty-Third Annual Meeting of the American Psychological Association, Washington, D.C., 1924.

Madison Bentley (1870–1955)

PhD, Cornell University, 1899 (under E. B. Titchener).

The Major Categories of Psychology. *Psychological Review*, 1926, *33*, 71–105.

Presented at the Thirty-Fourth Annual Meeting of the American Psychological Association, Ithaca, New York, 1925.

Bentley remained at Cornell after he received his degree until he was invited to the University of Illinois as professor of psychology and director of the psychological laboratory (1912–1928). After Titchener's death, Bentley was given Titchener's chair at Cornell until his retirement (1940). He then accepted a courtesy office at Stanford University, where he continued editorial duties and writing until shortly before his death. His systematic textbook, *The Field of Psychology* (1924), appeared in revision under the title, *The New Field of Psychology* (1933).

In his address, Bentley first criticized behaviorism for neglecting experience, then recognized that prior treatments of experience were inadequate and that the category therefore required careful examination. Bentley's address was the first of the APA presidential addresses to deal seriously with Gestalt psychology. He found it unsatisfactory because Gestalt psychologists limited phenomenology to configuration. In the end, Bentley accepted three basic psychological approaches: objective, experiential, and conceptual. This acceptance allowed all psychologists to work side by side, without accepting an eclecticism that can lead only to confusion.

Harvey Carr (1873–1954)

PhD, University of Chicago, 1905 (under J. R. Angell).

The Interpretation of the Animal Mind. *Psychological Review*, 1927, *34*, 87–106.

Presented at the Thirty-Fifth Annual Meeting of the American Psychological Association, Philadelphia, Pennsylvania, 1926.

After spending some years at the Pratt Institute in Brooklyn, New York, Carr returned to the University of Chicago (1908). He was in charge of the animal laboratory and then became departmental chairman until his retirement in 1938. His textbook, *Psychology: A Study of Mental Activity* (1925), although never revised, remained in use by his students for many years as a representative text preserving the functionalist position against the dominant behaviorism. His later book, *An Introduction to Space Perception* (1935) carried on the tradition with an emphasis on the contribution of learning to perception.

In his address, Carr noted that M. F. Washburn, a previous APA president, had argued in her book *Animal Mind* that it is necessary to be anthropomorphic in order to be psychological. Carr believed it to be necessary to come to grips with the behaviorist's denial of consciousness. Carr ended his address as a cautious nonbehaviorist, for he believed that it is possible to make limited inferences as to consciousness in animals based on the degrees of similarity to humans in behavior and in structure.

Harry Levi Hollingworth (1880–1956)

PhD, Columbia University, 1909 (under J. McK. Cattell).

Sensuous Determinants of Psychological Attitude. *Psychological Review*, 1928, *35*, 93–117.

Presented at the Thirty-Sixth Annual Meeting of the American Psychological Association, Columbus, Ohio, 1927.

Although Hollingworth received his PhD under Cattell, he was also indebted to R. S. Woodworth and E. L. Thorndike. His academic career was spent teaching at Barnard College of Columbia University (1909–1946), where the laboratories were named in his honor in 1954. Three of his books were published close to the time of his election to the APA presidency: *The Psychology of Thought* (1926), *Mental Growth and Decline* (1927), and *Psychology, Its Facts and Principles* (1928).

In his address, Hollingworth classified the warring psychologists as interoceptists (sensationists) and exteroceptists (behaviorists), but objected to both, particularly in their handling of the concept of meaning. Hollingworth believed that we have to rid ourselves of the trinity of experience, body, and stimulus, and he introduced his own way of considering psychological problems according to the redintegrative theory that appeared in his book *Psychology, Its Facts and Principles*. The principal modes of redintegrative sequence were partiality, concurrence, and reduction. Instead of the terms stimulus and response, Hollingworth used the terms antecedent and consequent, terms that became popular among later writers who were sometimes unfamiliar with his introduction of them.

Edwin Garrigues Boring (1886–1968)

PhD, Cornell University, 1914 (under E. B. Titchener).

The Psychology of Controversy. *Psychological Review*, 1929, *36*, 97–121.

Presented at the Thirty-Seventh Annual Meeting of the American Psychological Association, New York, New York, 1928. *(See Chapter 13.)*

Boring taught at Cornell University (1913–1918) and at Clark University (1919–1922) before coming to Harvard University (1922) for the remainder of his academic career. He retired in 1956 but remained active as an editor in his emeritus years. His best-known book was *A History of Experimental Psychology* (1929; revised, 1950). He also authored *The Physical Dimensions of Consciousness* (1933) and *Sensation and Perception in the History of Experimental Psychology* (1942). Two collections of his papers have been published, *Psychologist at Large* (1961) and *History, Psychology and Science* (1963) and he co-authored *Source Book in the History of Psychology* (1965) with R. J. Herrnstein. He was also the first editor of APA's book review journal, *Contemporary Psychology*, and was responsible for its style and tone.

Boring's address showed both his skill as a historian and his desire to be the mediator between the clashes of opinion that advance science. As specific illustrations he chose the history of animal magnetism and hypnosis, a controversy between C. Stumpf and W. Wundt over musical intervals and the E. B. Titchener–J. M. Baldwin controversy over muscular and sensorial reaction times.

Wolfgang Köhler (1887–1967)

PhD, University of Berlin, 1909 (under C. Stumpf).

. Gestalt Psychology Today. *American Psychologist*, 1959, *14*, 727–734.

Presented at the Sixty-Seventh Annual Meeting of the American Psychological Association, Cincinnati, Ohio, 1959. *(See Chapter 14.)*

Köhler was at the University of Frankfurt (1910–1913) when, with Max Wertheimer and Kurt Koffka, Gestalt psychology was initiated. At the Anthropoid Station in Tenerife (1913–1919), he performed experiments on apes that became well-known through his book, *The Mentality of Apes* (published in German, 1917; in English, 1924). He taught for a year at the University of Göttingen, then taught at the University of Berlin for the rest of his stay in Germany (1922–1935). Because of his objections to Hitler's regime, he moved to the United States and joined the faculty of Swarthmore College and remained there until retirement (1935–1958), when he became a research professor at Dartmouth College. His most important book *Die Physischen Gestalten in Ruhe und in Stationären Zustand* (1920) has never been fully translated into English. *Gestalt Psychology* (1929; revised, 1947) is representative of his books written in English.

In his address, Köhler refuted the idea that Gestalt psychology succeeded because its message became assimilated within conventional psychology. He pointed out that much could be learned from Gestalt psychology; he also expressed admiration for American psychology because of its respect for method and caution. At the same time, he warned young psychologists that if these virtues were to become too strong, they might bring forth a spirit of skepticism and thus prevent new work. Köhler believed that psychologists should not limit their studies to areas already familiar from previous research. He criticized the restrictiveness of "methodological behaviorism" as represented in the work of Hull. *(See Chapter 17.)* (Köhler's address is placed here because Gestalt psychology became most influential in the 1920s, when both Koffka and Köhler lectured in America and their books were published in English. Many subsequent presidential addresses refer to Gestalt psychology but none, strictly speaking, is fully representative of the Gestalt viewpoint. It was a historical accident that Köhler's election to the APA presidency was delayed until he was in his retirement years.)

Karl Spencer Lashley (1890–1958)

PhD, Johns Hopkins University, 1914 (under J. B. Watson).

Basic Neural Mechanisms in Behavior. *Psychological Review*, 1930, *37*, 1–24.

Presented at the Ninth International Congress of Psychology, New Haven, Connecticut, 1929. *(See Chapter 15.)*

After receiving his degree, Lashley was associated with S. I. Franz at St. Elizabeth's Hospital in Washington, D.C. He began his teaching career at the University of Minnesota (1917) and went to the Behavior Research Fund in Chicago (1926), where he was affiliated at the time of his presidential address. He was associated with the University of Chicago as a professor (1929–1935) and moved to Harvard University (1935–1942). He then became director of the Yerkes Laboratories of Primate Biology in Orange Park, Florida, where he remained (beyond retirement age) in emeritus status until shortly before his death in France. His major book, *Brain Mechanisms and Intelligence* (1929) was published the same year that he presented his presidential address.

In his address, Lashley summarized the conclusions he had drawn after many years of research on the white rat: (a) he was against the conditioned reflex and in favor of Gestalt notions of equivalence of patterns and reactions to ratios of stimulation; (b) he believed in the equipotentiality of different parts of the cortex; and (c) he held to the principle of mass action—that the disturbances of function depended on the quantity of brain tissue destroyed rather than its location. An important sentence in his address served those who wished to declare psychology's independence from neurological explanation: "Psychology is more advanced than neurology."

Herbert Sidney Langfeld (1879–1958)

PhD, University of Berlin, 1909 (under C. Stumpf).

A Response Interpretation of Consciousness. *Psychological Review*, 1931, *38*, 87–108.

Presented at the Thirty-Eighth Annual Meeting of the American Psychological Association, Iowa City, 1930.

Langfeld taught at Harvard University (1910–1924), then moved to Princeton University for the remainder of his academic career (1924–1947). His best-known book is *The Esthetic Attitude* (1920). He was co-editor, with E. G. Boring, and H. P. Weld, of the textbook *Foundations of Psychology* (1935 and later editions).

Langfeld developed the motor theory of consciousness under the name of response interpretation. He believed behaviorism to be simply one among many methods of study, all valuable in the development of psychology. According to Langfeld, the response theory includes an interpretation of mind beyond a method of inquiry. The perception of a lifted weight as *heavy* provides an empirical illustration: "according to the response theory, at least incipient motor responses do occur, and the efferent impulse in connection with these is a physiological factor underlying the peculiar object called weight, and without such responses there would be no perception of weight." Langfeld considered also the relation of motor responses to visual perception.

Walter Samuel Hunter (1889–1954)

PhD, University of Chicago, 1912 (under H. A. Carr and J. R. Angell).

The Psychological Study of Behavior. *Psychological Review*, 1932, 39, 1–24.

Presented at the Thirty-Ninth Annual Meeting of the American Psychological Association, Toronto, Ontario, Canada, 1931.

Hunter taught at the University of Texas (1912–1916), the University of Kansas (1916–1925), and Clark University (1925–1936), where he was affiliated at the time of his APA presidential address. In 1936 he moved to Brown University for the remainder of his life. In his best-known book, *Human Behavior* (1928), he proposed the term *anthroponomy* to replace *psychology*.

In addition to his research and teaching he served many editorial and administrative roles. He was the first editor of *Comparative Psychology Monographs* and of *Psychological Abstracts*. He was the chief psychological examiner at several military camps during World War I and was chairman of the Applied Psychology Panel of the National Defense Research Committee during World War II. The psychology building at Brown University has been named for him.

In his address, Hunter noted that the problems that most clearly separate psychology from other sciences are (a) the study of learning, (b) the utilization of tests, (c) the analysis of social behavior, and possibly (d) the analysis of language behavior. Some important topics in psychology, such as receptor functions and behavior disorders, overlap with various other sciences. After critical discussion of the limits of experimental psychology, Hunter arrived at this definition: "Psychology seeks to describe and explain, to predict and control, the extrinsic behavior of the organism to an external environment which is predominantly social."

Walter Richard Miles (1885–1978)

PhD, University of Iowa, 1913 (under C. E. Seashore).

Age and Human Ability. *Psychological Review*, 1933, *40*, 99–123.

Presented at the Fortieth Annual Meeting of the American Psychological Association, Ithaca, New York, 1932.

After teaching at Wesleyan University (1913–1914) Miles was employed by the Carnegie Nutrition Laboratory in Boston (1914–1922) until he became a professor at Stanford University, (1922–1932). In 1932 he moved to Yale University, where he remained until he became emeritus in 1953. Thereafter he taught at the University of Istanbul and served for many years at the U.S. Navy Submarine Medical Research Laboratory in Groton, Connecticut. In tribute to Raymond Dodge, who influenced Miles at Wesleyan, at the Carnegie Laboratory, and at Yale, Miles edited a Dodge commemorative volume entitled, *Psychological Studies of Human Variability* (1936).

Miles stated in his address that psychologists show interest in the first two and a half decades of human life and neglect the remaining five or six decades. Miles reported data from his Stanford Later Maturity Study (1930–1932), in which some 2,500 persons were studied at ages ranging from 6 to 95 years. He focused on perceptual ability, motor ability, memory, imagination, comparison, judgment, combination, and abstraction and concluded that although most abilities decline with age, some show no average decline. Even among those abilities that do decline, about one-fourth of those persons over 70 years of age do as well as the average of the total group.

Louis Leon Thurstone (1887–1965)

PhD, University of Chicago, 1917.

The Vectors of the Mind. *Psychological Review*, 1934, *41*, 1–32.

Presented at the Forty-First Annual Meeting of the American Psychological Association, Chicago, Illinois, 1933. *(See Chapter 16.)*

Thurstone's academic career began at the Carnegie Institute of Technology in Pittsburgh where he was one of a distinguished group in the field of applied psychology under the direction of Walter V. Bingham (1917–1924). He then taught at the University of Chicago (1924–1952), where he was affiliated at the time of his APA presidential address. When he reached retirement age in 1952 he moved to the University of North Carolina, where he died. He is best known for his books on factor analysis, *The Vectors of the Mind*

(1934) and *Multiple-Factor Analysis* (1947), and he made many significant contributions to more conventional psychophysical measurement and to test procedures in areas such as attitudes and personality.

Thurstone began his address by giving credit to C. E. Spearman, who initiated the factor problem and made a significant contribution toward its solution. Thurstone believed, however, that Spearman's formulation, based on a single common factor, was inadequate for the multidimensionality of mental abilities. Thurstone commented that an alternate view, represented in the work of T. L. Kelley, began with the assumption that there may be several independent or dependent mental abilities, and it is a question of fact for each study how many factors are needed to account for the observed correlations. Thurstone explained the multiple-factor method and illustrated the method by factor analyses of personality, psychotic symptoms, vocational interests, radical attitudes, and an intelligence battery, including performance tests. Thurstone also discussed the centroid method, according to which the factors can be plotted to show their relationships. This proved to be an elegant and very influential development.

Joseph Peterson (1878–1935)

PhD, University of Chicago, 1907 (under J. R. Angell).

Aspects of Learning. *Psychological Review*, 1935, *42*, 1–27.

Presented at the Forty-Second Annual Meeting of the American Psychological Association, New York, New York, 1934.

Peterson taught at Brigham Young University (1907–1911), the University of Utah (1911–1915), and the University of Minnesota (1915–1918), before he began a long career at the George Peabody College for Teachers (1918–1935), where he was affiliated at the time of his APA presidential address. His interests focused on animal and human studies of learning and perception, but he is perhaps best known for his historical book, *Early Conceptions and Tests of Intelligence* (1925). He was co-author of *The Handling of Men in the Army* (1918, with Q. J. David) and *Comparative Ability of Whites and Negroes* (1929, with L. H. Lanier).

In his address, Peterson elucidated a principle of learning that he had earlier proposed called the "completeness of response" principle. According to this principle, which was his substitute for the law of effect, the consummatory response completes the series of tendencies by giving the whole act a unity that facilitates its reproduction under appropriate circumstances. Peterson used data from maze learning and other experiments to support the principle.

Albert Theodore Poffenberger (1885–1977)

PhD, Columbia University, 1912 (under J. McK. Cattell and R. S. Woodworth).

Psychology and Life. *Psychological Review*, 1936, *43*, 9–31.

Presented at the Forty-Third Annual Meeting of the American Psychological Association, Ann Arbor, Michigan, 1935.

Poffenberger spent his academic life at Columbia University (from 1914 until his retirement in 1950), where he headed the psychology department (1927–1941). He is well known in the field of applied psychology for his books *Psychology of Advertising* (1932) and *Principles of Applied Psychology* (1942).

Although other presidents had recognized psychology's public responsibility in wartime, Poffenberger was the first to take note of the great economic depression that had been marked by the stock market collapse in 1929. He deplored the lack of representation by psychologists in the new agencies that President Franklin Roosevelt had set up to combat unemployment. After discussing standards by which to hallmark adequate psychologists (representing *Homo psychologicus*), he made concrete proposals for extending psychological service within the community and emphasized the necessity of protecting the public from the misinterpretation of scientifically sound conclusions.

Clark Leonard Hull (1884–1952)

PhD, University of Wisconsin, 1918 (under V. A. C. Henmon and D. Starch).

Mind, Mechanism and Adaptive Behavior. *Psychological Review*, 1937, *44*, 1–32.

Presented at the Forty-Fourth Annual Meeting of the American Psychological Association, Hanover, New Hampshire, 1936. *(See Chapter 17.)*

After teaching at the University of Wisconsin (1916–1929), Hull moved to Yale University to complete his academic career (1929–1952). Best known for the elegant theoretical structure that he developed as a theory of learned behavior, he had earlier written the significant books *Aptitude Testing* (1928) and *Hypnosis and Suggestibility* (1933). His major theoretical book, *Principles of Behavior* (1943), is anticipated in his presidential address, and his final book was entitled *A Behavior System* (1952).

The style of representation of Hull's theory, a series of constructs carefully tied to observable reality at both ends, is well represented in his presidential address. The address shows the systematic elegance with which he presented his theories, using a hypothetico-deductive model that is familiar in geometry and is in some respects borrowed from Newton's *Principia*.

Edward Chace Tolman (1886–1959)

PhD, Harvard University, 1915 (under H. Münsterberg and E. B. Holt).

The Determiners of Behavior at a Choice Point. *Psychological Review*, 1938, *45*, 1–41.

Presented at the Forty-Fifth Annual Meeting of the American Psychological Association, Minneapolis, Minnesota, 1937. *(See Chapter 18.)*

After teaching at Northwestern University (1915–1918), Tolman spent the remainder of his academic life at the University of California, Berkeley (from 1918 until his retirement in 1954). His major book, *Purposive Behavior in Animals and Men* (1932), was followed by a small book on motivation, with its title modified by World War II, *Drives Toward War* (1942).

The type of behaviorism discussed by Tolman in his address stressed inferred intervening variables in a manner that has influenced more recent cognitive psychology. Because of his emphasis on *molar* rather than *molecular* behavior, Tolman felt that he had departed more than Hull from Watson's position; Tolman's position was often contrasted with Hull's despite some of the overlaps pointed out in the address.

John Frederick Dashiell (1888–1975)

PhD, Columbia University, 1913 (under J. McK. Cattell).

Some Rapprochements in Contemporary Psychology. *Psychological Bulletin*, 1939, *36*, 1–24.

Presented at the Forty-Sixth Annual Meeting of the American Psychological Association, Columbus, Ohio, 1938.

Dashiell taught philosophy at Waynesburg College (1913–1914) and at Princeton University (1914–1915) before having a psychology title at the University of Minnesota (1915–1917) and at Oberlin College (1917–1919). He then moved to the University of North Carolina, where he remained from 1919 until he became emeritus in 1958. After his retirement, he continued to teach at Wake Forest University (1958–1961), and then a year each at Florida State University, Emory University, Florida Presbyterian College, and the University of Oregon. His textbook *Fundamentals of Objective Psychology* (1928) was widely influential as a nonstrident behaviorism. His chapter on experimental social psychology in C. Murchison's *Handbook of Social Psychology* (1935) encouraged developments in that area.

Using interactions across modalities as an analogy, Dashiell argued that "gravitational" tendencies pull together the "tangential" influences in contemporary psychology: for example, a welcome concern for appropriate methodology (by way of logic, psychology's proper link with philosophy); also a better rapport with biology, and developments within learning and personality. Additionally significant was the rapprochement between the *experimental* and *clinical* attitudes.

Gordon Willard Allport (1897–1967)

PhD, Harvard University, 1922 (under E. B. Holt).

The Psychologist's Frame of Reference. *Psychological Bulletin*, 1940, *37*, 1–28.

Presented at the Forty-Seventh Annual Meeting of the American Psychological Association, Stanford University and University of California, Berkeley, 1939. *(See Chapter 19.)*

Allport's teaching career began at Harvard University as an instructor in social ethics (1924–1926) with R. C. Cabot. After a short period of teaching at Dartmouth College (1926–1930), the rest of his career was spent at Harvard as a professor of psychology, first in the department of psychology and then in the newly created department of social relations (1946–1966), after which he was named as the R. C. Cabot professor of social ethics. Although he authored many books, the one that most clearly established his reputation was *Personality, A Psychological Interpretation* (1937). Others included *Studies in Expressive Movement* (1933, with P. E. Vernon), *The Psychology of Radio* (1935, with Hadley Cantril), *The Psychology of Rumor* (1947, with Leo Postman), *The Individual and His Religion* (1950), *The Nature of Prejudice* (1954), and *Pattern and Growth in Personality* (1961). His contributions to tests of personality included an early test for ascendance–submission (1928), published jointly with his older brother, F. H. Allport, and *A Study of Values* (1931, with P. E. Vernon), later revised with the help of Gardner Lindzey (1960).

In his address, Allport content analyzed journal articles in psychology over a 50-year period and noted the trends. He criticized some trends because of their neglect of the individual case in preference for statistical (or nomothetic) findings.

Leonard Carmichael (1898–1973)

PhD, Harvard University, 1924 (under W. F. Dearborn).

The Experimental Embryology of Mind. *Psychological Bulletin*, 1941, *38*, 1–28.

Presented at the Forty-Eighth Annual Meeting of the American Psychological Association, State College, Pennsylvania, 1940.

After teaching at Tufts University (1923–1924), Princeton University (1924–1927), Brown University (1927–1936), and the University of Rochester (1936–1938), Carmichael became president of Tufts University (1938–1952). He then was Secretary of the Smithsonian Institution (1953–1964) and ended his career as an officer of the National Geographic Society. He became best known for the research that led to his chapter on the origin and prenatal growth of behavior in the second edition of C. Murchison's *Handbook of Child Psychology* (1933). He updated the chapter in later editions, two of which he edited under the title *Manual of Child Psychology* (1946, 1954). He co-authored *Elements of Human Psychology* (1930, with H. C. Warren) and *Reading and Visual Fatigue* (1947, with W. F. Dearborn) and authored *Basic Psychology* (1957).

The substance of Carmichael's address was similar to that in his chapter in *Handbook of Child Psychology*. The address included 64 titles in its list of references. To find the "zero" of behavior, Carmichael believed that it is necessary to look for the first significant response to stimulation. Because muscles respond to stimulation before neural control is established, ambiguity does exist, but it is best to look for the first true reflex response. In work with fetal guinea pigs, Carmichael and C. S. Bridgman had found the first signs of a reflex response to be a localized flexion of the neck, sometimes involving a forelimb. Carmichael illustrated other aspects of fetal development with detailed reports of what was known regarding the early development of special senses and the development of motor responses. He ended his address with a discussion of the implications of the study of fetal behavior for psychology.

Herbert Woodrow (1883–1974)

PhD, Columbia University, 1909 (under J. McK. Cattell).

The Problem of General Quantitative Laws in Psychology. *Psychological Bulletin*, 1942, *39*, 1–27.

Presented at the Forty-Ninth Annual Meeting of the American Psychological Association, Evanston, Illinois, 1941.

Woodrow taught at the University of Minnesota (1909–1927) and at the University of Oklahoma (1927–1928) before being invited to head the psychology department at the University of Illinois, where he remained until his retirement (1950). His major book was *Brightness and Dullness in Children* (1919; second edition, 1923).

Woodrow attempted in his address to derive a truly general quantitative law to express the relationship between the attributes of performance and the environmental variables on which they depend. He demonstrated that his law could be made to fit the data from 14 very different kinds of experimental relationship. Because the law had five parameters to be determined by curve fitting, and no truly theoretical basis, it was not influential in later quantitative psychology.

Calvin Perry Stone (1892–1954)

PhD, University of Minnesota, 1921 (under K. S. Lashley).

Multiply, Vary, Let the Strongest Live and the Weakest Die—Charles Darwin. *Psychological Bulletin*, 1943, *40*, 1–24.

Prepared for the Fiftieth Annual Meeting of the American Psychological Association, New York, New York, 1942. *(The address was not delivered in response to a request from the Office of Emergency Management that meetings be postponed for the duration of World War II.)*

Stone's academic career, after a year's teaching at the University of Minnesota, was spent entirely at Stanford University (1922–1954). He was very active in research, particularly in animal behavior. Representative of his work is the book *Comparative Psychology* (1951), which was edited by him and which contains a chapter by him on maturation and "instinctive" functions. He also taught abnormal psychology and one of the first university courses in Freudian psychology. He was the first editor of *Annual Review of Psychology* (1950–1954).

After reviewing the work of Charles Darwin and J. B. Lamarck, Stone turned to the issue of inheritance of acquired characters, a persistent problem in psychology. The rediscovery of Mendel led to new experiments on the inheritance of discontinuous changes in behavior, as distinct from modified somatic characters. Careful studies of egg laying as a result of selective breeding provided an example. Stone concluded his address with the observation that animal psychologists have neglected the study and appraisal of behavioral ecology and recommended it as the topic for the future.

John Edward Anderson (1893–1956)

PhD, Harvard University, 1917 (under H. Münsterberg).

Freedom and Constraint or Potentiality and Environment. *Psychological Bulletin,* 1944, *41,* 1–19.

Prepared for the Fifty-First Annual Meeting of the American Psychological Association, Evanston, Illinois, 1943. *(The address was not delivered in response to a request from the Office of Emergency Management that meetings be postponed for the duration of World War II.)*

Anderson began his teaching career at Yale University (1919–1926) then transferred to the University of Minnesota as director of the Institute of Child Welfare, where he remained until his retirement. Although he preferred journal publication to book writing, he co-authored a textbook, which reflects his interest in child development, entitled *Experimental Child Study* (1931, with Florence L. Goodenough).

Anderson's presidential address was the first to consider the lessons of World War II, which was then in progress. He noted how invention and scientific discovery stimulated by the war solved problems that under ordinary conditions would take more time. Constraints are removed, individuals are freed for new functions, and society itself is freed for new organizations. These observations provided a background for departing from the usual nature–nurture studies; instead Anderson considered in detail how the environment provides resources, incentives, and constraints that operate over a period of time. To answer the questions of what the person does to the environment and what the environment does to the person, Anderson believed that psychologists should give up their preoccupation with the person to examine more carefully the extraindividual surrounds that affect what the person does.

Gardner Murphy (1895–   )

PhD, Columbia University, 1923.

The Freeing of Intelligence. *Psychological Bulletin,* 1945, *42,* 1–19.

Presented at the Fifty-Second Annual Meeting of the American Psychological Association, Cleveland, Ohio, 1944.

After a long and productive assistant professorship at Columbia University (1929–1940), Murphy became a professor at the College of the City of New York (1940–1952). He then became research director for the

Menninger Foundation in Topeka, Kansas, until his retirement, although he continued to be active in his affiliation with George Washington University in Washington, D.C. Well known for his research and numerous books in the areas of personality, social psychology, history of psychology, and parapsychology, the early book *Experimental Social Psychology* (1931, written in collaboration with his wife, Lois Barclay Murphy), was influential (second edition, 1937, with Theodore Newcomb as an added collaborator). He also authored the impressive book *Personality* (1947).

Representative of his other books are *An Historical Introduction to Modern Psychology* (1928; latest revision with Joseph Kovach, 1972), *General Psychology* (1933), *Human Potentialities* (1958), *Development of the Perceptual World* (1960, with Charles Solley), *Challenge of Psychical Research* (1961, with L. Dale), and *Outgrowing Self-Deception* (1975, with Morton Leeds).

Murphy selected the dynamics of the thought process to illustrate how necessary it is to integrate mankind's thought patterns in their natural settings with the work of the laboratory. Murphy believed that if experimental psychologists reach to meet those who have studied thinking in natural settings, they may strive to integrate the findings within a single systematic effort. The autisms, whether individual or socially shared, have to be understood. Fortunately, the "standardization of error" is corrected by the scientist's curiosity. Murphy hoped that the new divisional structure of the APA would not produce more isolation by specialties, when integration was needed.

Edwin Ray Guthrie (1886–1959)

PhD, University of Pennsylvania, 1912 (under E. A. Singer).

Psychological Facts and Psychological Theories. *Psychological Bulletin*, 1946, *43*, 1–20.

Presented at the Fifty-Third Annual Meeting of the American Psychological Association, Evanston, Illinois, 1945.

Although he received his PhD under Singer, Guthrie attributed his interest in psychology more to H. K. Wolfe, who had received a PhD under W. Wundt and under whom Guthrie had studied at the University of Nebraska. Guthrie taught high school (1912–1914) and then began his service at the University of Washington (1914–1951), where he also served as dean of the graduate school (1943–1951). After his first retirement in 1951 he continued to teach part-time and to serve the university in other ways until retiring finally in 1956. He wrote an early behaviorist textbook, *General Psychology in Terms of Behavior* (1921, with Stevenson Smith). He is best known for his book *Psychology of Learning* (1935; second edition, 1952).

His other books included *The Psychology of Human Conflict* (1938; republished in paperback, 1962), which is very deferential to Pierre Janet. With the assistance of his wife, Helen M. Guthrie, he also translated Janet's *Principles of Psychotherapy* (1924). He co-authored *Cats in the Puzzle Box* (1946, with G. P. Horton), which covers the experiments described in his presidential address; later he co-authored *Psychology, a First Course in Human Behavior* (1949, with A. L. Edwards) and *Educational Psychology* (1950, with F. F. Powers).

Guthrie's address began with an exposition of the theory of conditioning with which he was already identified. This theory, based on the principle of associative learning, states that an organism, confronted with a situation, attempts to repeat what it last did in that same situation or in one similar to it. Guthrie bolstered this theory of one-trial learning by the experiments that were reported later in his book *Cats in a Puzzle Box*. Guthrie advised psychologists to observe behavior rather than the outcomes that behavior produces.

Reprinted with permission
from *Psychological Review*,
1918, *25*, 85–115.

Chapter 11

Psychology in Relation to the War

Major Robert M. Yerkes

Sanitary Corps, National Army,
Surgeon General's Office,
Washington, D.C.

It is my agreeable duty as President of the American Psychological Association to present to you in outline the history of the organizing of psychological military service. I shall limit myself strictly to the activities of the present year, 1917.

In Europe, psychologists have served conspicuously in the great war but psychology has done little. In this country, for the first time in the history of our science, a general organization in the interests of certain ideal and practical aims has been effected. Today American psychology is placing a highly trained and eager personnel at the service of our military organizations. We are acting not individually but collectively on the basis of common training and common faith in the practical value of

---

Address of the President before the American Psychological Association, Pittsburgh Meeting, December, 1917.

our work. At the first call American psychologists responded promptly and heartily, therefore the length to which the development of our work has progressed and the measure of service which has been attained.

On April 6, 1917, in connection with a meeting of a group of psychologists known as the "Experimentalists" which was at the time being held in Emerson Hall, Cambridge, Massachusetts, a session was arranged by Messrs. Langfeld and Yerkes with the approval of the chairman of the meeting, Mr. Titchener, for discussion of the relations of psychology to national defense. Captain Bowen, instructor in military science and tactics, Harvard University, attended this meeting and made valuable suggestions concerning the possible rôle of psychology. Notable suggestions were made also by Messrs. Bingham, Troland, Langfeld, Doll, Reeves, Burtt, Wells and others. At the conclusion of the discussion, which clearly indicated confidence in the preparedness of psychology for military service, it was moved by Mr. Warren that a committee consisting of Messrs. Yerkes, Bingham and Dodge be appointed to gather information concerning the possible relations of psychology to military affairs and to further the application of psychological methods to military problems.

On the evening of the same day at an informal conference of the members of this committee (Mr. Bingham's place being taken by Mr. Ogden), it was decided that the matter should be placed before the council of the American Psychological Association, so that our national organization, rather than any restricted or local group, might take action. Following this conference, the president of the American Psychological Association prepared the following letter, which on April 7 was dispatched to the members of the council of the association.

Emerson Hall, Cambridge, Mass.
April 6, 1917

To the Council of the American Psychological Association,

Gentlemen: In the present perilous situation, it is obviously desirable that the psychologists of the country act unitedly in the interests of defense. Our knowledge and our methods are of importance to the military service of our country, and it is our duty to cooperate to the fullest extent and immediately toward the increased efficiency of our Army and Navy. Formalities are not in order. We should act at once as a professional group as well as individually.

As president of the American Psychological Association, I apparently have choice of two lines of action: either I may recommend to the council that a special meeting of the association be called at once to consider the general situation, or I may, instead, ask the council to authorize the appointment, by the president, of such committee or committees from the association membership as seem desirable.

After consultation with a number of members of the association, I have chosen the second alternative, and I hereby request the council's authorization to appoint such necessary and desirable committee or committees.

The duties of any group or groups of members appointed to represent and act for us would evidently consist, first, in gathering all useful information concerning the varied aspects of the actual and possible practical relations of psychology to military affairs; second, to cooperate, as circumstances dictate, with governmental agencies, with the National Council of Defense, with local psychological groups or individuals, and with such other agencies as may develop; third, to further the development and application of methods to the immediate problems of military selection.

Already many of us are working for national defense in our respective communities. It is my thought that this action by our council should, far from interfering with individual initiative, tend to unite us as a professional group in a nation-wide effort to render our professional training serviceable.

I urge you, gentlemen, to give this matter your immediate consideration, and I trust that you will write freely concerning your own activities, plans and opinions, for your advice and suggestions concerning all aspects of the problem will be quite as welcome as your vote on the above recommendation.

Yours faithfully,

Robert M. Yerkes,

President, American Psychological Association

It was deemed desirable by two members of the council that a meeting be called immediately for consideration of the situation and decision concerning desirable action. Such meeting was called by the president in Philadelphia on the evening of April 21.

In the meantime the writer, in order to obtain pertinent information concerning actual and possible applications of psychology to military problems and, by request, to advise the Military Hospitals' Commission of Canada concerning the use of psychological methods, proceeded to the Dominion of Canada and made careful inquiry concerning psychological activities in Montreal, Ottawa and Toronto. The following memorandum report of observations in Canada was prepared especially for the Council of the American Psychological Association. It will serve to indicate both the general nature of the writer's inquiries and information and the personal sources of the same.

**Memorandum of Trip to Canada, April 10–14, for Consultation with
Military Hospitals' Commission Concerning Applications
of Psychological Methods to Soldiers**

From Boston to Montreal, Tuesday night, April 10. On Wednesday, April 11, called on Professor William Caldwell, McGill University, and after conference with him was introduced to Major Muchleston, with whom I talked concerning the use of psychological methods in examining recruits. Later lunched with Major Muchleston and Captain Robertson at University Club, and discussed with them possible relations of psychology to varied aspects of the military situation. Also, received the opinions of Captain Ross, a returned officer, who had been wounded in France and who was strongly of the opinion that psychologists and psychiatrists should be of great service in the present situation.

Left at four o'clock for Ottawa, arriving about seven-thirty. Was met by Messrs. E. H. Scammell and T. B. Kidner, of the Military Hospitals' Commission staff, and also by Captain Farrar and Doctor Brigham. We later for two hours discussed the organization and pyschological relations of the commission.

Thursday morning, April 12, I spent two hours in conference with Doctor Brigham, describing tests in use at the Psychopathic Hospital, Boston, and offering suggestions concerning their application to the military hospitals situation. The remainder of the morning was spent at the offices of the commission, in discussion of various psychological problems with the staff and in the examination of various reports concerning the condition and treatment of incapacitated soldiers.

Lunched at the Rideau Club with Messrs. Scammell, Kidner, Farrar, Brigham and W. L. McKenzie King. From this group I received valuable information. One of the most impressive things about the conversation was the constant emphasis of the spiritual as contrasted with the material in human life and the evident feeling that for the sake of material development certain essential aspects of the human have been neglected.

The afternoon was spent at the offices of the commission in further analysis of data and study of the relation of the organization to psychological methods and in conference with Senator McClennan, a member of the commission.

Later, Doctors Farrar and Brigham took me to the office of Major Dodd, who as member of the Board of Pension Commissioners, has very evident appreciation of the need of psychological information, but, like most of his colleagues, is unable to obtain the desired data.

The evening was spent with Doctors Farrar and Brigham in further discussion of the relations of psychologists to the problems of mental disease and defect as they appear in soldiers who are discharged from the army.

Lieut.-Colonel Alfred Thompson was absent from Ottawa, but I met and conferred with Captain Chipman and various civilian authorities connected with the Military Hospitals' Commission and obtained printed materials and various typewritten reports.

The general impression which my conferences in Ottawa gave me was that of urgent and rather generally appreciated psychological needs.

At eleven o'clock Doctor Brigham and I left for Toronto. Arriving there in the morning, we got in touch with Captain Ryan, of the Military Hospitals' Commission, and were taken by him to Doctor Clark, of Toronto University, who is superintendent of the university hospital and dean of the medical school. He, after telling us of the psychiatric work in his institution and of his interest in the problem of feeblemindedness, took us to the psychological laboratory of the University of Toronto, and there introduced us to Mr. Bott, who exhibited and explained to us most varied and interesting forms of home-made apparatus for the reeducation of crippled soldiers. The entire laboratory is given up to this work, and Mr. Bott, together with a number of assistants, gives practically all of his time to the task of reeducation.

This work is evidently the most important, from the social and economic standpoints, necessitated by the great war, since hundreds of thousands of soldiers are being returned to society partially incapacitated by paralysis or by the loss or injury of members. The relations of psychology to methods of reeducation, and in general to the treatment of these victims of war, are numerous and obviously important, but at present too little is being done in Canada or elsewhere toward utilizing either psychological knowledge or technical psychological methods.

After lunching with Doctor Clark at the university hospital, we were taken by Captain Ryan to visit two military hospitals. During this trip I especially inquired about the examination of recruits for the aviation corps and learned that no especially significant psychological tests are included in the examination.

In the military hospitals, which for the most part are buildings temporarily converted for the purpose, we saw in a general way the facilities for after-care and treatment of the men who are being returned to the Dominion now at the rate of about one hundred per day.

The chief work of the Military Hospitals' Commission, as indicated by its bulletins and other reports, is the proper distribution and medical care of returned soldiers and their vocational reeducation.

At five o'clock Friday, April 13, I left Toronto for Philadelphia. On the way I had opportunity to examine my Canadian materials and notes and to make memoranda concerning my observations.

While in Ottawa the writer received a telegram from Dr. George E. Hale, chairman of the National Research Council, requesting a conference in Philadelphia on April 14. In accordance with this request the president of the association met Dr. Hale and briefly reported to him the action which had been taken by American psychologists and the results of observations in Canada. President Hale requested that a psychology committee be organized in connection with the National Research Council and that the president of the American Psychological Association act as chairman of the committee and as member of the council.

He further invited the president of the association to attend the semi-annual meeting of the National Research Council in Washington on April 19, as a representative of psychological interests.

At a special meeting of the council of the American Psychological Association which was held on the evening of April 21 and the morning of April 22 in Philadelphia, there were present, in addition to the president, the secretary of the association, Mr. Langfeld, Messrs. Angier, Bingham, Dunlap and Scott of the council, and by invitation Mr. Dodge. Messrs. Carr and Hollingworth were unable to attend. The action of the council upon the original recommendations of the president are recorded in the following minutes of the meeting.

Minutes of Special Meeting of the Council of the
American Psychological Association

The president reported his investigations concerning the possibility of the cooperation of psychologists in a scientific capacity in the present emergency. He described his trip to Ottawa, Toronto, and Montreal, where he found the authorities very much interested in the possibility of psychological assistance. His impression was that they realized that they had made a mistake in not using psychological methods for the selection of recruits and for reeducation from the beginning of the war. The president later went to Washington to consult with the National Research Council.

It was voted that the president be instructed to appoint committees from the membership of the American Psychological Association to render to the government of the United States all possible assistance with psychological problems arising from the present military emergency. The following committees were authorized and their chairmen named.[1]

1. Committee on psychological literature relating to military affairs. A bibliography should be prepared and the important pertinent literature digested, so that the desirable information may be available to individuals who are interested in various lines of service or are undertaking the solution of special problems.

Chairman, Professor Madison Bentley.

2. Committee on the psychological examination of recruits. It is necessary to prepare a plan for this task, to arrange methods of examining, and if arrangements are made with the War Department, to organize a corps of examiners.

Chairman, Professor Robert M. Yerkes.

3. Committee on the selection of men for tasks requiring special aptitude, as for example various kinds of artillery service, signaling, etc.

Chairman, Professor E. L. Thorndike.

4. Committee on psychological problems of aviation, including the pertinent literature, the psychological classifications of an aviator, and the relations of these classifications to mechanical problems.

Chairman, Doctor H. E. Burtt.

5. Committee on psychological problems of incapacity, including those of shell shock, reeducation, etc.

Chairman, Doctor S. I. Franz.

6. Committee on psychological problems of vocational characteristics and vocational advice. These problems are related to those of reeducation and incapacity.

Chairman, Professor John B. Watson.

---

1. For membership of committees see "Psychology and National Service," *Psychol. Bull.*, 1917, *14*, 259–262.

7. Committee on recreation in the army and navy.

Chairman, Professor George A. Coe.

8. Committee on the pedagogical and psychological problems of military training and discipline.

Chairman, Professor Charles H. Judd.

9. Committee on problems of motivation in connection with military activities.

Chairman, Professor Walter D. Scott.

10. Committee on problems of emotional characteristics, self-control, etc., in their relations to military demands.

Chairman, Professor Robert S. Woodworth.

11. Committee on acoustic problems and characteristics of the sense of hearing in relation to military service; for example, the significance of localization of sounds, auditory acuity, the possibility of developing ability to discriminate different projectiles by their sound, etc.

Chairman, Professor Carl E. Seashore.

12. Committee on problems of vision which have military significance.

Chairman, Professor Raymond Dodge.

It was voted that, in order to provide the necessary funds for the development of the plans for national service, the council instruct the president of the association to appoint a special finance committee of three, which shall be empowered to raise and disburse a special fund, without authorization of the council. If the fund is not sufficient, said committee shall be empowered to present itemized bills, not to exceed the sum of one thousand dollars, which the council at the next annual meeting of the association shall recommend to be paid from the funds of the association.

It was moved and seconded that the secretary be instructed to formulate a letter to the members of the association describing the action of the council at this special meeting, in the hope that the members will communicate with the president concerning the best methods of offering their own resources and the resources of their laboratories to the government.

The council made certain suggestions to the president concerning the presentation to the proper government authorities of a plan for the psychological examination of recruits, and authorized the president to proceed with such presentation.

Herbert S. Langfeld,
Secretary, American Psychological Association.

Following this council meeting and by authorization already indicated, a psychology committee of the National Research Council was organized with the following membership: Messrs. Cattell, Hall, and

Thorndike from the National Academy of Sciences; Messrs. Dodge, Franz and Whipple from the American Psychological Association; and Messrs. Seashore, Watson and Yerkes from the American Association for the Advancement of Science.[2]

At the first meeting of this committee, it was voted

that whereas psychologists in common with other men of science may be able to do invaluable work for national service and in the conduct of the war, it is recommended by this committee that psychologists volunteer for and be assigned to the work in which their service will be of the greatest use to the nation. In the case of students of psychology, this may involve the completion of the studies on which they are engaged.

It is the function of this general committee to organize and, in a general way, supervise psychological research and service in the present emergency. Problems suggested by military officers or by psychologists are referred by the committee to appropriate individuals or institutions for immediate attention.

Several of the committees originally appointed by the Council of the American Psychological Association were subsequently accepted as sub-committees of the psychology committee of the National Research Council.

After the meeting of the National Research Council which the president of the American Psychological Association was privileged to attend in Washington, and at which he made a brief statement concerning the possible service of psychology to the military organizations, a circular letter was addressed to the members of the American Psychological Association in which their cooperation with the government in the interest of national defense was suggested. It was especially indicated that psychological laboratories might be made available and that offers of personal service would materially assist the council in formulating and furthering plans for the development of national service.

During the last week in April, in pursuance of the suggestions of the council of the American Psychological Association, the president acting as chairman of the committee on methods for the psychological examining of recruits, prepared for transmission to the proper military authorities the following plan for the examining of recruits.

Plan for the Psychological Examining of Recruits to Eliminate the Mentally Unfit

Whereas the Council of the American Psychological Association is convinced that in the present emergency American psychologists can substantially serve the government under the medical corps of the Army

---

2. Mr. Cattell resigned from the committee in October. Messrs. Angell and Scott have been added to the membership.

and Navy by examining recruits with respect especially to intellectual deficiency, psychopathic tendencies, nervous instability, and inadequate self-control, it has voted to present to the proper military authorities the following plan and suggestions for psychological service.

This is not intended as a reflection on the work of the military medical examiner, but instead as an offer of special professional aid in a time of unusual strain, pressure and haste. Psychologically incompetent recruits are peculiarly dangerous risks with respect to disaster in action, incapacity, and subsequent pension claims. For this reason and because few medical examiners are trained in the use of modern methods of psychological examining, our profession should be of extreme value to the medical corps.

It is proposed:

1. That the psychological examining be conducted in the training camps and, if possible, before men are finally accepted for the service. It is assumed that there will be ten to fifteen thousand men per camp.

2. That a chief psychological examiner, who shall be also an officer in the Medical Reserve Corps[3] and responsible to the chief medical officer, be located in each camp, to organize, direct and engage in the psychological work.

3. That the chief psychologist be allowed an assistant examiner for each twenty-five hundred men in the camp.

4. That each assistant psychological examiner be given a commission in the Medical Reserve Corps, in order that the psychological work may be conducted with proper decorum and with due respect of private for examiner. The service of civilians as psychological examiners would appear to be undesirable.

5. That properly trained privates, non-commissioned and commissioned officers, be assigned to psychological examining as need requires and given rank in the Medical Reserve Corps. This provides for the contingency that a large number of the men who are especially qualified for this work may have enlisted or accepted commissions in army or navy prior to the organizing of psychological corps.

6. That an appropriate private examining room with floor space of approximately 10 by 12 feet be provided for each psychological examiner. For a camp of ten to fifteen thousand men, five such rooms would be required. A table, flat-top desk with locked drawers, and two or three chairs would be needed in each room.

7. That the necessary materials for psychological examining and the requisite record blanks and filing cards be supplied by the Government. It is estimated that the materials would cost approximately five dollars per examiner, wholesale, and the record sheets not more than a cent per man examined.

---

3. Since most psychological examiners do not hold medical degrees, it would be necessary probably to commission them as civilian experts under the Medical Corps.

8. That the procedure of examining be substantially as follows:

(a) In consultation with medical officers and company officers the psychologist should prepare a list of all men in a given company for whom special psychological examination is indicated by exceptional or unsatisfactory behavior.

(b) With this special list before him the psychological examiner should summon the men of the company to appear, one at a time, in his examining room. Each should there be subjected to a short series of mental measurements, the necessary time for which should not exceed ten minutes. The result of these measurements should be a rough estimate of the mental status and chief characteristics of the individual and consequent classification as mentally *inferior, normal,* or *superior.* Special attention should be given to men whose mental fitness had been questioned by medical or other officers.

(c) The normal group (probably 80 to 90 per cent. of all) should be passed, without further examination, as mentally competent. The inferiors should be given a special examination at once to decide whether they should be eliminated from the service. The superiors, time permitting, should be systematically examined for indications of their special value in the military organization.

(d) The special examination for inferiors (or superiors) would require from thirty to sixty minutes. It should consist of measurements of various forms and aspects of response, among which should appear motor characteristics (for example, quickness, steadiness, and fatigability), observation, memory, suggestibility, adaptability or rapidity of learning, judgment, reasoning power, instinctive and emotional traits.

(e) The psychological staff should discuss the examination record of each inferior man and vote on the question of recommending to the medical officer his rejection or discharge from the service.

9. Further, this plan should be elaborated and perfected by a competent group of psychological examiners in conference and in cooperation with military authorities.

Robert M. Yerkes,
Chairman, Psychology Committee, National Research Council.

Early in May this plan was submitted to the president of the National Research Council, who in turn referred it to the chairman of the Committee on Medicine and Hygiene of the Council, Dr. Victor C. Vaughan. With Dr. Vaughan's support and cooperation the plan was promptly placed before the Surgeon General of the Army.

The evident necessity for developing methods of psychological examining especially adapted to military needs stimulated the chairman of the committee on methods of examining recruits to seek such financial aid as would render possible the organizing of an active committee for this special task. About the middle of May this need and opportunity were brought to the attention of the Committee on Provision for the Feebleminded (Philadelphia), whose secretary, Mr. Joseph P. Byers, immediately presented the matter to his board. It was promptly voted by this organization to offer the committee on methods facilities for work at The Training School, Vineland, New Jersey, and to meet the expenses of the work to an amount not to exceed five hundred dollars. This sum was later increased to seven hundred dollars. On the basis of this offer of assistance, a committee consisting of Messrs. Bingham, Goddard, Haines, Terman, Wells, Whipple and Yerkes was assembled at The Training School, Vineland, New Jersey, on May 28. It remained in session until June 9 when it adjourned for two weeks to make certain trial of methods which had been devised.

During the first two weeks it was decided to arrange a method of examining recruits in groups of twenty-five to fifty, as an initial psychological survey. The group method, as finally agreed upon and printed for preliminary trial, consists of ten different measurements.

From June 10 to 23, the various members of the committee conducted examinations by the above method in several parts of the country. In all, about four hundred examinations were made, chiefly upon United States Marines and candidates in officers' training camps. These measurements were carefully analyzed by the committee and used as a basis for revision and the devising of methods of scoring.

On June 25, the committee resumed its sessions at Vineland and continued its work until Saturday, July 7, when it adjourned, on the completion of tentative methods of group and individual examining. At this time the committee had in press five forms of group examination record blanks; an individual examination record blank, which provides special forms of measurement for illiterates, those who have difficulty with the English language, those who exhibit irregularities suggestive of psychopathic condition, those who are intellectually subnormal or inferior, and finally, those who are distinctly supernormal; an examiner's guide, which contains directions for the conduct of examination; and various types of special record sheet.

Before its adjournment, the committee, through a joint committee of psychiatrists and psychologists, consisting of Doctors Copp, Meyer, Williams, Terman, Haines (Bingham, alternate) and Yerkes received assurance from the committee on furnishing hospital units for nervous and mental disorders to the United States government[4] that the above committee would finance to the extent of twenty-five hundred dollars the trial of the above methods of psychological examining in various army and navy organizations, the work to be so planned as to test thoroughly the reliability and serviceableness of the methods and to supply materials for their improvement and for the development of satisfactory methods of scoring and reporting data of examinations.

This offer of assistance resulted in the prompt formulation of the following plan, which was successfully carried out.

Outline of Plan for Trial of Methods of Examining Recruits

Five groups of three men each to be organized for immediate work in four different military establishments, each group to consist of a chief

---

4. Mental Hygiene War Work Committee.

examiner and two assistants. The fifth group to be organized for statistical work.

The four examining groups are to work for one month in either naval stations, army reorganization camps, or officers' training camps. It is proposed that approximately one thousand men be examined at each place by the group method, and approximately two hundred by the individual method. Further, that so far as possible, the results of these examinations be correlated with industrial and military records or histories.

This work is to begin as soon after July 15 as possible. Toward the expense $2,500 has been appropriated.

The estimated cost of the work is as follows:

Printing	$ 500.00
Stencils	25.00
Maintenance and travelling expenses of fifteen men, $75 each ...	1,125.00
Examiners' materials, including lock-boxes for shipment and storage	290.00
Furnishings for four examining rooms	250.00
Total	$2,190.000

Records of examinations are to be shipped to the statistical unit in New York City as rapidly as possible, so that they may be scored and the results evaluated and correlated with a view to determining the best methods of scoring and desirable changes in methods of examining.

Personnel of Units

Examining unit, Fort Benjamin Harrison, Indianapolis, Ind.: Chief examiner, G. M. Whipple, succeeded by T. H. Haines; Assistant examiners, J. E. Anderson, W. K. Layton.

Examining unit, Camp Jackson, Nashville, Tenn.: Chief examiner, E. K. Strong; assistant examiners, B. R. Simpson, D. G. Paterson.

Examining unit, Reorganization Camp, Syracuse, N. Y.: Chief examiner, J. W. Hayes; assistant examiners, J. C. Bell, W. S. Foster.

Examining unit, Naval Training Base No. 6, Brooklyn, N. Y.: Chief examiner, R. S. Woodworth; assistant examiners, N. J. Melville, G. C. Myers.

Statistical unit: Statistician, E. L. Thorndike; assistants, A. S. Otis, L. L. Thurstone.

The examining of approximately four thousand soldiers in accordance with the plan described above and the comparison of the results with officer's ratings of the men revealed correlation of about .5, and in general justified the belief that the new methods would prove serviceable to the Army.

On July 20, after the adjournment of the Committee on Methods and as a direct result of its work, the following substitute plan for the psychological examining of recruits was forwarded to the Surgeon General of the Army.

Plan for the Psychological Examining of Recruits to Eliminate the Mentally Unfit

This replaces a plan earlier submitted, action on which has been postponed by request.

The committee on methods of the psychology committee of the National Research Council, having completed the preparation of methods especially adapted to the selection of a "first-line army" and the elimination of bad mental risks, respectfully submits the following plan to the Surgeon General of the Army.

I. *Personnel:* It is proposed,

(1) That six (6) qualified experts, designated hereafter as chief psychological examiners, be recommended immediately for commissions in the Sanitary Corps. One chief examiner shall be located in each camp to organize, direct, and participate in the psychological work. (Pending action on commissions, these men might be employed under the Civil Service Commission as provided in (2) below.)
(2) That eighteen (18) men be employed immediately as assistant psychological examiners under the provision of the Civil Service Commission for the employment of unlisted scientific experts. This will not involve delay, since examination is not required.

Supplementary Memorandum Concerning Personnel

If this plan should be acted upon favorably, a list of names for commissions in the Sanitary Corps and for civil service employment, will be submitted promptly upon request.

The committee has a list of 150 men who have signified their willingness to serve the government as psychological examiners or investigators. Of these it is estimated that not more than 75 are both properly qualified and able to undertake this work within a month.

It is further estimated, from information which we have at hand, that within a week 24 men can be made available for service as recommended under sections (1) and (2).

II. *Apparatus and Other Equipment:* It is further proposed,

(1) That there be provided in connection with each camp in which psychological examining is to be conducted:
  (a) One room for group examinations with floor space approximately 28 by 40 feet, and door at each end. The same to be furnished with 56 tablet-arm chairs (or small tables and chairs), and examiner's table.
  (b) Not fewer than two rooms with floor space at least 10 by 12 feet, to be used as private examining rooms. Each to be furnished with table and three chairs.
(2) That the following apparatus and supplies be furnished:
  (a) For each examiner:
      (1) Cube construction,
      (2) Cube imitation,
      (3) Cheap clock,   Estimated cost,
      (4) Stop watch, $15
      (5) Pencils and paper,
      (6) Examiner's guide or manual
  (b) For each camp, or examining unit:
      (1) Pencil sharpener,   Estimated cost,
      (2) Stock of pencils and paper $10
  (c) For each recruit examined:
      Group record blank, and in certain instances also individual record blanks. Estimated cost, 2 to 4 cents according to number printed.

Memorandum Concerning Examining Outfits

Fifteen complete sets of examining materials are at present in use in various army and navy camps and stations. These can promptly be turned over to the government, in case this plan is acted upon favorably.

III. *Procedure in Examination:* It is proposed,

(1) That all recruits be subjected, in groups of about 50, to a general mental examination which shall require not less than 20 nor more than 40 minutes per group. It is the expectation of the committee that this time can be reduced to 20 minutes. If so, the average time per man would be less than ½ minute.
(2) That all recruits, on the results of the group examinations, be tentatively classified as mentally (a) low; (b) high; (c) average; (d) irregular, and that as time permits the lowest 10 per cent., the highest 5 per cent., and irregular individuals shall be subjected to more searching individual examination, on the basis of which, report shall be made by the psychological examiner to the proper medical officer.
(3) That all psychological examining be done under authority of the Army Medical Corps, and immediately under the direction of those medical officers who are specially designated to deal with nervous and mental cases.

(4) That the chief purpose of psychological examination be classification of all recruits as first, second or third class mentally, so that the War Department may use the data of examination as a basis for elimination or for service classification, as policy or necessity dictate.

Copies of the Examiner's Guide, of Form A of the group examination record blank, of the individual examination record blank, and of a special four-page record sheet, are submitted with this plan. These materials have been printed in several hundred copies, and are now being used in an extensive test of the usefulness of the method of examining recruits which is recommended.

Respectfully submitted,

Robert M. Yerkes,
Chairman, Psychology Committee, National Research Council.

July 20, 1917

Early in August report of the trial of methods of psychological examinations in Army and Navy stations was prepared and on the basis thereof it became possible definitely to recommend to the Medical Department of the Army official trial in the drafted Army of the methods prepared by the committee.

The chairman of the committee was, upon recommendation of Doctors Vaughan and Welch, of the National Research Council, appointed with the rank of major in the Sanitary Corps, National Army, to organize and direct psychological examining for the Medical Department.

It was later decided by the Medical Department to authorize an initial experiment in the following National Army cantonments: Camp Lee, Petersburg, Virginia; Camp Zachary Taylor, Louisville, Kentucky; Camp Dix, Wrightstown, New Jersey and Camp Devens, Ayer, Massachusetts. Arrangements were made for the necessary personnel and equipment, and instructions to commanding generals of the divisions were issued by the War Department.

The Psychological Staffs of the Several Cantonments

Camp Lee: First Lieutenants Clarence S. Yoakum, George O. Ferguson, Jr., Walter S. Hunter, Edward S. Jones, and the following civilians: Leo T. Brueckner, Donald G. Paterson, A. S. Edwards, Rudolph Pintner, Benjamin F. Pittenger, Ben D. Wood.

Camp Taylor: First Lieutenants Marion R. Trabue, Karl T. Waugh, Heber B. Cummings, Edgar A. Doll and the following civilians: James W. Bridges, J. Crosby Chapman, John K. Norton, Eugene C. Rowe, J. David Houser, C. P. Stone.

Camp Dix: First Lieutenants Joseph W. Hayes, Harold A. Richmond,

Herschel T. Manuel, Carl C. Brigham, and the following civilians: Thomas H. Haines, Norbert J. Melville, H. P. Shumway, Thomas M. Stokes, J. J. B. Morgan, C. C. Stech.

Camp Devens: First Lieutenants William S. Foster, John E. Anderson, Horace B. English, John T. Metcalf, and the following civilians: Raymond H. Wheeler, Harold C. Bingham, Carl R. Brown, Chester E. Kellogg, Ralph S. Roberts and Charles H. Toll.

The work of psychological examining proceeded rapidly, and in December, on the basis of statistical data and reports of inspectors, it was decided by the Medical Department to recommend the extension of psychological examining to the entire Army.

On December 24, 1917, this recommendation was approved by the General Staff and the Medical Department was requested to present a plan for the examining of all newly appointed officers and all drafted and enlisted men. The Section of Psychology, Office of the Surgeon General is now engaged in preparing a plan for the extension of the work.

Official reports of the results of psychological examining will be issued from time to time by the office of the Surgeon General. In this connection it will suffice to quote briefly from the recommendation of the Medical Department.

The purposes of psychological tests are: (a) to aid in segregating the mentally incompetent, (b) to classify men according to their mental capacity, (c) to *assist* in selecting competent men for responsible positions.

In the opinion of this office these reports (accompanying recommendation) indicate very definitely that the desired results have been achieved.

The success of this work in a large series of observations, some 5,000 officers and 80,000 men, makes it reasonably certain that similar results may be expected if the system be extended to include the entire enlisted and drafted personnel and all newly appointed officers.

In view of these considerations I recommend that all company officers, all candidates for officers' training camps and all drafted and enlisted men be required to take the prescribed psychological tests.

The work in question has thus far justified itself in the opinion of military authorities on the following practical counts:

(1) As a means of eliminating certain types of mentally incompetent men; (2) as a prompt and convenient method of obtaining for the use of company commanders information which leads to the intelligent assignment and training of men; (3) as a guide to such assignment of men as will result in organizations approximately equal in mental strength; (4) as an aid in the selection of candidates for officers' training groups, for promotion and for special assignment.

The account of the work of this single committee is inordinately lengthy and for the moment it may tend to give an unjust estimate of the significance of other lines of work which have led to important service. It is now proposed to present briefly an account of the development of certain of the more important of these lines of work. They will be considered under the head of committees.

The committee, which under the chairmanship of Dr. Thorndike was charged with problems concerning the selection of men for tasks requiring special skill, has rendered conspicuous service to the committee on methods of examining recruits and the committee on aviational problems. It further has the special distinction of having indirectly furthered the organization of the Committee on Classification of Personnel of the War Department.

The latter organization is due directly to the activities of Dr. Scott who shortly after the special meeting of the council of the American Psychological Association began work in collaboration with his colleagues of the department of psychology, Carnegie Institute of Technology, Pittsburgh, on the preparation of a rating scale for the selection and promotion of officers. Dr. Scott, during July, by personal representation succeeded in introducing this scale in several of the first series of officers' training camps. The trials of the method resulted in favorable and extremely enthusiastic reports from commanding officers to the War Department, consequently the rating scale in revised form was ordered to use in all of the second series of training camps and the Secretary of War, convinced by results already achieved, of the serviceability of psychologists and psychological methods, requested that a special committee be organized to be known as the Committee on Classification of Personnel of the War Department. This committee was organized early in August, 1917.

The need which led to this development is thus briefly stated in Dr. Scott's response to the request of the Secretary of War.

The attached memorandum makes it apparent that the chiefs of the War Department Bureaus are not wholly satisfied with present methods of classifying personnel and making recommendation for commissions and that they desire to try out the plan outlined below.

The first aim of this committee is to bring to the aid of the various bureaus the combined judgment and experience of specialists in methods of employing, examining, rating and classifying men according to their native abilities and their relative value to different branches of the service. The second aim is to provide a means for bringing to a focus the combined experience of the various branches of the Army organization in selecting, classifying and assigning men and in recommending them for commission.

This double purpose requires that the committee consist of (1) a scientific staff of specialists with civilian status, and (2) a board of cooperating members consisting of a representative from the War College and one officer designated by each chief of a War Department Bureau who chooses to share in the work of this committee. This plan would call for a staff of ten specialists with assistants and a board of cooperating members consisting of ten Army officers.

Psychologists who have served on this committee are Messrs. Angell, Bingham, Dodge, Scott, Shepard, Strong, Terman, Thorndike, Watson and Yerkes. A brief statement concerning the work of the committee prepared by its director, Dr. Scott, on November 12 follows:

My dear Major Yerkes: The work of the committee on classification of personnel in the Army is of such a nature that it is very difficult to state the exact date on which any work begins and is ended. In fact, practically all of our work has developed gradually and so far as we can see now, will never end. It is therefore difficult to give any report.

The following statement, however, will, in a way, conform with your request of November 6:

1. The Rating Scale was made the form for recommending candidates for promotion in eight of the first series of officers' training camps.

2. In the second series of officers' training camps, a permanent record and a rating scale and a pocket rating card were introduced and made a regular part of the system.

3. For selecting candidates for the third series of officers' training camps, the rating scale, a special form of making reports and a pocket rating card are made the official forms.

4. A personnel department has been established in each of the thirty-one divisions now in the United States. Sixteen civilian experts have been employed by the committee to install the personnel department and these sixteen civilians are cooperating with possibly two thousand officers and enlisted men who are devoting their time to this army work. In some of the divisions, this personnel work is developing very rapidly. This is notably true in the case of Camp Upton, where as many as seventy-two officers and three hundred enlisted men have been employed on the work at the same time.

5. The committee has cooperated in the work of psychological examining which is being conducted in four of the cantonments by the Surgeon General's Department under the direct supervision of Major Yerkes.

6. The committee is cooperating in the work of selecting men for the Signal Corps.

7. The committee is inaugurating a series of trade tests with the hope of making them a regular part of the work in each of the training camps.

8. The committee has formulated a qualification record card for use of officers in the army.

9. The committee has formulated a plan for securing data concerning the eight million registrants who have not as yet been called to the colors.

10. The committee has formulated a plan for promoting, transferring and demoting officers in the army.

11. The committee is formulating a plan to reduce the paper work in the army.

12. The committee has an office in Room 526, War Building, at which place current data are kept concerning all of the men in the National Army and the National Guard. This information is kept on file for the benefit of the Adjutant General of the Army and the Chief of Staff.

13. Seventy-five thousand, six hundred dollars has been appropriated by the War Department for the use of the committee.

Walter Dill Scott,
Director, Committee on Classification of Personnel in the Army

The committee on classification of personnel is not a direct outgrowth of the activities of the psychology committee of the National

Research Council, but has resulted from the individual efforts of Doctors Scott and Thorndike who acted as members of an original committee appointed by the council of the American Psychological Association. The work of the committee, as Dr. Scott's summary report indicates, has attained a scope and magnitude which renders adequate account in this connection impracticable. I have endeavored therefore to give such an outline of the work as may serve as a suitable introduction to the more detailed statement which Dr. Scott will make at our meeting tomorrow and so to interest you in this important psychological service that you may all be present to listen to his address.

The original committee on psychological problems of aviation, began the preparation and trial of tests in April under the chairmanship of Dr. Burtt who was assisted by Doctors Miles and Troland. Subsequently Dr. Burtt, because of the need of a vacation, resigned the chairmanship of the committee and Dr. Stratton was appointed in his stead with Dr. Thorndike as executive secretary. Doctors Watson, Maxfield and McComas were added to the membership of the committee.

A large number of measurements on aviational cadets were made in the ground flying schools in Massachusetts, Pennsylvania and California. It is probable that these measurements will ultimately lead to significant practical application.

Meantime, Professor Watson, who in August became a member of the committee on classification of personnel in the Army, accepted appointment as major in the Signal Corps and was placed on duty in the division of personnel. He has been responsible for the organizing of methods, other than the medical, of the aviational examining boards, and has further been charged with the direction of the work of a group of research psychologists.

His own summary statement concerning this work, which pertains to the effects of high altitude, is presented herewith:

The work of the Oxygen Committee is being carried out under the general supervision of Major Lewis, Major Wilmer, Major Watson and Captain Yandel Henderson.

Preliminary investigations are being undertaken at the Bureau of Mines, American University, Washington. Several men in physiology, psychology, and general medicine have been commissioned and are undertaking the actual experimentation. Captain Dunlap is in immediate charge of the laboratory work in psychology. Captain Schneider is in immediate charge of the work in physiology. On January 1, the work will be continued at Mineola, Long Island, where a small laboratory has been built. At present, the work is being carried out upon re-breathing apparatus. A steel tank which can be exhausted will be used in later experiments. In this way, the factor of barometric pressure can be controlled and the aerial conditions more closely simulated.

Psychological members at present on aviational examining boards are: Messrs. Wells, Bentley, Hamilton, Stratton and Henmon.

The work of the aviational committee and of Major Watson, its military representative, is clearly of great importance but it is utterly impossible in this brief address to report results or even to indicate satisfactorily the directions in which psychologists are contributing and may hope to contribute to the success of aerial warfare.

The committee on psychological literature relating to military affairs consists of the chairman only, Dr. Bentley, who for weeks sought out pertinent publications and forwarded to the sub-committees references and summaries of articles. In this way substantial aid was rendered psychologists who were engaged in the development of new methods and in the attempt to make practical application of existing methods of psychological research to special military problems.

The committees on the psychological problems of incapacity, including those of shell-shock, reeducation, etc., under the chairmanship of Dr. Franz, and on the psychological problems of vocational characteristics and vocational advice under the chairmanship of Dr. Watson were subsequently combined under the chairmanship of Dr. Franz who with the assistance of Doctors Watson and Lashley has furthered the development of reeducational methods and has attempted to cooperate in various ways with the appropriate committees of the Council of Defense and with the Division of Special Hospitals, Office of the Surgeon General.

This field of work is obviously of extreme importance and will doubtless demand the services of many psychologists, among whom women may be numbered, as the war continues and incapacitated men are returned to this country.

Dr. Coe, chairman of the committee on psychological problems of recreation in the Army and Navy, promptly organized his committee and instituted investigations which should lead to the establishment of proper cooperative relations between his group and the various agencies actively concerned with recreational activities in military stations. Dr. Coe's latest report indicates that his committee is attempting so to formulate psychological problems of military recreation as to decide wisely on lines of work which should be prosecuted immediately for the assistance of the recreational organizations.

Pedagogical and psychological problems of military training and discipline, in the interest of which Dr. Judd was named as chairman of the committee, received no attention because of the chairman's inability to find time for additional work. Dr. Judd finally resigned the chairmanship and the Psychology Committee of the National Research Council elected Dr. Bagley in his place. As yet no report concerning plans for the organization of the committee or for the prosecution of possible work has been received from Dr. Bagley. It is believed that this committee should be able to render signal service to the War Department by carefully analyzing various forms of military training and discipline and by suggesting new methods or modifications of old methods in the light of pedagogical and psychological knowledge.

The chairman of the committee on problems of motivation of military service, Dr. Scott, has been so far occupied with work on his rating scale and with his duties as director of the committee on classification of personnel that he has been unable to give special attention to the tasks outlined for his original committee. It is hoped that in the future opportunity may be found for special studies of motivation.

Similarly the committee on problems of emotional stability, fear and self-control, whose chairman is Dr. Woodworth, has thus far been unable to find suitable opportunity for practical work. According to the latest statement received from the chairman an attempt is being made to develop methods which shall aid in the elimination of men who are emotionally unstable.

Dr. Seashore's committee on acoustic problems of military importance has recently been invited to advise concerning methods suitable for military use and the chairman has submitted suggestions which promise to be of practical importance.

One of the first psychological problems suggested to the psychology committee of the National Research Council for solution was referred in May to Dr. Dodge, chairman of the committee on visual problems of military significance. This had to do with the needs of the Navy and its prompt and successful solution by Dr. Dodge led to increasingly important demands for his professional services. Much of the work which this committee has furthered is strictly secret. I therefore shall make use of a statement concerning the work of his committee which Dr. Dodge has prepared for me. Otherwise, I might make the mistake of telling something which I do not know!

Navy activities of the Psychology Committee: The Psychology Committee has been of service to various enterprises, two of which, involving more than one of our subcommittees, may not be mentioned at this time.

In addition to these the committee on personnel has prepared a qualification record adapted from the qualifications record of the army to the particular requirements of naval service. This has not yet been officially adopted, but preliminary trials have been ordered to ascertain its defects in operation, if there are any.

For the psychology committee of the National Research Council Dr. Dodge undertook the analysis of the reactions and coordinations which are involved in gun-pointing, for the purpose of devising tests to discover special fitness for the several tasks with a minimum loss of time. From this analysis a set of tests for the fire control party was elaborated with the cooperation of interested naval officers. This is now in practical use in the Atlantic Fleet.

Also with the cooperation of various naval officers he devised a graphic instrument to record the pointing reactions, the accuracy of coordinations in keeping on a moving target, and the accuracy of fire. This instrument was put through a severe trial on two of the major fighting units of the navy. It proved its value and has been elaborated into a robust and fool-proof land training instrument. This has already proved highly satisfactory in one of the training stations and has been ordered reproduced for general use.

Recently the psychology committee of the National Research Council has appointed two additional subcommittees, the functions of which are of such nature that they may not be discussed without lessening the prospective value of the work of the committees.

The obvious and significant trend of our psychological military work is toward service. Psychologists who develop methods or accumulate information which promises to aid us in winning the war are shortly appointed to positions which give them opportunity to apply their special knowledge effectively. At present our profession is importantly represented in the Department of the Adjutant General, in the Navy, the Signal Corps, the Medical Corps, the Sanitary Corps and the Quartermaster Corps. In some of these bureaus men have been commissioned. In others, psychologists are serving under civil appointment.

As we look ahead and attempt to prophesy future needs in the light of occurrences of the past six months, it is clear that the demand for psychologists and psychological service promises, or threatens, to be overwhelmingly great. In the Sanitary Corps alone, for the conduct of psychological examining, it is safe to assume that at least one hundred and fifty men will be needed for military appointments during 1918. For reeducational work during the same period it is probable that at least one hundred men or women, trained in the use of psychological and educational methods, will be required by special hospitals. In the aviational section of the Signal Corps the chances are that all psychologists properly qualified by scientific training who are available can be utilized to advantage. The Navy makes no personnel demands but it is using to very great advantage the professional advice of psychologists properly qualified to give such advice. The committee on classification of personnel has needs which cannot possibly be met by the available supply of well-trained psychologists. It behooves us therefore to maintain, and if possible improve, the facilities for psychological training in our educational institutions and the quality of instructional work. There should be no attempts at short cuts, but instead capable students should be encouraged to train themselves thoroughly for military positions which demand professional competence in addition to sound common-sense, good judgment and strong personalities.

Our profession has brought to the front the desirability and the possibility of dealing scientifically and effectively with the principal human factors in military organization and activity. It is by no means improbable that the work which has been initiated by the council of the American Psychological Association, by the psychology committee of the National Research Council and by the committee on classification of personnel will ultimately lead to the organization of a new bureau or corps within the military department. This bureau would be responsible for the varied human problems which experimental psychology has revealed to the military authorities and has dealt with in effectively practical ways.

It has been my desire in this historical account of our psychological services to give personal credit so far as possible. I cannot close without making grateful acknowledgment to those who have prepared the way for various lines of psychological work and materially furthered our progress. The list is necessarily incomplete. The authorities of the Military Hospitals' Commission of Canada rendered substantial aid at the outset by revealing needs of psychological assistance. Dr. George E. Hale, chairman of the National Research Council, opened the way to service by recognizing our science and by giving it a place in the Council of Defense. Major Victor C. Vaughan and Major William H. Welch foresaw the possibilities of value in psychological examining and took the risk of recommending psychological service to the Medical Department of the Army. Major Edgar King and Major Pearce Bailey materially assisted in the formulation of plans which made possible the proper coordination of psychological work with military training. Colonel Henry A. Shaw, through his thorough inspection of psychological examining and his personal interest in the extension of psychological methods to the entire Army, hastened the latter achievement and greatly encouraged the psychological staff. Surgeon General Gorgas and his staff hospitably received us and supplied ample opportunities for service.

Finally, it remains for me to say that from the very start there has been conspicuous enthusiasm for psychological military service and loyalty in the service. The work has been arduous, the discouragements often numerous and serious but in spite of them our various lines of work have been carried forward satisfactorily and in most instances with surprising rapidity. Everyone who has had opportunity to share in the work obviously feels that he has contributed to our military progress and has rendered more substantial service through the application of his professional training than would have been possible in any other line.

Reprinted with permission
from *Psychological Review*,
1924, *31*, 93–117.

Chapter 12

The Mental Test as a Psychological Method

Lewis M. Terman

Stanford University

I

However much one may dislike to "embark upon the troubled waters of definition," as President Angell once picturesquely phrased it, it seems necessary to begin by trying to come to some understanding with regard to what a mental test—or, if you prefer, a psychological test—is.

The English term "mental test" was first used, so far as I can learn, by Professor Cattell in 1890.[1] The tests he described were brief samplings of such abilities as strength of grip, reaction time, color naming, and memory span. A year earlier, in a discussion of intellectual disturbances following upon cerebral injury, C. Rieger made suggestions looking toward what he called *"Eine allgemein anwendbare Methode der Intelligenzprüfung."*[2] The idea, however, is implicit in an article by Galton

---

Address of the President, before the American Psychological Association, Madison Meeting, December, 1923.

1. In an article on "Mental and Physical Measurements" which appeared in *Mind*, 1890.

2. Stern, "Differentielle Psychologie," p. 89, 1911.

published ten years earlier 1879.[3] The earliest formulated definition I find is that of Binet and Henri, in 1896.[4] The method of mental tests, they say, "consists in the selection of a number of tasks designed to give detailed information on individual differences." One here notes the implication that other psychological methods do not use "tasks" and are not intended to give information on individual differences. Later definitions have usually followed along similar lines, but have tended to distinguish rather more explicitly between the mental test and the psychological experiment. Thus Whipple, in the introductory chapter of his "Manual of Mental and Physical Tests," 1910, says:

The mental test is some respects resembles, in some respects differs from the typical experiment of the psychological laboratory. Like this latter, the test is superior to the casual observation of everyday life because it is purposeful and methodical; it thus possesses all the merits common to experimental investigation at large, viz: the control of conditions (including the elimination of disturbing, and the systematic isolation of contributory factors), the possibility of repetition, and the possibility of subjecting the obtained results to quantitative treatment. Unlike the typical experiment of the psychological *laboratory*, the mental test ordinarily places little or no emphasis upon introspective observation by the subject, in part because of its relatively short duration, in part because it is frequently applied to inexperienced subjects who are incapable of aught but the most elementary introspection, but more especially because it is concerned less with the qualitative examination or structural analysis of mental processes than with the quantitative determination of mental efficiency; because, in other words, it studies mental performance rather than mental content.

In the 1914 edition of his "Manual," Whipple repeats what he said in 1910, but makes a significant insertion. His statement differentiating the test from the experiment now begins:

The primary difference between the research-experiment and the test-experiment is really one of aim. The test has a diagnostic, rather than a theoretical aim: its purpose is not to discover new facts, principles or laws for the science of psychology—though such a result may indirectly be attained—but to analyze, measure and rank the status or the efficiency of traits and capacities in the individual under examination.

That is, whereas the distinction drawn in 1910 was based entirely on the nature of the method itself, the distinction of 1914 is based first of all on aim.

---

3. "Psychometric Experiments," *Nineteenth Century*, 1879. Republished in "Inquiries into the Human Faculty," 1883.

4. *L'année psychologique*, 1896, p. 464.

This insertion seems to have been influenced by the distinction drawn by Stern in the 1911 edition of his "Differentielle Psychologie,"[5] which runs as follows:

The standpoint of the test-experiment (*Prüfungsexperiment*), which always characterizes individual psychology, is somewhat different from that of the research-experiment (*Forschungsexperiment*). We give it the English designation "Test," in the sense of "*Stichprobe*," but limit its use to the true test-experiment, although by others the term is sometimes extended to include the research-experiment. A test is thus an experiment which is designed to determine the individual mental character of a person or one of his special mental traits. Its immediate aim is, therefore, not a purely scientific-theoretical one, but a diagnostic one; its purpose is not to discover unknown laws or new relationships, but to classify a particular case with reference to known phenomena. To be sure, the goal of such diagnostic tests is the drawing of conclusions; if possible, conclusions of scientific value. The logical presuppositions of the test are, first, that it shall afford a real indication (*Zeichen*) of a significant trait; second, that in respect to this trait it shall give the individual tested a definite rank in a variational series. An experiment can only be called a test if, in spite of its acute character, it possesses a chronic symptom-value.

Dunlap, in his "Elements of Scientific Psychology," 1922,[6] states the difference as follows:

In mental measurement, the mental capacities and performances of individuals are measured with a view to the comparisons of individuals with one another, either for the purpose of selecting certain types of persons for certain purposes, or else for the rating of these individuals for some other practical ends. In Experimental Psychology, although measurements are always made on individuals, the purpose is to discover and analyze traits common to all of the group investigated, the differences being difficulties to be overcome by experimental technique, rather than being the main objective.

I do not know whether any significance is to be attached to the fact that in the passage just quoted *Experimental Psychology* is printed with initial caps while *mental measurements* is not! A later passage in the same text[7] leads me to suspect that the inconsistency in orthography may not have been accidental. The passage runs as follows: "In certain cases"— the author is discussing the measurement of sensory discrimination—

it is important and possible to make determinations in which small units of measurement are not demanded, and in which the reactor is not required to determine just perceptible and just imperceptible values. Such determinations

---

5. Pp. 87–88.
6. P. 19.
7. P. 131.

are called *tests*; and although in each case certain details of technique are indispensable, this technique is neither as detailed nor as difficult of acquisition as the technique of exact measurements.

That is, if the measurement is exact, it is an experiment; if only an approximation, it is a test. If such is the implication, I have no reason to suppose that Dunlap is the only Experimentalist of capital E persuasion.

As the above quotations indicate, there is a tendency to stress the following differences between a mental test and a psychological experiment: the mental test is primarily concerned with individual differences, rather than with the universals of psychology; it is applied to a large number of subjects; it studies mental behavior rather than mental content; it makes little use of apparatus; it is intended to accomplish a quick determination of an individual's status with respect to established names [norms]; its results, although at times they may have scientific value, are usually less exact than those of the experiment.

Without meaning to imply that all of these distinctions are groundless, I would raise the question whether to the extent that they hold at all, they reflect fundamental and necessary pre-suppositions of the mental test or only the accidents of its history. As for myself, I have never been able to see why one who employs the test method should confine himself to the study of individual differences; why he should dispense with introspection, if he considers it important for his purpose; why his aim should necessarily be practical; or why his results should be less exact or less capable of verification than those of the experimentalist.

When a few weeks ago I undertook to set down some of the considerations which seemed to me to justify this view, I found myself hesitating. After all, idols of the den are no mere figure of speech, and I realized that, with the exception of a few youthful forays which I made under the tutelage of Bergstrom and Sanford, I had lived my psychological life pretty much in the test den. I therefore decided to wait until I could take a few soundings; or, to keep the figure more consistent, until I could question the oracles of other psychological dens. My decision finally expressed itself in the form of three questions, which I addressed to twenty-two members of this Association. The first ran as follows: *What are the essential characteristics of a mental test? By this is meant, what (if anything) distinguishes it from any other psychological experiment?* The second question had to do with the contributions of the test method; the third called for a rating of its value in a way presently to be described.

My letter was submitted to two groups of psychologists, which we may designate the "random" group and the "interested" group. The "random" group (random, at least, for the present purpose) included all the eleven surviving presidents of this Association since 1910. In chronological order they are: Seashore, Thorndike, Warren, Woodworth, Watson, Dodge, Yerkes, Scott, Franz, Washburn, and Dunlap. The "interested" group was made up of eleven individuals selected because of their contributions to test psychology, and in such a way that they would represent various fields of interest, including industrial, educational, clinical, statistical, and experimental psychology. The names are: Bingham, Boring, Burtt, Cattell, Goddard, Kelley, Kuhlman, Pintner, Thurstone, Wells, and Whipple. No one in either group failed to reply. In response to the first question—what a mental test is, and how it differs from a psychological experiment—the two groups did not show any characteristic differences and have therefore been thrown together. The distinctions most often mentioned fall into three classes, which we may characterize in substance as follows:

1. Tests are intended to throw light upon individual differences; the experiment, to establish general principles. (Mentioned by ten.)

2. The test, in contrast to the experiment, is characterized by simplicity, or brevity, or less elaborateness, or the use of paper and pencil instead of apparatus. (Mentioned by nine.)

3. The test has a practical aim, usually individual diagnosis and guidance; it has to do with technology rather than with science. (Mentioned by seven.)

Other distinctions mentioned by one or more include the following: the test does not control conditions and vary the factors as an experiment must; the experiment is an analytic investigation, while the test merely samples functions to ascertain their presence or amount; the significance of a test depends upon the use of norms; the test ordinarily deals with the higher mental processes.

You will note that the distinctions drawn are for the most part in line with the quotations which I have cited from the literature, with perhaps a little more emphasis upon the greater simplicity of test procedure. However, there are five of my correspondents who point out the essential methodological identity of the test and the experiment. These are Boring, Goddard, Thorndike, Warren, and Woodworth. Watson's statement might perhaps justify including him in the same group. I quote their replies.

Boring:

(a) Methodologically there is no essential difference between a mental test and a scientific psychological experiment. (b) Historically in actual usage there is a difference. I should attempt to summarize the history of the tests as follows: A mental test is an *abbreviated experiment* upon an *individual* in which his *behavior* is observed in order to determine his *capacity* with respect to some *biological use*. Its motivation is, therefore, biologically and often socially *practical*. The loss of precision, due to its abbreviation, is usually offset by its application to a large number of individuals, so that it becomes a precise measure for a *group*.

Goddard: "Nothing distinguishes the mental test from any other psychological experiment. The difference is in the use we make of the data."

Thorndike:

There is no sharp line, in my opinion, between what we call a mental test and any other psychological experiment. A mental test usually seeks to measure the amount of some one thing which is supposed to increase in amount without changing its essential nature.

Warren, quoting the judgment of his department faculty:

We are unable to agree on any characterization which will differentiate the mental test from *all* other experiments. As compared with ordinary laboratory research it is objective rather than introspective—but so is the conditioned reflex method, yet the latter is evidently not "mental testing."

Watson: "The first time a test is given to a sufficiently large group to bring out its essential points it is like any other psychological experiment. If repeated it becomes a tool or a routine.

Woodworth:

A distinction some have drawn is that a test appertains to applied psychology, an experiment to pure psychology. This is obviously on the wrong track, since, first, experiments can be and are made in applied psychology (e.g., on advertisements), and since, second, the ultimate aim of the investigator who employs tests may be to solve a problem in pure science (e.g., mental heredity). Nor could you always tell a test from an experiment by watching the two in progress, since both might use the same apparatus and procedure and give identical data. The difference lies neither in the immediate procedure, nor in the ultimate end in view, but in something in between; namely, in the direct use to be made of the data, whether as general in reference, or whether as individual. However, [Woodworth continues,] what I have said applies to the *use* of the test rather than to the process of standardization and obtaining of norms. The latter would itself be an experiment, according to my distinction, and would also be a result in pure psychology.

It is the purpose of this paper to try to convince you of the essential correctness of the position which these half dozen psychologists have joined me in taking, though I am unable to accept without qualification all of the statements they have made. As I proceed you may feel that I am emphasizing differences of opinion which are more apparent than real; that the views to which I shall take exception would hardly be open to criticism if one took account of the definitions which they presuppose. In this you would be partly correct; but even so, my problem remains. I wish to show that psychologists have too often conceived of the mental test as a mere practical device; that it has a large value as an instrument of research; and that its kinship to other psychological methods is much closer than either the average tester or the average laboratory worker appears to assume. First, let us examine further the grounds of the distinctions which have been drawn.

II

1. *Use of tests in individual psychology*. That mental tests are the method *par excellence* of individual psychology does not mean either that they may not be used for other purposes or that individual differences may not be studied by other than test methods. That there exist quick-determination tests which can be applied to large numbers does not mean that tests of more searching character may not profitably be carried on with as small a number of subjects as you please. Binet's three year mental test study of his two daughters shows how unessential to the method large numbers are. On the other hand, that experimental psychology has usually dealt with so few subjects may be due less to deliberate choice than to the natural limitations imposed by its technique, and to its early relationships with physiology, a science which has always worked chiefly with small numbers. The view that in experimental psychology individual differences are to be regarded as "difficulties to be overcome by experimental technique," seems to me indefensible if psychology is conceived as a science of all the facts rather than of part of them. It harks back to the ancient confusion of errors of observation with supposed errors of nature in creating types or realizing an ideal. Experimental psychology is finding, just as physiology is finding, that the neglect of apparent departures from the norm is likely to result in a totally erroneous conception of the norm itself.

2. *Pencil and paper character*. In the little use it makes of apparatus the test is not alone. A fairly large number of investigations in the experimental field have been made in the last twenty years with no other aids than pencil and paper, nor is the practice becoming less common. On the other hand, fairly complicated apparatus is sometimes used for test purposes; for example, in tests of flying ability or of honesty of report.

3. *Omission of introspection*. Although resort to introspection in the use of mental tests is exceptional, this fact offers no basis for a distinction between a test and an experiment, unless we wish to classify all behavior methods as tests. The historical fact is that subjective and objective methods in psychology have existed side by side since the very beginning of the science. Weber and Fechner laid its foundations by methods which were rather more behavioristic than introspective, in any true sense of the term. The objective investigation of memory by Ebbinghaus was undertaken in 1879, the very year in which Wundt established at Leipzig the first psychological laboratory. From the middle eighties on through the nineties objective experimental work was carried on very actively by the psychologists of Germany, France, and America.

And, just as objective and subjective methods grew up side by side in experimental psychology, so in mental tests have both methods been employed; for example, by Binet,[8] Sharp, Meumann, and Whipple. That the practice has not been more general is of course due in part to the frequent use of tests with subjects for whom introspection is out of the question; but over and above this is the fact that mental tests represent one aspect of a fairly widespread movement away from the atomistic psychology of Wundt and his immediate followers.

4. *Exactness, verifiability of results, control of conditions, and possibilities of analysis.* As affording a cross-section picture of the individual's efficiency in this or that trait, or of the relationship obtaining among given traits, the accuracy of the test result depends, if the usual precautions of experimental procedure have been observed, entirely upon the appropriateness and adequacy of the sampling which the test affords. The sampling can of course, be made as extensive as may be necessary; how extensive it needs to be, is always a matter for statistical determination. This holds not only with respect to sampling for the diagnosis of "acute" conditions, but also with respect to sampling for "chronic" traits. That the latter could be revealed by any ordinary amount of sampling was long beyond the hope of many psychologists. However, as validity data are showing, some of our tests are diagnostic of chronic traits to a high degree. A fifty-minute intelligence test of high school freshmen yields as valid a prediction of the marks these pupils will receive five years hence in a university, as is yielded by their scholastic performance in high school during four years of a thousand hours each. The validity of our best tests holds not only for a group, as a group, but also, to a considerable extent, for the individual.

Whether these "chronic" traits reflect primarily the influence of endowment or of environment, is a question to which no certain answer can at present be given. As far as intelligence is concerned, there is no convincing evidence that such differences as we find among children of a given nationality who have had the ordinary advantages offered by the public school and by other common social contacts are due, in any considerable degree, to environmental factors. That there is no possibility of creating high I.Q.'s artificially is a proposition which, like any other universal negative, is not open to experimental proof. On the other hand, if the I.Q. *is* largely the product of environment, it should be easy to prove the fact beyond cavil. The oft-quoted proof offered by Cyril Burt that Binet scores are, to the extent of three-fourths, due to other factors than intelligence loses all significance when we note that by "intelligence" Burt means nothing more than scores on his syllogism test. It will be better evidence if someone can show that foster sibs (of unknown parentage) adopted early resemble each other or their foster parents as

---

8. Binet, in his earlier years, was even ready to rule out of psychology any kind of experimental work which did not make use of introspection. ("Introduction à la Psychologie expérimentale," p. 18. 1894.)

much as true sibs resemble each other or their true parents; or if it can be shown that by special treatment from an early age the I.Q.'s of a group of fifty or a hundred children can be raised significantly above the I.Q.'s of their untreated sibs. The issue here is one of the most important humanity faces, and one that will some day be decided on the evidence of mental tests.

With regard to the control of conditions and the verifiability of results, the test psychologist can point to numerous published arrays of probable errors and coefficients of reliability. These are not always as he would have them, but that he does have them is the significant fact. I am not aware that anyone has ever computed a probable error of an introspective report. In the use of any standardized psychological test, different investigators can readily control the conditions sufficiently to get practically identical results. At the opposite extreme is the condition depicted by one of my friends, a man who has made notable contributions to introspective psychology, that probably not more than a half dozen individuals in this country are able to give a dependable introspective account of their mental experiences. Possibly my friend is unduly pessimistic, but we are all aware of the difficulties which the introspectionist encounters because of the influence of expectation, interest, and suggestion. Whether, for example, a given observer finds that he has imageless thoughts, depends entirely too much on whether imageless thoughts are supposed to inhabit the particular laboratory in which he works.

To the test psychologist, the most exasperating thing about the average published introspective report is its indefiniteness. If you met it five minutes afterwards "on the street" you would not recognize it. Perhaps, as in Messer's experiments, the observer is trying to describe his mental experiences provoked by the stimulus question "Is eternal peace possible?"[9] One might report that he saw himself in a graveyard; or heard a solemn voice that he associated with Jesus; or experienced an aesthetic appreciation of the poetic value of the phrase "eternal peace"; or that he felt himself inclining the head in attitude of affirmation. Now if we were to translate mental test scores into this kind of description we should have something like this: "Saw an analogy relationship"; "a word occurred to me that was the opposite of something"; "solved a problem that had some numbers in it"; "appreciated the resemblance between a funny shaped block and an inset in a board"; etc. Imagine the test psychologist trading his objective scores for this kind of evidence, especially if he found that the stimulus which aroused in one observer the analogy experience, aroused in another the arithmetical or form board experience!

The contrast between objective test and subjective observation is in some respects like the contrast between phototelescopic and oculoteles-

---

9. "Experimentalpsychologische Untersuchungen über das Denken," *Archiv f. d. ges. Psychol., 8,* p. *41, 1908.*

copic study of the stars. The phototelescopic method, like the mental test, gives a permanent objective record which can be studied at leisure and subjected to various kinds of quantitative treatment that cannot be applied to the fleeting visual impression. It is largely freed from the influence of the personal equation.

It may be objected, however, that the exactness of the test score, even apart from any question as to the soundness of its statistical presuppositions, is illusory, because it stands for an unanalyzed complex of Heaven knows what contributing elements; that the attempt to test intelligence, or mechanical ability, or moral judgment, or psychopathic predisposition in our present state of ignorance of what these traits are is rather worse than folly; that it is the business of experimental science to isolate factors, and that this is something which the test method fails to accomplish.

Certainly no one can deny the difficulties the psychologist encounters in meeting all the conditions of ideal experimental procedure. But are these difficulties peculiar to the test method? I do not think they are. That investigators of animal learning, for example, have not succeeded in ruling out all disturbing factors is shown by the relatively low correlations which have been found for learning records made by the same animals in different series of experiments.[10] Fortunately, in this case, the very fact that reliabilities of learning scores are obtainable affords a guarantee that whatever refinement of procedure is necessary will ultimately be attained. Whether introspection holds out any such hope is a question. In the experiment of Messer to which I have referred, the uncontrolled and uncontrollable factors are so many that there is no predicting what conscious content will be produced if the stimulus is repeated a second or third or fourth time.

In reply to the psychologists who insist that we should first define what we would attempt to measure, one might retort by demanding a generally acceptable definition of a few "simple" terms like *sensation, feeling, attitude,* or *instinct.* This would not dispose of the problem, but it ought to lend a touch of mutual forbearance, if not of sympathy. It may be pointed out, furthermore, that the test method is by no means lacking in technique for ascertaining what factors contribute to a score. I refer especially to the method of partial correlation, which is probably as analytic as any technique the laboratory psychologist is accustomed to employ. In other words, the test itself will furnish ultimately the definitions which our critical friends are so impatient for. One might add, in passing, that the partial correlation method and the method of correction for attenuation would prove as valuable in the experiment as in the test, provided large enough numbers were used to permit of generalization.

5. *Practical vs. theoretical aim.* Here, some will say, we have at last a

---

10. See Wm. T. Heron and Walter S. Hunter, "Studies of the Reliability of the Problem Box and the Maze with Human and Animal Subjects," *Comp. Psychol. Monog.,* 1, 1922.

valid basis of distinction. It is the method of tests that has brought psychology down from the clouds and made it useful to men; that has transformed the "science of trivialities" into the "science of human engineering." The psychologist of the pre-test era was, to the average layman, just a harmless crank, but now that psychology has tested and classified nearly two million soldiers; has been appealed to in the grading of several million school children; is used everywhere in our institutions for the feeble-minded, delinquent, criminal and insane; has become the beacon light of the eugenics movement; is appealed to by congressmen in the reshaping of national policy on immigration; is furnishing high-powered explosives for the social reformers of one wing, while serving at the same time as the target drawing the hottest fire from the other wing,—no psychologist of to-day can complain that his science is not taken seriously enough. And is not most of this change, you will say, due to the mental test?

It is true that the practical usefulness of mental tests is one of their outstanding characteristics. This was recognized long before the first psychological laboratory was established, as is illustrated by Solomon's test of the rival claimants for possession of the disputed child (a group test of the maternal instinct!); or by the ancient ordeal that required the accused to prove his innocence by salivating and swallowing mouthfuls of desiccated rice (test of honesty of report by the conditioned reflex method!); or by the tests that primitive tribes have sometimes employed in the selection of a chieftain (test of leadership). In all of these the practical aim is evident enough. It is no wonder that the average individual, especially since he himself has from the earliest childhood used tests as a means of increasing his knowledge of those around him— applying a stimulus or setting a condition to see how another would react to it,—can see nothing in a modern psychological test but a useful device.

However, when one looks into the history of tests over the last thirty years, one finds that the psychologists who devised and used them were by no means always governed by practical considerations. Admittedly, one is often at a loss to unravel the motives which have actuated his fellow scientists, or for that matter even himself, and I cannot be sure that you would agree with me in regard to any particular individual. I do believe, however, that almost anyone will, by a careful study of the literature of test psychology, be led to the conclusion that a considerable number, if not a majority, of the psychologists who have worked with tests, have had as much of a theoretical as a practical interest in the outcome. For example, I would so classify Binet, Cattell, Spearman, Stern, and Thorndike.

The inclusion of Binet's name in this list may be questioned, but the history of his life and work justifies it. His interest was in the science of psychology. His intelligence scale was in a sense a by-product, even if all his earlier work did contribute toward it. In the four years he lived after completing the 1908 scale he made not a single application of it to practical problems and attempted no really serious revision. By 1911 he had moved on to new fields. Had he lived he would no doubt have continued to use tests, but he would have used them primarily for purposes of research. In the account of his extended test study of his two daughters he suggests no applications of this type of mental analysis, but is interested rather in the elucidation of the functional and dynamic point of view in general psychology.[11] One sees the same thing again in his 1909 article, "L'intelligence des imbeciles."[12] As the last twenty-five pages of that article show, Binet was far more interested in imageless thought than in imbeciles. His work heads up in a scheme of the higher mental processes, rather than in any scheme of segregating or teaching the mentally defective.

Stern's "Individual Psychology" is only an approach to a systematic psychology of personality. Mental tests as such he at first had little use for. At the 1904 Congress of Experimental Psychology in Giessen, commenting on a statement by Henri which he misinterpreted to mean that Binet and Henri had given up mental tests, Stern expressed satisfaction that these investigators had at last abandoned a method which could "bring nothing but discredit upon scientific psychology." Spearman no one would accuse of neglecting the theoretical implications of test results, and I think the same could be said of Thorndike and Cattell. And is not this true, in varying degrees, of most of us? Certainly many of the recent contributions by members of this Association would suggest far less interest in the diagnosis of cases for practical purposes than in questions of such general interest to psychology as mental development, mental inheritance, I.Q. constancy, race and sex differences, and the nature of intelligence.

Some would lay down the principle that investigations which use tests belong to experimental psychology as long as they are in search of fundamental laws, whether these are sought for their own sake or in order to establish a basis for improved methods of testing; but that when the end-product of such experiments—the perfected test—is put to use we no longer have to do with experimental psychology or with psychology at all. From this point of view, the mental test might be defined as "canned science," and would be typified by the Seashore phonograph records.

It must be admitted that when the test has been perfected, and, I am afraid, sometimes before, hordes of untrained workers are likely to use it for all kinds of purposes that have nothing to do with science. The fact remains, however, that if the test has been properly constructed and validated it may at once become a tool for the investigation of important scientific problems, such as mental growth, educability, individual differences, or mental organization. *It is only because tests are capable of practical application that we overlook their research possibilities and come to think of them as something to be contrasted with other methods of psychological investigation.*

---

11. "L'étude expérimentale de l'intelligence," 1903.
12. *L'année psychologique*, 1909.

After all, who can distinguish between the theoretical and the practical or draw a clear line between pure and applied science? As Watson has pointed out, the fact that a psychologist has discovered explanatory facts and principles capable of ready application does not make him an applied psychologist; and on the other hand, the mere fact that one is moved by practical motives is no evidence that his work may not prove of capital importance for the advancement of his science. It was in researches on such homely, practical problems as chicken cholera, swine fever, rabies, the diseases of swine, the diseases of silkworms, and the manufacture of alcohol and vinegar that Pasteur created out of hand the science of bacteriology. The enormously rapid development of theoretical chemistry, electrical science, and histology under the stimulus of human needs is a no less significant object lesson. A sufficiently keen realization of the fact that a full-grown science of psychology would enable us to add to the efficiency, happiness and morality of mankind, perhaps even to his average native endowment, and an abiding faith that these ends are actually attainable, might in the long run carry us farther toward the goal of pure science than millions for research without the dynamic effect of these incentives.

III

If time were available to recount the history of mental tests it would be easy to show how intimately the growth of test psychology has been connected with that of experimental psychology generally. The one is almost as old as the other, and the names associated with the two lines of development are in large part identical. For example, one can hardly say whether Galton is more connected with the history of experimental psychology by his study of mental imagery, published in 1880,[13] than he is connected with mental tests by his "Psychometric Experiments" published in 1879.[14] In the latter paper Galton tells how he made out a list of 75 words and used them in a free-association test. His method was to expose a word and then write down the first two words it suggested. What a little step to Jung, to Kent and Rosanoff, and to the Wyman association test of interests! And if the name of Ebbinghaus were used in such an experiment with psychologists as subjects, who can say whether the response frequency of *nonsense syllables* would be greater or less than that of *completion test?* Kraepelin, who must be named in any history of experimental psychology, worked chiefly with tests. That he confined himself to tests of the simpler processes may have been due in part to German caution, but it was more probably due to the experimental traditions engendered by Weber, Fechner, and Wundt. In his lively and

---

13. In *Mind*.
14. *Nineteenth Century.* Republished in "Inquiries into the Human Faculty," 1883.

prophetic introduction to the first volume of his *Arbeiten*, in 1894,[15] he made it clear that he looked forward to the time when it would be possible to make "a comprehensive determination of every kind of mental process."

In the land of Charcot, Ribot, Janet, and Binet, psychological interests centered about the larger problems of mental integration and personality, and as a result, mental tests in France, almost from the beginning, dealt with the more complex mental processes. This background colors the entire work of Binet, as one can see in his book, "Psychologie des grands calculateurs et joueurs d'echecs" and in his article, in *Revue philosophique*, "De la suggestibilité naturelle chez les enfants," both published in 1894; in his two articles, "La psychologie individuelle," 1895,[16] and "La mésure en psychologie individuelle," 1898; [17] and in his book, "L'étude experimentale de l'intelligence," 1903.

In America, Cattell founded our first psychological laboratory and gave us our first series of mental tests. In him the Wundtian and the Galtonian influences combined in a way to put the science of individual differences on its feet and to give the mental test movement in America an auspicious beginning. For twenty years the test was cultivated in this country primarily as a method of experimental psychology. One recalls the correlational studies based upon Cattell's tests of Columbia students; [18] Bolton's report of memory tests given to Worcester school children in 1891; [19] Münsterberg's series of ten tests described in 1891; [20] Jastrow's extensive preoccupation with tests in the early nineties, and especially his article on the "Community of Ideas in Men and Women," 1894; [21] Miss Calkins' article of 1896 on a repetition of this test; [22] and the interesting contribution by Royce the same year describing a test of inventive ability. [23] These are but samples.

Of the thirteen presidents of this Association since 1910, I think that all but two have worked with mental tests, and that even these have sponsored dissertations based upon test data. Of the nineteen presidents of the Association from its founding in 1892 up to 1910, the names of nine would belong in any reasonably complete bibliography of mental tests. The founder and first president of the Association, to whom so many of us are indebted for priceless inspiration, seems to have been the first in America to use a mental test for purposes of research. I refer to

---

15. Vol. 1, p. 43.

16. *L'année psychologique*, 2, 411–465.

17. *Revue philosophique*, 1898.

18. See Cattell, "Mental and Physical Measurement," *Mind*, 1890, 373–381; Cattell and Farrand, "Physical and Mental Measurements of Students of Columbia University," *Psychol. Rev.*, 3, 618–648, 1896; and Wissler, "The Correlation of Mental and Physical Tests," *Psychol. Rev. Monog.* 3, 1901.

19. "Growth of Memory in School Children," *Amer. J. Psychol.*, 4, 362–380, 1892.

20. "Zur Individualpsychologie," *Zentbl. f. Nervenheilk. u. Psychiatrie*, 1891.

21. *Psychol. Rev.*, 1, 152, and *Psychol. Rev.*, 3, 68–71.

22. *Psychol. Rev.*, 3, 426–430.

23. "The Psychology of Invention," *Psychol. Rev.*, 5, 111–143.

Hall's study made in the fall of 1880 on "The Contents of Children's Minds," a study which may be regarded as the lineal ancestor of our many present-day tests of information and vocabulary.[24] Some of you may share my regret that so "intrepid a devotee to concrete human nature," to use Thorndike's apt characterization, should not have turned his attention to the refinement and extension of the promising method with which he began.

This Association previous to fifteen years ago had had two committees on mental and physical tests. The first was appointed at the 1895 meeting on the suggestion of Baldwin, and included Jastrow, Sanford, Witmer, and Cattell (chairman). The recommendations of this committee were presented at the 1897 meeting by Jastrow and Cattell.[25] In a discussion of this report Baldwin described three memory tests which he had devised. The second committee was authorized in 1906 and was called the Committee on Standardizing Procedure in Experimental Tests. It consisted of Judd, Pillsbury, Seashore, Woodworth, and J. R. Angell (chairman). The committee's report of 1910 contained an article by Pillsbury, on "Methods of Determination of Sound Intensity"; one by Seashore, on "Measurement of Pitch Discrimination"; and one by Angell, on "Determination of Mental Imagery." Yerkes and Watson, who were invited to work with the committee, prepared a monograph on tests of color vision in animals; Woodworth and Wells in collaboration produced their well-known monograph on tests of association.

We see, therefore, that historically the mental test grew up as a fairly integral part of experimental psychology. One must not be misled by the fact that it has often been cultivated for its immediate usefulness, and that its problems have compelled it to develop a technique of its own. Objectively, the psychological test is a method of sampling mental processes or mental behavior, and so, in a sense, is any method of psychological experiment. The investigations of animal intelligence have been based almost entirely upon what might legitimately be called the test method; have, indeed, often used the same kind of material as is used in mental tests, such as the maze, the puzzle box, and the multiple choice apparatus. The present-day animal studies are coming more and more to resemble the test-experiments, and to deal with such problems as individual differences, mental inheritance, and the interaction of mental functions. Both with human and with animal subjects, experimental investigations of memory are samplings of memory ability; those of skill acquisition are samplings of habit formation; those of attitude, instinct or will are samplings of these mental and behavior phenomena.

As regards the complexity of processes studied, we have seen that both the test and the experiment show a fairly wide diversity of practice

---

24. *Princeton Rev.*, 1893. This is a refinement of an experiment carried out in Berlin in 1870. For an account of the many repetitions of this experiment see B. Hartman, "Die Analyse des kindlichen Gedankenkreiss," fifth edition, 1909, pp. 61-139.

25. *Psychol. Rev.*, 1898.

from their earliest beginnings to the present. On the whole, perhaps one can say that for a decade or so the simpler processes played in the test a rather predominant rôle, and that during the last quarter century the situation has been reversed.[26] For example, Oehrn's article on tests of individual differences, first published in 1889,[27] gives the rank orders of his ten subjects by name, not omitting himself and his teacher, Kraepelin. The psychological student of today may well lament that test literature no longer possesses this element of biographical interest, but the fact that it does not is eloquent tribute to the increasing success of mental tests in affording a picture of the subject's *"innere Persönlichkeit."* But if the test somewhat more quickly than the laboratory experiment moved on to the more complex processes, the experiment was not far behind. The invasion was part of a general movement in which all psychology shared. Binet in 1909[28] calls attention to the fact that he first set forth his ideas on the "scheme of thought" in 1900, and intimates that they were taken up by the Würzburg school without due credit to their source. Whatever the extent of this debt, one can say that for some fifteen years now experimental psychology in Germany, like the mental test everywhere, has concerned itself chiefly with the higher thought processes. One would probably be safe in predicting that the next decade will see a large interaction between the psychology of mental tests and the experimental psychology of thinking. On the one hand, the opening up of problems of individual differences by means of tests will inevitably lead to the more intensive study of such differences by the usual laboratory methods; and, on the other hand, the success attained by tests in the diagnosis of abilities for useful purposes is likely in turn to have a considerable effect upon the technique of experimental psychology. Woodworth, for example, has shown how a simple test of memory for paired associates may challenge the whole doctrine of association by contiguity, and how a test of incidental memory may cast doubt upon the testimony of trained introspectionists as to the sensory nature of their recalls.[29]

IV

I think we may conclude that the attempt to distinguish between the method of tests and the method of experiment is not warranted either on logical or historical grounds. The mental test is part and parcel of experimental psychology. How important a part, only the future can tell. Nevertheless, there is an abundance of opinion, which it may be

---

26. The terms "simple" and "complex" are of course used in a relative sense, as we now know that no mental process is really simple.

27. Five years later republished in Kraepelin's *"Psychologische Arbeiten,"* Vol. I, 1894.

28. "L'intelligence des imbeciles," *L'année psychologique*, 15, p. 143.

29. "A Revision of Imageless Thought," *Psychol. Rev.*, 22, p. 11 and 18 ff. 1915.

interesting to sample. A census of opinion may not carry the stamp of finality, but it does divest the issue of individual bias and is the nearest approach we can make to the probable facts.

You will recall that the letter which I sent to twenty-two representative psychologists called for a rating, on a crude seven point scale, of the value of the test method to psychological science. The task given to each was to check one of seven given statements, which ran as follows:

1.   *Value less than zero (more a liability than an asset).*
2.   *Value zero.*
3.   *Value positive, but slight compared with that of other accepted methods.*
4.   *Value considerable, but distinctly less than that of other accepted methods.*
5.   *Value compares well with that of other accepted methods.*
6.   *Value greater than that of most other methods.*
7.   *The most important (or promising) psychological method.*

In the "random" group presidents of the Association since 1910, seven checked the statement "value compares well with that of other methods"; one, "value greater than that of most other methods"; three, "value considerable, but distinctly less, etc." In the "interested" group contributors to test psychology, six checked the statement "value compares well, etc."; one, the statement "value distinctly less than etc."; one, "value greater than"; and three, "the most important (or promising) psychological method." The "interested" group, therefore, gives somewhat higher ratings, but the mean rating of the two groups combined expresses an opinion slightly more favorable than the statement "value compares well with that of other accepted methods," five rating the test higher than this and four lower.

The above figures at best can but serve to show a trend of opinion among fallible judges. They harbor a certain degree of ambiguity due to the fact that those who replied did not all define "mental test" in the same way. Naturally, those who gave a larger connotation to the term tended to give the highest ratings. However, making due allowances, it is evident that in the opinion of these twenty-two judges the mental test has come to occupy an important place in psychological methodology. If we could have a similar expression from all the psychologists of the last twenty or thirty years, it is possible that the scattering of ratings would be greater. One can easily imagine that for Wundt mental tests must have held even a lower place than what he called the *"Scheinexperimente"* of Marbe and Bühler. On the other hand, Spearman regards them as "the most alive and futureful shoot of all contemporary psychology."[30]

At this point I am reminded that a good many of you harbor a profound distrust of the "verbal report" and would probably prefer to

30. "The Nature of Intelligence and the Principles of Cognition," p. 35, 1923.

have a verdict based upon a census of "behavior." Very well. In the 1923 Year Book of our Association I find some 362 members recorded as carrying on psychological research. Of these, 147, or 40 percent, are doing research in the field of tests. The actual number, however, is much greater than this, since 94 others, or 27 percent of all, are doing research in a field in which the use of tests is almost inevitable, such as clinical, educational, or applied psychology. Probably the total number working with tests is somewhere between 50 percent and 65 percent of our psychologists engaged in research. In the same Year Book there are 117 members who have received the degree of Ph.D. since the beginning of 1915 and are recorded as carrying on psychological research. Of these, 53 percent are doing research with tests; and, exclusive of these, 30 percent more are carrying on research in educational, clinical, or industrial psychology. Of the 34, or 30 percent, who are recorded as doing research in experimental psychology, all but 14 are also working with tests or in a field that involves the use of tests. The trend is too evident to require comment.

Another sampling of performance may be had from the programs of our annual meetings. I have examined that of the last meeting I attended—1921. That year, so far as I could make out, 33 papers were presented which summarized data of original investigations. Of these, about twenty, or 60 percent, were based either wholly or in part on the test method.

The above figures are not offered in the spirit of a patent-medicine testimonial. It must be admitted that their meaning is far from clear. Some would say that they merely reflect popular demand and present-day professional opportunities. I doubt the correctness of this interpretation. Anyone who has canvassed our universities within the last five years to find suitable candidates for an instructorship or assistant professorship in experimental psychology will probably agree with me that in this field the supply is less adequate to the demand than in the field of tests and measurement. I am inclined to attribute a good deal to the relative human interest of the problems in the respective fields, and to the relative promise they are deemed to offer with respect to significance of results. If such is the motive, it is conceivable, of course, that it rests upon an error judgment. Whether the scientific value of test contributions at the present time is in full proportion to the labor expended upon them, is a question on which there may well be a difference of opinion. Certainly the value is less than it might be, and less than in time it will be.

That the labors thus far have not been entirely fruitless, however, is indicated very definitely in the statements made by our twenty-two psychologists in reply to question 2 of my circular letter: *Have mental tests opened up, or thrown light upon, any problem or problems of substantial importance to psychology as a science?* Nineteen of the twenty-two replies received to this question were affirmative without qualification, and the three exceptions were evidently based upon a more limited definition of the test than was presupposed by the others. The greatest number (thirteen) mention individual differences, including differences due to age, race, and sex. Eleven say that mental tests have thrown light upon such problems as mental organization, mental types, the nature of intelligence, and the intercorrelations of mental traits. Other contributions mentioned by two or more have to do with heredity and endowment; personality, character, and emotional traits; the higher thought processes; fatigue and other factors which influence efficiency; mental development; the function of language in thinking; educability; the rôle of intelligence in every day life; and, finally, the use of the test as a supplement to, or as an introduction to, more intensive forms of experimentation. As stated by Cattell,

Psychology as a science consists *largely* of the knowledge obtained by quantitative psychological tests. This knowledge is in itself of substantial importance and is interrelated with the whole field of psychology. It is as ultimate, both as description and in its application, as any other part of psychology.

In conclusion, I do not believe that anyone interested in the whole science of psychology can weigh lightly such problems as individual and race differences, the interrelation of mental traits, the phenomena of mental growth, the limitations of educability, or the psychology of genius, mental deficiency and insanity. Upon all these, the mental test has thrown light. It is proving itself applicable not only to the problems of intelligence, but also to those of emotion, volition, temperament, and character. It has become one of the important methods of psychological research; some would say, the most important. Not the least of its contributions is the fact that it has broadened and intensified our incentives to research, enlarged the public support of our science, and attracted new hosts of workers to the psychological vineyard.

Reprinted with permission
from *Psychological Review*,
1929, *36*, 97–121.

Chapter 13

The Psychology
of Controversy

Edwin G. Boring

Harvard University

Ideally, it might be argued, the psychologist is a superior being, for over all other scientists he has the advantage of being a psychologist. He alone, the argument would continue, knows the human mind without which there could be no science. The work of the exact sciences, as they are sometimes called, involves not only precise observation but also a loose admixture of personal prejudice, ambition and conviction. The psychologist, however, knows the human mind that is both the object and the subject of his work, and is superior to prejudice, to exaggeration, to vanity, and consequently to quarrelsomeness. Thus without these constant errors he serenely pursues his way, at peace with his fellow-workers, his hand alone grasping at fundamental truth with the personal equation of observation accounted for and eliminated by corrections. Psychology would thus be the one perfect exact science.

And it might be, though it is not clear that it could be. Certainly psychology has not been above personal bias. It is true that when psychologists battle they may hurl Freudian explanations of each other at each other. They may rise with scientific magnanimity against oppo-

Address of the President before the American Psychological Association at New York, December 28, 1928.

nents and suggest that falsification is involuntary and unconscious, or that stupidity is inherited and therefore not a matter of individual responsibility. All this is, perhaps, delightfully scientific, and yet there nevertheless remains in such controversy a seeming lack of objectivity. For instance, some psychologists in writing for publication place the mystic symbol Ph.D. after their names, but none, as far as I know, has yet seen the value of adding the statement of his own I.Q. Stanford University now does that sort of thing posthumously for the great, but it has not yet undertaken a handbook of the living. The classical method of psychology is introspection, yet not the behaviorist, nor the "gestaltist," nor the purposivist, nor the late functionalist, nor even the introspectionist himself has yet succeeded in maintaining clear vision with the eye rotated through 180° to see the mind that is at work. From this point of view we would seem to have a long way to go, and yet I must confess to you, attractive as my picture is, that I am not sure that we want to go, or can go, all that way. The scientific eye sees dimly when it turns through half a circle to look behind itself. The scientist, it seems to me, is limited by certain paradoxes of human nature and the psychologist shares these limitations with other scientists. It is therefore to two of these paradoxes that I ask your attention. The second follows from the first.

I

The history of science, like Hegel's view of the history of thought, is one long series of theses, set off by ardently advocated antitheses, with ultimate syntheses terminating controversy and marking a step forward. This picture, it seems to me, holds, not only for speculative, philosophical psychology, but also for the most rigorously observational work. Controversy has always been part of the method of science. A judge, or even a lawyer, might accept the statement that controversy, the clash of prosecution and defense, is the fundamental method for getting at truth. However, I do not think that the scientist would be quite so ready to subscribe whole-heartedly to this principle. He expects controversy as part of the scientific "game," but he generally engages in it under the principle that "'I am right and you are wrong." We hear little in science of an able defense of a lost case. Only correct discoveries are held to measure scientific ability. There is little applause for the investigator who, by being brilliantly wrong, prevents his antagonist from being wrong at all, and thus contributes to the truth. Unfortunately this situation makes scientists tend to hold to lost causes, when they might know better, for no other reason—unconscious reason—than that the laurel commands no acclaim when shown to be artificial.

After much thought about the matter, I have come reluctantly to the conclusion that scientific truth, like juristic truth, must come about by controversy. Personally this view is abhorrent to me. It seems to mean that scientific truth must transcend the individual, that the best hope of science lies in its greatest minds being often brilliantly and determinedly wrong, but in opposition, with some third, eclectically minded, middle-of-the-road nonentity seizing the prize while the great fight for it, running off with it, and sticking it into a textbook for sophomores written from no point of view and in defense of nothing whatsoever. I hate this view, for it is not dramatic and it is not fair; and yet I believe that it is the verdict of the history of science.

The paradox then in science would seem to be that the more you fight for the truth the less you see it. If you are always trying to see it, you have no time to fight, and without fighting you get science nowhere; you are just the cautious critic who is afraid to venture research. Perhaps I can improve this doleful picture before it is done. Let us, however, turn our attention first to famous controversies, and, since discretion behooves us, chiefly to those of the dead.

If we are looking for controversy, there is of course the case of Mesmer, who participated in a battle royal with the conservative scientists of Paris at the end of the eighteenth century.[1] Certainly the egotistic, opinionated Mesmer was an uncomfortable person for the scientific contemporary who did not believe in his theory; but, if science is, as is so often claimed, quite impersonal, Mesmer's personality ought to have nothing to do with the question of his demonstration of the truth of animal magnetism. Nobody knows whether Mesmer in young manhood was more conceited than the average of men who later became famous. It is quite clear, however, that, even had he been a modest and retiring person when young, his great theory that an important beneficent power resided in his own person would have made him into the sort of man that his opponents would regard as vain. In fact, conceit was involved in his scientific theory, since the theory had to do specifically with Mesmer. Yet nobody in the various investigating committees or in the Académie des Sciences was objective enough to see this crucial point. They denounced Mesmer, largely, so it seems to me, because of his personality, and thus mingled their own personalities with their scientific criticism.

The facts can be restated briefly. Mesmer was a physician in Vienna. As a physician he could not ignore the obvious influence of the celestial bodies upon human well-being, a fact well known then although not now. Mesmer asked himself how these remote bodies can act upon human beings from a distance, and it occurred to him that the astrological influence might be mediated by magnetism, a force that is capable of penetrating space. This was Mesmer's first theory, and if he had, then and there, written a book about it we could have put him down with all those persons, from the Greeks to the present day, who have held and advanced theories without resort to experimental proof. Mesmer, however, in good scientific fashion, used his happy thought as the basis for

---

1. In general on F. A. Mesmer, see Binet, A., and Féré, C., "Le magnétisme animal," 1887, Eng. trans. 1888, Chap. 1; Moll, A., "Hypnotism," various eds., Chap. 1.

an experiment. He got himself magnets and tried passing them over the bodies of his patients with remarkable effects; the persons were bene-fited by the magnets or even cured of diseases. "By the magnets"—it is a proper phrase to have used, and yet so often the supposed analysis of an effect into its causes turns out to be wrong. Presently Mesmer met a Swiss priest who was practicing the same kind of therapeutics as Mesmer, passing his hands over the bodies of his patients *without* the magnets. Mesmer had fixed upon the wrong cause of his effect.

There were two things for Mesmer to do. The more probable thing—so I am obliged by the history of science to conclude—would have been for Mesmer to have denounced the priest or at least to have tried to prove that he had concealed magnets up his sleeves, to have come out more vigorously in favor of magnets, insisting that they were essential to the true Mesmeric method, and to have enlarged, by the advertising that dogmatic assertion in the face of controversy gives, his medical practice. Mesmer, however, did the improbable thing: he discarded the magnets. It would have been lucky for all the people who have wrangled over this matter for a century after him, if he had discarded the word "magnet-ism" also. Unfortunately Mesmer had begun with the notion that a mysterious influence without contact is likely to be magnetic, and the physiologist, van Helmont, a century earlier had expounded a theory of animal magnetism. So Mesmer called his new therapeutic means "animal magnetism," allowing the implication to stand that the influence was something like mineral magnetism. He now knew that he could cure people of certain diseases, or make them think themselves cured, which, in certain cases, is the same thing from the physician's point of view. Others could not effect these cures. Undoubtedly Mesmer's personality and his growing confidence in his power were the reasons for his power, but Mesmer did not know this. Not all minerals are magnetic; why should all persons be magnetic? Mesmer came to believe that he, unlike most other persons, was magnetic, and thus capable of influencing others. All this happened before Mesmer left Vienna for Paris in 1778.

Up to this point, it seems to me, we have nothing more than the account of the genesis of a scientific discovery that is without reproach. Mesmer's personality is irrelevant to the scientific fact. The Church opposed him; the scientific academies ignored him; his followers wor-shipped him; but none of these things matter. He had discovered hypnotism, that is to say, he had discovered the state of hypnosis, had arrived at a vague notion of its therapeutic significance, and was possessed of the practical means of inducing the state, although he had an incorrect theory as to the nature of the means. Thus Mesmer occupies a definite position in the history of the knowledge of hypnosis. Without him knowledge could not have advanced as it did advance, for it was the travelling mesmerists who interested both Elliotson and Braid, it was Elliotson who interested Esdaile and many others in England, it was Braid who started Liebault on hypnotic work and Liebault who con-vinced Bernheim who began the Nancy school. Mesmer, ordinarily neglected, occupies the important place at the beginning of the genetic chain of events. That his knowledge of the conditions, the nature, and the effects of hypnosis was incomplete is a situation that applies to almost all scientific discoveries at first; moreover our knowledge of these facts is still incomplete.

After Mesmer went to Paris it is not quite so clear that his discoveries can be divorced from his personality. Here he developed further the conditions of hypnosis, the mysterious baquet with its rods of iron that the patients held (iron, of course, because of its magnetic properties), the circle of sitters about the baquet connected by cords or hands (a circuit, because of magnetic analogy), the subdued light, the soft music, the hocus-pocus of Mesmer's speech and his magician's attire. It is no wonder that the scientific world was disgusted, but my question is whether this disgust interfered with its perception of the truth. Mesmer was the talk of Paris. There was a large band of enthusiastic disciples. The scientists appointed investigating committees, which investigated and found, so it is always said, "against Mesmer." Actually there was no denying the phenomena; all the committees did was to disapprove Mesmer's theory which he had formally embodied in twenty-seven propositions, and in particular to deny the identity of this influence with mineral magnetism and the existence of "a responsive influence between the heavenly bodies, the earth, and animated bodies." The view then developed that Mesmer, since he was not using mineral magnetism, was employing some secret force that he would not divulge. His disciples, who thought that they had been promised this secret, finally turned against Mesmer because he would not reveal it. Mesmer was discredited, driven from Paris by public opinion, and died shortly afterward. He had, of course, no secret to reveal. Everybody, the committees and his disciples, knew all that he did, but could not realize that a man can know how to use a power without understanding its nature.

The question of Mesmer's personality comes in here because we wonder whether he merited rebuke. The technique of the baquet was certainly an aid to the technique of hypnotizing, and Mesmer in a sense made this discovery. But was he sincere? Did he believe that all this mystery was an aid to animal magnetism, or did he induce it quite consciously to attract the crowds? The concept of sincerity is a dangerous one. Psychologists could well do without it, substituting the notion of dissociation. At any rate, it seems to me that psychologists who have thought about the problems of personality will have to agree with Mesmer's defenders that Mesmer at least thought he was sincere; and who but a psychologist could undertake to distinguish between a man's sincerity and his belief in his sincerity? However, the conviction or the exoneration of Mesmer hardly matters to us. What about the scientists who repudiated him? They shut their eyes to an important scientific discovery because they could not stomach the conditions of its demonstration. Mesmer was a nuisance. He was a propagandist and a demagogue, and, behold, the whole world had gone after him. Moreover he was making money out of his discovery. He was vain and opinionated, and had even achieved that summit of conceit of making the new force a property of his own person. It is thus no wonder that the scientists repudiated him, and it is also no wonder that the use of hypnosis passed from the hands of scientists to charlatans for nearly half a century. This is the scientific dilemma that I am discussing: does science preserve its purity and thus retard its progress by shutting its eyes to partial truths, and does it thus sometimes cut off its nose to spite its face?

I have dealt with Mesmer at length because I want you to be quite clear as to my problem. I could now go on with other instances from the history of our science keeping you here until early morning, unless, in spite of being psychologists, you should develop free wills and leave. As it is, my love of determinism is too great to risk such an *experimentum crucis*. I shall be brief with my other cases.

The history of Mesmer was repeated with John Elliotson in the forties of the last century, except for the fact that there can be no doubt of Elliotson's complete sincerity, that is to say, of the complete integration of his personality, with no divided knowledge about what he claimed to be the truth.[2] Elliotson was a physician of exceptional native ability who was a member of the faculty of University College in London in the thirties of the last century. Nowadays we should call him a radical. He was always, to the resentment of his colleagues, advocating some new idea, like the use of the stethoscope, just invented, of which they said, "It's just the thing for Elliotson to rave about," or the maintenance of a hospital in connection with a medical school, an idea which, however, he advocated successfully. He made some important contributions to *materia medica*, and did not hesitate to ridicule the fallacies of current medical dogma. He was too ardent to be tactful, and consequently he was disliked by most of his colleagues. In 1837 Elliotson acquired the inheritance of Mesmer by witnessing the demonstration of a travelling mesmerist. Within a few days he was mesmerizing the patients of the new University College Hospital and getting what he regarded as beneficial therapeutic results. He was urged to desist on the ground that he was injuring the reputation of the Medical School, but he refused on the opposite ground that truth is more important than a reputation. Within a year the Council of University College had passed a resolution forbidding "the practice of mesmerism or animal magnetism within the Hospital," and Elliotson had resigned from the Hospital and from University College never to enter either again. He kept up his crusade. No medical journal, would print his papers so he founded the *Zoist* as an organ of free speech about new things, especially mesmerism. He was denounced. Medical men would not associate with him. He lost his practice. Feeling ran into intimate channels and he also lost most of his personal friends. Yet Elliotson kept on. Mesmeric hospitals sprang up all

---

2. In general on John Elliotson, see Bramwell, J. M., "Hypnotism, Its History, Practice, and Theory," 1903, 3–30.

over England. He had a group of supporters, but the group did not include many of the reputable medical practitioners of his day.

How far this controversy penetrated into the emotional lives of its participants is illustrated by the following instance. Like Mesmer, Elliotson saw in mesmerism mostly a therapeutic agent, but it was also obvious that the new state might be used as an anesthetic—in those days just before the discovery of the modern anesthetics. In 1842 Ward, a surgeon, amputated a leg of a patient under mesmeric trance.[3] The patient had been suffering excruciating torture from the least motion of an ulcerated knee-joint, and could sleep little. A mesmerist, Topham, one of Elliotson's disciples, found that he could give this patient rest by mesmeric sleep. Later Ward amputated the leg at the thigh after Topham had mesmerized the patient, and tried, in the course of the operation, bruising the cut end of the sciatic nerve. The patient remained in relaxed sleep and denied all memory of the operation afterward.

Ward then reported the case to the Royal Medical and Chirurgical Society of London. The report aroused a storm of protest. Marshall Hall, whom we now honor for the discovery of reflex action, described mesmerism as "trumpery which pollutes the temple of science," and fell back on his own theory, arguing that the report was false because it did not show that the sound leg twitched reflexly when the other leg was cut. Eight years later Hall informed the Society that the patient had confessed to collusion, although the patient then signed a deposition stating that the operation had been painless. Other members at this first meeting of the Society contended that,

if the account of the man experiencing no agony during the operation were true, the fact was unworthy of their consideration because pain is a wise provision of nature, and patients ought to suffer pain while their surgeon is operating.

At the next meeting of the Society, after violent discussion, it was voted to strike from the minutes the statement that such a paper had been read.[4]

Well? Intolerance does not beget tolerance. That is all. Hypnosis may

---

3. The full description of the Ward case and of the action of the R. M. C. S. upon it are given in a little pamphlet by John Elliotson, "Numerous Cases of Surgical Operations without Pain in the Mesmeric States; with Remarks," 1843. The "remarks" are numerous and caustic. The pamphlet I have seen was published in Philadelphia, but I think it was also printed in London.

4. I have omitted all mention of James Braid, the reputed discoverer of hypnosis, on account of lack of time. See Braid, J., "Neurypnology," 1843, reprinted 1899. Braid also met opposition, but he did not break with the medical profession because he refrained from criticizing it, because he laid no claim to a peculiar personal power but sought to explain hypnosis in normal physiological terms, because he avoided the word "mesmerism," because he opposed Elliotson, and because Elliotson attacked him. See my remarks on this situation in *Amer. J. Psychol.*, 1927, *39*, 83–86.

not be the ideal surgical anesthetic, but it is a great deal better than none, as Esdaile, inspired by Elliotson, was in the same years proving in hundreds of cases in India, and against opposition almost as strong as was to be found in England.[5] The medical men almost let the world suffer on in surgical operations for an indefinite period. They might have done so but for the fortunate discovery of the anesthetic effects of nitrous oxide in 1845, three years after Ward's use of mesmerism, and of ether, and chloroform a couple of years later.[6] Against these anesthetics there is a story of similar opposition and of the contention that anesthesia interferes with God's plan for the universe; but I have cited enough instances of this sort.

In fact the history of science is full of such examples. Elliotson made them his text when, after much opposition, he was finally invited in 1846 to deliver the Harveian Oration before the Royal College of Physicians. He could begin most aptly with the story of the opposition to Harvey's discovery of the circulation of the blood.[7]

In modern psychology we have so far been spared the violent controversy that engages public attention, except in psychic research, which represents today a case almost exactly like that of mesmerism. It seems impossible to undertake psychic research without emotion, and the emotions of the investigators are present in part because it is an egotistic hypothesis. Like mesmerism it claims that a peculiar power is localized only in certain individuals, and it defines this power in terms of its effects and omits the causal term that is necessary to every scientific correlation or fact.

However, although modern psychology lacks these dramatic controversies that enlist the lay public on one side or the other, it is lacking neither in controversy nor in intolerance. I trust that I am still treading safe ground if I ask you to recall with me the famous controversy between Wundt and Stumpf about the tonal distances.

Into the elaborate intricacies of this controversy we cannot enter, nor do we need to do so. As is well known, musical interval follows a law like Weber's Law. A given interval is divided into two equal portions by a stimulus which is, in vibration rate, the geometric mean of the stimuli for the two extremes. Stumpf, with a musical background, believed that musical interval bore a close relation to the simple sensory properties of tones. Wundt, basing his view on experiments in the Leipzig laboratory by his pupil Lorenz, regarded sense-distances as less closely related to musical interval. Lorenz's results showed that observers in bisecting a tonal interval tended toward the arithmetical mean and not the geometric. About this difference the controversy waxed.

We should perhaps bear in mind the fact that the difference in

---

5. The secondary source for James Esdaile is Bramwell, *loc. cit.*

6. For an interesting account of the controversy that the discovery of anesthesia aroused, see Smith, C. A. H., *Scient. Mo.*, 1927, 24, 64-70.

7. Elliotson, "The Harveian Oration," 1846.

question is small with respect to the tonal distances involved. On the other hand—and this was Wundt's ground for assurance—these seemingly small differences were large with respect to the scatter of the judgments, much larger than modern statisticians are accustomed to require. Stumpf, however, could not accept this view. For one thing he appealed to the extreme case as a *reductio ad absurdum*; if tonal distance is directly proportional to vibration rate, as Wundt claimed, then a major second like c^3-d^3, must include the same distance as the entire octave, c-c^1, three octaves below. This proposition seems so manifestly absurd that we can understand why Stumpf felt that Lorenz's results must be capable of being explained away, as he undertook to do argumentatively, in part by questioning the meaning of Lorenz's observers in judging tonal distance and the degree to which they were influenced by musical relationships.

Wundt had espoused Lorenz's results by publishing some of them in the third edition of the "Physiologische Psychologie" in 1887.[8] Lorenz's paper came out in 1890.[9] Then followed controversy, altogether of 141 pages. Each published thrice. First Stumpf printed sixty-seven pages, in which he reprinted portions of many of Lorenz's tables and sought to reinterpret them.[10] There was almost no personal invective in the paper; nevertheless it is hardly impersonal to reprint another man's results and, in a paper almost as long as the original, argue elaborately to opposite conclusions. It is easy to imagine Wundt's feelings when the significance of the observations was thus called in question. Wundt, therefore, replied with a paper which included some personal advice to Stumpf.[11] Stumpf's rejoinder adopted more nearly Wundt's tone.[12] It was called "Wundt's Antikritik." Then Wundt printed "Eine Replik C. Stumpf's."[13] Finally the controversy closed in verbal exhaustion with Stumpf's "Mein Schlusswort gegen Wundt"[14] and Wundt's "Auch ein Schlusswort."[15] The discussion became less calm as it progressed. The two final *Schlusswörter* dealt each almost as much with the psychological problem of how the other psychologist conducted argument as with the psychological problem of tonal distances.

This controversy must be read to be appreciated, but I can perhaps give you the flavor of it. As I have said, Stumpf in his original criticism had little to say to which Wundt or Lorenz could have objected, except that they were wrong and should have drawn exactly the opposite conclusions. The only definite resort to the method of psychologizing opponent psychologists that I have found in the entire paper is this:

---

8. Wundt, W., "Physiologische Psychologie," 1887, *1*, 428*f*.

9. Lorenz, G., *Philos. Stud.*, 1890, *6*, 26–103.

10. Stumpf, C., *Zsch. f. Psychol.*, 1890, *1*, 419–485.

11. *Philos. Stud.*, 1891, *6*, 605–640.

12. *Zsch. f. Psychol.*, 1891, *2*, 266–293.

13. *Philos. Stud.*, 1891, *7*, 298–327.

14. *Zsch. f. Psychol.*, 1891, *2*, 438–443.

15. *Philos. Stud.*, 1892, *7*, 633–636.

This extension, however, certainly does not amount to as much as it should according to Wundt, who here, as he so often does, has exaggerated a correct idea into another that is falsely inverted with respect to it.

Wundt in his reply studied to be calm. He said twice that he would test Stumpf's conclusions "sine ira et studio," without anger and vehemence. Such a statement, however, carries a latent as well as a manifest content. When the orator says, "I will call my opponent neither a liar nor a fool," he is not doing just exactly what he says he is doing. There is not the least doubt at all that Stumpf had hurt Wundt's feelings, and that Wundt was thus moved to many of his remarks, including his final sentences, which read as follows:

Stumpf knows, I hope, as well as I, that whoever would further the psychology of tone must have something more than musical experience. However, it can do no harm, I believe, if he will strengthen himself in this conviction by the result which he now achieves (as the consequence of this criticism). Somewhat sooner then will this polemic also have for him the further result, that he will learn to value, not only as the best but also as the most useful virtue for a scientific researcher, this: to be just toward others, to be severe toward himself.

This peroration does not seem to me to clinch the problem of the tonal distances. I suppose, however, that Wundt thought it did.

I have not time to cull numerous examples from the remaining four articles. You can imagine what was said after Wundt has thus advised Stumpf "without anger and vehemence." To Wundt's personal advice about being just toward others and severe toward himself, Stumpf, everything considered, replied quite calmly. He said, "Wundt is accustomed to imprint on his polemics a kind of moral stamp. . . . It is distasteful to me to make many words about the matter." Wundt reiterated that he found nothing in Stumpf's rejoinder "from beginning to end but distortion and fictions. 'I have studied these things and you have not!' Upon these words I restrain myself from judgment," he concluded.

Finally Stumpf, who had been consistently the more reluctant to pursue the personal side of this controversy, was goaded in his *Schlusswort* into a frank characterization of Wundt's polemical method. He wrote:

I abstain from a detailed rejoinder to the new voluminous reply of Wundt. For it, which pours out his expression of blind thoughts, any word would be too much. Those, however, who wish to compare, point for point, his new article with mine and especially with the earlier one upon which it is based, will find therein for themselves, as in his preceding article, the same mixture of untrue assertions, of confusions, of mutilations of the course of my thought, of obscure imputations and negligences, of infirm evasions, of fallacies of every kind, and of frequent assurances of the incapacity and ignorance of his adversary.

Each of the first six items of the list Stumpf supported with long footnotes, omitting only citations of his own alleged incapacity and ignorance.

Stumpf started the controversy, but Wundt made it personal. It is plain that Stumpf was drawn into this aspect of it with reluctance, and that, being more tender-minded than Wundt, he felt it keenly. More than thirty years later, in writing a short account of his life and thought, the affair still rankled. He devoted to the controversy a paragraph, which he placed in the biographical half of his article.[16] Stumpf regarded the controversy as an event in his life more than as a psychological contribution; but Wundt, the tough-minded, made no reference to this little affair in his "Erlebtes und Erkanntes."

Now I feel that most of you will be disposed to condemn this controversy and to blame Wundt the more for the part he took, and yet I believe that there are not so many of us who, on the next occasion when our work is attacked in print, will in reply studiously avoid trying to make our antagonist seem to our readers like the fool that we believe him to be. We have not yet solved my fundamental dilemma; we have only illustrated it.

However, before I discuss the major issue, let me point out that controversy of this kind is not limited to Germany. In the nineties there was the American controversy about reaction times, with Titchener and Baldwin the chief protagonists.[17] Titchener was upholding the Leipzig view that the muscular reaction is always about one tenth of a second shorter than the sensorial, provided you have subjects so well practiced that they can assume the two attitudes at will. Baldwin was contending that people are of different types and that some react more quickly in a sensory manner and some in a motor manner. Baldwin thought that Titchener was misrepresenting the truth by selecting subjects that would fit his theory. Titchener thought that Baldwin had wandered from the straight scientific path in concerning himself with a problem of human nature instead of the scientific problem of the generalized human mind. Of course, as Angell and Moore showed eventually, both were right; yet neither seemed to be able to see how the other was right, obvious as the matter is now. If Baldwin wanted to work with individual differences in true American fashion, what matter if Titchener thought that personal idiosyncrasies are not the problem of science. If Titchener got his difference with *general* practice (not, of course, with practice for giving the desired result), why did Baldwin mind that training in the direction of attention should counteract the effect of natural modes of attention? Yet each was so sure of his view that neither ever seemed in publication to understand the other. Each, like Wundt and Stumpf, made a moral

---

16. Schmidt, R., "Philosophie der Gegenwart in Selbstdarstellungen," 5, 1924, 218.

17. The chief controversial papers are: Baldwin, J. M., *Psychol. Rev.*, 1895, 2, 259–273; Titchener, E. B., "Mind," 1895, N.S. 4, 74–81, 506–514; Baldwin, *ibid.*, 1896, N.S., 5, 81–89; Titchener, *ibid.*, 236–241.

judgment. Titchener thought Baldwin unscientific because he used subjects untrained, in the Leipzig sense, to precise observation. Baldwin thought Titchener unscientific because he closed his eyes to a problem of the natural world.

Nor is controversy of this sort limited to the ancients of the late nineteenth century. I could have taken my examples from the present decade, but I have thus far forborne because it must be hard for you to believe that my remarks carry with them no whit of praise or blame. Perhaps I can briefly make my point that the styles have not greatly changed by a few citations in which I obscure the source.

Only a few years ago one psychologist complained, in a long critical article, about the practice of a colleague, who, he asserted, would praise the work of his friends and condemn similar work by others. This controversy is full of instances germane to my subject-matter, but I shall content myself by citing only the closing sentence of the paper I have mentioned. It reads:

We live close to one another with our similar problems, which approach today as nearly as does all the community of work. If here, as in a thickly planted forest, conflicting growth occurs, it is a thing of the natural order. If, however, it falls out as in a horse-race, where someone uses the whip in order to lash the noses of the neighboring horses, then I must raise a protest against it in the name of fair play.[18]

Recently a psychologist, usually very conservative in his utterances, actually likened a colleague to "a soap-box evangelist." Within the year another psychologist has said, in print, of still another: "To the charge of misunderstanding must now be added the charges of misreading, misinterpreting, and misquoting," and then, like Stumpf in his *Schlusswort* to Wundt, has proceeded in two pages to document these items. It sounds scandalous, that a scientist should not only misread and misinterpret, but actually misquote. Yet I doubt if either author is less well-intentioned than the other.

You may say, of course, that all this is but the scientific "game," that it is the way things are done. I submit, however, that these expressions are not mere stylistic conventions of writing; often there is even more real feeling than the words express. Wundt's moral prescriptions for Stumpf in 1891 were still disagreeing with him in 1924. We have all known psychologists who were supposed not to be able to meet each other socially lest something should happen. Most of us know what it is to feel bitter about published criticism, especially when it is personal; yet, if science is the dispassionate search for truth by the empirical method, can it flourish in the face of passion?

Let us go back to Wundt and Stumpf. The argument is, so far as it dealt with the tonal distances, very evenly balanced. Titchener said that

_____

18. The quotation is as literal as anonymity permits.

he read the controversy three times, and decided twice for Wundt and once for Stumpf.[19] Since we still do not know the correct answer to their problem, we might say that the chances are even for either of them being right; and thus the chances are even for either being wrong. It was a battle of giants; why discriminate? But, if scientists are seeking only for the truth and not to prove themselves right, then there are even chances that Stumpf would have convinced Wundt, or Wundt Stumpf, and only a twenty-five per cent chance that each would have convinced the other and have thus continued the controversy. I make this ludicrous use of the elementary principles of probability in order to show you how certain you would have been from the start that neither was going to be convinced. They both could not be right; each knew that; each, as a psychologist, knew about human fallibility and prejudice even in the pre-Freudian days, and could therefore realize that there was a good chance of his being somewhere in the wrong. Plainly there is a perseverative tendency in scientific thinking.

It would be easy now to draw the moral that the scientific value of an investigator varies inversely with his emotionality in scientific matters, but I do not believe that such a conclusion would be true. It is not only the lesser men who quarrel. The great are particularly adept at it, and the lesser may perhaps only be copying them. Rather it seems to me that we have a true dilemma, that the drive that urges men to laborious research and to the braving of public criticism with their conclusions, is the drive which perseveres and makes them persist against criticism. Thus the same thing that drives them toward the truth may also keep them from it. We still face, then, the uncomfortable picture with which I began. However, before I attempt even an incomplete solution, I want to deal briefly with the second of my scientific paradoxes, which I promised you long ago.

II

This second paradox is that new movements in psychology, and presumably in thought at large, are most obviously negative. That which claims to be progress, that which is presently accepted as progress, is nevertheless most patently an undoing of the progress of the past. How then is there any real progress in what appears on inspection to be a regress? The answer, I think, is psychological, but before I come to it, let me try to establish my point about the negativism of progress.

Recently I have tried to show for psychology that trite historian's point that nothing which is supposed to be new is ever really new.[20] The course of scientific thought is gradual, as it is in individual thought. In

---

19. Titchener, "Experimental Psychology," 2, ii, 1905, 242.
20. *Amer. J. Psychol.*, 1927, 39, 70–90.

the individual it is hard to distinguish imagination from memory; careful scrutiny of a creative imagination seems to reveal little that is brand-new. So it is in scientific thought. The ideas occur as the result of individual thinking, or the facts are found as the result of experiment, both are put forward, and nothing much happens. Then, perhaps many years later, someone comes along, sees relationships, puts things together, and formulates a great theory or founds a great movement. Often the formulator or founder is not even the compounder, but another man, who because of his personality or because of the times in which he speaks, has the capacity for gaining attention. So he originates, as we say, a step in progress, lending his name to a theory or a school, and it is left to dull historians to discover and reiterate the fact that de Moivre discovered the Gaussian law and Charles Bell the Müllerian doctrine of the specific energy of nerves. Founders are generally promoters, in science as elsewhere, and we have therefore here to consider the mechanisms of public attention.

With respect to scientific movements there seems to exist something like Newton's third law of motion: action equals reaction. You cannot move—in the sense of starting a movement—unless you have something to push against. The explanation of this law, I think, lies in the relation of movements to public attention. Science can actually, by the empirical method, so I am disposed to believe, lift itself by its own boot straps, but the result is not what we call a "movement" because motion can be defined only with respect to a frame of reference. A movement must move with respect to something, and progress must move away from something, if the movement is to command observational attention. It is therefore the business of the founders of new schools, the promoters and propagandists, to call persistent attention to what they are not, just as one political party is forever emphasizing the short-comings of the other.

Thus we see that movements are founded upon controversy, and that all we have been saying about the effect of controversy on controversialists applies also to the schools. A school may be flexible and disposed toward change and growth in all directions except those against which it has set itself. Here it is hardened by its own drive. A movement cannot move backwards and persist, and the question as to which direction is backwards is decided by the opposition which brought the movement into being. Moreover the drive forward leads to an over-estimation of the distance moved. The negativism of progress is thus essential to observed progress.

Now let me illustrate.

The greatest foundation within modern psychology is Wundt's promotion of experimental psychology itself. The question is often asked: Did Fechner or Wundt found experimental psychology? Fechner came first and may be its father, but Wundt is certainly its founder. Fechner with his psychophysics was trying to found, not experimental psychology, but a spiritualistic metaphysics. Wundt, from within physiology, arrived at his view from a study of the relationships of the sciences, in a day when physiology was as self-conscious as psychology is now.

In the interests of the new movement Wundt had to overcome many obstacles. He had to write a scientific handbook for experimental psychology. He had to get himself a chair of philosophy and pervert it to experimental practices. He had to found a laboratory, a real laboratory of rooms with instruments in them. He had to get the experiments going, and then to found a journal for their publication. To make his point it was necessary for him, in all sincerity, to exaggerate. The new experimental science must be exhibited to the world as a lusty infant with none of its organs missing. Thus Wundt, when experimental results were lacking, resorted in his handbook to speculation to fill the chapters. There was certainly an over-emphasis on apparatus, peculiarly psychological apparatus. If psychology was an independent science, it must have apparatus to distinguish if from philosophy, and special apparatus to distinguish it from physiology.

All this we can readily understand because we ourselves are still of this self-conscious school of Wundt's. The struggle to separate psychology from philosophy in American universities is still not quite yet over. The habit of writing complete text-books in the face of incomplete knowledge still persists. There is still, I believe, a tendency to collect and exhibit much psychological apparatus without regard to the immediate needs of research. If you do not know what it is like to be on the inside of a new movement, consult therefore your own minds.

Yet this movement for a scientific psychology was largely negativistic. It was primarily directed against philosophy. It was a long time before Wundt had done any experimental work equal in importance to Fechner's, and yet Fechner thought he was working in experimental philosophy. The experimental work of the sixties and seventies was performed mostly by physiologists. Of course, we say now that the final result has demonstrated the positive nature of the original idea, although there remain philosophers who do not agree. I do not believe, however, that the present outcome reacts upon the situation of sixty years ago. Whatever has happened since, there was a chance then that experimental psychology might prove sterile. But it is difficult to argue clearly where our own prejudices are involved. Let us consider the movements within psychology.

In the nineties there was the school of *Gestaltqualität*. It was a reaction against the current elementarism, although it did not itself avoid elementarism as successfully as does the modern *Gestalt*. The chemical combination of sensations was obviously inadequate for the explanation of perceptions. Nevertheless the form-qualities, the founded contents, the superiora, and the act of founding turned out to have no empirical definition and the movement failed. Or did it not fail, but live on to be reborn in *Gestaltpsychologie*? The answer does not matter. My point is that it would not have been a movement if it had not been directed against something.

So it was also with Külpe's school of imageless thought. The very word "imageless" is a negative term. The movement was nothing more than a protest against sensationism. It is easy to say this now, but what of the enthusiasm of the Würzburgers for the *Bewusstseinslagen* and *Bewusstheiten*? They did not think that their movement was negative. They thought they had discovered a new kind of mental stuff. You have only to read the controversial literature to see how the love of self-preservation sustained each side.

In America we used to have functionalism. It was a revolt of the colonial psychologists against Germany, their mother-country. The controversy between Titchener and Baldwin was a phase of the whole. Germany was more philosophical and America more practical, as America's rôle in the history of mental tests has shown. Chicago functionalism was the explicit movement, but I think it was but symptomatic of what was quietly going on all over America, except in some protected places like Ithaca, where Penelope still remained faithful to the marriage vow. Functionalism centered attention upon the individual and the individual organism. Leipzig could still work with the generalized human mind; in Chicago, and in Columbia too, they had *minds*. I think of this revolt as the most radical since Wundt's original heterodoxy, and I also recall that the explicit functional movement itself was largely negative and got little further along positively than did the school at Würzburg.

In those days the opposite of functionalism was structuralism, but nobody—except perhaps some graduate students—ever called himself a "structuralist." Titchener adopted the phrase "structural psychology" and abandoned it long before it went out of use. No, the functionalists had to have something definite to push against, and it was they only who talked about "structuralists."

We have this same phenomenon in behaviorism. For years the American tendency has been to have two behaviorists growing where one grew before. Any number of psychologists have been willing to call themselves behaviorists and to be proud of it, but they missed badly a definite opposition to set them off. Words have been coined for the opponent school, words like "introspectionism" or "introspectionalism," but I have never heard anyone apply such a term to himself. Someone once suggested "Titchenerism," which had the advantage of seeming to indicate at least one Titchenerist definitely. My point is that all along behaviorism has been seeking an enemy so that it could disprove the charge that it is fighting windmills, for it must fight something; it is a movement.

I know it is not fair to leave behaviorism so casually, but I must do so. Behaviorism is not new; this has been shown more than once. Yet Watson is right in thinking that he founded it. He could not have founded it if it had been new; it would not yet have been ready to found. It denies consciousness as the subject-matter of investigation, and therefore the so-called introspective method for investigating it. In this it is negative. It goes on investigating what is left, bereft of an enemy since many of those whom it woos for enemies would also investigate the same problems. It is unfortunately limited by its parental inheritance, for it cannot get over trying to translate consciousness and the sensory quale into behavioristic terms, as it has already translated association into the conditioned reflex. Respect for parents may be laudable and yet hinder the free development of youth. Behaviorism is already past its prime as a movement, because movements exist upon protest and it no longer needs to protest. Had it been less successful it might have lived longer as a movement and a shorter time as a method.

Gestaltpsychologie is in the same box with behaviorism. Born at the same time its development was hindered by the war, so that it is now less mature. Its infant cries of protest against an unkind world still persist. Everybody must know now what *Gestaltpsychologie* is not. It is not elementaristic or associationistic. It eschews the vague concepts of the past, like attention and attitude, and cultivates new vague concepts in their place, like insight, closure, and level. When Wertheimer and Koffka were describing it, they worked largely in negative terms. There is no general positive content of *Gestaltpsychologie* with which anybody disagrees. Still the voice cries in the wilderness, whereas the kingdom of God is already with man. *Gestaltpsychologie* was not new in 1912; it was quite ready to be founded. It is now a movement. Presently, I think, it too will become simply psychology.

I am now ready to form a conclusion.

I believe that I have shown that movements and the rise of schools are a form of controversy, often one-sided because directed against no particular antagonist. Thus, as controversy, the movement introduces all the psychological advantages and disadvantages of personal controversy.

Discussion is relevant to scientific work, but controversy is more than discussion. It involves emotion; and passion, while of itself irrelevant to scientific procedure, enters to prejudice reason and to fix the debaters more firmly in their opinions. If it were possible, scientific discussion should be dispassionate, not only in form but in spirit, for otherwise progress toward the truth is hindered.

Since the controversy of a movement is apt to be less personally pointed, especially when there is only one active party to the quarrel, participation in a movement may have the advantage of blinding the scientist less than participation in a personal controversy. On the other hand, movements, in so far as they are blind, have the further disadvantage of lending to blindness the social support of the group within the school.

As psychologists, we cannot, however, afford to condemn controversy, be it ever so emotional. If we could read out of the body scientific every investigator who lost his temper with an opponent and kept it lost, we should read out those very men who, because of their drives or prejudices or whatever we like to call that conative component of their personalities, had made the positive contributions to the science. Research is something more than a habit and it requires something more than patience. It requires, among other things, an irresistible urge, bolstered up, I think, not so much by curiosity, as by egotism. This urge may carry one to the truth, beyond it, or even directly away from it. Vision and blindness are here alike, for both are attention, and attention to one thing is inattention to another. The same urge helps and hinders progress.

Must the truth then forever transcend the individual? Is the stage of science like the court of law, where attorneys contend and only the judge speaks the truth? This is the view of research that I find so personally abhorrent and yet seem forced to accept.

There is, however, an incomplete solution for the dilemma. A scientist should, I think, cultivate dissociation. Too much has been said in favor of the integration of the personality, and too little in favor of dissociation. The scientist needs to be a dual personality. He needs to be able to become the prosecutor or the judge at will. He can then stand off and evaluate himself at times, and perhaps even arrange things so that the prosecuting personality will fare more happily when it returns to dominate his person. But I would not have him be the judge too often, for then the assured, prejudiced, productive personality might get "squeezed out," and science would be the loser.

I recommend this dissociation, not because it will make us happier, not merely because it is fun to be the judge as well as the prosecutor, but because I have no expectation that it could be so complete that there would be no interaction between the two personalities. I should hope for a tempering of the prosecutor by the judge so that there would really be more vision and less blindness, and so that psychology would benefit thereby. Then we should have less futile controversy, fewer people devoting their lives to lost causes, even more candid and thus more fruitful discussion, less talk and more research.

I have asked you to-night to play the judge with me. I think it is important for psychology, still so talkative a science, that we should all be practiced in being judge as well as prosecutor. Do I dare in closing to point you a moral, as Wundt so ungraciously did to Stumpf? If there is any precept that comes out of all this talk, it is rather that we should beware of precepts. Psychology needs both judiciousness and effective prejudices; and I cannot resist the impression that we shall do well to cultivate and welcome both.

Reprinted with permission
from *American Psychologist,*
1959, *14*, 727–734.

Chapter 14

Gestalt Psychology Today

Wolfgang Köhler

Dartmouth College

In 1949, the late Herbert Langfeld gave a lecture in Europe in which he described what appeared to him to be the major trends in American psychology. He also mentioned Gestalt psychology; but he added that the main observations, questions, and principles characteristic of this school had become part of every American psychologist's mental equipment. I was not so optimistic. And, in fact, the very next year attempts were made to explain the molar units in perception by processes which gradually connect neural elements. Soon afterwards, a theory of conditioning was developed, according to which more and more components of a stimulus object are gradually conditioned, and the course of the whole process can be explained in this fashion. Such theories may prove to be very useful, but one can hardly say that, at the time, their authors were greatly influenced by Gestalt psychology. It is for this and similar reasons that a new discussion of old questions seems to me indicated.

Address of the President at the sixty-seventh Annual Convention of the American Psychological Association, Cincinnati, Ohio, September 6, 1959.

I should like to begin with a few remarks about the history of Gestalt psychology—because not all chapters of this history are generally known. In the eighties of the past century, psychologists in Europe were greatly disturbed by von Ehrenfels' claim that thousands of percepts have characteristics which cannot be derived from the characteristics of their ultimate components, the so-called sensations. Chords and melodies in hearing, the shape characteristics of visual objects, the roughness or the smoothness of tactual impressions, and so forth were used as examples. All these "Gestalt qualities" have one thing in common. When the physical stimuli in question are considerably changed, while their relations are kept constant, the Gestalt qualities remain about the same. But, at the time, it was generally assumed that the sensations involved are individually determined by their individual stimuli and must therefore change when these are greatly changed. How, then, could any characteristics of the perceptual situation remain constant under these conditions? Where did the Gestalt qualities come from? Ehrenfels' qualities are not fancy ingredients of this or that particular situation which we might safely ignore. Both positive and negative esthetic characteristics of the world around us, not only of ornaments, paintings, sculptures, tunes, and so forth, but also of trees, landscapes, houses, cars—and other persons—belong to this class. That relations between the sexes largely depend on specimens of the same class need hardly be emphasized. It is, therefore, not safe to deal with problems of psychology as though there were no such qualities. And yet, beginning with Ehrenfels himself, psychologists have not been able to explain their nature.

This holds also for the men who were later called Gestalt psychologists, including the present speaker. Wertheimer's ideas and investigations developed in a different direction. His thinking was also more radical than that of Ehrenfels. He did not ask: How are Gestalt qualities possible when, basically, the perceptual scene consists of separate elements? Rather, he objected to this premise, the thesis that the psychologist's thinking must begin with a consideration of such elements. From a subjective point of view, he felt, it may be tempting to assume that all perceptual situations consist of independent, very small components. For, on this assumption, we obtain a maximally clear picture of what lies behind the observed facts. But, how do we know that a subjective clarity of this kind agrees with the nature of what we have before us? Perhaps we pay for the subjective clearness of the customary picture by ignoring all processes, all functional interrelations, which may have operated before there is a perceptual scene and which thus influence the characteristics of the scene. Are we allowed to impose on perception an extreme simplicity which, objectively, it may not possess?

Wertheimer, we remember, began to reason in this fashion when experimenting not with perceptual situations which were stationary, and therefore comparatively silent, but with visual objects in motion when corresponding stimuli did not move. Such "apparent movements," we would now say, occur when several visual objects appear or disappear in certain temporal relations. Again in our present language, under these circumstances an interaction takes place which, for instance, makes a second object appear too near, or coincident with, a first object which is just disappearing, so that only when the first object, and therefore the interaction, really fades, the second object can move toward its normal position. If this is interaction, it does not, as such, occur on the perceptual scene. On this scene, we merely observe a movement. That movements of this kind do not correspond to real movements of the stimulus objects and must therefore be brought about by the sequence of the two objects, we can discover only by examining the physical situation. It follows that, if the seen movement is the perceptual result of an interaction, this interaction itself takes place outside the perceptual field. Thus, the apparent movement confirmed Wertheimer's more general suspicion: we cannot assume that the perceptual scene is an aggregate of unrelated elements because underlying processes are already functionally interrelated when that scene emerges, and now exhibits corresponding effects.

Wertheimer did not offer a more specific physiological explanation. At the time, this would have been impossible. He next turned to the problem of whether the characteristics of stationary perceptual fields are also influenced by interactions. I need not repeat how he investigated the formation of molar perceptual units, and more particularly of groups of such objects. Patterns which he used for this purpose are now reproduced in many textbooks. They clearly demonstrate that it is *relations* among visual objects which decide what objects become group members, and what others do not, and where, therefore, one group separates itself from another. This fact strongly suggests that perceptual groups are established by interactions; and, since a naive observer is merely aware of the result, the perceived groups, but not of their dependence upon particular relations, such interactions would again occur among the underlying processes rather than within the perceptual field.

Let me add a further remark about this early stage of the development. Surely, in those years, Gestalt psychologists were not satisfied with a quiet consideration of available facts. It seems that no major new trend in a science ever is. We were excited by what we found, and even more by the prospect of finding further revealing facts. Moreover, it was not only the stimulating newness of our enterprise which inspired us. There was also a great wave of relief—as though we were escaping from a prison. The prison was psychology as taught at the universities when we still were students. At the time, we had been shocked by the thesis that all psychological facts (not only those in perception) consist of unrelated inert atoms and that almost the only factors which combine these atoms and thus introduce action are associations formed under the influence of mere contiguity. What had disturbed us was the utter senselessness of this picture, and the implication that human life, apparently so colorful and so intensely dynamic, is actually a frightful bore. This was not true of our new picture, and we felt that further discoveries were bound to destroy what was left of the old picture.

Soon further investigations, not all of them done by Gesalt psychologists, reinforced the new trend. Rubin called attention to the difference between figure and ground. David Katz found ample evidence for the role of Gestalt factors in the field of touch as well as in color vision, and so forth. Why so much interest just in perception? Simply because in no other part of psychology are facts so readily accessible to observation. It was the hope of everybody that, once some major functional principles had been revealed in this part of psychology, similar principles would prove to be relevant to other parts, such as memory, learning, thinking, and motivation. In fact, Wertheimer and I undertook our early studies of intellectual processes precisely from this point of view; somewhat later, Kurt Lewin began his investigations of motivation which, in part, followed the same line; and we also applied the concept of *Gestaltung* or organization to memory, to learning, and to recall. With developments in America, Wertheimer's further analysis of thinking, Asch's and Heider's investigations in social psychology, our work on figural aftereffects, and eventually on currents of the brain, we are probably all familiar.

In the meantime, unexpected support had come from natural science. To mention only one point: Parts of molar perceptual units often have characteristics which they do not exhibit when separated from those units. Within a larger visual entity, a part may, for instance, be a corner of this entity, another part its contour or boundary, and so on. It now seems obvious; but nobody in psychology had seen it before: the same happens in any physical system that is pervaded by interactions. These interactions affect the parts of the system until, eventually, in a steady state, the characteristics of all parts are such that remaining interactions balance one another. Hence, if processes in the central nervous system follow the same rule, the dependence of local perceptual facts on conditions in larger entities could no longer be regarded as puzzling. Comparisons of this kind greatly encouraged the Gestalt psychologists.

In America, it may seem surprising that enthusiastic people such as the Gestalt psychologists were intensely interested in physics. Physics is generally assumed to be a particularly sober discipline. And yet, this happened to us most naturally. To be sure, our reasoning in physics involved no changes in the laws of physics, and no new assumptions in this field. Nevertheless, when we compared our psychological findings with the behavior of certain physical systems, some parts of natural science began to look different. When reading the formulae of the physicist, one may emphasize this or that aspect of their content. The particular aspect of the formulae in which the Gestalt psychologists became interested had, for decades, been given little attention. No mistake had ever been made in applications of the formulae, because what now fascinated us had all the time been present in their mathematical form. Hence, all calculations in physics had come out right. But it does make a difference whether you make explicit what a formula implies or merely use it as a reliable tool. We had, therefore, good reasons for being surprised by what we found; and we naturally felt elated when the new reading of the formulae told us that organization is as obvious in some parts of physics as it is in psychology.

Incidentally, others were no less interested in this "new reading" than we were. These other people were eminent physicists. Max Planck once told me that he expected our approach to clarify a difficult issue which had just arisen in quantum physics—if not the concept of the quantum itself. Several years later, Max Born, the great physicist who gave quantum mechanics its present form, made almost the same statement in one of his papers. And, only a few weeks ago, I read a paper in which Bridgman of Harvard interprets Heisenberg's famous principle in such terms that I am tempted to call him, Bridgman, a Gestalt physicist.

We will now return to psychology. More particularly, we will inspect the situation in which American psychology finds itself today. The spirit which we find here differs considerably from the one which characterized young Gestalt psychology. Let me try to formulate what members of this audience may have been thinking while I described that European enterprise. "Enthusiasm?" they probably thought.

Feelings of relief when certain assumptions were found less dreary than those of earlier psychologists in Europe? But this is an admission that emotional factors and extrascientific values played a part in Gestalt psychology. We know about the often pernicious effects of the emotions in ordinary life. How, then, could emotions be permitted to influence scientific judgments and thus to disturb the objectivity of research? As we see it, the true spirit of science is a critical spirit. Our main obligation as scientists is that of avoiding mistakes. Hence our emphasis on strict method in experimentation and on equally strict procedures in the evaluation of results. The Gestalt psychologists seem to have been guilty of wishful thinking. Under the circumstances, were not some of their findings unreliable and some of their concepts vague?

I will at once admit two facts. Almost from its beginning, American psychology has given more attention to questions of method and strict proof than Gestalt psychology did in those years. In this respect, American psychology was clearly superior. Secondly, sometimes the Gestalt psychologists did make mistakes. Not in all cases was the reliability of their findings up to American standards, and some concepts which they used were not immediately quite clear. I myself once used a certain concept in a somewhat misleading fashion. I had better explain this.

What is insight? In its strict sense, the term refers to the fact that, when we are aware of a relation, of any relation, this relation is not experienced as a fact by itself, but rather as something that follows from the characteristics of the objects under consideration. Now, when primates try to solve a problem, their behavior often shows that they are aware of a certain important relation. But when they now make use of this "insight," and thus solve their problem, should this achievement be called a *solution by insight*? No—it is by no means clear that it was also insight which made that particular relation *emerge*. In a given situation, we or a monkey may become aware of a great many relations. If, at a certain moment, we or a monkey attend to the right one, this may happen for several reasons, some entirely unrelated to insight. Consequently, it is misleading to call the whole process a "solution by insight."

This will be particularly obvious when the solution of the problem is arbitrarily chosen by the experimenter. Take Harlow's excellent experiments in which primates are expected to choose the odd item in a group of objects. "Oddity" is a particular relational fact. Once a monkey attends to it, he will perceive it with insight. But why should he do so during his first trials? His first choices will be determined by one factor or another, until he happens to attend, once or repeatedly, to the oddity relation just when he chooses (or does not choose) the right object. Gradually, he will now attend to this particular relation in all trials; and he may do so even when entirely new objects are shown. Surely, such a process should not simply be called "learning by insight." If Harlow were to say that, under the circumstances, it is learning of one kind or another which gives the right relation and corresponding insight their chance to operate, I should at once agree. What, I believe, the monkeys do not learn is insight into which object in a given group is the odd one; but they must learn to pay attention to the oddity factor in the first place. I hope that this will clarify matters. They have not always been so clear to me.

When the solution of a problem is not arbitrarily chosen by the experimenter, but more directly related to the nature of the given situation, insight may play a more important role. But, even under these circumstances, it is not insight alone which brings about the solution. The mere fact that solutions often emerge to the subjects' own surprise is clear proof that it cannot be insight alone which is responsible for their origin.

But I intended to discuss some trends in American psychology. May I confess that I do not fully approve of all these trends?

First, I doubt whether it is advisable to regard caution and a critical spirit as *the* virtues of a scientist, as though little else counted. They are necessary in research, just as the brakes in our cars must be kept in order and their windshields clean. But it is not because of the brakes or of the windshields that we drive. Similarly, caution and a critical spirit are like tools. They ought to be kept ready during a scientific enterprise; however, the main business of a science is gaining more and more new knowledge. I wonder why great men in physics do not call caution and a critical spirit the most important characteristics of their behavior. They seem to regard the testing of brakes and the cleaning of windshields as mere precautions, but to look forward to the next trip as the business for which they have cars. Why is it only in psychology that we hear the slightly discouraging story of mere caution over and over again? Why are just psychologists so inclined to greet the announcement of a new fact (or a new working hypothesis) almost with scorn? This is caution that has gone sour and has almost become negativism—which, of course, is no less an emotional attitude than is enthusiasm. The enthusiasm of the early Gestalt psychologists was a virtue, because it led to new observations. But virtues, it has been said, tend to breed little accompanying vices. In their enthusiasm, the Gestalt psychologists were not always sufficiently careful.

In American psychology, it is rightly regarded as a virtue if a man feels great respect for method and for caution. But, if this virtue becomes too strong, it may bring forth a spirit of skepticism and thus prevent new work. Too many young psychologists, it seems to me, either work only against something done by others or merely vary slightly what others have done before; in other words, preoccupation with method may tend to limit the range of our research. We are, of course, after clear evidence. But not in all parts of psychology can evidence immediately be clear. In some, we cannot yet use our most exact methods. Where this happens, we hesitate to proceed. Experimentalists in particular tend to avoid work on new materials resistant to approved methods and to the immediate application of perfectly clear concepts. But concepts in a new field can only be clarified by work in this field. Should we limit our studies to areas already familiar from previous research? Obviously, this would mean a kind of conservatism in psychology. When I was his student, Max Planck repeated this warning over and over again in his lectures.

Our wish to use only perfect methods and clear concepts has led to Methodological Behaviorism. Human experience in the phenomenological sense cannot yet be treated with our most reliable methods; and, when dealing with it, we may be forced to form new concepts which, at first, will often be a bit vague. Most experimentalists, therefore, refrain from observing, or even from referring to, the phenomenal scene. And yet, this is the scene on which, so far as the actors are concerned, the drama of ordinary human living is being played all the time. If we never study this scene, but insist on methods and concepts developed in research "from the outside," our results are likely to look strange to those who intensely live "inside."

To be sure, in many respects, the graphs and tables obtained "from the outside" constitute a most satisfactory material; and, in animal psychology, we have no other material. But this material as such contains no direct evidence as to the processes by which it is brought about. In this respect it is a slightly defective, I am tempted to say, a meager, material. For it owes its particular clearness to the fact that the data from which the graphs and tables are derived are severely selected data. When subjects are told to say no more than "louder," "softer," and perhaps "equal" in certain experiments, or when we merely count how many items they recall in others, then we can surely apply precise statistical techniques to what they do. But, as a less attractive consequence, we never hear under these circumstances how they do the comparing in the first case and what happens when they try to recall in the second case.

Are such questions now to be ignored? After all, not all phenomenal experiences are entirely vague; this Scheerer has rightly emphasized. And, if many are not yet accessible to quantitative procedures, what of it? One of the most fascinating disciplines, developmental physiology, the science investigating the growth of an organism from one cell, seldom uses quantitative techniques. And yet, nobody can deny that its merely qualitative description of morphogenesis has extraordinary scientific value. In new fields, not only quantitative data are relevant. As to the initial vagueness of concepts in a new field, I should like to add an historical remark. When the concept of energy was first introduced in physics, it was far from being a clear concept. For decades, its meaning could not be sharply distinguished from that of the term "force." And what did the physicists do? They worked and worked on it, until at last it did become perfectly clear. There is no other way of dealing with new, and therefore not yet perfect, concepts. Hence, if we refuse to study the phenomenal scene, because, here, few concepts are so far entirely clear, we thereby decide that this scene will never be investigated—at least not by us, the psychologists.

Now, I had better return to Gestalt psychology. Let me try to show you how Gestalt psychology tends to work today by discussing a more specific issue, an issue on which scores of American psychologists have worked for years. We shall thus be enabled to compare the way in which they approach this issue with the Gestalt psychologists' approach.

The issue in question refers to the concepts of conditioning and motivation. One school seems to regard conditioning as almost *the* process with which the psychologist has to deal. In a famous book with the general title *Principles of Behavior,* the late Clark Hull, then the most influential member of the school, actually dealt with little else—although he often used other terms. He felt that even such facts as thinking, insight, intentions, striving, and value would eventually be explained by a consistent investigation of the various forms of conditioning. We are all familiar with the basic concepts of his theory. Hence I will say only a few words about it. When conditions in an animal's tissue deviate from an optimal level, a state of need is said to exist in this tissue. Such needs produce, or simply are, drives—which means that they tend to cause actions in the nervous system, some more or less prescribed by inherited neural connections, others of a more random nature. Drives are also called motivations. None of these terms is to be understood in a phenomenological sense. They always refer to assumed states of the tissue. The main point is that, for biological reasons, states of need must, if possible, be reduced and that this may be achieved by certain responses of the organism to the given situation. In case first responses are of a random character, learning or conditioning will often select such responses as do reduce the needs in question. In a simple formulation, the well-known rule which governs such developments is as follows: when a response has repeatedly occurred in temporal contiguity with the neural effects of a certain stimulus, then this stimulus will tend to evoke the same response in the future—provided the response has caused a reduction of the need. I will not define such further concepts as habit strength, reaction potential, afferent stimulus interaction, reactive inhibition, and so forth, because they will play no role in my discussion.

But one term seems to me particularly important. Many recent, and important, investigations are concerned with so-called "learned drives," an expression which has, of course, this meaning: if a neutral stimulus is repeatedly followed by conditions which cause a primary state of drive such as pain, and the corresponding fear, then the fear with its usual effects on behavior will gradually become connected with that neutral stimulus, so that the stimulus alone now evokes the fear and its overt consequences. Certain drives are therefore said to be "learnable" in the sense that they can be attached to facts which, as such, are not related to the drive and hence would originally not evoke corresponding responses.

Some experiments in the field of conditioning in general are most interesting. I will only discuss the concepts used in the interpretation of this work and the conclusions which it is said to justify.

To begin with these conclusions: They refer to certain human experiences which, if the conclusions were justified, would have to be regarded as strange delusions. I mean our cognitive experiences. Suppose somebody discovers by accident that, every time he subtracts the square of a given integer from the square of the next integer in the series, the result is an odd number. A more learned friend now explains to him why this is a necessary rule, undoubtedly valid beyond any tests ever done by a person. The explanation refers to simple relations and to relations among relations—all readily understandable—and the final outcome is convincing. Now, is the understanding of the relations involved to be explained in terms of conditioning? Nothing in conditioning seems to give us access to the psychological fact which I just called understanding; and, since an understanding of relations is essential to all cognitive achievements, the same applies to the whole field.

Explanation of our intellectual life in terms of conditioning would simply mean: its reduction to the operations of an often most practical, but intrinsically blind, connection of mere facts. Promises that such an explanation will nevertheless be achieved cause in the present speaker a mild, incredulous horror. It is not the business of science to destroy evidence. Behaviorists would perhaps answer that arguments which refer to human thinking as an experience are irrelevant, because science is only concerned with facts observable from the outside, and therefore objective. This answer would hardly be acceptable. The Behaviorist's own objective observations are invariably observations of facts in his perceptual field. No other form of objective observation has ever been discovered. Consequently, the Behaviorist cannot, without giving more particular reasons, reject reference to other individual experiences merely because they are such experiences.

Thus we are justified in considering a further example of human experience. A need or drive, we are sometimes told, is a motivation. I do not entirely agree with this statement for the following reasons. A need or drive, we remember, is supposed to be a particular state in the tissue. There is no indication in Hull's writings that such a state "points beyond itself" toward any objects—although it may, of course, cause movements, or actions of glands. Now it is true that the same holds for certain needs as human experiences; because, when a need is felt, it does not always point toward an object, attainment of which would satisfy the need. At the time, no such object may be in sight; in fact, no such object may yet be known. But when the proper object appears, or becomes known, then the situation changes. For, now the subject feels attracted or (in certain instances) repelled by this object. In other words, an object may have characteristics which establish a dynamic relation between the subject and that object. According to common experience, it is this dynamic relation which makes the subject move toward, or away from, the object. We ought to use different terms for a mere need *per se* and the situation in which a subject is attracted or repelled by an object. Otherwise, the dynamic aspect of the latter situation might easily be ignored. I suggest that we reserve the term "motivation" for this dynamic situation. Here we are, of course, on familiar ground. Motivation as just described was Kurt Lewin's main concern in psychology. He clearly recognized the part which certain characteristics of an object play in establishing the dynamic relation between this object and the subject. He called such characteristics of objects *Aufforderungscharaktere*, a term which then became "valences" in English.

So far as I know, there are no valences in objects, no attractions and no repulsions between objects and subjects in the Behaviorist's vocabulary. I am afraid that, in this fashion, he misses a point not only important in human experience but also relevant to what he regards as true science.

How would a Gestalt psychologist handle motivation in the present sense? He would begin with the following psychological facts. I do not know up to what point Lewin would have accepted what I am now going to say. My facts are these: (a) In human experience, motivation is a dynamic vector, that is, a fact which has a direction and tends to cause a displacement in this direction. (b) Unless there are obstacles in the way, this direction coincides with an imaginary straight line drawn from the object to the subject. (c) The direction of the experienced vector is either that toward the object or away from it. In the first case, the vector tends to reduce the distance in question; in the second, to increase it. (d) The strength of both the need present in the subject and of the valence exhibited by the object can vary. Both in man and in animals it has been observed that, when the strength of the valence is low, this reduction can be compensated for by an increase of the need in the subject; and, conversely, that, when the need is lowered, an increase of the strength of the valence may compensate for this change.

When considering these simple statements, anybody familiar with the elements of physics will be reminded of the behavior of forces. (a) In physics, forces are dynamic vectors which tend to change the distance between one thing (or event) and another. (b) Unless there are obstacles in the way, a force operates along a straight line drawn from the first object (or event) to the other. (c) The direction in which a force operates is either that of an attraction or of a repulsion, of a reduction or of an increase of the given distance. (d) The formula by which the intensity of a force between two objects is given contains two terms which refer to the sizes of a decisive property (for instance, an electric charge) in one object and in the other. It is always the product of these two terms on which, according to the formula, the intensity of the force depends. Consequently, a reduction of the crucial term on one side can be compensated for by an increase of the term on the other side.

We have just seen that the behavior of vectors in motivational situations is the same as the behavior of forces in nature. Gestalt psychologists are, therefore, inclined to interpret motivation in terms of such forces, or, rather, of forces which operate between certain perceptual processes and processes in another part of the brain, where a need may be physiologically represented. We have no time to discuss the question how cortical fields or forces would cause overt movements of the organism in the direction of these forces.

Now, not everybody likes the term "force." Its meaning, it has been said, has anthropomorphic connotations. But, in human psychology, we simply must use terms which—if I may use this expression—"sound human." If we refused to do so, we would not do justice to our subject matter which (to a high degree) is human experience. To be sure, in physics, Heinrich Hertz once tried to do without the concept "force." He actually wrote a treatise on mechanics in which he avoided this term. And what happened? He had to populate the physical world with unobservable masses, introduced only in order to make their hidden presence substitute for the much simpler action of forces. Ever since that time, physicists have happily returned to the old concept "force," and nobody has ever been harmed by the fact.

The present reasoning leads to a conclusion which distinguishes this reasoning from the treatment of motivation in the Behaviorist's system. Clark Hull was a great admirer of science; but, to my knowledge, he hardly ever used the concepts characteristic of field physics. The fundamental distinction between physical facts which are scalars (that is, facts which have a magnitude but no direction) and vectors (which have both an intensity and a direction) played no decisive part in his theorizing. His main concepts were obviously meant to be scalars. There is no particular spatial direction in a habit strength, none in a reaction potential, and none even in what he called a drive state. Hence, the core of modern physics as developed by Faraday and Maxwell had no influence on his system. For this reason, and also because he refused to consider motivation as an experienced vector, he could not discover that the operations of motivation appear to be isomorphic with those of fields or forces in the brain.

But, if motivation is to be interpreted in this fashion, certain assumptions often made by Behaviorists may no longer be acceptable. Take the concept of learned drives. As I understand this term, it means that learning can attach a drive state to a great variety of stimuli which, as such, are neutral facts. Now, so long as a drive is not regarded as a vector, this seems indeed quite possible. But, if the drive in Hull's sense is replaced by a motivational force which operates between a subject and some perceptual fact, no arbitrary connections of this kind can be established. For, now motivation becomes the experienced counterpart of a force in the brain, and this force depends entirely upon the relation between conditions in the subject and the characteristics of the perceived object. There can be no such force if the object is, and remains, a neutral object. Forces only operate between objects which have the right properties. Any example of a force in nature illustrates this fact.

How, then, are the observations to be explained which are now interpreted as a learning of drives? After all, some learning must be involved when an originally neutral object gradually begins to attract or repel a subject. From the present point of view, only one explanation is possible. Supposing that the subject's need does not vary, learning must change the characteristics of the object, and thus transform it into an adequate motivation object. One instance would be what Tolman calls a sign Gestalt; in other words, the neutral object would become the signal for the appearance of something else which is a proper motivational object. This expected object would now be the object of the motivation. Or also, when a neutral object is often accompanied by facts which are natural motivational objects, the characteristics of such facts may gradually "creep into" the very appearance of the formerly neutral object and thus make it a proper motivational object. Years ago, comparative psychologists in England stressed the importance of such processes, to which they gave the name "assimilation." They regarded assimilation as a particularly effective form of an association. And is it not true that, as a consequence of learning, a coffin *looks* forbidding or sinister? I also know somebody to whom a bottle covered with dust and just brought up from the cellar *looks* most attractive.

As a further and particularly simple possibility, the subject might just learn more about the characteristics of the given object itself than he knew in the beginning; and the characteristics revealed by this learning might be such that now the same object fits a need. It seems to me that all these possibilities ought to be considered before we accept the thesis that motivations in the present sense can be attached to actually neutral objects. Incidentally, similar changes of objects may also be responsible for the developments which Gordon Allport once regarded as evidence of "functional autonomy."

You will ask me whether my suggestions lead to any consequences in actual research. Most surely, they do. But, since I have lived so long in America, and have therefore gradually become a most cautious scientist, I am now preparing myself for the study of motivation by investigating, first of all, the action of dynamic vectors in simpler fields, such as cognition and perception. It is a most interesting occupation to compare motivational action with dynamic events in those other parts of psychology. When you do so, everything looks different, not only in perception but also in certain forms of learning. Specific work? There is, and will be, more of it than I alone can possibly manage. Consequently, I need help. And where do I expect to find this help? I will tell you where.

The Behaviorist's premises, we remember, lead to certain expectations and experiments. What I have just said invites us to proceed in another direction. I suggest that, in this situation, we forget about schools. The Behaviorist is convinced that his functional concepts are those which we all ought to use. The Gestalt psychologist, who deals with a greater variety of both phenomenal and physical concepts, expects more from work based on such premises. Both parties feel that their procedures are scientifically sound. Why should we fight? Many experiments done by Behaviorists seem to me to be very good experiments. May I now ask the Behaviorists to regard the use of some phenomenal facts, and also of field physics, as perfectly permissible? If we were to agree on these points, we could, I am sure, do excellent work together. It would be an extraordinary experience—and good for psychology.

Reprinted with permission
from *Psychological Review*,
1930, 37, 1-24.

Chapter 15

Basic Neural Mechanisms in Behavior

K. S. Lashley

Behavior Research Fund, Chicago

Among the systems and points of view which comprise our efforts to formulate a science of psychology, the proposition upon which there seems to be most nearly a general agreement is that the final explanation of behavior or of mental processes is to be sought in the physiological activity of the body and, in particular, in the properties of the nervous system. The tendency to seek all causal relations of behavior in brain processes is characteristic of the recent development of psychology in America. Most of our text-books begin with an exposition of the structure of the brain and imply that this lays a foundation for a later understanding of behavior. It is rare that a discussion of any psychological problem avoids some reference to the neural substratum, and the development of elaborate neurological theories to "explain" the phenomena in every field of psychology is becoming increasingly fashionable.

Address of the President of the American Psychological Association before the Ninth International Congress of Psychology at New Haven, September 4, 1929.

In reading this literature I have been impressed chiefly by its futility. The chapter on the nervous system seems to provide an excuse for pictures in an otherwise dry and monotonous text. That it has any other function is not clear; there may be cursory references to it in later chapters on instinct and habit, but where the problems of psychology become complex and interesting, the nervous system is dispensed with. In more technical treatises the neurological explanations are made up mostly of assumptions concerning the properties of the nerve cell which have no counterpart in physiological experiment. Thus we find the superiority of distributed over concentrated practice seriously "explained" by the "fact" that successive passage of neural impulses over a synapse reduces its resistance least when the impulses come in quick succession.

There is no direct evidence for any function of the anatomical synapse: there is no evidence that synapses vary in resistance, or that, if they do, the resistance is altered by the passage of the nerve impulse. If the explanation is to be given in terms of established facts, as it must be, then it is limited to the following form: the superiority of distributed practice is due to the discontinuity of the neurons, the polarity of conduction, the fact of learning, and the superiority of distributed practice.

This is a typical case of the neurological explanations to be found in our psychological literature. With such conditions prevailing, it seems time to examine critically the relations between psychology and neurology and to attempt an evaluation of current notions concerning the mechanisms of the brain.

Inadequacy of Current Theories

The starting point for our attempts to account for behavior in terms of nervous processes has been either the cerebral localization of functions or the theory that all nervous integration is patterned after the spinal reflex. I need scarcely point out the difficulties encountered by the older doctrine of cerebral localization. It expresses the fact that destruction of definite areas results in definite symptoms and the probable inference that these different parts have diverse functions, but it has given us no insight into the manner in which the areas or centers exercise their functions or the way in which they influence one another. It is only by applying psychological conceptions like that of association, or by turning to the theory of reflexes that the doctrine of localization is made to express the dynamic relations of behavior.

The extension of the theory of reflex conduction, first derived from studies of the spinal cord, to problems of cerebral function provided a welcome addition to the psychophysical doctrine of localization. It gave a clear interpretation of localized areas as relay points or centers along the course of the reflex arc and seemed to explain the functional relations of the areas. However, the theory has not worked well in application to the details of behavior. To understand the difficulties we should have clearly in mind the form and limitations of the theory. It states that the mechanism of cerebral function is essentially the same as that of the spinal reflexes, involving the conduction of nerve impulses from the sense organs over definite, restricted paths to the effectors. The performance of a habit, whether of speech or of manipulative movement, is determined by the existence of definite connections between a limited number of nerve cells, which are always functional in that habit. The model for the theory is a telephone system. Just as two instruments can be connected only by certain wires, so the sense organs and muscles concerned in any act are connected by nerve fibers specialized for that act.

Perhaps few neurologists would agree to such a bare statement. They point to the incalculable number of nerve cells, the interplay of inhibition and facilitation, and suggest that in so complex a system there are limitless possibilities. But the fact remains that the essential feature of the reflex theory is the assumption that individual neurons are specialized for particular functions. The explanatory value of the theory rests upon this point alone, and no amount of hypothetical elaboration of connections alters the basic assumption.

Both the doctrines of localization and of conditioned reflexes imply the correspondence of structural and functional units—the specialization of minute areas or of single cells for definite limited functions. Recent experimental and clinical evidence seems to show that there is no such correspondence, and thus to present fatal difficulties to both theories. I shall sketch the main lines of this evidence, then turn to a consideration of other possible mechanisms.

Analysis of the Adequate Stimulus

The notion of the reflex arc was developed in studies of spinal preparations in which protopathic stimuli or muscle tensions are the chief sources of excitation. Under these simple conditions something like a point for point correspondence between receptor cells and muscle groups could be demonstrated, as in the case of the scratch reflex.

We first attempted the extension of this conception to instinctive behavior, on the assumption that the adequate stimulus to nursing, to the recognition of the mate or young, to the recognition of the nest site, to sexual excitment might be expressed in terms of the excitation of such and such receptor cells. This proved to be a vain hope. The adequate stimulus in such cases may be described in terms of a pattern having definite proportions but always, within wide limits, it is a matter of indifference to what receptor cells this pattern is applied.

A survey of various types of behavior shows that this is an almost universal attribute of the adequate stimuli.[1] It is most obvious in pattern vision and can be demonstrated in animals with a rather primitive cortex. I have recently improved the technique for study of vision in the rat so that habits of pattern vision may be established in 20 or 30 trials. It is thus easy to test the equivalence of stimuli under conditions where previous associations are ruled out. Not only do we find transposition as Köhler has described it for chimpanzees, but even more striking equivalencies. An animal trained to discriminate patterns of solid white on a black ground is undisturbed by reversal of the brightness relations, by substitution of outlines for the solid figures, or even by partial outlines which retain some of the proportions of the original figures.

In many cases it is clear that the equivalent stimuli involve none of the retinal elements which were activated during learning. Here we have a situation where a habit is formed by the activation of one set of receptors and executed immediately upon stimulation of an entirely different and unpracticed group. The equivalence of stimuli is not due to the excitation of common nervous elements. The equivalent patterns have in common only ratios of intensity or of proportion in the spacial distribution of excited points. I might multiply examples of this sort indefinitely, but the studies of the Gestalt psychologists leave little doubt that such a condition is the rule for all stimuli with which we deal in the study of behavior.

Analysis of Reactions

Turning to motor activity, we are confronted by an identical problem. If we train an animal in a maze and observe carefully his subsequent errorless running, we find little identity of movement in successive trials. He gallops through in one trial, in another shuffles along, sniffing at the cover of the box. If we injure his cerebellum, he may roll through the maze. He follows the correct path with every variety of twist and posture, so that we cannot identify a single movement as characteristic of the habit.[2]

I have earlier reported cases of the direct adaptive use in the performance of motor habits of limbs which were paralyzed throughout training and whose motor paths consequently could not have been exercised during training.[3] It is not helpful to say that previously formed general habits are utilized in such performances, for the preexisting

1. K. Goldstein, Die Topik der Grosshirnrinde in ihrer klinischen Bedeutung, *Dtsch. Zsch. f. Nervenheilk.*, 1923, 77, 7-124.

2. K. S. Lashley and D. A. McCarthy, The survival of the maze habit after cerebellar injuries, *J. Comp. Psychol.*, 1926, 6, 423-433.

3. K. S. Lashley, The theory that synaptic resistance is reduced by the passage of the nerve impulse, *Psychol. Rev.*, 1924, 31, 369-375.

habits have not been associated with the new situation and the problem of the spontaneous association of the new patterns remains unsolved.

The problem of equivalence of motor responses has been less studied than that of equivalence of stimuli, but the phenomenon seems to be equally common. Activities ranging from the building of characteristic nests by birds to the so-called purposive activities of man show the absence of stereotyped movements in the attainment of a predetermined goal. The most familiar and most striking example is that of grammatical form in speech. Once we learn a new word, we use it in correct grammatical relations in limitless combinations with other words, without having to form new associations for each new setting.

It is only in certain acts of skill that stereotyped movements are recognizable and the uniformity of these is a result of long practice. We seem forced to conclude that the same motor elements are not necessarily used in the learning and performance of motor habits and that motor elements can be utilized directly when no specific associations have been formed with them.

Plasticity in Central Organization

Studies of the central nervous system give a similar picture. The functions are relatively independent of the structural elements. I can only cite a few of the lines of evidence, but sufficient, I believe, to establish the point.

First with respect to the specificity of conduction paths. The final motor neurons have been studied by Weiss.[4] He grafted additional limbs on salamanders, cutting the nerve which supplied the original limb so that the regenerating fibers came to innervate both the original and the new limb. The two limbs innervated by the same nerve showed synchronization of movements in corresponding muscle groups. Histological examination showed that the axons of the original nerve had branched so that the muscles of the two limbs were supplied by fibers from the same axons. There is no selective outgrowth of regenerating fibers and the branches of the same axon do not necessarily go to corresponding muscles. It seems, then, that the coordination of the two limbs is not a function of the particular fibers which innervate each muscle, but is due to some property of the nerve impulse such that the same fiber can selectively elicit either of two antagonistic movements. These experiments are still the subject of controversy, but the objections raised against the results are not particularly impressive and, though they may raise some doubt of this conclusion, they certainly do not establish the specificity of the axon. The results of Weiss are in harmony with many facts revealed by the study of the central nervous system.

---

4. P. Weiss, Die Funktion transplantierter Amphibienextremitäten. *Arch. f. mik. Anat.*, 1924, 52, 645–672.

In work with injuries to the spinal cord Miss Ball and I[5] have found that orientation of the rat in the maze is undisturbed by interruption in the cervical cord of either the pyramidal, rubrospinal, or any other of the long descending tracts. The impulses controlling turning and threading the maze somehow get down the cord after the destruction of any half of the descending fibers. I have more recently been working with double hemisections of the cord. In these preparations one half of the cord is divided in the upper cervical region, the other half below the nucleus of the phrenic nerve, so that all the long fibers are interrupted above the motor centers for the limbs. After three months such preparations show coordinated movements in walking and are able to control the limbs for orientation in response to stimuli applied to the head. The control is established in spite of the permanent interruption of all the long spinal paths.

We have also been accumulating evidence upon the functions of the projection and association tracts of the cerebrum in the rat. The data are not yet complete, but it seems fairly certain that the interruption of the projection fibers to a part of a functional area produces far less pronounced symptoms than destruction of the cortical area supplied by those fibers. We have now a large number of cases in which linear lesions sever the connections between the different anatomical areas of the cortex or divide the association fibers within single areas. It is rare that any symptoms can be detected in such cases, unless there is involved a considerable destruction of cortical tissue. The most capable animal that I have studied was one in which the cortex and underlying association fibers had been divided throughout the length of each hemisphere. His I.Q., based on ten tests, was 309.

In higher forms there is evidence for a somewhat greater specificity of long tracts in the central nervous system, but even in man the evidence is unequivocal only for the pyramidal system, which we have reason to believe is a part of the postural system and not especially concerned in the higher integrative functions of the brain, and for sensory paths of the cord. Although I would not venture the opinion that the association tracts of the cerebrum are a skeletal structure, there is certainly no direct evidence for the existence in them of any sharply defined reflex paths whose interruption results in the loss of isolated elementary functions.

What is the evidence that the cortex itself contains the definite specialized synapses which are demanded by the reflex theory? The data from extirpation experiments are somewhat ambiguous, but taken as a whole, fairly conclusive. Small lesions either produce no symptoms or very transient ones, so that it is clear that the mechanisms for habits are not closely grouped within small areas. When larger areas are involved, there are usually amnesias for many activities. Some of our experiments

---

5. K. S. Lashley and J. Ball, Spinal conduction and kinaesthetic sensitivity in the maze habit, J. Comp. Psychol., 1929, 9, 70–106.

show that the degree of amnesia is proportional to the extent of injury and, within wide limits, independent of the location of the injury. This may mean that the cells differentiated for the habits are widely and uniformly scattered, or that there are no especially differentiated cells. After injuries to the brain, the rate of formation of some habits is directly proportional to the extent of injury and independent of the position within any part of the cortex. This shows that the rate of learning is not dependent upon the properties of individual cells, but is somehow a function of the total mass of tissue. Rate of change in individual synapses does not express the facts of learning unless we postulate some means by which the capacity for change in any cell is modified by the activity of all other cells of the cortex. Finally, when such habits have been formed after brain injury, their retention correlates with the amount of functional tissue. This can be interpreted only as evidence that memory is not a function of individual cells, but is a property of the total mass of tissue.[6]

The reflex theory is not helpful for an understanding of such facts, nor do they seem consistent with it. If we consider the whole reaction, from sense-organ to effector, the impossibility of a theory of specialized intercellular connections becomes apparent. Let us analyze a visual reaction, for here the anatomical localization of paths seems best established. The observations of Marie and Chatelain,[7] and of Holmes and Lister[8] suggest a detailed projection of the retina upon the cortex, the macula represented in the posterior calcarine region, and successive radial zones along the borders of the fissure. (I am not sure that this interpretation is correct. Poppelreuter[9] has pointed out that the forms of scotoma are not as varied as the manifold shapes of lesion should lead us to expect, and that all the forms of scotoma can be interpreted as radiating or converging disturbances of the functional balance within the entire area. I have observations of a migraine scotoma in which the blind area retained a characteristic shape but drifted from the macula to the periphery of the visual field in the course of half an hour.) But granting a cortical retina, the problem of integration is only moved back a step. I have cited evidence to show that the retinal cells used in the formation of a habit need not be excited in order to reinstate the habitual response. This must be equally true, then, for the cortical retina. The same cells may not be twice called upon to perform the same function. They may be in a fixed anatomical relation to the retina, but the functional organization plays over them just as the pattern of letters plays over the bank of lamps in an electric sign.

---

6. K. S. Lashley, Brain mechanisms and intelligence, Chicago, Univ. Press, 1929, pp. 186.

7. P. Marie, et C. Chatelin, Les troubles visuels dus aux lésions des voies optiques intracérébrales et de la sphère visuelle corticale dans les blessures du crâne pai coup de feu, *Rev. neurol.*, 1914–15, *28*, 882–925.

8. G. Holmes, and W. T. Lister, Disturbances of vision from cerebral lesions with special reference to the macula, *Brain*, 1916, *39*, 34–73.

9. W. Poppelreuter, Die psychischen Schädungen durch Lopfschuss, Leipzig, 1917.

We find then at the point of projection on the cortex a variable pattern shifting over a fixed anatomical substratum. How can this elicit a response from a definite set of motor cells? It can not do so by excitation over definite association paths, for there is evidence against the existence of such paths and, besides, there are no fixed points of origin for them. Nor is it certain that there are any fixed motor points. We have found in studies of the motor cortex that a point which will elicit a primary movement of the fingers on one day may, a week later, produce a movement of the shoulder and at another time even movements of the face.[10] And the motor cortex, with its somewhat definite localization, is probably not concerned in habitual activity, anyway.

There does not seem to be a possibility of a constant anatomical localization at any point from receptor surface to effectors. Somehow the motor system must be sensitized to respond to the sensory patterns, but the phenomena cannot be expressed in terms of definite anatomical connections. This is the fundamental problem of neural integration and must serve as the starting point for any adequate theory of cerebral function.

The Doctrine of Circular Reflexes

An essential element of the reflex theory as applied to psychological problems is the doctrine that all the effects of stimulation are immediately observable in the motor systems. The James-Lange theory of emotion, the idea that mental attitudes are an expression of bodily postures or "sets," the theory that instincts and serial habits are chains of sensory-motor activity, the doctrine that implicit speech or gesture forms the basis of thinking: these are all expressions of the belief that the nervous system serves merely for the rapid switching and conduction of impulses from receptor to effector, without long-continued intraneural sequences of activity. This notion has been attractive, as offering a possibility of direct objective study of mental activity, but attempts to verify it experimentally have given disappointingly negative results.

The problem of emotion is still in such confusion that one can draw no conclusions with confidence, but the accumulation of evidence upon the variability of expressive reactions and the repeated failure to find any consistent correlations between bodily changes and either exciting situations or reported subjective states lends little support to the visceral theory.

On the question of maintained attitude or set we have some recent evidence which seems significant. Studying the influence of bodily posture upon the movements elicited by stimulation of the motor cortex

---

10. K. S. Lashley, Temporal variation in the function of the gyrus precentralis in primates, *Amer. J. Physiol.*, 1923, 65, 585–602.

Dr. Jacobsen and I mapped the motor area and selected for study a point giving extension of the fingers. We changed the posture of the limbs, head, and body of the preparation, stimulated muscles and nerve points electrically and in other ways sought to alter the conditions of peripheral stimulation. The excitability of the point was unaltered by this treatment and the same movement was elicited at five-minute intervals for two hours. We then altered the excitability of the point by stimulation of another distant point, changing the primary movement from extension to flexion. This new primary movement persisted for 55 minutes in spite of repeated changes in the posture of the animal, then reverted spontaneously to the original movement of extension. The experiment suggests that the pattern of organization of the motor cortex can be altered by central excitation and that the altered condition can be maintained for long periods without reinforcement from peripheral organs. It seems to fulfill the conditions for demonstration of a centrally maintained attitude.

Miss Ball and I have tested the effects on serial habits of sectioning the afferent paths of the cord, together with removal of all external directive clues after the animal is oriented in the starting box. Under these conditions the habits are run off without disturbance. With external and internal sensory cues eliminated it seems that the series of acts must be controlled by some wholly central mechanism.

The work of Thorson on tongue-movements[11] and unpublished observations on eye-movements during thinking, together with reports of the recovery of speech with use of an artificial larynx, oppose the doctrine of the completed reflex and point to some continued intraneural process as the basis of thinking. The weight of evidence, I believe, favors the view that in emotion, in all persistence of attitudes, in all serial activity there are continuously maintained central processes which, if they become intense, may irradiate to motor centers and produce expressive movements, implicit speech, and the like. The pattern of irradiation varies from subject to subject according to chance variations in the excitability of the motor or vegetative nervous systems, and the peripheral activities are not an essential condition for the maintenance of the central processes.

I have devoted so much time to criticism of the reflex theory of behavior because it seems to be deeply rooted in our thinking and to have had an important influence in the development of almost every phase of psychology. It has been valuable in counteracting certain trends toward vitalism and mysticism, but I believe that it is now becoming an obstacle rather than a help to progress. In the youth of a science there is virtue in simplifying the problems so that some sort of decisive experiments may be formulated, but there is a danger that oversimplification will later blind us to important problems. In the study of cerebral functions we seem to have reached a point where the reflex theory is no

---

11. A. M. Thorson, The relation of tongue movements to internal speech, *J. Exper. Psychol.*, 1925, *8*, 1–32.

longer profitable either for the formulation of problems or for an understanding of the phenomena of integration. And if it is not serviceable here, it can scarcely be of greater value for an understanding of the phenomena of behavior.

The Alternative to the Reflex Theory

What is the alternative to the doctrine of the specialization of nervous elements for definite reactions? It is possible that the modes of organization in the brain are not less numerous and diverse than the types of behavior to which they give rise. We have little direct evidence as to the nature of these central processes, but can deduce some laws from the effects of cerebral injury which may point the way to the significant investigations of the future.

Dynamic Aspects of Localization

Specialization of functions in the cerebral cortex is an indisputable fact, but we have yet to find an adequate interpretation of it. We have asked, Where are psychological functions localized in the brain? and have gained a meaningless answer. We should ask, How do specialized areas produce the details of behavior with which they are associated: what are the functional relationships between the different parts and how are they maintained?

Variable degrees of localization. If we survey the disturbances produced by brain injuries in a wide range of activities we are forced to the conclusion that the accuracy of localization or the degree of specialization varies greatly. Definitely limited defects appear in the visual and tactile and to a lesser extent in the motor fields after limited lesions to the calcarine, postcentral and precentral gyri. In other sensory spheres and in all the more elaborate organizations of behavior, there is little evidence for an equal fineness of differentiation. The visual cortex probably represents the maximum of specialization of small units. In the somesthetic field there is also a cortical projection, but less finely differentiated. In other functions we find every degree of specialization up to the limit where all parts of the cortex participate equally in the same function. The latter is apparently the condition for the maze habit in the rat. Destruction of any part of the cortex produces a partial loss of the habit and equal amounts of destruction produce equal amounts of loss, regardless of locus within the cortex.

An area which is highly specialized for one function may play a more generalized rôle in another. The habit of brightness discrimination in the rat is abolished by injury to the area striata, and by injury to no other part of the cortex. Here is a clear case of specialization. But the maze habit is abolished by destruction of this same area or of any other of equal size. Is it because the maze habit is dependent on vision? No, for blinding trained animals does not affect the habit, whereas destruction of the area striata abolishes the habit in animals which were blind during training. The deterioration does not differ in any observable way from that following lesions to other parts of the brain.

Except in projection areas there is no evidence for anatomical specialization within the general areas of localization. Thus in the aphasias showing predominantly a loss of naming ability or of memory for words there is not a selective effect upon memories for specific words, but a general difficulty of recall which embraces all words of a functional group.

The evidence on localization suggests that where the relations of stimuli in space are of importance for behavior, there exists in the cortex a spacial distribution of points corresponding to the sensory surfaces, but that for all other functions a similar spacial arrangement is lacking. In terms of the reflex theory such a spacial arrangement has little meaning, but in terms of the hypothesis to which I am leading it is of prime importance.

Functional levels of organization. Turning to the dynamics of localization, we find that loss or partial loss of functions may find expression in various ways. In some cases it seems that the fundamental organization for a function has been very little disturbed but that the ease of arousal is markedly altered. Thus in monkeys and probably in man, the severity of cerebral paralysis varies somewhat with the current emotional state, and during great excitement the power of voluntary movement may be temporarily restored. The paralysis seems to consist of a greater or lesser difficulty in initiating movements, whose organization is undisturbed.[12] The emotional facilitation can restore the capacity for movement. It clearly does not supply the specific integrations but only makes the final common paths more excitable or increases the intensity of activity in the integrating mechanisms. Here we have the energy for activity supplied, as it were, from an outside source. Some of the symptoms of cerebellar ataxia and the conditions described as pure motor aphasia present the same sort of picture. I have used the term energy here with reluctance, for the notion of nervous energy has led to many extravagant speculations, yet it seems impossible to deal with such phenomena except in terms of some general factor which may influence the ease of functioning of a system of activities without changing the specific integrations.

In another type of quantitative reduction in efficiency, the integrative mechanism itself seems affected, but without disintegration into elementary functions. In the rat, destruction of the occipital cortex abolishes the habit of brightness discrimination in the Yerkes box. Brightness vision is actually undisturbed, as can be demonstrated by other methods, but the association with the specific activities of the

12. M. Minkowski, Etude physiologique des circonvolutions rolandique et pariétal, *Arch. Suisse de neurol. et psychiat.*, 1917, 1,389-459.

training box is disturbed. The amount of practice necessary to reestablish the association is closely proportional to the extent of lesion. Here we are dealing with some function akin to the memory trace of Ebbinghaus. Just as the memory trace grows weaker with the passage of time, so it is weakened by cerebral injury. Recall may be impossible, yet a persisting trace of the former training may be demonstrated by the "savings method." The strength of the trace is determined by the quantity of tissue. The efficiency of performance is determined by the summated action of all parts of the area.

We cannot here use the accepted theories of summation or reinforcement, for these theories are based upon the phase relations of nerve impulses and we seem to be dealing with a continuous summation. It seems impossible to express the facts in other terms than simple variation in energy.

The relative fragility of functions. I have pointed out that the same area may be involved in quite diverse functions. These may be differently affected by lesions. Thus the habit of threading a complex maze is seriously disturbed by destruction of any part of the cortex, provided the lesion involves more than 15 per cent. The habit of a simpler maze is unaffected by lesions involving as much as 50 per cent of the cortex. We do not have an extensive series of tests with different mazes, but a comparison of Cameron's cases[13] with my own indicates that there is a definite relationship between the complexity of the maze habit and the minimal lesion which will produce a measurable disturbance of it.

Dr. Jacobsen has similar evidence from experiments with monkeys.[13a] Animals were trained to open a series of simple puzzle boxes and also a box in which the latches of the simple boxes were combined. After destruction of the frontal or parietal lobes, the ability to open the simple boxes was retained, but the same latches in combination could not be opened.

We have similar results on the limits of training for both the rat and monkey. Simple problems may be learned at almost normal rate after brain injuries; complex problems are learned slowly, if at all. Further, the greater the brain injury, the greater is the disproportion between the learning of simple and complex habits. In such cases the brain injuries seem to limit the complexity of organization which may be acquired, without disturbing the capacity for the simple acts which are mediated by the same areas.

The clinical literature presents many comparable cases. The aphasic patient may be able to understand and execute simple commands and yet be unable to grasp the same instructions when several are given at the same time. Head cites numerous instances of this limitation in complexity of organization.[14] In pattern vision, the stages through which the patient passes during recovery from cortical blindness form a series with

---

13. N. Cameron, Cerebral destruction in its relation to maze learning, *Psychol. Monog.*, 1928, *39*, (No. 1), 1-68.

13a. To be reported soon in *J. Comp. Neur.*

14. H. Head, Aphasia and kindred disorders of speech, New York, 1926.

respect to complexity. It seems probable that the great fragility of color vision and of the perception of depth is due to the high degree of organization required for these functions, rather than to their separate localization in the cortex.

Both the animal experiments and the clinical material point to the conclusion that a given area may function at different levels of complexity, and lesions may limit the complex functions without disturbing the simpler ones. Further, we cannot ascribe this limitation to the loss of some necessary elementary functions or to disturbances of nutrition or to shock, for it has been shown in some cases to be solely a function of the quantity of tissue. In this respect the limitation of complexity seems to accord with Spearman's view[15] that intelligence is a function of some undifferentiated nervous energy.

The Relational Framework in Cerebral Function

Let us turn now to another important aspect of cerebral function. A review of symptoms suggests that no logically derived element of behavior can be shown to have a definite localization; no single sensation, memory, or skilled movement is destroyed alone by any lesion. On the contrary the various parts of the functional areas seem equipotential for such elements, and either a whole constellation of them is affected by the lesion, or none at all. In these constellations of activities the grouping is determined, not by associative bonds, but by similarities of organization. Let me illustrate this point. In an hysterical amnesia we may find a loss of memory for all events associated with some emotional experience. The constellation is here determined by the grouping of habits. In organic amnesias the grouping is quite different. The speech most commonly retained in aphasia is that related to emotional expression, as was pointed out by Hughlings Jackson. Ejaculations, words of affirmation or negation, profanity, and words having a deep personal significance make up the residual vocabulary. The determining factor here seems to be the relation to emotional facilitation. Head's work shows other groupings, the loss of words involving the object-name relation, or of those concerned with the relations of space, time, and logical order.[16] The defects can in every case be related to ways of thinking about things, but not to loss of specific associations.

Many disturbances of vision show the same characteristics. An apparent word-blindness, for example, may be due, not to a loss of visual memory for the words, but to an inability to see the letters in a definite spacial arrangement.

Even in experiments with animals there are suggestions of similar conditions. We find rather frequently a picture which suggests loss of the general sense of direction, with retention of associations with the specific turns in the maze.

15. C. Spearman, The abilities of man, New York, 1927.

16. H. Head, op. cit.

I have not time to multiply examples, but I believe that there is ample evidence to show that the units of cerebral function are not single reactions, or conditioned reflexes as we have used the term in America, but are modes of organization. The cortex seems to provide a sort of generalized framework to which single reactions conform spontaneously, as the words fall into the grammatical form of a language.

The Mutual Influence of Cerebral Activities

Every statement concerning independence of functions must be made with certain reservations. The early students of aphasia, using the crudest of examining methods, were able to identify a great variety of types involving entirely different defects in the use of language. More careful study of the aphasias with finer methods of examination has failed to reveal such clear-cut distinctions, and today we have no accepted classification of the aphasias. Marie concluded that all types are the result of a common intellectual defect. Head denies that the intellectual defect is primary but admits that in all cases intellect suffers to the extent that it employs symbolism in thinking. All investigators seem now agreed that the disturbance of speech is only one symptom of a disorder which can be traced through the whole fabric of thought.

This is typical of recent developments in the clinical field. With improvement in methods of examination, the complete isolation of functions becomes more and more questionable, until it seems as though disturbance in any function implies lesser, but recognizable changes in every other.

This interdependence is not merely an expression of the subtraction of elementary functions by brain injuries. It seems to involve a genuine fusion of different processes, such as is shown in the observations of Poppelreuter[17] on the "totalizing function" of the visual area, and those of Gelb on the mutual influence of normal and hemiamblyopic areas. Poppelreuter reports the completion of simple figures in the cortically blind field, much like the normal filling in of the blind spot. Gelb[18] describes a case in which objects were judged smaller when seen in one half of the visual field than when seen in the other. When exposed so as to include both fields they were judged intermediate in size. Evidently in such cases as this there is fusion rather than summation of elements.

Self Regulation in Neural Function

This unity of action seems to be more deeply rooted than even the structural organization. In working with animals and with human

---

17. W. Poppelreuter, *op. cit.*

18. A. Gelb. u. K. Goldstein, Psychologische Analysen hirnpathologischer Fälle, Leipzig, 1920.

patients I have been more and more impressed by the absence of the chaotic behavior which we might expect from the extent and irregular form of the lesions. There may be great losses of sensory or of motor capacities, amnesias, emotional deterioration, dementia—but the residual behavior is still carried out in an orderly fashion. It may be grotesque, a caricature of normal behavior, but it is not unorganized. There are certain apparent exceptions to this rule, such as the loss of control of laughter in certain thalamic and lenticular cases, jargon in aphasia, the loss of spacial organization in some cases of visual agnosia, but even here the disturbances are not chaotic. Even dementia is not wholly unintelligent. It involves reduction in the range of comprehension, in the complexity of the relations which may be perceived, but what falls within the patient's range is still dealt with in an orderly and intelligible fashion.

There seems always to be a certain spontaneous compensation or adaptive reorganization. The most definite example of this sort is the observations of Fuchs[19] on pseudofovea. He finds that in cases of complete hemianopsia there is a shift of the center of fixation from the anatomical fovea to a variable point in the peripheral retina which acquires a greater visual acuity than can be demonstrated in the anatomical macula.

Such phenomena suggest that the nervous system is capable of a self-regulation which gives a coherent logical character to its functioning, no matter how its anatomical constituents may be disturbed. If we could slice off the cerebral cortex, turn it about, and replace it hind side before, getting a random connection of the severed fibers, what would be the consequences for behavior? From current theories we could predict only chaos. From the point of view which I am suggesting we might expect to find very little disturbance of behavior. Our subject might have to be reeducated, perhaps not even this, for we do not know the locus or character of habit organization—but in the course of his reeducation he might well show a normal capacity for apprehending relationships and for the rational manipulation of his world of experience.

This may sound like a plunge into mysticism, but an example from another field will show that such self-regulation is a normal property of living things. Wilson and later Child[20] have crushed the tissues of sponges and hydroids, sifted the cells through sieves of bolting cloth and observed their later behavior. The cells are at first suspended independently in the water, but may be brought into aggregates by settling or centrifuging. Starting as flat sheets, they round up into spherical masses and begin differentiation. Embryonic stages may be simulated and eventually adult individuals with characteristic structures, mouth, hy-

---

19. W. Fuchs, Untersuchungen über das Sehen der Hemianopiker und Hemiamblyopiker. In Gelb und Goldstein, *op. cit.*

20. C. M. Child, Axial development in aggregates of dissociated cells from Cory morpha palma, *Physiol. Zool.*, 1928, *1*, 419–461.

postome, tentacles, and stalk in normal relative positions are produced. In spite of the abnormal conditions to which it is subjected, the formless mass of cells assumes the structure characteristic of the species. Of course many abnormal forms appear, but even these follow the characteristic scheme of organization.

Many lines of evidence show a close parallelism between the facts of morphogenesis and those of the organization of the nervous system. In both we have given as the fundamental fact an organization which is relatively independent of the particular units of structure and dependent upon the relationships among the parts. In both there is a capacity for spontaneous readjustment after injury, so that the main lines of organization are restored; in both there is evidence that every part may influence every other; in both there is a possibility of dissociation and independent activity of some parts.

The Mechanisms of Organization

This brings us to the question of the mechanisms by which organization of behavior is brought about. There is, I think, nothing mysterious about the problem. There is no need to assume an emergence of new properties, a transcendent influence of the whole upon the parts, a subordination of substance to form, or the like; there is certainly no need to look for nonphysical agencies. We are dealing with a complex system in which there is an influence of every part upon every other, with all degrees of intimacy in the relations and various degrees of dominance and subordination. Our problem is to discover the means by which these influences are exerted.

We have seen that the notion of isolated reflex paths, exerting mutual inhibition and facilitation and conducting nervous impulses over pathways determined by the specific resistance of synapses, is not only inadequate to account for the simplest facts of behavior, but is also opposed by direct neurological evidence. The greatest progress in neurophysiology within the past decade has been made in the study of conduction in peripheral nerves, but the results have as yet little bearing upon the problems of central organization. At most they offer a basis for speculation concerning the behavior of nerve impulses at intercellular junctions, and recent negative results upon conduction with decrement throw some doubt upon the value of these speculations. Students of nerve conduction have taken for granted the doctrine of anatomical specialization, and their work has not been developed, in the direction of our problems. Lapicque[21] has recently pointed out some of the difficulties of the anatomical hypothesis and has suggested the substitu-

---

21. L. Lapicque, The chronaxic switching in the nervous system, *Science*, 1929, *70*, 151–154.

tion of temporal for spacial factors in organization, but the study of chronaxie is not far enough advanced for application to the problems of psychology. The laws of conduction in nerve fibers thus far revealed are not alone sufficient for an understanding of integration. The nervous unit of organization in behavior is not the reflex arc, but the mechanism, whatever be its nature, by which a reaction to a ratio of excitations is brought about. We have as yet no direct evidence upon this problem, but the similarities of the problems of nervous function and of growth should direct our interest toward the processes which have been found important in the control of structural development.

The work of many students of experimental embryology has shown the importance of the restriction of gaseous interchange, of gradients in chemical diffusion, metabolic activity or rate of growth, the influences of chemical and electrical polarization and of the flow of action currents in determining the course of development. During its first differentiation the nervous system is subject to the same influences as any other developing tissue and the mechanisms of diffusion and of polarization play an important rôle in the determination of its structures and inherent organization. It would be strange if, with the completion of growth, these factors should no longer be important in the life of the cells. Rather, we should expect the neurons to be continuously modified by the same influences. The structure of the nervous system is such as to allow of this. The interconnections of distant parts are well insulated, where correlated functions without influence of intermediate parts is required, but within the gray matter the cell bodies and processes are not so protected. They are directly exposed in a liquid medium capable of conducting diffuse chemical and electrical changes which may readily influence the excitability of the neurons. The arrangement of the gray matter in thin sheets and the projection of the receptor and motor surfaces upon these sheets may have a real functional significance. Child[22] has shown that distance of separation favors the development of independently polarized systems, and the arrangement of cell bodies in the gray matter offers the optimal condition for this and for the development of systems in which the spacial arrangement of stresses can be effective. Although the distant intercommunications of cells may be solely through the conduction of nerve impulses, the more immediate coordinations within the gray matter may depend upon relative amounts of excitation, the spacial arrangement of excited points, stress patterns resulting from the total mass of excitation, which may be more important for behavior than the connections of individual cells. It is here, I believe, that we must look for the next significant development in our knowledge of the functions of the brain.

Cerebral organization can be described only in terms of relative masses and spacial arrangements of gross parts, of equilibrium among

---

22. C. M. Child, Studies on the axial gradients in Corymorpha palma. iii, *Biologia Generalis*, 1926, 2, 771–798.

the parts, of direction and steepness of gradients, and of the sensitiza-
tion of final common paths to patterns of excitation. And the organization must be conceived as a sort of relational framework into which all
sorts of specific reactions may fit spontaneously, as the cells of the polyp
fit into the general scheme of development.

Such notions are speculative and vague, but we seem to have no
choice but to be vague or to be wrong, and I believe that a confession of
ignorance is more hopeful for progress than a false assumption of
knowledge.

Conclusion

I have devoted my time to-night to problems which are not strictly
psychological, yet I believe that these problems are of real significance
for the progress of psychology. Certainly the development of the science
up to the present has been strongly influenced by neurological theory.
The frantic search for sources of motivation and of emotion in visceral
activity, though initiated by introspective analysis, has been supported
by the faith that the nervous system is only a conductor having no
sources of energy within itself. Our preoccupation with analysis of
learning by trial and error, the denial of association by similarity, the
belief that transfer of training can occur only through the training of
common synapses—these are a result of the belief that learning is simply
a linking together of elementary reflexes. The doctrine that the intelligent
solution of problems results only through random activity and selection,
and that intelligence itself is an algebraic sum of multitudinous capacities, is largely a deduction from the reflex theory.

I shall not pretend to evaluate such doctrines from the standpoint of
psychological evidence. They may or may not be true, but their truth
must be demonstrated by experiment and cannot be assumed on a
background of questionable neurology. Psychology is today a more
fundamental science than neurophysiology. By this I mean that the latter
offers few principles from which we may predict or define the normal
organization of behavior, whereas the study of psychological processes
furnishes a mass of factual material to which the laws of nervous action
in behavior must conform.

The facts of both psychology and neurology show a degree of
plasticity, of organization, and of adaptation in behavior which is far
beyond any present possibility of explanation. For immediate progress it
is not very important that we should have a correct theory of brain
activity, but it is essential that we shall not be handicapped by a false
one.

The value of theories in science today depends chiefly upon their
adequacy as a classification of unsolved problems, or rather as a
grouping of phenomena which present similar problems. Behaviorism

has offered one such classification, emphasizing the similarity of psychological and biological problems. Gestalt psychology has stressed a
different aspect and reached a different grouping; purposive psychology
still another. The facts of cerebral physiology are so varied, so diverse, as to suggest that for some of them each theory is true, for all of
them every theory is false.

Reprinted with permission
from *Psychological Review*,
1934, *41*, 1–32.

Chapter 16

The Vectors
of Mind

L. L. Thurstone

The University of Chicago

Under the title of this address, "The Vectors of Mind," I shall discuss one of the oldest of psychological problems with the aid of some new analytical methods. I am referring to the old problem of classifying the temperaments and personality types and the more recent problem of isolating the different mental abilities.

Until very recently the only attempt to solve this problem in a quantitative way seems to have been the work of Professor Spearman and his students. Spearman has formulated methods for dealing with the simplest case, in which all of the variables that enter into a particular study can be regarded as having only one factor in common. The factor theory that I shall describe starts without this limitation, in that I shall make no restriction as to the number of factors that are involved in any particular problem. The resulting factor theorems are quite different in form and in their underlying assumptions, but it is of interest to discover that they are consistent with Spearman's factor theory, which turns out to be a special case of the present general factor theory.

Address of the president before the American Psychological Association, Chicago meeting, September, 1933.

In this paper I shall first review the single-factor theory of Spearman. Then I shall describe a general factor theory. Those who have only a casual interest in the theoretical aspects of this problem will be more interested perhaps in the applications of the new factor theory to a number of psychological problems. These psychological applications will constitute the major part of this paper.

It is thirty years ago that Spearman introduced his single-factor method and the hypothesis that intelligence is a central and general factor among the mental abilities. The literature on this subject of factor analysis has tended temporarily to obscure his contribution, because the controversies about it have frequently been staged about rather trivial or even irrelevant matters. Professor Spearman deserves much credit for initiating the factor problem and for his significant contribution toward its solution, even though his formulation is inadequate for the multi-dimensionality of the mental abilities.

Spearman's theory has been called a two-factor method or theory. The two factors involved in it are, first, a general factor common to all of the tests or variables, and second, a factor that is specific for each test or variable. It is less ambiguous to refer to this method as a single-factor method, because it deals with only one common or general factor. If there are five tests with a single common factor and a specific for each test, then the method involves the assumption of one common and five specific factors, or six factors in all. We shall refer to his method less ambiguously as a single-factor method.

We must distinguish between Spearman's method of analyzing the intercorrelations of a set of variables for a single common factor and his theory that intelligence is such a common factor which he calls "g". If we start with a given table of intercorrelations it is possible by Spearman's method, and also by other methods, to investigate whether the given coefficients *can* be described in terms of a single common factor plus specifics and chance errors. If the answer is in the affirmative, then we *can* describe the correlations as the effect of (1) a common factor, (2) a factor specific to each test, and (3) chance errors. In factor theory, the last two are combined because they are both unique to each test. Hence the analysis yields a summation of a common factor and a factor unique to each test. About this aspect of the single-factor method there should be no debate, because it is straight and simple logic.

But there can be debate as to whether we should describe the tests by a single factor even though one factor is sufficient. It is in a sense an epistemological issue. Even though a set of intercorrelations *can* be described in terms of a single factor, it is possible, if you like, to describe the same correlations in terms of two or three or ten or any number of factors.

The situation is analogous to a similar problem in physical science. If a particle moves, we designate the movement by an arrow-head, a vector, in the direction of motion, but if it suits our convenience we put two arrowheads or more so that the observed motion may be expressed in terms that we have already been thinking about, such as the x, y, and

z axes. Whether an observed acceleration is to be described in terms of one force, or two forces, or three forces, that are parallel to the x, y, and z axes, is entirely a matter of convenience for us. In exactly the same manner we may postulate two or more factors in a correlation problem instead of one, even when one factor would be sufficient. To ask whether there "really" are several factors when one is sufficient, is as indeterminate as to ask how many accelerations there "really" are that cause a particle to move. If the situation is such that one factor is not adequate while two factors would be adequate, then we may think of two factors, but we may state the problem in terms of more than two factors if our habits or the immediate context makes that more convenient.

Spearman believes that intelligence can be thought of as a factor that is common to all the activities that are usually called intelligent. The best evidence for a conspicuous and central intellective factor is that if you make a list of stunts, as varied as you please, which all satisfy the common sense criterion that the subjects must be smart, clever, intelligent, to do the stunts well, and that good performance does not depend primarily upon muscular strength or skill or upon other non-intellectual powers, then the inter-stunt correlations will all be positive. It is quite difficult to find a pair of stunts, both of which call for what would be called intelligence, as judged by common sense, which have a negative correlation. This is really all that is necessary to prove that what is generally called intelligence can be regarded as a factor that is conspicuously common to a very wide variety of activities. Spearman's hypothesis, that it is some sort of energy, is not crucial to the hypothesis that it is a common factor in intellectual activities.

There is a frequently discussed difficulty about which more has been written than necessary. It has been customary to postulate a single common factor (Spearman's "g") and to make the additional but unnecessary assumption that there must be nothing else that is common to any pair of tests. Then the tetrad criterion is applied and it usually happens that a pair of tests in the battery has something else in common besides the most conspicuous single common factor. For example, two of the tests may have in common the ability to write fast, facility with geometrical figures, or a large vocabulary. Then the tetrad criterion is not satisfied and the conclusion is usually one of two kinds, depending on which side of the fence the investigator is on. If the investigator is out to prove "g," then he concludes that the tests are bad becasue it is supposed to be bad to have tests that measure more than one factor! If the investigator is out to disprove "g," then he shows that the tetrads do not vanish and that therefore there is no "g." Neither conclusion is correct. The correct conclusion is that more than one general factor must be postulated in order to account for the intercorrelations, and that one of these general factors may still be what we should call intelligence. But a technique for multiple factor analysis has not been available and consequently we have been stumbling around with "group factors" as the trouble-making factors have been called. A group factor is one that is common to two or more of the tests but not to all of them. I use the term common factor for all factors that extend to two or more of the variables. We see therefore that Spearman's criterion, limited as it is to a single common factor, is not adequate for proving or disproving his own hypothesis that there is a conspicuous factor that is common to all intelligence tests. If his criterion gives a negative answer it simply means that the correlations require more than one common factor. We do not need any factor methods at all to prove that a common factor of intelligence is a legitimate postulate. It is proved by the fact that all intelligence tests are positively correlated.

There is only one limited problem for which Spearman's method is adequate, namely, the question whether a single factor is sufficient to account for the intercorrelations of a set of tests. The usual answer is negative. His criterion that the tetrads shall vanish is rarely satisfied in practice. One might wonder then why it is that numerous examples have been compiled in which the tetrad criterion is satisfied. The reason is simply this—that in order to satisfy the criterion, the tests must be carefully selected so as to have only one thing in common. Another way by which the criterion is satisfied is to throw out of the battery those tests which do not agree with the criterion. The remaining set will then satisfy it. The reason for these difficulties is that Spearman's tetrad difference criterion demands more than his own hypothesis requires. His hypothesis does not state that there shall be only one common factor or ability. He himself deals with many factors. But his tetrad difference criterion requires that there shall be only one common factor.

Now it happens that one can readily put together several batteries of tests such that *within each battery* the criterion is satisfied and therefore we have a common factor "g" in each battery. But if we take a few tests from each of these batteries and put together a new composite, then the criterion is not satisfied and we then require more than one factor. We are then faced with the ambiguity that we have several batteries of tests each with its own single common factor. Which of these common factors shall we call the general one? Which is it that we should call "g"? Spearman's answer is that we should use a set of perceptual tests as a reference and that if we are dealing with that particular common factor, then we should call it general but that if we are dealing with one of the other common factors, then we should call it a special ability, a group factor, a sub-factor of some sort. It would be more logical to assign a letter or a name to each of these mental abilities and to treat them as related dependent abilities. If we choose one of them, such as facility in dealing with perceptual relations, as an axis of reference (Spearman's "g"), then it should be frankly acknowledged that the choice is statistically arbitrary, for we could equally well start with verbal ability or with arithmetical ability as an axis of reference. The choice of the perceptual axis of reference might be made from purely psychological considerations, but it would not rest on statistical evidence.

The multi-dimensionality of mind must be recognized before we can make progress toward the isolation and description of separate abilities. It remains a fact, however, that since all mental tests are positively correlated, it is possible to describe the intercorrelations in terms of several factors in such a manner that one of the factors will be conspicuous in comparison with the others. But the exact definition of this factor varies from one set of tests to another. If it is this factor that Spearman implies in his theory of intelligence, then his criterion is entirely inadequate to define it, because the tetrad criterion merely tells us whether or not any given set of intercorrelations can be described in terms of one and only one common factor.

Let us start with the assumption that there may be several independent or dependent mental abilities, and let it be a question of fact for each study how many factors are needed to account for the observed intercorrelations.[1] We also make the assumption that the contributions of several independent factors are summative in the individual's performance on each one of the psychological tests. If we do not make this assumption, the solution seems well-nigh hopeless, and it is an assumption that is either explicit or implicit in all attempts to deal with this problem.

We may start our analysis of the generalized factor problem by considering the many hundreds of adjectives that are in current use for describing personalities and temperaments. We have made such a list. Even after removing the synonyms we still had several hundred adjectives. It is obvious at the start that all these traits are not independent. For example, people who are said to be congenial are also quite likely to be called friendly, or courteous, or generous, even though we do not admit that these words are exactly synonymous. It looks as though we were dealing with a large number of dependent traits.

The traditional methods of dealing with these psychological complexities have been speculative, bibliographical, or merely literary in character. The problem has been to find a few categories, called personality types or temperaments, in terms of which a longer list of traits might be described. Psychological inquiry has not yet succeeded in arriving at a list of fundamental categories for the description of personality. We are still arguing whether extraversion and introversion are scientific entities or simply artifacts, and whether it is legitimate even to look for any personality types at all.

In the generalized factor method we have one of the possible ways in which a set of categories for the scientific study of personality and temperament may be established on experimental grounds as distinguished from literary verbosity about this subject. It is our belief that the problem can be approached in several rational and quantitative ways and that they must agree eventually before we have a satisfactory foundation for the scientific description of personality.

The problem has geometrical analogies that we shall make use of. If we have a set of n points, defined by r coordinates for each point, we may discover that they are dependent in that some of these points can be

---

1. This point of view is represented by the work of T. L. Kelley as distinguished from the work of Spearman and his students.

described linearly in terms of the coordinates of the rest of the points. If the adjectives were represented by these points, it is as though we were to describe most of them in terms of a limited number of adjectives. But such a solution is not unique, because if we have ten points in space of three dimensions, then it is possible, in general, to describe any seven of the points in terms of the remaining three. It is just so with the personality traits, in that a unique solution is not given without additional criteria.

But before demanding this sort of reduction it would be of great psychological interest to know *how many* temperaments or personality types we must postulate in order to account for the differentiable traits that we use in describing people. Again the geometrical analogy is useful. If we have a table of three coordinates for each one of ten points and if that matrix has the rank 2, then we know that all ten points lie in a plane and consequently they can all be described by two coordinates in that plane instead of by three. The application of this analogy would be the description of ten traits in terms of two independent traits which would then become psychological categories or fundamental types. They would constitute the frame of reference in terms of which the other traits would be described and in terms of which interrelations could be stated.

But since we have no given frame of reference to begin with, we do not have the coordinates of the points that might represent the adjectives. We therefore let each adjective represent its own coordinate axis, so that with *n* traits we shall have as many axes. These coordinate axes will be oblique, since the traits are known to be at least not all independent. The projection of any one of these traits *A* on the oblique axis through another trait *B* is the cosine of their central angle, but this is also the correlation between the two traits *A* and *B*. The correlations can be ascertained by experiment, and then our problem becomes that of finding the smallest number of orthogonal coordinate axes in terms of which we can describe all of the traits whose intercorrelations are known.

The actual data that we must handle are subject to chance errors. It is therefore profitable to see how the geometrical manner of thinking about this problem is affected by the chance errors. It can be shown that each test may be thought of as a vector in space of as many dimensions as there are independent mental factors. If the test is perfect, then it is represented geometrically by a unit vector. If the test has a reliability less than unity, then the length of the vector is reduced. In fact, the length of a test vector in the common factor space is the square root of its reliability. If the test has zero reliability, then it determines nothing and this fact has its geometrical correspondence in that the test vector is then of zero length so that it determines no direction at all in the space of mental abilities.

The obtained correlation between two tests is the scalar product of the two test vectors. If the two tests are perfect, then their scalars are both unity so that the true correlation between the two tests is the cosine of the angular separation between the two vectors.

	1	2	3
A	a_1	a_2	a_3
B	b_1	b_2	b_3
C	c_1	c_2	c_3
D	d_1	d_2	d_3
E	e_1	e_2	e_3
F	f_1	f_2	f_3
G	g_1	g_2	g_3

A	B	C	D	E	F	G
a_1	b_1	c_1	d_1	e_1	f_1	g_1
a_2	b_2	c_2	d_2	e_2	f_2	g_2
a_3	b_3	c_3	d_3	e_3	f_3	g_3

	A	B	C	D	E	F	G
A		r_{ab}	r_{ac}	r_{ad}	r_{ae}	r_{af}	r_{ag}
B	r_{ab}		r_{bc}	r_{bd}	r_{be}	r_{bf}	r_{bg}
C	r_{ac}	r_{bc}		r_{cd}	r_{ce}	r_{cf}	r_{cg}
D	r_{ad}	r_{bd}	r_{cd}		r_{de}	r_{df}	r_{dg}
E	r_{ae}	r_{be}	r_{ce}	r_{de}		r_{ef}	r_{eg}
F	r_{af}	r_{bf}	r_{cf}	r_{df}	r_{ef}		r_{fg}
G	r_{ag}	r_{bg}	r_{cg}	r_{dg}	r_{eg}	r_{fg}	

Figure 1. Factorial matrix A. Transpose of factorial matrix A'. Correlational matrix R. Factor theorem: $AA' = R$. Example: $r_{ab} = a_1b_1 + a_2b_2 + \cdots + a_rb_r$.

We shall consider next two of the fundamental theorems in a generalized theory of factors.[2] Let us take a table of seven variables as an example. In Figure 1 we have shown such a table toward the right side of the diagram. We may call it the correlational matrix. In a table of this kind we show the correlation of each test with every other test. For example, the correlation between the two tests A and B is indicated in the customary cell.

In the diagonal cells of a table of intercorrelations we are accustomed to record the reliabilities, but that is incorrect in factor theory unless the tests have been so chosen that they contain no specific factors. It is necessary for us to make a distinction between that part of the variance of a test which is attributable to the common factors and that part of the variance which is unique for each test. The part which is unique for each test may again be thought of as due to two different sources, namely, the chance errors in the test and the ability which is specific for the test. The reliability of a test is that part of the total variance which is due to the common factors as well as to the specific factor. It differs from unity only by that part of the variance which is due to chance errors. We need in factor theory another term to indicate that part of the total variance which is attributable only to the common factors and which eliminates not only the variance of chance errors but also the specific variance. We have used the term *communality* to indicate that part of the total variance of each test which is attributable to the common factors. It is always less than the reliability unless a specific factor is absent, in which case the communality becomes identical with the reliability. It is these communalities that should be recorded in the diagonal cells, but they are the unknowns to be discovered by the factorial analysis.

At the extreme left of the diagram we have a table of factor loadings. Here the seven tests are listed vertically and there are as many columns

---

2. The present generalized factor theory has been described in two lithographed pamphlets by the writer. These are: "The theory of multiple factors," The University of Chicago Bookstore, Chicago, Ill., and "A simplified multiple factor method," The University of Chicago Bookstore.

as there are factors. In the present example we have assumed three factors, so that we have three columns and seven rows. Let us suppose that the first factor represents verbal ability and that the second factor represents arithmetical ability. These particular abilities are not independent, but we may ignore that for the moment. Then the entry a_1 indicates the extent to which the test A calls for verbal ability and the entry a_2 indicates the extent to which it calls for arithmetical ability. Since we have assumed three factors in this diagram we have three factor loadings for each test. A table in which the factor loadings are shown for each test we have called a *factorial matrix*, while the square table containing the intercorrelations we have called a *correlational matrix*.

The experimental observations give us the correlational matrix, so that it may be regarded as known. The object of a factorial analysis is to find a factorial matrix which corresponds to the given intercorrelations. There is a rather simple theoretical relation between the given correlational matrix and the factorial matrix. This relation constitutes the fundamental theorem of the present factor theory. It is illustrated by an example under the correlation table and it can also be stated in very condensed form by matrix notation in that *the factorial matrix multiplied by its transpose reproduces the correlational matrix* within the observational errors of the given correlation coefficients.

When we want to make an analysis of a table of intercorrelations, the first thing we want to know is how many independent common factors we must postulate in order to account for the given correlation coefficients. One of our fundamental theorems states that *the smallest number of independent common factors that will account exactly for the given correlation coefficients is the rank of the correlational matrix*. Although this theorem is of fundamental significance it is not possible to apply it in its theoretical form, because of the fact that the given coefficients are subject to experimental errors and the rank is therefore in general equal to the number of tests. It is always possible to account for a table of intercorrelations by postulating as many abilities as there are tests, but that is simply a matter of arithmetical drudgery and nothing is thereby accomplished. The only situation which is of scientific and psychological interest is that in which a table of intercorrelations can be accounted for by a relatively small number of factors compared with the number of tests.

There is no conflict between the present multiple factor methods and the tetrad difference method. When a single factor is sufficient to account for the given coefficients, then the rank of the correlational matrix must be 1, but the necessary and sufficient condition for this is that all of the second order minors shall vanish. Now if you expand the second order minors in a table of correlation coefficients you find that you are in fact writing the tetrads. Hence the tetrad difference method is a special case of the present multiple factor theorem.

It would be possible to extend the tetrad difference method by writing the expansions of the minors of higher order and in that manner to write formulae for any number of factors which correspond to the

TABLE 1   *List of Adjectives Used for Factor Study*

persevering	religious	haughty	eccentric
crafty	impetuous	submissive	ingenious
awkward	fickle	suspicious	accommodating
self-important	domineering	courageous	tactful
determined	frank	stern	careless
friendly	pessimistic	headstrong	tidy
patient	spiteful	jealous	precise
sarcastic	quiet	generous	systematic
congenial	disagreeable	dependable	cheerful
hard-working	reserved	faithful	conscientious
stubborn	refined	reserved	grasping
capable	unnatural	solemn	satisfied
tolerant	bashful	earnest	cynical
calm	self-reliant	talented	courteous
peevish	broad-minded	frivolous	unconventional
			quick-tempered

tetrads for the special case when one factor is sufficient. Such a procedure is unnecessarily clumsy. In fact, there should be no excuse for ever computing any more tetrads. Several better methods are available which give much more information with only a fraction of the labor that is required in the computation of tetrads.

We return now to the multiple factor analysis of personality. In Table 1 we have a list of sixty adjectives that are in common use for describing people. These adjectives together with their synonyms were given to each of 1300 raters. Each rater was asked to think of a person whom he knew well and to underline every adjective that he might use in a conversational description of that person. Since it was not necessary for the rater to reveal the name of the person he was rating it is our belief that the ratings were relatively free from the inhibitions that are usually characteristic of such a task. With 1300 such schedules we determined the tetrachoric correlation coefficient for every possible pair of traits. Since there were sixty adjectives in the list we had to determine 1770 tetrachoric coefficients. For this purpose we developed a set of computing diagrams which enable one to ascertain the tetrachoric coefficients with correct sign by inspection.[3] Each coefficient can be ascertained in a couple of minutes by these computing diagrams.

The table of coefficients for the sixty personality traits was then analyzed by means of multiple factor methods[4] and we found that five factors are sufficient to account for the coefficients. We reproduce in Figure 2 the distribution of discrepancies between the original tetrachoric coefficients and the corresponding coefficients that were calcu-

---

3. "Computing diagrams for the tetrachoric correlation coefficient," The University of Chicago Bookstore.
4. "A simplified multiple factor method," Univ. Chicago Bookstore, 1933.

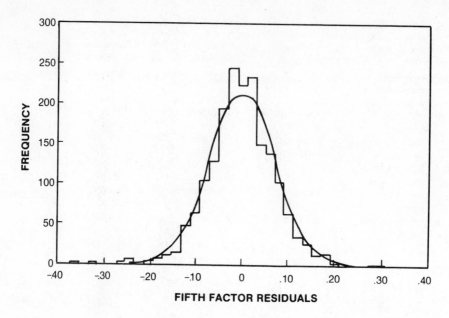

Figure 2. Frequency distribution of fifth factor residuals in a study of sixty personality traits.

lated by means of the five factors. It has a standard deviation of .069. The average standard error of thirty tetrachoric coefficients chosen at random in this table is .052.

It is of considerable psychological interest to know that the whole list of sixty adjectives can be accounted for by postulating only five independent common factors. It was of course to be expected that all of the sixty adjectives would not be independent, but we did not foresee that the list could be accounted for by as few as five factors. This fact leads us to surmise that the scientific description of personality may not be quite so hopelessly complex as it is sometimes thought to be.

Next comes the natural question as to just what these five factors are, in terms of which the intercorrelations of sixty personality traits may be described. Each of the adjectives can be thought of as a point in space of five dimensions and the five coordinates of each point represent the five factor components of each adjective.

We shall consider a three-dimensional example in order to illustrate the nature of the indeterminacy that is here involved (Figure 3). Let us suppose that three factors are sufficient to account for a list of traits. Then each trait can be thought of as a point in space of three dimensions. In fact, each trait can be represented as a point on the surface of a ball. If two traits A and B tend to coexist, the two points will be close together on the surface of the ball. If they are mutually exclusive, so that when one is present the other is always absent and vice versa, then the two traits are represented by two points that are diametrically opposite on the surface of the ball such as A and D. If the two traits are independent

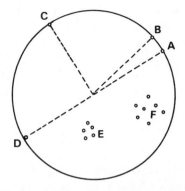

Figure 3. Correlation *AB* is high and positive. Correlation *AC* is zero. Correlation *AD* is −1. *E* and *F* represent constellations. Location of the orthogonal axes is arbitrary.

and uncorrelated, such as *A* and *C*, then they will be displaced from each other in the same way as the north pole and a point on the equator, namely by ninety degrees.

Now suppose that the traits have been allocated to points on the surface of the sphere in such a manner that the correlation for each pair of traits agrees closely with the cosine of the central angle between the corresponding points on the surface of the sphere. Then we want to describe each of these traits in terms of its coordinates, but we should first have to decide where to locate at least two of the three coordinate axes. This is an arbitrary matter, because the internal relations between the points, that is, the intercorrelations of the traits, remain exactly the same no matter where in the sphere we locate the coordinate axes. That is, when the points have been assigned on the surface of the ball, we have not thereby located the respective coordinate axes. It is possible to determine uniquely how many independent common factors are required to account for the intercorrelations without thereby determining just what the factors are. We may therefore use any arbitrarily chosen set of orthogonal axes.

It is psychologically more illuminating to investigate constellations of the traits. In the factor analysis of the adjectives, constellations of traits reveal themselves in that the points which represent some of the traits lie close together in a cluster on the surface of a five-dimensional sphere. One or two examples will illustrate this type of analysis with respect to the personality traits. We find, for example, that the following traits lie close together in a cluster, namely, *friendly, congenial, broad-minded, generous,* and *cheerful*. It would seem, therefore, that as far as the five basic factors are concerned, whatever be their nature, these several traits are very much alike as far as can be determined by the way in which we actually use these adjectives in describing people.

Another such cluster of adjectives which are used as though they signified the same fundamental trait are the adjectives *patient, calm, faithful,* and *earnest*. They cling close together in the factorial analysis. Another small group is found in the three traits *persevering, hard-working,* and *systematic*, which lie close together. Still another one is the cluster of traits *capable, frank, self-reliant,* and *courageous*.

It is of psychological interest to note that the largest constellation of traits consists of a list of derogatory adjectives. Such a cluster is the following: *self-important, sarcastic, haughty, grasping, cynical, quick-tempered,* and several other derogatory traits that lie close by. It clearly indicates that if you describe a man by some derogatory adjective you are quite likely to call him by many other bad names as well. This lack of objectivity in the description of the people we dislike is not an altogether unknown characteristic of human nature.

The schedules used in this study contained 120 adjectives, since every one of the 60 adjectives in the principal list was represented also by a synonym. This enabled us to ascertain the correlation between each pair of synonyms and we used it as an index of the consistency with which the trait was judged. Let us consider this correlation to be an estimate of the reliability of the judgments of the trait. By factor analysis we know the communality of each trait. It is that part of its total variance which it has in common with the other adjectives, namely, the five common factors. The difference between these two variances is the specificity. It shows the magnitude of the specific factor in each adjective.

We have listed these differences for each adjective in Table 2 and they yield some psychologically interesting facts. We find, for example, one adjective which has a surprisingly high specificity of nearly .60, and we want to know, of course, what kind of trait it represents. We find that it is the adjective *talented*. It seems reasonable to guess that this adjective refers largely to the intellectual abilities which are not represented by this list. When this study is repeated, we shall include several adjectives of this type, so that intelligence may be investigated as a vector in relation to the personality traits.

Another item with a high specificity is the adjective *awkward.* This means that the trait *awkward* has something about it which is unique in our list of sixty and which is not represented by the five common factors. This trait is probably ease and facility in body movement, which is certainly not represented in the rest of the sixty traits. When this study is repeated we may or we may not include several adjectives of this type, depending on whether we want to include this additional factor in a study of personality. Another adjective with high specificity is *religious* and the explanation is undoubtedly along the same lines because this is the only adjective in the list that refers to any kind of religiousness.

Studies of this sort should be repeated until every important trait is represented by several adjectives. The analysis should yield as many independent factors as may be required. When the factorial analysis is complete, the specifics should all vanish or they should be relatively small. Then the communalities and the reliabilities will have nearly the same value. The constellations to be found in such an analysis will constitute the fundamental categories in terms of which a scientific description of personality may be attained.

There is no necessary relation between the number of factors and the number of constellations. A system of tests might be found which can be

TABLE 2

Specificity	Adjective	Specificity	Adjective
.18	persevering	.05	broad-minded
.40	crafty	.00	haughty
.46	awkward	.07	submissive
.10	self-important	.17	suspicious
.16	determined	.27	courageous
.14	friendly	.01	stern
.02	patient	.01	headstrong
.16	sarcastic	.25	jealous
.16	congenial	.16	generous
.34	hard-working	.17	dependable
.34	stubborn	.13	faithful
.16	capable	.00	solemn
.04	tolerant	.04	earnest
.27	calm	.59	talented
.09	peevish	.39	eccentric
.58	religious	.23	ingenious
.36	impetuous	.30	accommodating
.07	fickle	.26	tactful
.19	domineering	.34	tidy
.40	frank	.22	precise
.22	pessimistic	.22	systematic
.04	spiteful	.03	cheerful
.12	quiet	.11	conscientious
.19	disagreeable	.30	grasping
.08	reserved	.68	satisfied
.27	refined	.29	cynical
.18	unnatural	.12	courteous
.48	bashful	.14	unconventional
.14	self-reliant	.41	quick-tempered

accounted for by several factors even though it contains no constellations. Fortunately the constellations can be isolated in a very simple manner when the coefficients have been corrected for attenuation.

I turn next to a factor study of the insanities. I have used a very elaborate set of data which Dr. Thomas Verner Moore of Washington, D.C., collected and investigated by other factor methods. Dr. Moore worked with a list of forty-eight symptoms, thirty-seven of which are listed in Table 3. He recorded the presence–absence, or a rating or test measure of each symptom for each of several hundred patients. With these records it was possible to ascertain to what extent any two symptoms tend to coexist in the same patient. For example, the extent to which the two symptoms *excited* and *destructive* tend to coexist in the same patient is indicated by the tetrachoric correlation of +.71. The records were sufficiently complete so that we could prepare a table of intercorrelations of the tetrachoric form for thirty-seven symptoms or 666 coefficients. These computations were also made by the computing diagrams.

The multiple factor method was then applied to the table of 666

TABLE 3   *Multiple Factor Analysis of Psychotic Symptoms*

Code No.	Psychotic Symptom	Code No.	Psychotic Symptom
1.	Alcoholism of Parents	28.	Memory Ratio
2.	Anxious	29.	Mutism
3.	Attacks, Number of Previous	30.	Negativism
6.	Delusions, Bizarre	31.	Neurasthenia
9.	Depression	32.	Perception Defect
10.	Destructive	33.	Reasoning
11.	Disorientation in Space	34.	Refusal of Food
13.	Euphoria	35.	Retardation
14.	Excited	36.	Sensibilities, Loss of Finer
15.	Fallacies, Autistic	37.	Shut In
16.	Fallacies, Logical	38.	Stereotypism of Actions
17.	Giggling	39.	Stereotypism of Any Kind
18.	Hallucinations, Auditory	40.	Stereotypism of Attitudes
19.	Hallucinations, Others	41.	Stereotypism of Words
23.	Homicidal	42.	Suicidal
24.	Insane Relatives	43.	Tantrums
25.	Insight, Absence of	44.	Tearful
26.	Irritable	45.	Voices, Speaking to
27.	Memory, Total Defect		

References: (1) Moore, T. V., *Amer. J. Psychiat.*, 1930, *9*, 719–738. (2) Moore, T. V., Series of Research Publications of *Ass'n for Research in Nervous and Mental Diseases*, Vol. *9*, 324–339; Baltimore, Williams and Wilkins.

coefficients and we found that five factors are sufficient to account for the correlations, with residuals small enough so that they can be ignored. The communalities were then computed for each one of the symptoms and we found that about ten of the symptoms do not contain enough in common with the other symptoms to warrant their retention in a factor study. In other words, about ten of the symptoms are either so specific in character or so unreliable as to estimates that they do not yield significant correlations with the several other symptoms. This left twenty-six symptoms which are more or less related and for which the factorial clusters of symptoms could be profitably investigated.

In Table 4 we have listed the psychotic symptoms which lie in each of several constellations. We find, for example, that the following symptoms are functionally closely related, namely, *mutism, negativism, being shut-in, stereotypism of action, stereotypism of attitudes, stereotypism of words,* and *giggling.* These seven traits are evidently related in that they tend to be found in the same patients and we recognize the list as descriptive of the catatonic group. Another constellation consists in the presence of *logical fallacies, defect in memory, defect in perception,* and *defect in reasoning.* This is a constellation of symptoms that indicates a derangement of the cognitive functions of the patient as contrasted with derangements of the affective aspects of his mentality. Another group of three symptoms that lie close together in the factorial analysis consists of the traits *destructive, irritable,* and *having tantrums.* A fourth cluster

TABLE 4   *Psychotic Symptoms*

Cluster A, Catatonic Group	*Cluster B, Cognitive Group*
Mutism	Logical fallacies
Negativism	Total memory defect
Shut in	Perception defect
Stereotypism of action	Reasoning
Stereotypism of attitudes	Disorientation in space
Stereotypism of words	
Giggling	

Cluster C, Manic Group	*Cluster D, Hallucinatory Group*
Destructive	Bizarre delusions
Excited	Auditory hallucinations
Irritable	Other hallucinations
Tantrums	Speaking to voices

Cluster E, Depression
Anxious
Depression
Tearful
Retardation in movement

contains the symptoms *delusions,* auditory and other types of *hallucinations,* and *speaking to voices.* A fifth group contains the symptoms *anxious, depressed,* and *tearful.*

It is not likely that this analysis of the tetrachoric correlations between symptoms has given us anything like a dependable classification of the insanities, because the study can be much improved when it is done the next time. But our results indicate that by the multiple factor methods it should be possible to arrive at a rational classification of the insanities and of personality types.

Another application of the present factor methods is an analysis to ascertain whether the vocational interests of college students can be classified in constellations and whether they can be described in terms of vocational interest types, small in number compared with the list of available occupations. These should eventually be related to the temperamental and personality traits and to the constellations of mental abilities.

We asked three thousand students in four universities to indicate their likes and dislikes on a list of eighty of the better known occupations (Table 5) which are available for college students. The tetrachoric correlations indicate the extent to which those who are interested in engineering, for example, can also be expected to have some interest in physics, or in chemistry. Those who are interested in engineering tend to dislike law and journalism and salesmanship, so that these correlations are negative. Our first question will be to ascertain the number of factors that are necessary to account for the observed intercorrelations. Previous inquiry indicates that the number of types may not exceed six or eight.

The scoring of the individual schedules might be reduced to a

TABLE 5

Actor	Explorer	Pharmacist
Advertiser	Factory Manager	Philosopher
Architect	Farmer	Photographer
Army Officer	Florist	Physician
Art Critic	Foreign Correspondent	Physicist
Artist	Forest Ranger	Poet
Astronomer	Fruit Grower	Press Agent
Athletic Director	Geologist	Printer
Auctioneer	High School Teacher	Private Secretary
Auto Salesman	Historian	Professional Athlete
Banker	Insurance Salesman	Psychologist
Biologist	Inventor	Public Speaker
Botanist	Jeweler	Radio Announcer
Building Contractor	Journalist	Railway Conductor
Business Manager	Judge	Real Estate Salesman
Cattle Rancher	Landscape Gardener	Retail Merchant
Certified Public Accountant	Lawyer, Criminal	Sales Manager
Chemist	Lawyer, Corporation	Scientist
Civil Engineer	Librarian	Sculptor
Clergyman	Manufacturer	Secret Service Man
Club Secretary	Mathematician	Ship Officer
College Professor	Mechanical Engineer	Sociologist
Congressman	Musician	Stockbroker
Dentist	Newspaper Reporter	Surgeon
Diplomatic Service	Novelist	Tax Expert
Economist	Office Manager	Vocational Counselor
Electrical Engineer	Orchestra Conductor	

number of scores equal to the number of factors. These scores would be the coordinates of a point which represent the subject in a space of as many dimensions as there are factors required by the intercorrelations. The occupational likes and dislikes of the subject might be estimated by the coordinates of the point which represent his own interests. In this manner it may be possible to make a limited list of occupations that are typical of the interests of each student.

The question might be raised whether a student should be advised to enter that occupation for which his interests are typical. It might well be argued that he has a better chance of success if he enters a profession for which his interests are unusual. But that question refers, of course, to educational and vocational guidance while our present problem concerns the methodology of isolating types or constellations of traits. If we should find that vocational interests group themselves into a relatively small number of types it would have psychological interest in relation to the personality traits and mental abilities of the same subjects. It would be another question to decide how such data could or should be used in guidance.

An application of the factor methods has recently been made by Mrs. Thurstone. Her problem was to ascertain whether radicalism is a common factor in people's attitudes on various disputed social issues. She

Figure 4. Factor study of radicalism with attitude scales by Thelma Gwinn Thurstone.

gave eleven attitude scales to about 380 students in several universities. Records of the intelligence examination of the American Council on Education were available for the majority of these students, so that the study includes twelve variables. The factorial analysis reveals a conspicuous common factor that we recognize as radicalism. The second factor residuals were comparable with the standard errors of the given coefficients. The standard error of the mean correlation coefficient was .047 while the standard error of the second factor residuals was .056.

Since the two factors were sufficient to account for the intercorrelations, we have plotted in Figure 4 the factor loadings as the two coordinates for each of the twelve variables. Several psychological interpretations can be made from this diagram. The variables which are heavily loaded with radicalism are attitudes favorable to evolutionary doctrines, favorable to birth control, favorable to easy divorce, favorable to communism, and it is of interest to note that intelligence is positively correlated with these radical or liberal attitudes. In the opposite direction we find conservatism in attitudes favorable to the church, favorable to prohibition, the observance of Sunday, and belief in a personal God. Inspection of the original coefficients as well as the factorial analysis shows the more intelligent college students tend to be radical or liberal on social questions and that they tend to be atheistic or agnostic on religious matters.

In naming the common factor which is most prominent in these attitude scales there may be some question as to whether it should be called conservatism or religion. The most pious people are likely to be against evolutionary doctrines, against birth control, and against easy divorce. It may also be that what we have called radicalism–conservatism is a factor which is nearly the same as the religious factor. It is a psychological question of considerable interest to ascertain whether this conspicuous common factor is to be attributed to temperamental and intellectual differences in people or merely to religious training.

One or two observations may be made about the second factor. We note first that patriotism and communism are diametrically opposite in the factorial diagram and this is what we should expect. It is surprising that intelligence should correlate negatively with patriotism among college students; but when we inspect the original coefficients we find that the strongest correlation with intelligence is negative .44 with patriotism. In other words the most intelligent college students tend to be lukewarm in their patriotism as judged by the attitude scale for this trait. It is unfortunate that we did not have a scale for measuring attitude toward pacifism, because it is a more disputed object than war. As is to be expected, the second factor of nationalism is most heavily represented in patriotism and in the glorification of war, while the opposite attitude, namely, international-mindedness, is represented by the attitudes of those Americans who are friendly toward communism and toward Germany. These examples will suffice to illustrate the possibilities of factorial analysis in dealing with the affective and temperamental attributes of people.

Until recently practically all of the studies that have been made by factor methods have been confined to the cognitive traits and especially to the mental abilities that are represented by psychological tests. It is on this type of material that Professor Spearman and his students have worked extensively with the tetrad difference method. I shall describe the analysis of a set of nine psychological tests which have been investigated by Mr. W. P. Alexander of the University of Glasgow and I reproduce here with his permission a section of his unpublished data (Table 6). The nine tests are all well known except the new performance test which he has recently devised. When we apply the multiple factor methods to this correlational matrix we find that most of the variance of each test can be accounted for by postulating only two factors. These we have plotted in Figure 5.

In this diagram the abscissae represent the first factor that was extracted and the ordinates represent the second factor. As is to be expected the centroid of the whole system is on the x-axis since this is implied in the approximation procedure that was used for this problem. Even in a first glance at this diagram we are struck by the fact that the nine tests divide themselves into two groups or clusters. We turn immediately to the tests to see what psychological abilities may be found in the tests that constitute each of these two constellations. We then find that all of the verbal tests fall in one of these constellations and that all of the performance tests fall in the other constellation. This suggests a rational method of establishing the psychological categories that we

TABLE 6   *Correlations of Nine Tests Used by W. P. Alexander*
Westfield State Farm—71 Cases
Correlation Matrix

Test	1	2	3	4	5	6	7	8	9
1	—	451	373	337	717	750	768	786	612
2	451	—	428	470	277	393	407	557	616
3	373	428	—	362	255	402	415	334	415
4	337	470	362	—	189	304	257	203	528
5	717	277	255	189	—	695	752	800	335
6	750	393	402	304	695	—	834	850	478
7	768	407	415	257	752	834	—	917	433
8	786	557	334	203	800	850	917	—	450
9	612	616	415	528	335	478	433	450	—

Description of Tests: (1) Stanford-Binet; (2) Pintner-Paterson Scale; (3) Healy Puzzle II–Picture Completion; (4) Porteus Maze Test; (5) Thorndike Reading Test; (6) Otis Group Test; (7) Otis Self-Administering Test; (8) Terman Group Test; (9) Alexander Performance Scale.

should call *mental abilities.* There seems to be little doubt in naming one of these constellations *verbal ability* and we shall name the other one tentatively as *manipulation,* since that is common to all of the performance tests. The verbal tests that cling together in this analysis are the Stanford-Binet, the Thorndike reading test, the Otis group test, the Otis self-administering test, and the Terman group test. The performance tests that group themselves apart from the verbal tests are the Pintner-Paterson scale, the Healy Puzzle II (picture completion), the Porteus maze test, and Alexander's new performance test.

It is to be noted that these two constellations are entirely independent of the location of the two orthogonal axes through this sytem of nine tests. A characteristic of the multiple factor problem is that the location of the axes is arbitrary and that hence the factorial components are to that extent arbitrary and without fundamental psychological significance.

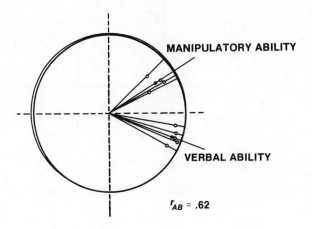

Figure 5. Two factor analysis of nine tests used by W. P. Alexander.

This limitation is entirely obviated if we center our interest on the constellations of mental traits that are revealed in the factorial analysis. The relations between the constellations are invariant under rotation of the orthogonal axes, and hence we have here something more or less permanent in terms of which we may define psychological categories and mental abilities.

As illustrative of this method we have found the centroid of each of the two constellations in Alexander's nine tests. These centroids are indicated by the small black circles. If we had a fairly large number of tests in each constellation we could attach some confidence to the centroid of the constellation as a definition of a mental ability. I am here using the term *mental ability* to identify a constellation of tests which lie in the same cluster in the factorial analysis and which correlate nearly unity when they are corrected for attenuation.

In Alexander's data we find that the two constellations are not independent. This is seen on the diagram by the fact that the central angle between the two constellations is not a right angle. Since all mental abilities are positively correlated, we should expect that all of the constellations of mental abilities will be positively correlated also, and that is the case in the present data. Now if we are to use these constellations of traits as the categories for psychological description and if we are to define mental abilities and personality types in terms of constellations, then it is immediately apparent that our categories will not all be independent. This indicates that we must look eventually to still more fundamental categories in terms of which to describe the mental abilities. In the meantime it will be useful to describe them in terms of constellations of known degrees of dependence and we shall

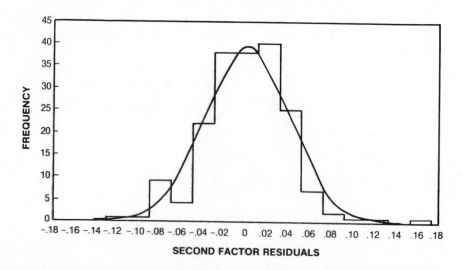

Figure 6. Frequency distribution of second factor residuals for 20 tests used by Dr. William Brown. "A test of the theory of two factors," *Brit. J. Psychol.*, April, 1933. Approximate solution by multiple factor methods.

then be using a system of oblique coordinates instead of the orthogonal coordinates of conventional mathematics. Ultimately we shall want to find that particular location of the orthogonal axes which corresponds to independent genetic elements.

I shall now describe briefly the results of a multiple factor analysis of a set of twenty tests that were recently used by Dr. William Brown in support of the Spearman single-factor hypothesis of intelligence. We can sympathize with Dr. Stephenson who computed all of the fifteen thousand tetrad differences for this table and we shall not even venture to guess how long it must have taken to make the computations.

The multiple factor method in its simplest approximation form was applied to this set of data, and we find that two factors are sufficient to account for the given coefficients. The distribution of second factor residuals is shown in Figure 6. The standard deviation of the distribution of residuals is .039. In Figure 7 we have plotted the two-factor coordinates for these twenty tests and we then see that they fall into two constellations. Reference to the tests shows that all of the verbal tests are in one group and that all of the perceptual tests are found in the other group. We might regard these two groups as representing two mental abilities, one of which we should call verbal ability, while the other one might be called visual form perception. The correlation between pure

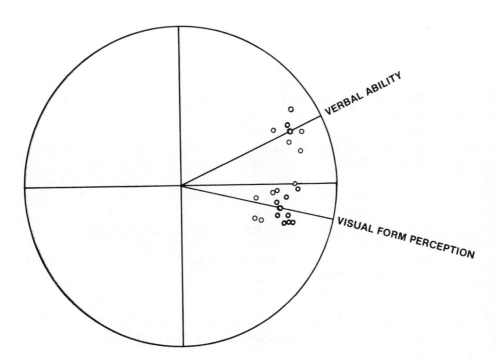

Figure 7. Two-factor analysis of the 20 tests used by Dr. William Brown in "A test of the theory of two factors," *Brit. J. Psychol.*, April, 1933.

measures of these two abilities is the cosine of the angular separation between the two centroids.

Brown's interpretation of these relations which he has investigated with the tetrad difference method is that one of these two clusters represents Spearman's "g" and that whatever is left over is attributable to verbal ability. It seems to us that it would be just as logical to call the verbal cluster the general one and to attribute the residuals to a special perceptual factor. In that case the verbal constellation would be called the general "g." This reasoning might be extended to each one of the many constellations of abilities which are represented by groups of psychological tests. But the evidence is as yet entirely insufficient to demonstrate that any one of the constellations of mental abilities is a principal intellective factor.

Since all mental tests are positively correlated, it follows that the tests must lie in a limited quadrant or octant of the geometrical representation of the mental abilities. Instead of adopting one of the constellations as a reference it might be more logical to find a point in the octant of the mental abilities such that the most diversified series of tests all correlate positively with the imaginary test at this central point. It is not inconceivable that a point might be located by this means with some degree of certainty. It would then represent the central intellective factor and those tests would be the best tests of intelligence which correlate highest with the imaginary pure test, which is represented by this central vector. It would not be the centroid of any particular set of tests unless these should happen to be evenly distributed over the space of the mental abilities and that is a condition which can not be guaranteed beforehand. It is not inconceivable that the constellation of perceptual relations of Spearman will lie close to this central vector, because we may expect those tests to lie close to it which correlate best with judgments of intelligence, and that is the practical criterion by which intelligence tests have been constructed. If that should turn out to be the case, then Spearman's "g" would be a close representation of a principal intellective factor even though his tetrad criterion is ambiguous and inadequate. If we follow Spearman's procedure in carefully picking out a list of tests, as diversified as possible, which all satisfy his criterion, then we should be defining a common factor which is close to the center of the space of mental abilities.

But this procedure necessarily leads to at least some negative factor loadings in all but the first factor, and it is difficult to make a psychological interpretation of negative abilities. It is much more likely that the opposite procedure will give a solution that makes sense for psychology and for genetics. This solution would be to find a set of orthogonal axes through the fringe of the space of mental abilities rather than through the middle of it. The geometrical representation of the solution will probably be as follows. The mental abilities can be represented as points within a cone. The axis of the cone will represent a fictitious central intellective factor. The fundamental abilities which have genetic meaning will be represented by a set of orthogonal elements of the cone in space of as many dimensions as there are genetic factors. All mental tests will then be described in terms of positive orthogonal coordinates, corresponding to the independent genetic factors. Negative loadings will disappear. For rough and practical descriptive purposes the axis of the cone of mental abilities may be used as an axis of reference which is central in the space of mental abilities. It will be a fictitious central intellective factor but it will probably have no fundamental psychological or genetic meaning.

In conclusion I want to suggest the course of investigation which is likely to lead to a scientific description and understanding of mental abilities and personality traits and their aberrations. Our first task is to establish the identity of the several mental abilities which reveal themselves as distinct constellations in factorial analysis. Among these abilities it is quite likely that we shall find verbal ability, perceptual relations, and arithmetical ability to be distinct, though positively correlated.

In these studies it is probably best not to pivot on any single constellation as fundamental to all of the rest. It is better to use an analysis which allows as many factors to appear as are necessary to account for each new set of tests and to name the constellations when they appear. These categories should be frankly regarded as temporary and subject to redefinition in successive experiments. Eventually we should be able to work with a rather limited number of mental abilities and trait constellations. These categories will be either more or less conventionalized, or else they will be so consistent that some physical or even genetic significance may be attached to them.

In extracting each constellation it is essential to make sure that the specific variance in each variable has vanished or that it is small enough so that it can be ignored. If one of the variables retains a considerable specific variance after the common factors have been extracted, it is necessary to repeat the experiments with additional tests which are similar to the one which has shown a specific variance. Only when the reliability and the communality are nearly equal can we be sure that the common factors account for the total variance in each test. In order to favor this outcome it is best to assemble the test batteries in such a way that there are several similar tests of each kind that are to be investigated. This is in a sense the opposite of the precautions which have been current in factor studies where the experimenters have been careful to avoid similar tests simply because they disturb the tetrad criterion. Instead of concealing the specific variance with the chance errors, as is done in tetrad analysis, it is more illuminating to investigate the nature of the specific variance of each test by including several similar tests of each kind in the test battery.

When the mental abilities have been defined in terms of a large number of elementary tests for each ability, it will be of considerable interest to ascertain experimentally the extent to which training of one ability transfers to another ability and to relate such transfer effects to the known correlations between the abilities.

It is my conviction that the isolation of the mental abilities will turn out to be essentially a problem in genetics. It will be profitable to ascertain what part of the variance of each ability can be attributed to the parents. It is not unlikely that this type of genetic research will constitute one of the means for identifying the independent elements in the mental abilities.

We hope that the development of factorial methods of analysis will give us the tools by which to reduce the complexities of social and psychological phenomena to a limited number of elements. These methods should be useful not only for developing the theory of mental abilities and temperamental traits but also in meeting the practical demands of educational and psychological guidance.

Reprinted with permission
from *Psychological Review*,
1937, 44, 1-32.

Chapter 17

Mind, Mechanism, and Adaptive Behavior

Clark L. Hull

*Institute of Human Relations,
Yale University*

Introduction

Since the time of Charles Darwin it has become clear not only that living organisms have gradually evolved through immense periods of time, but that man is evolution's crowning achievement. It is equally clear that man's preeminence lies in his capacity for adaptive behavior. Because of the seemingly unique and remarkable nature of adaptive behavior, it has long been customary to attribute it to the action of a special agent or substance called "mind." Thus "mind" as a hypothetical entity directing and controlling adaptive behavior attains biological status possessing survival value and, consequently, a "place in nature." But what is this mysterious thing called

---

Presidential Address delivered before the American Psychological Association, Hanover, New Hampshire, September 4, 1936.

The author is indebted to Professor Max Wertheimer for a critical reading of this paper.

mind? By what principles does it operate? Are these principles many or are they few? Are they those of the ordinary physical world or are they of the nature of spiritual essences—of an entirely different order, the non-physical?

It will, perhaps, be most economical to begin our examination of this important problem by passing briefly in review some typical phenomena of adaptive behavior which have led to the assumption of a special psychic entity. Among these may be mentioned the following: When obstacles are encountered, organisms often persist in making the same incorrect attempt over and over again; they vary their reactions spontaneously; they display anticipatory reactions antedating the biological emergencies to which the reactions are adaptive; they present the phenomena of disappointment and discouragement; they strive to attain states of affairs which are biologically advantageous; they transfer to new problem situations adaptive behavior acquired in situations which, objectively considered, are totally different. The behavior of organisms is purposive in that they strive for goals or values, and in so doing manifest intelligence or insight and a high degree of individual freedom from current coercion of the environment. Whatever may be the final conclusion as to the ultimate nature of these phenomena, their biological significance in terms of survival must be immense. The task of understanding and controlling them is surely worthy of the best cooperative efforts of the biological and social sciences.

The Controversy Regarding Adaptive Behavior Is Theoretical, Not Factual

Historically, two main views have been held as to the ultimate nature of adaptive behavior. The most widely accepted of these, at the present time, is also the most ancient; its roots lie far back in primitive animism. According to this view, the principles governing adaptive behavior are essentially non-physical, mental, or psychic. The second view, despite its austerity, has received a certain amount of favor among men of science. It assumes that adaptive behavior operates ultimately according to the principles of the physical world. In our consideration of these contrasting views, it will be convenient to begin with the latter.

The physical or mechanistic view of the nature of adaptive behavior can best be stated by quoting the beautiful presentation of the raindrop analogy written by the late Albert P. Weiss:

We may best visualize the relationship between the responses that make up the so-called purposive behavior category by the raindrop analogy. We may start with the assumption that every drop of rain in some way or other gets to the ocean. . . . Anthropomorphizing this condition we may say that it is the *purpose* of every drop of rain to get to the ocean. Of course, this only means that virtually every drop *does* get there eventually. . . . Falling from the cloud it may strike the leaf of a tree, and drop from one leaf to another until it reaches the ground. From here it may pass under or on the surface of the soil to a rill, then to a brook, river, and finally to the sea. Each stage, each fall from one leaf to the next, may be designated as a *means* toward the final end, the sea, . . . Human behavior is merely a complication of the same factors.[1]

The nub of Weiss's statement lies in his concluding remark that adaptive behavior is merely a "complication" of the same factors as those which are involved in the behavior of a drop of water finding its way from an inland cloud to the sea. Obviously, Weiss did not mean to say that the several forms of seeking and striving behavior characteristic of the higher organisms are brought about by the various compoundings of such processes as evaporation, condensation, splashing, and flowing. The context of the quotation shows that he meant that ultimately the complex forms of purposive behavior would be found to derive from the same *source* as those from which the raindrop phenomena are derived; i.e., from the basic entities of theoretical physics, such as electrons and protons. He discusses these latter concepts explicitly and at length.

Passing to the more orthodox view, that adaptive behavior is essentially non-physical, or psychic, the words of A. S. Eddington may be taken as a point of departure. In his book, "The nature of the physical world,"[2] Eddington remarks:

Conceivably we might reach a human machine interacting by reflexes with its environment; but we cannot reach rational man morally responsible. [P. 343.] . . . In a world of aether and electrons we might perhaps encounter *nonsense*; we could not encounter *damned nonsense*.

The significance of Eddington's statement centers around the word *reach*. From the present point of view, he seems to be saying that we cannot reach the highest forms of adaptive behavior, such as complex problem solution (rational behavior) and certain complex forms of social behavior involving the implicit verbal coercion of the behavior of the individual (moral behavior) if we start out merely with aether and electrons; we must begin with something non-physical, or psychic—presumably consciousness.

Thus the issue is joined. We are presented with the paradox of Eddington, the physicist, apparently insisting that the higher forms of behavior are at bottom non-physical, whereas Weiss, the psychologist, insists that they are fundamentally non-psychological!

But what, exactly, is the issue? Is it, for example, a difference as to an ordinary matter of observed fact? Do Eddington and those who share

---

1. Albert P. Weiss, A theoretical basis of human behavior, Columbus, Ohio: R. G. Adams and Company, 1925, pp. 346–347.

2. New York: The Macmillan Company, 1929, p. 345.

his view claim to have made certain observations which are in conflict with a corresponding set of observations supposed to have been made by Weiss and those with a mechanistic leaning? The dispute involves nothing of this nature. It is clear that the controversy is definitely a theoretical one. Eddington seems to be implying that we *can not* reach a sound theory of rational, purposive and moral behavior if we set out with nothing but aether and electrons. Weiss is saying, by implication, that a sound theory of such behavior *can* be reached by setting out with nothing but electrons and protons.

The Methodology of Scientific Theory Differentiated from That of Philosophical Speculation

Having located definitely in the field of theory the contrasted views represented in a general way by Weiss and Eddington, we face at once the critical question of whether the problem lies within the range of the operation of scientific methodology. If it does, what is that methodology? How is it to be applied to the question before us in a way which will avoid the interminable wrangles and philosophical futilities so long associated with the mind-body problem? It will be necessary to go into the matter of methodology rather thoroughly, in part because of its central importance for our present problem, but in part also because of the widespread misconceptions regarding it due to our early associations with philosophy. With the question of methodology clarified we shall return to Weiss and Eddington in the hope of demonstrating its concrete application.

The essential characteristics of a sound scientific theoretical system, as contrasted with ordinary philosophical speculation, may be briefly summarized under three heads:

1. A satisfactory scientific theory should begin with a set of explicitly stated postulates accompanied by specific or "operational" definitions of the critical terms employed.

2. From these postulates there should be deduced by the most rigorous logic possible under the circumstances, a series of interlocking theorems covering the major concrete phenomena of the field in question.

3. The statements in the theorems should agree in detail with the observationally known facts of the discipline under consideration. If the theorems agree with the observed facts, the system is probably true; if they disagree, the system is false. If it is impossible to tell whether the theorems of a system agree with the facts or not, the system is neither true nor false; scientifically considered, it is meaningless.

Since concrete example is more illuminating and more convincing than abstract statement, there is reproduced below a small scientific theoretical system in which an attempt has been made to conform to the above principles. There may be found (p. 320) a number of definitions, which are followed (p. 321) by six postulates. The system concludes with a series of thirteen theorems (p. 322), each derived from the postulates by a process of reasoning analogous to that ordinarily employed in geometry.

At first sight the formal characteristics of scientific theory look very much like those of philosophical speculation and even of ordinary argumentation, from which philosophical speculation can scarcely be distinguished. At their best, both scientific theory and philosophical speculation set out from explicit postulates; both have definitions of critical terms; both have interlocking theorems derived by meticulous logic. Consider, for example, Spinoza's "Ethic," a philosophical work of the better sort. This has all of the above characteristics in almost exactly the same form as the miniature scientific system which is presented below. Where, then, lie the great difference and superiority of the scientific procedure?

The answer, while extending into many complex details, rests upon a single fundamental principle. The difference is that *in philosophical speculation there is no possibility of comparing a theorem with the results of direct observation*. An obvious example of this impossibility is seen in Spinoza's famous pantheistic theorem, Proposition XIV, from Part One of his "Ethic":

Besides God no substance can be, nor can be conceived.

It is difficult to imagine subjecting such a theorem as that to an observational test.

Consider, by way of contrast, a really scientific procedure, one carried out by Galileo at about the same time that Spinoza was writing. The Copernican hypothesis concerning the nature of the solar system was then in violent dispute. From this hypothesis, together with a few familiar principles concerning the behavior of light, it follows logically as a theorem that the planet Venus, like the moon, should show the crescent and all the other stages between the full and dark phases. Presumably led by this deduction, Galileo, with a telescope of his own construction, made the necessary observations on Venus and found the phases exactly as demanded by the theorem. Here we have the indispensable observational check demanded by science but lacking in philosophy.

But why, it will be asked, is it so imperative to have an observational check on the theorems of a system if the system is to merit serious consideration by scientists? To answer this question adequately it will be necessary to consider in a little detail the characteristics of postulates, the procedure in selecting them, and the methodology of their substantiation.

It is important to note at the outset that in scientific theory postulates tend to be of two kinds. First, there are postulates which are mere matters of fact; i.e., they are matters of relatively simple and direct observation. Second, there are postulates which by their nature cannot conceivably be matters of direct observation. The classical investigation of Galileo just considered contains examples of both types. The principles of light and shadow upon which lunar and planetary phases depend are obviously matters of ordinary, everyday, direct terrestrial observation, and so represent postulates of the first type. On the other hand, the Copernican hypothesis as to the relative movements of the several components of the solar system is not susceptible to direct observation, and so represents postulates of the second type.

In scientific theory, owing to the continuous checking of theorems arrived at deductively against the results of direct observation, both types of postulates are constantly receiving *indirect* verification or refutation. Thus postulates capable of the direct approach are susceptible of two independent kinds of test, the direct and the indirect. But the continuous indirect test is of special importance for the postulates incapable of the direct approach. Were it not for this they would be subject to no observational verification at all, and scientific theory would in this respect have no more safeguard against erroneous basic assumptions than has philosphical speculation. Thus Galileo's brilliant observations of the phases of Venus not only gave the scientific world some new facts but, of far greater importance, they substantiated in a convincing, though indirect, manner the fundamental Copernican hypothesis.[3]

Whenever a theorem fails to check with the relevant facts, the postulates which gave rise to it must be ruthlessly revised until agreement is reached. If agreement cannot be attained, the system must be abandoned. In this constant revision there is a definite tendency to choose and formulate the postulates in a way which will make them yield the deductions desired. Such a procedure involves an obvious element of circularity. This is particularly the case where the system is small and where the postulates are purely symbolic constructs or inventions and therefore not subject to direct investigation. Even so, the choice of postulates to fit the facts is methodologically legitimate and, upon the whole, desirable. One important reason for this is that a postulate or hypothesis so arrived at may lead to a *direct*, experimental confirmation in case it is capable of the direct approach.[4] In such an event, of course, all circularity disappears.

---

3. Many persons have been puzzled by the paradox that in science a deduction frequently sets out with postulates which are by no means securely established, whereas in ordinary argumentation there is the greatest insistence upon the certainty of the premises upon which the argument is based. The explanation of this paradox lies largely in the difference of objective in the two cases. Argument ordinarily seeks to convince by a deductive procedure of something which under the circumstances is not directly observable; otherwise there would be no point in performing the deduction. It is clear that if the person to whom the argument is directed does not agree with the premises he will not agree with the conclusion and the whole procedure will be futile. In science, on the other hand, the situation may be almost completely reversed; the conclusion (or theorem) may be known observationally at the outset, but the premises (or postulates) may at first be little more than conjectures and the logical process quite circular. For the methodology of resolving this circularity, see the following.

4. From the experimental point of view the process of developing systematic theory thus leads in two directions. On one hand it leads to the investigation of theorems derived from postulates of the system, and on the other to the direct investigation of postulates

But if the system is truly scientific in nature, the circularity just considered is only a temporary phase even when one or more of the postulates are insusceptible to direct investigation. It is precisely in this connection that scientific method shows its incomparable superiority over philosophical speculation. A sound set of postulates should lead to the deduction of theorems representing phenomena never previously investigated quite as logically as of theorems representing phenomena already known when the postulates were formulated. When a theorem representing novel phenomena receives direct observational confirmation there is no possibility of circularity; as a consequence the probability that the postulates directly involved are sound is very definitely increased.[5] Thus the fact that Venus shows lunar phases could not have been known to Copernicus when he formulated his epoch-making hypothesis, because the telescope had not yet been invented. Accordingly their discovery by Galileo constituted strong positive evidence of the essential soundness of the Copernican hypothesis regarded as a postulate. This classical example of the observational but indirect confirmation of the soundness of postulates will serve as a fitting conclusion for our general consideration of theoretical methodology.

The Recognized Scientific Methodology Has Not Been Applied to the Behavior Controversy

We turn now to the question of whether the recognized scientific methodology is really applicable to a resolution of the controversy concerning the basic nature of adaptive behavior. At first glance the prospect is reassuring. It becomes quite clear, for example, what Weiss and Eddington should have done to substantiate their claims. They should have exhibited, as strict logical deductions from explicitly stated postulates, a series of theorems corresponding in detail to the concrete

---

which appear to be required as assumptions for the deductive explanation of facts already known. Since phenomena of the latter type are fundamental in a strict sense, their investigation is of the highest significance. A background of systematic theory thus often directly suggests fundamental investigations which might be indefinitely delayed under the usual procedure of random, and even of systematic, exploration.

5. A single unequivocal disagreement between a theorem and observed fact is sufficient to assure the incorrectness of at least one of the postulates involved. But even if the postulates of a system generate a very long series of theorems which are subsequently confirmed without exception, each new confirmation merely adds to the *probability* of the truth of such postulates as are incapable of direct observational test. Apparently this indirect evidence never reaches the crisp certainty of a deductive conclusion in which the postulates are directly established, except in the highly improbable situation where all the possible deductions involving a given postulate have been tested with positive results. According to the theory of chance, the larger the sample from this possible total which has been tried and found without exception to be positive, the greater the probability that a new deduction based on the same set of postulates will be confirmed when tested.

manifestations of the higher forms of human behavior. Then, and only then, they might proceed to the examination of the postulates of such system. To substantiate his position Weiss would have to show that these postulates concern essentially the behavior of electrons, protons, etc.; and Eddington to support his assertions would need to show that the postulates of a successful system are primarily phenomena of consciousness.[6] The formal application of the methodology is thus quite clear and specific.

But here we meet an amazing paradox. In spite of the calm assurance of Weiss as to the truth of his statement that purposive behavior is at bottom physical, we find that he neither presents nor cites such a system. Indeed, he seems to be quite oblivious of such a necessity. Turning to Eddington, we find exactly the same paradoxical situation. Notwithstanding his positive, even emphatic, implications that moral behavior must be conscious or psychic in its ultimate nature, we find him neither presenting nor citing a theoretical system of any kind, much less one derived from psychic or conscious postulates. This paradox is particularly astonishing in the case of Eddington because he has been active in the field of physical theory and should, therefore, be sophisticated regarding the essential methodology involved in scientific theory in general. Surely the same logic which demands strict deduction from explicitly stated postulates in physical theory demands it for the theory of adaptive and moral behavior. And surely if we demand it of a mechanistic theory of the more recondite forms of human behavior, as Eddington seems emphatically to do, there is no hocus-pocus whereby a psychic view of such behavior may be maintained without the same substantial foundation.

A Demonstration of the Application of Theoretical Methodology to Adaptive Behavior

But if neither Weiss nor Eddington, nor any other writer in this field, has been able to bring forward the indispensable systematic theory as a prerequisite of the logical right to express a valid conclusion concerning the ultimate nature of higher adaptive behavior, may this not mean that the attainment of such a system is impossible, and that, consequently, the problem still remains in the realm of philosophical speculation? There is reason to believe that this is not the case. The ground for optimism lies in part in the small theoretical system which is presented below (p. 320).

By way of introduction to the system we may begin with the consideration of Theorem 1 (p. 322). In brief, this theorem purports to show that Pavlov's conditioned reactions and the stimulus-response

---

6. It is here assumed as highly probable that if the two approaches are strictly in conflict, only one would be successful. In the course of the development of scientific theoretical systems, however, it is to be expected that during the early stages several different systems may present appreciable evidences of success. See The conflicting psychologies of learning—A way out, *Psychol. Rev.*, 42, 1936; especially pp. 514–515.

"bonds" resulting from Thorndike's so-called "law of effect" are in reality special cases of the operation of a single set of principles. The major principle involved is given in Postulate 2. Briefly, this postulate states the assumption of the present system concerning the conditions under which stimuli and reactions become associated. The difference in the two types of reaction thus turns out to depend merely upon the accidental factor of the temporal relationships of the stimuli to the reactions in the learning situation, coupled with the implication that R_G, which in part serves to mark a reinforcing state of affairs, is also susceptible of being associated with a new stimulus.[7] The automatic, stimulus-response approach thus exemplified is characteristic of the remainder of the system.

A consideration of Theorem 2 will serve still further as an orientation to the system before us. We find this theorem stating that both *correct* and *incorrect* reaction tendencies may be set up by the conditioning or associative process just referred to. Our chief interest in this theorem, as an introduction to the system, concerns the question of whether the terms "correct" and "incorrect" can have any meaning when they refer to reaction tendencies which are the result of a purely automatic process of association such as that presented by Postulate 2. It is believed that they have a very definite meaning. Definitions 7 and 8 state in effect that correctness or incorrectness is determined by whether the reaction tendency under given conditions is, or is not, subject to experimental extinction. Such purely objective or behavioral definitions of numerous terms commonly thought of as applying exclusively to experience, as distinguished from action, are characteristic of the entire system.

With this general orientation we may proceed to the theorems more specifically concerned with adaptive behavior. The proof of the first of these, Theorem 3, shows that under certain circumstances organisms will repeatedly and successively make the same incorrect reaction. At first sight this may seem like a most commonplace outcome. However, when considered in the light of the definition of correctness given above it is evident that this theorem differs radically from what might be deduced concerning the behavior of a raindrop or a pebble moving in a gravitational field.[8]

---

7. In effect this deduction purports to show that the Pavlovian conditioned reflex is a special case under Thorndike's "law of effect," though Thorndike might not recognize his favorite principle as formulated in Postulate 2. For a fuller but less formal discussion of this point see *Psychol. Bull.*, 1935, 32, 817–822.

8. It may be suggested that if water should fall into a hollow cavity on its way to the sea, it might at first oscillate back and forth vigorously and then gradually subside, each oscillation corresponding to an unsuccessful attempt and the gradual cessation, to experimental extinction. In all such cases the discussion as to whether the observed parallelism in behavior represents an essential similarity or a mere superficial analogy requires that both phenomena possess a thorough theoretical basis. *If the two phenomena are deducible from the same postulates and by identical processes of reasoning, they may be regarded as essentially the same, otherwise not.* But if one or both lacks a theoretical basis such a comparison cannot be made and decision can ordinarily not be reached. Much futile argument could be avoided if this principle were generally recognized.

Theorem 4 states that after making one or more incorrect reactions an organism will spontaneously vary the response even though the environmental situation remains unchanged. This theorem is noteworthy because it represents the classical case of a form of spontaneity widely assumed, as far back as the Middle Ages, to be inconceivable without presupposing consciousness.

Theorem 5 states that when an organism originally has both correct and incorrect excitatory tendencies evoked by a single stimulus situation, the correct tendency will at length be automatically selected in preference to stronger incorrect ones.[9] This theorem, also, has been widely regarded as impossible of derivation without the presupposition of consciousness. Otherwise (so it has been argued) how can the organism know which reaction to choose?

Theorem 6 represents the deduction that in certain situations the organism will give up seeking, i.e., cease making attempts, and thus fail to perform the correct reaction even when it possesses in its repertoire a perfectly correct excitatory tendency. The substance of this proof lies in the expectation that the extinction resulting from repeated false reactions will cause indirectly a critical weakening of a non-dominant but correct reaction tendency. This theorem is of unusual importance because it represents the deduction of a phenomenon not as yet subjected to experiment. As such it should have special significance as a test of the soundness of the postulates.

With Theorems 7 and 8 we turn to the problem of anticipatory or preparatory reactions. The proof of Theorem 7 derives, from the principles of the stimulus trace and conditioning (Postulates 1 and 2), the phenomenon of the antedating reaction. The substance of this theorem is that after acquisition, learned reactions tend to appear in advance of the point in the original sequence at which they occurred during the conditioning process.[10] Pursuing this line of reasoning, Theorem 8 shows that in the case of situations demanding flight, such antedating reactions become truly anticipatory or preparatory in the sense of being biologically adaptive to situations which are impending but not yet actual. Thus we arrive at behavioral foresight, a phenomenon evidently of very considerable survival significance in animal life and one frequently regarded as eminently psychic, and inconceivable without consciousness.[11]

Passing over Theorem 9, which lays some necessary groundwork, we come to Theorem 10. Here we find a deduction of the existence of the fractional anticipatory goal reaction. Of far greater significance from our present point of view, the deduction purports to show that through the

---

9. See Simple trial-and-error learning: A study in psychological theory, *Psychol. Rev.*, 1930, *37*, 241–256: especially pp. 243–250.

10. See A functional interpretation of the conditioned reflex, *Psychol. Rev.*, 1929, *36*, 498–511; especially pp. 507–508.

11. See Knowledge and purpose as habit mechanisms, *Psychol. Rev.*, 1930, *37*, 511–525; especially pp. 514–516.

action of mere association the fractional anticipatory reaction tends automatically to bring about on later occasions the state of affairs which acted as its reinforcing agent when it was originally set up. For this and other reasons it is believed that the anticipatory goal reaction is the physical basis of expectation, of intent, of purpose, and of guiding ideas.[12]

Theorem 11 represents a deduction of the phenomenon of behavioral disappointment[13] as manifested, for example, by Tinklepaugh's monkeys. When these animals had solved a problem with the expectation of one kind of food they would tend to refuse a different kind of food, otherwise acceptable, which had been surreptitiously substituted.[14]

Theorem 12 purports to be the deduction of the principle that organisms will strive actively to attain situations or states of affairs which previously have proved to be reinforcing. The automaticity deduced in the proof of Theorem 10 has here reached a still higher level. This is the capacity to surmount obstacles. But with the ability to attain ends in spite of obstacles comes automatically a genuine freedom (Definition 18), of great biological value but in no way incompatible with determinism.[15]

Theorem 13 is also derived with the aid of the fractional anticipatory goal reaction. This theorem represents the phenomenon of the adaptive but automatic transfer of learned reactions to situations having, as regards *external* characteristics, nothing whatever in common with the situations in which the habits were originally acquired. This, once more, is a form of adaptive behavior of the greatest survival significance to the organism, and one supposed in certain quarters to be impossible of derivation from associative principles. This is believed to be a low but genuine form of insight and a fairly high order of the "psychic."

This concludes the list of formally derived theorems. They have been selected from a series of fifty or so which are concerned with the same subject. None of these theorems "reaches" Eddington's "rational man morally responsible." They accordingly are not offered as a basis for deciding the ultimate nature of such behavior. They *are* offered as a concrete and relevant illustration of the first and most essential step in the methodology which must be followed by Eddington, or anyone else who would determine the basic nature of the higher forms of behavior. Incidentally they are offered as specific evidence that such problems,

---

12. See Goal attraction and directing ideas conceived as habit phenomena, *Psychol. Rev.*, 1931, *38*, 487–506.

13. It is to be observed from a comparison of Definitions 9 and 16 that *Disappointment* necessarily presupposes a specific expectation or intent (r_G), whereas *Discouragement* does not.

14. O. L. Tinklepaugh, An experimental study of representative factors in monkeys, *J. Comp. Psychol.*, 1928, *8*, 197–236. See especially p. 224 ff.

15. An additional element of interest in this theorem is the fact that the fundamental phenomenon of motivation seems to have been derived from the ordinary principle of association (Postulate 2). If this deduction should prove to be sound, it will have reduced the two basic categories of motivation and learning to one, the latter being primary.

long regarded as the peculiar domain of philosophy, are now susceptible of attack by a strictly orthodox scientific methodology.

Adaptive Behavior—A Scientific Theoretical System in Miniature[16]

Definitions

1. A *reinforcing state of affairs* (Postulate 3) is one which acts to give to the stimulus-trace component (Postulate 1) of preceding or following temporal coincidences consisting of a stimulus trace and a reaction, the capacity to evoke the reaction in question (Postulate 2).

2. *Experimental extinction* is the weakening of a conditioned excitatory tendency resulting from frustration or the failure of reinforcement (Postulate 4).

3. *Frustration* is said to occur when the situation is such that the reaction customarily evoked by a stimulus complex cannot take place (Postulate 4).

4. *Seeking* is that behavior of organisms in trial-and-error situations which, upon frustration, is characterized by varied alternative acts all operative under the influence of a common drive (S_D).

5. An *attempt* is a segment of behavior the termination of which is marked by either reinforcement or extinction.

6. A *simple trial-and-error situation* is one which presents to an organism a stimulus complex which tends to give rise to multiple reaction tendencies which are mutually incompatible, one or more of them being susceptible to reinforcement and one or more of them not being so susceptible.

7. A *correct* or "right" reaction is a behavior sequence which results in reinforcement.

8. An *incorrect* or "wrong" reaction is a behavior sequence which results in experimental extinction.

9. *Discouragement* is the diminution in the power of one excitatory tendency to evoke its normal reaction, this diminution resulting from one or more unsuccessful attempts involving a second reaction.

10. A behavior sequence is said to be *directed* to the attainment of a particular state of affairs when there appears throughout the sequence a characteristic component (r_G) of the action (R_G) closely associated with the state of affairs in question and this component action (r_G) as a stimulus tends to evoke an action sequence leading to the total reaction (R_G) of which the component constitutes a part.

11. Striving is that behavior of organisms which, upon frustration, displays varied alternative action sequences, all *directed* by an intent (r_G) to the attainment of the same reinforcing state of affairs.

12. A *goal* is the reinforcing state of affairs towards the attainment of which a behavior sequence of an organism may be directed by its intent (r_G).

13. An organism is said to *anticipate* a state of affairs when there is active throughout the behavior sequence leading to the state of affairs a fractional component (r_G) of the action associated with the state of affairs in question.

16. The author is greatly indebted to Dr. E. H. Rodnick and Mr. D. G. Ellson for detailed criticisms and suggestions during the original preparation of the system which follows. Thanks are also due Professor K. F. Muenzinger, Dr. R. T. Ross, and Dr. R. K. White for criticisms given since the presentation at Hanover.

14. *Success* is the culmination of striving which is characterized by the occurrence of the full reaction (R_G) of which the fractional anticipatory component (r_G) is a part.

15. *Failure* is the culmination of striving which is characterized by the lack of the enactment of the full reaction (R_G) of which the fractional component (r_G) is a part.

16. *Disappointment* is the diminution in the power of one reinforcing situation to evoke appropriate consummatory reaction, this diminution (Postulate 4) resulting from the failure of a second reaction sequence directed (by an intent, or r_G) to a different reinforcing situation from that to which the first was directed, both being based on the same drive (S_D).

17. A *habit-family hierarchy* consists of a number of habitual behavior sequences having in common the initial stimulus situation and the final reinforcing state of affairs.

18. *Individual freedom* of behavior, so far as it exists, consists in the absence of external restraint.

Postulates

1. The adequate stimulation of a sense organ initiates within the organism a neural reverberation which persists for some time after the stimulus has ceased to act, the absolute amount of the reverberation diminishing progressively to zero but at a progressively slower rate. (Stimulus trace.)

2. When a reaction and a given segment of a stimulus-trace (Postulate 1) repeatedly occur simultaneously and this coincidence occurs during the action of a drive (S_D) and temporally close to a reinforcing state of affairs (Definition 1), this and stronger segments of the stimulus trace tend progressively to acquire the capacity to evoke the reaction, the strength of the association thus acquired manifesting a negatively accelerated diminution with distance of the associates from the reinforcing state of affairs. (Positive association.)

3. A characteristic stimulus-reaction combination ($S_G \; {-}{-}\!\rightarrow R_G$) always marks reinforcing states of affairs (Definition 1). The particular stimulus-response combination marking the reinforcing state of affairs in the case of specific drives is determined empirically, i.e., by observation and experiment. (Mark of reinforcing state of affairs.)

4. When a stimulus evokes a conditioned (associative) reaction (Postulate 2) and this event does not occur within the range of the reinforcing state of affairs (Definition 1 and Postulate 3), or when an excitatory tendency in a behavior sequence encounters a situation which makes the execution of the act impossible (Definition 3), the excitatory tendency in question undergoes a diminution in strength with a limit below the reaction threshold (Definition 2), this diminution extending in considerable part to other excitatory tendencies which may be operative at the same time or for some time thereafter. (Negative association or experimental extinction.)

5. The strength of any given increment of either positive or negative association (Postulates 2 and 3) diminishes with the passage of time, and the portion remaining shows a progressively greater resistance to disintegration with the increase in time since its acquisition, a certain proportion of each increment being permanent. (Negative retention or forgetting.)

6. Each reaction of an organism gives rise to a more or less characteristic internal stimulus. (Internal stimulation.)

Key to Diagrams

S = an adequate stimulus together with the resulting trace (Postulate 1).

S_D = the stimulus associated with a drive, such as hunger.

S_G = the stimulus associated with the goal or reinforcing state of affairs.

s = an internal stimulus resulting from a reaction.

R = a reaction.

R_G = the reaction associated with the goal or reinforcing state of affairs.

r_G = a fractional component of the goal reaction.

$-- \rightarrow$ = excitatory tendency from stimulus to reaction.

$\leadsto \rightarrow$ = causal connection of a non-stimulus-reaction nature.

$. . .$ = a continuation or persistence of a process, as of a drive (S_D).

Distance from left to right represents the passage of time.

Theorems

1

The Pavlovian conditioned reaction and the Thorndikian associative reaction are special cases of the operation of the same principles of learning.

1. Suppose that in the neighborhood of a sensitive organism stimuli S_C and S_G occur in close succession, that these stimuli in conjunction with the drive (S_D) evoke reactions R_C and R_G respectively, that S_m coincides in time with S_C while S_n coincides in time with S_G, and that (Postulate 1) the stimulus trace of S_m extends to R_C, and the stimulus trace of S_n extends to R_G.

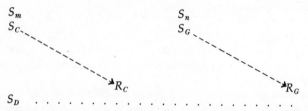

2. From (1) and Postulate 1, it follows that one phase of the stimulus trace of S_m will coincide with R_C, and one phase of the stimulus trace of S_n will coincide with R_G.

3. Now, by Postulate 3, the combination $S_G -- \rightarrow R_G$ marks a reinforcing state of affairs.

4. From (1), (2), (3), and Postulate 2 it follows, among other things, that the trace of S_n will become conditioned to R_G, and the trace of S_m will be conditioned to R_C, yielding the following excitatory tendencies:

$$S_m -- \rightarrow R_C$$
$$S_n -- \rightarrow R_G$$

5. But by (3) and (4) the reaction of the newly acquired excitatory tendency $S_n -- \rightarrow R_G$ is that intimately associated with the reinforcing state of affairs, which identifies it as a conditioned reaction of the Pavlovian type.

6. On the other hand, by (3) and (4) the reaction of the excitatory tendency $S_m \relbar\relbar\rightarrow R_C$ is a reaction distinct from that of the reinforcing state of affairs, which identifies it as an associative reaction of the Thorndikian type.

7. By (5) and (6) both the Pavlovian and the Thorndikian types of reaction have been derived from (1), (2), (3), and (4) jointly, and these in turn from the same principles of learning (Postulates 1, 2, and 3).

8. From (7) the theorem follows.

Q.E.D.

2

Both correct (right) and incorrect (wrong) reactions may be set up by the conditioning (associative) process.

1. Let it be supposed that an organism capable of acquiring associative reactions (Postulate 2) is, a number of times, stimulated simultaneously by S_A, S_B, S_C, and S_D; the S_C evokes reaction R_C; that the stimulus trace (Postulate 1) of S_A and S_B extend as far as R_C; that the object represented by S_B, in conjunction with act R_C, produces (causes) in the external world the event yielding the stimulus S_G; and finally that S_G evokes R_G.

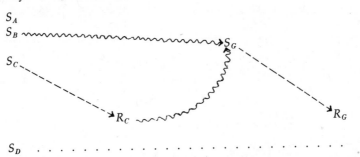

2. By Postulate 3, $S_G \relbar\relbar\rightarrow R_G$ marks a reinforcing state of affairs.

3. From (1), (2), and Postulates 1 and 2, it follows that among other associative tendencies the following must be set up:

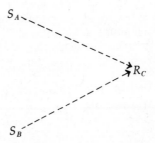

4. Now suppose that at a later time, S_B *alone* should evoke R_C. It follows from (1) that S_B, in conjunction with R_C, will cause to occur the event in the external world which will yield the stimulus S_G which, in turn, will evoke R_G.

5. But, once more, by Postulate 3, $S_G \relbar\relbar\rightarrow R_G$ marks a reinforcing state of affairs from which it follows that under the special new conditions of (4) the reaction tendency $S_B \relbar\relbar\rightarrow R_C$ will still be reinforced.

6. From (5) and Definition 7 it follows that $S_B \relbar\relbar\rightarrow R_C$ must be a correct or "right" reaction.

7. Let us suppose, on the other hand, that S_A *alone* should evoke R_C. It follows from (1) that the external event giving rise to S_G will not occur (S_B being absent), and the excitatory tendency $S_A \mathrel{-\!-\!\rightarrow} R_C$ will not be reinforced and, by Postulate 4, will suffer experimental extinction.

8. From (7) and Definition 8 it follows that $S_A \mathrel{-\!-\!\rightarrow} R_C$ will be an incorrect or "wrong" reaction.

9. From (6) and (8) the theorem follows.

Q.E.D.

3

Simple trial-and-error situations may arise in which the organism will make repeated incorrect reactions.

1. Let it be supposed that we have the simultaneous stimulus situation $S_T S_B S_D$ with the component S_B (step 3, Theorem 2) evoking R_C; that S_B and R_C when operating jointly cause S_G, S_G evoking R_G, whereas S_T evokes R_V with an excitatory tendency exceeding that of S_B to R_C by an amount greater than the weakening effect (Postulate 4) of several unreinforced attempts (Definition 5); that R_V is not followed by its usual reinforcing sequence ($S'_G \mathrel{-\!-\!\rightarrow} R'_G$); and that the external stimulus situation after each attempt becomes exactly the same as before.

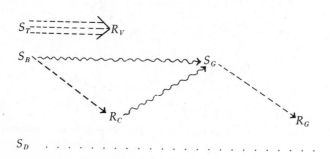

2. From (1) it follows that reaction R_V will take place at once after the organism encounters the compound stimulus $S_T S_B S_D$.

3. Now, by (1) the situation is such that R_V cannot be followed by its accustomed reinforcing sequence, so that this behavior sequence must be interrupted.

4. From (3) and Postulate 4, the excitatory tendency from S_T to R_V will be weakened by experimental extinction.

5. By (4) and Definition 8, R_V is an incorrect reaction.

6. By (1) and (2) the stimulus situation after the first R_V reaction must be the same as at the beginning, and the excitatory tendency to R_V must still be considerably in excess of that to R_C, from which it follows that R_V will occur a second time, and so on.

7. But, by (2), we have a first reaction (R_V), which, by (5) is incorrect and by (6) we have a repetition of this incorrect reaction, from which the theorem follows.

Q.E.D.

4

Organisms in simple trial-and-error situations may manifest spontaneous variability of reaction, the objective situation remaining constant.

1. Suppose the situation in (1) of Theorem 3 with the additional assumption that excitatory tendency $S_B \text{ ---} \rightarrow R_C$ shall be strong enough to resist all generalized inhibitory effects (Postulate 4) sufficiently to escape becoming subliminal.

2. By (1) and Theorem 3, it follows that reaction R_V will take place repeatedly.

3. By (1) and (2), reaction $S_T \text{ ---} \rightarrow R_V$ will not be followed by reinforcement (neither $S'_G \text{ ---} \rightarrow R'_G$ nor $S_G \text{ ---} \rightarrow R_G$), which failure (Postulate 4) will progressively weaken the tendency to R_V.

4. From (1) and (3) it follows that the reaction tendency to R_V must finally become weaker than that to R_C, at which point the stimulus complex $S_T S_B S_D$ will evoke reaction R_C.

5. But the shift from reaction R_V (2) to R_C (4) constitutes a variability of reaction.

6. Meanwhile, by (1) the objective situation has not changed.

7. From (5) and (6) the theorem follows.

Q.E.D.

5

Organisms in simple trial-and-error situations beginning with erroneous reactions may, after a sufficiently large number of attempts, come to give an indefinitely long series of successive correct reactions.

1. Let us assume the situation in step (1) of the deduction of Theorem 4.

2. By (1) and steps (2), (3), and (4) of Theorem 4, reaction tendency R_V will be progressively weakened by extinction until it is below the level of R_C, when the latter will take place.

3. Moreover, by (1), R_C in conjunction with S_B causes S_G; and S_G evokes R_G which, by Postulate 3, marks a reinforcing state of affairs.

4. It follows from (2), (3), and Postulate 2 that the excitatory tendency $S_B \text{ ---} \rightarrow R_C$ will be reinforced, and therefore strengthened.

5. But a certain amount of time must elapse while reaction R_C is taking place; by Postulate 5, this time must permit a certain amount of spontaneous recovery from experimental extinction on the part of R_V.

6. Now, the rate of the spontaneous recovery of R_V (5) may be either (A) more rapid than the gain in strength of R_C through the latter's reinforcement, or (B) it may be less rapid, or (C) the two processes may take place at the same rate. If it is less rapid, or if the two processes take place at the same rate, R_C will maintain its dominance, thus giving an indefinitely long series of correct reactions (Definition 7); from which the theorem follows.

7. But suppose, on the other hand, that the rate of the spontaneous recovery of R_V from its experimental extinction is faster than the gain in strength of R_C through its reinforcement (6). It follows that on this alternative R_V must again become dominant.

8. From (7) it follows by reasoning analogous to that in (2) that R_V will occur

repeatedly until depressed by further experimental extinction below the strength of R_C when the latter will again occur, to be further reinforced, and so on.

9. Now it follows from (4) and (8) together with Postulate 5, that after each complete cycle of reversal of R_V and R_C, the former will retain a certain amount of its weakening which will not yield to spontaneous recovery and the latter will retain a certain amount of the strengthening which will not yield to forgetting.

10. It follows from (9) that if the cyclical alternation were to go on indefinitely, the tendency to R_V must be weakened to zero and that to R_C must be strengthened to its maximum.

11. It is evident from (10) that at some point in the progressive shift in the basic strengths of R_V and R_C the two movements must cross, at which point R_C will be permanently dominant over R_V irrespective of spontaneous recovery or forgetting, and there will then follow an indefinitely long series of successive correct reactions.

12. From (6) and (11) the theorem follows.

Q.E.D.

6

In simple trial-and-error learning situations, failure of final correct reaction will, under certain conditions, result from discontinued effort.

1. Suppose the situation in (1) of Theorem 3 except that the excitatory tendency $S_B \text{---} \to R_C$ is at the outset only a little above the reaction threshold.

2. From (1) and Theorem 3, false reaction R_V will be made repeatedly.

3. By (1) and (2), reaction tendency $S_T \text{---} \to R_V$ will not be followed by reinforcement, which failure (by Postulate 4) will, if not interrupted, gradually weaken $S_T \text{---} \to R_V$ to zero.

4. By (3) and Postulate 4, the weakening of $S_T \text{---} \to R_V$ will extend in considerable part to $S_B \text{---} \to R_C$.

5. Now, by (1) the super-threshold margin of strength of $S_B \text{---} \to R_C$ may be smaller than any assigned finite value, from which it follows that it may be smaller than the depressing effects (4) arising from the extinction of $S_T \text{---} \to R_V$.

6. It follows from (5) that before $S_T \text{---} \to R_V$ may be extinguished beneath the level of $S_B \text{---} \to R_C$ the latter will also have been depressed below the reaction threshold so that when $S_T \text{---} \to R_V$ reaches zero and ceases action, the potentially correct reaction tendency, $S_B \text{---} \to R_C$, will also be unable to function even though without any competition whatever.

7. But the depression of both the tendency to R_V and R_C as shown in (6) will bring about a cessation of attempts (Definition 5), the latter of which (1) would have been a correct reaction (Definition 7).

8. From (3), (4), and (7) the theorem follows.

Q.E.D.

Corollary 1.

Organisms capable of acquiring competing excitatory tendencies will manifest discouragement.

This follows directly from Theorem 6 and Definition 9.

7

Reactions conditioned to a late segment of a stimulus trace will subsequently occur as antedating reactions.

1. Suppose that stimulus S_B precedes stimulus S_C by several times the latency of conditioned reactions; that S_C evokes reaction R_C; that the stimulus trace of S_B extends as far as R_C; that the physical event responsible for S_C, jointly with reaction R_C, causes S_G; that S_G evokes R_G; and that S_D begins at S_C and persists throughout the remainder of the process.

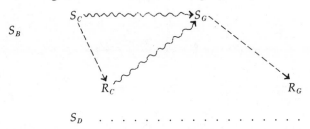

2. From (1) and Postulate 1, a segment of the stimulus trace initiated by S_B will coincide with R_C.

3. By (1) and Postulate 3, S_G — — → R_G marks a reinforcing state of affairs and follows the coincidence of R_C with the trace of S_B.

4. By (2), (3), and Postulate 2, reaction R_C will become conditioned to a late coinciding segment of the trace of stimulus S_B, i.e., that portion which coincides temporally with R_C.

5. Now, by Postulate 1, stimulus trace S_B at the point of the onset of the stimulus is substantially the same as at the segment conditioned to R_C, except that it is stronger.

6. From (5) and Postulate 2 it follows that once R_C has been conditioned to a late segment of the trace of stimulus S_B with a supraliminal strength, the reaction will be evoked by any portion of the same trace which is as strong as, or stronger than, the segment conditioned.

7. But since, by (1), the initial portion of the stimulus trace of S_B will occur several times the latency of such a reaction in advance of the original point of the occurrence of R_C, it follows from (5) and (6) that after conditioning, R_C will be evoked in advance of the point of its original occurrence.

8. From (7) the theorem follows.

Q.E.D.

8

Organisms capable of acquiring trace conditioned reactions will be able to execute successful defense reactions.

1. Let it be supposed that an organism capable of acquiring trace conditioned reactions is stimulated by S_B, that the external world event responsible for S_B initiates a causal sequence several times the length of a conditioned reaction latency, which sequence terminates in S_G and S_D, the two latter jointly constituting an injury and evoking R_G, a flight reaction, which terminates their impact on

the organism; and that the stimulus trace of S_B reaches well beyond the point at which R_G occurs.

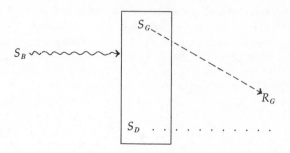

2. From (1) and Postulates 1 and 2 it follows that R_G will be conditioned to the trace of S_B.

3. From (1), (2), and Theorem 7 it follows that if S_B occurs on a later occasion, reaction R_G will occur in advance of situation S_GS_D, which, if it impinges on the organism, will be injurious.

4. But, by (1), R_G is a flight reaction. It follows from (3) that the organism will not be present when the situation otherwise giving rise to S_GS_D occurs and so will escape the injury, thus:

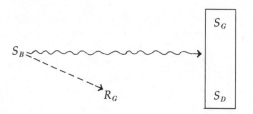

5. From (1) and (4) the theorem follows.

Q.E.D.

9

In stable behavior sequences terminating in reinforcement, each reaction, in general, becomes conditioned (A) to the proprioceptive stimulus arising from the action immediately preceding it, and (b) to the drive stimulus (S_D), each with an intensity diminishing according to a negatively accelerated rate with distance from the reinforcing state of affairs.

1. Let it be supposed that there impinges on an organism a uniform sequence of external stimuli S_1, S_2, S_3, etc.; that these stimuli evoke in the organism reactions R_1, R_2, R_3, etc.; that these reactions produce (Postulate 6) proprioceptive stimuli s_1, s_2, s_3, etc.; that R_3 by an external causal sequence produces a state of affairs which includes S_G; that S_G evokes R_G; that the

combination S_G — — → R_G marks (Postulate 3) a reinforcing state of affairs; and that throughout the sequence there occurs the persisting drive stimulus S_D.

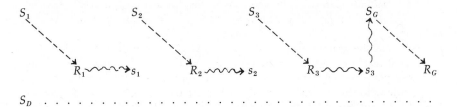

2. By Postulates 1 and 2 the situation supposed in (1) will give rise to an association between each proprioceptive stimulus and the reaction immediately following thus:

$$s_1 \text{— — →} R_2$$
$$s_2 \text{— — →} R_3$$
$$s_3 \text{— — →} R_G$$

3. Also, since by (1) S_D occurs at every point throughout the series, it follows from (1) and Postulate 2 that S_D will be conditioned to every reaction in the series, thus:

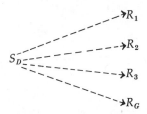

4. By (2) and Postulate 2,

$$s_3 \text{——→} R_G > s_2 \text{——→} R_3 > s_1 \text{——→} R_2$$

and

$$(s_3 \text{——→} R_G) - (s_2 \text{——→} R_3) > (s_2 \text{——→} R_3) - (s_1 \text{——→} R_2)$$

5. Also by (3) and Postulate 2,

$$S_D \text{——→} R_G > S_D \text{——→} R_3 > S_D \text{——→} R_2 > S_D \text{——→} R_1$$

and

$$(S_D \text{——→} R_G) - (S_D \text{——→} R_3) > (S_D \text{——→} R_3)$$
$$- (S_D \text{——→} R_2) > (S_D \text{——→} R_2) - (S_D \text{——→} R_1)$$

6. But the expressions in (4) and (5) represent negatively accelerated excitatory gradients diminishing with distance from the reinforcing state of affairs.

7. From (2), (3), and (6) the theorem follows.

Q.E.D.

10

A fractional anticipatory goal reaction as a stimulus will tend to bring about the reinforcing state of affairs with which the total goal reaction, of which it is a constituent part, is associated.

1. Suppose the situation in (1) of Theorem 9 with the additional assumption that the goal reaction (R_G) is composed of two components, a major one which cannot take place without the aid of the object represented by S_G and which is incompatible with the several acts of the sequence preceding it, and a minor one (r_G) which is not mechanically dependent on S_G and which may take place simultaneously with the antecedent reactions of the series.

2. Now, by Theorem 9, S_D is conditioned to R_G and, since by (1) r_G is a constituent part of R_G, S_D is also conditioned to r_G.

3. Since, by (1), S_D occurs throughout the series, it follows that it will evoke r_G at all points in the behavior sequence R_1, R_2, R_3, etc.

4. From (3) and Postulates 1 and 6 it follows that the trace of the internal stimulus produced by r_G, i.e., s_G, will tend to occur in conjunction with all the reactions of the sequence R_1, R_2, R_3, etc.

5. Now, each time the situation represented in (4) occurs it is followed (1) by the reinforcing state of affairs marked by S_G — — → R_G, from which it follows by Postulate 2 that s_G will ultimately become associated with all of the reactions of the sequence, thus:

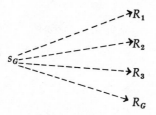

very much as in the case of S_D (Theorem 9).

6. From (5) it follows that s_G will tend, on subsequent occasions, to bring about reactions R_1, R_2, R_3. By (1), R_3 causes S_G, and S_G evokes R_G.

7. But by (1), r_G is a constituent part of R_G which, with its S_G, marks (i.e., is associated with) the reinforcing state of affairs.

8. But if (6 and 7) r_G, through the action of s_G, brings about the inevitable mark of its reinforcing state of affairs (S_G — — → R_G), it must at the same time bring about the reinforcing state of affairs itself.

9. From (7) and (8) the theorem follows.

Q.E.D.

11

Organisms capable of acquiring functionally potent anticipatory reactions intimately associated with the reinforcing state of affairs, will manifest a weakened tendency to the consummatory reaction if, at the completion of the action sequence, the state of affairs then presented does not permit the occurrence of the complete reaction of which the anticipatory reaction is a constituent part.

1. Suppose that an organism which has been in a situation such as (1) in Theorem 9 later finds itself in the same situation with the exception that the terminal conditions, instead of permitting reaction $S_G \dashrightarrow R_G$, permit a different reaction, $S'_G \dashrightarrow R'_G$, which is appropriate to the same drive (S_D) and is in the repertoire of the organism in question but has a strength only slightly above the reaction threshold.

2. By step (1) of the proof of Theorem 9, together with Theorem 9 itself, the customary stimulus complex giving rise to the terminal reaction must be:

3. Now, by (1) and Theorem 9, the s_G of (2) represents r_G, and r_G (Definition 13) is both a reaction anticipatory of, and a fractional component of, R_G.

4. On the other hand, by (1), (2), and Theorem 9, the excitatory tendencies under the changed conditions of the present theorem will be:

$$S'_G \dashrightarrow R'_G$$
$$s_G \dashrightarrow$$
$$S_D \dashrightarrow R_G$$

5. From (1) and (4) it follows that the excitatory tendencies leading to R_G must be frustrated (Definition 3) which (by Postulate 4) will set up experimental extinction at the point in question.

6. From (5) and Postulate 4 it follows that as a result of the extinction of the tendencies to R_G there will occur simultaneously a weakening of the tendency to reaction R'_G.

7. But by (1) the tendencies to R'_G may be as small as desired and therefore smaller than the generalized extinction of (6), from which it follows that under these circumstances the excitatory tendencies to R'_G will pass below the reaction threshold.

8. From (3) and (7) the theorem follows.

Q.E.D.

Corollary 1.
Organisms will display disappointment.
This follows directly from Theorem 11 and Definition 16.

12

Organisms capable of acquiring anticipatory goal reactions will strive to bring about situations which are reinforcing.

1. Let it be assumed that an organism has acquired a habit-family hierarchy (Definition 17) of two distinct action sequences of the type described in (1) of Theorem 10, both originating in the external stimulus situation S_1, terminating in the reinforcing situation $S_G \dashrightarrow R_G$ and associated with the drive S_D; that the initial acts of one of the sequences are R_I, R_{II}, etc., and those of the other are R_1, R_2, etc.; that the excitatory tendency initiating the sequence beginning with R_1 is

dominant over that beginning with R_I, but that the tendency to R_I is far enough above the reaction threshold to survive the weakening effect which would result (Postulate 4) from the frustration of the tendency to R_1.

2. Now suppose that an obstacle is interposed which effectually prevents the completion of R_1 and the remainder of that sequence (1). It follows from Postulate 4 that this excitatory tendency will suffer extinction, with no limit above zero.

3. From (1) and (2) it follows that the sequence beginning with R_I and terminating with R_G will be executed after the frustration of the excitatory tendency leading to R_1.

4. Now, from (1) it follows by reasoning strictly analogous to steps (2), (3), (4), (5), and (6) of the deduction of Theorem 10, that s_G will acquire during the acquisition of the habit family the tendency to evoke (A) reaction sequence R_1 and all those acts following it in the sequence leading to R_G, and (B) reaction sequence R_I together with all those leading from it to R_G.

5. From (2), (3), (4), and Definition 10 it follows that under these circumstances the introduction of a barrier will cause the organism to shift from one behavior sequence *directed* to a reinforcing state of affairs to another *directed to the same* reinforcing state of affairs.

6. But by (5) and Definition 11, when the interposition of an obstacle leads an organism to choose an alternative action sequence *directed* to the same reinforcing state of affairs as that interrupted by the obstacle, the behavior in question is striving.

7. From (6) the theorem follows.

Q.E.D.

Corollary 1.

Organisms will strive for goals.

This follows directly from Theorem 12 and Definitions 11 and 12.

13

When an organism has attained a reinforcing state of affairs in a situation which, objectively considered, is totally novel, but by means of a member of a previously established habit-family hierarchy, there may follow without specific practice a tendency to a transfer to the new situation of the behavior tendencies represented by one or another of the remaining members of the habit-family hierarchy in question.

1. Let it be assumed that an organism has acquired a habit-family hierarchy (Definition 17) of two distinct action sequences of the type described in (1) of Theorem 10, both originating in the external stimulus situation S_1, terminating in the reinforcing situation S_G — — $\rightarrow R_G$ and associated with the drive stimulus S_D; that the initial act of one of the sequences is R_I and that of the other is R_1.

2. From (1) it follows by reasoning strictly analogous to steps (2), (3), (4), (5), and (6) of the deduction of Theorem 10, that s_G will acquire during the acquisition of the habit family the tendency to evoke (A) reaction sequence R_1 and all those acts following it in the sequence leading to R_G, and (B) reaction sequence R_I together with all those leading from it to R_G.

3. Now, suppose that this same organism in a novel external situation S'_1 and acting under the same drive stimulus S_D reaches, a few times, by the process of trial and error the reinforcing state of affairs marked by S_G — — $\rightarrow R_G$, by an action sequence the same as that beginning with R_1 of one of the members of the habit-family hierarchy of (1).

4. From (3) it follows by reasoning similar to steps (2) and (3) of the deduction leading to Theorem 10, that r_G will be present throughout the behavior sequence beginning with S'_1.

5. It follows from (4) that there will be a coincidence of r_G and the stimulus trace of S'_1.

6. Since by (3) the coincidence of the stimulus trace of S'_1 and r_G (5) is followed by $S_G \; -\!-\!\to R_G$, it follows by Postulates 1 and 2 that there will be set up the excitatory tendency $S'_1 \; -\!-\!\to r_G$.

7. From (6), (2), and Postulate 6 it follows that S'_1 will tend to initiate the behavior sequence (omitting internal stimuli after R_1):

$$S'_1 \; -\!-\!\to r_G \leadsto s_G \; -\!-\!\to R_1 \; -\!-\!\to R_2 \; -\!-\!\to R_3 \leadsto S_G \; -\!-\!\to R_G$$

and also

$$S'_1 \; -\!-\!\to r_G \leadsto s_G \; -\!-\!\to R_I \; -\!-\!\to R_{II} \; -\!-\!\to R_{III} \leadsto S_G \; -\!-\!\to R_G$$

or, combining the two sequences,

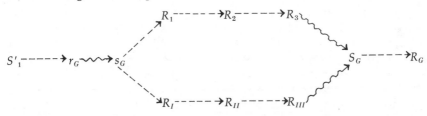

8. Now, suppose that at this point an obstacle is interposed such that R_1 cannot take place, and that $s_G \; -\!-\!\to R_I$ is far enough above the reaction threshold to resist the weakening effect of the frustration of the excitatory tendency to R_1. With the competition of R_1 thus removed from the excitatory tendency to R_I, s_G will initiate R_I (7); this will lead to R_{II}, this to R_{III}, etc., and finally to $S_G \; -\!-\!\to R_G$.

9. But the shift from the sequence beginning with R_1 to that beginning with R_I as in (8) is a transfer without specific practice from an old to a new situation because R_I, R_{II}, etc., have never taken place in the external stimulus situation beginning with S'_1.

10. From (9) the theorem follows.

Q.E.D.

The Nature of Adaptive Behavior as Indicated by the Postulates of the Present System

We come now to the second step in our exposition of the procedure which should have been carried out by Eddington and Weiss before they presumed to state the ultimate nature of the more complex forms of adaptive and moral behavior. In this step we turn, mainly for purposes of illustration, to the direct examination of the postulates which gave rise to the system, to see whether they are, in fact, physical or psychic. Let us pass them in review. Postulate 1 states that the physiological effects of a stimulus persist for a certain time even after the stimulus has ceased. Postulate 2 indicates the conditions under which stimuli and reactions become associated or conditioned. Postulate 3 gives the marks of reinforcing situations. Postulate 4 states the conditions under which associations are unlearned. Postulate 5 gives the conditions under which positive and negative learning are lost. Postulate 6 states the well-known fact of internal stimulation.

At first glance most persons would probably say that these postulates represent the behavior of what has always been regarded as physical. Moreover, the postulates appear to be phenomena of physical structures which most theoretical physicists believe will ultimately be derived, i.e., deduced, by them from electrons, protons, deutrons, etc. According to this view the theoretical physicists will ultimately deduce as theorems from electrons, protons, etc., the six postulates which we have employed as the basis for the deduction of adaptive behavior. If this deduction were accomplished we should have an unbroken logical chain extending from the primitive electron all the way up to complex purposive behavior. Further developments may conceivably extend the system to include the highest rational and moral behavior. Such is the natural goal of science. This is the picture which a complete scientific monism would present. Unfortunately, theoretical physics is very far from this achievement, and judgment regarding its ultimate accomplishment must be indefinitely suspended. At most such a view, attractive as it is, can be regarded only as a working hypothesis.[17]

But What of Consciousness?

But what of consciousness, of awareness, of experience—those phenomena of which the philosophers and theologians have made so much and upon the priority of which they are so insistent? An inspection of the postulates of the miniature system of adaptive behavior presented above certainly shows no trace of any such phenomena. It is clear, therefore, that so far as that considerable array of complex behavior is concerned,

---

17. There is conceivable, however, a kind of experimental shortcut to the determination of the ultimate nature of adaptive behavior. Suppose it were possible to construct from inorganic materials, such as the theoretical physicists have already succeeded in deriving from electrons and protons, a mechanism which would display exactly the principles of behavior presented in the six postulates just examined. On the assumption that the logic of the above deductions is sound, it follows inevitably that such a "psychic" machine, if subjected to appropriate environmental influences, must manifest the complex adaptive phenomena presented by the theorems. And if, upon trial, this *a priori* expectation should be verified by the machine's behavior, it would be possible to say with assurance and a clear conscience that such adaptive behavior may be "reached" by purely physical means. A beginning in the direction of such constructions has already been made. See R. G. Krueger and C. L. Hull, An electro-chemical parallel to the conditioned reflex, *J. Gen. Psychol.*, 1931, 5, 262–269; G. K. Bennett and L. B. Ward, Synthesis of conditioned reflex, *Amer. J. Psychol.*, 1933, 45, 339; D. G. Ellson, A mechanical synthesis of trial-and-error learning, *J. Gen. Psychol.*, 1935, 13, 212–218.

consciousness or experience has no logical priority. In the field of scientific theory no other form of priority is of primary significance.

What, then, shall we say about consciousness? Is its existence denied? By no means. But to recognize the existence of a phenomenon is not the same thing as insisting upon its basic, i.e., logical, priority. Instead of furnishing a means for the solution of problems, consciousness appears to be itself a problem needing solution. In the miniature theoretical system, no mention of consciousness or experience was made for the simple reason that no theorem has been found as yet whose deduction would be facilitated in any way by including such a postulate. Moreover, we have been quite unable to find any other scientific system of behavior which either has found consciousness a necessary presupposition or, having assumed it, has been able to deduce from it a system of adaptive behavior or moral action.[18] There is, however, no reason at all for not using consciousness or experience as a postulate in a scientific theoretical system if it clearly satisfies the deductive criteria already laid down. If such a system should be worked out in a clear and unambiguous manner the incorporation of consciousness into the body of behavior theory should be automatic and immediate. The task of those who would have consciousness a central factor in adaptive behavior and in moral action is accordingly quite clear. They should apply themselves to the long and grinding labor of the logical derivation of a truly scientific system. Until such a system has been attained on a considerable scale, the advancement of science will be favored by their limiting their claims to statements of their hopes and wishes as such. Meanwhile, one cannot help recalling that for several centuries practically all psychological and philosophical theorists have set out precisely with the assumption of the priority of consciousness or experience. Considering the practically complete failure of all this effort to yield even a small scientific system of adaptive or moral behavior in which consciousness finds a position of logical priority as a postulate, one may, perhaps, be pardoned for entertaining a certain amount of pessimism regarding such an eventuality.

In view of the general lack of the kind of evidence which would be necessary to show the logical priority of consciousness, it may naturally be asked why there is such insistence upon its central significance.

---

18. It is rather hoped and expected that this statement will be challenged. In the interest of the clarification of an important problem, it is desirable that the challenge be accompanied by a formal exhibition of the structure of the system supposed to manifest the critical characteristics. As illustrated above, a theoretical system is a considerable sequence of interlocking theorems, all derived from the same set of postulates. Too often what pass as systems in psychology are merely informal points of view containing occasional propositions which, even if logically derived, would be nothing more than isolated theorems. Some authors are prone to the illusion that such propositions could be deduced with rigor in a few moments if they cared to take the trouble. Others assert that the logic has all been worked by them "in their heads," but that they did not bother to write it out; the reader is expected to accept this on faith. Fortunately, in science it is not customary to base conclusions on faith.

While there are many contributing factors, it can scarcely be doubted that an important element in the situation is found in the perseverative influences of medieval theology. During the Middle Ages, and for centuries thereafter, social or moral control was supposed to be effected largely through promises of rewards or punishments after death. Therefore something had to survive death to reap these rewards. Consciousness as a non-physical entity was considered incorruptible and thus immune to the disintegration of the flesh. Consequently it offered a logical possibility of something surviving physical death upon which scores might be evened among the shadows beyond the river Styx. But to be convincing, it was necessary for the thing rewarded or punished to be an essentially causal element in the determination of moral conduct or behavior. Thus it was imperative not only that consciousness be non-physical, but also that it be the basic factor in determining action. Such a view is incompatible with the belief that the more complex forms of human behavior could be derived without any reference whatever to consciousness. Tradition is strong, especially when fostered by powerful institutions. Accordingly, the frequent insistence on the logical priority of consciousness is not surprising, even when coming from persons who have no clear notion as to the origin of their feelings in the matter.

Thus it can hardly be doubted that psychology in its basic principles is to a considerable degree in the thrall of the Middle Ages, and that, in particular, our prevailing systematic outlook in the matter of consciousness is largely medieval. The situation depicted in a remarkable panel of the fresco by Orozco in the Dartmouth Library gives a powerful artistic representation of this. There, lifeless skeletons in academic garb assist solemnly at the gruesome travail of a reclining skeleton in the act of reproducing itself. What a picture of academic sterility! Fortunately the means of our salvation is clear and obvious. As ever, it lies in the application of scientific procedures. The methodology is old and tried; it goes back even to the time of Galileo. The present paper is, in reality, an exposition of the specific application of this technique in a systematic manner to the problems of complex adaptive behavior. Galileo practiced this methodology at the imminent risk of imprisonment, torture, and death. For us to apply the methodology, it is necessary only to throw off the shackles of a lifeless tradition.

Reprinted with permission
from *Psychological Review*,
1938, *45*, 1–41.

Chapter 18

The Determiners of Behavior at a Choice Point

Edward Chace Tolman

University of California

T he question I am going to discuss is the very straightforward and specific one of "why rats turn the way they do, at a given choice-point in a given maze at a given stage of learning."

The first item in the answer is fairly obvious. They turn the way they do because they have on the preceding trials met this same choice-point together with such and such further objects or situations, down the one path and down the other, for such and such a number of preceding trials. Let me, however, analyze this further, with the aid of a couple of diagrams. First, consider a diagram of a single choice point (Figure 1).

In this figure the point of choice itself is designated as O_C; the complex of stimulus-objects met going down the left alley, as O_L, that met going down the right alley, as O_R; the goal at the left, as O_{GL}; and that at the right, as O_{GR}. The behavior of turning to the left is represented by the arrow B_L; and that of turning to the right, by the arrow B_R. And

---

Presidential address delivered before the American Psychological Association, Minneapolis, September 3, 1937.

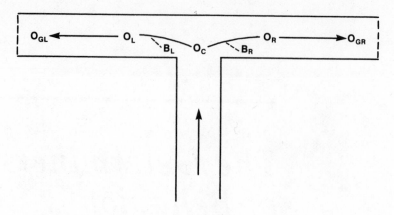

Figure 1.

the point I am now making is that the relative strength of the tendency to turn, say, left (rather than right) will be, first of all, a result not only of the present presentation of O_C but also of all the previous presentations of it together with the O_L, O_{GL}, O_R, and O_{GR} consequences of having behaved by B_L and B_R on all these preceding occasions. In short, I would schematize this feature of the causal determination of the left-turning tendency by the diagram shown in Figure 2.

The expression $B_L/(B_L + B_R)$ at the right-hand side of Figure 2 is the "dependent variable" (we may call it the behavior-ratio). It is the percentage tendency at any given stage of learning for the group as a whole to turn left. And the hieroglyphic at the left-hand side of this figure is the "independent variable" which determines this behavior-ratio. This hieroglyphic is to be read as meaning: the *sum* of all the preceding occasions in which O_C has, by virtue of B_L, been followed by O_L and O_{GL} and by virtue of B_R been followed by O_R and O_{GR}. This diagram is thus no more than a schematic way of representing the, shall we say, (to use the term we theoretical psychologists have of late taken so violently to our bosoms) "operational" facts. The expression at the left is

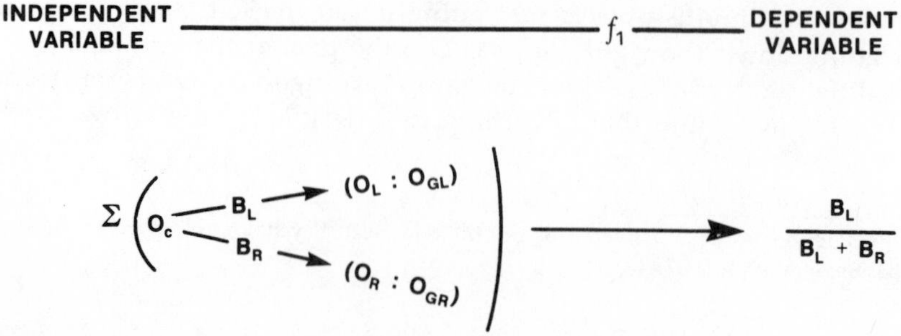

INDEPENDENT VARIABLE ———————————— f_1 ———— DEPENDENT VARIABLE

$$\Sigma \left(O_c \overset{B_L}{\underset{B_R}{\rightrightarrows}} \begin{matrix} (O_L : O_{GL}) \\[2pt] (O_R : O_{GR}) \end{matrix} \right) \longrightarrow \frac{B_L}{B_L + B_R}$$

Figure 2.

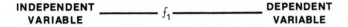

INDEPENDENT ————————— f_1 ————————— DEPENDENT
VARIABLE   VARIABLE

$$\Sigma \text{(OBO)} \longrightarrow \frac{B_L}{B_L + B_R}$$

Figure 3.

an "operationally defined" independent variable and that at the right, an "operationally defined" dependent variable.

For brevity's sake, I shall often substitute, however, an abbreviated symbol for the left-hand term, viz.: simply $\Sigma(OBO)$, as shown in Figure 3.

One further point—the f_1 in each of these figures indicates merely the fact of the functional dependence of the dependent variable upon the independent variable. To indicate the "form" of this function we would require a more analytical diagram, such as that shown in Figure 4.

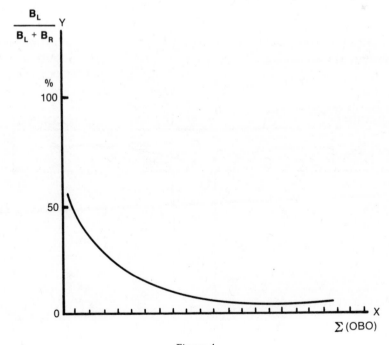

Figure 4.

But this, or course, is no more than our old friend, the learning curve. It results when we plot the independent variable along an X axis and the dependent variable along a Y axis. Nothing very new so far. It seems surprising, however, that in spite of the thousands, not to say millions, of such learning curves which have been obtained in the last four decades in American rat laboratories there are still a variety of quite simple things about this function which we do not yet know or with regard to which we are still in dispute.

For example, we are still in dispute, first of all, as to the relative importance of the occurrences of the two alternative behaviors B_L and B_R, where B_L is "wrong" and B_R is "correct." (See Figure 5.)

Thorndike (118, 119) and Lorge (69) and their co-workers, as you all know, working with human beings in analogous, though verbal, set-ups have now concluded that the occurrence of the wrong behavior has no such general causative effect. They find that learning appears only as a result of the occurrences of the rewarded sequence O_C—B_R→$(O_R:O_{GR})$. On the other hand, still more recently, Muenzinger and Dove (95), working with set-ups similar to Thorndike's have found that the occurrence of the wrong response O_C—B_L→$(O_L:O_{GL})$ does weaken its tendency to re-occur. Also Carr, as a result of a series of experiments done by his students (54, 72, 132, 135, 137) some time since in the Chicago laboratory, was finally forced to conclude that

. . . a certain number of errors must be made and eliminated before the subject is ever able to run the maze correctly. Correct modes of response are established in part by learning *what not to do* (16, p. 98, italics mine).

A second point about which we are still surprisingly ignorant is that we do not yet know the importance of the rat's being permitted, or not

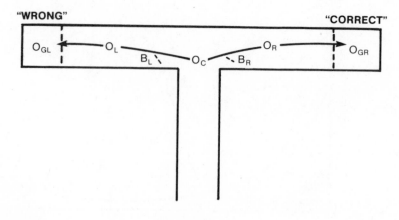

Figure 5.

permitted, to return out of the wrong choice. In some experiments, when the animal takes the wrong alley, he passes through a one-way gate and is started over again. In others, he is allowed to treat it as a blind and back out. But, so far as I know, there has been no carefully controlled comparison between these two procedures.

Thirdly, the question of the relative effects of concentrated versus distributed repetitions has not as yet received the thoroughgoing experimental analysis that it deserves. But I understand that Professor Stone and his co-workers are now directing their attention to it and are getting some very significant findings.

Fourthly, we are ignorant concerning the difference between animals which have an initial left-hand bias and those which have an initial right-hand bias.[1] We usually lump the results for both types together in a single curve. But we might well separate them and study them independently.

Fifthly, Brunswik (14) has recently brought to light a new point in our ignorance. He has been trying the effect of rewarding on the right and rewarding on the left different proportions of times. In other words, it was no God-given rule but apparently some merely human predilection on our part which made us heretofore tend almost invariably to make one of the alternative behaviors always rewarded and the other always punished. But other frequencies of reward and punishment are equally possible and equally deserving of study.

Sixthly, experiments by Krechevsky (59, 60, 61), seem to indicate that there may be certain general features about the content of the OBO's such, for example, as their containing variable or non-variable paths, which are very important in determining the resultant behavior-ratios and about which we need more information.

Seventhly, a further point which needs more investigation is, as Muenzinger and his co-workers (87, 88, 89, 90, 91, 92, 93) have beautifully brought out, the fact that punishment or obstacles to be overcome, *even on the correct side,* may sometimes seem to aid rather than hinder learning. (See also Tolman, 125, and Tolman, Hall and Bretnall, 127.)

Eighthly, there is the question of what happens when $\Sigma(OBO)$, the number of trials, has become very great. This seems to induce a special sort of result for which the term fixation has been suggested.[2] And further studies of such "fixations" are needed.

Ninthly, the problem as to the effect of temporal intervals between O_C and the resultant O_{GL} and O_{GR} are still by no means altogether completely worked out in spite of all the beautiful work of Hunter and

---

1. For one of the first experiments indicating that there are such biases, see Yoshioka (149).

2. See the original experiments on fixation by Gilhousen (31, 32), Krechevsky and Honzik (62) and Hamilton and Ellis (28, 38, 39).

his students, and others who have followed after, on the "delayed reaction" and on "double alternation."[3]

Finally, however, there is a point with regard to which we are not altogether ignorant but the importance of which we usually overlook—namely, the fact that any such function—any such learning curve, actually, is always obtained within the matrix of a larger number of other independent variables in addition to $\Sigma(OBO)$. The following is a tentative list of such other variables together with $\Sigma(OBO)$:

1. Environmental Variables
        M—Maintenance Schedule
        G—Appropriateness of Goal Object
        S—Types and Modes of Stimuli Provided
        R—Types of Motor Response Required
    $\Sigma(OBO)$—Cumulative Nature and Number of Trials
        P—Pattern of Succeeding and Succeeding Maze Units
2. Individual Difference Variables
        H—Heredity
        A—Age
        T—Previous Training
        E—Special Endocrine, Drug or Vitamin Conditions

As you will see, I have divided such independent variables into two groups which I have called: (1) Environmental Variables, and (2) Individual Difference Variables. The *environmental variables* are M, the maintenance schedule, by which I mean time since food, water, sex, parturition, or the like, which in common parlance we would call the drive condition; G, the appropriateness of the goal-object provided at the end of the maze relative to this drive; S, the specific types and modes of stimuli which the maze provides; R, the specific kinds of motor response required of the animal in the maze; $\Sigma(OBO)$, the cumulative sum and manner of trials; and P, the general pattern of the maze, that is to say, the number and sorts of preceding and succeeding units. The individual difference variables are: H—heredity, A—age; T—previous training, and E—any special endocrine, drug, or vitamin conditions.

But if, now, we are to include all these independent variables together with $\Sigma(OBO)$, we must have a new causal picture. I suggest the one shown in Figure 6.

A main causal line has been drawn, as you see, issuing from each environmental variable. And the individual difference variables, H, A, T, and E, have been arranged as possible modifiers of each such main causal line. And what I have hereby tried to indicate is merely the actual types of experiment which we maze-psychologists go in for.

---

3. The literature on these matters is, of course, already enormous and I can not pretend to quote it here. It will suffice to refer to Munn's chapter on "Symbolic Processes" (95, Ch. 7) and to Heron's chapter on "Complex Learning Processes" (40).

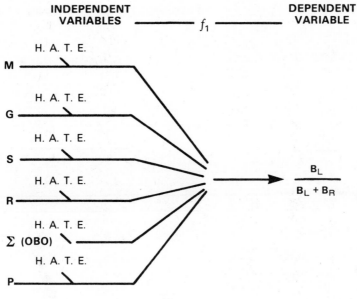

Figure 6.

I wish now, however, to pass from the above outline of experiments to a consideration of theories. But why, you may ask, can we not be satisfied with just experiments and the "facts" resulting from them?[4] I find that there are two reasons. In the first place, an entirely factual, empirical establishment of the complete functional relation, f_1, to cover the effects on $B_L/(B_L + B_R)$ of all the permutations and combinations of M, G, S, etc., etc., would be a humanly endless task. We have time in this brief mortal span to test only a relatively limited number of such permutations and combinations. So, in the first place, we are forced to propose theories in order to use such theories to extrapolate for all these combinations for which we have not time to test.

But I suspect that there is also another reason for theories. Some of us, psychologically, just demand theories. Even if we had all the million and one concrete facts, we would still want theories to, as we would say, "explain" those facts. Theories just seem to be necessary to some of us to relieve our inner tensions.

But what is a theory? According to Professor Hull (49), a theory is a set of definitions and postulates proposed by the theorist (on the basis presumably of some already found facts) from which other empirically testable facts, or as he calls them, theorems, can be logically deduced. These deduced theorems will be new empirical relationships which the

---

4. That the facts must be obtained first of all and that we psychologists have for the most part been both extremely lazy and extremely shoddy in our pursuit of the "facts" has been eloquently pointed out by Brown (12).

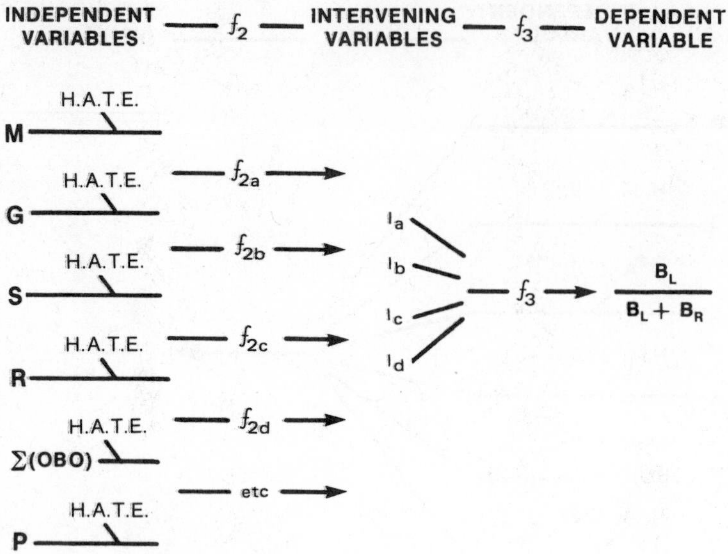

Figure 7.

theorist—or more often, his research assistants—can, then and there, be set to look for.

For my own nefarious purposes, however, I wish to phrase this matter of the relationship of a theory to the empirical facts out of which it arises and to which it leads in somewhat other terms. A theory, as I shall conceive it, is a set of "intervening variables." These to-be-inserted intervening variables are "constructs" which we, the theorists, evolve as a useful way of breaking down into more manageable form the original complete f_1 function. In short, I would schematize the nature of our psychological theories by Figure 7. In place of the original f_1 function, I have introduced a set of intervening variables, I_a, I_b, I_c, etc., few or many, according to the particular theory. And I have conceived a set of f_2 functions to connect these intervening variables severally to the independent variables, on the one hand, and an f_3 function to combine them together and connect them to the final dependent variable, on the other.[5]

But turn, now, to some of the actual theories. I shall restrict myself to the discussion of three—Professor Thorndike's, Professor Hull's, and my own. This, or course, will hardly be a fair survey of the field. There are many other doctrines of learning, as, for example, Professor Guthrie's (33), and those of the other conditioned reflex psychologists (145)[6] and those of the Gestalt school, (2), (45), (55), (56), (143), which are of as great

---

5. For previous presentations of this notion of "intervening variables" see Tolman (124, 126).

6. For a superb presentation and summary of all the conditioned reflex theories of learning see Hilgard (44).

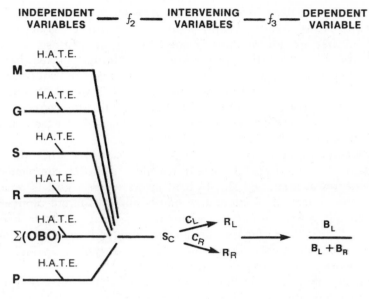

Figure 8.

importance and which have equally affected by own thinking. But I shall have to omit a discussion of them here.

Professor Thorndike's "intervening variables" are quite simple. They are "stimuli," "bonds" or "connections," and "response-tenden-cies." His theory I would represent, therefore, by the diagram shown in Figure 8. It is Thorndike's conception of the nature of the f_2 function which seems to be the crux of his theory. Originally, his statement of this function included both a Law of Exercise and a Law of Effect. But now, as we all know, it includes a Law of Effect only, and a truncated law at that. For, as now stated, Thorndike finds that it is the repetitions of the rewarded sequence $O_C - B_R \rightarrow (O_R:O_{GR})$ which alone are important. These strengthen the C_R connection. The repetitions of the punished $O_c - B_L \rightarrow (O_L:O_{GL})$ sequence do not, he says, correspond-ingly weaken the C_L connection.

I have quite a number of quarrels with this theory. I would like to say first, however, that it seems to me that this theory of Thorndike's either in its present or in its earlier form, is *the* theory relative to which the rest of us here in America have oriented ourselves. The psychology of animal learning—not to mention that of child learning—has been and still is primarily a matter of agreeing or disagreeing with Thorndike, or trying in minor ways to improve upon him. Gestalt psychologists, condition-reflex psychologists, sign-gestalt psychologists—all of us here in America seem to have taken Thorndike, overtly or covertly, as our starting point. And we have felt very smart and pleased with ourselves if we could show that we have, even in some very minor way, developed new little wrinkles of our own.

Let me now, nonetheless, try to present my criticisms. First, Thorndike's theory, as I see it, identifies stimuli (S's) with gross objects (O's) and identifies specific muscular responses (R's) with gross means-end behaviors (B's). And this procedure seems to me to require more justification than he gives it. It raises the problem of "equivalence of stimuli" and "equivalence of response" which Klüver *(53)*, Waters *(138)*, and others have been concerned with. It is also probably connected with the problem of perception-constancy which the Gestalt psychologists and other Europeans have dealt with at such length.[7]

My second objection is that the theory as stated by Thorndike does not allow for the facts of "latent learning," of the complementary phenomenon of a sudden shoot-up in errors when a goal is removed, and of the utilization of alternative habits under different motivations. That, to allow for these facts, a distinction must be made between "learning" and "performance" has indeed already been emphasized by Lashley *(63)*, Elliott *(27)*, Leeper *(64)* and myself *(122, 123)*. But Thorndike's theory allows no such distinction.

Finally, my third objection is that the theory does not, for the most part, make anything of the other circumambient variables M, G, S, etc., in addition to $\Sigma(OBO)$. No doubt Thorndike, if this were pointed out to him, would try to work all these other independent variables in as further conditions tending to favor or hinder the respective strengths of C_R and C_L. But my suspicion is that he would have difficulty.

Turn, now, to Professor Hull's theory. For Hull the intervening variables are "conditionings" of the running responses to successive aggregates of exteroceptive, proprioceptive, and interoceptive stimuli. In order to explain this, first let me present another picture of the simple T-maze (Figure 9).

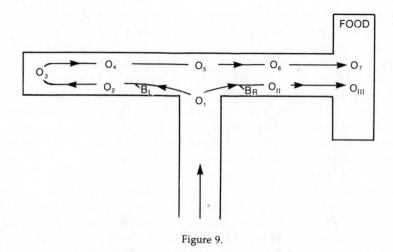

Figure 9.

---

7. For a resume of this work see Koffka *(56,* Ch. 6).

Two alternative routes are shown—one in which the animal goes directly down the true path and one in which he first chooses the blind to the left. Successive points along these two paths are indicated as successively numbered O's. The true path involves three such O's, the blind alley, seven, and, to explain the tendency which develops in such a situation to go right rather than left, Hull's theory postulates the intervening variables shown in Figure 10.

What I have done, as you will see, is to insert one of Hull's *own* diagrams *(48, 44)* in the middle and to call it his set of intervening variables. You are all familiar with such diagrams. They are very clever and can be invented, as I know to my cost, to explain practically any type of behavior, however far distant from an instance of conditioning such a behavior might at first sight appear. I have, therefore, the greatest respect for them. And, even though I argue against them, I find myself continually being intrigued and almost ready to change my mind and accept them and Hull after all.

It must be noted further, however, that there are certain other concepts besides conditioning involved in these diagrams which help to make them work. These seem to be: (1) anticipatory goal-responses, i.e., the little r_G's with their little resultant proprioceptive or interoceptive s_G's whereby the character of the goal is brought back into the aggregates of conditioned stimuli at the different points along the maze; (2) the continuous drive stimulus S_D which also appears at all points and thus also becomes part of the total conditioned stimulus-aggregate at each point along the maze paths; (3) the goal-gradient hypothesis whereby all conditionings are stronger the nearer they are to the goal; and (4) habit-family hierarchies whereby, if one path or route is blocked, the rat readily switches over to any alternative chain of conditionings which he has at his command. By virtue of these concepts, in addition to that of conditioning *per se*, Professor Hull is able to bring into his diagram the influences not only of $\Sigma(OBO)$ but also of M, maintenance schedule; G, goodness of goal; and P, maze-pattern, in a rather remarkable way. He has not, on the other hand, as I see it, especially considered as yet the variables S, and R, and H, A, T, and E.

I have four rather specific criticisms of Hull's theory. First, Hull, like Thorndike, passes from O's and B's to S's and R's with no clear statement of his justification for doing so. And, again, I feel, as I did relative to Thorndike, that, if such simple S-R formulations are to have cogency, we must be told why and how the actual gross O's can be reduced to simple S's, and the actual gross means-end B's to simple R's.

My second criticism lies in the fact that I doubt that the supposed laws of conditioning are as simple and as well-known as Hull assumes. Many of the actual workers in the field, for example Loucks *(70, 71)*, Liddell *(67)*, Culler *(21)*, Schlosberg *(105, 106)*, Hilgard *(42, 43)* seem to find conditioning a very variable and complicated phenomenon. To explain maze behavior by conditioning seems to me, therefore, like asking the halt to lead the blind. Or to put this another way, what Skinner *(108)* (see Figure 11) calls his Type 1 sort of conditioning (which

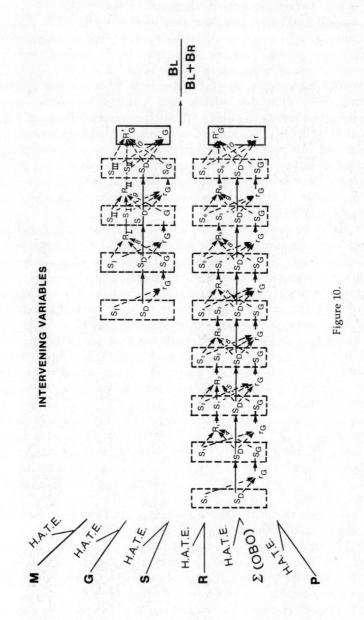

Figure 10.

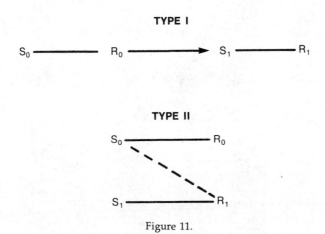

Figure 11.

for me is not conditioning at all) seems to be at the present stage of the game, just as well and perhaps better understood than the more classical, or what he calls his Type 2, sort of conditioning.

Finally, when it comes to using one of Hull's diagrams for actually predicting, on any given occasion, the value of $B_L/(B_L + B_R)$ I find that the difficulty of determining the actual strengths to be assigned to the various S-R connections an almost insuperable one. But, then, perhaps an analogous sort of criticism will be raised against my diagrams. So, in conclusion, let me repeat that I have a tremendous respect for Professor Hull's theory and that I am not by any means as yet altogether certain that mine is better.

I come, now finally, to my own theory. But first, I would like to make it clear that however complicated what I am actually going to present may appear, it will be in reality an *over-simplified and incomplete* version. Partly for the sake of simplicity and partly also, I suppose, because I have not as yet completely thought the whole thing through, the diagrams I shall present will not contain as many "intervening variables" nor as complicated interfunctional relations as, I suspect, will finally actually prove necessary. They will, however, indicate the general picture.

My first diagram would be that shown in Figure 12.

Note the list of *intervening variables*: "demand," "appetite," "differentiation," "skill," "hypotheses," and "biases."[8] Such concepts are, I am sure, irritating in that they appear subjective and not the sort to be

_____

8. In addition to these the final version of the theory would, I suspect, have to add other intervening variables such as: "general activity," for the best discussion of this which I know see Munn (97, Ch. 2); General attentivity or "vigilance," see Krechevsky (58); and demand for "parsimony"—i.e., demand against "distance" and "barriers," see, for example, Tolman (122, Ch. 7), Gengerelli (30), McCulloch (84), Tsai (133), Waters (140), Wheeler (143) and Wright (148).

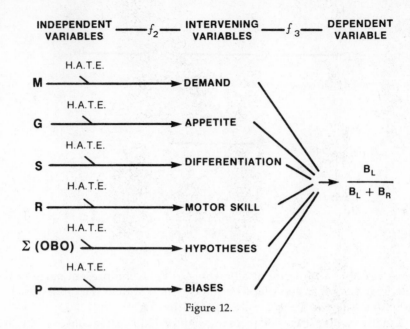

Figure 12.

permitted in an honest behaviorism. Each of them is, nonetheless, I would claim, capable of a perfectly objective definition and measurement. Thus, you will note that each is depicted as resulting from its own correlative environmental variable plus the controlling effects of H, A, T, and E. "Demands" result from M's; "appetites" from G's; "differentiations" from S's; "skills" from R's; "hypotheses" from $\Sigma(OBO$'s); and "biases" from P's. And I am now going to assert that each such "intervening variable" is defined by a standard experiment in which its correlative independent environmental variable is systematically varied. Further, in each such experiment all the other independent variables are held constant while the one in question is systematically changed. Under such conditions the resultant variations in $B_L/(B_L + B_R)$ are, *by definition*, to be said to mirror directly the variations in the one given intervening variable.

For example, the intervening variable—"demand"—(say for food) shall, by definition, be measured by the variations in the behavior-ratio which occur in a standard experiment when G and S and R and $\Sigma(OBO)$ and P and H, and A, and T, and E, that is, all the independent variables *other than M*, are held constant at certain "standard" values, while M, itself, is systematically varied. For example, as standard values for these other variables I should probably choose: for G the regular standard living diet of the colony, for S an elevated maze in which all possible visual, olfactory, auditory, tactual and kinaesthetic stimuli would be available, for R a maze which involved running rather than swimming, or climbing, or going hand over hand, or pulling strings, or what not, for $\Sigma(OBO)$, that set-up which makes the left-hand side a blind and a distribution of one trial every 24 hours, and a number of trials which, for

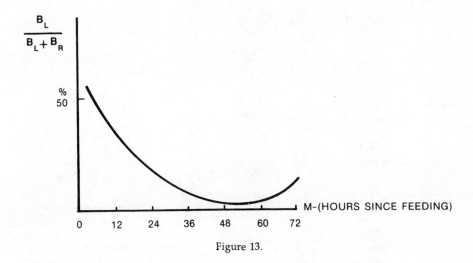

Figure 13.

an average value of M, would bring the learning curve about down to the base line—say some 10 trials—and for P a single-unit T with no preceding or succeeding units. With such a set-up in which all the other independent variables would thus be given these standard values and held constant, I would then vary M and study the correlated variations in $B_L/(B_L + B_R)$. And the sort of results one would get are shown in Figure 13.

But the demand should really be defined as *inversely* related to this $B_L/(B_L + B_R)$ ratio, so that replotting one would have as one's final defining function that shown in Figure 14. And having, thus at last, this

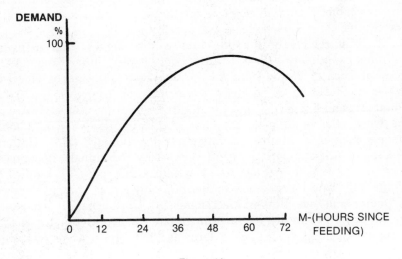

Figure 14.

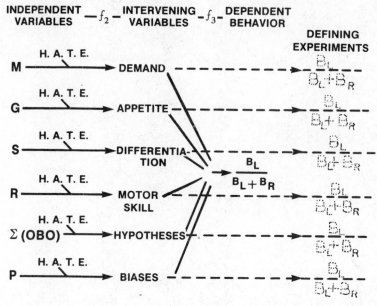

Figure 15.

curve—this f_2 function—between M and "demand" one would use it for defining the to-be-assumed value of the demand for any given value of M on all future occasions.

But this procedure, which I have thus outlined in some detail for demand, could also be used in analogous fashion for defining each of the other intervening variables. For each of them, also, we could set up a defining experiment in which all the independent variables other than the correlative one, would be held constant while that one was systematically varied. And we would obtain in each case a resultant defining curve or table. Figure 15 schematizes the fact of such possible defining procedures.

A brief review of the literature would suggest that many such defining experiments have already been done. Under "demand" we think at once of Warden and his co-workers (136), and of Elliott (26). Under the heading of "appetite" we think of Young (151, 152, 153), Elliott (25) and Bruce (13), and for an extraordinarily good summary of all the work relative to both demands and appetites we would look to Stone's chapter in Moss's "Comparative Psychology" (115). Under the heading of "differentiation" we think of many individuals: Watson (141), Carr (17, 18, 19), Hunter (50, 51), Dennis (24), Casper (20), Lindley (68), Wolfle (147), and Honzik (46), to mention only a few. Under the heading of "motor skill" we think of Macfarlane (73). Under that of "hypotheses" we think of practically all rat-runners in the world but for the final indignity of suggesting such a term as "hypotheses" we must blame

Krechevsky (57).[9] And finally, under "biases" we think of Dashiell (22), Bayroff (6), Dashiell and Bayroff (23), Schneirla (107), Yoshioka (149, 150), Ballachey and Krechevsky (5), Spence (110), Spence and Shipley (111), Spragg (112, 113), Buel (7, 8), Ballachey and Buel (3, 4), Buel and Ballachey (10, 11), Ruch (100, 101, 102, 103), Waters (139), and Witkin and Schneirla (146); and not even this completes the list.

Finally, turn to the f_3 function. It is by means of this f_3 function (if we but knew what it was) that we would be able to predict the final outcome for all possible values of the intervening variables. It would allow us to predict the result of every possible strength of "demand" combined with every possible degree of "appetite," with every possible goodness of "differentiation," and so on. That is to say, the f_3 function, if we but knew it, would provide a set of rules by which to predict for all these million and one possible combinations. It would consist in some equation, geometrical picture, or what not, which would give the way of adding together the different values of these different variables. But here, alas, I confess is the feature of my doctrine about which I am, to date, haziest. I would venture, however, a few suggestions.

First I would assert that the implicit assumption of most other psychologists is to the effect that their f_3 functions are in the nature of simple algebraic summations. That is to say, these others seem to assert that a poor demand would be compensated for by a good hypothesis, a poor skill by a strong differentiation, a poor differentiation by a strong appetite, and the like. Indeed it seems to me that *all* the associationistic psychologies, whether they be of the trial-and-error variety or of the conditioned reflex variety really imply just such simple algebraic summations. What I have distinguished as "demands," "appetites," "differentiations," "skills," "hypotheses," and "biases" the associationistic psychologies have lumped together, one and all, as mere S-R's. If the rat be very hungry (have a strong demand) this, for them, is but an enhancement of some S-R connection; if he have a strong appetite as a result of the type of goal presented, this also is but some S-R, stronger than it otherwise would have been; if the given maze-bifurcation present lots of stimuli (leads to clear differentiations) again, merely some S-R's are stronger; if the maze be constructed to require unusual motor skill from the animal, this again means merely a strengthening (or in this case probably a weakening) of some bond or other; if $\Sigma(OBO)$ has become large—if, that is to say, the hypotheses have become "developed and sure" this also means but better S-R connections; and finally, if the maze be shaped to induce, say, a strong centrifugal swing to the right or a strong forward-going tendency to the left, this, also is for them, but a matter of the strengthening of one or another S-R bond. And the final

---

9. See also the problems concerning this f_2 function between $\Sigma(OBO)$ and hypotheses already discussed above.

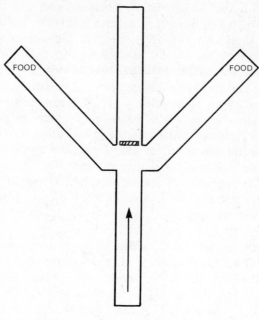

Figure 16.

value of the resultant behavior-ratio is then obtained by all such psychologies by a simple toting up of these plus and minus, strong and weak, S-R bonds. But I am very doubtful of the adequacy of any such simple type of additions.

Let me recall again the facts of "latent learning." During latent learning the rat is building up a "condition" in himself, which I have designated as a set of "hypotheses," and this condition—these hypotheses—do not then and there show in his behavior. S's are presented, but the corresponding R's do not function. It is only later, after a goal has been introduced which results in a strong appetite, that the R's or as I would prefer to say, the B's, appropriate to these built-up hypotheses appear. So long as there is no appetite for what is found at the end of the maze, strong demands, plus strong hypotheses do not add up at all. A strong hypothesis and a strong demand do not compensate for a weak appetite. And a strong demand and a strong appetite cannot in their turn overcome a weak hypothesis. And so on. The ways of combination of the intervening variables do not seem those of simple scala addition.

Or consider, as another example, the addition of two hypotheses. And suppose that instead of the usual two-way choice-point, we had one such as that shown in Figure 16. In this set-up after a long series of preliminary training in which only the two side-paths were open, the middle path was also opened up (I refer here to an actual experiment devised and carried out at California by Mr. R. S. Crutchfield). As a result of the preliminary training the two hypotheses of food to the left and food to the right were built up. It appeared, however, in the test

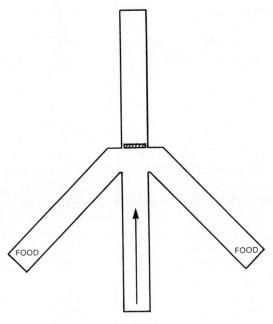

Figure 17.

runs, that these then added together in such a way as to make a very strong resultant tendency to go straight ahead when the third central path was opened—in short, a very much stronger tendency to go ahead than was found to have resulted from the two hypotheses which got built up when in another set-up the two side paths were as shown in Figure 17. The laws of the addition of hypotheses here appeared, in short, not as scala and algebraic, but as vectorial.

Or, again consider the facts of rat behavior which ordinarily go under the names of "insight" and reasoning, that is to say, such facts as have been gathered by Honzik and myself (128, 47) and by Maier (74, 75, 76, 77).[10] These are again, as I see it, also primarily facts concerning the addition of hypotheses. The addition here also is anything but simple and algebraic.

And so I am brought finally to my present confession of faith— namely, that Professor Lewin's topological and dynamic concepts (65, 66) now seem to me the best lead that I have at present for conceiving the nature of this f_3 function. I neither understand nor approve them in their entirety. And, if I were clever enough, I should undoubtedly try in many ways to improve upon them. But nonetheless, even as they are, they seem to me by far the most stimulating and important ideas which have appeared in psychology (that is, in pure psychology, as distinct from physiology or embryology) in the past decade.

10. For a summary of most of these facts see Munn (97, Ch. 7) and Heron (40).

One final point, concerning my thinking about the f_3 function. I am at present being openly and consciously just as anthropomorphic about it as I please. For, to be anthropomorphic is, as I see it, merely to cast one's concepts into a mold such that one can derive useful preliminary hunches from one's own human, everyday experience. These hunches may then, later, be translated into objective terms. But there seems to me every advantage in *beginning* by conceiving the situation loosely and anthropomorphically. I might never have arrived at this point of view of accepting anthropomorphism as a perfectly proper heuristic procedure all by myself. And I certainly would hardly have dared advance such a view publicly, if it had not been for the counsels of several other psychologists, especially Professors Liddell and Zener. But, in any case, I in my future work intend to go ahead imagining how, *if I were a rat*, I would behave as a result of such and such a demand combined with such and such an appetite and such and such a degree of differentiation; and so on. And then, on the basis of such imaginings, I shall try to figure out some sort of f_3 rules or equations. And then eventually I shall try to state these latter in some kind of objective and respectable sounding terms such as vectors, valences, barriers, and the like (to be borrowed for the most part from Professor Lewin).

Also, of course, I shall try to do experiments similar to those of Lewin and his students in which these intervening variables (as extrapolated from their correlative independent variables) are given such and such supposed values and then the final behavioral outcomes measured.[11]

But many of you must have been asking yourselves all this time: what about the H, A, T, and E variables? In the defining experiments I have suggested so far, which have been concerned primarily with the environmental variables, these "individual difference variables" are assumed to have been given average standard values. We rat-workers have always done this, perhaps unconsciously. We have tried to keep heredity normal by using large groups, age normal by using rats between 90 and 120 days old, previous training normal by using fresh rats in each new experiment, and endocrine and nutritional conditions normal by avoiding special dosages and also again by using large groups.

But suppose, now, our intersts *be* in individual differences, *per se*. What experiments do we carry out then? It seems to me that individual-difference psychologists here tend to do two sorts of things.

On the one hand, they attempt (as do we environmental psychologists) to manipulate their independent variables for whole groups of animals and to get correlated variations in $B_L/(B_L + B_R)$. Thus they vary

11. As a beginning in this direction we already have some rat experiments by Hall (34, 35, 36) and Hall and Ballachey (37), and a recent set of experiments by Wright (148), but the latter were done unfortunately, from my point of view, not upon rats but upon children. But analogous experiments could, I believe, be done with rats.

heredity, H, as Tryon *(129)* and Heron *(41)*, and Rundquist *(104)* have done in controlled ways for large groups and get corresponding variations in this behavior-ratio, for such groups. Or, they vary age, A, as Stone and his students have done *(114)*, also for large groups and again get corresponding variations in the behavior-ratio. Or, they vary previous training, T, that is, they study the effects of transfer—and here we have all taken pot shots—the first important experiment was, perhaps, that of Webb *(142)* and the last seems to be that of Bunch and Rogers *(15)*—and again attempt to get corresponding variations in the behavior-ratio. Or, finally, they vary drugs, endocrines and vitamins, E, and get correlated variations in $B_L/(B_L + B_R)$. Here there are too many experiments for me to attempt to list them.[12]

Secondly, however, the individual difference psychologists have also done another *more characteristic* type of experiment. They have accepted from God, and from the accidents of miscegenation and of nursery schools, very large heterogeneous samples of rats and then they have put each such sample through a miscellaneous assortment of experiments (i.e., the different types of mazes that, in American rat-culture, are required of young rats in school, and also the different types of maze, discrimination-box, food, times since eating, and the like, which are required of old rats in polite society); and then they have obtained correlations and worked out factor analyses. And, finally, these individual-difference psychologists have ended up with their notions concerning the number and nature of the fundamental traits or capacities—"The Vectors of Mind" *(120)*. These traits or capacities are, of course, but a new type of intervening variable and it would be nice, for me, if they fitted in neatly with the sort of intervening variables already suggested. They could then be put into my diagram as shown in Figure 18. But, alas, at present the results of factor analysis do not seem to suggest any such simple or agreed-upon results. You all know how the controversy rages from Spearman's one or two factors *(109)* through Kelley's *(52)* and Thurstone's *(120)* three to nine factors, differing somewhat in each set-up[13] to Thorndike's *(116, 117)* and Tryon's *(131)*—God only knows how many.[14]

By way of conclusion, I want now, however, to turn to one wholly new point. I want to suggest that there also appear in maze behavior types of activity other than the simple B_L's and B_R's which we have thus

---

12. One of the best known early experiments was that of Anderson and Smith *(1)* on the effect of insufficient diets. And recent further important experiments on diet are those of Maurer *(78, 79, 80)*, and Maurer and Tasi *(82, 83)*, Bernhardt *(7)*, Muenzinger and the Poes *(96, 98, 99)*. For recent important experiments on drugs, see Miller and Miles *(85)* and Williams and O'Brien *(144)*. Also for a summary, see Moss's own chapter in "Comparative Psychology" *(86)*.

13. I think here of Vaughn's recent important monograph *(120)* in which he finds eight factors governing maze behavior.

14. For a general discussion of the problem of individual differences in animals see, also, Tryon *(130)*.

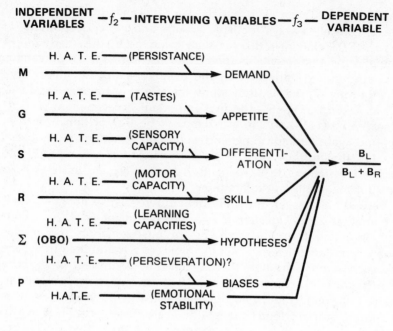

Figure 18.

far talked about. If these latter be called "achievement behaviors," then these new types of activity which I now have in mind, may be called "catalyzing behaviors." And it seems that we rat psychologists have to date rather pigheadedly (i.e., like Professor Liddell's pigs) ignored such catalyzing behaviors.

I have two instances which I would here like to call to your attention, although I believe that in the future technological advances in recording will bring to the fore many others for study. The first of these two examples consists of those "lookings or runnings back and forth" which often appear at the choice-point and which all rat-runners have noted, but few have paid further attention to. And the second type is that disrupted sort of activity which appears when a previously obtained goal object is removed or blocked. Let me begin with the former.

A few years ago (121; 122, Chap. 13) I had the temerity to suggest that such "lookings back and forth" might be taken as a behavioristic definition of *conscious awareness*. This was, no doubt, a silly idea. I would hardly dare propose it now. But, at any rate, such behavior is interesting and deserving of further study. Anthropomorphically speaking, it appears to be a "looking before you leap" sort of affair. Klüver (53) and Gellerman (29) have recorded it in connection with the behavior of monkeys, chimpanzees and children. And, further, I have recently learned that Professor Muenzinger and his students have also been keeping records of it in rats and that they have called it "vicarious trial and error"—or, more briefly, VTE. I shall, therefore, designate such behavior as VTE or B_{VTE} from here on.

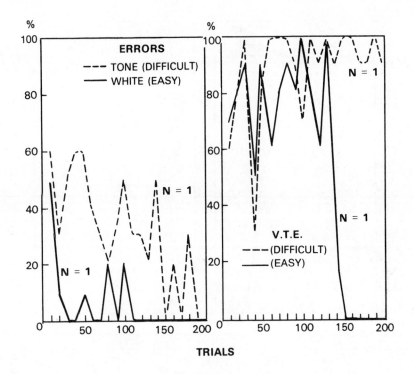

Figure 19.

First, let me show you some individual rat curves obtained by Dr. Evelyn Gentry (94) in Muenzinger's laboratory. The one rat had a difficult discrimination—namely, to go left when a tone is sounded; the other had an easy discrimination—to go towards the white in a white-black discrimination box (Figure 19).

At the left are the error curves and at the right the *VTE* curves. Whenever the rat looked one or more times before making his overt choice in a given trial that trial was recorded as having involved a *VTE*. The points on the curves are averages for ten trials. The solid curves are for the easy discrimination and the dash curves are for the difficult discrimination. As you see, there tended to be more *VTE* and the latter persisted longer for the difficult discrimination than for the easy one.

Next, let me present some recent data on *VTE* obtained by Mr. M. F. Friedman at California on the effect of moderate amounts of cortical lesion[15] (see Figure 20). The problem was learning to turn left on a simple elevated *T* where one arm led to food and the other did not. The dash curves are for the brain lesion group and the solid curves are for the control group. Each point is an average of 4 trials. The normal animals exhibited more *VTE* and learned faster than did those with cerebral insults.

---

15. The histology necessary for determining the actual amounts of these lesions has not yet been done.

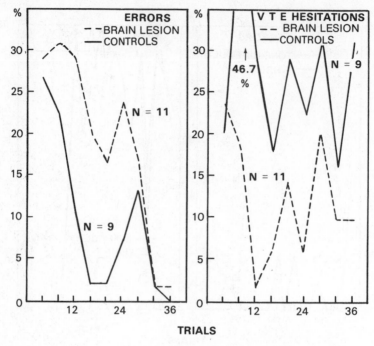

Figure 20.

Next, I present some curves obtained by Honzik with an elevated discrimination set-up. The animal had to discriminate between a black and a white face-on door. There was a partition projecting out between the doors. White was the positive stimulus. One group ran over a continuous platform and could run back around the projecting partition if they chose the wrong door first. The other group had to jump a gap of $8\frac{1}{2}$ inches to a 4-inch ledge just in front of the doors. If this jump group chose incorrectly, they had to jump back again to the starting platform and then make a second jump to the correct door (Figure 21). The solid curves are for the jump group and the dash curves for the non-jump group. Each point represents an average of 10 trials. The jumpers made more *VTE*'s and learned faster.

Finally, let me present a set of curves also obtained by Honzik, in a similar set-up, but for two different jump-groups (Figure 22). The conditions for the one-jump group were those just described. We may call them here the near-jump group. For the others, which we may call the far-jump group, the farther side of the gap was 15 inches from the to-be-discriminated doors and the taking off platform $23\frac{1}{2}$ inches from these doors. Solid curves are for the near jumpers, dash curves for the far-jumpers. Each point represents an average of 10 trials.

The near-jump group learned faster and exhibited more *VTE* than did the far-jump group. It is to be noted that the far-jump group probably could not see the differences between the two doors at the place

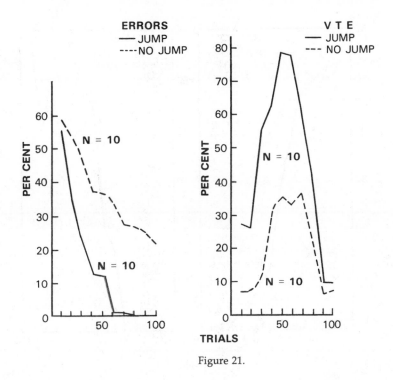

Figure 21.

of "taking off" very well. Hence their poor error score. Further, because they could not see very well, it did them little good to "go in for" "looking before they leapt." And, in fact, the *VTE*'s for this far-jump group were decidedly less than for the near-jump group.

Let me briefly summarize: (1) For a difficult discrimination such as learning to turn left when a tone is sounded there was slower learning but more *VTE* than for an easy, white-black discrimination; (2) on a simple *T*, normal rats showed faster learning and exhibited more *VTE* than did brain lesion rats; (3) with a near-jump, jump rats learned faster and showed more *VTE* than did non-jump rats; (4) near-jump rats learned faster and exhibited more *VTE* than did far-jump rats.

What, now, is to be our theoretical envisagement? Obviously, the question divides into two: (1) What effect do *VTE*'s, when evoked, have upon learning; (2) what are the conditions of learning which favor the evoking of such *VTE*'s?

In answer to the first question I shall postulate that *VTE*'s always aid the learning which they accompany. In the sole case, that of the difficult discrimination, where the poorer learning was accompanied by more *VTE*'s I believe that this learning was nonetheless faster than it would have been if it had not been for these greater *VTE*'s. And in all the other three experiments the greater *VTE*'s did accompany the faster learning.

Turn now, to the second question. What are the learning conditions which tend to evoke *VTE*'s? Here I believe we are not yet ready for any general answer. I shall therefore merely re-enumerate for your benefit the

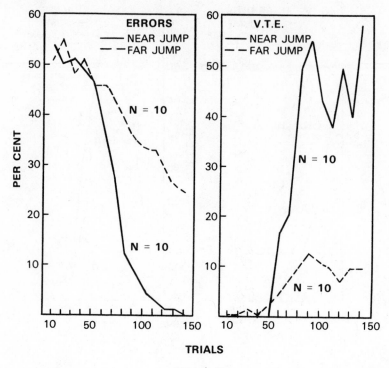

Figure 22.

conditions of the four experiments. The conditions favorable to *VTE*'s in these experiments were: (1) a difficult discrimination; (2) a normal brain; (3) a gap to be jumped which induced caution; and (4) a nearness of the jumping platform such that the extra caution exposed the animal longer to the critical stimuli.

Finally, let me by another figure suggest how I would propose to fit this catalyzing *VTE* behavior into my general causal diagram (Figure 23). You will note that I have shown the *VTE* behavior—symbolized as B_{VTE}— as an auxiliary result of the "intervening variables." These latter are to be conceived as tending to produce their usual "achievement behavior" $B_L/(B_L + B_R)$. But, in addition, they produce more or less B_{VTE}, and the further catalyzing effect of such B_{VTE} is, I have assumed, in some way to enhance the values of one or more of the independent variables them-selves—in this case especially of *S* and of $\Sigma(OBO)$—and thus to help induce new values of certain of the intervening variables and a new final value of the achievement behavior. That is to say, as shown in the figure, the achievement behavior takes some new value $B_L'/(B_L' + B_R')$.

Turn now briefly to the case of the disruption behavior which occurs when an expected goal is not obtained. I have as yet no curves or detailed data concerning either the causes or the results of such disrup-tion behaviors. I believe, however, that they also are to be conceived as auxiliary, catalyzing sorts of affair which react back upon the independ-

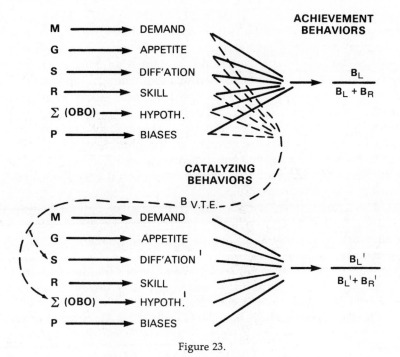

Figure 23.

Figure 24.

ent variables and make the final values of the resultant behavior-ratios different from what the latter originally would have been.

The rat's disrupted behavior is a surprised sort of hunting about and exploring. And it is my contention as shown in Figure 24 that this surprised hunting and exploring brings about new values of the independent variables—especially of G and $\Sigma(OBO)$,—and thus causes a different outcome in the final behavior-ratio. The disrupted behavior enhances a new negative aspect in what was originally a positive goal. In short, I am assuming that because of this disrupted searching the rats are better in the next trials about not continuing to go to that side where the goal has been blocked than they would have been if this, their disrupted searching, had not appeared.

Let me close, now, with a final confession of faith. I believe that everything important in psychology (except perhaps such matters as the building up of a super-ego, that is everything save such matters as involve society and words) can be investigated in essence through the continued experimental and theoretical analysis of the determiners of rat behavior at a choice-point in a maze. Herein I believe I agree with Professor Hull and also with Professor Thorndike.

So in closing let me borrow a verse written by Alexander Meiklejohn in a copy of his book as he gave it me. He wrote, and I would now repeat:

> To my ratiocinations
> I hope you will be kind
> As you follow up the wanderings
> Of my amazed mind.

REFERENCES

1. Anderson, J. E., & Smith, A. H.   The effect of quantitative and qualitative stunting upon maze learning in the white rat, *J. Comp. Psychol.*, 1926, *6*, 337–361.
2. Adams, D. K.   A restatement of the problem of learning, *Brit. J. Psychol.*, 1931, *22*, 150–178.
3. Ballachey, E. L., & Buel, J.   Centrifugal swing as a determinant of choice-point behavior in the maze running of the white rat, *J. Comp. Psychol.*, 1934, *17*, 201–223.
4. Ballachey, E. L., & Buel, J.   Food orientation as a factor determining the distribution of errors in the maze running of the rat, *J. Genet. Psychol.*, 1934, *45*, 358–370.
5. Ballachey, E. L., & Krechevsky, I.   "Specific" vs. "general" orientation factors in maze running, *Univ. Calif. Publ. Psychol.*, 1932, *6*, 83–97.
6. Bayroff, A. G.   Direction orientation and the forward-going tendency in white rats, *J. Comp. Psychol.*, 1933, *15*, 211–228.
7. Bernhardt, K. S.   The effect of vitamin B deficiency during nursing on subsequent learning in the rat, *J. Comp. Psychol.*, 1934, *17*, 123–148.
8. Buel, J.   The linear maze. I. "Choice-point expectancy," "correctness," and the goal gradient, *J. Comp. Psychol.*, 1934, *17*, 185–199.
9. Buel, J.   Differential errors in animal mazes, *Psychol. Bull.*, 1935, *32*, 67–99.
10. Buel, J., & Ballachey, E. L.   Choice-point expectancy in the maze running of the rat, *J. Genet. Psychol.*, 1934, *45*, 145–168.

11. Buel, J., & Ballachey, E. L.   Limiting factors in the effect of the reward upon the distribution of errors in mazes, *Psychol. Rev.*, 1935, *42*, 28–42.

12. Brown, W., Facing the facts, *Univ. South. Calif. Proc. 25th Anniv. Inauguration Grad. Studies*, Los Angeles, 1936, 116–121.

13. Bruce, R. H.   A further study of the effect of variation of reward and drive upon the maze performance of rats, *J. Comp. Psychol.*, 1935, *20*, 157–182.

14. Brunswik, E.   Reaction of rats to probability and danger situations (in preparation).

15. Bunch, M. E., & Rogers, M.   The relationship between transfer and the length of the interval separating the mastery of the two problems, *J. Comp. Psychol.*, 1936, *21*, 37–51.

16. Carr, H. A.   Psychology, a study of mental activity, New York: Longmans, Green and Co., 1925.

17. Carr, H. A.   Maze studies with the white rat. I. Normal animals, *J. Anim. Behav.*, 1917, *7*, 259–275.

18. Carr, H. A.   Maze studies with the white rat, II. Blind animals, *J. Anim. Behav.*, 1917, *7*, 276–294.

19. Carr, H. A.   Maze studies with the white rat. III. Anosmic animals, *J. Anim. Behav.*, 1917, *7*, 295–306.

20. Casper, B.   The normal sensory control of the perfected double-alternation spatial-maze habit of the albino rat, *J. Genet. Psychol.*, 1933, *43*, 239–292.

21. Culler, E., Finch, F., Girden, E., & Brogden, W.   Measurements of acuity by the conditioned-response technique, *J. Gen. Psychol.*, 1935, *12*, 223–227.

22. Dashiell, J. F.   Direction orientation in maze running by the white rat, *Comp. Psychol. Monog.*, 1930, *7*, No. 72.

23. Dashiell, J. F., & Bayroff, A. G.   A forward-going tendency in maze running, *J. Comp. Psychol.*, 1931, *12*, 77–94.

24. Dennis, W.   The sensory control of the white rat in the maze habit, *J. Genet. Psychol.*, 1929, *36*, 59–90.

25. Elliott, M. H.   The effect of change of reward on the maze performance of rats, *Univ. Calif. Publ. Psychol.*, 1928, *4*, 19–30.

26. Elliott, M. H.   The effect of appropriateness of reward and of complex incentives on maze performance, *Univ. Calif. Publ. Psychol.*, 1929, *4*, 91–98.

27. Elliott, M. H.   Some determining factors in maze performance, *Amer. J. Psychol.*, 1930, *42*, 315–317.

28. Ellis, W. D., & Hamilton, J. A.   Behavior constancy, *J. Gen. Psychol.*, 1933, *8*, 421–429.

29. Gellermann, L. W.   Form discrimination in chimpanzees and two-year-old children: I. Discrimination of form per se. II. Form versus background, *J. Genet. Psychol.*, 1933, *42*, 3–50.

30. Gengerelli, J. A.   The principle of maxima and minima in animal learning, *J. Comp. Psychol.*, 1930, *11*, 193–236.

31. Gilhousen, H. C.   An investigation of "insight" in rats, *Science*, 1931, *73*, 711.

32. Gilhousen, H. C.   Fixation of excess distance patterns in the white rat, *J. Comp. Psychol.*, 1932, *16*, 1–24.

33. Guthrie, E. R.   The psychology of learning, New York: Harper and Brothers, 1935.

34. Hall, C. S.   Emotional behavior in the rat. I. Defecation and urination as measures of individual differences in emotionality, *J. Comp. Psychol.*, 1934, *18*, 385–403.

35. Hall, C. S.   Emotional behavior in the rat. II. The relationship between need and emotionality, *J. Comp. Psychol.*, 1936, *22*, 61–68.

36. Hall, C. S.   Emotional behavior in the rat. III. The relationship between emotionality and ambulatory activity, *J. Comp. Psychol.*, 1936, *22*, 345–352.

37. Hall, C. S., & Ballachey, E. L.   A study of the rat's behavior in a field: A contribution to method in comparative psychology, *Univ. Calif. Publ. Psychol.*, 1932, *6*, 1–12.

38. Hamilton, J. A., & Ellis, W. D.   Behavior constancy in rats, *J. Genet. Psychol.*, 1932, *41*, 120–139.

39. Hamilton, J. A., & Ellis, W. D.   Persistence and behavior constancy, *J. Genet. Psychol.*, 1932, *41*, 140–153.

40. Heron, W. T.   Complex learning processes, in "Comparative Psychology," F. A. Moss (Ed.), New York: Prentice-Hall, Inc., 1934, pp. 335-366.

41. Heron, W. T.   The inheritance of maze learning ability in rats, *J. Comp. Psychol.*, 1935, *19*, 77-90.

42. Hilgard, E. R.   The nature of the conditioned response: I. The case for and against stimulus-substitution, *Psychol. Rev.*, 1936, *43*, 366-385.

43. Hilgard, E. R.   The nature of the conditioned response: II. Alternatives to stimulus substitution, *Psychol. Rev.*, 1936, *43*, 547-564.

44. Hilgard, E. R.   The relationship between the conditioned response and conventional learning experiments, *Psychol. Bull.*, 1937, *34*, 61-102.

45. Holt, E. B.   Animal drive and the learning process, New York: Henry Holt and Company, 1931, Vol. I., p. 151 f.

46. Honzik, C. H.   The sensory basis of maze learning in rats, *Comp. Psychol. Monog.*, 1936, *13*, Serial No. 64.

47. Honzik, C. H., & Tolman, E. C.   The perception of spatial relations by the rat: a type of response not easily explained by conditioning, *J. Comp. Psychol.*, 1936, *22*, 287-318.

48. Hull, C. L.   The concept of the habit-family hierarchy and maze learning. Part I., *Psychol. Rev.*, 1934, *41*, 33-54.

49. Hull, C. L.   Mind, mechanism, and adaptive behavior, *Psychol. Rev.*, 1937, *44*, 1-32.

50. Hunter, W. S.   The sensory control of the maze habit in the white rat, *J. Genet. Psychol.*, 1929, *36*, 505-537.

51. Hunter, W. S.   A further consideration of the sensory control of the maze habit in the white rat, *J. Genet. Psychol.*, 1930, *38*, 3-19.

52. Kelley, T. L.   Crossroads in the mind of man, Stanford University: Stanford University Press, 1928.

53. Klüver, H.   Behavior mechanisms in monkeys, Chicago: University of Chicago Press, 1933.

54. Koch, H. C.   The influence of mechanical guidance upon maze learning, *Psychol. Monog.*, 1923, *32*, No. 147.

55. Köhler, W.   Gestalt psychology, New York: Horace Liveright, 1929.

56. Koffka, K.   Principles of gestalt psychology, New York: Harcourt, Brace and Company, 1935.

57. Krechevsky, I.   "Hypotheses" in rats, *Psychol. Rev.*, 1932, *39*, 516-532.

58. Krechevsky, I.   Brain mechanisms and brightness discrimination learning, *J. Comp. Psychol.*, 1936, *21*, 405-446.

59. Krechevsky, I.   Brain mechanisms and variability. I. Variability within a means-end-readiness, *J. Comp. Psychol.*, 1937, *23*, 121-138.

60. Krechevsky, I.   Brain mechanisms and variability. II. Variability where no learning is involved, *J. Comp. Psychol.*, 1937, *23*, 139-163.

61. Krechevsky, I.   Brain mechanisms and variability. III. Limitations of the effect of cortical injury upon variability, *J. Comp. Psychol.*, 1937, *23*, 351-364.

62. Krechevsky, I., & Honzik, C. H.   Fixation in the rat, *Univ. Calif. Publ. Psychol.*, 1932, *6*, 13-26.

63. Lashley, K. S.   Learning: I. Nervous-mechanisms of learning, in "The Foundations of Experimental Psychology," Worcester, Mass.: Clark University Press, 1929, pp. 524-563.

64. Leeper, R.   The rôle of motivation in learning: A study of the phenomenon of differential motivational control of the utilization of habits, *J. Genet. Psychol.*, 1935, *46*, 3-40.

65. Lewin, K.   A dynamic theory of personality, New York: McGraw-Hill Book Company, Inc., 1935.

66. Lewin, K.   Principles of topological psychology, New York: McGraw-Hill Book Company, Inc., 1936.

67. Liddell, H. S.   The conditioned reflex, in "Comparative Psychology," F. A. Moss (Ed.), New York: Prentice-Hall, Inc., 1934, pp. 247-296.

68. Lindley, S. B.   The maze-learning ability of anosmic and blind anosmic rats, *J. Genet. Psychol.*, 1930, *37*, 245–267.

69. Lorge, I.   Irrelevant rewards in animal learning, *J. Comp. Psychol.*, 1936, *21*, 105–128.

70. Loucks, R. B.   An appraisal of Pavlov's systematization of behavior from the experimental standpoint, *J. Comp. Psychol.*, 1933, *15*, 1–45.

71. Loucks, R. B.   Reflexology and the psychobiological approach, *Psychol. Rev.*, 1937, *44*, 320–338.

72. Ludgate, K. E.   The effect of manual guidance upon maze learning, *Psychol. Monog.*, 1923, *33*, No. 148.

73. Macfarlane, D. A.   The rôle of kinesthesis in maze learning, *Univ. Calif. Publ. Psychol.*, 1930, *4*, 277–305.

74. Maier, N. R. F.   Reasoning in white rats, *Comp. Psychol. Monog.*, 1929, *6*, 3.

75. Maier, N. R. F.   In defense of reasoning in rats, *J. Comp. Psychol.*, 1935, *19*, 197–206.

76. Maier, N. R. F.   Age and intelligence in rats, *J. Comp. Psychol.*, 1932, *13*, 1–16.

77. Maier, N. R. F.   The effect of cerebral destruction on reasoning and learning in rats, *J. Comp. Neur.*, 1932, *54*, 45–75.

78. Maurer, S.   The effect of partial depletion of vitamin B (B^1) upon performance in rats. III., *J. Comp. Psychol.*, 1935, *20*, 309–318.

79. Maurer, S.   The effect of early depletion of vitamin B_2 upon the performance in rats. IV., *J. Comp. Psychol.*, 1935, *20*, 385–388.

80. Maurer, S.   The effect of acute vitamin A depletion upon performance in rats. V., *J. Comp. Psychol.*, 1935, *20*, 389–392.

81. Maurer, S.   The effect of a diet of pasteurized milk upon performance in rats. VI., *J. Comp. Psychol.*, 1935, *20*, 393–396.

82. Maurer, S., & Tsai, L. S.   Vitamin B deficiency and learning ability, *J. Comp. Psychol.*, 1930, *11*, 51–62.

83. Maurer, S., & Tsai, L. S.   The effect of partial depletion of vitamin B complex upon learning ability in rats, *J. Nutrition*, 1931, *4*, No. 4.

84. McCulloch, T. L.   Performance preferentials of the white rat in force-resisting and spatial dimension, *J. Comp. Psychol.*, 1934, *18*, 85–111.

85. Miller, N. E., & Miles, W. R.   Effect of caffeine on the running speed of hungry, satiated, and frustrated rats, *J. Comp. Psychol.*, 1935, *20*, 397–412.

86. Moss, F. A.   The effect of drugs and internal secretions on animal behavior, in "Comparative Psychology," F. A. Moss (Ed.), New York: Prentice-Hall, Inc., 1934, pp. 113–148.

87. Muenzinger, K. F.   Motivation in learning. I. Electric shock for correct response in the visual discrimination habit, *J. Comp. Psychol.*, 1934, *17*, 267–277.

88. Muenzinger, K. F.   Motivation in learning. II. The function of electric shock for right and wrong responses in human subjects, *J. Exper. Psychol.*, 1934, *17*, 439–448.

89. Muenzinger, K. F., & Newcomb, H.   Motivation in learning. III. A bell signal compared with electric shock for right and wrong responses in the visual discrimination habit, *J. Comp. Psychol.*, 1935, *20*, 85–93.

90. Muenzinger, K. F., & Wood, A.   Motivation in learning. IV. The function of punishment as determined by its temporal relation to the the act of choice in the visual discrimination habit, *J. Comp. Psychol.*, 1935, *20*, 95–106.

91. Muenzinger, K. F., & Newcomb, H.   Motivation in learning. V. The relative effectiveness of jumping a gap and crossing an electric grid in a visual discrimination habit, *J. Comp. Psychol.*, 1936, *21*, 95–104.

92. Muenzinger, K. F., & Fletcher, F. M.   Motivation in learning. VI. Escape from electric shock compared with hunger-food tension in the visual discrimination habit, *J. Comp. Psychol.*, 1936, *22*, 79–91.

93. Muenzinger, K. F., & Fletcher, F. M.   Motivation in learning. VII. The effect of an enforced delay at the point of choice in the visual discrimination habit, *J. Comp. Psychol.*, 1937, *23*, 383–392.

94. Muenzinger, K. F., & Gentry, E.   Tone discrimination in white rats, *J. Comp. Psychol.*, 1931, *12*, 195–206.

95. Muenzinger, K. F., & Dove, C. C.   Serial Learning: I. Gradients of uniformity and variability produced by success and failure of single responses, *J. Gen. Psychol.*, 1937, *16*, 403–414.

96. Muenzinger, K. F., Poe, E., & Poe, C. F.   The effect of vitamin deficiency upon the acquisition and retention of the maze habit in the white rat. II. Vitamin B$_2$ (G), *J. Comp. Psychol.*, 1937, *23*, 59–66.

97. Munn, N. L.   An introduction to animal psychology, the behavior of the rat, New York: Houghton Mifflin Company, 1933.

98. Poe, E., Poe, C. F., & Muenzinger, K. F.   The effect of vitamin deficiency upon the acquisition and retention of the maze habit in the white rat. I. The vitamin B complex, *J. Comp. Psychol.*, 1936, *22*, 69–77.

99. Poe, E., Poe, C. F., & Muenzinger, K. F.   The effect of vitamin deficiency upon the acquisition and retention of the maze habit in the white rat. III. Vitamin B^1, *J. Comp. Psychol.*, 1937, *23*, 67–76.

100. Ruch, F. L.   Goal direction orientation, generalized turning habit and goal gradient as factors in maze learning in the rat, *J. Comp. Psychol.*, 1934, *17*, 225–232.

101. Ruch, F. L.   Experimental studies of the factors influencing the difficulty of blind alleys in linear mazes. I. Experiments with the maze patterns RLRLLRLRRLRL and LRLRRLRLLRLR, *J. Comp. Psychol.*, 1935, *20*, 21–34.

102. Ruch, F. L.   Experimental studies of the factors influencing the difficulty of blind alleys in linear mazes. II. Generalized-turning habits, *J. Comp. Psychol.*, 1935, *20*, 35–52.

103. Ruch, F. L.   Experimental studies of the factors influencing the difficulty of blind alleys in linear mazes. III. Is there an anticipatory tendency in maze learning?, *J. Comp. Psychol.*, 1935, *20*, 113–124.

104. Rundquist, E. E.   Inheritance of spontaneous activity in rats, *J. Comp. Psychol.*, 1933, *16*, 415–438.

105. Schlosberg, H.   Conditioned responses in the white rat, *J. Genet. Psychol.*, 1934, *45*, 303–335.

106. Schlosberg, H.   The relationship between success and the laws of conditioning, *Psychol. Rev.*, 1937, *44*, 379–394.

107. Schneirla, T. C.   Learning and orientation in ants, *Comp. Psychol. Monog.*, 1929, *6*, No. 30, pp. 143.

108. Skinner, B. F.   Two types of conditioned reflex and a pseudo type, *J. Gen. Psychol.*, 1935, *12*, 66–77.

109. Spearman, C.   The nature of "intelligence" and the principles of cognition, London: Macmillan and Co., 1927.

110. Spence, K. W.   The order of eliminating blinds in maze learning by the rat, *J. Comp. Psychol.*, 1932, *14*, 9–27.

111. Spence, K. W., & Shipley, W. C.   The factors determining the difficulty of blind alleys in maze learning by the white rat. *J. Comp. Psychol.*, 1934, *17*, 423–436.

112. Spragg, S. D. S.   Anticipation as a factor in maze errors, *J. Comp. Psychol.*, 1933, *15*, 319–329.

113. Spragg, S. D. S.   Anticipatory responses in the maze, *J. Comp. Psychol.*, 1934, *18*, 51–73.

114. Stone, C. P.   The age factor in animal learning: I. Rats in the problem box and the maze. II. Rats on a multiple light discrimination box and a difficult maze, *Genet. Psychol. Monog.*, 1925, *5*, 1–130; *6*, 125–202.

115. Stone, C. P.   Motivation: drives and incentives, in "Comparative Psychology," F. A. Moss (Ed.), New York: Prentice-Hall, Inc., 1934, pp. 73–112.

116. Thorndike, E. L.   Educational psychology, Vol. III.; mental work and fatigue; Individual differences and their causes, New York: Teachers College, Columbia University, 1923.

117. Thorndike, E. L.   The measurement of intelligence, New York: Teachers College, Columbia University, 1927.

118. Thorndike, E. L.   The fundamentals of learning, New York: Teachers College, Columbia University, 1932.

119. Thorndike, E. L.   Wants, interest and attitudes, New York: The Century Co., 1935.

120. Thurstone, L. L.   The vectors of mind, Chicago: University of Chicago Press, 1935.

121. Tolman, E. C.   A behaviorist's definition of consciousness, *Psychol. Rev.*, 1927, *34*, 433–439.

122. Tolman, E. C.   Purposive behavior in animals and men, New York: The Century Co., 1932, Ch. 13.

123. Tolman, E. C.   The law of effect: a reply to Dr. Goodenough, *J. Exper. Psychol.*, 1933, *16*, 459–462.

124. Tolman, E. C.   Psychology vs. immediate experience, *Philos. Science*, 1935, *2*, 356–380.

125. Tolman, E. C.   Distance-preferentials. A new apparatus and some results, *Psychol. Bull.*, 1936, *33*, 727.

126. Tolman, E. C.   Operational behaviorism and current trends in psychology, *Proc. 25th Anniv. Celebration Inaug. Grad Stud.*, Los Angeles: The University of Southern California, 1936, pp. 89–103.

127. Tolman, E. C., Hall, C. S., & Bretnall, E. P.   A disproof of the law of effect and a substitution of the laws of emphasis, motivation and disruption, *J. Exper. Psychol.*, 1932, *15*, 601–614.

128. Tolman, E. C., & Honzik, C. H.   "Insight" in rats, *Univ. Calif. Publ. Psychol.*, 1930, *4*, 215–232.

129. Tryon, R. D.   The genetics of learning ability in rats: preliminary report, *Univ. Calif. Publ. Psychol.*, 1929, *4*, 71–89.

130. Tryon, R. C.   Individual differences, in "Comparative Psychology," F. A. Moss (Ed.), New York: Prentice-Hall, Inc., 1934, pp. 409–448.

131. Tryon, R. C.   A theory of psychological components—an alternative to "mathematical factors," *Psychol. Rev.*, 1935, *42*, 425–454.

132. Tsai, L. S.   Gradual vs. abrupt withdrawal of guidance in maze learning, *J. Comp. Psychol.*, 1930, *10*, 325–332.

133. Tsai, L. S.   The laws of minimum effort and maximum satisfaction in animal behavior, *Monog. Nat. Instit. Psychol.*, 1932, No. 1, pp. 49, (seen in *Psychol. Abst.*, 1936, *6*, No. 4329).

134. Vaughn, C. L.   Factors in rat learning—an analysis of the intercorrelations between 34 variables, *Comp. Psychol. Monog.*, 1937, *14*, Serial No. 69.

135. Wang, T. L.   The influence of tuition in the acquisition of skill, *Psychol. Monog.*, 1925, *33*, No. 154.

136. Warden, C. J.   Animal motivation, Experimental studies on the Albino Rat. New York: Columbia University Press, 1931.

137. Waters, R. H.   The influence of large amounts of manual guidance upon human maze learning, *J. Gen. Psychol.*, 1930, *4*, 213–228.

138. Waters, R. H.   Equivalence of response in learning, *Psychol. Bull.*, 1936, *33*, 798–799.

139. Waters, R. H.   The wall-seeking tendency and maze learning in the white rat, *J. Psychol.*, 1937, *4*, 23–26.

140. Waters, R. H.   The principle of least effort in learning. *J. Gen. Psychol.*, 1937, *16*, 3–20.

141. Watson, J. B.   Kinaesthetic and organic sensations: Their rôle in the reactions of the white rat, *Psychol. Rev. Monog.*, 1917, *8*, 2.

142. Webb, L. W.   Transfer of training and retroaction, *Psychol. Rev. Monog.*, 1917, *24*, No. 3.

143. Wheeler, R. H.   The science of psychology, New York: Thomas Y. Crowell Company, 1929.

144. Williams, G. W., & O'Brien, C.   The effect of sodium phenobarbital on the learning behavior of white rats, *J. Comp. Psychol.*, 1937, *23*, 457–474.

145. Wilson, W. R.   Principles of selection in "trial and error" learning, *Psychol Rev.*, 1924, *31*, 150–160.

146. Witkin, H. A., & Schneirla, T. C.   Initial maze behavior as a function of maze design, *J. Comp. Psychol.*, 1937, *23*, 275–304.

147. Wolfle, D. L.   The effects of continuous interchange of alley sections on the maze behavior of rats, *J. Comp. Psychol.*, 1935, *19*, 91–106.

148. Wright, H. F.   The influence of barriers upon strength of motivation, *Contrib. Psychol. Theory*, Vol. I, No. 3, Duke Univ. Press, 1937.
149. Yoshioka, J. G.   Direction as a factor in maze solution in rats, *J. Genet. Psychol.*, 1930, *38*, 307–320.
150. Yoshioka, J. G.   A study of orientation in a maze, *J. Genet. Psychol.*, 1933, *42*, 167–183.
151. Young, P. T.   Preferential discrimination of the white rat for different kinds of grain, *Amer. J. Psychol.*, 1928, *40*, 372–400.
152. Young, P. T.   Relative food preferences of the white rat, *J. Comp. Psychol.*, 1932, *14*, 297–319.
153. Young, P. T.   Relative food preferences of the white rat. II., *J. Comp. Psychol.*, 1933, *15*, 149–166.

Reprinted with permission
from *Psychological Bulletin*,
1940, 37, 1–28.

Chapter 19

The Psychologist's Frame of Reference

Gordon W. Allport

Harvard University

For the first time in the forty-seven years of its history this Association has elected to assemble on the coast of the Pacific. This meeting at two great centers of learning and research is not only proof of the ocean-to-ocean sweep of our membership, of our influence and prosperity, but may be taken to symbolize as well the westward trek of culture in America; or to those who like epic perspective, it may signify the westward march of Mind from Asia, to Europe, to America. But whether we think in terms of historical symbolism or not, we can hardly deny, at a time when heavy darkness has descended over the European continent, that this Forty-seventh Annual Meeting finds the burden of scientific progress in psychology resting as never before upon the membership of this Association.

Presidential address delivered at the Forty-seventh Annual Meeting of the American Psychological Association, Berkeley, California, September 7, 1939.

Fortunate we are in assuming this burden to have the support of gifted émigrés who have come so recently to join their strength to ours.

With the responsibility for the preservation and eventual rehabilitation of world psychology falling upon our shoulders, we do well to examine our credentials. Are we American psychologists equipped for the versatile leadership demanded by our comprehensive discipline; are we prepared to develop the potentialities of all its parts? These are not rhetorical questions but questions of such immediate, practical import for our science that I propose from this unusual vantage point today to seek answers as definite and unequivocal as possible. By charting the course American psychology has taken in its recent past we can determine whether the signs we observe augur the wholesome growth of psychology under our leadership and the extension of its beneficial influences to humanity at large.

Fifty Years of Change

Since psychology is whatever competent psychological workers make of it, I am asking, first, what it is that competent psychologists in America have been making of our science in the past fifty years, and seek to answer the question by the well-known method of combing our professional journals.

Thirty colleagues rated fifty journals according to their significance for, and devotion to, the advancement of psychology as science. The fourteen journals at the top of the list were chosen for analysis. For every tenth year, beginning 1888 and ending 1938, the entire periodical literature of these fourteen journals was read and analyzed.[1] To be sure, only two journals extend as far back as the decade beginning 1888,[2] and some of them did not come into existence until 1938. Yet, if the sample is smaller for the earlier years, it is likewise more exhaustive, since virtually no periodicals were omitted from the earlier years.

The selected journals contained over sixteen hundred articles in all, each of which was read and fitted to a system of thirty-two rubrics. Since many of these rubrics, especially those pertaining to the theoretical predilections of the authors of the articles, required subjective judgment, for a generous sample of the material independent judgments were secured from two classifiers. Mr. Jerome Bruner was my collaborator, and our agreement for all our separate judgments was 91%. At a later date the

---

1. The journals were the *Psychological Review; Journal of Experimental Psychology; American Journal of Psychology; Journal of Abnormal and Social Psychology; Journal of General Psychology; Psychological Bulletin; Journal of Psychology; Pedagogical Seminary and Journal of Genetic Psychology; Journal of Social Psychology; Character and Personality; Journal of Educational Psychology; Psychometrika; Journal of Comparative Psychology; Journal of Applied Psychology.*

2. The *Psychological Review*, founded 1888, and the *Pedagogical Seminary*, founded 1891.

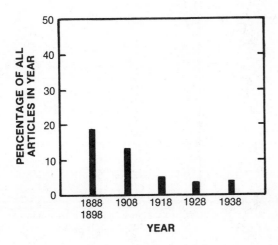

Figure 1. Facultative treatments of mental functions.

results of our analysis will be published in detail *(9)*. For my purposes this afternoon a few of the most representative results will serve.

First, we note the decline in "facultative" treatments of mental functions. Figure 1 reflects the diminution in the *deus ex machina* type of explanation. Owing to the fewness of cases in the earlier years, we combine 1888 and 1898, and find that 19% of all articles in these years lean for their interpretation upon instinct, the "power" of attention, synthetic apperceptive unity, and kindred concepts. In successive years the falling off is gradual but almost complete. Offsetting it in part, however, is the rise of a modern facultative treatment, different in terminology, but kindred in spirit. Here we place some of the contributions, though by no means all, that deal with factors, abilities, or the libido, as if they, too, were gods of a machine. On the whole, however, this latter tendency is not marked.

Another declining interest, so far as its explicit treatment in periodical literature is concerned, is the body–mind problem. Figure 2 shows the irregular decline. To a certain extent, however, this figure masks a significant shift in viewpoint. In the earlier literature solutions to the problem were boldly offered in monistic or dualistic terms; today the fashion is to deny the existence of the body–mind problem, the denial being generally effected with the aid of Vienna logic.

Figure 3 demonstrates the rise and fall of the unconscious. True, psychoanalytic journals are not included in our survey, but the point is here established that the principal periodicals written and read by our own Association reflect a loss of faith in the causal efficacy of the unconscious as well as of faculties in general.

Another decreasing interest is in speculation concerning the true and essential nature of this or that mental *process*. The two parts of Figure 4 bring into contrast what might be called *process as entity* and *process as construct*, or the "realistic" view of the nature of process *versus* the "nominalistic" view. Nowadays we care less than formerly what the

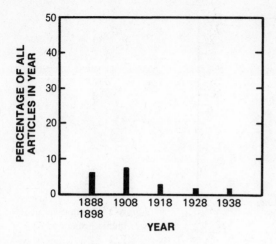

Figure 2. Explicit treatments of the body–mind problem.

nature of "intelligence," "learning" "attention," or "drive" may be, but at the same time we care more about avoiding the hypostatization of mental processes. In the white bars are entered all articles dealing with what might broadly be called methodological formalism—methods for determining constructs from operations, postulational and geometric substitutes for mental entities, criticisms of "verbal magic," and the case for "intervening variables."

Turning from rational interpretation to experimental studies, in Figure 5 we encounter a distinct change in the manner of attacking the higher mental processes (excluding from this count perception, but including learning). In black we see a decline in studies based on language behavior, as involved in learning, reasoning, concept-forma-tion, reverie, or creative thinking. Every study of higher mental pro-cesses requiring the verbal cooperation of the subject, excepting those based on standard intelligence tests, is here included. Note how few

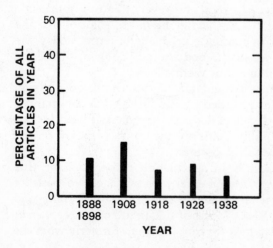

Figure 3. Appeals to the ex-planatory efficacy of uncon-scious mechanisms.

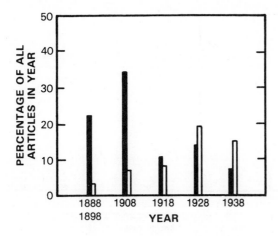

Figure 4. Speculations regarding the nature of mental processes. Black: "entity"; white: "construct."

there are in 1938. Shaded bars represent all studies of cognitive functions and abilities based on the application of mental tests. Even these have declined in recent years. White bars include maze learning in animals and men, conditioning experiments, and all other investigations of higher mental processes by means of non-verbal methods. It is clear that the distinctively human function of language has a decreasing appeal for psychologists, even when the language expression is in the form of standardized tests. Note that the only increase is in those studies of higher mental processes conducted with animal subjects or with human subjects who for the duration of the experiment are rendered totally speechless.

Interest in the single case has also lessened. Included in Figure 6 are articles directed toward the understanding of the individual event, based upon intensive studies of clinical cases, individual persons, or single

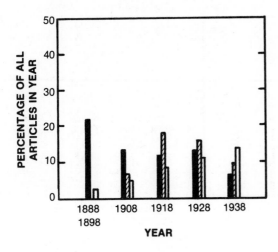

Figure 5. The higher mental processes. Black: language behavior; shaded: mental tests; white: animal and non-verbal behavior.

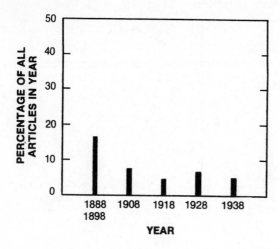

Figure 6. Understanding the single case.

historical events, stressing the setting of the case in its life-environment. Formerly the idiographic view of the single case was fairly popular; in recent years it has almost been ruled out of court. We seem now relatively uninterested in what the individual case can teach us, or in checking our scientific schemes against the obdurate concrete event.

In Figure 7 we see a decline in the percentage of contributions dealing with applied psychology as well as of those concerned with social betterment. In view of the flourishing activity of the American Association for Applied Psychology and the Society for the Psychological Study of Social Issues, it is surprising to find a distinct falling off in articles applying psychology to life or pointing it in the interests of social amelioration. The conclusion to be drawn, I think, is not that our membership as a whole is less interested in the usefulness of psychology, but that a certain professional cleavage is developing. Psychologists using the fourteen journals studied are, in their writings, becoming more and more remote from living issues and more abstract in the presenta-

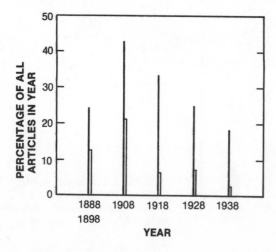

Figure 7. Applied psychology (black); social betterment (white).

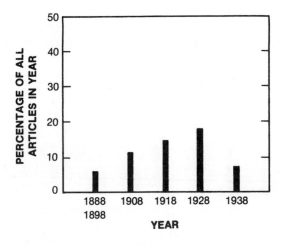

Figure 8. Historical surveys of literature.

tion of their subject matter. The consulting, applied, and socially-minded psychologists are turning to other, more specialized, journals not included within our survey. Thus, the indication is that "pure" and "applied" psychology are parting ways to some extent—an event which some will deplore and others welcome.

A decline of another sort is seen in the diminution of historical surveys. After steadily increasing their recognition and acknowledgment of antecedent studies, it looks now as if psychologists have started to declare their independence of the past. There are fewer historical reviews, as such, in our journals, and fewer historical preludes to experimental reports. Whether the fault lies with the authors who no longer feel respect for past work in their special lines of research, or with the editorial guillotine that decapitates articles to fit our crowded journals, I cannot say. But the fact remains that as research accumulates in our archives it is cited less frequently in our current publications.

Turning from negative to positive trends, we find, first, striking

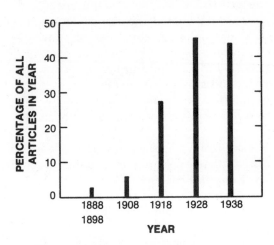

Figure 9. Employment of statistical aids.

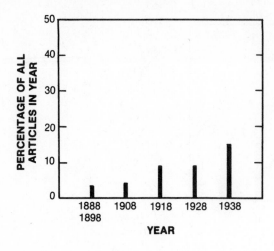

Figure 10. Use of animal subjects.

evidence of the increased use of statistical aids in the treatment of research data. Formerly, statements of central tendency were sufficient. Nowadays, measures of range, variability, correlation, and still more elaborate quantitative treatment of data are increasingly employed, until nearly half of all our periodical literature shows dependence upon them.

It is still too early to tell whether or not the decline in 1938 reflects a substantial growth of interest in more intensive work with fewer subjects, though there seem to be promises of this change not only among clinical psychologists but among animal psychologists as well.

Another decidedly upward trend is the use of animal subjects in psychological research. In 1888 and 1898, taken together, only 3.5% of all studies employed animals—and this always with the intent of finding out how animals *as animals* behave; whereas last year over 15% of all articles were based upon investigations with animals and with no such modest expectation. Today it seems animals are not studied for their own sakes, but rather for what Fabre, the naturalist, called the "universal psychology" revealed by all animals from insects to *Homo sapiens*.

Another rise is seen in the growth of studies dealing specifically with physiological functions. Figure 11 shows the trend. The earlier studies for the most part sought physiological correlates of conscious experience. The reviving interest in physiological research, accompanied by incomparably greater proficiency in such techniques as extirpation and electrical recording, centers less often upon the parallelism of bodily functions and experience, but studies bodily functions directly in a manner that makes the line between psychophysiology and physiology increasingly difficult to draw.

Somewhat more elusive for classification is the growing tendency to regard processes or events as differentiated within a total context. Figure 12 shows a decline and rise in this point of view. Most of the earlier entries did mere lip-service to the proposition that all factors in the total situation must be considered. Only a few of them actually demonstrated

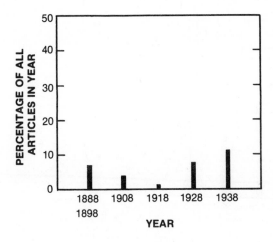

Figure 11. Studies in physiological psychology.

the truth of this proposition as recent researches have done. The latter show unmistakably the influence of both modern neurology and Gestalt theory. Entries include studies of physical and mental growth, the figure-ground relationship, field theory, situational determination. In a variety of ways these investigations recognize the importance of dynamic segregation, of the determination of the part by the whole.

Next, though in a way the point is repetitious, I call your attention to the general upswing in methodological studies. Making no distinction as to what kind of methodology is under discussion, we see the trend in Figure 13. As a matter of fact, the earlier methodological articles dealt chiefly with the metaphysical nature of psychological data and asked how we should set about our studies of attention, intelligence, and thought, viewed as real processes. Later studies, on the other hand, are concerned primarily with getting rid of entities, giving the necessary arguments for constructs, intervening variables, rational learning curves,

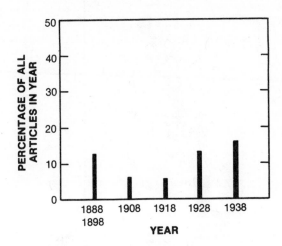

Figure 12. Differentiation of
events within a total context.

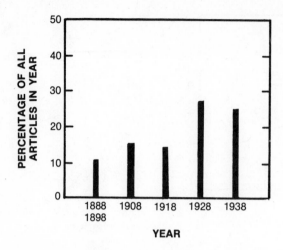

Figure 13. Methodological studies of all kinds.

and the like. More specifically, the modern methodologists generally subscribe to some form of logical empiricism, increasingly to operationism.

Concerning operationism itself, the term, though new, has a special lure. Figure 14 shows its upward path. In 1928, close on the heels of Bridgman's book, one article mentioning operationism appeared. To bring the trend to date, the percentage for the first six months of 1939 has been added.

A close-up shows that the course of this magic concept is onward and upward, leading somewhere into the world of tomorrow.

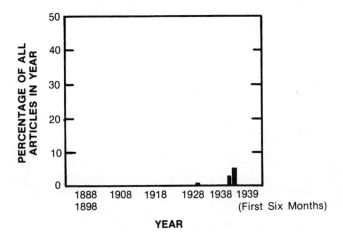

Figure 14. Mentions of operationism.

Such are some of the waxing and waning fashions of the day. The story is incomplete, but even from the few points just plotted, we can draw a significant perspective. Reviewing the evidence, we find mental faculties and hypostasized psychic processes vanishing rapidly, though here and there still masquerading behind new terms. The body–mind problem, never solved, has been declared popularly null and void. Dualism evokes rejection responses of considerable vehemence. (Indeed, of all philosophical pollens, psychologists seem most allergic to this.) The appeal of the unconscious is dwindling. Higher mental processes as exhibited in the speech of human beings are relatively neglected, marked preference being shown for studies of non-verbal behavior and for animal subjects. A schism is apparent between pure and applied psychology, and there is a growing disregard for studies of single cases. It also looks as if modern psychology were becoming appreciably unhistorical.

Among accelerated trends we find a striking rise in the employment of statistical aids, in the use of animal subjects, in the spread of physiological research. At the same time there is a growing recognition of the importance of context, which has led to many fruitful studies of dynamic segregation. Methodological studies have mounted, characterized especially by philosophical theorizing concerning the nature of psychological constructs. Operationism is the current watchword of an austere empiricism. Synoptic systems, such as those of McDougall and Stern, have given way to miniature systems, and embracing theories expounded in the grand manner have yielded to diminutive theories implemented with great precision. Immediate experience is rigidly excluded from most modern systems, and in its place surrogate operational functions are sought. Needless to say, all these trends have staunch and able advocates, but our task today is not to extol them—

rather, to view them in perspective and to anticipate their long-range effects on our science.

Perspective

The psychologial system-builders of the Nineteenth and early Twentieth Centuries were filled with the lingering spirit of the Enlightenment which hated mystery and incompleteness. They wanted a synoptic view of man's mental life. If moral and metaphysical dogmatism were needed to round out their conception of the complete man, they became unblushing dogmatists. Yet even while their synoptic style flourished, the very experimental psychology which they helped to create was leading others into new paths. Their own students, in the very process of enhancing their experimental proficiency, came to admire not the work of their masters, but the self-discipline of mathematics and of the natural sciences. Willingly they exchanged what they deemed fruitless dialectics for what to them was unprejudiced empiricism. Nowadays, for one experimentalist to proclaim another "superior to controversy about fundamentals" is considered high tribute (8, p. 133).

There are with us still, of course, stubborn apostles of the Enlightenment who have not been pleased with this turn of events. They complain that we are putting too little architectonic into our work; that, though not everyone should be a myth maker, we must have a few whose weighty influence will keep the rest of us keyed to the necessity of seeing larger significance in what we do. They say we have become a craft overstuffed with techniques and that, preoccupied with minutiae, we are in danger of losing perspective. They even say that Leipzig in labor brought forth a mere mouse (36, p. 429). But the modernist says à bas! with such nostalgia, and down, too, with synoptic systems, and down with the dated subjective categories derived from immediate experience that are invoked to sustain these systems. We will have no more of them!

Fierce and portentous is the modern attack upon immediate experience.[3] While it is commonly granted that the immediate experience of the investigator is the source of the subject matter of psychology, as of all other sciences, yet it is said that like the older sciences psychology should instantly supplant this direct experience by indirect objective formulations. Subjective immediatism must give way to a public outdoor attitude toward our knowledge. It is said that the very claim made by some psychologists that their work remains true to life, close to untrammeled common sense, is the very thing that disqualifies this work from

---

3. A full explanation of this attack would have to include an account of many influences, among them (a) long frustration with the body-mind problem, (b) cumulative attacks upon the reliability of introspection, (c) imitative strivings after the "monism" of the natural sciences, (d) slight success in empirical studies of thinking, reasoning, volition, (e) correspondingly greater (felt) success with animal experimentation.

being scientific (26, p. 178). There is no need for a curve of sensory intensity to *feel* like sensory intensity, for the obstruction method to *feel* like a desire, nor for a curve of conforming behavior to look like a crowd at a traffic intersection (19, p. 33).

So it comes about that after the initial take-off we, as psychological investigators, are permanently barred from the benefit and counsel of our ordinary perceptions, feelings, judgments, and intuitions. We are allowed to appeal to them neither for our method nor for our validations. So far as *method* is concerned, we are told that, because the subject is able to make his discriminations only after the alleged experience has departed, any inference of a subjectively unified experience on his part is both anachronistic and unnecessary (6). If the subject protests that it is evident to him that he had a rich and vivid experience that was not fully represented in his overt discriminations, he is firmly assured that what is vividly self-evident to him is no longer of interest to the scientific psychologist. It has been decided, to quote Boring, that "in any useful meaning of the term existence," "private experience does not exist" (7).

When it comes to *validating* his work, the modernist follows a logic all his own. He certainly *implies* that his findings overspread the problem initially formulated from experience—that thresholds of discrimination correspond to thresholds of consciousness,[4] that crossings of a grid correspond to desire, and that PGR deflections correspond to felt emotions. But should he return to the initial experience from which he started in order to validate or to apply these findings, he would probably be startled—even as the layman is startled—by the grotesque lack of fit. Fortunately for him, however, his creed forbids him to consult more than his skeletonized operations—the full-bodied experience he started with is never appealed to.

The consequences of the raid on immediate experience have already been shown in the graphs: disbelief in the existence or approachability of mental processes as such, a flight from linguistic functions, loss of interest in the single case, as well as in the historical background of psychology, and at the same time the development of a notable schism between the psychology constructed in a laboratory and the psychology constructed on the field of life.

An increasing number of investigators now pin their faith upon experimentation with animals. Our program tells us that 25% of the papers delivered at this year's meetings are based upon animal research. In 1914, twenty-five years ago, the corresponding percentage was 11.

A colleague, a good friend of mine, recently challenged me to name a single psychological problem not referable to rats for its solution. Considerably startled, I murmured something, I think, about the psychology of reading disability. But to my mind came flooding the historic problems of the aesthetic, humorous, religious, and cultural behavior of

---

4. A point concerning which J. G. Miller's experiment has raised considerable doubt (23).

men. I thought how men build clavichords and cathedrals, how they write books, and how they laugh uproariously at Mickey Mouse; how they plan their lives five, ten, or twenty years ahead; how, by an elaborate metaphysic of their own contrivance, they deny the utility of their own experience, including the utility of the metaphysic that led them to this denial. I thought of poetry and puns, of propaganda and revolution, of stock markets and suicide, and of man's despairing hope for peace. I thought, too, of the elementary fact that human problem-solving, unlike that of the rat, is saturated through and through with verbal function, so that we have no way of knowing whether the delay, the volition, the symbolizing and categorizing typical of human learning are even faintly adumbrated by findings in animal learning.[5]

One should not prejudge this issue; but before we wander much farther down the road we are traveling might we not with profit hold a symposium for the purpose of discovering to what extent infrahuman analogues have given us power to predict, understand, and control human behavior? It is not, of course, a question of the parallels from anatomy and physiology obviously valuable for medical science, but of parallels in gross molar conduct applicable in a sphere where the culture and peculiar genius of humanity prevail. We need to ask ourselves point-blank whether the problems we frame with our rats are unquestionably of the same order as the problems we envisage for human kind; and further, if we succeed in solving a problem for rats, how we are to make sure the findings hold for man unless we repeat the whole investigation on man himself; and if we are forced to verify our principles by a separate study of man, whether we have the right to inveigh against the psychologist who prefers to study human manners and morals, since it is upon his work that the validation of our own will ultimately rest.

At the present time there can be little doubt that it is not altogether the demonstrated value of animal research that accounts for its vogue, but in large part its delightful suitability for the exercise of objective and approved methods. By studying rats, not men, we gain status as scientists, for like the natural sciences we can, in this line of investiga-

---

5. In a valuable paper on the experimental analysis of instinctive behavior K. S. Lashley tells of the activity of the microstoma, a tiny marine worm, that, having no stinging cells of its own, captures and ingests hydras that have, until it is sated and has incorporated in itself the nettles it needs for its own protection. Regarding this remarkable performance Lashley has written: "Here, in the length of half a millimeter, are encompassed all of the major problems of dynamic psychology. There is a specific drive or appetite, satisfied only by a very indirect series of activities, with the satisfaction of the appetite dependent upon the concentration of nettles in the skin" (20, p. 446). One wonders whether the only major problems of dynamic psychology are those having to do with specific drive and its satisfaction through an indirect series of activities performed by an uncorticated organism. Does a cortex bring no major problems of its own? Are symbols, dreams, autism, irreality, guilt feelings, the ego ideal, of no essential significance? Does culture create no major problems for dynamic psychology? And has the microstoma, one wonders, that curious type of scientific motivation that requires it to view itself as a mechanism devoid of immediate experience and volition?

tion, employ precision techniques and operational modes of communication. This desire for status on our part is understandable, but because of it we are in danger of losing sight of the true source of the eminence of the elder sciences. Their enviable glory does not consist in their fidelity to a set of conventional methods, but rather in the unexampled power they have given mankind in *predicting, understanding,* and *controlling* the course of nature for mankind's own benefit. As a mature science psychology, too, will find its justification, not in performing a ritual of method, but in contributing to humanity the power to achieve these ends.

Prediction

Considering, then, man's interest in his own well-being, let us ask how matters stand with psychological prediction. Is it not true that apart from a narrow range of segmental reactions in the laboratory we psychologists can predict very little concerning human conduct? It is argued, of course, that sophistication in methodology will improve matters. Yet there are two grounds for doubting this claim. First, since the current methodological trend will not take direct experience as a model for its constructs nor return to it for a validation of its results, it seems unlikely that the utility of its predictions will be great. Or to state the point affirmatively, in order to predict events of pressing significance for human life one must *deal* with these events (not with some simplified surrogate or analogue), studying them at a suitable level of complexity and checking one's predictions by the actual lives men lead.

The second ground for misgiving lies in the fact that the modern methodologist, no less than his predecessors throughout the history of psychological science, fails to see the peculiar need in psychology for the prediction of the individual event. Of the two kinds of prediction appropriate to psychology—the actuarial and the individual—the former only, up to now, has received the attention it deserves.

Suppose we set out to discover the chances of John Brown to make good on parole, and use for the purpose an index of prediction based upon parole violations and parole successes of men with similar histories. We find that 72% of the men with John's antecedents make good, and many of us conclude that John, therefore, has a 72% chance of making good. There is an obvious error here. The fact that 72% of the men having the same antecedent record as John will make good is merely an actuarial statement. It tells us nothing about John. If we knew John sufficiently well, we might say not that he had a 72% chance of making good, but that he, as an individual, was almost certain to succeed or else to fail. Indeed, if we believe in determinism at all, his chances are either zero or else 100; he is bound to succeed or else to violate because the germs of his future are already contained in his attitudes, in the meaning to him of his antecedent life, and in the specific psychological environment that molds him. Even admitting the possibility of unforeseeable accidents, as scientific determinists we ought to strive for a prediction more accurate than the senseless 72% that is derived from a table of norms based on the antecedents of paroled men *en masse*. Or again, if seven in ten Americans go to the movies each week, it does not follow that I have seven in ten chances of attending. Only a knowledge of *my* attitudes, interests, and environmental situation will tell you my chances, and bring your prediction from a 70% actuarial statement to a 100% certain individual prediction.

The upshot of the matter is this: psychology will become *more* scientific, i.e. better able to make predictions, when it has learned to evaluate single trends in all their intrinsic complexity, when it has learned how to tell what will happen to *this* child's IQ if we change his environment in a certain way, whether *this* man will make a good executive, whither *this* social change is tending.

For certain purposes actuarial predictions have their uses. They are based on the type of law that transcends geographical-historical context. Yet in many cases we find that human conduct is so utterly modified by geographical-historical context, and by all concurrent internal trends accompanying the behavior in question, that laws ignoring context do not entirely meet our need.[6]

Our survey has shown that an increasing number of psychologists are becoming aware of the importance of context. The time is therefore ripe to seek more assiduously those laws that define the influence of ground upon figure, context upon judgment, traits upon behavior, frames of reference upon attitudes and activity, situational fields upon performance. These contextual laws are stepping stones toward that form of synthetic understanding on the basis of which truly serviceable predictions concerning individual happenings are made.

One large section of our profession will claim success in the line of approach I have indicated. Clinical psychologists will say that their daily work requires all manner of individual predictions, and that guidance is based upon it. In principle they are right, but two admonitions are in order. First, clinicians need to check their judgments rigorously, for the validity of clinical predictions is rarely known. Further, they need to make explicit the basis on which their correct predictions are made. Urgently we need to know the way in which successful predictions in individual cases are arrived at. In the meantime psychologists in general might do worse than study the bases of correct predictions made by statesmen, psychiatrists, lawyers, and even head waiters, whose skill in forecasting important aspects of human behavior is greater than ours. If

---

6. It does no good to object that everything in the universe supplies a context for everything else, that "if a man is ever to utter the whole truth about a natural event, he must not shut his mouth until he has expressed all nature" (7, p. 445). It is still a question of *what degree* of limitation upon the system chosen for study is most serviceable. Because some limitation is obviously required it does not follow that the most fruitful level to adopt is that of the most isolated possible motor automatism (the elementary discrimination).

we can first learn from them, we may ultimately teach them and ourselves more. To raise our level of prediction above that achieved by common sense, even by superior common sense, should be our steadfast aim.

Understanding

To the power of prediction science adds the capacity to understand what we observe. By understanding I mean the ability that human beings have to place details of information within a pattern of thought. Psychologists have long known that no fact apprehended ever stands alone, for it cannot be a fact until it is embedded within, and interpreted by, a context to which it is in some way related. With the advent of dynamic psychology it became common knowledge that what is accepted as fact depends very largely upon the individual's sense of the importance of fact, each individual carrying with him convictions concerning what is important for him.[7] Sometimes we call these convictions his values. Unless we can first comprehend our subject's value-context, we are unable to know the significance of his behavior as he performs it, for the simple reason that the behavior we perceive is instantly ordered to *our* own presuppositions without any regard to what *his* presuppositions may be. In other words, our frame, not his, supplies the context.

Let me give an illustration. Suppose a psychologist sets about to study learning. Suppose, too, he brings to his task a firm sense of the importance of mechanical connectedness. He observes the subject's behavior, and since fact depends upon the sense of the importance of fact, he interprets this observed behavior in terms of his own presuppositions concerning mechanical connectedness. Now, the learning itself was achieved by an individual who had a very different sense of values. He was not learning in order to demonstrate mechanical connectedness to himself, but in order to acquire something important to him. Shall the psychologist understand this behavior with the aid of his own imperatives or strive to understand it in the light of the subject's imperatives? In the former case mechanical connectedness becomes the chief law of learning; in the latter case interest and importance become the chief law.[8]

Instead of attempting to understand the other organism's point of

---

7. Especially instructive is A. N. Whitehead's discussion of the relation between matter-of-fact and the sense of importance of fact (35, Ch. 1).

8. To be sure, the organism has a way of insistently making its point of view apparent, trying, as it were, to tell the psychologist that the primary law of learning lies in this sense of importance. So the psychologist then postulates demands or drives to account for learning, but continues to view these within his (the psychologist's) own frame of importance. Our current conceptions of motivation are not framed from the subject's point of view. If they were, we should study less often mechanical retroaction, and more often the classificatory power that interest confers on memory; less often the effects of specific incentives or drives, and more often the mature interest systems in accordance with which human beings acquire their knowledge and skill.

view and interpreting his activity in reference to this, it is our custom early in our investigations to disregard or even to disrupt his context of behavior, and, instead of comprehending his activity within his frame of importance, to interpret his behavior in terms of our own. Moreover, when we make rational reconstructions of our findings (constructs), we do so from the point of view of our presuppositions and communicate them to other scientists sharing these same presuppositions. In the course of this procedure the pattern of trends peculiar to the organism, what the organism is trying by himself to do, is almost completely lost to sight.

You will recognize that I have here been skirting the problem of *Verstehen* formulated and explored by German psychology; and you will admit that it is one of the leads from German psychology that has not been followed very far by Americans. Our own psychology would profit if we undertook to apply to it our genius for clarification. There are, of course, in America a few theoretical skirmishes with the problem (2, 17), and some native experiments that point the way, among them the investigations of Murray and his collaborators (25), L. B. Murphy (24), Allport, Walker, and Lathers (1), Estes (14), Cartwright and French (11).[9] In various ways all these experiments have shed light upon the process of understanding the contexts and imperatives that determine behavior from the subject's point of view.

Let us turn back for a moment from the subject's sense of importance to the experimenter's. To some extent it is inevitable that in striving for system each of us plan his experiment in his own way, select his instruments and subjects, and draw his interpretations in accordance with his own presuppositions, excluding what is not consistent with his frame of importance. Such natural pedantry is not necessarily an evil, for specialization must be allowed within our extensive subject matter. But it follows that, unless we have a diversity of presuppositions and interests in our science, we shall lose all those forms of experience that are automatically excluded when but one set of presuppositions is followed. Especially today variety is needed, for limited and miniature systems are in fashion, from which exclusions are exceedingly strict.

Our survey has shown that this is an age of interest in methodology. What it has not so clearly shown is that the purveyor of methods is necessarily asking you to accept his own frame of presuppositions. It is for this reason that it becomes necessary to scrutinize the consequences

---

9. The importance of this last-named experiment, soon to be published, lies in its demonstration that in judgments of personality the validity attained by each of two judges can be in excess of their reliability. That is, two investigators may have demonstrable correctness that exceeds their agreement with one another, because each understands different *aspects* of the subject's personality. It follows that when we pare down our acceptable data until only that portion remains upon which all investigators agree, we are left with less than our just scientific reward. What is needed is a method of combining demonstrably valid insights rather than a reduction of our data to the bare bones upon which all observers may objectively agree.

of any commitment of method. Even so harmless a methodological doctrine as operationism is fraught with unexpected entanglements.

In an age of turmoil, one hundred and seventy years ago, Voltaire made the demand: "If you would converse with me, you must first define your terms." In our present age of turmoil, operationism is making the same refreshing demand (31). It is a demand that appeals to all sensible men. Now, the best way to define a term is by the use of the typical instance or event. When we speak operationally we say, in effect, "I mean something which is illustrated by the following actions." In this way, through the telling illustration, we communicate a prior understanding in ourselves in order to arouse a like understanding in others. Operationism thus may become a useful tool of understanding.

But when the operationist goes further and insists that "a concept is synonymous with the corresponding set of operations," can he mean what he says? If so, there must be an infinitude of discrete concepts. Think, for instance, of all the different operations that have gone into the study of learning. To prevent complete and senseless pluralism operations have to be grouped by classes, and there is ultimately no way of grouping them except by relational thought. The most austere operationist communicates not operations, but a prior concept, for operational symbolizing depends upon prior ideas of entities and relations that are symbolized. Even if we try to rely upon the "standard experiment," as Tolman proposes, to serve as the operation by which a concept is defined (32), it is only by virtue of some act of understanding that the equivalence of this experiment with others can be established.[10]

It is not to operationism's demand for illustrative definitions that objection can be made, but to the fact that its hidden metaphysical presuppositions of extreme nominalism beckon us away from the fundamental problem of how we know things together. Hyperaesthesia for our operations and anaesthesia for understanding make us lose our way in an infinitude of detail. Synoptic views become more and more difficult; an entropy of scientific energy sets in. Fearful lest we imply that we did something more than our experiments indicate, we are tempted to give up our search for useful generalizations and to disclaim responsibility for the wider application of our work.

Along this path lies skepticism which—as historians have noted—sends forth its pallid bloom at the end of eras of great intellectual

---

10. Critics have pointed out that the agreements under the operational creed do not go deep, and that the unity of science is after all not just around the corner. Some advocates of operationism maintain that it readily includes both immediate experience and the introspective technique within its view, some think the opposite; some would admit purposive interpretations within operationism, others would exclude them; some think that field theory fits, some that it does not. And if, as some say, its sole objective is to separate the rational criteria of inquiry from the positive and experimental criteria, then there is but temporary gain, since we have to return to understanding in order to know-together the rational and empirical ingredients of the analysis.

advance. Permit me to quote two passages from a recent methodological book written by an able experimentalist:

Science after all is only one of the games played by the children of this world, and it may very well be that those who prefer other games are in their generation wiser. It must be remembered, however, that *science is a game* and those who play it have a right to insist that it be played according to rule. If some of the players, or the bystanders, try to change the rules, the game will go to pieces, or at least, it will not be the same game. (26, p. 57)

And again:

Science is a vast and impressive tautology. Its laws are summaries of observations, its hypotheses involve arguments that are circular. Since its explanations are true only if they can be demonstrated empirically, they explain nothing that is not already known. The mystery which surrounds the life of man is as dark today as it was when man first came out of the jungle, and will be just as impenetrable when the last surviving scientist thinks his concluding thought or writes his final sentence. (26, p. 154)

Such weariness is inevitable so long as we make the test of psychology one of fidelity to method rather than to understanding, prediction, and control. Methodism as the sole requirement of science means that all the faithful crowd onto a carpet of prayer, and with their logical shears cut more and more inches off the rug, permitting fewer and fewer aspirants to enjoy status. Two debilitating attitudes result: that of the playboy who likes his childish games, and that of the fatalist who sees no duty devolving upon a scientist other than that of formal ritual. The survival value of either attitude is zero, for both lead us, and all those who look to psychology for help, to believe that psychology has no essential relation to life, and that human events lie entirely beyond our control. Such a belief undermines the very civilization that has endowed psychology with its freedom, in return charging it with the contribution of useful knowledge.[11]

Control

Until our deficiencies in prediction and understanding are repaired, it is unlikely that psychology can go far in meeting the third and supreme

---

11. Not infrequently the skeptic derides applied psychology. Outside the laboratory he lives a cultured and varied life of a free agent and useful citizen. Yet his methodical work in the laboratory overspreads very little of his daily experience and prevents integration in his life. Though he generally repudiates a dualism of mind and body, he welcomes the equally stultifying dualism of laboratory and life.

criterion of validity for science—that of practical control of human affairs. The clinician is most active in this direction. He and other consultants, educators, and technicians are controlling human events, but whether more successfully than unaided common sense could do depends on evidence still to be supplied in conscientious records of success and failure.

Outside of the clinical field little control is attempted. The man of common sense approaching our treatises for help finds that a large portion of his daily conduct is not only left unexplained, but is not represented at all. From agencies of government, industry, education, and human welfare come daily appeals for assistance in their service to mankind. Psychology, as science—may I repeat?—can be justified only by giving mankind practical control over its destinies, not by squatting happily on a carpet of prayer.[12]

Frame of Reference

Fortunately, currents engender countercurrents. The flow in psychology today is not altogether toward the shoals and reefs of formalism and of skepticism. Our evidence (Figure 12) shows a strong revival of interest in the problems of context, which of necessity include the structure of the human personality and its activity within its social surroundings. To study highly integrated functions at levels where serviceable prediction and understanding result is, of course, a most difficult undertaking, requiring inventions of method not dreamed of today; requiring, also, the borrowing of many tools of precision and safeguards of measurement from the experimentalist's storehouse. It is characteristic of this new movement that its concepts have a realistic and humanistic flavor, for it is vital in this new work to believe that something real and substantial is under investigation.

An example of the trend is the growing interest in the *frame of reference*, a concept which I have appropriated for the title of this address. It is of recent origin and may for that reason be viewed with suspicion. Yet it is, I feel sure, the legitimate offspring of the flourishing principle of dynamic differentiation. It expresses the importance of context; it repairs the ravages that result from viewing the behavior of other organisms exclusively within the investigator's frame of presuppositions; it aids in understanding. Its fruitfulness is seen in many experimental studies of the past five years, including those of Ansbacher

---

12. It seems only fair to add that there are signs of a growing demand among psychologists for significant and useful research. The demand is clearly apparent among social psychologists, and elsewhere as well. T. L. Kelley, speaking recently to mathematical psychologists, has urged them to invent and employ "measures of utility" in order that the factors they conjure into being may turn out not to be factors of just no importance at all (16).

(4), Cantril *(10)*, Darley *(12)*, Kornhauser *(18)*, McGregor *(22)*, Sells *(28)*, Sherif *(29)*, Stagner *(30)*, Watson and Hartmann *(34)*, and others.

Frame of reference has to do with any context whatever that exerts a demonstrable influence upon the individual's perceptions, judgments, feelings, or actions. Often the influence is—to use Köhler's term—"silent." Of the existence of frames the subject himself is only partially aware, and unless he is well warned the investigator too may overlook them entirely. At the present time it is especially the social and dynamic psychologists who are ardent on the trail, although much pertinent related work is found wherever there is research upon problems of equivalence, aspiration level, life space, constancy phenomena, and psychophysical judgment.

Many frames, of course, especially those encountered in psychophysics, are neutral and impersonal in type, providing simple spatial and temporal orientations. Others are personal and ego-involving.[13] The position of college buildings upon a campus is an impersonal spatial system that orients and directs our excursions to and from our classes; but our status within the collegiate hierarchy is of a more personal order, charged with intimate importance to ourselves, and determining affective attitudes of motivational significance. Dynamic and social psychologists are especially concerned with these personal, ego-involving frames, and are often able to show that what are sometimes thought to be neutral-perceptual judgments, even the judgments of scientists themselves, are not wholly determined by an objectively established frame, but are entangled deep in the web of personality.

The relation of frames to *attitudes* and to *traits* is a problem yet to be worked out. These concepts all refer in various gradations to complex and relatively persistent forms of mental organization. Their popularity, together with that of *trend, need, sentiment,* and other kindred concepts, gives support to McDougall's claim, expressed in one of his last papers, that the most indispensable doctrine in modern psychology is that of *tendency (21)*. All are frankly class concepts, and can be defended, I think, for the superior promise they hold in our triple task of predicting, understanding, and controlling behavior.

Class concepts though they are, they do not necessarily exclude considerations of cultural influence nor the situational field. It is especially those frames of reference adopted as the "wise prejudices" of our own station, class, and culture that reflect prevailing social norms. We are now making progress in the detailed study of conforming behavior, in the composition of ideological thought, and in the genesis and development of frames in childhood.[14] We are beginning to sort out that

---

13. In making the distinction between personal and impersonal frames, T. A. Ryan *(27)* confines the former to certain self-referred systems of space, time, or meaning, neglecting to consider the emotional frames that are ego-involving.

14. Especially fascinating are the problems in this area. Consider, for example, the question which frames the child adopts from his playmates and which from his parents. Matters of politics and religion he ordinarily seems to refer to frames taken from parents, but standards of speech and clothing to frames acquired from his contemporaries. Why does he do so?

monstrously tangled heap our Councils have christened "personality and culture." Not yet, however, are we able to tell what makes a mauve decade mauve, or a skeptical age skeptical, or psychology in the 1880's soulful and in the 1930's soulless. Nor do we know the extent to which a man can shake himself free of the influence of his times, or even recreate them to his liking. Freud, we know, had something to do with Queen Victoria's downfall; but was he consequence or cause? Who can say?

Speaking on this very campus forty years ago, John Dewey, later to become the eighth president of our Association, made what for that time was a striking observation (13). Psychology, he held, cannot help but be politically conditioned. He had in mind, for example, the fact that doctrines of the fixedness of human nature flourish in an aristocracy and perish in a democracy. The privileges of the elite in ancient Greece, and the doctrines of the Church in mediaeval times, provided the setting for psychological theories of their day. Under modern conditions theories of statehood play a major role.[15]

The president of the *Deutsche Gesellschaft*, addressing that organization last year, praised typological studies that enabled psychology, in matters of heredity, race, and education, to pick out the national *Gegentypus* whose unwelcome qualities are individualism and intellectualism. In passing, he warned against using the mental tests that one of the great figures in psychology, William Stern, a Jew, had introduced, and said that he wondered not at all that some of his colleagues had been censured for pursuing a pre-revolutionary course of thought. At the same time he added:

> Antagonistic foreign countries speak of coordination (*Gleichschaltung*) whenever conformity of science and politics is perceived. No, this conformity is certainly not based on coordination, but upon the fact that politics and science, now for the first time, strive after truth even in the basic questions of existence, over which heretofore darkness and error reigned. (15, p. 14)

And what is the situation with us? Do we American psychologists lack politically determined attitudes? At first thought it would seem so, for are we not entirely free in our individual researches, and may we not hold any fantastic view that we choose? We may, and that proves the point for the political determinist, for only in a democracy can anything like a "socially detached intelligentsia" be realized. On the theory that democracy will ultimately gain by giving each thinker all the space he wants, we American psychologists are subsidized, encouraged, and defended. Each worker may elect, as he pleases, any section or subsection of psychology that he finds suited to his taste and abilities.

The desirability of keeping alive diversified investigation and a diversified sense of importance is the generous lesson that democracy teaches us. Now, if ever, must we learn it well and apply it to ourselves.

---

15. In this connection the striking fusion of John Dewey's own psychological theories with his allegiance to democracy is well worth special study (cf. 3, Ch. 9).

If we rejoice, for example, that present-day psychology is—as Bills has pointed out (5) and as our survey has shown—increasingly *empirical, mechanistic, quantitative, nomothetic, analytic,* and *operational,* we should also beware of demanding slavish subservience to these presuppositions. Why not allow psychology as a science—for science is a broad and beneficent term—to be also *rational, teleological, qualitative, idiographic, synoptic,* and even *non-operational?* I mention these antitheses of virtue with deliberation, for the simple reason that great insights of psychology in the past—for example, those of Aristotle, Locke, Fechner, James, Freud—have stemmed from one or more of these unfashionable presuppositions.

My plea, therefore, is that we avoid authoritarianism, that we keep psychology from becoming a cult from which original and daring inquiry is ruled out by the application of one-sided tests of method; that we come to evaluate our science rather by its success in enhancing—above the levels achieved by common sense—our powers of *predicting, understanding,* and *controlling* human action. As an aid to progress I have tried especially to strengthen the case for research upon complex patterns of human mental organization, frames of reference, the subject's point of view, and the act of understanding.

If we but watch with amused humility our own personal frames affect our perceptions and our deeds, we will then enjoy and profit from our disagreements. Best of all, we shall be able to sink these disagreements into a common determination that the vast horizons of our science shall not prematurely close down, neither through bigotry, nor surrender to authoritarianism, nor through our failure to pay our way in the civilization that is sustaining us.

BIBLIOGRAPHY

1. Allport, F. H., Walker, L., & Lathers, E.   Written composition and characteristics of personality. *Arch. Psychol., N. Y.,* 1934, *26,* No. 173.
2. Allport, G. W.   *Personality: A psychological interpretation.* New York: Holt, 1937.
3. Allport, G. W.   The individual and social psychology of John Dewey. In P. A. Schlipp (Ed.), *The philosophy of John Dewey.* Evanston: Northwestern Univ. Press, 1939. Ch. 9.
4. Ansbacher, H.   Perception of number as affected by the monetary value of the objects. *Arch. Psychol., N. Y.,* 1937, *30,* No. 215.
5. Bills, A. G.   Changing views of psychology as a science. *Psychol. Rev.,* 1938, *45,* 377–394.
6. Boring, E. G.   Temporal perception and operationism. *Amer. J. Psychol.,* 1936, *48,* 519–522.
7. Boring, E. G.   A psychological function is the relation of successive differentiations of events in the organism. *Psychol. Rev.,* 1937, *44,* 445–461.
8. Boring, E. G.   Review of R. S. Woodworth's *Experimental psychology. Amer. J. Psychol.,* 1939, *52,* 131–138.
9. Bruner, J. S., & Allport, G. W.   Fifty years of change in American psychology. (Forthcoming in the *Psychol. Bull.)*
10. Cantril, H.   The prediction of social events. *J. Abnorm. Soc. Psychol.,* 1938, *33,* 364–389.

11. Cartwright, D., & French, J. R. P.   The reliability of life-history studies. *Character & Pers.*, 1939, *8.*

12. Darley, J. G.   Changes in measured attitudes and adjustments. *J. Soc. Psychol.*, 1938, *9*, 189–199.

13. Dewey, J.   Psychology as philosophic method. Berkeley: Univ. Chronicle, 1899; reprinted as Consciousness and experience, in his *Influence of Darwin on philosophy and other essays*. New York: Holt, 1910. Pp. 242–270.

14. Estes, S. G.   Judging personality from expressive behavior. *J. Abnorm. Soc. Psychol.*, 1938, *33*, 217–236.

15. Jaensch, E.   Wozu Psychologie? *Ber. XVIth Kongr. dtsch. Ges. Psychol.*, Leipzig, 1939, 7–30.

16. Kelley, T. L.   Mental factors of no importance. *J. Educ. Psychol.*, 1938, *30*, 139–142.

17. Klein, D. B.   Scientific understanding in psychology. *Psychol. Rev.*, 1932, *39*, 552–569.

18. Kornhauser, A. W.   Attitudes of economic groups. *Publ. Opin. Quart.*, 1938, *2*, 260–268.

19. Lashley, K. S.   The behavioristic interpretation of consciousness. *Psychol. Rev.*, 1923, *30*, 237–272.

20. Lashley, K. S.   Experimental analysis of instinctive behavior. *Psychol. Rev.*, 1938, *45*, 445–471.

21. McDougall, W.   Tendencies as indispensable postulates of all psychology. *Proc. XIth int. Congr. Psychol.*, Paris, 1937, 157–170.

22. McGregor, D.   The major determinants of the prediction of social events. *J. Abnorm. Soc. Psychol.*, 1938, *33*, 179–204.

23. Miller, J. G.   Discrimination without awareness. *Amer. J. Psychol.*, 1939, *52*, 562–578.

24. Murphy, L. B.   Social behavior and child personality: an exploratory study of some roots of sympathy. New York: Columbia Univ. Press, 1937.

25. Murray, H. A., et al.   Explorations in personality. New York: Oxford Univ. Press, 1938.

26. Pratt, C. C.   *The logic of modern psychology*. New York: Macmillan, 1939.

27. Ryan, T. A.   Dynamic, physiognomic, and other neglected properties of perceived objects: a new approach to comprehending. *Amer. J. Psychol.*, 1938, *51*, 629–650.

28. Sells, S. B.   The atmosphere effect: An experimental study of reasoning. *Arch. Psychol.*, N. Y., 1936, *29*, No. 200.

29. Sherif, M.   The psychology of social norms. New York: Harper, 1936.

30. Stagner, R.   Measuring relationships among group opinions. *Publ. Opin. Quart.*, 1938, *2*, 622–627.

31. Stevens, S. S.   Psychology and the science of science. *Psychol. Bull.*, 1939, *36*, 221–263.

32. Tolman, E. C.   Operational behaviorism and current trends in psychology. *Proc. 25th Anniv. Celeb. Inaug. Grad. Stud.*, Univ. So. Calif., Los Angeles, 1936, 89–103.

33. Tolman, E. C.   Psychology versus immediate experience. *Phil. Sci.*, 1938, *2*, 356–380.

34. Watson, W. S., & Hartmann, G. W.   Rigidity of a basic attitudinal frame. *J. Abnorm. Soc. Psychol.*, 1939, *34*, 314–336.

35. Whitehead, A. N.   *Modes of thought*. New York: Macmillan, 1938.

36. Zangwill, O. L.   Review of R. S. Woodworth's *Experimental psychology. Brit. J. Psychol.*, 1939, *29*, 429–431.

Part Three

Psychology After World War II

Presidents of the
American Psychological Association
1946–1967

Henry E. Garrett, *1946*

Carl R. Rogers, *1947*

Donald G. Marquis, *1948*

Ernest R. Hilgard, *1949*

J. P. Guilford, *1950*

Robert R. Sears, *1951*

J. McVickers Hunt, *1952*

Laurance F. Shaffer, *1953*

O. Hobart Mowrer, *1954*

E. Lowell Kelly, *1955*

Theodore M. Newcomb, *1956*

Lee J. Cronbach, *1957*

Harry F. Harlow, *1958*

Wolfgang Köhler, *1959**

D. O. Hebb, *1960*

Neal E. Miller, *1961*

Paul E. Meehl, *1962*

Charles E. Osgood, *1963*

Quinn McNemar, *1964*

Jerome S. Bruner, *1965*

Nicholas Hobbs, *1966*

Gardner Lindzey, *1967*

---

* Köhler's address appears earlier (see Chapter 14).

Chapter 20

The Presidents
and
Their Messages
1946-1967

Most of the APA presidents from 1946 to 1967 served in World War II, either in uniform or as civilians in government agencies. They worked with others of dissimilar training, performed unfamiliar tasks, and were relocated to new geographical areas. While the presidential addresses seldom reflected these war experiences directly, secondary signs can be found, such as confidence in psychology's broadened role in public affairs. Some of the younger members of the profession of psychology, who grew up in the atmosphere of the Vietnam War, are not likely to understand the satisfaction that psychologists felt by serving the nation in World War I or World War II. Those involved in World War I fought the tyranny of the German Kaiser and "made the world safe for democracy"; those serving in World War II fought the excesses of Hitler. Loyalty to this war effort was enhanced by the shock of the surprise attack by Japan on Pearl Harbor.

In the period from 1946 to 1967, World War II was over, psychologists were reunited under their new constitution, and the few references to the war were made by the majors and colonels among those elected to the APA presidency.

All of the presidents in this period were university connected at the time of their addresses. Most had returned from war service and were setting their sights on their wishes for and expectations of psychology.

D. G. Marquis reflected the new outlook by noting that in an era of large-scale cooperative research (the kinds of research learned during the war), psychologists must continue to plan research in previously unfamiliar areas.

The presidents in this period showed a sharp decline of interest in the excitements of the preceding period. The controversial aspects of large systems were by this time of little interest to the presidents; learning theory was seldom the primary interest even for those psychologists who had once been strongly identified with it. The issues between clinical and experimental psychology still existed but were somewhat tempered. L. J. Cronbach contrasted not clinical and experimental psychology but correlational and experimental methods. The newcomer psycholinguistics emerged, a portent of future research. This new field, represented by both O. H. Mowrer and C. E. Osgood was earlier proposed by Hunter as an important topic. D. O. Hebb urged the study of thought processes and thus anticipated the development of cognitive psychology.

The address of Carl Rogers was selected as a chapter in this section to represent the interest in clinical psychology that emerged during World War II. The address is a reminder that Rogers' theory was the first important American development of a theory and a method of psychotherapy. Clinical psychology was accelerated and received the enthusiastic postwar support of the universities through financing by the Veterans Administration and the National Institute of Mental Health. Other addresses that focused on clinical psychology were given by P. E. Meehl and N. Hobbs. Some addresses, though not directly clinical, were of clinical interest, especially G. Lindzey's; his address was the only presidential address to use the term "psychoanalytic" in its title, although several other addresses showed a friendliness to psychoanalysis.

H. E. Garrett's address was the first of several in this period that dealt with tests and their utility; others who spoke on this topic were J. P. Guilford, J. McV. Hunt, L. F. Shaffer, E. L. Kelly, and Q. McNemar. L. J. Cronbach generalized the problem created by the division of correlational methods and experimental methods.

Personality and social psychology were treated from very different vantage points by C. R. Rogers, E. R. Hilgard, R. R. Sears, E. L. Kelly, and T. M. Newcomb, with a comparative picture from H. F. Harlow. Developmental psychology was also discussed by Harlow as well as by R. R. Sears, J. S. Bruner, and G. Lindzey.

D. O. Hebb and N. E. Miller represented physiological psychology. Miller's analytic studies of drive and rewards, including the results of electrical stimulation of the brain, specified experimentation that investigated the neurophysiological basis of behavior.

Henry Edward Garrett (1894–1973)

PhD, Columbia University, 1922 (under R. S. Woodworth and A. T. Poffenberger).

A Developmental Theory of Intelligence. *American Psychologist*, 1946, *1*, 372–378.

Presented at the Fifty-Fourth Annual Meeting of the American Psychological Association, New York, New York, 1946.

Garrett spent his academic career (1922-1956) at Columbia University where he was head of the department of psychology from 1941 until retirement; he then moved to the University of Virginia (1956-1964). His textbook *Statistics in Psychology and Education* (1926; final revision, 1966) and his book *Great Experiments in Psychology* (1930) were both well known. His last book published was *The Art of Good Teaching* (1965).

Garrett used the term intelligence to include at least the abilities demanded in the solution of problems that require the comprehension and use of symbols. In brief, this component is *symbol* or *abstract* intelligence. Garrett proposed that intelligence, so defined, changes in its organization with increasing maturity; for example, homogeneity between the verbal factor and memory is reduced as age increases. Garrett also offered implications for theory and practice.

Carl Ransom Rogers (1902–   )

PhD, Teachers College, Columbia University, 1931 (under G. Watson; influenced by L. S. Hollingworth and H. S. Elliott of Union Theological Seminary).

Some Observations on the Organization of Personality. *American Psychologist*, 1947, *2*, 358–368.

Presented at the Fifty-Fifth Annual Meeting of the American Psychological Association, Detroit, Michigan, 1947. (*See Chapter 21.*)

Carl Rogers was the first APA president born in the twentieth century. He began his professional career in Rochester, New York (1931-1950), where he worked with the Society for the Prevention of Cruelty to Children and with the Rochester Guidance Center. His book *Clinical Treatment of the Problem Child* (1939) antedated the introduction of the nondirective therapy for which he became known. His academic career began at Ohio State University (1940-1945), where he introduced nondirective therapy in his book *Counseling and Psychotherapy* (1942). He moved to the University of Chicago (1945-1957) where he was affiliated at the time of his APA presidency. His nondirective therapy was renamed in his book *Client-Centered Therapy* (1951). His later career included periods at the University of Wisconsin (1958–1963) and at the Western Behavioral Sciences Institute at La Jolla. He has continued in research writing and lecturing; his other books include *Psychotherapy and Change* (1954, with others) and, *On Becoming a Person* (1961).

In his address, Rogers noted that the kinds of observations made in nondirective (or client-centered) therapy bear on personality organization. The counselor attitude of warmth and understanding maximizes the freedom of expression of the individual. Rogers believed that the findings should modify psychology in many areas other than those identified formally as clinical and personality psychology.

Donald George Marquis (1908–1973)

PhD, Yale University, 1932 (under H. S. Burr; influenced by L. M. Terman).

Research Planning at the Frontiers of Science. *American Psychologist*, 1948, *3*, 430–438.

Presented at the Fifty-Sixth Annual Meeting of the American Psychological Association, Boston, Massachusetts, 1948.

Marquis began his graduate study at Stanford University before receiving his degree at Yale. After a year's fellowship in neurophysiology, he became an instructor in psychology at Yale University, and eventually departmental chairman (1933–1945). He then moved to the University of Michigan as departmental chairman (1945–1957), where he was affiliated at the time of his APA presidential address. After a year at the Social Science Research Council, he became professor of management at the Massachusetts Institute of Technology (1959–1973). His early research on learning and neuropsychology led to the book *Conditioning and Learning* (1940, with E. R. Hilgard). He also co-authored the fifth edition of Woodworth's *Psychology* (1947) and later wrote *Successful Industrial Innovations* (1969, with S. Meyers) and *Factors in the Transfer of Technology* (1969, with W. H. Gruber).

In his address, Marquis stated that research is always at the frontier of knowledge, but science itself has frontiers. In psychology these frontiers are in the fields of interpersonal relations and social psychology, with extensions into anthropology, sociology, economics, and political science. Marquis noted that, with philanthropic foundations and governmental agencies providing large sums of money for research, the need is evident for policy planning of research—planning of distribution of effort among programs, areas, or fields. He also pointed out that psychology and other sciences have had little experience with this type of planning.

Ernest Ropiequet Hilgard (1904–   )

PhD, Yale University, 1930 (under R. Dodge; influenced by R. P. Angier and E. S. Robinson).

Human Motives and the Concept of the Self. *American Psychologist*, 1949, *4*, 374–382.

Presented at the Fifty-Seventh Annual Meeting of the American Psychological Association, Denver, Colorado, 1949.

E. Hilgard undertook his academic career at Yale University (1929–1933), then moved to Stanford University where he remained until retirement (1933–1969). With the help of funding support, he has remained active in research in motivation and hypnosis.

His books include *Conditioning and Learning* (1940, with D. G. Marquis), *Theories of Learning* (1948; fourth edition, with Gordon H. Bower, 1975), *Introduction to Psychology* (1953; sixth edition, with Richard C. Atkinson and Rita L. Atkinson, 1975), *Hypnotic Susceptibility* (1965), *Hypnosis in the Relief of Pain* (1975, with his wife, Josephine R. Hilgard), and *Divided Consciousness* (1977).

Hilgard's presidential address was uncharacteristic at the time, but anticipated his later work. He suggested that human motives of any consequence usually involve some kind of self-reference, as in the motivated defenses recognized by psychoanalysts. Defenses can be interpreted as motivated by the desire to reduce anxiety or to enhance self-esteem. Although the self-concept is puzzling, Hilgard believed that it is possible to approach it according to self-perception, on the one hand, or according to the inferred self, as interpreted by others.

Joy Paul Guilford (1897–   )

PhD, Cornell University, 1927 (under K. M. Dallenbach).

Creativity. *American Psychologist*, 1950, *5*, 444–454.

Presented at the Fifty-Eighth Annual Meeting of the American Psychological Association, State College, Pennsylvania, 1950.

After teaching at the University of Illinois and the University of Kansas, Guilford remained at the University of Nebraska (1928–1940) until he moved to the University of Southern California until his retirement (1940–1967). He has been active as an emeritus professor since 1967. His books include *Psychometric Methods* (1936; revised, 1954), *General Psychology* (1939; revised, 1952), *Personality* (1959), *The Nature of Intelligence* (1967), and *The Analysis of Intelligence* (1971, with R. Hoepfner).

Guilford noted the neglect of the study of creativity and recognized its social importance. In his address he reported on a research project that he had initiated in 1949. He selected the factor-analytic method as the most promising and proposed some tentative hypotheses that might direct the development of creativity tests. He believed that pertinent individual differences must exist in *sensitivity to problems*, in *degree of novelty* of which the person is capable, in *flexibility* of mind, in *synthesizing* and *analyzing* ability, and in *evaluation skill*, thus permitting a person to select the ideas that are to survive. (The historically minded will note that the search process discussed here resulted a few years later in the important distinction between *convergent* and *divergent* thought processes, the latter referring to creative thinking. The tests that survived the factor-analytic process reflect some of the early hypotheses, with modification: *fluency, flexibility, originality,* and *elaboration.*)

Robert Richardson Sears (1908–   )

PhD, Yale University, 1932 (under H. S. Burr and R. P. Angier; influenced by C. L. Hull).

A Theoretical Framework for Personality and Social Behavior. *American Psychologist,* 1951, 6, 476–483.

Presented at the Fifty-Ninth Annual Meeting of the American Psychological Association, Chicago, Illinois, 1951.

After teaching at the University of Illinois (1932–1936), Sears returned to teach at Yale University (1936–1942) and then directed the Iowa Child Welfare Research Station at the University of Iowa (1942–1949). He was also director of the Laboratory of Human Development at Harvard University (1949–1953), where he was affiliated at the time of his APA presidential address. He then accepted an appointment at Stanford University as head of the department of psychology (1953–1961), and later as dean of humanities and sciences (1961–1970). He retired in 1974 but remains active as an emeritus professor. His books include *Frustration and Aggression* (1939, with J. Dollard, O. H. Mowrer, Neal E. Miller, and others), *Objective Studies of Psychoanalytic Concepts* (1943), *Patterns of Child Rearing* (1957, with Eleanor Maccoby and Harry Levin), and *Identification and Child Rearing* (1965, with Lucy Rau and Richard Alpert); he also wrote numerous research articles and monographs.

To combine individual and social behavior into a single theoretical system, Sears distinguished between *monadic* (single-person) and *dyadic* (two-person) units. He presented diagrams to show the instigation-action system when a single person is engaged in goal-directed behavior and when two persons, in a dyadic relationship, interact in their motivated behavior. The *expectancy* of the environmental event is responsible for maintaining stability of the dyadic unit. In this framework, personality is a description of those properties of a person that specify his or her potentialities for action. Sears provided a concrete example of the conceptualization by an experiment relating the aggressive acts of children in interpersonal relations in school and in fantasy (doll play) to the punitiveness of the mother.

Joseph McVickers Hunt (1906–   )

PhD, Cornell University, 1933 (under M. Bentley; influenced by J. P. Guilford).

Psychological Services in the Tactics of Psychological Science. *American Psychologist*, 1952, 7, 608–627.

Presented at the Sixtieth Annual Meeting of the American Psychological Association, Washington, D.C., 1952.

Hunt was awarded fellowships at the New York Psychiatric Institute, Worcester State Hospital and at St. Elizabeth's Hospital (1933–1936), taught at Brown University (1936–1946), and served as research director of the Institute of Welfare Research in New York (1946–1951). He returned to academic life at the University of Illinois, Urbana, until his retirement (1951–1974). He was affiliated with the University of Illinois at the time of his APA presidential address. He became well known initially as editor of the two-volume book *Personality and the Behavior Disorders* (1944). His book *Intelligence and Experience* (1961) was influential in setting Piaget's views of cognitive development against more conventional views derived from intelligence test measurements. He also authored several monographs on social casework and its outcomes.

Hunt noted in his address four obstacles that prevent relying solely on field observations to study human relations and social problems: first, interference from emotions connected with personal behavior; second, the gap separating those who have to make the actual decisions for action and those who do the conceptualizing; third, the long time span between the initiation of important actions and their ultimate consequences; and, fourth, the inherent complexity of the influences upon action. For these reasons he believed that the simplification that the laboratory provides can be helpful and that an interdependence exists between psychological services and psychological science.

Laurance Frederic Shaffer (1903–1976)

PhD, Teachers College, Columbia University, 1930 (under H. Rugg; A. I. Gates and P. M. Symonds were on dissertation committee).

Of Whose Reality I Cannot Doubt. *American Psychologist*, 1953, *8*, 608–622.

Presented at the Sixty-First Annual Meeting of the American Psychological Association, Cleveland, Ohio, 1953.

Shaffer worked with the Carnegie Institute of Technology (1928–1941) until he left for service in World War II. At Teachers College, Columbia University, he was professor of psychology and education (1945–1963) and was associate dean (1963–1968), until he became emeritus. His dissertation, *Children's Interpretations of Cartoons*, has recently been reprinted, and his book *Psychology of Adjustment* (1936; revised with E. J. Shoben, 1956), was widely adopted as a textbook.

The title of Shaffer's address was from a quotation of William James: "Whatever things have intimate and continuous connection with my life are things of whose reality I cannot doubt." Shaffer believed that a pervasive issue exists between two attitudinal frames of references, the *intuitive* observations of those who value immediate experience and the *objective* attitude of those who prefer mediated experiences (reflected in tables and graphs and correlation coefficients). He reported a questionnaire study of the members of Division 12, then the Division of Clinical and Abnormal Psychology, that elicited responses related to biographical data. The responses fell into the two clusters that he predicted. Intuitivists had direct experience in face-to-face contacts with people; objectivists had direct experience with experimental designs and statistical analysis. From either viewpoint there is no mediated experience; each of us believes in the immediate.

Orval Hobart Mowrer (1907–   )

PhD, Johns Hopkins University, 1932 (under K. Dunlap).

The Psychologist Looks at Language. *American Psychologist*, 1954, *9*, 660–694.

Presented at the Sixty-Second Annual Meeting of the American Psychological Association, New York, New York, 1954.

Mowrer received postdoctoral fellowships at Northwestern University and Princeton University, then began research and teaching at Yale University (1934–1940). He authored *Frustration and Aggression* (1939, with

Dollard and others) and wrote numerous books, including *Learning Theory and Personality Dynamics* (1950), *Psychotherapy: Theory and Research* (1953), *Learning Theory and the Symbolic Processes* (1960), and *The New Group Therapy* (1964).

Mowrer recognized the upsurge of interest in language in the previous two decades and attempted to formulate interesting questions that were still incompletely answered. The published version of his address is an extension of the address as orally presented. Its 90 references are a useful source of information on the "state of the art" in 1954. Mowrer relied on a conditioning model in which mediation was involved and in which the sentence itself was considered to be a conditioning device. (Mowrer's address was taken as a point of departure a decade later by C. E. Osgood; see Seventy-First Annual Meeting, 1963. Mowrer's address was delivered before and Osgood's address was delivered after Noam Chomsky's theory became influential.)

Everett Lowell Kelly (1905–   )

PhD, Stanford University, 1930 (under W. R. Miles; influenced by L. M. Terman and C. C. Miles).

Consistency of the Adult Personality. *American Psychologist*, 1955, *10*, 659–681.

Presented at the Sixty-Third Annual Meeting of the American Psychological Association, San Francisco, California, 1955.

Kelly taught at the University of Hawaii (1930–1932), studied in Germany and Austria (1932–1933), and then taught at the University of Connecticut (1933–1939) and at Purdue University (1939–1942). During World War II he served in the U.S. Naval Reserve. He moved to the University of Michigan (1946) and was a professor and a department chairman until retirement in 1975. His best-known book is *The Prediction of Performance in Clinical Psychology* (1951, with D. W. Fiske).

Although most psychologists do not anticipate that humans change in personality after the first few years of life, Kelly indicated that the possibility of change is implicit on the part of some people engaged in advertising, public relations, and psychotherapy. He described a long-range investigation of changes in personality that take place over a period of approximately 20 years in adult life. A sample of 300 engaged couples were first studied from 1935 to 1938 and again from 1953 to 1954. Of the 521 subjects located among the original 600, 86% completed the retest forms. Although intelligence, values, and vocational interests remain relatively stable, other aspects of personality, such as self-ratings and attitudes, change more. Although changes were found to be neither so large nor so sudden as to threaten the continuity of the self-percept or to impair one's day-to-day efficiency, they were sufficient to give hope for continued psychological growth during the adult years.

Theodore Mead Newcomb (1903–   )

PhD, Teachers College, Columbia University, 1929 (under G. Watson; influenced by P. M. Symonds).

The Prediction of Interpersonal Attraction. *American Psychologist,* 1956, *11,* 575–586.

Presented at the Sixty-Fourth Annual Meeting of the American Psychological Association, Chicago, Illinois, 1956.

After a year at Lehigh University and a short period at Cleveland College (1930–1934), Newcomb moved to Bennington College (1934–1941) and then completed his career at the University of Michigan, first in the field of sociology and then as professor of sociology and psychology, until he retired in 1973. His books include *Experimental Social Psychology* (revised edition; 1937, with G. Murphy and L. Murphy), *Personality and Social Change* (1943), *Social Psychology* (1950), *The Acquaintance Process* (1961), *Persistence and Change* (1967), and *Impact of College on Students* (1969, with Kenneth Feldman).

Newcomb believed that insofar as communication results in the perception of increased similarity of attitude toward important and relevant objects, it will also be followed by an increase in positive attraction between the communicators. He derived this general formulation from a review of previous studies and theoretical considerations and subjected it to experimental testing. A student house was rented and free room for a semester was offered to 17 male transfer students who did not know each other and who had not lived in the same city or ever attended the same schools. The experiment was repeated a second year. Changes in attraction could be predicted based on such independent variables as propinquity (through rooming together), reciprocal attraction between pairs, and within-pair agreement with respect to others. The results led Newcomb to believe that a limited theory about a class of objects (in this case, persons) can profit by taking account of the significant properties of those objects and in particular those properties closely related to the fact of human dependence upon communication. (The full report of Newcomb's study is in his book *The Acquaintance Process* [1961].)

Lee Joseph Cronbach (1916–   )

PhD, University of Chicago, 1940 (under G. T. Buswell; influenced by R. W. Tyler).

The Two Disciplines of Scientific Psychology. *American Psychologist,* 1957, *12,* 671–684.

Presented at the Sixty-Fifth Annual Meeting of the American Psychological Association, New York, New York, 1957. *(See Chapter 22.)*

Cronbach taught at the State College of Washington (1940-1946), the University of Chicago (1946-1948), and the University of Illinois, Urbana (1948-1964), where he was affiliated at the time of his APA presidential address. Since 1964 he has been professor of education at Stanford University. Among his books are *Educational Psychology* (1954; third edition, 1977), *Psychological Tests and Educational Decisions* (1965, with G. C. Gleser), *Essentials of Psychological Testing* (1949; third edition, 1970), *Research for Tomorrow's Schools* (1969, co-edited with Patrick Suppes), *Mental Tests and Cultural Adaptation* (1972, edited with P. J. Drenth), *Aptitudes and Instructional Methods* (1977, with R. E. Snow).

In his address, Cronbach discussed the two historic streams of method, thought, and affiliation that run through the last century of psychological science: *experimental psychology* and *correlational psychology*. In his view, psychology continues to this day to be limited by the dedication of its investigators to one or the other method of inquiry rather than to scientific psychology as a whole. (For a later supplement to his position, see Cronbach's article, "Beyond the Two Disciplines of Scientific Psychology," *American Psychologist*, 1975, *30*, 116-127.)

Harry Frederick Harlow (1905–   )

PhD, Stanford University, 1930 (under C. P. Stone; influenced by L. M. Terman and W. R. Miles).

The Nature of Love. *American Psychologist*, 1958, *13*, 673–685.

Presented at the Sixty-Sixth Annual Meeting of the American Psychological Association, Washington, D.C., 1958. *(See Chapter 23.)*

Harlow spent his academic career at the University of Wisconsin (1930-1974). After much experimentation with rhesus monkeys, he became director of a regional primate center on the campus (1961). He left Wisconsin to join the psychology faculty at the University of Arizona as a research professor (1974). Prolific in research in many areas of neurophysiology, learning, and development, his publications are primarily in journals, monographs, and chapters of edited books. He is the author of *Psychology* (1971, with J. L. McGaugh and R. F. Thompson), and *Learning to Love* (1973).

Harlow discussed the nature of love as manifested in mother-infant relations that were shown in his experiments with rhesus monkeys. These relations included the infant's reaction to an artificial mother-surrogate. He countered the idea that affection or love is derived by learning through the reduction of primary drives—particularly hunger, thirst, and pain. Instead, Harlow believed that love is based on a multiplicity of affectional bonds. He illustrated the important role of contact by convincing (and amusing) illustrations from other species.

Wolfgang Köhler (1887–1967)

(See Chapter 10 for biographical information and abstract, and see Chapter 14 for complete address.)

Donald Olding Hebb (1904–   )

PhD, Harvard University, 1936 (under K. S. Lashley).

The American Revolution. *American Psychologist*, 1960, *15*, 735–745.

Presented at the Sixty-Eighth Annual Meeting of the American Psychological Association, Chicago, Illinois, 1960.

Hebb remained at Harvard for one year after receiving his degree, then accepted a Rockefeller Fellowship at the Montreal Neurophysiological Institute, McGill University (1937–1939) before going to Queen's University, Ontario (1939–1942). After performing research at the Yerkes Laboratories of Primate Biology (1942–1947), he became a professor of psychology at McGill University (1947–1972). He served also as chancellor of the university (1970–1974). He wrote *A Textbook of Psychology* (1958; revised, 1966); and his *Organization of Behavior* (1959), along with other developments within his laboratory, brought him into prominence as a neuropsychological theoretician.

Hebb stated in his address that the revolution in psychology, largely in North America, had proceeded in two stages. The first, in the form of behaviorism and learning, was almost completed and the second phase was about to begin: a behavioristic or learning-theory analysis of the thought process. He dealt with a special aspect of this phase: self-awareness and certain fantasies about the self. He believed that mind and consciousness are intervening variables or constructs and are properly part of a behavioristic psychology. The mental processes of self-perception are the same processes, in large part, that constitute the perception of another person. Hebb also believed that the mediational postulate, which permits a behavioral approach to these matters, is a powerful tool that was ready for use.

Neal Elgar Miller (1909–   )

PhD, Yale University, 1935 (under W. R. Miles; influenced by C. L. Hull).

Analytic Studies of Drive and Reward. *American Psychologist*, 1961, *16*, 739–754.

Presented at the Sixty-Ninth Annual Meeting of the American Psychological Association, New York, New York, 1961. (*See Chapter 24.*)

Miller's postdoctoral fellowship year (1935–1936) was spent at the Psychoanalytic Institute in Vienna. He then returned to Yale University (1936–1966), where he was affiliated at the time of his APA presidential address. Since 1966 he has been at Rockefeller University. He co-authored *Frustration and Aggression* (1939, with Dollard and others) and published two other books with Dollard, *Social Learning and Imitation* (1941) and *Personality and Psychotherapy* (1951). He also collected many of his research papers in a volume entitled *Neal E. Miller, Selected Papers* (1971).

In his address, Miller reviewed some of his earlier behavioral studies and some later ones that combined behavioral and physiological techniques. All of the studies concentrated on drive and reward, including the effects of electrical stimulation of the "feeding area" of the brain. In the new view that he represented, the brain is an active organ that exerts considerable control over its sensory input.

Paul Everett Meehl (1920–   )

PhD, University of Minnesota, 1945 (under S. R. Hathaway; influenced by B. F. Skinner and D. G. Paterson).

Schizotaxia, Schizotypy, Schizophrenia. *American Psychologist*, 1962, *17*, 827–838.

Presented at the Seventieth Annual Meeting of the American Psychological Association, St. Louis, Missouri, 1962.

Meehl became a member of the faculty at the University of Minnesota in 1944, became a professor in 1955, and was chairman of the department (1951–1957). His book *Clinical vs. Statistical Prediction* (1954) received wide attention. In the same year he authored, with others, *Modern Learning Theory*. His clinical experience and research on personality measurement resulted in his *Atlas for Clinical Use of the MMPI* (1951, with S. A. Hathaway) and *Psychodiagnosis* (1973).

In his address, Meehl used the term *schizotaxia* to refer to the neural integrative defect that he believed was predisposing to schizophrenia. Whether pathological symptoms appear depends on the history of social learning, which leads in the less disturbed *schizotype* to some signs of *cognitive slippage* (a better term than *thought disorder*), interpersonal aversiveness, anhedonia, and ambivalence. A subset of the schizotypes decompensate into clinical *schizophrenia*. Hence Meehl believed that schizotaxia is a necessary condition for schizophrenia but is not itself sufficient. He maintained that schizophrenia is fundamentally a neurological disease of genetic origin.

Charles Egerton Osgood (1916–   )

PhD, Yale University, 1945 (under D. G. Marquis; influenced by I. L. Child).

On Understanding and Creating Sentences. *American Psychologist*, 1963, *18*, 735–751.

Presented at the Seventy-First Annual Meeting of the American Psychological Association, Philadelphia, Pennsylvania, 1963.

After one year of service connected with World War II, Osgood taught at the University of Connecticut (1946–1949) and then moved to the University of Illinois, Urbana, where he has been a professor of psychology with various assignments in the department, in the Institute of Communication Research, and in the Center for Advanced Study. He wrote *Method and Theory in Experimental Psychology* (1953) and developed the semantic differential that led to his books *The Measurement of Meaning* (1957, with G. J. Suci and P. H. Tannenbaum), and *Semantic Differential Technique* (1969, edited with J. G. Snider). He has long been interested in psycholinguistics and in psychological aspects of international relations.

Osgood indicated in his address the advances that had been made in psycholinguistics in the decade since Mowrer's address, and he mentioned the influence of Noam Chomsky's transformational grammar. Osgood proposed a learning-theory model that he described as a three-stage mediation model; in opposing Chomsky, he wished to avoid a "special" theory of psycholinguistics.

Quinn McNemar (1900–   )

PhD, Stanford University, 1932 (under L. M. Terman).

Lost: Our Intelligence? Why? *American Psychologist*, 1964, *19*, 871–882.

Presented at the Seventy-Second Annual Meeting of the American Psychological Association, Los Angeles, California, 1964.

McNemar's academic life, except for some brief periods, was spent at Stanford University, where he began an instructorship (1931) and retired as an emeritus professor of psychology (1965). He spent one year (1937–1938) at Fordham University and served on the staff of the Social Science Research Council (1941–1943). After retiring from Stanford, he accepted an invitation as a professor at the University of Texas at Austin (1965–1971). He collaborated in the revision of the Stanford-Binet scale and wrote the definitive report on its sampling and scaling procedures, *The Revision of the Stanford-Binet Scale* (1942). He became well known for his book *Psychological Statistics* (1949; fourth edition, 1969).

McNemar noted in his address that L. L. Thurstone's centroid factor method appeared to disprove Spearman's concept of a general factor *g*, and replaced it with seven primary abilities. The test scores for the primary abilities all correlated positively, however, so that something like a general factor was needed. In the end, McNemar believed that the criterion of social usefulness must serve as a basis for deciding whether it is wise to discard general intelligence. When intelligence tests are studied according to social usefulness, differential or multiple-aptitude batteries, based on factor analysis, do not live up to their promises. McNemar noted that in most instances a test of general intelligence is as useful (or more useful) a predictor of special performances as specific subscores, and is more economical to administer.

McNemar criticized tests that are designed to measure creativity as a component of intelligent behavior not reflected in general intelligence scores. His criticism was based on the faulty statistical logic used in experiments conducted with the help of such tests. The scatter diagram between IQ and creativity is probably triangular in shape, with a wider range of creativity at high IQ levels. Hence, McNemar stated, it is not surprising if, with selected high IQs, there will be low correlations with creativity properly assessed. McNemar recognized that the nature of general intelligence is not well understood, but he believed that it still has a rightful place in the practical affairs of mankind.

Jerome Seymour Bruner (1915–   )

PhD, Harvard University, 1941 (under G. W. Allport).

The Growth of the Mind. *American Psychologist*, 1965, *20*, 1007–1017.

Presented at the Seventy-Third Annual Meeting of the American Psychological Association, Chicago, Illinois, 1965. *(See Chapter 25.)*

After service in World War II Bruner returned to Harvard University (1945) and was director of the center for cognitive studies (1961–1971). He then accepted an appointment to Oxford University, England, where he is still active. His many books include *Mandate from the People* (1941), *A Study of Thinking* (1956, with J. J. Goodnow and G. A. Austin), *The Process of Education* (1960), and *Studies in Cognitive Growth* (1966, with R. R. Olver and P. M. Greenfield).

Bruner dealt in his address with the problem of transmission of culture to the young—of equipping the young with amplifiers of the sensory and action systems that they possess as a result of biological development. He described a course of study for 10-year-olds that was being constructed, tested, and evaluated. The course served as an opportunity to portray the inherent difficulties of assisting the growth of mind in children in the special setting of the school.

Nicholas Hobbs (1915–   )

PhD, Ohio State University, 1946 (under S. L. Pressey; influenced by C. R. Rogers).

Helping Disturbed Children: Psychological and Ecological Strategies. *American Psychologist*, 1966, *21*, 1105–1115.

Presented at the Seventy-Fourth Annual Meeting of the American Psychological Association, New York, New York, 1966.

Hobbs taught at Teachers College, Columbia University (1946–1950) and at Louisiana State University (1950–1951), until he became professor and chairman of the division of human development at George Peabody College for Teachers (1951–1967), where he was affiliated at the time of his APA presidential address. In 1967 he became the provost of Vanderbilt University.

He edited *Psychological Research in Flexible Gunnery Training* for the Aviation Psychology Program (1947). He wrote numerous research papers and essays, and his book *The Future of Children* (1975) summarizes his long experience with the exceptional child.

In his address, Hobbs described a planful effort at social invention to meet an acute national problem, the problem of emotional disturbance in children. Residential schools were established for children of normal or superior intelligence who were in serious trouble in school. The children were permitted to go home on weekends in order to keep family relations intact. Cure was abandoned as a goal; the problem was defined as trying to make a small social system work in a reasonably satisfactory manner. The success was sufficient to lead to the hope that similar schools would be established elsewhere.

Gardner Lindzey (1920–   )

PhD, Harvard University, 1949 (under G. W. Allport).

Some Remarks Concerning Incest, the Incest Taboo, and Psychoanalytic Theory. *American Psychologist*, 1967, *22*, 1051–1059.

Presented at the Seventy-Fifth Annual Meeting of the American Psychological Association, Washington, D.C., 1967.

Lindzey's education was interrupted for one year as a result of World War II (1944–1945) and, after some teaching and research at Pennsylvania State University and Western Reserve University, he turned to graduate study at Harvard University. After completing his degree, he remained at Harvard and eventually was placed in charge of the Psychological Clinic (1953–1956). He then took a position as professor at Syracuse University, accepted a professorship at the University of Minnesota (1957–1964), and then moved to the University of Texas at Austin, where he was affiliated at the time of his APA presidential address. At Texas, Lindzey served as professor and chairman of the psychology department and vice-president for academic affairs (1968–1975) and dean of graduate studies. He interrupted his stay at Texas for one year to serve as chairman of the department of psychology and social relations at Harvard University (1972–1973), and in 1975 left Texas to become Director of the Center for Advanced Study in the Behavioral Sciences, Stanford, California.

Among his published books are *Projective Techniques and Cross-Cultural Research* (which he edited, 1961), *Handbook of Social Psychology* (1954; second edition, with Elliot Aronson, 1968), *Theories of Personality* (1957, with Calvin S. Hall; latest revision, 1978), *Contributions to Behavior-Genetic Analysis* (1970, edited with D. D. Thiessen), *Race Differences in Intelligence* (1975, with J. C. Loehlin and J. N. Spuhler), and *Psychology* (1975, with others; revised, 1978).

Lindzey's address is the only presidential address to mention psychoanalysis in its title, although other presidents were friendly to, or were influenced by, psychoanalysis. The address reflects other interests, including behavior genetics and sociobiology. Prohibitions against nuclear incest (sexual relations between members of the nuclear family other than mother and father) have long been observed to be one of the few regularities in complex human behavior that transcend time and culture. Lindzey advanced the formulation that the biological consequence of inbreeding is a decrease in fitness. The evidence from modern studies of behavior genetics supports the position, especially in the observance of pathologies among the offspring of nuclear incest matings.

Despite the powerful incest taboo, strong incestuous impulses continue to exist, with supporting evidence from various sources, including the studies directed by A. C. Kinsey. With the taboo and the impulses both operative, their conflict represents an important developmental crisis. Lindzey credited Freud with identifying this transcultural crisis that was ignored or minimized by other theorists.

Reprinted with permission
from *American Psychologist*,
1947, 2, 358–368.

Chapter 21

Some Observations on the Organization of Personality

Carl R. Rogers

University of Chicago

In various fields of science rapid strides have been made when direct observation of significant processes has become possible. In medicine, when circumstances have permitted the physician to peer directly into the stomach of his patient, understanding of digestive processes has increased and the influence of emotional tension upon all aspects of that process has been more accurately observed and understood. In our work with nondirective therapy we often feel that we are having a psychological opportunity comparable to this medical experience—an opportunity to observe di-

---

Address of the retiring President of the American Psychological Association delivered at the September 1947 Annual Meeting.

rectly a number of the effective processes of personality. Quite aside from any question regarding nondirective therapy as therapy, here is a precious vein of observational material of unusual value for the study of personality.

Characteristics of the Observational Material

There are several ways in which the raw clinical data to which we have had access is unique in its value for understanding personality. The fact that these verbal expressions of inner dynamics are preserved by electrical recording makes possible a detailed analysis of a sort not heretofore possible. Recording has given us a microscope by which we may examine at leisure, and in minute detail, almost every aspect of what was, in its occurrence, a fleeting moment impossible of accurate observation.

Another scientifically fortunate characteristic of this material is the fact that the verbal productions of the client are biased to a minimal degree by the therapist. Material from client-centered interviews probably comes closer to being a "pure" expression of attitudes than has yet been achieved through other means. One can read through a complete recorded case or listen to it, without finding more than a half-dozen instances in which the therapist's views on any point are evident. One would find it impossible to form an estimate as to the therapist's views about personality dynamics. One could not determine his diagnostic views, his standards of behavior, his social class. The one value or standard held by the therapist which would exhibit itself in his tone of voice, responses, and activity, is a deep respect for the personality and attitudes of the client as a separate person. It is difficult to see how this would bias the content of the interview, except to permit deeper expression than the client would ordinarily allow himself. This almost complete lack of any distorting attitude is felt, and sometimes expressed by the client. One woman says:

It's almost impersonal. I like you—of course I don't know why I should like you or why I shouldn't like you. It's a peculiar thing. I've never had that relationship with anybody before and I've often thought about it. . . . .A lot of times I walk out with a feeling of elation that you think highly of me, and of course at the same time I have the feeling that "Gee, he must think I'm an awful jerk" or something like that. But it doesn't really—those feelings aren't so deep that I can form an opinion one way or the other about you.

Here it would seem that even though she would like to discover some type of evaluational attitude, she is unable to do so. Published studies and research as yet unpublished bear out this point that counselor responses which are in any way evaluational or distorting as to content are at a minimum, thus enhancing the worth of such interviews for personality study.

The counselor attitude of warmth and understanding, well described by Snyder (9) and Rogers (8), also helps to maximize the freedom of expression by the individual. The client experiences sufficient interest in him as a person, and sufficient acceptance, to enable him to talk openly, not only about surface attitudes, but increasingly about intimate attitudes and feelings hidden even from himself. Hence in these recorded interviews we have material of very considerable depth so far as personality dynamics is concerned, along with a freedom from distortion.

Finally the very nature of the interviews and the techniques by which they are handled give us a rare opportunity to see to some extent through the eyes of another person—to perceive the world as it appears to him, to achieve at least partially, the internal frame of reference of another person. We see his behavior through his eyes, and also the psychological meaning which it had for him. We see also changes in personality and behavior, and the meanings which those changes have for the individual. We are admitted freely into the backstage of the person's living where we can observe from within some of the dramas of internal change, which are often far more compelling and moving than the drama which is presented on the stage viewed by the public. Only a novelist or a poet could do justice to the deep struggles which we are permitted to observe from within the client's own world of reality.

This rare opportunity to observe so directly and so clearly the inner dynamics of personality is a learning experience of the deepest sort for the clinician. Most of clinical psychology and psychiatry involves judgments *about* the individual, judgments which must, of necessity, be based on some framework brought to the situation by the clinician. To try continually to see and think *with* the individual, as in client-centered therapy, is a mindstretching experience in which learning goes on apace because the clinician brings to the interview no pre-determined yardstick by which to judge the material.

I wish in this paper to try to bring you some of the clinical observations which we have made as we have repeatedly peered through these psychological windows into personality, and to raise with you some of the questions about the organization of personality which these observations have forced upon us. I shall not attempt to present these observations in logical order, but rather in the order in which they impressed themselves upon our notice. What I shall offer is not a series of research findings, but only the first step in that process of gradual approximation which we call science, a description of some observed phenomena which appear to be significant, and some highly tentative explanations of these phenomena.

The Relation of the Organized Perceptual Field to Behavior

One simple observation, which is repeated over and over again in each successful therapeutic case, seems to have rather deep theoretical implications. It is that as changes occur in the perception of self and in the perception of reality, changes occur in behavior. In therapy, these perceptual changes are more often concerned with the self than with the external world. Hence we find in therapy that as the perception of self alters, behavior alters. Perhaps an illustration will indicate the type of observation upon which this statement is based.

A young woman, a graduate student whom we shall call Miss Vib, came in for nine interviews. If we compare the first interview with the last, striking changes are evident. Perhaps some features of this change may be conveyed by taking from the first and last interviews all the major statements regarding self, and all the major statements regarding current behavior. In the first interview, for example, her perception of herself may be crudely indicated by taking all her own statements about herself, grouping those which seem similar, but otherwise doing a minimum of editing, and retaining so far as possible, her own words. We then come out with this as the conscious perception of self which was hers at the outset of counseling.

I feel disorganized, muddled; I've lost all direction; my personal life has disintegrated.

I sorta experience things from the forefront of my consciousness, but nothing sinks in very deep; things don't seem real to me; I feel nothing matters; I don't have any emotional response to situations; I'm worried about myself.

I haven't been acting like myself; it doesn't seem like me; I'm a different person altogether from what I used to be in the past.

I don't understand myself; I haven't known what was happening to me.

I have withdrawn from everything, and feel all right only when I'm all alone and no one can expect me to do things.

I don't care about my personal appearance.

I don't know *anything* anymore.

I feel guilty about the things I have left undone.

I don't think I could ever assume responsibility for anything.

If we attempt to evaluate this picture of self from an external frame of reference various diagnostic labels may come to mind. Trying to perceive it solely from the client's frame of reference we observe that to the young woman herself she appears disorganized, and not herself. She is perplexed and almost unacquainted with what is going on in herself. She feels unable and unwilling to function in any responsible or social way. This is at least a sampling of the way she experiences or perceives her self.

Her behavior is entirely consistent with this picture of self. If we abstract all her statements describing her behavior, in the same fashion as we abstracted her statements about self, the following pattern emerges—a pattern which in this case was corroborated by outside observation.

I couldn't get up nerve to come in before; I haven't availed myself of help. Everything I should do or want to do, I don't do.

I haven't kept in touch with friends; I avoid making the effort to go with them; I stopped writing letters home; I don't answer letters or telephone calls; I avoid contacts that would be professionally helpful; I didn't go home though I said I would.

I failed to hand in my work in a course though I had it all done: I didn't even buy clothing that I needed; I haven't even kept my nails manicured.

I didn't listen to material we were studying; I waste hours reading the funny papers; I can spend the whole afternoon doing absolutely nothing.

The picture of behavior is very much in keeping with the picture of self, and is summed up in the statement that "Everything I should do or want to do, I don't do." The behavior goes on, in ways that seem to the individual beyond understanding and beyond control.

If we contrast this picture of self and behavior with the picture as it exists in the ninth interview, thirty-eight days later, we find both the perception of self and the ways of behaving deeply altered. Her statements about self are as follows:

I'm feeling much better; I'm taking more interest in myself.

I do have some individuality, some interests.

I seem to be getting a newer understanding of myself. I can look at myself a little better.

I realize I'm just one person, with so much ability, but I'm not worried about it; I can accept the fact that I'm not always right.

I feel more motivation, have more of a desire to go ahead.

I still occasionally regret the past, though I feel less unhappy about it; I still have a long ways to go; I don't know whether I can keep the picture of myself I'm beginning to evolve.

I can go on learning—in school or out.

I do feel more like a normal person now; I feel more I can handle my life myself; I think I'm at the point where I can go along on my own.

Outstanding in this perception of herself are three things—that she knows herself, that she can view with comfort her assets and liabilities, and finally that she has drive and control of that drive.

In this ninth interview the behavioral picture is again consistent with the perception of self. It may be abstracted in these terms.

I've been making plans about school and about a job; I've been working hard on a term paper; I've been going to the library to trace down a topic of special interest and finding it exciting.

I've cleaned out my closets; washed my clothes.

I finally wrote my parents; I'm going home for the holidays.

I'm getting out and mixing with people: I am reacting sensibly to a fellow who is interested in me—seeing both his good and bad points.

I will work toward my degree; I'll start looking for a job this week.

Her behavior, in contrast to the first interview, is now organized, forward-moving, effective, realistic and planful. It is in accord with the realistic and organized view she has achieved of her self.

It is this type of observation, in case after case, that leads us to say with some assurance that as perceptions of self and reality change, behavior changes. Likewise, in cases we might term failures, there appears to be no appreciable change in perceptual organization or in behavior.

What type of explanation might account for these concomitant changes in the perceptual field and the behavioral pattern? Let us examine some of the logical possibilities.

In the first place, it is possible that factors unrelated to therapy may have brought about the altered perception and behavior. There may have been physiological processes occurring which produced the change. There may have been alterations in the family relationships, or in the social forces, or in the educational picture or in some other area of cultural influence, which might account for the rather drastic shift in the concept of self and in the behavior.

There are difficulties in this type of explanation. Not only were there no known gross changes in the physical or cultural situation as far as Miss Vib was concerned, but the explanation gradually becomes inadequate when one tries to apply it to the many cases in which such change occurs. To postulate that some external factor brings the change and that only by chance does this period of change coincide with the period of therapy, becomes an untenable hypothesis.

Let us then look at another explanation, namely that the therapist exerted, during the nine hours of contact, a peculiarly potent cultural influence which brought about the change. Here again we are faced with several problems. It seems that nine hours scattered over five and one-half weeks is a very minute portion of time in which to bring about alteration of patterns which have been building for thirty years. We would have to postulate an influence so potent as to be classed as traumatic. This theory is particularly difficult to maintain when we find, on examining the recorded interviews, that not once in the nine hours did the therapist express any evaluation, positive or negative, of the client's initial or final perception of self, or her initial or final mode of behavior. There was not only no evaluation, but no standards expressed by which evaluation might be inferred.

There was, on the part of the therapist, evidence of warm interest in the individual, and thoroughgoing acceptance of the self and of the behavior as they existed initially, in the intermediate stages, and at the conclusion of therapy. It appears reasonable to say that the therapist established certain definite conditions of interpersonal relations, but since the very essence of this relationship is respect for the person as he is at that moment, the therapist can hardly be regarded as a cultural force making for change.

We find ourselves forced to a third type of explanation, a type of explanation which is not new to psychology, but which has had only partial acceptance. Briefly it may be put that the observed phenomena of change seem most adequately explained by the hypothesis that *given certain psychological conditions, the individual has the capacity to reorganize his field of perception, including the way he perceives himself, and that a concomitant or a resultant of this perceptual reorganization is an appropriate alteration of behavior.* This puts into formal and objective terminology a clinical hypothesis which experience forces upon the therapist using a client-centered approach. One is compelled through clinical observation to develop a high degree of respect for the ego-integrative forces residing within each individual. One comes to recognize that under proper conditions the self is a basic factor in the formation of personality and in the determination of behavior. Clinical experience would strongly suggest that the self is, to some extent, an architect of self, and the above hypothesis simply puts this observation into psychological terms.

In support of this hypothesis it is noted in some cases that one of the concomitants of success in therapy is the realization on the part of the client that the self has the capacity for reorganization. Thus a student says:

You know I spoke of the fact that a person's background retards one. Like the fact that my family life wasn't good for me, and my mother certainly didn't give me any of the kind of bringing up that I should have had. Well, I've been thinking that over. It's true up to a point. But when you get so that you can see the situation, then it's really up to you.

Following this statement of the relation of the self to experience many changes occurred in this young man's behavior. In this, as in other cases, it appears that when the person comes to see himself as the perceiving, organizing agent, then reorganization of perception and consequent change in patterns of reaction take place.

On the other side of the picture we have frequently observed that when the individual has been authoritatively told that he is governed by certain factors or conditions beyond his control, it makes therapy more difficult, and it is only when the individual discovers for himself that he can organize his perceptions that change is possible. In veterans who have been given their own psychiatric diagnosis, the effect is often that of making the individual feel that he is under an unalterable doom, that he is unable to control the organization of his life. When however the self sees itself as capable of reorganizing its own perceptual field, a marked change in basic confidence occurs. Miss Nam, a student, illustrates this phenomenon when she says, after having made progress in therapy:

I think I do feel better about the future, too, because it's as if I won't be acting in darkness. It's sort of, well, knowing somewhat why I act the way I do . . . and at least it isn't the feeling that you're simply out of your own control and the fates are driving you to act that way. If you realize it, I think you can do something more about it.

A veteran at the conclusion of counseling puts it more briefly and more positively: "My attitude toward myself is changed now to where I feel I *can* do something with my self and life." He has come to view himself as the instrument by which some reorganization can take place.

There is another clinical observation which may be cited in support of the general hypothesis that there is a close relationship between behavior and the way in which reality is viewed by the individual. It has been noted in many cases that behavior changes come about for the most part imperceptibly and almost automatically, once the perceptual reorganization has taken place. A young wife who has been reacting violently to her maid, and has been quite disorganized in her behavior as a result of this antipathy, says:

After I . . . discovered it was nothing more than that she resembled my mother, she didn't bother me any more. Isn't that interesting? She's still the same.

Here is a clear statement indicating that though the basic perceptions have not changed, they have been differently organized, have acquired a new meaning, and that behavior changes then occur. Similar evidence is given by a client, a trained psychologist, who after completing a brief series of client-centered interviews, writes:

Another interesting aspect of the situation was in connection with the changes in some of my attitudes. When the change occurred, it was as if earlier attitudes were wiped out as completely as if erased from a blackboard. . . . When a situation which would formerly have provoked a given type of response occurred, it was not as if I was tempted to act in the way I formerly had but in some way found it easier to control my behavior. Rather the new type of behavior came quite spontaneously, and it was only through a deliberate analysis that I became aware that I was acting in a new and different way.

Here again it is of interest that the imagery is put in terms of visual perception and that as attitudes are "erased from the blackboard" behavioral changes take place automatically and without conscious effort.

Thus we have observed that appropriate changes in behavior occur when the individual acquires a different view of his world of experience, including himself; that this changed perception does not need to be dependent upon a change in the "reality," but may be a product of internal reorganization; that in some instances the awareness of the capacity for reperceiving experience accompanies this process of reorganization; that the altered behavioral responses occur automatically and without conscious effort as soon as the perceptual reorganization has taken place, apparently as a result of this.

In view of these observations a second hypothesis may be stated, which is closely related to the first. It is that *behavior is not directly influenced or determined by organic or cultural factors, but primarily* (and perhaps only), *by the perception of these elements.* In other words the crucial element in the determination of behavior is the perceptual field of the individual. While this perceptual field is, to be sure, deeply influenced and largely shaped by cultural and physiological forces, it is nevertheless important that it appears to be only the field as it is *perceived*, which exercises a specific determining influence upon behavior. This is not a new idea in psychology, but its implications have not always been fully recognized.

It might mean, first of all, that if it is the perceptual field which determines behavior, then the primary object of study for psychologists would be the person and his world *as viewed by the person himself*. It could mean that the internal frame of reference of the person might well constitute the field of psychology, an idea set forth persuasively by Snygg and Combs in a significant manuscript as yet unpublished. It might mean that the laws which govern behavior would be discovered more deeply by turning our attention to the laws which govern perception.

Now if our speculations contain a measure of truth, if the *specific* determinant of behavior is the perceptual field, and if the self can reorganize that perceptual field, then what are the limits of this process? Is the reorganization of perception capricious, or does it follow certain laws? Are there limits to the degree of reorganization? If so, what are they? In this connection we have observed with some care the perception of one portion of the field of experience, the portion we call the self.

The Relation of the Perception of the Self to Adjustment

Initially we were oriented by the background of both lay and psychological thinking to regard the outcome of successful therapy as the solution of problems. If a person had a marital problem, a vocational problem, a problem of educational adjustment, the obvious purpose of counseling or therapy was to solve that problem. But as we observe and study the recorded accounts of the conclusion of therapy, it is clear that the most characteristic outcome is not necessarily solution of problems, but a freedom from tension, a different feeling about, and perception of, self. Perhaps something of this outcome may be conveyed by some illustrations.

Several statements taken from the final interview with a twenty year old young woman, Miss Mir, give indications of the characteristic attitude toward self, and the sense of freedom which appears to accompany it.

I've always tried to be what the others thought I should be, but now I am wondering whether I shouldn't just see that I am what I am.

Well, I've just noticed such a difference. I find that when I feel things, even when I feel hate, I don't care. I don't mind. I feel more free somehow. I don't feel guilty about things.

You know it's suddenly as though a big cloud has been lifted off. I feel so much more content.

Note in these statements the willingness to perceive herself as she is, to accept herself "realistically," to perceive and accept her "bad" attitudes as well as "good" ones. This realism seems to be accompanied by a sense of freedom and contentment.

Miss Vib, whose attitudes were quoted earlier, wrote out her own feelings about counseling some six weeks after the interviews were over, and gave the statement to her counselor. She begins:

The happiest outcome of therapy has been a new feeling about myself. As I think of it, it might be the only outcome. Certainly it is basic to all the changes in my behavior that have resulted.

In discussing her experience in therapy she states:

I was coming to see myself as a whole. I began to realize that I am *one* person. This was an important insight to me. I saw that the former good academic achievement, job success, ease in social situations, and the present withdrawal, dejection, apathy and failure were all adaptive behavior, performed by *me*. This meant that I had to reorganize my feelings about myself, no longer holding to the unrealistic notion that the very good adjustment was the expression of the real "me" and this neurotic behavior was not. I came to feel that I am the same person, sometimes functioning maturely, and sometimes assuming a neurotic role in the face of what I had conceived as insurmountable problems. The acceptance of myself as one person gave me strength in the process of reorganization. Now I had a substratum, a core of unity on which to work.

As she continues her discussion there are such statements as:

I am getting more happiness in being myself. I approve of myself more, and I have so much less anxiety.

As in the previous example, the outstanding aspects appear to be the realization that all of her behavior "belonged" to her, that she could accept both the good and bad features about herself and that doing so gave her a release from anxiety and a feeling of solid happiness. In both instances there is only incidental reference to the serious "problems" which had been initially discussed.

Since Miss Mir is undoubtedly above average intelligence and Miss Vib is a person with some psychological training, it may appear that such results are found only with the sophisticated individual. To counteract this opinion a quotation may be given from a statement written by a veteran of limited ability and education who had just completed counseling, and was asked to write whatever reactions he had to the experience. He says:

As for the consoleing I have had I can say this, It really makes a man strip his own mind bare, and when he does he knows then what he realy is and what he can do. Or at least thinks he knows himself party well. As for myself, I know that my ideas were a little too big for what I realy am, but now I realize one must try start out at his own level.

Now after four visits, I have a much clearer picture of myself and my future. It makes me feel a little depressed and disappointed, but on the other hand, it has taken me out of the dark, the load seems a lot lighter now, that is I can see my way now, I know what I want to do, I know about what I can do, so now that I can see my goal, I will be able to work a whole lot easer, at my own level.

Although the expression is much simpler one notes again the same two elements—the acceptance of self as it is, and the feeling of easiness, of lightened burden, which accompanies it.

As we examine many individual case records and case recordings, it appears to be possible to bring together the findings in regard to successful therapy by stating another hypothesis in regard to that portion of the perceptual field which we call the self. It would appear that *when all of the ways in which the individual perceives himself—all perceptions of the qualities, abilities, impulses, and attitudes of the person, and all perceptions of himself in relation to others—are accepted into the organized conscious concept of the self, then this achievement is accompanied by feelings of comfort and freedom from tension which are experienced as psychological adjustment.*

This hypothesis would seem to account for the observed fact that the comfortable perception of self which is achieved is sometimes more positive than before, sometimes more negative. When the individual permits all his perceptions of himself to be organized into one pattern, the picture is sometimes more flattering than he has held in the past, sometimes less flattering. It is always more comfortable.

It may be pointed out also that this tentative hypothesis supplies an operational type of definition, based on the client's internal frame of reference, for such hitherto vague terms as "adjustment," "integration," and "acceptance of self." They are defined in terms of perception, in a way which it should be possible to prove or disprove. When all of the organic perceptual experiences—the experiencing of attitudes, impulses, abilities and disabilities, the experiencing of others and of "reality"— when all of these perceptions are freely assimilated into an organized and consistent system, available to consciousness, then psychological adjustment or integration might be said to exist. The definition of adjustment is thus made an internal affair, rather than dependent upon an external "reality."

Something of what is meant by this acceptance and assimilation of perceptions about the self may be illustrated from the case of Miss Nam, a student. Like many other clients she gives evidence of having experienced attitudes and feelings which are defensively denied because they are not consistent with the concept or picture she holds of herself. The way in which they are first fully admitted into consciousness, and then organized into a unified system may be shown by excerpts from the recorded interviews. She has spoken of the difficulty she has had in bringing herself to write papers for her university courses.

I just thought of something else which perhaps hinders me, and that is that again it's two different feelings. When I have to sit down and do (a paper), though I have a lot of ideas, underneath I think I always have the feeling that I just can't do it. . . . I have this feeling of being terrifically confident that I can do something, without being willing to put the work into it. At other times I'm practically afraid of what I have to do. . . .

Note that the conscious self has been organized as "having a lot of ideas," being "terrifically confident" but that "underneath," in other words not freely admitted into consciousness, has been the experience of feeling "I just can't do it." She continues:

I'm trying to work through this funny relationship between this terrific confidence and then this almost fear of doing anything. . .and I think the kind of feeling that I can really do things is part of an illusion I have about myself of being, in my imagination, sure that it will be something good and very good and all that, but whenever I get down to the actual task of getting started, it's a terrible feeling of—well, incapacity, that I won't get it done either the way I want to do it, or even not being sure how I want to do it.

Again the picture of herself which is present in consciousness is that of a person who is "very good," but this picture is entirely out of line with the actual organic experience in the situation.

Later in the same interview she expresses very well the fact that her perceptions are not all organized into one consistent conscious self.

I'm not sure about what kind of a person I am—well, I realize that all of these are a part of me, but I'm not quite sure of how to make all of these things fall in line.

In the next interview we have an excellent opportunity to observe the organization of both of these conflicting perceptions into one pattern, with the resultant sense of freedom from tension which has been described above.

It's very funny, even as I sit here I realize that I have more confidence in myself, in the sense that when I used to approach new situations I would have two very funny things operating at the same time. I had a fantasy that I could do anything, which was a fantasy which covered over all these other feelings that I really couldn't do it, or couldn't do it as well as I wanted to, and it's as if now those two things have merged together, and it is more real, that a situation isn't either testing myself or proving something to myself or anyone else. It's just in terms of doing it. And I think I have done away both with that fantasy and that fear. . . . So I think I can go ahead and approach things—well, just sensibly.

No longer is it necessary for this client to "cover over" her real experiences. Instead the picture of herself as very able, and the experienced feeling of complete inability, have now been brought together into one integrated pattern of self as a person with real, but imperfect abilities. Once the self is thus accepted the inner energies making for self-actualization are released and she attacks her life problems more efficiently.

Observing this type of material frequently in counseling experience would lead to a tentative hypothesis of maladjustment, which like the other hypothesis suggested, focuses on the perception of self. It might be proposed that the tensions called psychological maladjustment exist when the organized concept of self (conscious or available to conscious awareness) is not in accord with the perceptions actually experienced.

This discrepancy between the concept of self and the actual perceptions seems to be explicable only in terms of the fact that the self concept resists assimilating into itself any percept which is inconsistent with its present organization. The feeling that she may not have the ability to do a paper is inconsistent with Miss Nam's conscious picture of herself as a very able and confident person, and hence, though fleetingly perceived, is denied organization as a part of her self, until this comes about in therapy.

The Conditions of Change of Self Perception

If the way in which the self is perceived has as close and significant a relationship to behavior as has been suggested, then the manner in which this perception may be altered becomes a question of importance. If a reorganization of self-perceptions brings a change in behavior; if adjustment and maladjustment depend on the congruence between perceptions as experienced and the self as perceived, then the factors which permit a reorganization of the perception of self are significant.

Our observations of psychotherapeutic experience would seem to indicate that absence of any threat to the self-concept is an important item in the problem. Normally the self resists incorporating into itself those experiences which are inconsistent with the functioning of self. But a point overlooked by Lecky and others is that when the self is free from any threat of attack or likelihood of attack, then it is possible for the self to consider these hitherto rejected perceptions, to make new differentiations, and to reintegrate the self in such a way as to include them.

An illustration from the case of Miss Vib may serve to clarify this point. In her statement written six weeks after the conclusion of counseling Miss Vib thus describes the way in which unacceptable percepts become incorporated into the self. She writes:

> In the earlier interviews I kept saying such things as, "I am not acting like myself," "I never acted this way before." What I meant was that this withdrawn, untidy, and apathetic person was not myself. Then I began to realize that I was the same person, seriously withdrawn, etc. now, as I had been before. That did

not happen until after I had talked out my self-rejection, shame, despair, and doubt, in the accepting situation of the interview. The counselor was not startled or shocked. I was telling him of all these things about myself which did not fit into my picture of a graduate student, a teacher, a sound person. He responded with complete acceptance and warm interest without heavy emotional overtones. Here was a sane, intelligent person wholeheartedly accepting this behavior that seemed so shameful to me. I can remember an organic feeling of relaxation. I did not have to keep up the struggle to cover up and hide this shameful person.

Note how clearly one can see here the whole range of denied perceptions of self, and the fact that they could be considered as a part of self only in a social situation which involved no threat to the self, in which another person, the counselor, becomes almost an alternate self and looks with understanding and acceptance upon these same perceptions. She continues:

Retrospectively, it seems to me that what I felt as "warm acceptance without emotional overtones" was what I needed to work through my difficulties. . . .The counselor's impersonality with interest allowed me to talk out my feelings. The clarification in the interview situation presented the attitude to me as a "ding an sich" which I could look at, manipulate, and put in place. In organizing my attitudes, I was beginning to organize me.

Here the nature of the exploration of experience, of seeing it as experience and not as a threat to self, enables the client to reorganize her perceptions of self, which as she says was also "reorganizing me."

If we attempt to describe in more conventional psychological terms the nature of the process which culminates in an altered organization and integration of self in the process of therapy it might run as follows. The individual is continually endeavoring to meet his needs by reacting to the field of experience as he perceives it, and to do that more efficiently by differentiating elements of the field and reintegrating them into new patterns. Reorganization of the field may involve the reorganization of the self as well as of other parts of the field. The self, however, resists reorganization and change. In everyday life individual adjustment by means of reorganization of the field exclusive of the self is more common and is less threatening to the individual. Consequently, the individual's first mode of adjustment is the reorganization of that part of the field which does not include the self.

Client-centered therapy is different from other life situations inasmuch as the therapist tends to remove from the individual's immediate world all those aspects of the field which the individual can reorganize except the self. The therapist, by reacting to the client's feelings and attitudes rather than to the objects of his feelings and attitudes, assists the client in bringing from background into focus his own self, making it easier than ever before for the client to perceive and react to the self. By offering only understanding and no trace of evaluation, the therapist removes himself as an object of attitudes, becoming only an alternate expression of the client's self. The therapist by providing a consistent atmosphere of permissiveness and understanding removes whatever threat existed to prevent all perceptions of the self from emerging into figure. Hence in this situation all the ways in which the self has been experienced can be viewed openly, and organized into a complex unity.

It is then this complete absence of any factor which would attack the concept of self, and second, the assistance in focusing upon the perception of self, which seems to permit a more differentiated view of self and finally the reorganization of self.

Relationship to Current Psychological Thinking

Up to this point, these remarks have been presented as clinical observations and tentative hypotheses, quite apart from any relationship to past or present thinking in the field of psychology. This has been intentional. It is felt that it is the function of the clinician to try to observe, with an open-minded attitude, the complexity of material which comes to him, to report his observations, and in the light of this to formulate hypotheses and problems which both the clinic and the laboratory may utilize as a basis for study and research.

Yet, though these are clinical observations and hypotheses, they have, as has doubtless been recognized, a relationship to some of the currents of theoretical and laboratory thinking in psychology. Some of the observations about the self bear a relationship to the thinking of G. H. Mead (7) about the "I" and the "me." The outcome of therapy might be described in Mead's terms as the increasing awareness of the "I," and the organization of the "me's" by the "I." The importance which has been given in this paper to the self as an organizer of experience and to some extent as an architect of self, bears a relationship to the thinking of Allport (1) and others concerning the increased place which we must give to the integrative function of the ego. In the stress which has been given to the present field of experience as the determinant of behavior, the relationship to Gestalt psychology, and to the work of Lewin (6) and his students is obvious. The theories of Angyal (2) find some parallel in our observations. His view that the self represents only a small part of the biological organism which has reached symbolic elaboration, and that it often attempts the direction of the organism on the basis of unreliable and insufficient information, seems to be particularly related to the observations we have made. Lecky's posthumous book (4), small in size but large in the significance of its contribution, has brought a new light on the way in which the self operates, and the principle of consistency by which new experience is included in or excluded from the self. Much of his thinking runs parallel to our observations. Snygg and Combs (11) have recently attempted a more radical and more complete emphasis upon the internal world of perception as the basis for all psychology, a statement which has helped to formulate a theory in which our observations fit.

It is not only from the realm of theory but also from the experimental laboratory that one finds confirmation of the line of thinking which has been proposed. Tolman (12) has stressed the need of thinking as a rat if fruitful experimental work is to be done. The work of Snygg (10) indicates that rat behavior may be better predicted by inferring the rat's field of perception than by viewing him as an object. Krech (Krechevsky, 3) showed in a brilliant study some years ago that rat learning can only be understood if we realize that the rat is consistently acting upon one hypothesis after another. Leeper (5) has summarized the evidence from a number of experimental investigations, showing that animal behavior cannot be explained by simple S-R mechanisms, but only by recognizing that complex internal processes of perceptual organization intervene between the stimulus and the behavioral response. Thus there are parallel streams of clinical observation, theoretical thinking, and laboratory experiment, which all point up the fact that for an effective psychology we need a much more complete understanding of the private world of the individual, and need to learn ways of entering and studying that world from within.

Implications

It would be misleading however if I left you with the impression that the hypotheses I have formulated in this paper, or those springing from the parallel psychological studies I have mentioned, are simply extensions of the main stream of psychological thinking, additional bricks in the edifice of psychological thought. We have discovered with some surprise that our clinical observations, and the tentative hypotheses which seem to grow out of them, raise disturbing questions which appear to cast doubt on the very foundations of many of our psychological endeavors, particularly in the fields of clinical psychology and personality study. To clarify what is meant, I should like to restate in more logical order the formulations I have given, and to leave with you certain questions and problems which each one seems to raise.

If we take first the tentative proposition that the specific determinant of behavior is the perceptual field of the individual, would this not lead, if regarded as a working hypothesis, to a radically different approach in clinical psychology and personality research? It would seem to mean that instead of elaborate case histories full of information about the person as an object, we would endeavor to develop ways of seeing his situation, his past, and himself, as these objects appear to him. We would try to see with him, rather than to evaluate him. It might mean the minimizing of the elaborate psychometric procedures by which we have endeavored to measure or value the individual from our own frame of reference. It might mean the minimizing or discarding of all the vast series of labels which we have painstakingly built up over the years. Paranoid, preschiz-ophrenic, compulsive, constricted—terms such as these might become irrelevant because they are all based in thinking which takes an external frame of reference. They are not the ways in which the individual experiences himself. If we consistently studied each individual from the internal frame of reference of that individual, from within his own perceptual field, it seems probable that we should find generalizations which could be made, and principles which were operative, but we may be very sure that they would be of a different order from these externally based judgments *about* individuals.

Let us look at another of the suggested propositions. If we took seriously the hypothesis that integration and adjustment are internal conditions related to the degree of acceptance or nonacceptance of all perceptions, and the degree of organization of these perceptions into one consistent system, this would decidely affect our clinical procedures. It would seem to imply the abandonment of the notion that adjustment is dependent upon the pleasantness or unpleasantness of the environment, and would demand concentration upon those processes which bring about self-integration within the person. It would mean a minimizing or an abandoning of those clinical procedures which utilize the alteration of environmental forces as a method of treatment. It would rely instead upon the fact that the person who is internally unified has the greatest likelihood of meeting environmental problems constructively, either as an individual or in cooperation with others.

If we take the remaining proposition that the self, under proper conditions, is capable of reorganizing, to some extent, its own perceptual field, and of thus altering behavior, this too seems to raise disturbing questions. Following the path of this hypothesis would appear to mean a shift in emphasis in psychology from focusing upon the fixity of personality attributes and psychological abilities, to the alterability of these same characteristics. It would concentrate attention upon process rather than upon fixed status. Whereas psychology has, in personality study, been concerned primarily with the measurement of the fixed qualities of the individual, and with his past in order to explain his present, the hypothesis here suggested would seem to concern itself much more with the personal world of the present in order to understand the future, and in predicting that future would be concerned with the principles by which personality and behavior are altered, as well as the extent to which they remain fixed.

Thus we find that a clinical approach, client-centered therapy, has led us to try to adopt the client's perceptual field as the basis for genuine understanding. In trying to enter this internal world of perception, not by introspection, but by observation and direct inference, we find ourselves in a new vantage point for understanding personality dynam-ics, a vantage point which opens up some disturbing vistas. We find that behavior seems to be better understood as a reaction to this reality-as-perceived. We discover that the way in which the person sees himself, and the perceptions he dares not take as belonging to himself, seem to have an important relationship to the inner peace which constitutes adjustment. We discover within the person, under certain conditions, a capacity for the restructuring and the reorganization of self, and consequently the reorganization of behavior, which has profound social implications. We see these observations, and the theoretical formulations which they inspire, as a fruitful new approach for study and research in various fields of psychology.

REFERENCES

1. Allport, Gordon W.   The ego in contemporary psychology. *Psychol. Rev.*, 1943, *50*, 451-478.
2. Angyal, Andras.   *Foundations for a science of personality.* New York. Commonwealth Fund, 1941.
3. Krechevsky, I.   Hypotheses in rats. *Psychol. Rev.*, 1932, *39*, 516-532.
4. Lecky, Prescott.   *Self-consistency: A theory of personality.* New York. Island Press, 1945.
5. Leeper, Robert.   The experimental psychologists as reluctant dragons. Paper presented at APA meeting, September 1946.
6. Lewin, Kurt.   *A dynamic theory of personality.* New York, McGraw-Hill, 1935.
7. Mead, George H.   *Mind, self, and society.* Chicago. University of Chicago Press, 1934.
8. Rogers, Carl R.   Significant aspects of client-centered therapy. *Amer. Psychologist,* 1946, *1*, 415-422.
9. Snyder, W. U.   "Warmth" in nondirective counseling. *J. abnorm. soc. Psychol.*, 1946, *41*, 491-495.
10. Snygg, Donald.   Mazes in which rats take the longer path to food. *J. Psychol.*, 1936, *1*, 153-166.
11. Snygg, Donald, & Combs, Arthur W.   Book manuscript, loaned to present author. In process of publication. New York. Harper and Bros.
12. Tolman, E. C.   The determiners of behavior at a choice point. *Psychol. Rev.*, 1938, *45*, 1-41.

Reprinted with permission
from *American Psychologist*,
1957, 12, 671–684.

Chapter 22

The Two Disciplines of Scientific Psychology

Lee J. Cronbach

University of Illinois

No man can be acquainted with all of psychology today, as our convention program proves. The scene resembles that of a circus, but a circus grander and more bustling than any Barnum ever envisioned—a veritable week-long diet of excitement and pink lemonade. Three days of smartly paced performance are required just to display the new tricks the animal trainers have taught their charges. We admire the agile paper-readers swinging high above us in the theoretical blue, saved from disaster by only a few gossamer threads of fact, and we gasp as one symposiast thrusts his head bravely between another's sharp toothed jaws. This 18-ring display of energies and talents gives plentiful evidence that psychology is going places. But whither?

In the simpler days of psychology, the presidential address provided a summing-up and a statement of destination. The President called the

Address of the President at the Sixty-Fifth Annual Convention of the American Psychological Association, New York, New York, September 2, 1957.

roll of the branches of psychology—praising the growth of some youngsters, tut-tutting patriarchally over the delinquent tendencies of others—and showed each to his proper place at the family table. My own title is reminiscent of those grand surveys, but the last speaker who could securely bring the whole of psychology within one perspective was Dashiell, with his 1938 address on "Rapprochements in Contemporary Psychology" (15). My scope must be far more restricted.

I shall discuss the past and future place within psychology of two historic streams of method, thought, and affiliation which run through the last century of our science. One stream is *experimental psychology*; the other, *correlational psychology*. Dashiell optimistically forecast a confluence of these two streams, but that confluence is still in the making. Psychology continues to this day to be limited by the dedication of its investigators to one or the other method of inquiry rather than to scientific psychology as a whole.

A stream of thought is identified by many features: philosophical underpinnings, methods of inquiry, topical interests, and loci of application. The experimental and correlational streams have all these aspects, but I am concerned with them as disciplines within scientific psychology. The job of science is to ask questions of Nature. A discipline is a method of asking questions and of testing answers to determine whether they are sound. Scientific psychology is still young, and there is rapid turnover in our interests, our experimental apparatus and our tests, and our theoretical concepts. But our methods of inquiry have become increasingly stable, and it is these methods which qualify us as scientists rather than philosophers or artists.

The Separation of the Disciplines

The experimental method—where the scientist changes conditions in order to observe their consequences—is much the more coherent of our two disciplines. Everyone knows what experimental psychology is and who the experimental psychologists are. Correlational psychology, though fully as old as experimentation, was slower to mature. It qualifies equally as a discipline, however, because it asks a distinctive type of question and has technical methods of examining whether the question has been properly put and the data properly interpreted.

In contrast to the Tight Little Island of the experimental discipline, correlational psychology is a sort of Holy Roman Empire whose citizens identify mainly with their own principalities. The discipline, the common service in which the principalities are united, is the study of correlations presented by Nature. While the experimenter is interested only in the variation he himself creates, the correlator finds his interest in the already existing variation between individuals, social groups, and species. By "correlational psychology" I do not refer to studies which rely on one statistical procedure. Factor analysis is correlational, to be sure, but so is the study of Ford and Beach (23) relating sexual behavior to differences along the phylogenetic scale and across the cultural spectrum.

The well-known virtue of the experimental method is that it brings situational variables under tight control. It thus permits rigorous tests of hypotheses and confident statements about causation. The correlational method, for its part, can study what man has not learned to control or can never hope to control. Nature has been experimenting since the beginning of time, with a boldness and complexity far beyond the resources of science. The correlator's mission is to observe and organize the data from Nature's experiments. As a minimum outcome, such correlations improve immediate decisions and guide experimentation. At the best, a Newton, a Lyell, or a Darwin can align the correlations into a substantial theory.

During our century of scientific psychology, the correlators have marched under many flags. In perhaps the first modern discussion of scientific method in psychology (1874), Wundt (54) showed how "experimental psychology" and "ethnic psychology" (i.e., cross-cultural correlations) supplement each other. In one of the most recent (1953), Bindra and Scheier (4) speak of the interplay of "experimental" and "psychometric" method. At the turn of the century, the brand names were "experimental" and "genetic" psychology, although experimenters were also beginning to contrast their "general psychology" with the "individual psychology" of Stern and Binet.

In 1913, Yerkes made the fundamental point that all the correlational psychologies are one. His name for this branch was "comparative psychology."

Although comparative psychology in its completeness necessarily deals with the materials of the psychology of infant, child, adult, whether the being be of human or infra-human; of animal or plant [!]—of normal and abnormal individuals; of social groups and of civilizations, there is no reason why specialists in the use of the comparative method should not be so distinguished, and, if it seems necessary, labelled (55).

Even in advocating research on animals (56), Yerkes is emphatic in defining the goal as correlation across species. In France, *la psychologie comparée* continues to include all of differential psychology; but in America, as Beach (2) has lamented, comparative psychology degenerated into the experimental psychology of the white rat and thereby lost the power of the correlational discipline.

Except for the defection of animal psychologists, the correlational psychologists have remained loosely federated. Developmental psychologists, personality psychologists, and differential psychologists have been well acquainted both personally and intellectually. They study the same courses, they draw on the same literature, they join the same divisions of APA.

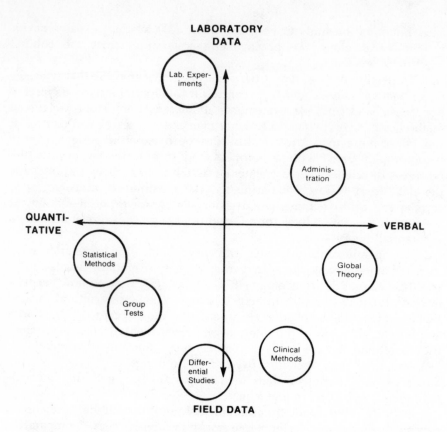

Figure 1. Factors accounting for esteem of leaders in psychology by American psychologists (based on correlations presented by Thorndike, 44, corrected for attenuation and refactored).

Experimental and correlational psychologists, however, grew far apart in their training and interests. It is now commonplace for a student to get his PhD in experimental psychology without graduate training in test theory or developmental psychology, and the student of correlational branches can avoid experimental psychology only a little less completely. The journals of one discipline have small influence on the journals of the other (14). Boring even dares to say (5, p. 578) that there is a personality difference between the fields: the distinction being that correlational psychologists like people!

Certainly the scientific values of psychologists are sharply divided. Thorndike (9, 44) recently asked American psychologists to rate various historic personages by indicating, on a forced-choice questionnaire, which have made the greatest contributions to psychology. A factor analysis of the ratings shows two distinct factors (Figure 1). One bipolar factor (irrelevant to our present discussion) ranges from verbal to quantitative psychologists. The other factor has at one pole the laboratory experimenters like Stevens, Dodge, and Ebbinghaus, and at the opposite pole those like Binet, May, and Goodenough who collect and correlate field data. A psychologist's esteem for the experimenters is correlated −.80 (−1.00, corrected for attenuation) with his esteem for scientists who use correlational methods.

There was no such schism in 1913 when Yerkes stated the program of correlational psychology. Genetic psychology and experimental psychology were hard at work on the same problems. Terman demonstrated in his 1923 presidential address (43) that the mental test was within the tradition of experimental, fundamental research in psychology, and had quotations to show that the contemporary experimentalists agreed with him. Wells and Goddard, in 1913, had been asked to lecture on mental tests within the Holy Temple itself, the Society of Experimental Psychologists. And, in 1910, the High Priest Titchener had said:

Individual psychology is one of the chief witnesses to the value of experiment. It furnishes the key to many, otherwise inexplicable differences of result, and it promises to allay many of the outstanding controversies. . . . There can be no doubt that it will play a part of steadily increasing importance (46).

But when Terman spoke in 1923, the common front had already been fatally breached. Watson had announced that experimental treatment could make and unmake individual differences at will, thus stripping them of scientific importance. Thurstone had taken the first firm stride in the opposite direction:

I suggest that we dethrone the stimulus. He is only nominally the ruler of psychology. The real ruler of the domain which psychology studies is the individual and his motives, desires, wants, ambitions, cravings, aspirations. The stimulus is merely the more or less accidental fact . . . (45, p. 364).

The personality, social, and child psychologists went one way; the perception and learning psychologists went the other; and the country between turned into desert.

During the estrangement of correlational and experimental psychology, antagonism has been notably absent. Disparagement has been pretty well confined to playful remarks like Cattell's accusation that the experimental psychologist's "regard for the body of nature becomes that of the anatomist rather than that of the lover" (7, p. 152), or the experimentalist Bartlett's (1, p. 210) satire on the testers emerging from World War I, "chanting in unaccustomed harmony the words of the old jingle

God has a plan for every man
And He has one for you.'"

Most correlationists have done a little experimenting in the narrow sense, and experimenters have contributed proudly to testing work under wartime necessity. But these are temporary sojourns in a foreign land. (For clear expressions of this attitude, see 5, pp. 570–578 and 52, p. 24.)

A true federation of the disciplines is required. Kept independent, they can give only wrong answers or no answers at all regarding certain important problems. It is shortsighted to argue for one science to discover the general laws of mind or behavior and for a separate enterprise concerned with individual minds, or for a one-way dependence of personality theory upon learning theory. Consider the physical sciences as a parallel. Physics for centuries was the study of general laws applying to all solids or all gases, whereas alchemy and chemistry studied the properties and reactions of individual substances. Chemistry was once only a descriptive catalogue of substances and analytic techniques. It became a systematic science when organized quantitative studies yielded principles to explain differences between substances and to predict the outcomes of reactions. In consequence, Mendeleev the chemist paved the way for Bohr the physicist, and Fermi's physics contributes to Lawrence's chemistry; the boundary between chemistry and physics has become almost invisible.

The tide of separation in psychology has already turned. The perceiver has reappeared in perceptual psychology. Tested intelligence and anxiety appear as independent variables in many of the current learning experiments. Factor analytic studies have gained a fresh vitality from crossbreeding with classical learning experiments (e.g., 18, 22). Harlow, Hebb, Hess, and others are creating a truly experimental psychology of development. And students of personality have been designing subtle combinations of experimental and correlational method (see, for example, 29) which may ultimately prove to be our parallel to the emergence of physical chemistry.

Characterization of the Disciplines

In the beginning, experimental psychology was a substitute for purely naturalistic observation of man-in-habitat. The experimenter placed man in an artificial, simplified environment and made quantitative observations of his performance. The initial problem was one of describing accurately what man felt, thought, or did in a defined situation. Standardization of tasks and conditions was required to get reproducible descriptions. All experimental procedures were tests, all tests were experiments. Kraepelin's continuous-work procedure served equally the general study of fatigue and the diagnosis of individuals. Reaction time was important equally to Wundt and to Cattell.

The distinctive characteristic of modern experimentation, the statistical comparison of treatments, appeared only around 1900 in such studies as that of Thorndike and Woodworth on transfer. The experimenter, following the path of Ebbinghaus, shifted from measurement of the average mind to measuring the effect of environmental change upon success in a task (51). Inference replaced estimation: the mean and its probable error gave way to the critical ratio. The standardized conditions and the standardized instruments remained, but the focus shifted to the single manipulated variable, and later, following Fisher, to multivariate manipulation. The experiment thus came to be concerned with between-treatments variance. I use the word "treatment" in a general sense; educational and therapeutic treatments are but one type. Treatment differences are equally involved in comparing rats given different schedules of reinforcement, chicks who have worn different distorting lenses, or social groups arranged with different communication networks.

The second great development in American experimental psychology has been its concern with formal theory. At the turn of the century, theory ranged far ahead of experiment and made no demand that propositions be testable. Experiment, for its part, was willing to observe any phenomenon, whether or not the data bore on theoretical issues. Today, the majority of experimenters derive their hypotheses explicitly from theoretical premises and try to nail their results into a theoretical structure. This deductive style has its undeniable defects, but one can not question the net gains from the accompanying theoretical sophistication. Discussions of the logic of operationism, intervening variables, and mathematical models have sharpened both the formulation of hypotheses and the interpretation of results.

Individual differences have been an annoyance rather than a challenge to the experimenter. His goal is to control behavior, and variation within treatments is proof that he has not succeeded. Individual variation is cast into that outer darkness known as "error variance." For reasons both statistical and philosophical, error variance is to be reduced by any possible device. You turn to animals of a cheap and short-lived species, so that you can use subjects with controlled heredity and controlled experience. You select human subjects from a narrow subculture. You decorticate your subject by cutting neurons or by giving him an environment so meaningless that his unique responses disappear (cf. 25). You increase the number of cases to obtain stable averages, or you reduce N to 1, as Skinner does. But whatever your device, your goal in the experimental tradition is to get those embarrassing differential variables out of sight.

The correlational psychologist is in love with just those variables the experimenter left home to forget. He regards individual and group variations as important effects of biological and social causes. All organisms adapt to their environments, but not equally well. His question is: what present characteristics of the organism determine its mode and degree of adaptation?

Just as individual variation is a source of embarrassment to the experimenter, so treatment variation attenuates the results of the correlator. His goal is to predict variation within a treatment. His experimental designs demand uniform treatment for every case contributing to a correlation, and treatment variance means only error variance to him.

Differential psychology, like experimental, began with a purely descriptive phase. Cattell at Hopkins, Galton at South Kensington, were simply asking how much people varied. They were, we might say, estimating the standard deviation while the general psychologists were estimating the central tendency.

The correlation coefficient, invented for the study of hereditary resemblance, transformed descriptive differential research into the study of mental organization. What began as a mere summary statistic quickly became the center of a whole theory of data analysis. Murphy's words, written in 1928, recall the excitement that attended this development:

> The relation between two variables has actually been found to be statable in other terms than those of experiment . . . [Moreover,] Yule's method of "partial correlation" has made possible the mathematical "isolation" of variables which cannot be isolated experimentally. . . . [Despite the limitations of correlational methods,] what they have already yielded to psychology . . . is nevertheless of such major importance as to lead the writer to the opinion that the only twentieth-century discovery comparable in importance to the conditioned-response method is the method of partial correlations (35, p. 410).

Today's students who meet partial correlation only as a momentary digression from their main work in statistics may find this excitement hard to comprehend. But partial correlation is the starting place for all of factor analysis.

Factor analysis is rapidly being perfected into a rigorous method of clarifying multivariate relationships. Fisher made the experimentalist an expert puppeteer, able to keep untangled the strands to half-a-dozen independent variables. The correlational psychologist is a mere observer of a play where Nature pulls a thousand strings; but his multivariate methods make him equally an expert, an expert in figuring out where to look for the hidden strings.

His sophistication in data analysis has not been matched by sophistication in theory. The correlational psychologist was led into temptation by his own success, losing himself first in practical prediction, then in a narcissistic program of studying his tests as an end in themselves. A naive operationism enthroned theory of test performance in the place of theory of mental processes. And premature enthusiasm[1] exalted a few measurements chosen almost by accident from the tester's stock as the ruling forces of the mental universe.

In former days, it was the experimentalist who wrote essay after anxious essay defining his discipline and differentiating it from competing ways of studying mind. No doubts plagued correlationists like Hall, Galton, and Cattell. They came in on the wave of evolutionary thought and were buoyed up by every successive crest of social progress or crisis.

---

1. This judgment is not mine alone; it is the clear consensus of the factor analysts themselves (see 28, pp. 321–325).

The demand for universal education, the development of a technical society, the appeals from the distraught twentieth-century parent, and finally the clinical movement assured the correlational psychologist of his great destiny. Contemporary experimentalists, however, voice with ever-increasing assurance their program and social function; and the fact that tonight you have a correlational psychologist discussing disciplinary identities implies that anxiety is now perched on *his* windowledge.

Indeed, I do speak out of concern for correlational psychology. Aptitude tests deserve their fine reputation; but, if practical, validated procedures are to be our point of pride, we must be dissatisfied with our progress since 1920. As the Executive Committee of Division 5 itself declared this year, none of our latter-day refinements or innovations has improved practical predictions by a noticeable amount. Correlational psychologists who found their self-esteem upon contributions to theory can point to monumental investigations such as the *Studies of Character* and *The Authoritarian Personality*. Such work does throw strong light upon the human scene and brings important facts clearly into view. But theories to organize these facts are rarely offered and even more rarely solidified (*30; 31*, p. 55).

Potential Contributions of the Disciplines to One Another

Perhaps it is inevitable that a powerful new method will become totally absorbing and crowd other thoughts from the minds of its followers. It took a generation of concentrated effort to move from Spearman's tetrad equation and Army Alpha to our present view of the ability domain. It took the full energies of other psychologists to move from S-R bonds to modern behavior theory. No doubt the tendency of correlationists to ignore experimental developments is explained by their absorption in the wonders and complexities of the phenomena their own work was revealing. And if experimentalists were to be accused of narrow-minded concentration on one particular style and topic of research, the same comment would apply.

The spell these particular theories and methods cast upon us appears to have passed. We are free at last to look up from our own bedazzling treasure, to cast properly covetous glances upon the scientific wealth of our neighbor discipline. Trading has already been resumed, with benefit to both parties.

The introduction of construct validation into test theory (*12*) is a prime example. The history of this development, you may recall, was that the APA's Committee on Psychological Tests discovered that available test theory recognized no way of determining whether a proposed psychological interpretation of a test was sound. The only existing theory dealt with criterion validation and could not evaluate claims that a test measured certain psychological traits or states. Meehl, capitalizing on the methodological and philosophical progress of the experimenters, met the testers' need by suggesting the idea of construct validity. A proposed test interpretation, he showed, is a claim that a test measures a construct, i.e., a claim that the test score can be linked to a theoretical network. This network, together with the claim, generates predictions about observations. The test interpretation is justified only if the observations come out as predicted. To decide how well a purported test of anxiety measures anxiety, construct validation is necessary; i.e., we must find out whether scores on the test behave in accordance with the theory that defines anxiety. This theory predicts differences in anxiety between certain groups, and traditional correlational methods can test those predictions. But the theory also predicts variation in anxiety, hence in the test score, as a function of experience or situations, and only an experimental approach can test those predictions.

This new theory of validity has several very broad consequences. It gives the tester a start toward the philosophical sophistication the experimenter has found so illuminating. It establishes the experimental method as a proper and necessary means of validating tests. And it re-establishes research on tests as a valuable and even indispensable way of extending psychological theory.

We may expect the test literature of the future to be far less saturated with correlations of tests with psychologically enigmatic criteria, and far richer in studies which define test variables by their responsiveness to practice at different ages, to drugs, to altered instructions, and to other experimentally manipulated variables. A pioneering venture in this direction is Fleishman's revealing work (21, 22) on changes in the factorial content of motor skills as a function of practice. These studies go far beyond a mere exploration of certain tests; as Ferguson has shown (19, 20), they force upon us a theory which treats abilities as a product of learning, and a theory of learning in which previously acquired abilities play a major role.

Perhaps the most valuable trading goods the correlator can offer in return is his multivariate conception of the world.

No experimenter would deny that situations and responses are multifaceted, but rarely are his procedures designed for a systematic multivariate analysis. The typical experimental design and the typical experimental law employ a single dependent variable. Even when more than one outcome is measured, the outcomes are analyzed and interpreted separately. No response measure, however, is an adequate measure of a psychological construct. Every score mixes general construct-relevant variance with variance specific to the particular measuring operation. It is all right for the agriculturist to consider size of crop as the fundamental variable being observed: that is the payoff for him. Our task, however, is to study changes in fundamental aspects of behavior, and these are evidenced only indirectly in any one measure of outcome.

The correlational psychologist discovered long ago that no observed criterion is truly valid and that simultaneous consideration of many criteria is needed for a satisfactory evaluation of performance. This same principle applies in experimentation. As Neal Miller says in a recent paper on experiments with drugs:

> Where there are relatively few facts it seems easy to account for them by a few simple generalizations. . . . As we begin to study the effects of a variety of drugs on a number of different behavioral measures, exceptions and complexities emerge. We are forced to reexamine and perhaps abandon common-sense categories of generalization according to convenient words existing in the English language. As new and more comprehensive patterns of results become available, however, new and more precise generalizations may emerge. We may be able to "carve nature better to the joint" and achieve the simplicity of a much more exact and powerful science (32, pp. 326–327).

Theoretical progress is obstructed when one restricts himself to a single measure of response (34). Where there is only one dependent variable, it is pointless to introduce intervening variables or constructs. When there are many response variables, however, it is mandatory to subsume them under constructs, since otherwise we must have a separate set of laws for every measure of outcome. Dealing with multiple response variables is, as Miller says (33), precisely the problem with which the factor analysts have been concerned. Factor analysis, by substituting formal for intuitive methods, has been of great help in locating constructs with which to summarize observations about abilities. It is reasonable to expect that multivariate treatment of response measures would have comparable value in experimental psychology.

Experimenters very probably have even more to gain from treating *in*dependent variables as a continuous multivariate system. The manifold treatment categories in a Fisherian design are established a priori. In agriculture, the treatment dimensions the farmer can manipulate are obvious: fertilizer, water, species of seed, and so on. In a more basic science, we require genotypic constructs to describe situations, constructs like the physical scientist's temperature and pressure. The conditions the psychologist most easily manipulates—stimulus form, injunction to the subject, strength of electric shock—are not chosen because we intend to apply these specific conditions when we get around to "controlling behavior." They are used because these conditions, we hope, embody scientifically useful constructs.

The experimenter has no systematic way to classify and integrate results from different tasks or different reinforcers. As Ferguson remarks (20, p. 130; see also 19, p. 100):

> No satisfactory methodology has emerged for describing particular learning tasks, or indicating how one task differs from another, other than by a process of simple inspection.

We depend wholly on the creative flair of the theorist to collate the experiments and to invent constructs which might describe particular situations, reinforcements, or injunctions in terms of more fundamental variables. The multivariate techniques of psychometrics are suited for precisely this task of grouping complex events into homogeneous classes or organizing them along major dimensions. These methods are frankly heuristic, but they are systematically heuristic. They select variables with minimal redundancy, and they permit us to obtain maximum information from a minimum of experimental investment.

In suggesting that examining treatment conditions as a statistical universe is a possible way to advance experimental thinking, I am of course echoing the recommendations of Egon Brunswik (6, esp. pp. 39–58). Brunswik criticized the Fisherian experimenter for his ad hoc selection of treatments and recommended that he apply the sampling principles of differential psychology in choosing stimuli and conditions. A sampling procedure such as Brunswik suggests will often be a forward step, but the important matter is not to establish laws which apply loosely to a random, unorganized collection of situations. The important matter is to discover the organization among the situations, so that we can describe situational differences as systematically as we do individual differences.

Research on stress presents a typical problem of organization. Multivariate psychophysiological data indicate that different taxing situations have different effects. At present, stressors can be described and classified only superficially, by inspection. A correlational or distance analysis of the data groups treatments which have similar effects and ultimately permits us to locate each treatment within a continuous multidimensional structure having constructs as reference axes. Data from a recent study by Wenger, Clemens, and Engel (50) may be used as an illustration. Figure 2 shows the means of standardized physiological scores under four different stress conditions: mental arithmetic, a letter association test, hyperventilation, and a cold pressor. The "profiles" for the four conditions are very significantly different. I have made a distance analysis to examine the similarity between conditions, with the

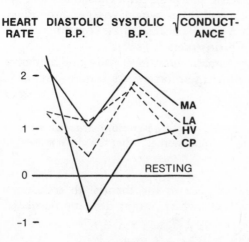

Figure 2. Mean response to four stressors expressed in terms of resting standard scores (data from 50).

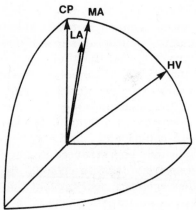

Figure 3. Multivariate diagram showing similarity between four stressors.

results diagrammed in Figure 3. There is a general factor among all the treatments, which distinguishes them from the resting state, and a notable group factor among three of them. According to these data, a mental test seems to induce the same physiological state as plunging one's foot into ice water!

Much larger bodies of data are of course needed to map the treatment space properly. But the aptness of an attempt in this direction will be apparent to all who heard Selye's address to the APA last year. His argument (40) that all stressful situations lead to a similar syndrome of physiological changes is strongly reminiscent of Spearman's argument regarding a general factor linking intellectual responses. The disagreement between Selye and other students of stress clearly reduces to a quantitative question of the relative size of specific and nonspecific or general factors in the effects of typical stressors.

Applied Psychology Divided Against Itself

Let us leave for the moment questions of academic psychology and consider the schism as it appears in applied psychology. In applied psychology, the two disciplines are in active conflict; and unless they bring their efforts into harmony, they can hold each other to a standstill. The conflict is especially obvious at this moment in the challenge the young engineering psychology offers to traditional personnel psychology.

The program of applied experimental psychology is to modify treatments so as to obtain the highest average performance when all persons are treated alike—a search, that is, for "the one best way." The program of applied correlational psychology is to raise average performance by treating persons differently—different job assignments, different therapies, different disciplinary methods. The correlationist is utterly antagonistic to a doctrine of "the one best way," whether it be the

heartless robot-making of Frederick Taylor or a doctrinaire permissiveness which tries to give identical encouragement to every individual.
The ideal of the engineering psychologist, I am told, is to simplify jobs
so that every individual in the working population will be able to
perform them satisfactorily, i.e., so that differentiation of treatment will
be unnecessary. This goal guides activities ranging from the sober to the
bizarre: from E. L. Thorndike and Skinner, hunting the one best
sequence of problems for teaching arithmetic, to Rudolf Flesch and his
admirers, reducing *Paradise Lost* to a comic book. If the engineering
psychologist succeeds: information rates will be so reduced that the most
laggard of us can keep up, visual displays will be so enlarged that the
most myopic can see them, automatic feedback will prevent the most
accident-prone from spoiling the work or his fingers.

Obviously, with every inch of success the engineer has, the tester
must retreat a mile. A slight reduction in information rate, accomplished
once, reduces forever the validity and utility of a test of ability to process
data. If, once the job is modified, the myopic worker can perform as well
as the man with 20/20 vision, Snellen charts and orthoraters are out of
business. Nor is the threat confined to the industrial scene. If tranquiliz-
ers make everybody happy, why bother to diagnose patients to determine which treatments they should have? And if televised lessons can
simplify things so that every freshman will enjoy and understand
quantum mechanics, we will need neither college aptitude tests nor final
examinations.

It is not my intention to warn testers about looming unemployment.
If test technology is not greatly improved, long before the applied
experimentalists near their goals, testing deserves to disappear. My
message is my belief that the conflicting principles of the tester and the
experimenter can be fused into a new and integrated applied psychology.

To understand the present conflict in purposes, we must look again
at historical antecedents. Pastore (36) argues with much justice that the
testers and classifiers have been political conservatives, while those who
try to find the best common treatment for all—particularly in education—
have been the liberals. This essential conservatism of personnel psychology traces back to the days of Darwin and Spencer.

The theory of evolution inspired two antagonistic movements in
social thought (10, 42). Darwin and Herbert Spencer were real determinists. The survival of the fittest, as a law of Nature, guaranteed man's
superiority and the ultimate triumph of the natural aristocrats among
men. As Dewey put it, Spencer saw "a rapid transit system of evolution
. . . carrying us automatically to the goal of perfect man in perfect
society" (17, p. 66). Men vary in their power of adaptation, and
institutions, by demanding adaptation, serve as instruments of natural
selection among men. The essence of freedom is seen as the freedom to
compete for survival. To Spencer, to Galton, and to their successors down
to the present day, the successful are those who have the greatest
adjustive capacity. The psychologist's job, in this tradition, is to facilitate

or anticipate natural selection. He seeks only to reduce its cruelty and wastage by predicting who will survive in schools and other institutions as they are. He takes the system for granted and tries to identify who will fit into it. His devices have a conservative influence because they identify persons who will succeed in the existing institution. By reducing failures, they remove a challenge which might otherwise force the institution to change (49).

The experimental scientist inherits an interpretation of evolution associated with the names of Ward, James, and Dewey. For them, man's progress rests on his intelligence; the great struggle for survival is a struggle against environment, not against competitors. Intelligent man must reshape his environment, not merely conform to it. This spirit, the very antithesis of Spencerian laissez-faire, bred today's experimental social science which accepts no institution and no tradition as sacred. The individual is seen as inherently self-directing and creative. One can not hope to predict how he will meet his problems, and applied differential psychology is therefore pointless (39, p. 37).

Thus we come to have one psychology which accepts the institution, its treatment, and its criterion and finds men to fit the institution's needs. The other psychology takes man—generalized man—as given and challenges any institution which does not conform to the measure of this standard man.

A clearer view of evolution removes the paradox:

> The entire significance of the evolutionary method in biology and social history is that every distinct organ, structure, or formation, every grouping of cells or elements, has to be treated as an instrument of adjustment or adaptation to a particular environing situation. Its meaning, its character, its value, is known when, and only when, it is considered as an arrangement for meeting the conditions involved in some specific situation (16, p. 15).

We are not on the right track when we conceive of adjustment or adjustive capacity in the abstract. It is always a capacity to respond to a particular treatment. The organism which adapts well under one condition would not survive under another. If for each environment there is a best organism, for every organism there is a best environment. The job of applied psychology is to improve decisions about people. The greatest social benefit will come from applied psychology if we can find for each individual the treatment to which he can most easily adapt. This calls for the joint application of experimental and correlational methods.

Interaction of Treatment and Individual in Practical Decisions

Goldine Gleser and the writer have recently published a theoretical analysis (11) which shows that neither the traditional predictive model of the correlator nor the traditional experimental comparison of mean

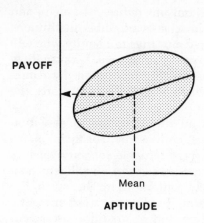

PAYOFF

Mean

APTITUDE

Figure 4. Scatter diagram and payoff function showing outcome as a function of individual differences.

differences is an adequate formulation of the decisions confronting the applied psychologist. Let me attempt to give a telescoped version of the central argument.

The decision maker has to determine what treatment shall be used for each individual or each group of individuals. Psychological data help a college, for example, select students to be trained as scientists. The aim of any decision maker is to maximize expected payoff. There is a payoff function relating outcome (e.g., achievement in science) to aptitude dimensions for any particular treatment. Figure 4 shows such a function for a single aptitude. Average payoff—if everyone receives the treatment—is indicated by the arrow. The experimentalist assumes a fixed population and hunts for the treatment with the highest average and the least variability. The correlationist assumes a fixed treatment and hunts for aptitudes which maximize the slope of the payoff function. In academic selection, he advises admission of students with high scores on a relevant aptitude and thus raises payoff for the institution (Figure 5).

Pure selection, however, almost never occurs. The college aptitude

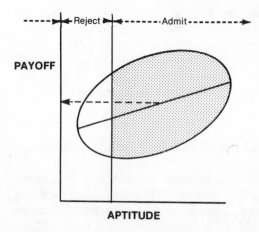

◀ Reject ▶◀ Admit ▶

PAYOFF

APTITUDE

Figure 5. Increase in payoff as a result of selection.

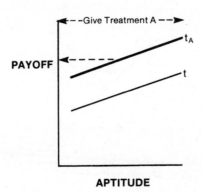

Figure 6. Payoff functions for two treatments.

test may seem to be intended for a selection decision; and, insofar as the individual college is concerned only with those it accepts, the conventional validity coefficient does indicate the best test. But from a societal point of view, the rejects will also go on into other social institutions, and their profit from this treatment must be weighed in the balance along with the profit or social contribution from the ones who enter college. Every decision is really a choice between treatments. Predicting outcome has no social value unless the psychologist or the subject himself can use the information to make better choices of treatment. The prediction must help to determine a treatment for every individual.

Even when there are just two treatments, the payoff functions have many possible relationships. In Figure 6 we have a mean difference between treatments, and a valid predictor. The predictor—though valid—is useless. We should give everyone Treatment A. In Figure 7, on the other hand, we should divide the group and give different treatments. This gives greater payoff than either treatment used uniformly will give.

Assigning everyone to the treatment with the highest average, as the experimentalist tends to recommend, is rarely the best decision. In

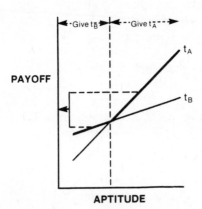

Figure 7. Payoff functions for two treatments.

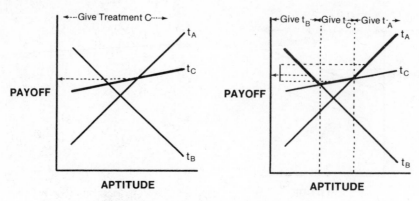

Figure 8. Payoff function for three treatments.

Figure 8, Treatment C has the best average, and we might assign everyone to it. The outcome is greater, however, if we assign some persons to each treatment. The psychologist making an experimental comparison arrives at the wrong conclusion if he ignores the aptitude variable and recommends C as a standard treatment.

Applied psychologists should deal with treatments and persons simultaneously. Treatments are characterized by many dimensions; so are persons. The two sets of dimensions together determine a payoff surface. For any practical problem, there is some best group of treatments to use and some best allocation of persons to treatments. We can expect some attributes of persons to have strong interactions with treatment variables. These attributes have far greater practical importance than the attributes which have little or no interaction. In dividing pupils between college preparatory and noncollege studies, for example, a general intelligence test is probably the wrong thing to use. This test, being general, predicts success in all subjects, therefore tends to have little interaction with treatment, and if so is not the best guide to differential treatment. We require a measure of aptitude which predicts who will learn better from one curriculum than from the other; but this aptitude remains to be discovered. Ultimately we should *design* treatments, not to fit the average person, but to fit groups of students with particular aptitude patterns. Conversely, we should seek out the aptitudes which correspond to (interact with) modifiable aspects of the treatment.

My argument rests on the assumption that such aptitude-treatment interactions exist. There is, scattered in the literature, a remarkable amount of evidence of significant, predictable differences in the way people learn. We have only limited success in predicting which of two *tasks* a person can perform better, when we allow enough training to compensate for differences in past attainment. But we do find that a person learns more easily from one *method* than another, that this best method differs from person to person, and that such between-treatments differences are correlated with tests of ability and personality. The studies showing interaction between personality and conditions of learning have burgeoned in the past few years, and the literature is much too voluminous to review in passing. Just one recent finding will serve in the way of specific illustration, a study done by Wolfgang Böhm at Vienna (38, pp. 58–59). He showed his experimental groups a sound film about the adventures of a small boy and his toy elephant at the zoo. At each age level, a matched control group read a verbatim text of the sound track. The differences in average comprehension between the audiovisual and the text presentations were trivial. There was, however, a marked interaction. For some reason yet unexplained, a general mental test correlated only .30 with text learning, but it predicted film learning with an average correlation of .77.[2] The difference was consistent at all ages.

Such findings as this, when replicated and explained, will carry us into an educational psychology which measures readiness for different types of teaching and which invents teaching methods to fit different types of readiness. In general, unless one treatment is clearly best for everyone, treatments should be differentiated in such a way as to maximize their interaction with aptitude variables. Conversely, persons should be allocated on the basis of those aptitudes which have the greatest interaction with treatment variables. I believe we will find these aptitudes to be quite unlike our present aptitude measures chosen to predict differences *within* highly correlated treatments.

The Shape of a United Discipline

It is not enough for each discipline to borrow from the other. Correlational psychology studies only variance among organisms; experimental psychology studies only variance among treatments. A united discipline will study both of these, but it will also be concerned with the otherwise neglected interactions between organismic and treatment variables (41). Our job is to invent constructs and to form a network of laws which permits prediction. From observations we must infer a psychological description of the situation and of the present state of the organism. Our laws should permit us to predict, from this description, the behavior of organism-in-situation.

There was a time when experimental psychologists concerned themselves wholly with general, nonindividual constructs, and correlational psychologists sought laws wholly within developmental variables. More and more, nowadays, their investigations are coming to bear on the same targets. One psychologist measures ego involvement by a personality test and compares the behavior of high- and low-scoring subjects. Another psychologist heightens ego involvement experimentally in one

---

2. Personal communication.

of two equated groups and studies the consequent differences in behavior. Both investigators can test the same theoretical propositions, and to the extent that their results agree they may regard both procedures as embodiments of the same construct.

Constructs originating in differential psychology are now being tied to experimental variables. As a result, the whole theoretical picture in such an area as human abilities is changing. Piaget (37) correlates reasoning processes with age and discovers a developmental sequence of schemata whose emergence permits operational thought; Harlow (24) begins actually to create similar schemata in monkeys by means of suitable training. It now becomes possible to pursue in the controllable monkey environment the questions raised by Piaget's unique combination of behavioral testing and interviewing, and ultimately to unite the psychology of intelligence with the psychology of learning.

Methodologies for a joint discipline have already been proposed. R. B. Cattell (8) has offered the most thorough discussion of how a correlationist might organize data about treatment and organism simultaneously. His factor analytic procedures are only one of many choices, however, which modern statistics offers. The experimenters, some of them, have likewise seen the necessity for a united discipline. In the very issue of *Psychological Review* where the much-too-famous distinction between S-R and R-R laws was introduced, Bergmann and Spence (3) declared that (at the present stage of psychological knowledge) the equation $R = f(S)$ must be expanded into

$$R = f(S, T, D, I)$$

The added variables are innate differences, motivation, and past experience—differential variables all. Hull (26, 27) sought general laws just as did Wundt, but he added that organismic factors can and must be accounted for. He proposed to do this by changing the constants of his equations with each individual. This is a bold plan, but one which has not yet been implemented in even a limited way. It is of interest that both Hull (27, p. 116) and Tolman (47, p. 26) have stated specifically that for their purposes factor analytic methods seem to have little promise. Tucker, though, has at least drawn blueprints of a method for deriving Hull's own individual parameters by factor analysis (48). Clearly, we have much to learn about the most suitable way to develop a united theory, but we have no lack of exciting possibilities.

The experimenter tends to keep his eye on *ultimate* theory. Woodworth once described psychological laws in terms of the S-O-R formula which specifically recognizes the individual. The revised version of his *Experimental Psychology* (53, p. 3), however, advocates an S-A-R formula, where A stands for "antecedent conditions." This formulation, which is generally congenial to experimenters, reduces the present state of the organism to an intervening variable (Figure 9). A theory of this type is in principle entirely adequate to explain, predict, and control the

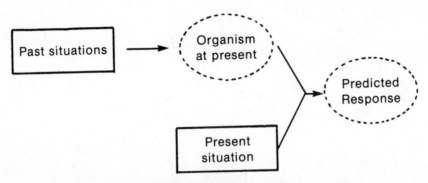

Figure 9. Theoretical model for prediction from historic data.

behavior of organisms; but, oddly enough, it is a theory which can account only for the behavior of organisms of the next generation, who have not yet been conceived. The psychologist turns to a different type of law (Figure 10) whenever he deals with a subject whose life history he has not controlled or observed in every detail. A theory which involves only laws of this type, while suitable for prediction, has very limited explanatory value. The theory psychology really requires is a redundant network like Figure 11. This network permits us to predict from the past experience or present characteristics of the organism, or a combination of the two, depending on what is known. Filling in such a network is

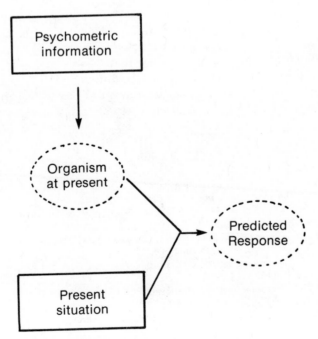

Figure 10. Theoretical model for prediction from historic data.

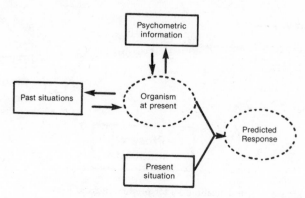

Figure 11. Theoretical network to be developed by a united discipline.

clearly a task for the joint efforts of experimental and correlational psychology.

In both applied work and general scientific work, psychology requires combined, not parallel, labors from our two historic disciplines. In this common labor, they will almost certainly become one, with a common theory, a common method, and common recommendations for social betterment. In the search for interactions we will invent new treatment dimensions and discover new dimensions of the organism. We will come to realize that organism and treatment are an inseparable pair and that no psychologist can dismiss one or the other as error variance.

Despite our specializations, every scientific psychologist must take the same scene into his field of vision. Clark Hull, three sentences before the end of his *Essentials of Behavior* (27, p. 116), voiced just this need. Because of delay in developing methodology, he said, individual differences have played little part in behavior theory, and "a sizeable segment of behavioral science remains practically untouched." This untouched segment contains the question we really want to put to Nature, and she will never answer until our two disciplines ask it in a single voice.

REFERENCES

1. Bartlett, F. C.   Fifty years of psychology. *Occup. Psychol.*, 1955, 29, 203–216.
2. Beach, F. A.   The snark was a boojum. *Amer. Psychologist*, 1950, 5, 115–124.
3. Bergmann, G., & Spence, K. W.   The logic of psychophysical measurement. *Psychol. Rev.*, 1944, 51, 1–24.
4. Bindra, D., & Scheier, I. H.   The relation between psychometric and experimental research in psychology. *Amer. Psychologist*, 1954, 9, 69–71.
5. Boring, E. G.   *History of experimental psychology.* (2nd ed.) New York: Appleton-Century-Crofts, 1950.
6. Brunswik, E.   *Perception and the representative design of psychological experiments.* Berkeley: Univer. California Press, 1956.
7. Cattell, J. McK.   The biological problems of today: Psychology. *Science*, 1898, 7, 152–154.

8. Cattell, R. B. *Factor analysis.* New York: Harper, 1952.

9. Clark, K. E. *America's psychologists.* Washington, D.C.: APA, 1957.

10. Corwin, E. S. The impact of the idea of evolution on the American political and constitutional tradition. In S. Persons (Ed.), *Evolutionary thought in America.* New Haven: Yale Univer. Press, 1950. Pp. 182–201.

11. Cronbach, L. J., & Gleser, Goldine C. *Psychological tests and personnel decisions.* Urbana: Univer. Illinois Press, 1957.

12. Cronbach, L. J., & Meehl, P. E. Construct validity in psychological tests. *Psychol. Bull.,* 1955, *52,* 281–302.

13. Cronbach, L. J., & Neff, W. D. Selection and training. In Com. on Undersea Warfare Panel on Psychology and Physiology, *Human Factors in Undersea Warfare.* Washington, D.C.: Nat. Res. Coun., 1949. Pp. 491–516.

14. Daniel, R. S., & Louttit, C. M. *Professional problems in psychology.* New York: Prentice-Hall, 1953.

15. Dashiell, J. F. Some rapprochements in contemporary psychology. *Psychol. Bull.,* 1939, *36,* 1–24.

16. Dewey, J. *Studies in logical theory.* Chicago: Univer. Chicago Press, 1903.

17. Dewey, J. *The influence of Darwin on philosophy and other essays.* New York: Holt, 1910.

18. Eysenck, H. J. Reminiscence, drive, and personality theory. *J. abnorm. soc. Psychol.,* 1956, *53,* 328–333.

19. Ferguson, G. A. On learning and human ability. *Canad. J. Psychol.,* 1954, *8,* 95–112.

20. Ferguson, G. A. On transfer and human ability. *Canad. J. Psychol.,* 1956, *10,* 121–131.

21. Fleishman, E. A. Predicting advanced levels of proficiency in psychomotor skills. In *Proc. Sympos. on Human Engng.* Washington, D.C.: Nat. Acad. Sci., 1956. Pp. 142–151.

22. Fleishman, E. A., & Hempel, W. E., Jr. Changes in factor structure of a complex psychomotor test as a function of practice. *Psychometrika,* 1954, *19,* 239–252.

23. Ford, C. S., & Beach, F. A. *Patterns of sexual behavior.* New York: Harper, 1952.

24. Harlow, H. F. The formation of learning sets. *Psychol. Rev.,* 1949, *56,* 51–65.

25. Harlow, H. F. Mice, men, monkeys, and motives. *Psychol. Rev.,* 1953, *60,* 23–32.

26. Hull, C. L. The place of innate individual and species differences in a natural-science theory of behavior. *Psychol. Rev.,* 1945, *52,* 55–60.

27. Hull, C. L. *Essentials of behavior.* New Haven: Yale Univer. Press, 1951.

28. Laugier, H. (Ed.) *L'analyse factorielle et ses applications.* Paris: Centre National de la Recherche Scientifique, 1955.

29. Lazarus, R. S., & Baker, R. W. Personality and psychological stress—a theoretical and methodological framework. *Psychol. Newsletter,* 1956, *8,* 21–32.

30. McCandless, B. R., & Spiker, C. C. Experimental research in child psychology. *Child Develpm.,* 1956, *27,* 75–80.

31. McClelland, D. C. Personality. In P. R. Farnsworth (Ed.) *Annu. Rev. Psychol.,* 1956. Stanford: Annual Reviews, 1956. Pp. 39–62.

32. Miller, N. E. Effects of drugs on motivation: The value of using a variety of measures. *Ann. N.Y. Acad. Sci.,* 1956, *65,* 318–333.

33. Miller, N. E. Liberalization of basic S–R concepts: Extensions to conflict behavior and social learning. In S. Koch (Ed.), *Psychology: A study of a science.* Vol. II. *General systematic formulations, learning, and special processes.* New York: McGraw-Hill, in press.

34. Miller, N. E. Objective techniques for studying motivational effects of drugs on animals. In E. Trabucchi (Ed.), *Proc. Int. Sympos. on Psychotropic Drugs.* Amsterdam, Netherlands: Elsevier Publishing Co., in press.

35. Murphy, G. *An historical introduction to modern psychology.* (3rd ed.) New York: Harcourt, Brace, 1932.

36. Pastore, N. *The nature-nurture controversy.* New York: Kings Crown Press, 1949.

37. Piaget, J. *Psychology of intelligence.* M. Piercy & D. E. Berlyne (Trans.). London: Routledge and Kegan Paul, 1950.

38. Rohracher, H.   Aus der wissenschaftlichen Arbeit des Psychologischen Institutes der Universität Wien. *Wiener Z. Phil., Psychol., Pädag.*, 1956, *6*, 1-66.
39. Scoon, R.   The rise and impact of evolutionary ideas. In S. Persons (Ed.), *Evolutionary thought in America*. New Haven, Yale Univer. Press, 1950. Pp. 4-43.
40. Selye, H.   Stress and disease. *Science*, 1955, *122*, 625-631.
41. Shen, E.   The place of individual differences in experimentation. In Q. McNemar & M. A. Merrill (Eds.), *Studies in personality*. New York: McGraw-Hill, 1942. Pp. 259-283.
42. Spengler, J. J.   Evolutionism in American economics. In S. Persons (Ed.), *Evolutionary thought in America*. New Haven: Yale Univer. Press, 1950. Pp. 202-266.
43. Terman, L. M.   The mental test as a psychological method. *Psychol. Rev.*, 1924, *31*, 93-117.
44. Thorndike, R. L.   The psychological value systems of psychologists. *Amer. Psychologist*, 1954, *9*, 787-790.
45. Thurstone, L. L.   The stimulus-response fallacy in psychology. *Psychol. Rev.*, 1923, *30*, 354-369.
46. Titchener, E. B.   The past decade in experimental psychology. *Amer. J. Psychol.*, 1910, *21*, 404-421.
47. Tolman, E. C.   The determinants of behavior at a choice point. *Psychol. Rev.*, 1938, *45*, 1-41.
48. Tucker, L. R.   Determination of parameters of a functional relation by factor analysis. *ETS Res. Bull.*, 1955, *55*, No. 10.
49. Tyler, R. W.   Can intelligence tests be used to predict educability? In K. Eells et al., *Intelligence and cultural differences*. Chicago: Univer. Chicago Press, 1951. Pp. 39-47.
50. Wenger, M. A., Clemens, T. L., & Engel, B. T.   Autonomic response patterns to four stimuli. Unpublished manuscript, 1957.
51. Woodworth, R. S.   *Dynamic psychology*. New York: Holt, 1918.
52. Woodworth, R. S.   *Experimental psychology*. New York: Holt, 1938.
53. Woodworth, R. S., & Schlosberg, H.   *Experimental psychology*. (2nd ed.) New York: Holt, 1954.
54. Wundt, W.   *Principles of physiological psychology*. Vol. 1. (5th ed.) E. B. Titchener (Trans.) New York: Macmillan, 1904.
55. Yerkes, R. M.   Comparative psychology: A question of definitions. *J. Phil. Psychol., and sci. Methods*, 1913, *10*, 580-582.
56. Yerkes, R. M.   The study of human behavior. *Science*, 1914, *29*, 625-633.

Reprinted with permission
from *American Psychologist*,
1958, *13*, 673–685.

Chapter 23

The Nature of Love

Harry F. Harlow

University of Wisconsin

Love is a wondrous state, deep, tender, and rewarding. Because of its intimate and personal nature it is regarded by some as an improper topic for experimental research. But, whatever our personal feelings may be, our assigned mission as psychologists is to analyze all facets of human and animal behavior into their component variables. So far as love or affection is concerned, psychologists have failed in this mission. The little we know about love does not transcend simple observation, and the little we write about it has been written better by poets and novelists. But of greater concern is the fact that psychologists tend to give progressively less attention to a motive

Address of the President at the sixty-sixth Annual Convention of the American Psychological Association, Washington, D. C., August 31, 1958.

The researches reported in this paper were supported by funds supplied by Grant No. M-722, National Institutes of Health, by a grant from the Ford Foundation, and by funds received from the Graduate School of the University of Wisconsin.

which pervades our entire lives. Psychologists, at least psychologists who write textbooks, not only show no interest in the origin and development of love or affection, but they seem to be unaware of its very existence.

The apparent repression of love by modern psychologists stands in sharp contrast with the attitude taken by many famous and normal people. The word "love" has the highest reference frequency of any word cited in Bartlett's book of *Familiar Quotations*. It would appear that this emotion has long had a vast interest and fascination for human beings, regardless of the attitude taken by psychologists; but the quotations cited, even by famous and normal people, have a mundane redundancy. These authors and authorities have stolen love from the child and infant and made it the exclusive property of the adolescent and adult.

Thoughtful men, and probably all women, have speculated on the nature of love. From the developmental point of view, the general plan is quite clear: The initial love responses of the human being are those made by the infant to the mother or some mother surrogate. From this intimate attachment of the child to the mother, multiple learned and generalized affectional responses are formed.

Unfortunately, beyond these simple facts we know little about the fundamental variables underlying the formation of affectional responses and little about the mechanisms through which the love of the infant for the mother develops into the multifaceted response patterns characterizing love or affection in the adult. Because of the dearth of experimentation, theories about the fundamental nature of affection have evolved at the level of observation, intuition, and discerning guesswork, whether these have been proposed by psychologists, sociologists, anthropologists, physicians, or psychoanalysts.

The position commonly held by psychologists and sociologists is quite clear: The basic motives are, for the most part, the primary drives—particularly hunger, thirst, elimination, pain, and sex—and all other motives, including love or affection, are derived or secondary drives. The mother is associated with the reduction of the primary drives—particularly hunger, thirst, and pain—and through learning, affection or love is derived.

It is entirely reasonable to believe that the mother through association with food may become a secondary-reinforcing agent, but this is an inadequate mechanism to account for the persistence of the infant-maternal ties. There is a spate of researches on the formation of secondary reinforcers to hunger and thirst reduction. There can be no question that almost any external stimulus can become a secondary reinforcer if properly associated with tissue-need reduction, but the fact remains that this redundant literature demonstrates unequivocally that such derived drives suffer relatively rapid experimental extinction. Contrariwise, human affection does not extinguish when the mother ceases to have intimate association with the drives in question. Instead, the affectional ties to the mother show a lifelong, unrelenting persistence and, even more surprising, widely expanding generality.

Oddly enough, one of the few psychologists who took a position counter to modern psychological dogma was John B. Watson, who believed that love was an innate emotion elicited by cutaneous stimulation of the erogenous zones. But experimental psychologists, with their peculiar propensity to discover facts that are not true, brushed this theory aside by demonstrating that the human neonate had no differentiable emotions, and they established a fundamental psychological law that prophets are without honor in their own profession.

The psychoanalysts have concerned themselves with the problem of the nature of the development of love in the neonate and infant, using ill and aging human beings as subjects. They have discovered the overwhelming importance of the breast and related this to the oral erotic tendencies developed at an age preceding their subjects' memories. Their theories range from a belief that the infant has an innate need to achieve and suckle at the breast to beliefs not unlike commonly accepted psychological theories. There are exceptions, as seen in the recent writings of John Bowlby, who attributes importance not only to food and thirst satisfaction, but also to "primary object-clinging," a need for intimate physical contact, which is initially associated with the mother.

As far as I know, there exists no direct experimental analysis of the relative importance of the stimulus variables determining the affectional or love responses in the neonatal and infant primate. Unfortunately, the human neonate is a limited experimental subject for such researches because of his inadequate motor capabilities. By the time the human infant's motor responses can be precisely measured, the antecedent determining conditions cannot be defined, having been lost in a jumble and jungle of confounded variables.

Many of these difficulties can be resolved by the use of the neonatal and infant macaque monkey as the subject for the analysis of basic affectional variables. It is possible to make precise measurements in this primate beginning at two to ten days of age, depending upon the maturational status of the individual animal at birth. The macaque infant differs from the human infant in that the monkey is more mature at birth and grows more rapidly; but the basic responses relating to affection, including nursing, contact, clinging, and even visual and auditory exploration, exhibit no fundamental differences in the two species. Even the development of perception, fear, frustration, and learning capability follows very similar sequences in rhesus monkeys and human children.

Three years' experimentation before we started our studies on affection gave us experience with the neonatal monkey. We had separated more than 60 of these animals from their mothers 6 to 12 hours after birth and suckled them on tiny bottles. The infant mortality was only a small fraction of what would have obtained had we let the monkey mothers raise their infants. Our bottle-fed babies were healthier and heavier than monkey-mother-reared infants. We know that we are better monkey mothers than are real monkey mothers thanks to synthetic diets, vitamins, iron extracts, penicillin, chloromycetin, 5% glucose, and constant, tender, loving care.

During the course of these studies we noticed that the laboratory-

Figure 1. Response to cloth pad by one-day-old monkey.

raised babies showed strong attachment to the cloth pads (folded gauze diapers) which were used to cover the hardware-cloth floors of their cages. The infants clung to these pads and engaged in violet temper tantrums when the pads were removed and replaced for sanitary reasons. Such contact-need or responsiveness had been reported previously by Gertrude van Wagenen for the monkey and by Thomas McCulloch and George Haslerud for the chimpanzee and is reminiscent of the devotion often exhibited by human infants to their pillows, blankets, and soft, cuddly stuffed toys. Responsiveness by the one-day-old infant monkey to the cloth pad is shown in Figure 1, and an unusual and strong attachment of a six-month-old infant to the cloth pad is illustrated in Figure 2. The baby, human or monkey, if it is to survive, must clutch at more than a straw.

We had also discovered during some allied observational studies that a baby monkey raised on a bare wire-mesh cage floor survives with difficulty, if at all, during the first five days of life. If a wire-mesh cone is introduced, the baby does better; and, if the cone is covered with terry cloth, husky, healthy, happy babies evolve. It takes more than a baby and a box to make a normal monkey. We were impressed by the possibility that, above and beyond the bubbling fountain of breast or bottle, contact comfort might be a very important variable in the development of the infant's affection for the mother.

At this point we decided to study the development of affectional responses of neonatal and infant monkeys to an artificial, inanimate mother, and so we built a surrogate mother which we hoped and believed would be a good surrogate mother. In devising this surrogate mother we were dependent neither upon the capriciousness of evolutionary processes nor upon mutations produced by chance radioactive fallout. Instead, we designed the mother surrogate in terms of modern human-engineering principles (Figure 3). We produced a perfectly pro-

portioned, streamlined body stripped of unnecessary bulges and ap-
pendices. Redundancy in the surrogate mother's system was avoided by
reducing the number of breasts from two to one and placing this
unibreast in an upper-thoracic, sagittal position, thus maximizing the
natural and known perceptual-motor capabilities of the infant operator.
The surrogate was made from a block of wood, covered with sponge
rubber, and sheathed in tan cotton terry cloth. A light bulb behind her
radiated heat. The result was a mother, soft, warm, and tender, a mother
with infinite patience, a mother available twenty-four hours a day, a
mother that never scolded her infant and never struck or bit her baby in
anger. Furthermore, we designed a mother-machine with maximal maintenance efficiency since failure of any system or function could be
resolved by the simple substitution of black boxes and new component
parts. It is our opinion that we engineered a very superior monkey
mother, although this position is not held universally by the monkey
fathers.

Before beginning our initial experiment we also designed and
constructed a second mother surrogate, a surrogate in which we deliberately built less than the maximal capability for contact comfort. This
surrogate mother is illustrated in Figure 4. She is made of wire-mesh, a
substance entirely adequate to provide postural support and nursing
capability, and she is warmed by radiant heat. Her body differs in no
essential way from that of the cloth mother surrogate other than in the
quality of the contact comfort which she can supply.

In our initial experiment, the dual mother-surrogate condition, a
cloth mother and a wire mother were placed in different cubicles
attached to the infant's living cage as shown in Figure 4. For four
newborn monkeys the cloth mother lactated and the wire mother did
not; and, for the other four, this condition was reversed. In either
condition the infant received all its milk through the mother surrogate as

Figure 2. Response to gauze pad by six-month-old monkey used in earlier study.

Figure 3. Cloth mother surrogate.

Figure 4. Wire and cloth mother surrogates.

soon as it was able to maintain itself in this way, a capability achieved within two or three days except in the case of very immature infants. Supplementary feedings were given until the milk intake from the mother surrogate was adequate. Thus, the experiment was designed as a test of the relative importance of the variables of contact comfort and nursing comfort. During the first 14 days of life the monkey's cage floor was covered with a heating pad wrapped in a folded gauze diaper, and thereafter the cage floor was bare. The infants were always free to leave the heating pad or cage floor to contact either mother, and the time spent on the surrogate mothers was automatically recorded. Figure 5 shows the total time spent on the cloth and wire mothers under the two conditions of feeding. These data make it obvious that contact comfort is a variable of overwhelming importance in the development of affectional responses, whereas lactation is a variable of negligible importance. With age and opportunity to learn, subjects with the lactating wire mother showed decreasing responsiveness to her and increasing responsiveness to the nonlactating cloth mother, a finding completely contrary to any interpretation of derived drive in which the mother-form becomes conditioned to hunger–thirst reduction. The persistence of these differential responses throughout 165 consecutive days of testing is evident in Figure 6.

One control group of neonatal monkeys was raised on a single wire mother, and a second control group was raised on a single cloth mother. There were no differences between these two groups in amount of milk ingested or in weight gain. The only difference between the groups lay in the composition of the feces, the softer stools of the wire-mother infants suggesting psychosomatic involvement. The wire mother is biologically adequate but psychologically inept.

We were not surprised to discover that contact comfort was an important basic affectional or love variable, but we did not expect it to overshadow so completely the variable of nursing; indeed, the disparity is so great as to suggest that the primary function of nursing as an affectional variable is that of insuring frequent and intimate body contact of the infant with the mother. Certainly, man cannot live by milk alone. Love is an emotion that does not need to be bottle- or spoon-fed, and we

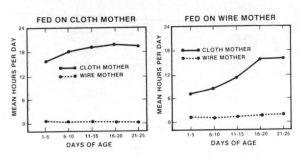

Figure 5. Time spent on cloth and wire mother surrogates.

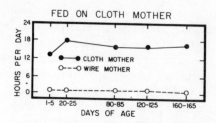

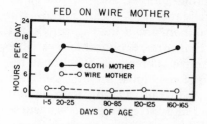

Figure 6. Long-term contact time on cloth and wire mother surrogates.

may be sure that there is nothing to be gained by giving lip service to love.

A charming lady once heard me describe these experiments; and, when I subsequently talked to her, her face brightened with sudden insight: "Now I know what's wrong with me," she said, "I'm just a wire mother." Perhaps she was lucky. She might have been a wire wife.

We believe that contact comfort has long served the animal kingdom as a motivating agent for affectional responses. Since at the present time we have no experimental data to substantiate this position, we supply information which must be accepted, if at all, on the basis of face validity:

The Hippopotamus

From *Look*, August 19, 1958.

This is the skin some babies feel
Replete with hippo love appeal.
Each contact, cuddle, push, and shove
Elicits tons of baby love.

From *Zoo Guide*, Zoological Society of London

The Rhinocerus

The rhino's skin is thick and tough,
And yet this skin is soft enough
That baby rhinos always sense,
A love enormous and intense.

From *All about Snakes* E. M. Hale & Co.

The Snake

To baby vipers, scaly skin
Engenders love 'twixt kith and kin.
Each animal by God is blessed
With kind of skin it loves the best.

The Elephant   Ylla

Though mother may be short on arms,
Her skin is full of warmth and charms.
And mother's touch on baby's skin
Endears the heart that beats within.

The Crocodile   Sponholz

Here is the skin they love to touch.
It isn't soft and there isn't much,
But its contact comfort will beguile
Love from the infant crocodile.

You see, all God's chillun's got skin.

One function of the real mother, human or subhuman, and presumably of a mother surrogate, is to provide a haven of safety for the infant in times of fear and danger. The frightened or ailing child clings to its mother, not its father; and this selective responsiveness in times of distress, disturbance, or danger may be used as a measure of the strength of affectional bonds. We have tested this kind of differential responsiveness by presenting to the infants in their cages, in the presence of the two mothers, various fear-producing stimuli such as the moving toy bear illustrated in Figure 13. A typical response to a fear stimulus is shown in Figure 14, and the data on differential responsiveness are presented in Figure 15. It is apparent that the cloth mother is highly preferred over the wire one, and this differential selectivity is enhanced by age and experience. In this situation, the variable of nursing appears to be of absolutely no importance: the infant consistently seeks the soft mother surrogate regardless of nursing condition.

Similarly, the mother or mother surrogate provides its young with a source of security, and this role or function is seen with special clarity when mother and child are in a strange situation. At the present time we have completed tests for this relationship on four of our eight baby monkeys assigned to the dual mother-surrogate condition by introducing

Figure 13. Typical fear stimulus.

them for three minutes into the strange environment of a room measuring six feet by six feet by six feet (also called the "open-field test") and containing multiple stimuli known to elicit curiosity-manipulatory responses in baby monkeys. The subjects were placed in this situation twice a week for eight weeks with no mother surrogate present during alternate sessions and the cloth mother present during the others. A cloth diaper was always available as one of the stimuli throughout all sessions. After one or two adaptation sessions, the infants always rushed to the mother surrogate when she was present and clutched her, rubbed their bodies against her, and frequently manipulated her body and face. After a few additional sessions, the infants began to use the mother surrogate as a source of security, a base of operations. As is shown in Figures 16 and 17, they would explore and manipulate a stimulus and then return to the mother before adventuring again into the strange new world. The behavior of these infants was quite different when the mother was absent from the room. Frequently they would freeze in a crouched position, as is illustrated in Figures 18 and 19. Emotionality indices such as vocalization, crouching, rocking, and sucking increased sharply, as shown in Figure 20. Total emotionality score was cut in half when the mother was present. In the absence of the mother some of the experimental monkeys would rush to the center of the room where the mother was customarily placed and then run rapidly from object to object, screaming and crying all the while. Continuous, frantic clutching of their

Figure 14. Typical response to cloth mother surrogate in fear test.

bodies was very common, even when not in the crouching position. These monkeys frequently contacted and clutched the cloth diaper, but this action never pacified them. The same behavior occurred in the presence of the wire mother. No difference between the cloth-mother-fed and wire-mother-fed infants was demonstrated under either condition. Four control infants never raised with a mother surrogate showed the same emotionality scores when the mother was absent as the experimen-

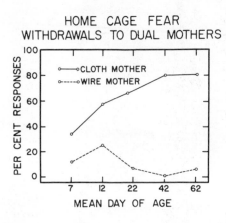

Figure 15. Differential responsiveness in fear tests.

Figure 16. Response to cloth mother in the open-field test.

tal infants showed in the absence of the mother, but the controls' scores were slightly larger in the presence of the mother surrogate than in her absence.

Some years ago Robert Butler demonstrated that mature monkeys enclosed in a dimly lighted box would open and reopen a door hour after hour for no other reward than that of looking outside the box. We now have data indicating that neonatal monkeys show this same compulsive visual curiosity on their first test day in an adaptation of the Butler apparatus which we call the "love machine," an apparatus designed to measure love. Usually these tests are begun when the monkey is 10 days of age, but this same persistent visual exploration has been obtained in a three-day-old monkey during the first half-hour of testing. Butler also

Figure 17. Object exploration in presence of cloth mother.

Figure 18. Response in the open-field test in the absence of the mother surrogate.

demonstrated that rhesus monkeys show selectivity in rate and frequency of door-opening to stimuli of differential attractiveness in the visual field outside the box. We have utilized this principle of response selectivity by the monkey to measure strength of affectional responsiveness in our infants in the baby version of the Butler box. The test sequence involves four repetitions of a test battery in which four stimuli—cloth mother, wire mother, infant monkey, and empty box—are presented for a 30-minute period on successive days. The first four subjects in the dual mother-surrogate group were given a single test sequence at 40 to 50 days of age, depending upon the availability of the apparatus, and only their data are presented. The second set of four subjects is being given repetitive tests to obtain information relating to

Figure 19. Response in the open-field test in the absence of the mother surrogate.

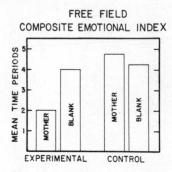

Figure 20. Emotionality index with and without the presence of the cloth mother.

the development of visual exploration. The apparatus is illustrated in Figure 21. The data obtained from the first four infants raised with the two mother surrogates are presented in the middle graph of Figure 22 and show approximately equal responding to the cloth mother and another infant monkey, and no greater responsiveness to the wire mother than to an empty box. Again, the results are independent of the kind of mother that lactated, cloth or wire. The same results are found for a control group raised, but not fed, on a single cloth mother; these data

Figure 21. Visual exploration apparatus.

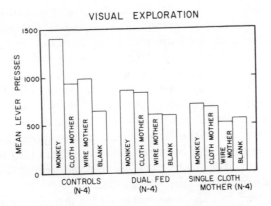

Figure 22. Differential responses to visual exploration.

appear in the graph on the right. Contrariwise, the graph on the left shows no differential responsiveness to cloth and wire mothers by a second control group, which was not raised on any mother surrogate. We can be certain that not all love is blind.

The first four infant monkeys in the dual mother-surrogate group were separated from their mothers between 165 and 170 days of age and tested for retention during the following 9 days and then at 30-day intervals for six successive months. Affectional retention as measured by the modified Butler box is given in Figure 23. In keeping with the data obtained on adult monkeys by Butler, we find a high rate of responding to any stimulus, even the empty box. But throughout the entire 185-day retention period there is a consistent and significant difference in response frequency to the cloth mother contrasted with either the wire mother or the empty box, and no consistent difference between wire mother and empty box.

Affectional retention was also tested in the open field during the first 9 days after separation and then at 30-day intervals, and each test condition was run twice at each retention interval. The infant's behavior

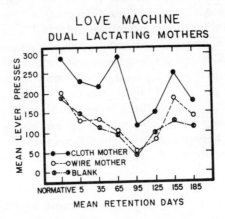

Figure 23. Retention of differential visual-exploration responses.

differed from that observed during the period preceding separation. When the cloth mother was present in the post-separation period, the babies rushed to her, climbed up, clung tightly to her, and rubbed their heads and faces against her body. After this initial embrace and reunion, they played on the mother, including biting and tearing at her cloth cover; but they rarely made any attempt to leave her during the test period, nor did they manipulate or play with the objects in the room, in contrast with their behavior before maternal separation. The only exception was the occasional monkey that left the mother surrogate momentarily, grasped the folded piece of paper (one of the standard stimuli in the field), and brought it quickly back to the mother. It appeared that deprivation had enhanced the tie to the mother and rendered the contact-comfort need so prepotent that need for the mother overwhelmed the exploratory motives during the brief, three-minute test sessions. No change in these behaviors was observed throughout the 185-day period. When the mother was absent from the open field, the behavior of the infants was similar in the initial retention test to that during the preseparation tests; but they tended to show gradual adaptation to the open-field situation with repeated testing and, consequently, a reduction in their emotionality scores.

In the last five retention test periods, an additional test was introduced in which the surrogate mother was placed in the center of the room and covered with a clear Plexiglas box. The monkeys were initially disturbed and frustrated when their explorations and manipulations of the box failed to provide contact with the mother. However, all animals adapted to the situation rather rapidly. Soon they used the box as a place of orientation for exploratory and play behavior, made frequent contacts with the objects in the field, and very often brought these objects to the Plexiglas box. The emotionality index was slightly higher than in the condition of the available cloth mothers, but it in no way approached the emotionality level displayed when the cloth mother was absent. Obviously, the infant monkeys gained emotional security by the presence of the mother even though contact was denied.

Affectional retention has also been measured by tests in which the monkey must unfasten a three-device mechanical puzzle to obtain entrance into a compartment containing the mother surrogate. All the trials are initiated by allowing the infant to go through an unlocked door, and in half the trials it finds the mother present and in half, an empty compartment. The door is then locked and a ten-minute test conducted. In tests given prior to separation from the surrogate mothers, some of the infants had solved this puzzle and others had failed. The data of Figure 24 show that on the last test before separation there were no differences in total manipulation under mother-present and mother-absent conditions, but striking differences exist between the two conditions throughout the post-separation test periods. Again, there is no interaction with conditions of feeding.

The over-all picture obtained from surveying the retention data is unequivocal. There is little, if any, waning of responsiveness to the

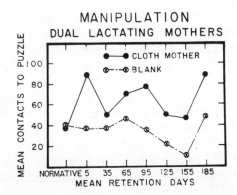

Figure 24. Retention of puzzle manipulation responsiveness.

mother throughout this five-month period as indicated by any measure. It becomes perfectly obvious that this affectional bond is highly resistant to forgetting and that it can be retained for very long periods of time by relatively infrequent contact reinforcement. During the next year, retention tests will be conducted at 90-day intervals, and further plans are dependent upon the results obtained. It would appear that affectional responses may show as much resistance to extinction as has been previously demonstrated for learned fears and learned pain, and such data would be in keeping with those of common human observation.

The infant's responses to the mother surrogate in the fear tests, the open-field situation, and the baby Butler box and the responses on the retention tests cannot be described adequately with words. For supplementary information we turn to the motion picture record. (At this point a 20-minute film was presented illustrating and supplementing the behaviors described thus far in the address.)

We have already described the group of four control infants that had never lived in the presence of any mother surrogate and had demonstrated no sign of affection or security in the presence of the cloth mothers introduced in test sessions. When these infants reached the age of 250 days, cubicles containing both a cloth mother and a wire mother were attached to their cages. There was no lactation in these mothers, for the monkeys were on a solid-food diet. The initial reaction of the monkeys to the alterations was one of extreme disturbance. All the infants screamed violently and made repeated attempts to escape the cage whenever the door was opened. They kept a maximum distance from the mother surrogates and exhibited a considerable amount of rocking and crouching behavior, indicative of emotionality. Our first thought was that the critical period for the development of maternally directed affection had passed and that these macaque children were doomed to live as affectional orphans. Fortunately, these behaviors continued for only 12 to 48 hours and then gradually ebbed, changing from indifference to active contact on, and exploration of, the surrogates. The home-cage behavior of these control monkeys slowly became similar to that of the animals raised with the mother surrogates from birth. Their manipulation and play on the cloth mother became progressively more vigorous to the point of actual mutilation, particularly during the morning after the cloth mother had been given her daily change of terry covering. The control subjects were now actively running to the cloth mother when frightened and had to be coaxed from her to be taken from the cage for formal testing.

Objective evidence of these changing behaviors is given in Figure 25, which plots the amount of time these infants spent on the mother surrogates. Within 10 days mean contact time is approximately nine hours, and this measure remains relatively constant throughout the next 30 days. Consistent with the results on the subjects reared from birth with dual mothers, these late-adopted infants spent less than one and one-half hours per day in contact with the wire mothers, and this activity level was relatively constant throughout the test sessions. Although the maximum time that the control monkeys spent on the cloth mother was only about half that spent by the original dual mother-surrogate group, we cannot be sure that this discrepancy is a function of differential early experience. The control monkeys were about three months older when the mothers were attached to their cages than the experimental animals had been when their mothers were removed and the retention tests begun. Thus, we do not know what the amount of contact would be for a 250-day-old animal raised from birth with surrogate mothers. Nevertheless, the magnitude of the differences and the fact that the contact-time curves for the mothered-from-birth infants had remained constant for almost 150 days suggest that early experience with the mother is a variable of measurable importance.

The control group has also been tested for differential visual exploration after the introduction of the cloth and wire mothers; these behaviors are plotted in Figure 26. By the second test session a high level of exploratory behavior had developed, and the responsiveness to the wire mother and the empty box is significantly greater than that to the cloth mother. This is probably not an artifact since there is every reason to believe that the face of the cloth mother is a fear stimulus to most

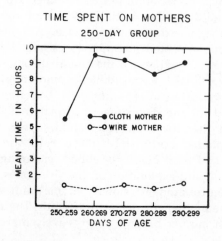

Figure 25. Differential time spent on cloth and wire mother surrogates by monkeys started at 250 days of age.

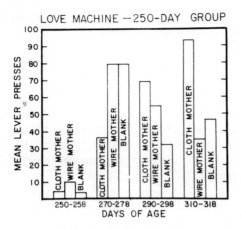

Figure 26. Differential visual exploration of monkeys started at 250 days of age.

monkeys that have not had extensive experience with this object during the first 40 to 60 days of life. Within the third test session a sharp change in trend occurs, and the cloth mother is then more frequently viewed than the wire mother or the blank box; this trend continues during the fourth session, producing a significant preference for the cloth mother.

Before the introduction of the mother surrogate into the home-cage situation, only one of the four control monkeys had ever contacted the cloth mother in the open-field tests. In general, the surrogate mother not only gave the infants no security, but instead appeared to serve as a fear stimulus. The emotionality scores of these control subjects were slightly higher during the mother-present test sessions than during the mother-absent test sessions. These behaviors were changed radically by the fourth post-introduction test approximately 60 days later. In the absence of the cloth mothers the emotionality index in this fourth test remains near the earlier level, but the score is reduced by half when the mother is present, a result strikingly similar to that found for infants raised with the dual mother-surrogates from birth. The control infants now show increasing object exploration and play behavior, and they begin to use the mother as a base of operations, as did the infants raised from birth with the mother surrogates. However, there are still definite differences in the behavior of the two groups. The control infants do not rush directly to the mother and clutch her violently; but instead they go toward, and orient around, her, usually after an initial period during which they frequently show disturbed behavior, exploratory behavior, or both.

That the control monkeys develop affection or love for the cloth mother when she is introduced into the cage at 250 days of age cannot be questioned. There is every reason to believe, however, that this interval of delay depresses the intensity of the affectional response below that of the infant monkeys that were surrogate-mothered from birth onward. In interpreting these data it is well to remember that the control monkeys had had continuous opportunity to observe and hear other monkeys housed in adjacent cages and that they had had limited opportunity to view and contact surrogate mothers in the test situations, even though they did not exploit the opportunities.

During the last two years we have observed the behavior of two infants raised by their own mothers. Love for the real mother and love for the surrogate mother appear to be very similar. The baby macaque spends many hours a day clinging to its real mother. If away from the mother when frightened, it rushes to her and in her presence shows comfort and composure. As far as we can observe, the infant monkey's affection for the real mother is strong, but no stronger than that of the experimental monkey for the surrogate cloth mother, and the security that the infant gains from the presence of the real mother is no greater than the security it gains from a cloth surrogate. Next year we hope to put this problem to final, definitive, experimental test. But, whether the mother is real or a cloth surrogate, there does develop a deep and abiding bond between mother and child. In one case it may be the call of the wild and in the other the McCall of civilization, but in both cases there is "togetherness."

In spite of the importance of contact comfort, there is reason to believe that other variables of measurable importance will be discovered. Postural support may be such a variable, and it has been suggested that, when we build arms into the mother surrogate, 10 is the minimal number required to provide adequate child care. Rocking motion may be such a variable, and we are comparing rocking and stationary mother surrogates and inclined planes. The differential responsiveness to cloth mother and cloth-covered inclined plane suggests that clinging as well as contact is an affectional variable of importance. Sounds, particularly natural, maternal sounds, may operate as either unlearned or learned affectional variables. Visual responsiveness may be such a variable, and it is possible that some semblance of visual imprinting may develop in the neonatal monkey. There are indications that this becomes a variable of importance during the course of infancy through some maturational process.

John Bowlby has suggested that there is an affectional variable which he calls "primary object following," characterized by visual and oral search of the mother's face. Our surrogate-mother-raised baby monkeys are at first inattentive to her face, as are human neonates to human mother faces. But by 30 days of age ever-increasing responsiveness to the mother's face appears—whether through learning, maturation, or both—and we have reason to believe that the face becomes an object of special attention.

Our first surrogate-mother-raised baby had a mother whose head was just a ball of wood since the baby was a month early and we had not had time to design a more esthetic head and face. This baby had contact with the blank-faced mother for 180 days and was then placed with two cloth mothers, one motionless and one rocking, both being endowed with painted, ornamented faces. To our surprise the animal would compulsively rotate both faces 180 degrees so that it viewed only a round, smooth face and never the painted, ornamented face. Further-more, it would do this as long as the patience of the experimenter in reorienting the faces persisted. The monkey showed no sign of fear or anxiety, but it showed unlimited persistence. Subsequently it improved its technique, compulsively removing the heads and rolling them into its cage as fast as they were returned. We are intrigued by this observation, and we plan to examine systematically the role of the mother face in the development of infant-monkey affections. Indeed, these observations suggest the need for a series of ethological-type researches on the two-faced female.

Although we have made no attempts thus far to study the generali-zation of infant-macaque affection or love, the techniques which we have developed offer promise in this uncharted field. Beyond this, there are few if any technical difficulties in studying the affection of the actual, living mother for the child, and the techniques developed can be utilized and expanded for the analysis and developmental study of father-infant and infant-infant affection.

Since we can measure neonatal and infant affectional responses to mother surrogates, and since we know they are strong and persisting, we are in a position to assess the effects of feeding and contactual schedules; consistency and inconsistency in the mother surrogates; and early, intermediate, and late maternal deprivation. Again, we have here a family of problems of fundamental interest and theoretical importance.

If the researches completed and proposed make a contribution, I shall be grateful; but I have also given full thought to possible practical applications. The socioeconomic demands of the present and the threat-ened socioeconomic demands of the future have led the American woman to displace, or threaten to displace, the American man in science and industry. If this process continues, the problem of proper child-rearing practices faces us with startling clarity. It is cheering in view of this trend to realize that the American male is physically endowed with all the really essential equipment to compete with the American female on equal terms in one essential activity: the rearing of infants. We now know that women in the working classes are not needed in the home because of their primary mammalian capabilities; and it is possible that in the foreseeable future neonatal nursing will not be regarded as a necessity, but as a luxury—to use Veblen's term—a form of conspicuous consumption limited perhaps to the upper classes. But whatever course history may take, it is comforting to know that we are now in contact with the nature of love.

Reprinted with permission
from *American Psychologist*,
1961, *16*, 739–754.

Chapter 24

Analytical Studies of Drive and Reward

Neal E. Miller

Yale University

I want to present some recent research which my students and I have been pursuing. These studies are interrelated, but they reflect a variety of my own interests as well as those of different students who have contributed greatly to them. Therefore, they cover quite a range, beginning with some purely behavioral studies, and ending with a combination of behavioral and physiological techniques.

In order to put these studies into proper context, I shall from time to time briefly summarize certain earlier work from my laboratory. For the benefit of those who have not had extensive experience with research, I

Address of the President to the sixty-ninth Annual Convention of the American Psychological Association, New York City, September 3, 1961.

Work on the studies cited in this paper was supported by Grants MY647 and MY2949 from the National Institute of Mental Health of the National Institutes of Health; United States Department of Health, Education, and Welfare; Bethesda, Maryland. The work of Angus A. Campbell and Donald Novin was supported by Grant G5818 from the National Science Foundation, Washington, D.C.

shall mention a few of the difficulties and failures, as well as those successes which ordinarily are all that is published and hence give a false impression of the actual process of groping forward into the unknown. But, even so, I shall not begin to do justice to the arduous exploration, only some of which has led forward.

While I realize all too well the difficulties of trying to prove the null hypothesis, I believe there should be more mention of negative results in publications, not only to give a truer picture of scientific research, but also to prevent later investigators, one after another, from proceeding in the same way into the same quagmires.

At the purely empirical level, drives and rewards obviously are important in the performance of learned behavior, be it individual or social, normal or abnormal. Thus all behavior theorists from Thorndike (1898) on have used the empirical law of effect in some form or other. Many advances have been made, and many more can be made, by staying at this level and applying the empirical law of effect to behavior in the laboratory and in the home, in the classroom, factory, and clinic. As you may know, I have made some such applications (Dollard & Miller, 1950; Miller, 1957b, 1959; Miller & Dollard, 1941). My present purpose, however, is to try to analyze some of the fundamental mechanisms involved in drive and reward.

Effect of Drive on Reward and Learning

Everyone agrees that the level of drive can affect performance, but there has been a long, vigorous controversy over whether it also affects learning. As you know, Tolman (1932) initiated this controversy which has been carried on by other expectancy theorists (Hilgard, 1956). He contended that animals exposed to a learning situation without any motivation learn "what leads to what," but do not display this "latent learning" until they are motivated to perform. One of the difficulties in resolving this controversy has been that in the complete absence of any motivation it is hard to get animals to expose themselves to the mazes and other types of learning situations commonly used. A completely unmotivated rat would be expected to sit completely still. But for the learning theorist there is not much future in watching rats sitting still. How can we surmount this difficulty?

As a means of exposing unmotivated rats to water, I asked one of my students, Donald Jensen, to try to develop a fistula into the mouth. With considerable ingenuity, he developed the polyethylene fistula illustrated in Figure 1. This enters in the back of the rat's neck (where it is hardest for him to bite or scratch it out), passes under the skin, is anchored by a blob of dental cement, plunges down through the snout, and emerges into a little metal tip on the top of the palate. With further perspicacity, Jensen suggested that this fistula might be used to elicit and record conditioned tongue licks. The tongue completes an electrical circuit with

Figure 1. The oral fistula used to elicit and record conditioned tongue licks.

the little metal tip. This technique was further developed with the help of another student, Richard C. DeBold, who performed with me the following experiment on the effects of thirst on conditioned tongue licks.

During the first, or learning, phase of the experiment, 64 male albino rats were given a total of 150 trials during which a flickering light was a signal for an injection of water into the mouth. Every fifth trial was an unpaired test trial. All rats were on a schedule of 22-hour water deprivation. Four experimental groups were run with different strengths of thirst achieved by the following treatments immediately before each day's training: (a) *strong thirst* with no drinking before training; (b) *moderate thirst*, allowed to drink before training 70% of amount usually consumed; (c) *satiated* by drinking ad lib. one hour before training; (d) *supersatiated* by preceding procedure plus injection via the mouth fistula of an additional 70% of daily water consumption, most of which the rat allowed to drool out of his mouth. We wanted to be absolutely sure that this last group was completely satiated. And it really was.

As a control for spontaneous level of licking and for pseudoconditioning, four similar control groups were run with exposure to the same number of lights and injections which never were paired with each other. Figure 2 shows the results for these control rats. There is a low

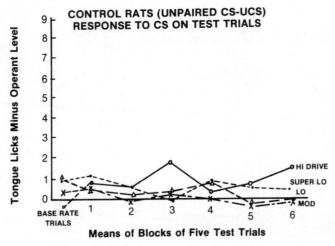

Figure 2. The four control groups for pseudoconditioning show a low level of spontaneous licking which is not consistently related to number of training trials or level of thirst.

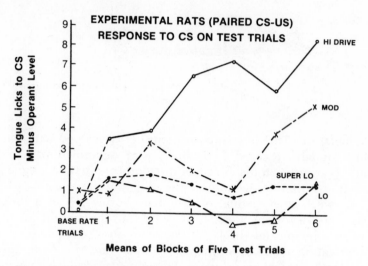

Figure 3. Performance during conditioning as a function of level of drive.

level of spontaneous licking which does not change throughout the training and is not markedly or consistently related to the level of thirst.

Figure 3 shows that, during test trials, the performance of the satiated (LO) and supersatiated animals was approximately the same as that of the pseudoconditioning controls. The moderately thirsty animals showed definitely better conditioning, and the highly thirsty ones obviously were the best of all. There seems to be a clear relationship between drive and learning. However, it is possible that the two nonthirsty groups actually were learning that the light led to the water, but were not performing because they were not motivated.

In order to test for such latent learning, half of the rats in each group were given five trials of exposure to the light alone (without water) when

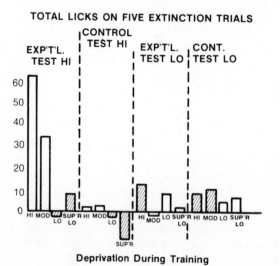

Figure 4. Performance during testing under high drive (22-hour water deprivation) or low drive (normal satiation), as a function of deprivation during training.

they were motivated by 22 hours of thirst. The other half were tested following normal satiation. The results are presented in Figure 4. Between the dotted lines just right of the center, we see that, when the experimental test is under low drive (actually satiation), the performance is within the range of the control test at the extreme right for spontaneous level and for pseudoconditioning. These results are yet another demonstration that performance is low under low drive.

On the left-hand side we see that when experimental animals were tested with high drive in order to bring out any latent learning, those originally conditioned with high drive gave many conditioned licks; those originally conditioned with moderate drive gave approximately half as many conditioned licks; and those conditioned with low or superlow drives were within the range of spontaneous licks, as indicated by the control groups. Thus, when the effects of drive on learning are separated from those on performance by tests designed to bring out any latent learning, a clear-cut relationship between strength of drive and learning remains. This result is contrary to the prediction from Tolman's (1932) expectancy theory. It emphasizes the importance of drive.

Figure 5 shows the effect of strength of drive on the unconditioned licks to the water during the training trials. It can be seen that the water elicited more licks in the thirstier rats. Contiguity theorists, following the Guthrie (1952) tradition, could use this relationship between the drive and the unconditioned response as a basis for explaining the superior learning of the more highly motivated group, without having to assume any relationship between the strength of thirst and the *rewarding* effects of water. Thus, while the results went against the expectancy theory, they did not differentiate between reinforcement based on contiguity alone and reinforcement based contiguity plus reward. How can we differentiate between these two possibilities?

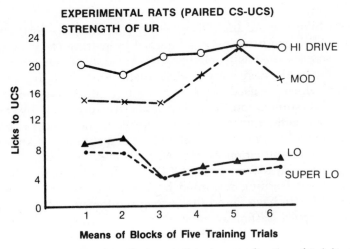

Figure 5. Unconditioned licks during conditioning as a function of training trials and strength of drive.

Unsuccessful Attempts to Condition Responses Elicited by
Electrical Stimulation of Motor Cortex of Rat

If one could elicit a response without motivation and reward, one might test between the contiguity and the reward theories of reinforcement. A considerable number of years ago, Roger Loucks (1935) apparently did this by implanting electrodes in the motor cortex of dogs. He paired a cue for over 600 trials with leg lifting elicited by stimulation of the motor cortex in three dogs without producing any conditioning. But by adding a food reward, he produced conditioning in two other dogs. This result seemed to show that contiguity alone was not sufficient for learning, while contiguity plus reward was.

I wanted to repeat this highly significant experiment and, in addition, to try a latent learning design to see whether, after pairing the cue with the motor response elicited by stimulating the cortex without reward, subsequent trials of pairing the motor response with reward (but without the cue), would cause the response to appear on final test trials with the cue but without motor stimulation or reward.

After considerable work, one of my students, Derek Hendry, found a place where leg movements could be elicited by stimulating the cortex of the rat, and also designed an apparatus for restraining the rat and recording the leg movements. But a large amount of additional effort yielded confusing and negative results.

Finally, we decided to see whether thirsty rats restrained in this way would learn the leg withdrawal as an instrumental response to get water without any central stimulation, much as they will learn to press a bar. They did not. Apparently rats react badly to restraint and are poor at learning discrete, leg retraction responses. We had achieved no results from almost a year of work on this project. Perhaps some radical, or even minor, change would make the procedure work, but it was time for Hendry to concentrate on a PhD thesis, so he prudently changed to a safer problem.

Meanwhile, I found that Giurgea (Doty & Giurgea, 1961) had been able to establish conditioning in an animal by pairing electrical stimulation of a sensory area with electrical stimulation of the motor cortex, provided the trials were very widely distributed. But did the motor stimulation which he used serve as a reward, either like the Olds and Milner (1954) stimulation in subcortical structures, or by relieving boredom? The latter hypothesis would explain the need for the wide distribution of trials since the novelty effect of a stimulus is known to be subject to rapid habituation by massed trials and, as would be expected from this fact, Arlo Myers and I (1954) have found that widely distributed trials favor learning rewarded by weak exploration. Furthermore, Bower and I (1960) have found that strong reinforcement is required the more resistance a response must overcome. Thus, if massed trials generate more reactive inhibition, they should require more reward. Such considerations suggest that Giurgea might get conditioning, even with less widely distributed trials, provided he added a reward.

I have just speculated that stimulating the motor cortex might have a mild rewarding effect. One could test for such a reward by determining whether the cortical stimulation will help to maintain some other response, such as bar pressing originally learned for food. If the cortical stimulation is rewarding, it should help to prevent the extinction of such a response (Miller, 1961a).

On the other hand, it is possible that the elicitation of an arousal response, rather than reward, is the basic requirement for effective learning. It is also possible that contiguity alone is sufficient, or that where an additional resistance must be overcome, a central excitatory state must also be conditioned by contiguity to serve as a booster.

Can Responses in the Sensory Cortex Be Strengthened by Reward?

At the moment I am shifting my efforts on this problem somewhat. I still am attempting to secure evidence on the effectiveness of contiguity alone compared with contiguity plus reward. But at the same time, I am exploring the possibility of objectively studying certain phenomena which may be relevant to imagery, hallucinations, and mediating responses. Various investigators have electrophysiologically recorded so-called sensory conditioning. For example, if a tone is a cue for a distinctive rhythm of flashes of light, the evoked potential to the flashes originally recorded from the visual cortex can sometimes be recorded to the tone alone. But such conditioning characteristically is variable and does not persist for a large number of trials. We are trying to see whether it can be strengthened by adding a reward after the flashes. Will anticipatory evoked potentials from the visual cortex be learned if they are rewarded by giving food to a hungry animal? Can the flashes then be omitted and the distinctive rhythm of cortical potentials be made instrumental to securing reward? If so, will the activity producing these potentials have all of the functional properties of a cue producing response, such as a visual image (Miller, 1961a)? I had hoped to have answers for you, but as often happens, the solution to various technical problems has required more time than I anticipated. It is also possible that this will be one of the trails that, instead of leading to a break through the barrier mountains, leads into a box canyon.

What Determines the Effective Point of Reinforcement in a Temporal Sequence?

To summarize our position so far, we have succeeded in securing a clear-cut demonstration of the effects of drive on learning, but have failed to solve a second problem and to complete a related third one. Let us now turn to a fourth problem. At what point in a temporal sequence does reward occur?

Experiments by Thorndike (1933) purported to demonstrate a bidirectional gradient of reinforcement affecting acts occurring both before and after the reward. Probable sources of artifact in his data were discovered and his interpretation was seriously questioned (Jenkins & Sheffield, 1946). Looking for a simpler, more direct, test, one of my students, Mohammed Nagaty (1951), trained hungry rats some years ago to press a bar as soon as it was inserted. Next he habituated them to receive a pellet immediately before, as well as immediately after, pressing the bar. Then he found that rats with only the pellet *after* pressing omitted, extinguished at the same rate as those with the pellet omitted *both* before and after pressing the bar. These results, and various controls, showed that the pellet before pressing the bar was not an effective reward. But under these conditions some of the food probably still was being chewed and swallowed, the taste lingered in the mouth, and food certainly was entering the stomach and being digested *after* the bar was pressed. In short, part of the chain of events of food ingestion and digestion followed pressing the bar. Why did these later events in the chain have no rewarding effect?

In a recent attempt to answer this question, David Egger and I (1962) advanced the hypothesis that reward occurs primarily at the point at which new information is delivered. Normally, delivery of food to the cup, and certainly food in the mouth, invariably means that it can be chewed, tasted, swallowed, will reach the stomach, and be digested. Therefore, feedback from these subsequent links in the sequence conveys no new information; it is completely redundant. According to our hypothesis, in Nagaty's experiment all of the new information, and hence the reward, came when the food was delivered.

In order to test this hypothesis, we worked on the learning of secondary reinforcement. We chose the learning of secondary reinforcement instead of the learning of a movement, since it is easier to control the interval between a cue and reward than it is the timing of a movement made by an animal. Our specific hypothesis was that the secondary reinforcement value of a cue is a function of its information value.

Figure 6 summarizes the experimental situation. Look at the diagram next to the bottom labeled "redundant." The first single pellet always predicts the delivery, 2 seconds later, of the trio of pellets. This is analogous to delivery of food predicting the taste, chewing, swallowing, and entry of food into the stomach. Thus, although the intervening stimulus is followed by additional pellets, it is redundant.

In the top diagram of simple conditioning, which represents the usual situation for learning secondary reinforcement, the stimulus is not redundant because there is no other way of predicting the trio of pellets.

But is there any other way of rendering the stimulus informative, while still having it always preceded by a pellet in order to control for any possible inhibitory aftereffect of the first bit of reward? Suppose we present unpredictably between trials a number of single free pellets, as is indicated in the diagram next to the top, labeled "informative." Then the

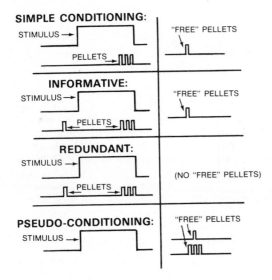

SIMPLE CONDITIONING:

INFORMATIVE:

REDUNDANT:

PSEUDO-CONDITIONING:

Figure 6. Diagrammatic representation of the conditions in the first experiment on secondary reinforcement as a function of the information value of the CS.

stimulus is no longer redundant: it is a more reliable predictor of the trio of pellets than is the single pellet. From our hypothesis, we predict that with such a group the stimulus should become a stronger secondary reinforcer than it will in the redundant group given exactly the same treatment in all other respects, but without the additional presentation of some free pellets not followed by the trio of pellets.

Finally, the bottom diagram represents a control for pseudoconditioning in which presentations of the stimulus and the pellets never were paired.

In order to achieve the most sensitive test for secondary reinforcement, we first trained rats to press a bar for pellets, then extinguished them by disconnecting the pellet feeder mechanism, and finally gave them test trials during which every third press delivered the stimulus, but no pellets. Thus the measure of secondary reinforcement was relearning after extinction and is shown by the amount of bar pressing for the stimulus in excess of that shown by the pseudoconditioning, control group.

Figure 7 presents the results. You can see that the informative group did as well as the group with the conventional simple conditioning procedure. The pellet of food a half-second before the stimulus had no obvious inhibitory aftereffect. Furthermore, as demanded by our hypothesis, the informative group performed significantly better than the redundant one.

Figure 8 summarizes the design of a similar experiment on the same problem. Since Stimulus 1 always precedes Stimulus 2, the latter is redundant and should acquire less secondary reinforcement value, even though it always precedes food. But there is a way to make S_2 informative. Present S_1 unpredictably a number of times without either S_2 or food. Then S_2 is a more reliable predictor of food than S_1 and is no longer redundant. From our hypothesis we predict that with a group given such

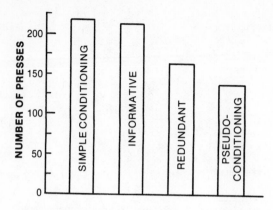

Figure 7. Food administered immediately before a CS does not interfere with the acquisition of secondary reinforcement, provided the stimulus is an informative predictor of additional food, but does produce a substantial reduction if it makes the CS redundant.

training S_2 will be a stronger reinforcer than it will in a group given exactly the same number of identical pairings of S_1 plus S_2 with food, but without the additional presentations of S_1 alone.

Figure 9 presents the results of such an experiment (Egger & Miller, 1962). The ordinate is the number of bar presses, followed by S_2 as a secondary reinforcer for relearning after experimental extinction. You can see that there were more bar presses for S_2 under the informative than under the redundant conditions. The results of this second experiment also are in line with the information hypothesis.[1]

But it is quite possible to interpret these results at a different level of analysis, using the drive-reduction hypothesis, which I have found it extremely fruitful to investigate, although I am not at all certain that it is true. According to the strong form of the drive-reduction hypothesis, the secondary reinforcer must produce a reduction in that part of the drive which can be modified by learning. Figure 10 presents a diagram of the

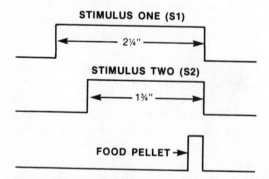

Figure 8. Design of stimulus sequence used in second experiment on secondary reinforcement as a function of the information value of the CS.

1. Since the measure was the ability of the cue to substitute for food in inducing recovery from experimental extinction, only the difference between the informative and redundant condition is relevant; the performance under the redundant condition may have represented disinhibition or spontaneous recovery.

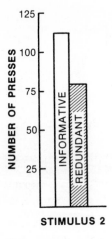

Figure 9. Results of a second experiment showing that a cue is a stronger secondary reinforcer when it is informative.

theoretical analysis. On the left-hand side of this diagram you can see that, if most of the learnable drive already has been reduced by S_1, little drive-reduction remains to be conditioned to S_2. On the other hand, if S_1 often fails to predict food, much of the conditioned drive-reduction to it should be extinguished. Hence, as is illustrated on the right-hand side of the diagram, more of the drive-reduction should occur to, and be conditioned to, S_2.

As you can see from the diagram, this type of an analysis demands that, if the secondary reinforcing value of our hitherto neglected stimulus, S_1, is tested, it should be greater under the conditions on the left-hand side when it is the reliable predictor (making S_2 redundant) than under those on the right-hand side when it is an unreliable predictor (making S_2 informative). Figure 11 shows that this is indeed the case.

Although the preceding experiment is in line with the deduction made by applying the drive-reduction hypothesis, it would be much more satisfying if we could test the hypothesis in this and in other situations by some more direct, independent measure of the moment-to-

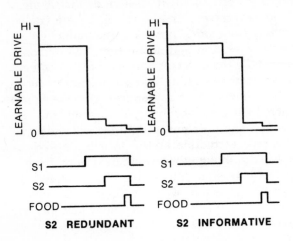

Figure 10. Diagram showing how the difference in acquisition under the redundant and informative conditions might be explained by the drive-reduction hypothesis of reinforcement.

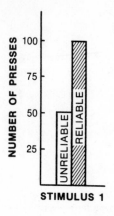

Figure 11. Confirmation of the prediction based on the theoretical analysis summarized in Figure 10. (Stimulus 1 is a stronger secondary reinforcer when it is a reliable than when it is an unreliable predictor.)

moment level of the drive. The need for such a measure in this and in many other experiments is one of the things that has motivated me to explore physiological techniques. My original hope was that, if the neural centers controlling hunger and satiation could be located, it might be possible to use direct recordings from such centers as a measure of drive. While I am less optimistic about this than when I started, the experimental program initiated by this hope has produced many interesting results.

Experiments on Sensory Feedback from the Mouth and Stomach

Before investigating the brain, however, I worked on some more peripheral mechanisms: the sensory feedback from the mouth and the stomach which I had speculated might be sources of reinforcement in puzzling over the results of Nagaty's experiment. Please fasten your seat belts while I summarize this old work quickly, in order to give the background for some new experiments.

If drive-reduction is the basis of reward, it is obvious that it must occur promptly after the food is received, or else it will be too late to reinforce the responses leading to food. Therefore, the reduction in hunger must occur long before digestion and absorption have restored the cellular deficit. In order to study the effect on hunger of feedback from various links in the chain between the eating and absorption of food, Martin Kohn and I spent the better part of a year trying to develop a simple fistula through which food could be injected directly into the stomach of the rat. After trying many different techniques, we ended up with a great respect for the rat's incredible ability to extrude various foreign devices from his body even though these were held in by flanges which seemed to make such extrusion impossible. Fortunately, we eventually heard that Evelyn K. Anderson of the National Institutes of Health had developed a stomach fistula for the rat. Now that various workers in our laboratory have made a few minor improvements of their own, this technique, which originally gave us so much trouble, can be taught to a good undergraduate student in a couple of days. Our experience in this particular case is representative of what often occurs in the development of new techniques. They are extremely difficult before certain problems are solved and quite easy afterwards.

Experiments by Kohn (1951), Berkun, Marion Kessen, and myself (1952) showed that food injected directly into the stomach produced a prompt reduction in hunger, and taken normally by mouth produced an even greater reduction. Similarly, Woodrow, Sampliner, and I (Miller, Sampliner, & Woodrow, 1957) found that water injected directly into the stomach produced a prompt reduction in thirst, but water taken normally by mouth produced an even greater reduction. With each of these drives the same results were secured by two different techniques for measuring drive: volume of food or water consumed, and rate of working for food or water by pressing a bar on a variable-interval schedule. Thus we were confident of the results which showed that the drive was regulated by immediate feedback from both the stomach and the mouth (Miller, 1957a). These prompt effects avoided the delay that would have been embarrassing to the drive-reduction hypothesis.

Meanwhile, Sheffield and Roby (1950) had shown that a nonnutritive but sweet substance, namely saccharine, could act as a reward for hungry animals even though all of it was excreted, so that it served no nutritional need. This finding has been used as an argument against the strong form of the drive-reduction hypothesis. But Edward Murray, Warren W. Roberts, and I showed that saccharine taken by mouth reduces the amount of food consumed immediately thereafter, which suggests that it temporarily reduces hunger as would be demanded by the drive-reduction hypothesis, and supplies additional evidence for an oral feedback controlling hunger (Miller, 1957a).

Recently, a student of mine, Derek Hendry, has observed that thirsty rats will lick at a cooling stream of air, and then has found that they will learn to press a bar to turn on the air briefly. Since the air increased evaporation, and hence the water deficit, he thought that this was evidence against the drive-reduction hypothesis. However, when at my suggestion he made the test for the effect of licking air on thirst, he found that a period of licking air not only reduced the immediately subsequent consumption of water, but also caused thirsty rats to reduce their rate of working for water by pressing a bar on a variable-interval schedule. Thus it appears that the feedback from the mouth produced by licking a jet of air may temporarily somewhat reduce thirst (Hendry & Rasche, 1961).

But to return to our original story, if food injected directly into the stomach produces a prompt reduction in hunger, it should serve as a reward. And indeed Marion Kessen and I (Miller & Kessen, 1952) found that rats would learn to turn to the side of the T maze in which they received milk via fistula directly into the stomach rather than isotonic saline.

Soon after that, we found that inflating a balloon in the rat's stomach

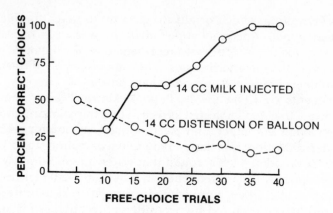

Figure 12. One group of hungry rats learns to choose the side of a T maze where their stomachs are distended by milk injected directly via fistula; another group learns to avoid the side where their stomachs are distended by injection of liquid into a balloon. (From Miller, 1957a)

would reduce the rate of bar pressing for food (Miller, 1955). We concluded that stomach distension probably reduced hunger. In that case, stomach distension should serve as a reward. But when we made the test, as Figure 12 shows, we found that the animals learned to avoid the side where their stomachs were distended by the balloon, in contrast to learning to go to the side where the stomach was distended by milk. This was nice in that the behavioral test showed up a qualitative difference, which otherwise might not have been suspected. But it complicated the theoretical picture (Miller, 1957a).

Design to Test Intervening Variable

Now for some time I had been advocating and also practicing the use of a variety of behavioral tests to cross-check each conclusion in order to avoid being misled by side-effects which might be specific to a given type of test (Miller & Barry, 1960). Indeed, I insistently pointed out (1959) that an intervening variable is meaningful only when one secures the expected type of agreement in experiments designed to use a variety of techniques to manipulate the assumed intervening variable and a variety of techniques for measuring it.

Recently, I have completed an experiment of this type to compare the effects of three methods of manipulating thirst—water by mouth, by fistula, and in a stomach balloon—on three different measures of thirst: the volume drunk immediately afterwards, the amount of quinine in the water required to stop drinking, and the rate of working at pressing a bar rewarded by water on a variable-interval schedule.

Figure 13 presents the results of this experiment. Let us look at the two diagrams to the left and in the center showing results for measuring

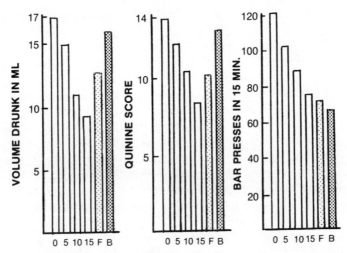

Figure 13. Comparison of three different measures of the effect on thirst of three different types of pretreatment: Water drunk normally by mouth (0, 5, 10, or 15 milliliters); 15 milliliters of water injected via stomach fistula (F); 15 milliliters of water injected into stomach balloon (B). (The patterns of results measured by volume consumed or by quinine score are highly similar; the results measured by rate of bar pressing are different.)

thirst by the volume of water drunk and by the amount of quinine required to stop drinking. In the open bars you can see that prefeeding increasing amounts of water—0, 5, 10 or 15 milliliters—produced progressive decrements in the scores on both tests. These decrements serve as a basis for calibrating the other effects.

Looking at the bar with single crosshatching and labeled F, you can see that using the fistula to inject 15 milliliters of water directly into the stomach produced an effect roughly comparable to that of drinking 10 milliliters normally by mouth. Allowing for sampling errors, the effects are roughly comparable in both the left and middle diagrams. Now looking at the double crosshatched bars labeled D, you can see that injecting into the balloon 15 milliliters of water to distend the stomach produced less effect than drinking 5 cubic centimeters normally by mouth. The effect is highly similar in both the left and middle diagrams. The general picture of agreement in these two diagrams is what might be expected if the different experimental operations—water via mouth, fistula, and in the balloon—all were manipulating a single intervening variable, namely, thirst, which was being measured by both of the tests: volume of water drunk, and amount of quinine required to stop drinking.

Now, shifting to the right-hand figure for results of the test which used rate of bar pressing as a measure, you can see that the effect of prefeeding various amounts of water was much like that in the preceding tests. The effect of injecting water by fistula was somewhat off. But the effect of inflating the balloon was grossly different. Instead of being almost negligible, *less* than drinking 5 cubic centimeters of water by mouth, it was *greater* than that of drinking 15 cubic centimeters of water by mouth.

From this result we draw two conclusions: First, in my previous work by relying on bar pressing as the sole test, I probably had been trapped into greatly overestimating the reduction in drive, if any, produced by inflation of a balloon in the stomach. Second, when the bar pressing test is also included, the overall results cannot be explained by the assumption of a single intervening variable, since the results of all three tests are not perfectly correlated, as they would have to be if they were all pure measures of the same unitary thing, namely, strength of thirst. Perhaps the bar pressing test is especially susceptible to distraction, pain, and nausea, possibly produced by inflating the balloon in the stomach. If so, this pain or nausea would be a second intervening variable.

In any event, the need for this particular type of experimental design is obvious. As I have pointed out before (Miller, 1957b), we have great confidence in the electron as an intervening variable, because electrons produced by a great variety of experimental operations: rubbing a cat's fur against amber, heating a metal in a vacuum, putting zinc and carbon in acid, or cutting a magnetic field with a wire, all have exactly the same charge when measured by a variety of techniques—repelling like charges on a droplet of oil, depositing silver in an electroplating bath, or creating magnetic lines of force when they move. It is this kind of agreement which gives us confidence.

In the behavioral sciences we need to make much more use of such cross-checking of hypotheses. With sufficient ingenuity, it is possible, not only in simple situations of the kind I have been describing, but also in dealing with many other problems. For example, in the area of personality development, certain clinical observations on children can be checked against controlled experiments on animals and also against anthropological observations on the effects of different conditions of child rearing in other cultures.

Brain Electrolytes and Thirst

To recapitulate briefly, I have described evidence that drive is important for learning. I have shown that the point in a temporal sequence, at which maximum reward effect is concentrated, can be described in terms of information theory and possibly explained in terms of the drive-reduction hypothesis of reinforcement. I have shown that the drives of both hunger and thirst are promptly reduced by feedback from both the mouth and the stomach. Now let me carry on the main story a bit further.

For some time, it has been believed that there are osmoreceptors in the brain which could be an additional mechanism involved in controlling thirst. A few years ago, Andersson (1953), in Stockholm, added convincing evidence by showing that minute injections in the region of the third ventricle of a satiated goat's brain, would elicit drinking if the solution injected (2% NaCl) had slightly more effective osmotic pressure than is normal for body fluids. My students and I confirmed this in the cat, and in addition showed that minute injections of pure water, which has less osmotic pressure than the body fluids, would have the opposite effect of reducing thirst. For both the increase and the reduction, we got the same results with two different measures: volume of water consumed and rate of performing a learned response to get water on a variable-interval schedule (Miller, 1961b). Thus we see that, in addition to being controlled by feedbacks from the mouth and stomach, thirst is controlled by receptors in the brain which respond to the state of the body fluid around them.

Still more recently a student of mine, Donald Novin (1962), has devised an ingenious technique for recording electrolyte concentration in the body fluids of normal rats free to move around in a small chamber. This is significant to our story because electrolyte concentration in the body is almost entirely due to the concentration of NaCl which in turn determines the effective osmotic pressure to which the "osmoreceptors" in the brain presumably respond.

Two platinum-black electrodes are chronically implanted in the rat's brain so that they can be connected to flexible leads. Since the electrolyte concentration of various body fluids presumably is the same, the placement in the brain is for convenience, rather than having crucial significance. With suitable bridge circuits, the resistance between these two electrodes is used to measure electrolyte concentration. Let us see some of the results which he has secured in our laboratory.

Figure 14 shows the results of water deprivation. As the animal becomes dehydrated, we expect the concentration of electrolytes (primarily salt) in his blood to increase, so that the conductivity should increase. We can see that this is exactly what occurred.

If a hungry animal is fed dry food, it makes him thirsty. Figure 15 shows that this procedure also increases the electrolyte concentration as measured by conductivity. But looking at the right-hand side of the

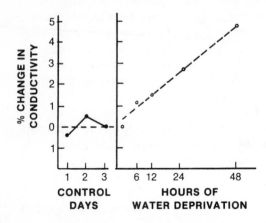

Figure 14. Electrolyte concentration, as measured by conductivity, increases with hours of water deprivation. (From Novin, 1962)

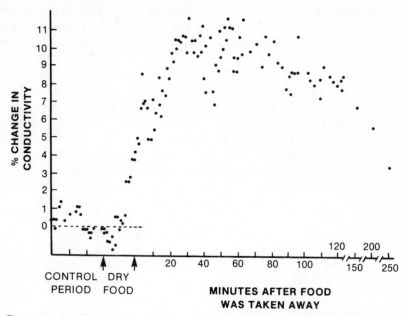

Figure 15. Feeding dry food to a hungry rat increases electrolyte concentration, as measured by conductivity, which then decreases during the subsequent interval without access to water. (From Novin, 1962)

figure, we see a peculiar thing. Several hours after eating dry food, and without any opportunity to drink, the conductivity begins going down. According to this, the animal should be less thirsty even though it is longer since his last drink. Figure 16 shows the results of separate tests for thirst, administered at different times after dry food without water. You can see that the rats do indeed drink less after the longer times. There is a striking parallelism between the curves of conductivity as a measure of electrolyte concentration and water-intake as a measure of thirst.

Figure 17 shows that an intravenous injection of a hypertonic saline (1 milliliter of 12%) solution into a satiated rat increases conductivity as would be expected, and when water is given after 10 minutes, causes him to start drinking as an indication of thirst. Drinking produces a drop in conductivity, which begins to occur rapidly enough so that it could be one of the factors involved in the eventual stopping of drinking.

The dotted theoretical curve of conductivity if water were not given is based on results of another experiment; the drop in it is produced by the excretion of salt by the kidneys. You should note for future reference that the empirical curve of conductivity comes back approximately to the same baseline level it had before the hypertonic saline was injected.

Looking at one type of experimental manipulation at a time, we have seen good qualitative agreement between the two measures: electrical conductivity and the volume of water drunk. If electrolyte concentration is the only intervening variable involved, we must expect a perfect

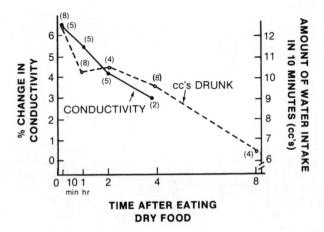

Figure 16. After thirst is induced by feeding dry food to hungry rats, longer rest intervals without water produce a great reduction in thirst as measured either by conductivity or by volume of water drunk. (Separate tests are given at the end of each interval.) (From Novin, 1962)

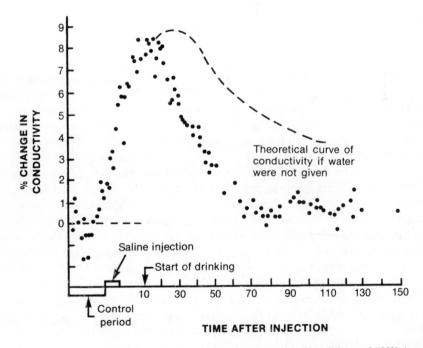

Figure 17. An intravenous injection of hypertonic saline (1 milliliter of 12%) into a satiated rat increases thirst as measured by conductivity, so that when water is introduced, the rat starts drinking which restores conductivity to the baseline level for satiation. (From Novin, 1962)

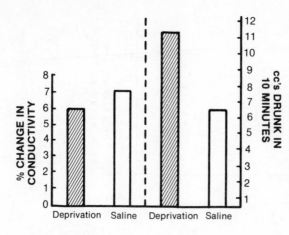

Figure 18. An injection of hypertonic saline which produces a greater increase in conductivity than does a period of water deprivation, elicits less drinking than does the deprivation. Therefore, the change in effective osmotic pressure, measured by conductivity, cannot be the sole factor involved in thirst. (From Novin, 1962)

positive correlation between these measures when the effects of different manipulations are compared. In order to test this, Novin performed an experiment, comparing the effects of normal deprivation and of intravenous injection of saline upon both measures.

Figure 18 shows the results. Looking to the left of the dotted line, we see that the water deprivation used produced a slightly *lower* level of conductivity than did the saline injection. But on the right-hand side of the dotted line, we see that the water deprivation induced considerably *more* drinking than did the saline injection. This is not a perfect positive correlation; in fact, it is a negative one. Thus the results show that electrolyte concentration, which produces effective osmotic pressure, cannot be the sole factor involved.

Additional evidence of a discrepancy comes from the effect of drinking on conductivity. In Figure 17 we have seen that, after an injection of saline, drinking brings conductivity back approximately to the base-line of the preceding satiated state. Figure 19 shows that, after normal deprivation, drinking brings conductivity far below the satiation baseline level depicted by the solid horizontal line out from the little square on the ordinate. This is the kind of result that would be expected if the animal is drinking to restore a water deficit, rather than to bring electrolyte concentration back to a given level. Perhaps the so-called osmoreceptors are reacting not solely to effective osmotic pressure, but to total amount of dehydration. Perhaps there are some other receptors that react to the volume of body fluid. At least we know that electrolyte concentration cannot be the whole story.

Again we see the advantage of testing an intervening variable with a design comparing the effects of at least two different experimental manipulations upon at least two different measures.

Unsuccessful Tests on Parabiotic Rats

There has been a good deal of speculation that, in addition to the osmoreceptors, the brain contains receptors which respond to a hunger

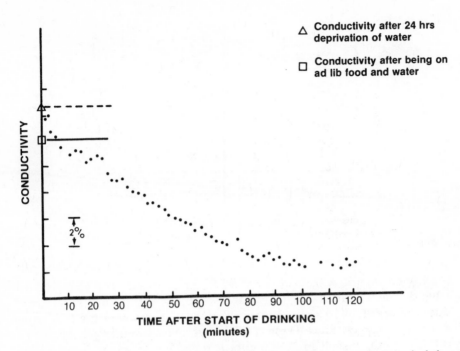

Figure 19. Ad lib. drinking following water deprivation reduces conductivity far below the normal predeprivation base level. (Represented by the little solid line out from the hollow square.) Contrast this with the effect of drinking induced by the hypertonic injection, as presented in Figure 17. (From Novin, 1962)

hormone, or the state of nutrients in the blood. In an attempt to locate some such humoral factor, Angus A. Campbell worked with me on parabiotic rats, or in other words, surgically created Siamese twins. But an extensive amount of labor failed to secure any evidence for a hunger hormone, or indeed for the transfer of appreciable amounts of nutrients across the parabiotic barrier. Since then I have learned that Teitelbaum also has secured somewhat similar negative results with such rats.[2] Perhaps we need some other type of preparation to study this problem.

Behavioral Analysis of Effects of Electrical Stimulation of the "Feeding Area" of the Brain

Now let us turn to a somewhat different approach to the problem. It has been known for some time that electrical stimulation of certain areas of

---

2. Our observation was that having a well-fed partner did not appreciably increase the starvation time of the unfed one or increase the food consumption of the fed one. In a personal communication, P. Teitelbaum has told us that, in a similar experiment, the food intake of the fed member of the pair did not increase during the first several days, although it perhaps may have increased approximately 24 hours before the unfed member died of starvation.

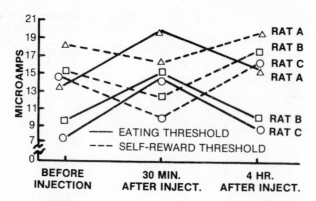

Figure 20. An injection of dexedrine (2 mg/k) raises the threshold for eating, but lowers it for self-reward. (Twenty-five tests were given to each rat at each point.) (Experiments by E. E. Coons from Miller, 1960)

the hypothalamus will cause a satiated animal to eat. Ted Coons and I have devised a series of behavioral tests to show that such stimulation does not merely arouse a gnawing reflex, but has many of the properties of normal hunger. Since these results have been summarized elsewhere (Miller, 1960), I shall merely mention them briefly as background for some new work. Stimulation of this area will elicit not only eating, but also will cause a satiated animal to perform learned responses reinforced by food. Such stimulation will cause a satiated rat to bite food, but not to lap up pure water. However, the rat will lap up sugar water or milk. Therefore the response is not defined primarily by the motor movements, but rather by a sensory feedback, namely, the taste of food. As would be expected from the drive-reduction hypothesis of reinforcement, turning *off* such stimulation will act as a reward to produce the learning of a T maze. But paradoxically, turning *on* such stimulation also will serve as a reward. This result is contrary to the prediction from the drive-reduction hypothesis of reinforcement.

In Figure 20 the center points of the solid lines show that the appetite reducing drug, dexedrine, *increases* the threshold (in microamperes) for eliciting eating. But as the center points of the dotted lines show, the same injection of the same drug *reduces* the threshold for bar pressing rewarded by a brief burst of stimulation. Both results are highly reliable for each of the three rats tested. Since the same drug has opposite effects on the two thresholds, perhaps the eating and rewarding effects are produced by different systems which are indiscriminately stimulated by the same electric current. If so, predictions from the drive-reduction hypothesis must be held in abeyance.

A Chemical Code in the Brain?

Another one of my students, Peter Grossman (1961), recently has devised a double cannula technique for stimulating the same "feeding area" of the rat's brain with minute amounts of crystalline substances. He has found that minute amounts of the adrenergic substances, adrenalin or noradrenalin, will cause satiated rats to eat and also to perform a learned response rewarded by food. By contrast, stimulation of the same area via the same cannula, by minute amounts of the cholinergic substances, acetylcholine or carbachol, will cause satiated rats to drink and also to perform learned responses rewarded by water.

Various control tests with other substances rule out Ph, vasoconstriction or vasodilation, and osmotic pressure as the primary sources of these effects. More convincing still is the fact that an intraperitoneal injection of ethoxybutamoxane, which is an adrenergic blocking agent, practically eliminates the eating elicited by inserting the adrenergic noradrenalin into the brain, while leaving the drinking elicited by the cholinergic carbachol, practically unaffected. Similarly, an intraperitoneal injection of the cholinergic blocking agent, atropine sulfate, leaves the eating to centrally administered noradrenalin relatively unaffected, while practically eliminating the drinking to carbachol. These effects of the blocking agents are an elegant control to show that the drugs elicit eating and drinking via their adrenergic and cholinergic effects, respectively.

In rats with a cannula into this area of the hypothalamus, we apparently have a good method of investigating new compounds suspected to have central, adrenergic, or cholinergic effects, or to function as central blocking agents.

But are the effects we have just described involved in normal hunger and thirst? That they probably are is indicated by the fact that administering the appropriate blocking agent, either peripherally by intraperitoneal injection or centrally via the cannula into the brain, produced the appropriate differential effects on rats made hungy or thirsty by deprivation of food or water. The effects of the blocking agents on normal hunger and thirst are somewhat less complete than those on eating and drinking elicited centrally, but they are unmistakable. The adrenergic blocking agent produces a reliably greater decrement in food consumption than does the cholinergic one; the cholinergic blocking agent produces a reliably greater decrement in water consumption than does the adrenergic one. Thus adrenergic and cholinergic effects seem to be involved in normal hunger and thirst, respectively. In short, this evidence, along with that of other more purely physiological studies, suggests a chemical code in the brain.

Basis of Antagonism Between Hunger and Thirst

The effects we have just described give us an opportunity to answer a theoretically interesting question. It is known that water deprived animals stop eating dry food. Is this because the drive of thirst is centrally incompatible with the drive of hunger, or because bodily dehydration interferes with peripheral aspects of the hunger mechanism—for example, a dry mouth making it difficult to eat dry food?

Similarly, food deprived animals drink less water. Is this because the

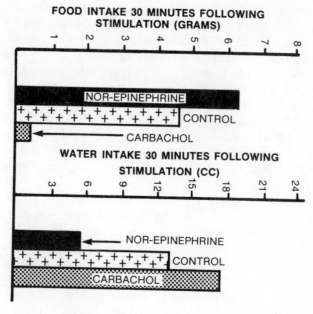

Figure 21. When introduced into the "feeding area" of the lateral hypothalamus, minute amounts of adrenergic norepinephrine potentiate food intake induced by 24-hour deprivation, while cholinergic stimulation by carbachol interferes with food consumption. The same substances via the same cannula have opposite effects in similar tests for water consumption. (From Grossman, 1961)

mechanism of the hunger drive is antagonistic to thirst or merely because animals not eating dry food do not require as much water?

In an attempt to answer these questions, Grossman secured the results shown in Figure 21. In the upper graph, you can see that direct stimulation of the hypothalamus by norepinephrine increased the food intake of normally hungry rats exposed only to food, while stimulation by carbachol markedly decreased it. Similarly, the lower graph shows that carbachol increased the drinking of normally thirsty rats exposed only to water, while norepinephrine decreased it. These results strongly suggest that there is some central way, analogous to reciprocal innervation, in which the drive mechanisms of hunger and thirst tend to inhibit each other.

These discoveries are being followed up in our laboratory. We have investigated the effects of injecting minute quantities of blood serum from hungry and satiated animals directly into the brain. Our preliminary results are negative. We are investigating the effects of other hormones and drugs, both in the feeding area and in the ventromedial nucleus, which is believed to be a satiation area. We are studying the effects of a bacterial toxin which seems to interfere with drinking (Dubos, 1961), and also we find with eating. We are testing the effects of adrenergic and cholinergic blocking agents on direct electrical stimulation of the brain. We are confronted with many more interesting problems than there possibly is time to investigate.

A New Conception of the Brain

The work that I have just described on drive and reward as well as the work on other topics by our Past President, Donald Hebb (1958), and by other laboratories in a number of nations, is opening up a new conception of the brain.[3] We no longer view the brain as merely an enormously complicated telephone switchboard which is passive unless excited from without. The brain is an active organ which exerts considerable control over its own sensory input. The brain is a device for sorting, processing, and analyzing information. The brain contains sense organs which respond to states of the internal environment, such as osmotic pressure, temperature, and many others. The brain is a gland which secretes chemical messengers, and it also responds to such messengers, as well as to various types of feedback, both central and peripheral. A combination of behavioral and physiological techniques is increasing our understanding of these processes and their significance for psychology.

REFERENCES

Andersson, B.   The effect of injections of hypertonic NaCl solutions into different parts of the hypothalamus of goats. *Acta physiol. Scand.*, 1953, *28*, 188–201.

Berkun, M. M., Kessen, M. L., & Miller, N. E.   Hunger-reducing effects of food by stomach fistula versus food by mouth measured by a consummatory response. *J. comp. physiol. Psychol.*, 1952, *45*, 550–564.

Bower, G. H., & Miller, N. E.   Effect of amount of reward on strength of approach in an approach-avoidance conflict. *J. comp. physiol. Psychol.*, 1960, *53*, 59–62.

Dollard, J., & Miller, N. E.   *Personality and psychotherapy.* New York: McGraw-Hill, 1950.

Doty, R. W., & Giurgea, C.   Conditioned reflexes established by coupling electrical excitation of two cortical areas. In J. Delafresnaye (Ed.), *Brain mechanisms and learning.* London: Blackwell, 1961.

Dubos, R. J.   The effect of bacterial endotoxins on the water intake and body weight of mice. *J. exp. Med.*, 1961, *113*, 921–934.

Egger, M. D., & Miller, N. E.   Secondary reinforcement in rats as a function of information value and reliability of the stimulus. *J. exp. Psychol.*, 1962, in press.

Field, J., Magoun, H. W., & Hall, V. E.   *Handbook of physiology. Sect. 1. Neurophysiology.* Washington, D. C.: American Physiological Society, 1960. 3 vols.

Grossman, S. P.   Behavioral effects of direct adrenergic and cholinergic stimulation of the hypothalamic mechanisms regulating food and water intake. Unpublished PhD thesis, Yale University, 1961.

Guthrie, E. R.   *The psychology of learning.* (Rev. ed.) New York: Harper, 1952.

Hebb, D. O.   *A textbook of psychology.* Philadelphia: Saunders, 1958.

Hendry, D. P., & Rasche, R.   Analysis of a new non-nutritive positive reinforcer based on thirst. *J. comp. physiol. Psychol.*, 1961, *54*, 477–483.

---

3. For an illuminating overview see Magoun (1958); for a comprehensive series of authoritative summaries, Field, Magoun, and Hall (1960).

Hilgard, E. R.   *Theories of learning.* (Rev. ed.) New York: Appleton-Century-Crofts, 1956.

Jenkins, W. O., & Sheffield, F. D.   Rehearsal and guessing habits as sources of the "spread of effect." *J. exp. Psychol.*, 1946, *36*, 316–330.

Kohn, M.   Satiation of hunger from food injected directly into the stomach versus food ingested by mouth. *J. comp. physiol. Psychol.*, 1951, *44*, 412–422.

Loucks, R. B.   The experimental delimitation of neural structures essential for learning: The attempt to condition striped muscle responses with faradization of the sigmoid gyri. *J. Psychol.*, 1935, *1*, 5–44.

Magoun, H. W.   *The waking brain.* Springfield, Ill.: Charles C Thomas, 1958.

Miller, N. E.   Shortcomings of food consumption as a measure of hunger: Results from other behavioral techniques. *Ann. N. Y. Acad. Sci.*, 1955, *63*, 141–143.

Miller, N. E.   Experiments on motivation: Studies combining psychological, physiological and pharmacological techniques. *Science*, 1957, *126*, 1271–1278. (a)

Miller, N. E.   *Graphic communication and the crisis in education. Audiovis. commun. Rev.,* 1957, *5*, 3. (b)

Miller, N. E.   Liberalization of basic S-R concepts: Extensions to conflict behavior, motivation and social learning. In S. Koch (Ed.), *Psychology: A study of a science.* Vol. 2. New York: McGraw-Hill, 1959.

Miller, N. E.   Some motivational effects of brain stimulation and drugs. *Fed. Proc.*, 1960, *19*, 846–854.

Miller, N. E.   Integration of neurophysiological and behavioral research. *Ann. N. Y. Acad. Sci.*, 1961, *92*, 830–839. (a)

Miller, N. E.   Learning and performance motivated by direct stimulation of the brain. In D. E. Sheer (Ed.), *Electrical stimulation of the brain: Subcortical integrative systems.* Houston: Univer. Texas Press, 1961. (b)

Miller, N. E., & Barry, H.   Motivational effects of drugs: Methods which illustrate some general problems in psychopharmacology. *Psychopharmacologia*, 1960, *1*, 169–199.

Miller, N. E., & Dollard, J.   *Social learning and imitation.* New Haven: Yale Univer. Press, 1941.

Miller, N. E., & Kessen, M. L.   Reward effects of food via stomach fistula compared with those of food via mouth. *J. comp. physiol. Psychol.*, 1952, *45*, 550–564.

Miller, N. E., Sampliner, R. I., & Woodrow, P.   Thirst-reducing effects of water by stomach fistula vs. water by mouth measured by both a consummatory and an instrumental response. *J. comp. physiol. Psychol.*, 1957, *50*, 1–5.

Myers, A. K., & Miller, N. E.   Failure to find a learned drive based on hunger: Evidence for learning motivated by "exploration." *J. comp. physiol. Psychol.*, 1954, *47*, 428–436.

Nagaty, M. O.   Effect of food reward immediately preceding performance of an instrumental conditioned response on extinction of that response. *J. exp. Psychol.*, 1951, *42*, 333–340.

Novin, D.   The relation between electrical conductivity of brain tissue and thirst in the rat. *J. comp. physiol. Psychol.*, 1962, in press.

Olds, J., & Milner, P.   Positive reinforcement produced by electrical stimulation of septal area and other regions of rat brain. *J. comp. physiol. Psychol.*, 1954, *47*, 419–427.

Sheffield, F. D., & Roby, T. B.   Reward value of a non-nutritive sweet taste. *J. comp. physiol. Psychol.*, 1950, *43*, 471–481.

Thorndike, E. L.   Animal intelligence: An experimental study of the associative processes in animals. *Psychol. Rev., Monogr. Suppl.*, 1898, *2*(4, Whole No. 8).

Thorndike, E. L.   A proof of the law of effect. *Science*, 1933, *77*, 173–175.

Tolman, E. C.   *Purposive behavior in animals and men.* New York: Appleton-Century, 1932.

Reprinted with permission
from *American Psychologist*,
1965, *20*, 1007–1017.

Chapter 25

The Growth of Mind

Jerome S. Bruner

Harvard University

These past several years, I have had the painful pleasure—and it has been both—of exploring two aspects of the cognitive processes that were new to me. One was cognitive development, the other pedagogy. I knew, as we all know, that the two were closely related, and it was my naive hope that, betimes, the relation would come clear to me. Indeed, 2 years ago when I first knew that in early September 1965 I would be standing here, delivering this lecture, I said to myself that I would use the occasion to set forth to my colleagues what I had been able to find out about this vexed subject, the relation of pedagogy and development. It seemed obvious then that in 2 years one could get to the heart of the matter.

The 2 years have gone by. I have had the privilege of addressing this distinguished audience (Bruner, 1964) on some of our findings concerning the development of cognitive processes in children, and I have similarly set forth what I hope are not entirely unreasonable ideas about pedagogy (Bruner, in press). I am still in a very deep quandary concerning the relation of these two enterprises. The heart of the matter

---

Address of the President to the Seventy-Third Annual Convention of the American Psychological Association, Chicago, September 4, 1965.

still eludes me, but I shall stand by my resolve. I begin on this autobiographical note so that you may know in advance why this evening is more an exercise in conjecture than a cataloguing of solid conclusions.

What is most unique about man is that his growth as an individual depends upon the history of his species—not upon a history reflected in genes and chromosomes but, rather, reflected in a culture external to man's tissue and wider in scope than is embodied in any one man's competency. Perforce, then, the growth of mind is always growth assisted from the outside. And since a culture, particularly an advanced one, transcends the bounds of individual competence, the limits for individual growth are by definition greater than what any single person has previously attained. For the limits of growth depend on how a culture assists the individual to use such intellectual potential as he may possess. It seems highly unlikely—either empirically or canonically—that we have any realistic sense of the furthest reach of such assistance to growth.

The evidence today is that the full evolution of intelligence came as a result of bipedalism and tool using. The large human brain gradually evolved as a sequel to the first use of pebble tools by early near-man. To condense the story, a near-man, or hominid, with a slightly superior brain, using a pebble tool, could make out better in the niche provided by nature than a near-man who depended not on tools but on sheer strength and formidable jaws. Natural selection favored the primitive tool user. In time, thanks to his better chance of surviving and breeding, he became more so: The ones who survived had larger brains, smaller jaws, less ferocious teeth. In place of belligerent anatomy, they developed tools and a brain that made it possible to use them. Human evolution thereafter became less a matter of having appropriate fangs or claws and more one of using and later fashioning tools to express the powers of the larger brain that was also emerging. Without tools the brain was of little use, no matter how many hundred cubic centimeters of it there might be. Let it also be said that without the original programmatic capacity for fitting tools into a sequence of acts, early hominids would never have started the epigenetic progress that brought them to their present state. And as human groups stabilized, tools became more complex and "shaped to pattern," so that it was no longer a matter of reinventing tools in order to survive, but rather of mastering the skills necessary for using them. In short, after a certain point in human evolution, the only means whereby man could fill his evolutionary niche was through the cultural transmission of the skills necessary for the use of priorly invented techniques, implements, and devices.

Two crucial parallel developments seem also to have occurred. As hominids became increasingly bipedal, with the freed hands necessary for using spontaneous pebble tools, selection also favored those with a heavier pelvic bony structure that could sustain the impacting strain of bipedal locomotion. The added strength came, of course, from a gradual closing down of the birth canal. There is an obstetrical paradox here: a creature with an increasingly larger brain but with a smaller and smaller birth canal to get through. The resolution seems to have been achieved through the immaturity of the human neonate, particularly cerebral immaturity that assures not only a smaller head, but also a longer period of transmitting the necessary skills required by human culture. During this same period, human language must have emerged, giving man not only a new and powerful way of representing reality but also increasing his power to assist the mental growth of the young to a degree beyond anything before seen in nature.

It is impossible, of course, to reconstruct the evolution in techniques of instruction in the shadow zone between hominids and man. I have tried to compensate by observing contemporary analogues of earlier forms, knowing full well that the pursuit of analogy can be dangerously misleading. I have spent many hours observing uncut films of the behavior of free-ranging baboons, films shot in East Africa by my colleague Irven DeVore with a very generous footage devoted to infants and juveniles. I have also had access to the unedited film archives of a hunting-gathering people living under roughly analogous ecological conditions, the !Kung Bushman of the Kalahari, recorded by Laurance and Lorna Marshall, brilliantly aided by their son John and daughter Elizabeth.[1] I have also worked directly but informally with the Wolof of Senegal, observing children in the bush and in French-style schools. Even more valuable than my own informal observations in Senegal were the systematic experiments carried out later by my colleague, Patricia Marks Greenfield (in press).

Let me describe very briefly some salient differences in the free learning patterns of immature baboons and among !Kung children. Baboons have a highly developed social life in their troops, with well-organized and stable dominance patterns. They live within a territory, protecting themselves from predators by joint action of the strongly built, adult males. It is striking that the behavior of baboon juveniles is shaped principally by play with their peer group, play that provides opportunity for the spontaneous expression and practice of the component acts that, in maturity, will be orchestrated into either the behavior of the dominant male or of the infant-protective female. All this seems to be accomplished with little participation by any mature animals in the play of the juveniles. We know from the important experiments of Harlow and his colleagues (Harlow & Harlow, 1962) how devastating a disruption in development can be produced in subhuman primates by

---

1. I am greatly indebted to Irven DeVore and Educational Services Incorporated for the opportunity to view his films of free-ranging baboons, and to Laurance and Lorna Marshall for the opportunity to examine their incomparable archives. DeVore and the Marshalls have been generous in their counsel as well.

interfering with their opportunity for peer-group play and social interaction.

Among hunting-gathering humans, on the other hand, there is *constant* interaction between adult and child, or adult and adolescent, or adolescent and child. !Kung adults and children play and dance together, sit together, participate in minor hunting together, join in song and story telling together. At very frequent intervals, moreover, children are party to rituals presided over by adults—minor, as in the first haircutting, or major, as when a boy kills his first Kudu buck and goes through the proud but painful process of scarification. Children, besides, are constantly playing imitatively with the rituals, implements, tools, and weapons of the adult world. Young juvenile baboons, on the other hand, virtually never play with things or imitate directly large and significant sequences of adult behavior.

Note, though, that in tens of thousands of feet of !Kung film, one virtually never sees an instance of "teaching" taking place outside the situation where the behavior to be learned is relevant. Nobody "teaches" in our prepared sense of the word. There is nothing like school, nothing like lessons. Indeed, among the !Kung children there is very little "telling." Most of what we would call instruction is through showing. And there is no "practice" or "drill" as such save in the form of play modeled directly on adult models—play hunting, play bossing, play exchanging, play baby tending, play house making. In the end, every man in the culture knows nearly all there is to know about how to get on with life as a man, and every woman as a woman—the skills, the rituals and myths, the obligations and rights.

The change in the instruction of children in more complex societies is twofold. First of all, there is knowledge and skill in the culture far in excess of what any one individual knows. And so, increasingly, there develops an economical technique of instructing the young based heavily on *telling* out of context rather than *showing* in context. In literate societies, the practice becomes institutionalized in the school or the "teacher." Both promote this necessarily abstract way of instructing the young. The result of "teaching the culture" can, at its worst, lead to the ritual, rote nonsense that has led a generation of critics from Max Wertheimer (1945) to Mary Alice White (undated) of Teachers' College to despair. For in the detached school, what is imparted often has little to do with life as lived in the society except insofar as the demands of school are of a kind that reflect *indirectly* the demands of life in a technical society. But these indirectly imposed demands may be the most important feature of the detached school. For school is a sharp departure from indigenous practice. It takes learning, as we have noted, out of the context of immediate action just by dint of putting it into a school. This very extirpation makes learning become an act in itself, freed from the immediate ends of action, preparing the learner for the chain of reckoning remote from payoff that is needed for the formulation of complex ideas. At the same time, the school (if successful) frees the child from the pace setting of the round of daily activity. If the school succeeds in avoiding a pace-setting round of its own, it may be one of the great agents for promoting reflectiveness. Moreover, in school, one must "follow the lesson" which means one must learn to follow either the abstraction of written speech—abstract in the sense that it is divorced from the concrete situation to which the speech might originally have been related—or the abstraction of language delivered orally but out of the context of an ongoing action. Both of these are highly abstract uses of language.

It is no wonder, then, that many recent studies report large differences between "primitive" children who are in schools and their brothers who are not: differences in perception, abstraction, time perspective, and so on. I need only cite the work of Biesheuvel (1949) in South Africa, Gay and Cole (undated) in Liberia, Greenfield (in press) in Senegal, Maccoby and Modiano (in press) in rural Mexico, Reich (in press) among Alaskan Eskimos.

What a culture does to assist the development of the powers of mind of its members is, in effect, to provide amplification systems to which human beings, equipped with appropriate skills, can link themselves. There are, first, the amplifiers of action—hammers, levers, digging sticks, wheels—but more important, the programs of action into which such implements can be substituted. Second, there are amplifiers of the senses, ways of looking and noticing that can take advantage of devices ranging from smoke signals and hailers to diagrams and pictures that stop the action or microscopes that enlarge it. Finally and most powerfully, there are amplifiers of the thought processes, ways of thinking that employ language and formation of explanation, and later use such languages as mathematics and logic and even find automatic servants to crank out the consequences. A culture is, then, a deviser, a repository, and a transmitter of amplification systems and of the devices that fit into such systems. We know very little in a deep sense about the transmission function, how people are trained to get the most from their potential by use of a culture's resources.

But it is reasonably clear that there is a major difference between the mode of transmission in a technical society, with its schools, and an indigenous one, where cultural transmission is in the context of action. It is not just that an indigenous society, when its action pattern becomes disrupted falls apart—at a most terrifying rate—as in uncontrolled urbanization in some parts of Africa. Rather, it is that the institution of a school serves to convert knowledge and skill into more symbolical, more abstract, more verbal form. It is this process of transmission—admittedly very new in human history—that is so poorly understood and to which, finally, we shall return.

There are certain obvious specifications that can be stated about how a society must proceed in order to equip its young. It must convert what is to be known—whether a skill or a belief system or a connected body of knowledge—into a form capable of being mastered by a beginner. The more we know of the process of growth, the better we shall be at such conversion. The failure of modern man to understand mathematics and science may be less a matter of stunted abilities than our failure to understand how to teach such subjects. Second, given the limited amount of time available for learning, there must be a due regard for saving the learner from needless learning. There must be some emphasis placed on economy and transfer and the learning of general rules. All societies must (and virtually all do) distinguish those who are clever from those who are stupid—though few of them generalize this trait across all activities. Cleverness in a particular activity almost universally connotes strategy, economy, heuristics, highly generalized skills. A society must also place emphasis upon how one derives a course of action from what one has learned. Indeed, in an indigenous society, it is almost impossible to separate what one does from what one knows. More advanced societies often have not found a way of dealing with the separation of knowledge and action—probably a result of the emphasis they place upon "telling" in their instruction. All societies must maintain interest among the young in the learning process, a minor problem when learning is in the context of life and action, but harder when it becomes more abstracted. And finally, and perhaps most obviously, a society must assure that its necessary skills and procedures remain intact from one generation to the next—which does not always happen, as witnessed by Easter Islanders, Incas, Aztecs, and Mayas.[2]

Unfortunately, psychology has not concerned itself much with any of these five requisites of cultural transmission—or at least not much with four of them. We have too easily assumed that learning is learning is learning—that the early version of what was taught did not matter much, one thing being much like another and reducible to a pattern of association, to stimulus-response connections, or to our favorite molecular componentry. We denied there was a problem of development beyond the quantitative one of providing more experience, and with the denial, closed our eyes to the pedagogical problem of how to represent knowledge, how to sequence it, how to embody it in a form appropriate to young learners. We expended more passion on the part-whole controversy than on what whole or what part of it was to be presented

---

2. I have purposely left out of the discussion the problems of impulse regulation and socialization of motives, topics that have received extended treatment in the voluminous literature on culture and personality. The omission is dictated by emphasis rather than evaluation. Obviously, the shaping of character by culture is of great importance for an understanding of our topic as it bears, for example, upon culture-instilled attitudes toward the uses of mind. Since our emphasis is upon human potential and its amplification by culturally patterned instrumental skills, we mention the problem of character formation in passing and in recognition of its importance in a complete treatment of the issues under discussion.

first. I should except Piaget (1954), Köhler (1940), and Vygotsky (1962) from these complaints—all until recently unheeded voices.

Our neglect of the economy of learning stems, ironically, from the heritage of Ebbinghaus (1913), who was vastly interested in savings. Our nonsense syllables, our random mazes failed to take into account how we reduce complexity and strangeness to simplicity and the familiar, how we convert what we have learned into rules and procedures, how, to use Bartlett's (1932) term of over 30 years ago, we turn around on our own schemata to reorganize what we have mastered into more manageable form.

Nor have we taken naturally to the issue of knowledge and action. Its apparent mentalism has repelled us. Tolman (1951), who bravely made the distinction, was accused of leaving his organisms wrapt in thought. But he recognized the problem and if he insisted on the idea that knowledge might be organized in cognitive maps, it was in recognition (as a great functionalist) that organisms go somewhere on the basis of what they have learned. I believe we are getting closer to the problem of how knowledge affects action and vice versa, and offer in testimony of my conviction the provocative book by Miller, Galanter, and Pribram (1960), *Plans and the Structure of Behavior*.

Where the maintenance of the learner's interest is concerned, I remind you of what my colleague Gordon Allport (1946) has long warned. We have been so concerned with the model of driven behavior, with drive reduction and the *vis a tergo* that, again, until recently, we have tended to overlook the question of what keeps learners interested in the activity of learning, in the achievement of competence beyond bare necessity and first payoff. The work of R. W. White (1959) on effectance motivation, of Harlow and his colleagues (Butler, 1954; Harlow, 1953) on curiosity, and of Heider (1958) and Festinger (1962) on consistency begins to redress the balance. But it is only a beginning.

The invention of antidegradation devices, guarantors that skill and knowledge will be maintained intact, is an exception to our oversight. We psychologists have been up to our ears in it. Our special contribution is the achievement test. But the achievement test has, in the main, reflected the timidity of the educational enterprise as a whole. I believe we know how to determine, though we have not yet devised tests to determine, how pupils use what they learn to think with later in life—for there is the real issue.

I have tried to examine briefly what a culture must do in passing on its amplifying skills and knowledge to a new generation and, even more briefly, how we as psychologists have dealt or failed to deal with the problems. I think the situation is fast changing—with a sharp increase in interest in the conversion problem, the problems of economy of learning, the nature of interest, the relation of knowledge and action. We are, I believe, at a major turning point where psychology will once again concern itself with the design of methods of assisting cognitive growth, be it through the invention of a rational technology of toys, of ways of enriching the environment of the crib and nursery, of organizing the activity of a school, or of devising a curriculum whereby we transmit an organized body of knowledge and skill to a new generation to amplify their powers of mind.

I commented earlier that there was strikingly little knowledge available about the "third way" of training the skills of the young: the first being the play practice of component skills in prehuman primates, the second the teaching-in-context of indigenous societies, and the third being the abstracted, detached method of the school.

Let me now become highly specific. Let me consider a particular course of study, one given in a school, one we are ourselves constructing, trying out, and in a highly qualitative way, evaluating. It is for schools of the kind that exist in Western culture. The experience we have had with this effort, now in its third year, may serve to highlight the kinds of problems and conjectures one encounters in studying how to assist the growth of intellect in this "third way."

There is a dilemma in describing a course of study. One begins by setting forth the intellectual substance of what is to be taught. Yet if such a recounting tempts one to "get across" the subject, the ingredient of pedagogy is in jeopardy. For only in a trivial sense is a course designed to "get something across," merely to impart information. There are better means to that end than teaching. Unless the learner develops his skills, disciplines his taste, deepens his view of the world, the "something" that is got across is hardly worth the effort of transmission.

The more "elementary" a course and the younger its students, the more serious must be its pedagogical aim of forming the intellectual powers of those whom it serves. It is as important to justify a good mathematics course by the intellectual discipline it provides or the honesty it promotes as by the mathematics it transmits. Indeed, neither can be accomplished without the other. The content of this particular course is man: his nature as a species, the forces that shaped and continue to shape his humanity. Three questions recur throughout:

> What is human about human beings?
> How did they get that way?
> How can they be made more so?

In pursuit of our questions we explore five matters, each closely associated with the evolution of man as a species, each defining at once the distinctiveness of man and his potentiality for further evolution. The five great humanizing forces are, of course, tool making, language, social organization, the management of man's prolonged childhood, and man's urge to explain. It has been our first lesson in teaching that no pupil, however eager, can appreciate the relevance of, say, tool making or language in human evolution without first grasping the fundamental concept of a tool or what a language is. These are not self-evident matters, even to the expert. So we are involved in teaching not only the role of tools or language in the emergence of man, but, as a necessary precondition for doing so, setting forth the fundamentals of linguistics or the theory of tools. And it is as often the case as not that (as in the case of the "theory of tools") we must solve a formidable intellectual problem ourselves in order to be able to help our pupils do the same. I should have said at the outset that the "we" I employ in this context is no editorial fiction, but rather a group of anthropologists, zoologists, linguists, theoretical engineers, artists, designers, camera crews, teachers, children, and psychologists. The project is being carried out under my direction at Educational Services, Incorporated, with grants from the National Science Foundation and the Ford Foundation.

While one readily singles out five sources of man's humanization, under no circumstances can they be put into airtight compartments. Human kinship is distinctively different from primate mating patterns precisely because it is classificatory and rests on man's ability to use language. Or, if you will, tool use enhances the division of labor in a society which in turn affects kinship. So while each domain can be treated as a separate set of ideas, their teaching must make it possible for the children to have a sense of their interaction. We have leaned heavily on the use of contrast, highly controlled contrast, to help children achieve detachment from the all too familiar matrix of social life: the contrasts of man versus higher primates, man versus prehistoric man, contemporary technological man versus "primitive" man, and man versus child. The primates are principally baboons, the prehistoric materials mostly from the Olduvai Gorge and Les Eyzies, the "primitive" peoples mostly the Netsilik Eskimos of Pelly Bay and the !Kung Bushmen. The materials, collected for our purposes, are on film, in story, in ethnography, in pictures and drawings, and principally in ideas embodied in exercises.

We have high aspirations. We hope to achieve five goals:

1. To give our pupils respect for and confidence in the powers of their own minds.

2. To give them respect, moreover, for the powers of thought concerning the human condition, man's plight, and his social life.

3. To provide them with a set of workable models that make it simpler to analyze the nature of the social world in which they live and the condition in which man finds himself.

4. To impart a sense of respect for the capacities and plight of man as a species, for his origins, for his potential, for his humanity.

5. To leave the student with a sense of the unfinished business of man's evolution.

One last word about the course of study that has to do with the quality of the ideas, materials, and artistry—a matter that is at once technological and intellectual. We have felt that the making of such a curriculum deserved the best talent and technique available in the world.

Whether artist, ethnographer, film maker, poet, teacher—nobody we have asked has refused us. We are obviously going to suffer in testing a Hawthorne effect of some magnitude. But then, perhaps it is as well to live in a permanent state of revolution.

Let me now try to describe some of the major problems one encounters in trying to construct a course of study. I shall not try to translate the problems into refined theoretical form, for they do not as yet merit such translation. They are more difficulties than problems. I choose them, because they are vividly typical of what one encounters in such enterprises. The course is designed for 10-year-olds in the fifth grade of elementary school, but we have been trying it out as well on the fourth and sixth grades better to bracket our difficulties.

One special point about these difficulties. They are born of trying to achieve an objective and are as much policy bound as theory bound. It is like the difference between building an economic theory about monopolistic practices and constructing policies for controlling monopoly. Let me remind you that modern economic theory has been reformulated, refined, and revived by having a season in policy. I am convinced that the psychology of assisted growth, i.e., pedagogy, will have to be forged in the policy crucible of curriculum making before it can reach its full descriptive power as theory. Economics was first through the cycle from theory to policy to theory to policy; it is happening now to psychology, anthropology, and sociology.

Now on to the difficulties. The first is what might be called *the psychology of a subject matter*. A learned discipline can be conceived as a way of thinking about certain phenomena. Mathematics is one way of thinking about order without reference to what is being ordered. The behavioral sciences provide one or perhaps several ways of thinking about man and his society—about regularities, origins, causes, effects. They are probably special (and suspect) because they permit man to look at himself from a perspective that is outside his own skin and beyond his own preferences—at least for awhile.

Underlying a discipline's "way of thought," there is a set of connected, varyingly implicit, generative propositions. In physics and mathematics, most of the underlying generative propositions like the conservation theorems, or the axioms of geometry, or the associative, distributive, and commutative rules of analysis are by now very explicit indeed. In the behavioral sciences we must be content with more implicitness. We traffic in inductive propositions: e.g., the different activities of a society are interconnected such that if you know something about the technological response of a society to an environment, you will be able to make some shrewd guesses about its myths or about the things it values, etc. We use the device of a significant contrast as in linguistics as when we describe the territoriality of a baboon troop in order to help us recognize the system of reciprocal exchange of a human group, the former somehow provoking awareness of the latter.

There is nothing more central to a discipline than its way of thinking. There is nothing more important in its teaching than to provide the child the earliest opportunity to learn that way of thinking— the forms of connection, the attitudes, hopes, jokes, and frustrations that go with it. In a word, the best introduction to a subject is the subject itself. At the very first breath, the young learner should, we think, be given the chance to solve problems, to conjecture, to quarrel as these are done at the heart of the discipline. But, you will ask, how can this be arranged?

Here again the problem of conversion. There exist ways of thinking characteristic of different stages of development. We are acquainted with Inhelder and Piaget's (1958) account of the transition from preoperational, through concrete operational, to propositional thought in the years from preschool through, say, high school. If you have an eventual pedagogical objective in mind, you can translate the way of thought of a discipline into its Piagetian (or other) equivalent appropriate to a given level of development and take the child onward from there. The Cambridge Mathematics Project of Educational Services, Incorporated, argues that if the child is to master the calculus early in his high school years, he should start work early with the idea of limits, the earliest work being manipulative, later going on to images and diagrams, and finally moving on to the more abstract notation needed for delineating the more precise idea of limits.

In "Man: A Course of Study," (Bruner, 1965) there are also versions of the subject appropriate to a particular age that can at a later age be given a more powerful rendering. We have tried to choose topics with this in mind: The analysis of kinship that begins with children using sticks and blocks and colors and whatnot to represent their own families, goes on to the conventional kinship diagrams by a meandering but, as you can imagine, interesting path, and then can move on to more formal and powerful componential analysis. So, too, with myth. We begin with the excitement of a powerful myth (like the Netsilik Nuliajik myth), then have the children construct some myths of their own, then examine what a set of Netsilik myths have in common, which takes us finally to Lévi-Strauss's (1963) analysis of contrastive features in myth construction. A variorum text of a myth or corpus of myths put together by sixth graders can be quite an extraordinary document.

This approach to the psychology of a learned discipline turns out to illuminate another problem raised earlier: the maintenance of interest. There is, in this approach, a reward in understanding that grows from the subject matter itself. It is easier to engineer this satisfaction in mathematics, for understanding is so utter in a formal discipline—a balance beam balances or it does not; therefore there is an equality or there is not. In the behavioral sciences the payoff in understanding cannot be so obviously and startlingly self-revealing. Yet, one can design exercises in the understanding of man, too—as when children figure out the ways in which, given limits of ecology, skills, and materials, Bushmen hunt different animals, and then compare their predictions with the real thing on film.

Consider now a second problem: *how to stimulate thought in the setting of a school.* We know from experimental studies like those of Bloom and Broder (1950), and of Goodnow and Pettigrew (1955), that there is a striking difference in the acts of a person who thinks that the task before him represents a problem to be solved rather than being controlled by random forces. School is a particular subculture where these matters are concerned. By school age, children have come to expect quite arbitrary and, from their point of view, meaningless demands to be made upon them by adults—the result, most likely, of the fact that adults often fail to recognize the task of conversion necessary to make their questions have some intrinsic significance for the child. Children, of course, will try to solve problems if they recognize them as such. But they are not often either predisposed to or skillful in problem finding, in recognizing the hidden conjectural feature in tasks set them. But we know now that children in school can quite quickly be led to such problem finding by encouragement and instruction.

The need for this instruction and encouragement and its relatively swift success relates, I suspect, to what pyschoanalysts refer to as the guilt-ridden oversuppression of primary process and its public replacement by secondary process. Children, like adults, need reassurance that it is all right to entertain and express highly subjective ideas, to treat a task as a problem where you *invent* an answer rather than *finding* one out there in the book or on the blackboard. With children in elementary school, there is often a need to devise emotionally vivid special games, story-making episodes, or construction projects to reestablish in the child's mind his right not only to have his own private ideas but to express them in the public setting of a classroom.

But there is another, perhaps more serious difficulty: the interference of intrinsic problem solving by extrinsic. Young children in school expend extraordinary time and effort figuring out what it is that the teacher wants—and usually coming to the conclusion that she or he wants tidiness or remembering or to do things at a certain time in a certain way. This I refer to as extrinsic problem solving. There is a great deal of it in school.

There are several quite straightforward ways of stimulating problem solving. One is to train teachers to want it and that will come in time. But teachers can be encouraged to like it, interestingly enough, by providing them and their children with materials and lessons that *permit* legitimate problem solving and permit the teacher to recognize it. For exercises with such materials create an atmosphere by treating things as instances of what *might* have occurred rather than simply as what did occur. Let me illustrate by a concrete instance. A fifth-grade class was working on the organization of a baboon troop—on this particular day, specifically on how they might protect against predators. They saw a brief sequence of film in which six or seven adult males go forward to intimidate and hold off three cheetahs. The teacher asked what the baboons had done to keep the cheetahs off, and there ensued a lively discussion of how the dominant adult males, by showing their formidable mouthful of teeth and making threatening gestures had turned the trick. A boy raised a tentative hand and asked whether cheetahs always attacked together. Yes, though a single cheetah sometimes followed behind a moving troop and picked off an older, weakened straggler or an unwary, straying juvenile. "Well, what if there were four cheetahs and two of them attacked from behind and two from in front. What would the baboons do then?" The question could have been answered empirically—and the inquiry ended. Cheetahs *do not* attack that way, and so we do not know what baboons *might* do. Fortunately, it was not. For the question opens up the deep issues of what might be and why it is not. Is there a necessary relation between predators and prey that share a common ecological niche? Must their encounters have a "sporting chance" outcome? It is such conjecture, in this case quite unanswerable, that produces rational, self-consciously problem-finding behavior so crucial to the growth of intellectual power. Given the materials, given some background and encouragement, teachers like it as much as the students.

I should like to turn now to the *personalization of knowledge*. A generation ago, the progressive movement urged that knowledge be related to the child's own experience and brought out of the realm of empty abstractions. A good idea was translated into banalities about the home, then the friendly postman and trashman, then the community, and so on. It is a poor way to compete with the child's own dramas and mysteries. A decade ago, my colleague Clyde Kluckhorn (1949) wrote a prize-winning popular book on anthropology with the entrancing title *Mirror for Man*. In some deep way, there is extraordinary power in "that mirror which other civilizations still hold up to us to recognize and study . . . [the] image of ourselves [Lévi-Strauss, 1965]." The psychological bases of the power are not obvious. Is it as in discrimination learning, where increasing the degree of contrast helps in the learning of a discrimination, or as in studies of concept attainment where a negative instance demonstrably defines the domain of a conceptual rule? Or is it some primitive identification? All these miss one thing that seems to come up frequently in our interviews with the children. It is the experience of discovering kinship and likeness in what at first seemed bizarre, exotic, and even a little repellent.

Consider two examples, both involving film of the Netsilik. In the films, a single nuclear family, Zachary, Marta, and their 4-year-old Alexi, is followed through the year—spring sealing, summer fishing at the stone weir, fall caribou hunting, early winter fishing through the ice, winter at the big ceremonial igloo. Children report that at first the three members of the family look weird and uncouth. In time, they look normal, and eventually, as when Marta finds sticks around which to wrap her braids, the girls speak of how pretty she is. That much is superficial—or so it seems. But consider a second episode.

It has to do with Alexi who, with his father's help, devises a snare and catches a gull. There is a scene in which he stones the gull to death. Our children watched, horror struck. One girl, Kathy, blurted out, "He's not even human, doing that to the seagull." The class was silent. Then another girl, Jennine, said quietly: "He's got to grow up to be a hunter. His mother was smiling when he was doing that." And then an extended discussion about how people have to do things to learn and even do things to learn how to feel appropriately. "What would you do if you had to live there? Would you be as smart about getting along as they are with what they've got?" said one boy, going back to the accusation that Alexi was inhuman to stone the bird.

I am sorry it is so difficult to say it clearly. What I am trying to say is that to personalize knowledge one does not simply link it to the familiar. Rather one makes the familiar an instance of a more general case and thereby produces awareness of it. What the children were learning about was not seagulls and Eskimos, but about their own feelings and preconceptions that, up to then, were too implicit to be recognizable to them.

Consider finally the problem of *self-conscious reflectiveness*. It is an epistemological mystery why traditional education has so often emphasized extensiveness and coverage over intensiveness and depth. We have already commented on the fact that memorizing was usually perceived by children as one of the high-priority tasks but rarely did children sense an emphasis upon ratiocination with a view toward redefining what had been encountered, reshaping it, reordering it. The cultivation of reflectiveness, or whatever you choose to call it, is one of the great problems one faces in devising curriculum. How lead children to discover the powers and pleasures that await the exercise of retrospection?

Let me suggest one answer that has grown from what we have done. It is the use of the "organizing conjecture." We have used three such conjectures—what is human about human beings, how they got that way, how they could become more so. They serve two functions, one of them the very obvious though important one of putting perspective back into the particulars. The second is less obvious and considerably more surprising. The questions often seemed to serve as criteria for determining where they were getting, how well they were understanding, whether anything new was emerging. Recall Kathy's cry: "He's not human doing that to the seagull." She was hard at work in her rage on the conjecture what makes human beings human.

There, in brief, are four problems that provide some sense of what a psychologist encounters when he takes a hand in assisting the growth of mind in children in the special setting of a school. The problems look

quite different from those we encounter in formulating classical developmental theory with the aid of typical laboratory research. They also look
very different from those that one would find in an indigenous society,
describing how children picked up skills and knowledge and values in
the context of action and daily life. We clearly do not have a theory of the
school that is sufficient to the task of running schools—just as we have
no adequate theory of toys or of readiness building or whatever the
jargon is for preparing children to do a better job the next round. It only
obscures the issue to urge that some day our classical theories of learning
will fill the gap. They show no sign of doing so.

I hope that we shall not allow ourselves to be embarrassed by our
present ignorance. It has been a long time since we have looked at what
is involved in imparting knowledge through the vehicle of the school—if
ever we did look at it squarely. I urge that we delay no longer.

But I am deeply convinced that the psychologist cannot alone
construct a theory of how to assist cognitive development and cannot
alone learn how to enrich and amplify the powers of a growing human
mind. The task belongs to the whole intellectual community: the behavioral scientists and the artists, scientists, and scholars who are the
custodians of skill, taste, and knowledge in our culture. Our special task
as psychologists is to convert skills and knowledge to forms and exercises
that fit growing minds—and it is a task ranging from how to keep
children free from anxiety and how to translate physics for the very
young child into a set of playground maneuvers that, later, the child can
turn around upon and convert into a sense of inertial regularities.

And this in turn leads me to a final conjecture, one that has to do
with the organization of our profession, a matter that has concerned me
greatly during this past year during which I have had the privilege of
serving as your President. Psychology is peculiarly prey to parochialism.
Left to our own devices, we tend to construct models of a man who is
neither a victim of history, a target of economic forces, or even a working
member of a society. I am still struck by Roger Barker's (1963) ironic
truism that the best way to predict the behavior of a human being is to
know where he is: In a post office he behaves post office, at church he
behaves church.

Psychology, and you will forgive me if the image seems a trifle
frivolous, thrives on polygamy with her neighbors. Our marriage with
the biological sciences has produced a cumulation of ever more powerful
knowledge. So, too, our joint undertakings with anthropology and
sociology. Joined together with a variety of disciplines, we have made
lasting contributions to the health sciences and, I judge, will make even
greater contributions now that the emphasis is shifting to the problems
of alleviating stress and arranging for a community's mental health.
What I find lacking is an alignment that might properly be called the
growth sciences. The field of pedagogy is one participant in the growth
sciences. Any field of inquiry devoted to assisting the growth of effective
human beings, fully empowered with zest, with skill, with knowledge,
with taste is surely a candidate for this sodality. My friend Philip

Morrison once suggested to his colleagues at Cornell that his department of physics grant a doctorate not only for work in theoretical, experimental, or applied physics, but also for work in pedagogical physics. The limits of the growth sciences remain to be drawn. They surely transcend the behavioral sciences cum pediatrics. It is plain that, if we are to achieve the effectiveness of which we as human beings are capable, there will one day have to be such a field. I hope that we psychologists can earn our way as charter members.

REFERENCES

Allport, G.   Effect: A secondary principle of learning. *Psychological Review*, 1946, *53*, 335–347.

Barker, R.   On the nature of the environment. *Journal of Social Issues*, 1963, *19*, 17–38.

Bartlett, F.   *Remembering*. Cambridge, England: Cambridge Univer. Press, 1932.

Biesheuvel, S.   Psychological tests and their application to non-European peoples. *Yearbook of Education*. London: Evans, 1949. Pp. 87–126.

Bloom, B., & Broder, L.   Problem solving processes of college students. *Supplementary Educational Monograph, No. 73*. Chicago: Univer. Chicago Press, 1950.

Bruner, J.   The course of cognitive growth. *American Psychologist*, 1964, *19*, 1–15.

Bruner, J.   Man: A course of study. *Educational Services Inc. Quarterly Report*, 1965, Spring-Summer, 3–13.

Bruner, J.   *Toward a theory of instruction*. Cambridge: Harvard Univer. Press, in press.

Butler, R. A.   Incentive conditions which influence visual exploration. *Journal of Experimental Psychology*, 1954, *48*, 19–23.

Ebbinghaus, H.   *Memory: A contribution to experimental psychology*. New York: Teachers College, Columbia University, 1913.

Festinger, L.   A theory of cognitive dissonance. Stanford: Stanford Univer. Press, 1962.

Gay, J., & Cole, M.   Outline of general report on Kpelle mathematics project. Stanford: Stanford University, Institute for Mathematical Social Studies, undated. (Mimeo)

Goodnow, Jacqueline, & Pettigrew, T.   Effect of prior patterns of experience on strategies and learning sets. *Journal of Experimental Psychology*, 1955, *49*, 381–389.

Greenfield, Patricia M.   Culture and conservation. In J. Bruner, Rose Olver, & Patricia M. Greenfield (Eds.), *Studies in cognitive growth*. New York: Wiley, in press. Ch. 10.

Harlow, H., & Harlow, Margaret.   Social deprivation in monkeys. *Scientific American*, 1962, November.

Harlow, H. F.   Mice, monkeys, men, and motives. *Psychological Review*, 1953, *60*, 23–32.

Heider, F.   *The psychology of interpersonal relations*. New York: Wiley, 1958.

Inhelder, Bärbel, & Piaget, J.   *The growth of logical thinking*. New York: Basic Books, 1958.

Kluckhorn, C.   *Mirror for man*. New York: Whittlesey House, 1949.

Köhler, W.   *Dynamics in psychology*. New York: Liveright, 1940.

Lévi-Strauss, C.   The structural study of myth. *Structural anthropology*. (Trans. by Claire Jacobson & B. Grundfest Scharpf) New York: Basic Books, 1963. Pp. 206–231.

Lévi-Strauss, C.   Anthropology: Its achievements and future. Lecture presented at Bicentennial Celebration, Smithsonian Institution, Washington, D.C., September 1965.

Maccoby, M., & Modiano, Nancy.   On culture and equivalence. In J. Bruner, Rose Olver, & Patricia M. Greenfield (Eds.), *Studies in cognitive growth*. New York: Wiley, in press. Ch. 12.

Miller, G., Galanter, E., & Pribram, K.   *Plans and the structure of behavior*. New York: Holt, 1960.

Piaget, J.   *The construction of reality in the child*. New York: Basic Books, 1954.

Reich, Lee.   On culture and grouping. In J. Bruner, Rose Olver, & Patricia M. Greenfield (Eds.), *Studies in cognitive growth*. New York: Wiley, in press. Ch. 13.

Tolman, E.   Cognitive maps in rats and men. *Collected papers in psychology*. Berkeley & Los Angeles: Univer. California Press, 1951. Pp. 241-264.

Vygotsky, L.   *Thought and language*. (Ed. & trans. by Eugenia Hanfmann & Gertrude Vakar) New York: Wiley, 1962.

Wertheimer, M.   *Productive thinking*. New York & London: Harper, 1945.

White, Mary A.   The child's world of learning. Teachers College, Columbia University, undated. (Mimeo)

White, R. W.   Motivation reconsidered: The concept of competence. *Psychological Review*, 1959, *66*, 297-333.

Part Four

The Recent Years

Presidents of the
American Psychological Association
1968–1977

Abraham H. Maslow, *1968*
George A. Miller, *1969*
George W. Albee, *1970*
Kenneth B. Clark, *1971*
Anne Anastasi, *1972*
Leona E. Tyler, *1973*
Albert Bandura, *1974*
Donald T. Campbell, *1975*
Wilbert J. McKeachie, *1976*
Theodore H. Blau, *1977*

Chapter 26

The Presidents and Their Messages
1968-1977

The presidential addresses in the decade from 1968 to 1977 reflect the social restlessness of the 1960s, commonly attributed in America to a revulsion with the Vietnam War. During this decade, the dissatisfaction with materialistic values, with injustice, and with problems of population, pollution, poverty, and peace (to quote the four "p's" of Harvey Brooks) and the search for a new life-style conforming to a new set of values both influenced the profession of psychology. This influence is reflected in those elected to the presidency and in the addresses that they chose to present.

A. H. Maslow represents the new trend even though he did not deliver a presidential address. He was the founder of humanistic psychology, which was concerned that psychology be value oriented. G. A. Miller, despite his commitment to experimental psychology, recognized his obligation to the spirit of the times and in his address discussed how to make psychology relevant to nonpsychologists by "giving psychology away." G. W. Albee, speaking for professional psychology, urged clinical psychologists, in particular, to give up the psychiatric model in order to fight racism, sexism, and poverty. K. B. Clark made a strong plea for those who possess power to share it with the powerless in our society. A. Anastasi and L. Tyler, elected in succession, the first female presidents in 51 years, both concerned themselves with a discussion of values. A. Bandura, a social learning theorist, criticized the older environmental reinforcement approach to learning and noted the obligation of psychology to provide individuals with their own choices for effecting personal and social change, with the end in view of a contribution by psychology to social betterment.

D. T. Campbell, also concerned for psychology's role in society, introduced an unusual note in defending the inhibitory prescriptions of conventional morality as valuable products of social evolution. W. J. McKeachie celebrated the changes in psychology, including cognitive psychology, that lead to a view of human nature as more human than in psychology's not so remote past—a view that in some respects is a return to Jefferson and the heritage of 1776. Finally, T. H. Blau, one of the few psychologists to be elected from the ranks of private practice, devoted his address to research findings bearing on the prediction of later schizophrenia based on childhood responses to a particular kind of test.

These addresses show that psychology is not immune to currents in contemporary society. Beneath the general optimism in the addresses cleavages can be recognized between the "science" and the "profession" of psychology, but the general desire is clearly expressed to keep psychology unified in the midst of diversity, with prestige distributed appropriately among those who represent psychology in different ways. More recent elections have been those of M. Brewster Smith, whose presidential address will be given in 1978, and Nicholas A. Cummings, in 1979—100 years after Wilhelm Wundt's laboratory was founded at the University of Leipzig.

Abraham Harold Maslow (1908–1970)

PhD, University of Wisconsin, 1934 (under H. F. Harlow).

(Maslow's illness prevented him from preparing or giving his address to the Seventy-Sixth Annual Meeting of the American Psychological Association, San Francisco, California, 1968.)

After receiving his PhD, Maslow remained at the University of Wisconsin (1934–1935), then took a fellowship at Teachers College, Columbia University (1935–1937) before moving to Brooklyn College (1937–1951). A large part of his academic career was spent at Brandeis University (1951–1969), where he was chairman of the department (1951–1961). In 1969 he became a resident fellow of the Laughlin Foundation in Menlo Park, California, until his death in 1970.

His books include *Principles of Abnormal Psychology* (1941, with B. Mittelman), *Motivation and Personality* (1954; revised, 1970), *Toward a Psychology of Being* (1962; revised, 1968), *Religion, Values, and Peak Experiences* (1964; revised, 1970); a number of his essays were published posthumously.

Maslow was known particularly for his motivational theory that distinguished between survival motives and higher motives, related to "being." Self-actualization and peak experiences, as he described them, are related to these higher motives. He was a leader in humanistic psychology and a founder of the *Journal of Humanistic Psychology*.

George Armitage Miller (1920–   )

PhD, Harvard University, 1946 (under S. S. Stevens; influenced by E. B. Newman).

Psychology as a Means of Promoting Human Welfare. *American Psychologist*, 1969, *24*, 1063–1075.

Presented at the Seventy-Seventh Annual Meeting of the American Psychological Association, Washington, D.C., 1969.

Miller's research fellowship at Harvard University, which began before he received his PhD, continued (1944–1948) until he became an assistant professor (1948–1951). He spent a few years at the Massachusetts Institute of Technology, then returned to Harvard (1955–1958). During his final year on appointment at Harvard he was visiting professor at Rockefeller University, where he has remained as professor (1968–present) and where he was affiliated at the time of his APA presidential address. His books include *Language and Communication* (1951), *Plans and the Structure of Behavior* (1960, with Eugene Galanter and Karl Pribram), *Psychology: The Science of Mental Life* (1962; second edition, with Robert Buckhout, 1973), *Communication, Language, and Meaning* (1973), and *Language and Perception* (1976, with P. N. Johnson-Laird).

Although Miller indicated that he would have been more comfortable in summarizing his own research, he decided to express his opinions about the current and potential role of psychology, a topic that was coherent with the theme of the convention at which he presided: "Psychology and the Problems of Society." He believed that scientific psychology is potentially one of the most revolutionary exercises ever conceived by the human mind. To Miller, the heart of the scientific revolution will be a new and scientifically based conception of man as an individual and as a social creature.

Miller stated that if psychologists take seriously the idea of a peaceful revolution based on a new conception of human nature, then scientific results will have to be instilled in the public consciousness in a practical and usable form so that what psychologists know can be applied by ordinary people. According to him, nothing could pose a greater challenge to the next generation of psychologists than to describe how best to give psychology away.

George Wilson Albee (1921–   )

PhD, University of Pittsburgh, 1949 (under C. A. Whitmer; influenced by W. Dennis and R. W. Russell).

The Uncertain Future of Clinical Psychology. *American Psychologist*, 1970, *25*, 1071–1080.

Presented at the Seventy-Eighth Annual Convention of the American Psychological Association, Miami Beach, Florida, 1970.

Albee served in the U.S. Army Air Force and the U.S. Navy before completing his graduate study. His career as a clinical psychologist began at the Western Psychiatric Institute, Pennsylvania (1949–1951), and he then served APA as assistant executive secretary (1951–1953). After a year as a Fulbright professor in Helsinki, in 1954 he became a professor at Case Western Reserve University, where he was affiliated at the time of his APA presidential address. He moved to the University of Vermont as professor of psychology in 1971. He is the author of *Mental Health Manpower* (1959) and is a frequent contributor to psychological journals.

In his address, Albee noted that clinical psychology is making the painful discovery that academic departments in the faculty of arts and sciences are not the best place to train professionals; therefore, a number of prestigious universities had dropped or curtailed their clinical programs at a time when the demand for training was high. Albee found the psychiatric setting an unsatisfactory place to learn the ideology of practice, and he suggested that psychologists step back and see what are truly the most pressing psychological problems that affect society. Clinical psychology, or some new field of applied psychology like community psychology, might select these most urgent human emotional problems after breaking free of psychiatric influence. Examples of these psychological problems are racism, sexism, and poverty.

Albee also discussed the incompatibility between the *science* of psychology and the *profession* of psychology and concluded that a separation or divorce may soon be required. In the light of these issues, he proposed several alternative APA organizational patterns.

Kenneth Bancroft Clark (1914–   )

PhD, Columbia University, 1940 (under O. Kline-berg; influenced by G. Murphy and R. S. Wood-worth).

The Pathos of Power: A Psychological Perspec-tive. *American Psychologist,* 1971, *26,* 1047–1057.

Presented at the Seventy-Ninth Annual Meeting of the American Psychological Association, Washington, D.C., 1971.

After a year at the Hampton Institute (1940–1941) and a year of war-related service, in 1942 Clark joined the faculty of the City College of New York, where he was affiliated at the time of his APA presidential address. Since 1967 he has been president of the Metropolitan Applied Research Center (later known as the MARC Corporation). His publications include a chapter based on the research conducted with his wife, Mamie P. Clark, *Racial Identifica-tion and Preference in Negro Children,* in T. Newcomb and E. L. Hartley's book *Readings in Social Psychology* (1947). His books include *Prejudice and Your Child* (1963), *Dark Ghetto* (1965), *A Relevant War Against Poverty* (1968), and *The Pathos of Power* (1974).

Clark's address reviewed briefly his research over the years, beginning with studies on the nature and development of the self and the problems of ego and racial identification. These studies invariably demonstrated the fragility of the ego. Clark's later studies showed the effects of social pressures and the consequences of rejection and acceptance of individual and group norms by the larger society. He also discussed a study of the federally funded antipoverty and community-based action programs that highlighted the unwill-ingness or inability of human beings with power to share with those who have been powerless. This study led Clark to a conceptual framework, influenced by the views of Alfred Adler, in which a theory of social power was the unifying concept.

According to Clark, psychotechnology cannot be avoided. Many provocative and suggestive findings emerge from neurophysiol-ogical, biochemical, and psychopharmacological research, and, therefore, psy-chotechnology must be used affirmatively, wisely, and with compassion. It must have a sound scientific, factual basis and be rooted in rational morality. Clark believed that if psychotechnology met these and related requirements, a rigor-ous, tough-minded science and technology of psychology would save humans from the consequences of their absurdities and propensities—the pathos of power.

Anne Anastasi (1908–   )

PhD, Columbia University, 1930 (under H. E. Garrett).

The Cultivation of Diversity. *American Psychologist*, 1972, 27, 1091–1099.

Presented at the Eightieth Annual Meeting of the American Psychological Association, Honolulu, Hawaii, 1972.

Anastasi began her academic career at Barnard College, Columbia University (1930–1939), then continued at Queens College, New York (1939–1946). She has been a professor at Fordham University since 1946 and was affiliated there at the time of her APA presidential address. Her books include *Differential Psychology* (1939; latest edition, 1958), *Psychological Testing* (1954; latest edition, 1976), *Fields of Applied Psychology* (1964), and *Individual Differences* (1965).

Anastasi emphasized in her address that psychologists need to exercise restraint, maintain a wholesome intellectual humility, and recognize the role of other disciplines if the potential contributions of psychologists are to have a genuine and lasting impact on society. Anastasi stressed that many values are common to psychologists as scientists, but psychologists must distinguish carefully between those assertions or recommendations that derive from their work as psychologists and those that stem from their individual values, beliefs, or prejudices. To present personal values in the guise of science is both ineffective and misleading.

In the process of "giving psychology away" (see G. A. Miller's address to the Seventy-Seventh Annual Meeting of the American Psychological Association, p. 531) Anastasi stated that psychologists need to share some well-established and thoroughly corroborated *orienting concepts*, such as multiplicity of variables, interaction, overlapping of distributions (regardless of mean differences), multidimensionality, modifiability, and effective decision making. Exposure to a multiplicity of intellectual traditions, value systems, and perceptual frames of reference frees the individual from narrow ideological constraints and permits the fullest development of individuality.

Leona Elizabeth Tyler (1906–   )

PhD, University of Minnesota, 1941 (under D. G. Paterson; influenced by R. M. Elliott).

Design for a Hopeful Psychology. *American Psychologist*, 1973, 28, 1021–1029.

Presented at the Eighty-First Annual Meeting of the American Psychological Association, Montreal, Canada, 1973.

Prior to completing her degree, Tyler began an instructorship at the University of Oregon (1940), where she remained as professor of psychology and as dean of the graduate school (1965–1971) until her retirement. Her books include *Psychology of Human Differences* (1947; revised, 1956), *The Work of the Counselor* (1953; latest edition, 1969), *Developmental Psychology* (1959, with Florence L. Goodenough), *Tests and Measurements* (1963; second edition, 1971), and *Individual Differences* (1974).

Tyler noted signs of change that may revitalize tarnished hopes for a psychology that contributes in a unique way to mankind's progress. Among these, Tyler included new ethical codes regarding research on human subjects and a shift in methods used to meet human problems—instead of relying on psychotherapy, psychologists were becoming consultants to people who were trying to help themselves. This shift was especially evident in the emerging field of community psychology. She noted that new orientations toward mental measurement and psychological testing were also in evidence. Tests were being designed for the benefit of the test taker rather than for the benefit of admissions officers or employers. The technical uses of these instruments had shifted from unidimensionality to multidimensionality. Another important sign that Tyler noted was the repudiation of elitism. She believed that this repudiation would modify the choice of research problems and emphasize communicating results to nonpsychologists.

The debate over freedom and determinism continued in Tyler's address. To her the issue was not free *will* but free *choice*. She made a strong case for the possibility of choice; the choices of psychologists should lead them to join with others in building a structure of rich human relationships.

Albert Bandura (1925–   )

PhD, University of Iowa, 1952 (under A. L. Benton; influenced by K. W. Spence).

Behavior Theory and Models of Man. *American Psychologist*, 1974, *29*, 859–869.

Presented at the Eighty-Second Annual Meeting of the American Psychological Association, New Orleans, Louisiana, 1974.

Bandura's academic career has been spent at Stanford University (1953–present) as professor of psychology and as chairman of the department of psychology. Among his books are *Adolescent Aggression* (1959, with R. H. Walters), *Social Learning and Personality Development* (1963, with R. H. Walters), *Principles of Behavior Modification* (1969), *Psychological Modeling: Conflicting Theories* (editor, 1971), *Aggression: A Social Learning Analysis* (1973), and *Social Learning Theory* (1977).

Bandura believed that modern learning theory does not rest on reflexive conditioning. Conditioning, simply a descriptive term for paired experiences, has turned out to be cognitively mediated. To Bandura, theories that explain human behavior as the product of external rewards and punishments present a truncated image because people partly regulate their actions by self-produced consequences. Bandura did not find it surprising that people change more rapidly if told what behaviors are rewardable and punishable than if they have to discover it from observing the consequences of their actions.

He believed that emphasis should be shifted away from the early behaviorist doctrine that learning can occur only by performing responses and experiencing their effects. The capacity to represent modeled activities symbolically enables humans to acquire new patterns of behavior observationally without reinforced enactment.

Bandura also noted that the issue of freedom and determinism has often been stated in misleading form. In backward causal analysis, conditions are usually portrayed as ruling people, whereas forward deterministic analysis of goal setting and attainment reveals how people can shape conditions for their purposes.

Bandura believed that psychology cannot tell people how they ought to live their lives, but it can provide them with the means for effecting personal and social change. In the end, psychology has an obligation to ensure that its findings are used in the service of human betterment.

Donald Thomas Campbell (1916–   )

PhD, University of California, Berkeley, 1947 (under H. E. Jones; influenced by R. C. Tryon, E. Frenkel-Brunswik, and R. N. Sanford).

On the Conflicts Between Biological and Social Evolution and Between Psychology and Moral Tradition. *American Psychologist*, 1975, *30*, 1103–1126.

Presented at the Eighty-Third Annual Meeting of the American Psychological Association, Chicago, Illinois, 1975.

Campbell's graduate study was interrupted by war service (1941–1946), but he received an assistantship in the Institute of Child Welfare while completing his degree. He began his academic career at Ohio State University (1947–1950), then moved to the University of Chicago (1950–1953). Since 1953 he has been a professor of psychology at Northwestern University, where he was affiliated at the time of his APA presidential address. His books include *Experimental and Quasi-Experimental Designs for Research* (1966, with J. C. Stanley), *Unobtrusive Measures* (1966), *Cross-Cultural Study of Perception* (1969, with M. H. Segall), and *Quasi-Experiments and True Experiments in Field Settings* (1976, with T. D. Cook).

Campbell maintained that present-day psychology and psychiatry, in all their major forms, are more hostile than is scientifically justified to the inhibitory messages of traditional religious moralizing. He defended this thesis in two arguments. First, validity can be found in recipes for living that have been evolved and tested through hundreds of generations of human social history. The argument rests on a natural-selectionist theory of social evolution.

Second, he defended his thesis by the theory of biological evolution, especially *group selection* and the *genetics of altruism*, which is prominent in sociobiology.

Campbell recognized that the wisdom produced by evolutionary processes (biological or social) is wisdom about past worlds. If grounds exist for believing that the relevant aspects of those worlds have changed, past adaptations may now be judged to be maladaptive. For example, the invention of modern military weaponry and related developments have outmoded ethnocentric military patriotism, a universal social evolutionary product. Still, the products of long tradition that have been adaptive in the past should lead to more respect for tradition than now exists.

Campbell defended two conclusions: (a) human urban social complexity has been made possible by social evolution rather than biological evolution; (b) this social evolution has had to counter individual selfish tendencies that biological evolution has continued to select as a result of the genetic competition among cooperators. (For correspondence aroused by the address, and invited by the editor, see the *American Psychologist*, 1976, *31*, 341–384.)

Wilbert James McKeachie (1921–   )

PhD, University of Michigan, 1949 (under D. G. Marquis; influenced by H. Guetzkow).

Psychology in America's Bicentennial Year. *American Psychologist*, 1976, *31*, 819–833.

Presented at the Eighty-Fourth Annual Meeting of the American Psychological Association, Washington, D.C., 1976.

McKeachie's graduate study was delayed by military service (1943–1945), but in 1948 he began teaching at the University of Michigan and has remained there as professor and as chairman of the department (1962–1971). In 1971 he was appointed director of the Center for Research in Learning and Teaching. His textbook *Psychology* (1966) is well known and widely adopted (third edition, 1976, with C. L. Doyle and M. M. Moffett). He has also published studies on the problems connected with effective teaching at the college level.

McKeachie traced American psychology from 1876 to 1900 and noted the initial optimism, so deeply rooted in American character since the days of the revolution. Ladd, in his presidential address of 1893, stated that psychology would make a great contribution to education and Dewey agreed in 1899. McKeachie cited William James' *Talks to Teachers* (1892) as a useful reference on early advice to teachers.

McKeachie believed that modern laws of learning have represented but a limited extension of James' ideas until recently, when the newer information-processing cognitive approaches have caused these "laws" to be reexamined. The newer approach is not *prescriptive* and is not oriented, as formerly, toward *behavioral control*. The new view of human nature is human, rather than mechanical, ratlike, or even computerlike. In that respect McKeachie believed that psychologists have returned to Thomas Jefferson and our forebears of 1776.

Theodore H. Blau (1928–   )

PhD, Pennsylvania State University, 1951 (under R. G. Bernreuter; influenced by B. V. Moore).

Torque and Schizophrenic Vulnerability: As the World Turns. *American Psychologist*, 1977, *32*, 997–1005.

Presented at the Eighty-Fifth Annual Meeting of the American Psychological Association, San Francisco, California, 1977.

Blau served a residency with the Veterans Administration at Perry Point, Maryland (1951–1952), then became director of clinical services and vice-president of Byron Harless and Associates, with headquarters in Miami, Florida (1953–1959). He then entered private practice in Tampa, Florida, which he has continued to the present. Since 1961 he has served also as adjunct professor at the University of South Florida. He is the author of the book *Private Practice in Clinical Psychology* (1959), and of several journal articles.

Blau noted the prevalence of "left-turning" in physical nature (e.g., the rotation of the earth in respect to the north–south axis) and its prevalence in living cells. He then reviewed a long-term study of a related tendency exhibited by children in relation to a number of other studies.

If a child is asked to draw a circle around each of three small Xs, the child of age 7 or older will, more often than not, draw the circles in a counterclockwise direction, regardless of which hand is used. If, however, the predominant direction is clockwise, the child is said to exhibit *torque*. Norms were provided on age changes in torque, indicating a gradual decrease in frequency from early childhood to adolescence.

In samples of emotionally disturbed children, aged 5–12, torque was found to be present at higher levels than expected from the normative data. Two samples of children (one sample with and one without torque), when initially tested at about 10 years of age, were followed for another 10 or more years. By the age of 21, of the 12 children diagnosed as schizophrenic in the meantime, 11 had exhibited torque at the earlier age. A much smaller proportion of the nonschizophrenics had shown torque at the earlier time. Blau proposed that torque may be a simple, external manifestation of a proposed neural integrative defect in the corpus callosum.

Name Index

Names in all CAPITALS are APA presidents. **Boldface**
page numbers indicate abstracts of presidential addresses;
italic page numbers indicate presidential addresses in full.

Subject Index